BLOOD, SWEAT AND EARTH

BLOOD, SWEAT AND EARTH

The Struggle for Control
over the World's Diamonds
Throughout History

TIJL VANNESTE

REAKTION BOOKS

For Nina and Sarah, two of the shiniest diamonds

Published by Reaktion Books Ltd
Unit 32, Waterside
44–48 Wharf Road
London N1 7UX, UK
www.reaktionbooks.co.uk

First published 2021
Copyright © Tijl Vanneste 2021

Printed and bound in Great Britain
by TJ Books Ltd, Padstow, Cornwall

A catalogue record for this book is available from the
British Library

ISBN 978 1 78914 435 2

CONTENTS

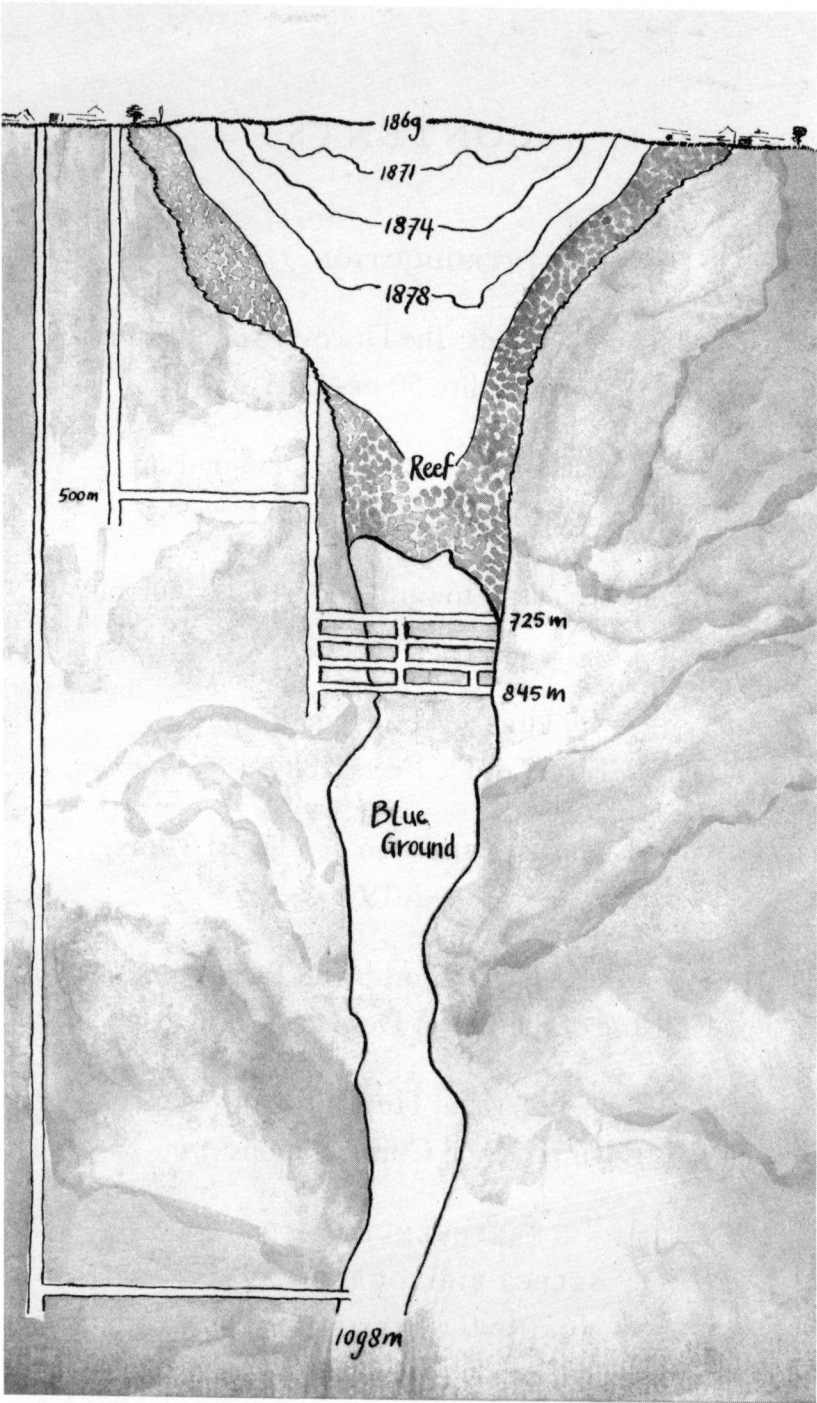

1 Kimberlite pipe based on Kimberley's Big Hole
and its historical evolution.

Introduction

The so-called volcanic pipes peculiar to all diamond-mines are simply
holes bored in the solid earth by the impact of monstrous meteors
... Bizarre as such a theory appears, I am bound to admit that there
are many circumstances which show that the notion of the Heavens
raining diamonds is not impossible.[1]

This description was written in 1908, and the man who wrote it believed in the possibility that diamonds came from outer space. Relying on the knowledge of his time, he could not have known that while he was not right, he was not exactly wrong either. Following the discovery of enormous diamond deposits in Kimberley, South Africa, during the 1870s, the theory that these gemstones occurred in deep underground pipes became well established in the scientific community. The 'so-called volcanic pipes' that contained diamonds, described in the article, soon became known as 'kimberlite pipes' after the town of Kimberley, where they had first been found (illus. 1). It was a revolutionary discovery with enormous consequences, as until that moment, diamonds had only been mined near the earth's surface, in or near riverbeds.

Today it is understood that kimberlite pipes are the remnants of volcanic eruptions that mostly took place during the geological period known as the Cretaceous (146 million to c. 65.5 million years ago).[2] Commercially viable deposits of diamonds are only found in a small fraction of them, 1 per cent of the 7,000 known pipes.[3] Diamonds are formed as carbon allotropes at high pressure and temperature in the earth's mantle, situated at least 150 kilometres (93 mi.) beneath the continental crust, or 200 kilometres (124 mi.) under the oceanic crust, after which they are carried to the surface within kimberlite, a type of magmatic rock (illus. 2).[4] A recent study has shown that these deep breeding grounds might contain many more diamonds than researchers previously thought.[5]

While no one doubts that the kimberlite pipes have their origins in the depths of our planet, astrophysicists discovered in 1987 that tiny presolar diamond grains existed in meteors.[6] The formation of diamonds in space is not yet fully understood, but more recent findings suggest that the size of diamonds found in meteors may be larger than has hitherto been thought, meaning that the 1908 article might be right after all.[7]

It is not hard to imagine why William Crookes, the article's author, was so taken with the idea of diamonds raining from the heavens. An origin in the stars fits the glamorous image carried by the most precious of gems much better than a genesis in the deep, muddy underground of our planet. Throughout history, the glitter that surrounds diamonds has been carefully constructed, using stories of large and famous diamonds possessed by the richest of the rich and tapping into Western orientalist fantasies about exotic diamond mines in mysterious locations. This imagery culminated in twentieth-century advertising campaigns that connected diamonds not only with glamour but with romantic ideals of fidelity and marriage. This modern branding made diamonds accessible to more consumers than ever before, a necessity after the hugely expanding production of diamonds in modern times.

Some argue that the success of the diamond, rated the most precious of all gems, is artificial, designed to accommodate those who are in control of them, and that its success came in spite of, and not because of, the

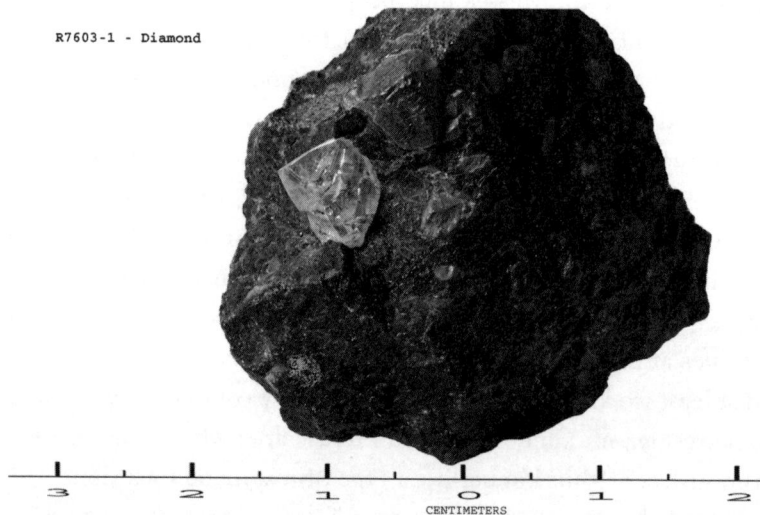

2 Kimberlite found at Dutoitspan mine.

intrinsic qualities of the stone. Unlike more colourful and unique gemstones, diamonds mostly look alike, often without colour and cut in the same form – the modern, round brilliant (illus. 17).[8] Yet while De Beers, the company that controlled both the production of and trade in diamonds for most of the twentieth century, succeeded so well in selling to the world unprecedented amounts of little colourless stones, the idea that diamonds are very precious goes back to antiquity. At first, though, diamonds were not appreciated for their beauty. An uncut, rough diamond does not look very special, but it is extremely hard, and that hardness, combined with their premodern rarity, led to the use of rough diamonds in amulets that provided magic protection to those wearing them, in Europe as well as in Asia. This symbolic use of diamonds all but disappeared in Europe during the Middle Ages following the spread of Christianity, and medieval lapidaries held the diamond in much lower esteem than other precious stones such as rubies and emeralds.[9]

One practice that did continue was medicinal, and diamond jewellery was used to ward off illness, as noted by the *Pharmacopoeia Londinensis* of 1691: 'the diamond is the hardest of all gems. It is never given inwardly, but only worn as Rings, Etc. So it's said to take away Fears, Melancholy, and to strengthen the heart.'[10] By that time, however, medicinal use was marginal in comparison to the establishment of diamonds as things of beauty. The development of cutting techniques, culminating in the invention of the brilliant, has given diamonds their highly appreciated lustre, which is the appearance of a diamond in reflected light, and attractive fire, which is the sparkle that one sees when light is travelling through the stone, deflected through its multiple facets, the polished surfaces of a cut stone. Indeed, consumers increasingly began to believe that diamonds could strengthen the heart, not as medicine, but as things of beauty that could last forever.

It is after the early modern development of cutting techniques and the parallel trends of growing production and consumption that the main role of diamonds solidified as gemstones set in jewellery, an appreciation that continues today. More than 12,000 categories exist to classify rough diamonds, crudely divided into three types: from high to low, these are gem quality, near-gem quality and industrial. Most commercial profit is, of course, made from selling gem-quality stones. These are what most people think of when considering diamonds. They are cut and polished to be used in jewellery or as single stones. Today, the value of such diamonds is based on the four Cs: the cut, the carat, the colour and the clarity.[11] The cut means the shape of the diamond after it has been transformed from rough diamond to finished stone. By far the most popular cut today is the round brilliant. Recently De Beers estimated that 40 per cent of the jewellery pieces containing diamonds sold in the United States, the world's most important consumer market for diamonds, are set with a round brilliant. Twenty-two per cent have a brilliant cut in the princess style, 12 per cent a cushion cut and 6 per cent contain a diamond in the shape of a heart.[12] The carat is a unit of weight, and one carat equals 200 milligrams.[13] The heavier the diamond the more it is worth, and a diamond of 42 carats is valued much higher than 42 diamonds of 1 carat, if all other Cs are the same. Colour ranges from white, the most valuable, to yellowish, and the so-called 'fancy diamonds', which are pink, red, brown, blue, yellow or green. These can be very valuable as well, depending on fashion and taste. Clarity measures the appearance of inclusions such as minerals, uncrystallized carbon or tiny fractures.

This categorization applies to only a small proportion of total diamond production, as only 20 per cent of the world's production falls in the gem-quality category. In 2016, 62 million carats of industrial diamonds were mined, about 49 per cent of the total production of diamonds that year.[14] Historically, these diamonds were of little use, except as 'diamond dust' that was mixed with oil and used on the diamond mills in the cutting process, but in the twentieth century, industrial-quality stones found new and widespread applications as abrasive in saw blades, grinding wheels and drill bits (illus. 3).

In 1941 the Dutch electronics company Philips smuggled industrial diamonds from France to Curaçao, to be used in the manufacture of tungsten wire for light bulbs.[15] In 1965 a Venezuelan scientist filed and obtained a u.s. patent for a diamond knife, which became a useful tool in eye surgery.[16] The fact that diamonds have good thermal conductivity but no electrical conductivity makes them useful in electronics and laser applications. Near-gem quality is a category in between the two extremes, and the boundary between this category and industrial stones is not always clear. Depending on demand, certain near-gem quality stones can be cut and polished into low-quality gemstones for use in jewellery at the lower end of the spectrum, but generally these also find their use in different industries.

Natural industrial diamonds are now only a tiny proportion of the total volume of diamonds used for industrial purposes, largely overtaken by the fabrication of synthetic diamonds, estimated at 4.4 billion carats in 2015.[17] Throughout history charlatans and scientists have been creating fake diamonds, but it was only in the early nineteenth century that scientists started to seriously attempt making synthetic diamonds that had the same physical attributes as natural ones. The creation of artificial diamonds was successfully achieved for the first time in the 1950s by ASEA, Sweden's largest electrical company (1953), and General Electric (1954).[18] After artificial diamonds proved to be a great success in the industry, the idea grew that they also could be used in jewellery. As the United States Federal Trade Commission judged in July 2018, 'lab-created products that have essentially the same optical, physical and chemical properties as mined diamonds are also diamonds.'[19] In the diamond sector itself, however, opinions are divided on how to deal with these so-called 'lab-grown' diamonds. Some see them as fake, and a threat to old monopolies. De Beers first criticized lab-grown diamonds, but has now created a company, Lightbox, to market them, although the name of De Beers is conspicuously absent from the website.[20] Several jewellers think lab-grown diamonds are the future of the industry, and one designer told the

3 Diamond-coated 2 mm bits.

New York Times that artificial diamonds offered 'the chance to create a high-end, ethical collection that stood for modernity'.[21]

Perhaps it is true that the current ability to grow diamonds in laboratories has begun to erode the glamorous reputation diamonds enjoyed for centuries, but it can easily be argued that it lays bare how much of a missed encounter with history it has been not to have deconstructed the glamour of diamonds earlier. By the end of the twentieth century the scandal of 'blood diamonds', stones mined in conflict zones and smuggled to Europe to finance wars in Africa, was exposed by NGOs, and the industry swiftly reacted by creating certificates to guarantee clean diamonds. In the end, however, these 'Kimberley Certificates' were the subject of abuse and falsification, and the mining of diamonds quickly resumed as usual. Consumption grew further, and the ever-continuing human and environmental abuse that has surrounded diamond mining since the very beginning disappeared once more from the public eye.

While revealing the practices underlying the trade in these blood diamonds did some good, it did not eradicate the historical wrongdoings, and, in a sense, it made them even less palpable. Despite efforts by certain NGOs and journalists to to show a more complex truth, most people identified blood diamonds exclusively with Africa and violent African warlords. Such a narrow interpretation vilifies African nations without fully acknowledging the involvement of Western governments, traders and mining managers, a way of thinking that fits outdated neocolonial, Eurocentrist and Western-superiority narratives. It is also an interpretation that is fundamentally ahistorical. The dark side of diamonds is very old, older than its brightly shining side. When one looks at the history of diamond mining and trading, one can see a long and exhausting narrative of wealth accumulation into a few hands, an accumulation fuelled by the blood and sweat of millions of anonymous miners and cutters, who were forced to work in tyrannical and unhealthy circumstances for little to no wage. The history of diamonds is a history of racial exploitation and social inequality, of a rich elite benefiting from the labour and doomed dreams of the poor, who continue to work in underground mines and dangerous rivers, in the hopes of one day finding a diamond that will set them free.

This book offers a narrative of that long history of oppression, by looking at the attempts of the few to limit the access to a commodity that is less rare than often believed, and to control the lives of the many anonymous miners who have so often been considered as dispensable. In 1934, when the British colonial authorities in Sierra Leone were thinking about how to deal with the newly found diamond deposits there, the assistant secretary of the colonial office in Freetown remarked that only two things needed to be taken into account. First, it was important to establish the precise boundaries of the mining area that was to be managed by a private company, and second, the question 'How can we protect the diamonds in the country from being worked or disposed of by others?' needed to be answered.[22] In other words, how to protect the colony's diamond deposits, and how to control the labour used there? This book narrates how regimes and companies have gone about answering those two issues in different temporal and spatial circumstances.

The continuity of this narrative is not only to be found in time, with exploitation of miners an ongoing tragedy, but in the strategies that were concocted by a peculiar mix of governments and private companies. It is remarkable how little has changed in the approach of those trying to maintain control of diamond mining. This can to a large extent be explained by the role played by European colonialism. Between the discovery of diamonds in Brazil in the early eighteenth century and the African independence movements of the 1950s, virtually all of the world's diamond production stood under some form of colonial control, and after the Asian and African countries that produced diamonds were able to claim political independence, continuing economic entanglements between the colonizers and the colonized ensured that the ghost of colonialism continued to haunt many men, women and children who worked in the diamond industry. The use of forced labour, a reliance on political oppression, the hoarding of diamonds to keep the price under control in spite of expanding production and efforts towards monopolization – all of these means have been applied for centuries, ensuring that diamonds, disregarding who actually mined them from the earth and how rare or pretty they really were, remained, in the eyes of an expanding consumer market, the most precious of all precious stones.

The exploitation of the workers in the mines and the recurrent attempts to monopolize the trading and mining of rough diamonds are the two main focal points of this book. Indian sultans enslaved whole families, while the Portuguese government brought millions of enslaved Africans to colonial Brazil, hundreds of thousands of whom were forced to dig for gold and diamonds. In South Africa, English industrialists separated their workforce on racial lines, and had no scruples in lodging black labourers in fenced-off compounds, often deprived of elementary human needs, a practice repeated elsewhere on the continent. No secret was made of the racist division of labour: 'this ceaseless toil of skilled and black labor – goes on day and night.'[23] The attempts at monopolization and hoarding were also of all times, and rulers on whose land diamonds were found often took the privilege of keeping the best ones to themselves. When new discoveries in Brazil upset the existing order in the early eighteenth century, monopolization in both trading and mining was attempted, with varying success. Later De Beers, starting in South Africa, successfully constructed a diamond empire that lasted until the beginning of the twenty-first century.

The decisions made on managing the flows of diamonds and the labour behind it had an impact on the consumption of polished diamonds, and vice versa, but the history of diamonds as jewellery is a different story that will not be told in this book.[24] When necessary, something will be said on changes in consumption patterns, demand for polished stones and developing cutting techniques, but essentially this book is about the management of the labour needed to extract rough diamonds from the earth and the efforts to monopolize the trade in them. The story told here is largely chronological, but sometimes parallel developments at different places in the world necessitate little diversions from this straightforward chronology.

From antiquity until the beginning of the eighteenth century, diamonds were mined in alluvial deposits in princely states in India and Borneo. Mining sites were almost always under direct control of local rulers, and a great deal of diamonds never left the region where they had been found. Asian diamonds had found their way to Europe at least as early as Roman times, but they became increasingly popular during the Renaissance, when Italian and Portuguese travellers started to write about the exotic mining sites in a way that sparked European fascination. Trade in Asian gemstones received a second and even stronger boost with the establishment of the various European East India companies in the first decade of the seventeenth century. The English East India Company in particular managed to institute almost complete control of the Indo-European diamond trade, although their dominance was not to last. The growing unification of India caused by Mughal conquests further fuelled the centralization of power over diamonds. The first chapter deals with the evolution of mining labour and the trade in diamonds in the Asian context, from the earliest traces until the discovery of diamond mines in Brazil during the first decades of the eighteenth century. While this chapter discusses the origins of diamond mining and trading, and although historical sources for this period are scant and provide little insight into the lives of the workers, enough evidence exists to indicate that miners were already exploited from the first moments mining labour was subjected to formal organization. It can also be asserted that the forces who tried to dominate the trade in rough diamonds were all aware of the importance of controlling the flow of rough diamonds as much as possible.

Attempts to master both labour and trade were perhaps for the first time truly successful in colonial Brazil, the subject of the second chapter. When diamonds were found in the riverbeds of the remote region of Serro do Frio, the fear arose that they would become too common. David Jeffries, an English jeweller who published a treatise on diamonds and pearls in 1751, remarked that the discovery of Brazilian diamonds 'occasioned many, even of the most capital traders in London, to believe, that Diamonds were likely to become as plenty as transparent pebbles; and they were so far influenced by this opinion, that most of them refused to buy Diamonds on any terms'.[25] Confronted with such worries, the Portuguese government decided to install a double monopoly. The right to mine diamonds in Brazil was sold to one company, which was allowed to use enslaved Africans to dig for diamonds in a number of well-designated areas, including the so-called 'diamond district' with Tejuco, present-day Diamantina, as capital. About fifteen years later, a second monopoly was established, which enabled a foreign company to sell the rough diamonds that the mining monopolists transported to Lisbon and from there onwards to merchants and diamond dealers in Europe. This attempt at control went further than the efforts made by the English East India Company, which held a monopoly over official trade routes bringing diamonds from India to Europe, but which was never able to exercise any control over labour. By the time the British had become territorial colonizers in India, able to manage labour, the produce of Indian diamond mines had already been reduced to negligible quantities.

The Portuguese king, on the contrary, was able to use his country's colonial domination over Brazil to shape the diamond region fully to his wishes. He maintained the right to keep the finest diamonds, a privilege also often taken by Indian rulers, and the Portuguese might have been the first to use hoarding of diamonds as a crucial strategy in the maintenance of artificially high prices, a tactic that has remained integral to the functioning of the diamond market ever since. Equally, even though the use of monopolies and enslaved labourers did not originate in Lisbon, the scale and international nature of their application in colonial Brazil made the Portuguese diamond administration a forerunner of the techniques used by De Beers in the twentieth century.

The alarmist messages that Brazilian production would ruin the market sparked the protective measures of hoarding and monopoly, but they also turned out to be quite wrong anyway. Half a century after diamonds were found in the New World, production in the old one had entered a downward spiral from which it never recovered. In the nineteenth century, this decline became more general, as Brazilian production also started to diminish. Even the takeover of mining management by the colonial administration in 1771 could not stop this Brazilian decline, which continued in the nineteenth century. That century turned out to be a pivotal period in the history of diamonds and is discussed in the third chapter. This chapter looks at how mining on the old alluvial fields of Brazil, Borneo and India became less and less organized to the point that the dire nature of the work was no longer characterized by the choice between either forced labour and slavery or illegality, but by the impossibility of making a living from mining for diamonds. Adventurers never gave up, though, and several mining rushes provided short-lived boosts to what looked like a dying industry. But history was to repeat itself, and this time salvation came from Africa. Diamonds were discovered in its southern tip in 1867, and it was quickly realized that diamonds were not just found in riverbeds, but that the true diamondiferous rocks were part of deep pipes, dubbed kimberlites after the town of Kimberley, where the first large pipe, the 'Big Hole' was discovered, leading to a diamond rush the world had never seen (illus. 37), and to a system in which black Africans were exploited in the most violent manner. Contemporaneous visual source material hardly ever captured violence against black miners, with the rare exception of a print published in the *London Evening News* in 1872 (illus. 4). Here, in the lower left corner, a white overseer is clearly kicking a black miner.

4 Racial violence at Kimberley's Big Hole, 1872.

The colonist's kick and the growing gorge were only the start. With the discovery of diamonds in South Africa began the modern industrial era of diamond mining.[26] Diamonds, alongside copper and gold, became an essential part of the construction of modern South Africa, and the mix of racial oppression and grotesque fantasies of imperialism were soon imitated elsewhere in Africa.[27] Dangerous underground mines, rather than alluvial fields, became the exclusive working terrain of underpaid, racially abused black labourers. Quickly, efforts to control the chaotic activities in South Africa's diamond mines intertwined with British dreams of adding a large and powerful African branch to its already vast colonial empire. Under the impulse of Cecil Rhodes, one company emerged as dominant in South Africa's diamond industry: De Beers, named after the two Dutch brothers who owned the farm on which land the diamond town of Kimberley would be built. The century following the establishment of the company in 1884 until the collapse of the Soviet Union in 1990 truly can be said to be the century of De Beers, propelled by the leadership of Ernest Oppenheimer, De Beers' main director in its most formative years. For the entire twentieth century, De Beers set the tone for the diamond industry, and Chapter Four will look at how that tone was built up, overcoming the different discords it met along the way, including the atrocities of the Second World War, which hit the diamond industry personnel mercilessly hard.

De Beers became notorious for its monopolistic position and distribution system, in which they selected a small group of jewellers, but it was their carefully crafted advertising campaigns that consolidated the image of diamonds as tokens of everlasting love. But while their romantic advertisements certainly convinced many consumers, they were unable to obscure the fact that De Beers actively participated in some of the darkest moments of twentieth-century history. De Beers established racially segregated labour environments, with black African miners forced to live in closed compounds, their most concretely visible contribution to the apartheid system. As South Africa's biggest company, they were complicit with the existing regime and tied to it in various ways. But De Beers was not only questioned over its dubious mining management in South Africa. It became, as a wholesaler, involved in the trade in blood diamonds, African stones that were mined and sold to finance some of the most atrocious wars that took place in the twentieth century.

The fifth chapter will analyse the context in which blood diamonds emerged, that of modern alluvial mining. Next to the development of industrial large-scale mining operations on the kimberlite pipes, dominated by De Beers, alluvial mining was continued, not only on the old diamond fields of Borneo, Brazil and India but in newly found deposits across sub-Saharan Africa, from Ghana and Sierra Leone, to the Democratic Republic of the Congo (DRC) and Angola, to Namibia, Tanzania and a handful of sites that escaped De Beers' control in South Africa. Alluvial mining was now also referred to as artisanal mining in order to distinguish it from industrial mining. Until the great African independence movements of the late 1950s and '60s, most of the areas where alluvial deposits occurred were part of Europe's colonial empires, and as such the English, French, Belgian and Portuguese authorities all benefitted from the presence of diamonds on territories they had claimed in the nineteenth century. But control over alluvial deposits was much harder as these were spread out over a much wider area than deposits found in kimberlite pipes. Alluvial fields crossed borders and were sometimes located in very remote areas. When new alluvial deposits were discovered, it often did not take long before they were invaded by thousands of adventurers, creating true diamond rushes that the authorities could not control.

This situation became even more complex with the wave of African independence spreading throughout the continent. The nascent local regimes had a hard time reconciling economic progress and nationalization with the persistent economic and political interests of their former colonizers. Furthermore, the new national regimes were regularly challenged by political opponents to the extent that civil war broke out in several African nations, with Sierra Leone, the DRC and Angola, fuelled by Cold War geopolitical considerations, as the most tragic examples. Because of the value of diamonds and the ease with which they could be smuggled, controlling the diamond fields became a crucial preoccupation of fighting factions. The involvement of these alluvially mined diamonds in armed conflict led to the coining of the term 'blood diamonds', and an engagement to no longer trade in them led to the almost globally adopted Kimberley Process (KP), an agreement to label all rough diamonds with certificates enabling buyers to trace their origins.

The development of the KP was a step forward, but the official end of the wars in Sierra Leone and Angola in 2002 was perhaps even more important. It was quickly realized that the KP did not solve all problems. It remained fairly easy to disguise a diamond's true origins – after the establishment of the KP, some African countries that never produced diamonds suddenly became important producers. Furthermore, a region might be considered as free of warfare and conflict in the eyes of the international community without it actually being the case. In the end, the KP was unable to regulate the diamond industry to the extent that all rough diamonds that circulated were indeed conflict-free. In Mugabe's Zimbabwe, officially at peace, mining labourers were suffering from low wages, forced labour, violence and unhealthy circumstances. The industry perhaps caught a lucky break with the discovery of rich diamond deposits in areas that were much less tarnished with bloody violence and colonial control, at least at first sight. The sixth and last chapter deals with the geographical diversification of diamond mining that began in the previous century but reached its apogee in our current one, following the loss of the De Beers cartel's monopoly. At the end of the twentieth century rich diamond deposits were found in unexpected and remote areas in Canada and Australia, while the existence of Russian diamonds, although known since the nineteenth century, would not face large-scale exploitation until after the Second World War. The decision of both post-Soviet

Russia and post-civil-war Angola to sell their diamonds outside of the De Beers cartel, and the impossibility for De Beers to do the same in Canada and Australia as they had done in Africa, created an oligopoly, a diamond industry in which a small number of mining giants control the market in rough diamonds. Several of these companies explicitly capitalized on the idea of selling 'clean diamonds', marketed as an ethical Western alternative for African blood diamonds.

In 2015 seven of the most important diamond mining enterprises set up a Diamond Producers Association in London to exercise wider control over the market after the demise of the De Beers cartel, under the motto 'real is rare.'[28] The largest absentee in this association is part state-controlled Endiama, the company that manages the diamond mines in Angola. In 2005, 177 million carats of rough diamonds were officially produced worldwide and sold for $11.6 billion. Ten years later production had decreased to 127 million carats, with a sales value of $13.8 billion.[29] In their 2019 report on the diamond market De Beers estimated that the previous year it occupied a 34.5 per cent share of the financial value of sales of rough diamonds, while Alrosa managed to gather a 26 per cent share. The other big producers, including Endiama, held a share of about 12.5 per cent; the informal sector and the small producers occupied the remaining share of 27 per cent.[30] Through their marketing branches established in old and new diamond centres, the mining companies sell most of their production to smaller enterprises and cutting firms, often located in India but also in Israel, Belgium and the USA. These buyers are part of one of the 31 members of the World Federation of Diamond Bourses (WFDB), founded in 1947 and headquartered in Antwerp. Bourses are found on all continents, with four located in Antwerp, and others in Mumbai, Ramat-Gan, New York, Moscow, Johannesburg, Amsterdam, London, Sydney, Dubai, Bangkok, Singapore, Hong Kong, Istanbul, Idar-Oberstein, Milan, Vienna, Toronto, Miami, Los Angeles, Tokyo, Seoul and Panama.[31] Ultimately, polished stones are sold by jewellers to the customer. According to De Beers, the top markets for jewellery in 2018 were the U.S., with a consumer demand of $36 billion out of a global demand of $76 billion, China, with a share of $10 billion, Japan with $5 billion, and India and the Gulf States with $3 billion.[32]

After the breakdown of the De Beers' monopoly, the grouping of the largest producers under one umbrella and the establishment of the WFDB are the twenty-first-century incarnations of the historical efforts to control the production and price levels of rough diamonds. It is tempting to think that the equally long history of attempting to control and exploit a cheap labour force has finally come to an end. After all, slavery has been abolished, and apartheid seems to belong to a different era. Racial and gender inequalities in labour, however, persist; in particular the abuse of labourers remains rife in the uncontrollable alluvial mining fields in remote regions. Nowadays concerns for the human rights of miners and workers are connected to the human rights of the people who lived on diamondiferous lands but were expelled from them, something that happened to various Brazilian tribes and to Aboriginals in Australia, as well as to a better understanding of the environmental damage created by diamond mining. Environmental impact of mining and unjust land appropriation have long been neglected in scholarly works, both in contemporary considerations as well as in studies that deal with the history of diamond mining.[33] I have opted to discuss both of these subjects in the epilogue: the endpoint of this book, which might well become the starting point of another.

The concerns discussed in the epilogue fit very well with our current apprehension about the negative consequences of human economic activities on the planet, and dreams of zero-impact are further motivating the development of diamonds grown in labs.[34] While this additional focus on the environment is most welcome, it should not be forgotten that the old dark side of diamond mining still persists.[35] One just has to look at the many impoverished artisanal diggers who hope that a lucky find on one of the many clandestine fields in Africa and South America might change their lives forever. The often inhumane circumstances in which men, women and children work serve as a reminder that, despite theories on the cosmic formation that so befit the shiny and eternal reputation of diamonds, they are still mined from the earth, with all the blood and sweat that comes with it.[36]

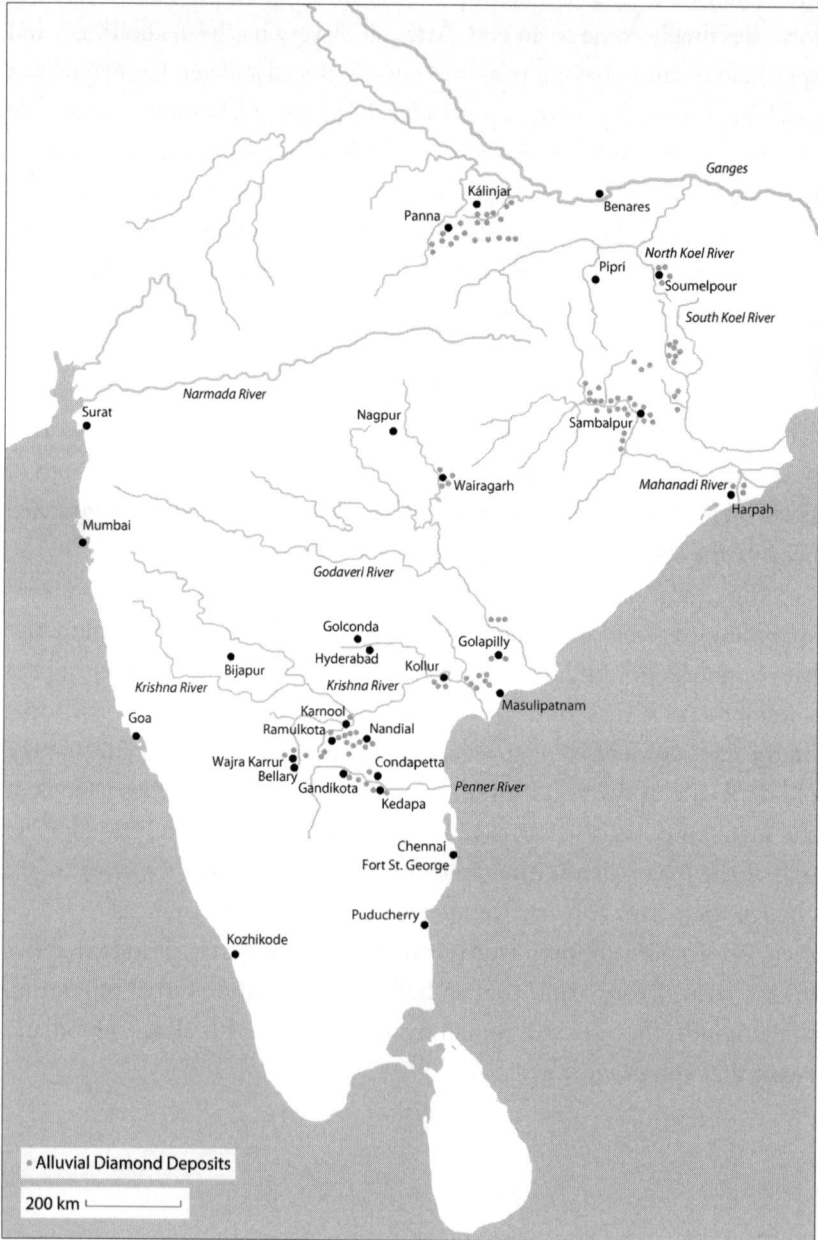

5 Diamond deposits in India.

1

Asian Diamonds: The Discovery of a Luxury Commodity, 50 CE–1785

Hast thou from the caves of Golconda, a gem
Pure as the ice-drop that froze on the mountain?
Bright as the humming-bird's green diadem,
When it flutters in sun-beams that shine through a fountain?

This is the opening verse of a poem by John Keats, 'On Receiving a Curious Shell, and a Copy of Verses, from the Same Ladies', published in 1817.[1] It is not surprising that Keats referred to the caves of Golconda as the finding place for the most majestic of gemstones. By the end of the nineteenth century 'Golconda' was included in English dictionaries as a noun meaning 'a source of great wealth'.[2] References to Indian diamonds had finally entered collective memory and language, after mines on the Indian peninsula had been the main source for these gemstones for many centuries. When Keats wrote his poem, there were only two other known areas where diamonds were found: Minas Gerais in Brazil and the island of Borneo. The city of Golconda, near present-day Hyderabad, was one of the main markets for diamonds mined in the hills and fields of the sultanate bearing the same name. While Golconda is the region most strongly identified with India's reserves of precious stones, the country had many other diamondiferous areas, some famous, others long forgotten (illus. 5). In 1425 the Indian historian Ferishta mentioned several exhausted mines in Madhya Pradesh, and his description probably included the Wairagarh mines.[3] One late seventeenth-century European traveller distinguished as many as 23 mines in the Golconda sultanate and fifteen in Bijapur, a sultanate conquered by the Mughal emperor Aurangzeb located in the southern state of Karnataka.[4]

This chapter starts at the very beginning, with ancient and mythical stories about diamonds found somewhere in Asia. That somewhere turned out to be the Indian peninsula, where a variety of local rulers (maharajahs), imperial potentates (Mughals) and the European maritime powers, particularly the English East India Company, strived for control over what was then thought to be the only spot where diamonds could be found, in spite of persistent rumours about a diamondiferous island – rumours that later turned out to be true.

Mythical Tales of Precious Stones

Most references to diamond fields in medieval and ancient sources are problematic, as they remain vague on the exact location and confound myth and reality. It is not an easy task to identify ancient and early modern mentions of Indian diamond mines with present-day localities. Several attempts have been made to classify the historical mining sites into different groups, and some of them are still helpful today. The German geographer Carl Ritter (1779–1859) distinguished five groups of diamondiferous regions: the Kedapa (formerly Cuddapah) group on the Penner river, located in the state of Andhra Pradesh, which included the mines of Condapetta and Wajra Karur; the nearby Nandial group, between the Krishna and Penner rivers, containing the Ramulkota mine; the Ellore or Golconda group in the northeast, on the Krishna river, with the well-known Kollur mine, but also the Malavilly; the Sambalpur group on the Mahanadi river, containing the Soumelpur and Wairagarh mines, located in the Chota Nagpur plateau in eastern India; and lastly, the Panna group in Bundelkhand, to the northwest of Chota Nagpur.[5] While this is a useful division of India's diamondiferous zones and helps to locate some of the better-known mines, it remains an impossible task to identify all of Ritter's mines with historical references. Locations sometimes remained vague in historical descriptions, names changed and nothing more is known of several mines than the moment they were abandoned.

One of the earliest references to diamonds can be found in a Sanskrit text, the *Arthaśāstra*, often attributed to Kauṭilya, an advisor to Candragupta, the first emperor of Maurya, who ruled over large parts of India between 321 and 297 BCE. The document specified the tasks of a superintendent of ocean mines, responsible for 'the collection of conch-shells, diamonds, precious stones, pearls, corals, and salt'.[6] The *Arthaśāstra* is also one of the oldest texts confirming the existence of a trade in diamonds, as it specified that merchants in gold, silver, pearls, coral, diamonds and other precious stones were to pay a commercial tax to the Maurya treasury.[7] It is difficult to assess the age of the manuscript, and of the sources it used, but Patrick Olivelle, author of a recent translation from Sanskrit into English, comes to the conclusion that the text must have been composed later than often thought, sometime between 50 and 125 CE.[8]

As with most ancient and medieval sources mentioning diamond mines, it has proven very difficult to identify these references with precise modern locations. The *Arthaśāstra* mentions six.[9] Arun Kumar Biswas, a specialist in minerals and gems in ancient times, has attempted to identify these six locations, and he managed to distinguish seven geographical areas: Wairagadh on the Sath river, near Nagpur, to the southwest of the Chota Nagpur plateau;[10] the Panna region; the Golconda mines; the Soumelpur area; alluvial fields in the Mahanadi valley; the Sambalpur district; and last, the Koel river area, all part of Ritter's five groups.[11] The problem of identification is further aggravated by different information in other texts.[12]

In his *Geographia*, Ptolemy (100–170 CE) made mention of a river where diamonds were mined, the 'Adamas' river, which has been identified with the Mahanadi river, although this claim has been disputed.[13] A recent article using Geographical Information System (GIS) methods to identify places in the *Geographia* with present-day localities suggests that the 'Adamas' river should be identified with the Subarnarekha river, north of the Mahanadi.[14] 'Adamas' is a Greek word used to refer to diamonds, but which literally means 'invincible by fire'. The linguistic relationship between different words that refer to diamonds says something about the geographical dispersion of knowledge about them. 'Diamond' is 'almaz' in Russian, 'alama' in Mongol, and in both Arabic and Kyrgyz it is translated as 'almas'.[15] The use of recent technology to identify Ptolemy's geographical references to diamonds is encouraging, but a heavy reliance on the diffusion of words, knowledge and the commodity itself in order to identify the exact locations of ancient Asian diamond mines is complicated by three problems. First, sources can be vague. The *Periplus of the Erythrean Sea*, a text on navigation and trade probably written around the middle of the first century CE, described diamond mines in India without being specific on location.[16] While the reference to diamonds in the text is still very important in order to better understand the chronology of diamond mining and trading, it does not allow for a more specific location of diamond mines than the rather vague 'India'.

Second, a positive identification of the word 'adamas' with the diamond is not always possible. In his *Natural History*, Pliny the Elder (23–79 CE) used the word to describe 'the substance that possesses the greatest value, not only among the precious stones, but of all human possessions.'[17] Pliny recorded the use of 'adamas' fragments to cut 'the very hardest substances known', but it remains doubtful whether he really referred to diamonds, as he mentioned that 'adamas' could be found in India, Ethiopia, Arabia, Macedonia and Cyprus.[18]

A third problem has to do with the fact that international trade could obscure knowledge about the original locations for finding diamonds, a problem that was aggravated by the classically secretive and often mysterious air that surrounded the commerce in diamonds and other precious stones. Even though diamonds are not found on Sri Lanka, a Chinese monk named Fa-Hien described in the fifth century CE how the Buddha went to the island, where he interrupted 'a prodigious trade in gemstones between Arab merchants and the island's aborigines'.[19] Considered as evidence for the existence of diamonds on Sri Lanka, Fa-Hien's remark at most demonstrates that traders sold Indian diamonds or other precious stones there. Nine hundred years later, in the fourteenth century, confusion about where to find diamonds still existed, and one wonders about the region a fourteenth-century Armenian traveller was describing when he mentioned a diamond-rich province named Sym.[20] Maybe he referred to the kingdom of Siam, where diamonds did not occur, but rubies and sapphires did. Diamonds – perhaps coming from Borneo – did pass through the kingdom, however, on their way to China.

Lack of information on the size of early Asian diamond trade renders identification of mining sites even more difficult. It is known that diamonds had crossed the Mediterranean since Alexander's campaigns in the East, but very few indications exist of a regular gem trade between the Greeks and the Indians.[21] There is more evidence of the development of a Eurasian diamond trade during Roman times. Archaeological material points to the inclusion of diamonds in trade relations between India and the Roman Empire at least since the first century CE, with the city of Arikamedu (historical Pondicherry and present-day Puducherry) playing a crucial role.[22] Technical analysis of a rock crystal found there suggests that it was worked using diamonds, sometime between 250 BCE and 300 CE, and Roman engravers might have learnt their techniques from there.[23] During the rule of Emperor Augustus (27 BCE–4 CE) references to gems were increasing, and sources demonstrate a growing Roman curiosity towards gemstones. The *Periplus of the Erythrean Sea* mentions Indo-Roman commerce in which precious stones were exchanged for items in silver and gold, tools and clothing.[24]

It is not clear whether China was trading in diamonds directly with India at that time, but it is known that trade connections between China under the Han dynasty (206 BCE–220 CE) and the Roman Empire did exist, and that it included a commerce in precious stones.[25] It remains equally unknown how far reaching diamond trading circuits were, but, according to Pliny, they extended all the way to include Ethiopia.[26] Most trade, however, was confined to India and its vicinities, due to the inclusion of payments in precious stones within local tributary systems and the privilege of local rulers who were able to keep the best diamonds. Most diamonds never made it to Europe, particularly when demand declined due to the rise of Christianity, which led to a diminishing cultural appreciation for the supernatural effects related to the hardness of diamonds.[27] Over time, however, overland routes developed that connected Asia with the Middle East and parts of Western Europe. The Persian scholar Al-Biruni (973–1048), born in Khwarazm, which was part of the Abbasid Empire, claimed that he had received diamonds by way of Isfahan and Fort Nandna (present-day Jelum in Pakistan).[28] Diamonds were transported westwards by way of the Red Sea, via the ports of Aden and Alexandria, and across the Persian Gulf, with Ormus as the main transit port, and subsequently transported through Aleppo and Constantinople. Cairo became an important trading centre, and the earliest presence of diamond merchants there dates from the eleventh century.[29] The place that connected these Middle Eastern circuits with Europe was Venice. The city had acted as the gateway for luxury items from Asia since at least the eighth century, and became the main commercial centre supplying Europe with Asian precious stones, including diamonds.[30] Venetian traders went in person to Alexandria and Aleppo to buy gemstones that they then sold to Frankish merchants in Pavia.[31] The further development of trade relations between northern Italian city states and Flanders, Brabant and France through the

Champagne fairs contributed to the spread of the diamond trade westwards. Venetians sold diamonds in Nuremberg, Paris and Bruges, and the latter became a very important diamond centre.[32]

The development of these overland trade networks was accompanied by growing Arab knowledge of diamonds, and many of the famous medieval Arab geographers wrote about diamonds and other gemstones.[33] Arab historian Al-Masudi (896–956) mentioned diamonds coming from the coasts of the Indian Ocean.[34] Al-Biruni, who discussed diamonds in an important work on mineralogy that he wrote in the early eleventh century, claimed that these precious stones were mined 'in Khwar which faces Serandib'.[35] Serandib was the old Arabic name for Sri Lanka, meaning 'Isle of Delight', and Al-Biruni hinted at diamonds occurring there as well. His work was one of the earliest known efforts to debunk existing mythology surrounding diamonds: he labelled stories of falcons and sparrows bringing diamonds from valleys to their nests, where they were picked up by adventurers, as false.[36] The myth of the Diamond Valley was famous and historians have traced its origins to the Hellenistic Orient, from where different versions spread to China, India, the Arabian peninsula, Persia and the Western world, all before the second half of the seventh century CE, a diffusion confirming that knowledge about diamonds was travelling, possibly following the commodity itself.[37] Most versions of the story agree that the diamonds were surrounded by snakes, but details on the location of the valley and how to get the diamonds differed greatly. One version of the story, mistakenly attributed to Aristotle and probably of Arabian origins, narrated that Alexander the Great had visited the valley, which lay beyond the frontier of Khorasan in Central Asia. The snakes in the valley had a gaze that killed men, but Alexander made them perish by using mirrors.[38] In the Chinese version of the Diamond Valley, recorded by Chang Yue (667–730), diamonds were found on the Mediterranean island of Fu-Lin.[39] Fu-Lin may have referred to the ancient city of Ctesiphon (or Al Mada'in) near Baghdad in Mesopotamia, known to the Chinese as a region where minerals and jewellery came from.[40]

One of the most popular versions of the story was told in the narrative of the second voyage of Sinbad the Sailor. It included Sinbad's visit to the site, where he saw merchants throwing chunks of meat down into the valley. Diamonds stuck to these chunks, and birds of prey picked up the meat and carried it to their nests, where merchants could easily collect the precious stones.[41] It is argued that tales of the island of Serandib, rich in gemstones, inspired this particular part of the story.[42]

In Europe, Marco Polo (*c.* 1254–1324) included the story's version of the snake-infested valley in his travel accounts, but was not as critical of them as Al-Biruni had been centuries earlier.[43] Later, Italian traveller Nicolò de' Conti (1395–1469) also mentioned the story, although his version, written down by the pope's secretary Poggio Bracciolini, was centred around a diamond-producing mountain surrounded by lagoons inhabited by snakes and other poisonous animals. Diamonds were secured by throwing the meat from an adjacent mountain.[44] De' Conti, like Polo, accepted the story at face value. Later scholars argued that the recognition of the story by various European travellers could be explained by local habits of making an animal sacrifice before opening a mine, a practice that attracted vultures.[45] De' Conti himself must have witnessed such an event, as he visited diamond mines situated at fifteen days' travel from the capital of the Vijayanagara Empire in southern India.[46]

Perhaps the oldest image of the myth can be found in the Catalan Atlas of 1375, made by Jewish cartographer Abraham Cresques and his son Jehuda for Prince Juan of Aragon (illus. 6).[47] The Catalan text accompanying the image of the Diamond Valley can be translated as follows:

> These men are chosen to pick diamonds. However, because they cannot climb the mountains where these are found, they cleverly toss pieces of meat where the precious stones lay. The stones adhere to the meat and detach [from the rocks]. Later the stones fall from the meat hoisted by the birds. Thus told it, Alexander.[48]

Cresques placed the Diamond Valley in the Baldassia Mountains, which can be identified with the Badakshan region, mainly situated in present-day Tajikistan. The region played an important role in ancient trade networks and was a stopover on the Silk Road. Al-Biruni mentioned it as a place where spinel could be found, while Ibn Battuta (1304–*c.* 1369) and Marco Polo stated that rubies were found there.[49] It seems that narratives on diamond mines in Central Asia cannot be confirmed by physical evidence and that these reports must refer to sites in present-day India. While the story of diamonds sticking to meat is generally accepted as a myth, there might be some truth in it after all. In 1897 an

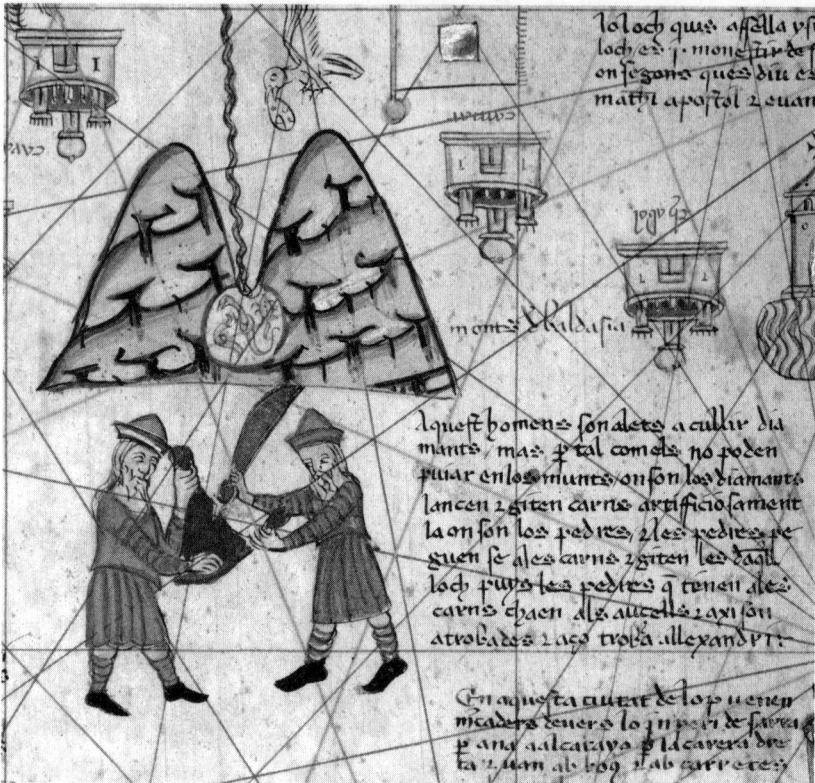

6 Detail from the Catalan Atlas, 1375.

employee working for De Beers at the Kimberley diamond mine found that diamonds stuck to grease, unlike the other minerals present in the diamondiferous earth dug up from the mine. This discovery led to the implementation of the grease table for sorting diamonds, which greatly enhanced efficiency in the diamond-finding process.[50]

Early European Travel Accounts

Set at the very end of the thirteenth century, Marco Polo's travel journal was one of the first works by a European traveller to mention Indian diamonds: 'and don't think that the good diamonds from there reach the Christians, they go to the Great Khan, and other kings and barons of those regions that have great wealth.'[51] At the time, the Deccan was ruled by the Vijayanagara emperors, and several other Europeans would follow Polo by describing Vijayanagara's diamond mines. The most important of these early European descriptions came from Polo's fellow Venetian de' Conti, who had visited diamond mines near the Krishna river, north of the Vijayanagara capital, during the 1420s, and the Portuguese explorer Duarte Barbosa (1480–1521).[52]

While the experiences of Polo and de' Conti fitted well within the Old World dominated by overland trade routes, the publication of Barbosa's work indicated that the commercial centre of gravity in Eurasia was shifting because of the establishment of the sea route between Europe and India via the Cape of Good Hope. Quickly maritime navigation replaced the land route through Venice, and the shift turned Lisbon into Europe's new gateway for the entry of Asian diamonds. Further north, Antwerp emerged as the main trading hub, after Bruges had lost its access to the North Sea when silt deposits filled the Zwin area. A growing amount of Italian and Portuguese traders settled in Antwerp, while Antwerp merchants established branches in Lisbon and Venice as well.[53] In the face of these developments, the role of Venice as international trading hub declined, but the city remained important as a diamond finishing centre, and during the first decades of the seventeenth century it still employed more craftsmen than Antwerp. This can largely be explained by the city's good connection to the Ottoman Empire, with Istanbul an important consumer market for diamonds polished in Venetian workshops.[54]

Portuguese vessels not only brought diamonds to Europe, they transported European clergymen, adventurers and traders the other way, and from the sixteenth century onwards European merchants started to appear in India, dealing in precious stones, jewellery and pearls. Some of these Europeans sold their merchandise as far as China and the Philippines, from where gemstones were exported to New Spain.[55] A man named Guylherme de Bruges had sapphires, rubies and jewels shipped to Lisbon by a merchant in Cochin in 1528. In the same period an agent for an Augsburg firm purchased diamonds from an Antwerp trader who had spent some time near the diamond mines in the Vijayanagara Empire.[56] A manuscript written in 1548 by Francisco Pereira, chief lapidary of the Portuguese king, contains several references to the Bellary, Kedapa and Wajra Karur mines. The Vijayanagara emperors sometimes gave diamonds as presents, such as the gift of sixteen stones, the biggest one weighing 162 carats, to the Bijapur sultan, an event that was recorded by Fernão Nunes in the travel accounts of his visit to the empire between 1535 and 1537.[57]

These early Portuguese reports greatly expanded European knowledge about Asian diamonds and were quickly complemented by eyewitness accounts of travellers coming from elsewhere in Europe, who provided even more details on the mining and trading activities that were taking place at diamondiferous sites in India. One of the best-known accounts of Indian diamond mines can be found in the *Itinerario*, written by Dutch merchant and traveller Jan Huyghen van Linschoten (1563–1611).[58] He discussed the Vijayanagara diamond mines with more detail than most of his predecessors, although he also borrowed extensively from the *Coloquios dos Simples e Drogas da India*, published in Goa in 1563 by the Portuguese Garcia da Orta.[59] According to Linschoten, the best diamonds were found in the Deccan on a mountain named Roça Velha ('Old Rock' in Portuguese) and transported to a city between Goa and Cambay where Gujarati merchants came to buy them.[60] Linschoten described how diamonds were mined in the same manner as gold, 'at a depth of a man's length'.[61] At times, mining holes were left idle for years before renewed efforts were made at the same place.

Another detailed report comes from Jacques de Coutre, a diamond trader from Bruges who spent more than thirty years in southern Asia and the Middle East. In 1611 he travelled to the diamond mine of Ramanacota, where he witnessed 50,000 men, women and children at work. He described them as poor, working practically nude, wearing nothing but a loincloth, which was a measure to prevent theft. Miners organized themselves in little companies financed by merchants, who paid for wages and expenses. These traders only paid small prices for the diamonds dug up by the miners' associations, and additionally a monthly tribute had to be paid to the 'lord of the mines', an overseer from the state, who, in de Coutre's time, was a nephew of the Vijayanagara emperor. Diamonds of seven carats or more that were unearthed, automatically belonged to him.[62] It was general practice in the Indian empires and sultanates to consider diamond mining as a monopoly belonging to the ruler that was either managed by officials on his behalf or sold to a contractor.[63] The produce of some mines, for instance at Currure, which became part of Golconda in the seventeenth century, was entirely preserved for the ruler.[64] Generally, however, merchants employing miners were able to get permission to mine in exchange for a fee. Rulers often demanded an additional tax on commercial diamond transactions.[65]

De Coutre described the mining methods, which, for alluvial mining, did not change over time. First, miners built a platform, surrounded by a small fence. Next to it they erected a small temple harbouring an idol smeared with saffron. After a sacrifice ritual, the miners started to extract diamondiferous earth, recognizable by its colour, using iron picks and shovels. This earth was dried on the platform, where the erosive force of the wind reduced the pile of earth, 'tall as a man', to a little heap of pebbles, out of which the diamonds could be easily picked. Diggers were constantly supervised and were not allowed to sell their finds to foreigners. Extracting earth was not without danger, and de Coutre described a tragic collapse of a digging hole due to heavy rainfall, burying 150 miners. Subsequently, thirty of their widows were burned alive, a ritual known as sati.[66]

One of the few known illustrations of an early modern Indian diamond mine comes from Dutch illustrator Romeyn de Hooghe (1645–1708) (illus. 7). While clearly romanticized, it shows several classic features of early modern Indian diamond mining, such as the proximity of merchants, the nakedness of the workers and the presence of a religious statue as well as 'priests'. De Hooghe was well-known and some of his images were bought by Pieter van der Aa, a Leiden-based publisher, who used them for several volumes of his own *Galerie agréable du monde*. The image of the diamond mine was printed in van der Aa's second volume on Persia and the Mughal Empire.[67] Neither van der Aa nor de Hooghe provided any details on the place where the diamond mine on the image was supposed to be, but in his first volume on *Les Indes Orientales*, van der Aa included a short description of the two kingdoms of Golconda and Orixa. Van der Aa described that Orixa, which can be identified with present-day Odisha, was so rich in diamonds that the nearby ruler of Golconda filled up the mine with debris in 1622 to ensure that there would be no abundance of diamonds, which would ruin their price. Van der Aa further specified that over 100,000 miners were working in Golconda, next to the presence of many merchants and more than 20,000 prostitutes, who were registered in special books.[68]

Van der Aa's volume on Persia and the Mughal Empire has only one other image related to diamonds, a copy of Abraham Bosse's representation of the twenty prettiest diamonds sold to the French king by Jean-Baptiste Tavernier (illus. 18). Tavernier (1605–1689), a jeweller working for the French court, was the most famous of the European travellers who

7 Diamond mine,
India, 1729.

wrote about diamond mines in India. He visited five mining areas, including one of the two diamondiferous rivers he knew existed. The first mine he described was Raolconda, in present-day Karnataka, later identified as the Ramulkota mine, which he visited in 1645 (see illus. 5).[69] Located in the Bijapur sultanate, the mine was discovered about two hundred years before Tavernier's visit, and the diamonds it contained were hidden in the veins of rocks.[70] This diamondiferous material was extracted by a group of miners that, according to the Frenchman, varied in number between fifty and a hundred. Tavernier, just like Linschoten, pointed to the presence on site of merchants who employed the miners, paying the ruler 2 pagodas (Indian currency) per day for a group of fifty miners.[71] While this tax covered the organized supervision, the government also took the privilege of keeping the best diamonds that were found. Tavernier's description confirmed Linschoten's picture of miners as poor people, working almost naked, making hardly any money and tempted to steal diamonds by swallowing them.[72] Miners were often impoverished peasants who mined for low wages and were partially paid in food and tobacco.[73] Theft was common, and Tavernier heard a story of a miner hiding a small diamond of two carats in the corner of his eye. As a prevention, merchants paid a group of up to fifteen miners a little extra to keep watch. Workers also received rewards, such as additional food, for finding bigger stones.[74]

Tavernier continued his travels by visiting the famous Kollur mine, near a river at seven days' travel from Golconda.[75] The site had been discovered by a millet planter about one hundred years earlier, and it carried a well-known reputation for yielding large stones, although they were not always of the purest quality.[76] In Tavernier's day it must have been one of the most intensively worked mines, as he mentioned a mass of 60,000 people working there. They, as elsewhere in India, began their work by praying to a statue and consuming a meal. After that, the men dug up to 4 metres (14 ft) deep, while the women and children transported the diamondiferous earth to a flattened and walled terrain where water was run through it, after which, similarly to de Coutre's description, workers raked and chopped the earth to reveal the diamonds contained in the samples brought for washing.[77] This method of extracting diamondiferous soil from riverbeds to a place where workers go through the earth to find diamonds has been virtually unchanged for alluvial mining everywhere and at all times, including the gendered division of labour (illus. 78 and 81).

The oldest mine described by the famous Frenchman was in Bengal, on the Koel river. From his description of operations there, it is clear that the mining in riverbeds was greatly influenced by the rhythm of the seasons.[78] In February, after the rainy season had ended and the water was cleared, about 8,000 people from Soumelpur and nearby villages arrived at the riverbeds. Their first action was to gain access to the river soil by drying up some parts of the river. This was a different method from that used at the dry diggings at Raolconda. The Koel river yielded pointed diamonds, and their absence on the European market at the time created the belief that these mines had been closed, although they might simply have never reached Europe.[79]

Tavernier's descriptions of this area can be supplemented with a report written by Dutch merchant Pieter de Lange about twenty years after Tavernier's passage. It had been compiled on behalf of the Dutch East India Company (voc) and reported information on four diamond mines, including several of the sites Tavernier had also visited.[80] First, de Lange described what he had heard about a diamond mine in Bengal, to

8 Diamond washing in Golconda, India, 1830.

the southeast of Pipri, in present-day Uttar Pradesh, which were said to contain old rock diamonds, but people steered clear of the mine because of the unhealthy climate and the bad government. The second mine was called the 'Rauvelecotte' or 'Roncoldael', in Bijapur, known since 'time immemorial'.[81] This might well have been Tavernier's Raolconda mine. The stones were taken from rocks, which produced a high amount of 'lasks', which were said to owe the irregularity of their cut to the fact that these rocks were heavily broken to expose the diamonds. 'Lask' was the name given to a particular cut of a rough diamond that was 'cut along its cleavage, producing a thin flat stone and losing less overall weight in the process'.[82] The 'lask' cut had originated in India, motivated by the desire of keeping as much of the rough stone's weight as possible, at the expense of its symmetry. Because of this different appreciation, 'lasks' were not very popular among European traders.[83] More generally, there was a tendency in Europe to consider Indian cuts as bad, leading a scholar such as Gedalia Yogev to conclude that 'lasks', which he defined as stones cut in India, differed a great deal in individual quality because 'Indian workmanship was bad', a rather Eurocentrist statement that fails to take taste differentials into account, and that has become fully outdated following twentieth-century developments.[84] The 'Rauvelecotte' mine was said to be exhausted at the time of de Lange's report. The third was a mine near the fortress of Gandikota, with a view of the Penner river, in the Kedapa region, but by the time de Lange reported on it it was in a state of decline, with both miners and merchants avoiding the place due to the existing government. It was a mine that yielded small and white diamonds, and the voc had made important purchases there in 1638.[85] Perhaps the

Gandikota mine was the same mine as the one described in a later report by Henry Howard, under the name 'Ganjeeconta', which was in private hands at that time.[86]

The last mine described was Kollur, already mentioned by Tavernier, covering 20 square miles, within which fourteen villages had been established, including the town of Kollur itself.[87] There, and in three other main towns, the *banyans* (merchants) resided, while the miners lived in the ten other villages. For every worker, a sum of money needed to be paid, while those working on their own account had to work one day in the week for the king, in exchange for a small wage.[88] Adventurers and merchants arriving in Kollur were allowed to employ as many miners as they wanted, paying for them by groups of ten. Miners used iron pickaxes and crowbars, digging through a layer of red stones until they reached the diamondiferous soil, which was transported for washing, up to six times in a row, until the remaining mass revealed its diamonds. As elsewhere, diamonds above a certain size automatically belonged to the local ruler. A common form of punishment for thieves was the enslavement of them and their families, forcing them to work for no remuneration in these mines. At Kollur, just as Tavernier had observed in Raolconda, the traders recruited the miners, but when a miner at Kollur was unable to find employment, he could be forced to work directly for the ruler.[89] The increasing amount of detailed official reports and eyewitness accounts by specialized personnel such as Tavernier and de Lange is indicative of a growing European desire to trade directly at the mining sites, and perhaps even of dreams to control them. The expanding power of the Mughals and restrictions on foreigners trading in Mughal territories prevented the full realization of such dreams and desires, although there are some occasional narratives of Europeans trading directly at the mining sites.[90]

The Time of the Mughals

At the same time as several early modern European travellers were putting their Indian experiences to paper, political turmoil was challenging ownership of various Indian mines. By the first decades of the seventeenth century several diamondiferous areas had been conquered by the Mughal emperors. In the north, Akbar (1542–1605) had already subjugated Bengal and its diamond mines before the end of the sixteenth century.

The *Ain-i-Akbari*, an extensive report on the state of Akbar's government in 1590, contains three references to diamond mines. The Harpah diamond mine in the district of Madáran in lower Bengal was said to produce very small stones. Alluvial fields near the Kálinjar fortress in the Bundelkhand region equally yielded small diamonds that were mined by local peasants. The third reference mentions a diamond mine named Bírágarh, near Kallam in Maharashtra.[91]

These references indicate Mughal interest in diamonds and confirm that conquering rulers were well aware of local gemstone riches. Later stories about Mughal conquests provide more details about diamond mines. In 1585 Akbar made Chota Nagpur and its capital Khokhra a tributary to the empire.[92] Its ruler Raja Durjan Sal, however, refused to pay any tribute. Aware of the presence of diamonds, Akbar's successor Jehangir (1569–1627) ordered an invasion with elephants of Chota Nagpur and its diamond mines in 1616, 31 years after Akbar's original attempt to control the area.[93] In his memoirs, Jehangir attributed this delay to the fact that the alluvial fields on the Koel and Sankh rivers were situated in thick jungle.[94] Following the invasion, Raja Sal was imprisoned, but received mercy when the emperor forced him to estimate the value of two diamonds that had been brought to him from Khokhra. The raja noticed that one of them was flawed, and an experiment proved him right. Both diamonds were attached to the horns of a ram, which was then made to fight with another ram. The flawed diamond split, and Jehangir allowed Durjan Sal to return to Chota Nagpur.[95]

Raja Sal's opposition was not the only resistance the Mughals encountered in diamondiferous lands. The Panna mines in Bundelkhand, south of the Ganges, had been conquered by Akbar in 1569, but the region proved hard to govern, and the Mughal emperors had to deal with chronic revolts. Partially in response to the intolerant religious policies of Jehangir's grandson Aurangzeb (1618–1707), the region rebelled under the leadership of a man named Chhatrasal, who raised an army against the Mughals in 1671. He used revenues from the local diamond mines to become raja of Bundelkhand, which remained independent until it came under Maratha control in the eighteenth century.[96]

In southern India the Vijayanagara Empire remained a strong political presence until they were beaten by an alliance of the Deccan sultanates, including Bijapur and Golconda, at the battle of Talikota in 1565, a defeat from which the empire never fully recovered. Following the battle, Vijayanagara's diamond mines fell into the hands of the Bijapur sultan. Although Bijapur and Golconda managed to remain independent sultanates throughout the sixteenth century, by 1636 Mughal emperor Shah Jahan (1592–1666) had turned them into vassal states.[97] The diamond mines in both sultanates were considered to be among the richest on the peninsula, and it was no surprise that the Mughals invaded both, in 1656 and 1687 respectively. Contemporary sources narrating the events surrounding these invasions have provided us with details of one of the only known administrators of diamond mines during the early modern period, a Persian named Muhammad Sayyid Ardestani (1591–1663), later known as Mir Jumla. Born near Isfahan, he was trained as a clerk for a diamond trader with connections in Golconda. He made a fortune when he supervised the Kollur mine under a different name and rose in the administrative ranks of Golconda. First, he became keeper of the royal records, later a military commander and governor.[98] Eventually he became prime minister (*wazir*) and expanded Golconda's territory at the expense of the Vijayanagara Empire, which had established a new dynasty and a new capital after its defeat at Talikota. As *wazir*, Mir Jumla led the Golcondan conquest of the Wajra Karur mine in 1640. When the new Vijayanagara capital fell in 1646, Golconda established a short-lived alliance with Bijapur, dividing the empire between them.[99] The diamond mines in Karnataka mostly came into Golcondan hands, but according to Tavernier, Mir Jumla closed six of them.[100] The famous and ancient Currure diamond mine was also incorporated into Golconda around that time.[101]

The final fall of the Vijayanagara Empire at the hands of the Golconda and Bijapur sultanates did not lead to peace in the Deccan. Soon the sultans started a war with each other, while both were threatened by Mughal emperor Shah Jahan and his son Aurangzeb, at that time Mughal viceroy of the Deccan.[102] Mir Jumla decided to switch allegiance and joined the Mughal ranks. Aurangzeb used this as a pretext to invade Golconda on behalf of his father.[103] Shah Jahan accepted Golconda's tributary submission, forcing Aurangzeb to retreat physically from Golconda's territory. The viceroy shifted his focus to Bijapur, where the sultan had died in 1656, and laid siege to the capital. Hostilities came to a temporary halt when the emperor called off the siege. A new Mughal invasion of both sultanates took place in 1687. Aurangzeb, who had become emperor in

1658, was impressed with Mir Jumla and decided to make him governor in Bengal.[104] Mir Jumla died in 1663, still, or again, as administrator of the Kollur mine, even though he had given day-to-day management to a *Brahmin* named Bimmassie.[105] When Jean-Baptiste Tavernier was allowed to see part of Aurangzeb's jewellery collection in November 1665, he was shown a 'grand diamant' that had been given to Shah Jahan by Mir Jumla.[106] It originally weighed 787.5 carats, but after cutting its weight was reduced to 280 carats. Tavernier seems to have been somewhat confused, because in his description of the Kollur mine he made a reference to the same diamond as given by Mir Jumla to Aurangzeb.[107] It has been suggested that the stone that Tavernier was shown at Aurangzeb's court was certainly not the diamond given to Shah Jahan, so Mir Jumla must have given at least two different diamonds as gifts, and Tavernier seems to have conflated both gifts, to Shah Jahan and Aurangzeb, into one.[108]

Mughal administration of the diamond mines instead of local control did not bring about any structural change in mining management. Important posts were now given to Mughal officials rather than to locals and additional tributes needed to be paid to the emperor, but otherwise existing systems remained in place. Even if the Mughals had wanted to change the structure of diamond mining, they barely had the time, as their control of the western Deccan was quickly challenged by the Marathas, who conquered large parts of Mughal territory during the eighteenth century.[109] By the mid-eighteenth century, Maratha rule had expanded to include the diamond mines at Panna, Wairagarh and Chota Nagpur.[110] Chhatrasal's rule of Bundelkhand was challenged when a Mughal army captured him in 1729. He escaped and joined the Maratha forces he had asked for help. Their assistance led to Chhatrasal's successful reinstatement on the Bundelkhand throne, and Chhatrasal married the daughter of one of the most important Maratha generals, Baji Rao 1. After his death, Bundelkhand came under Maratha control.[111]

Mughal power was already crumbling and was further eroded by the invasion of Nader Shah, the shah of Persia, who defeated Mughal forces near Karnal in February 1739 and led his troops into Delhi, which was sacked. In the subsequent negotiations between the Mughal emperor and the shah, the latter obtained not only the Mughal's Peacock throne, richly ornated with gemstones, but the famous Koh-i-Noor diamond.[112] The story of the Koh-i-Noor ('Mountain of Light'), just like Tavernier's confusion about Mir Jumla's two diamonds, points to a more general problem of identifying famous diamonds: some were lost, others were recut and reshaped. Additionally, European historians have found it tempting to fill in gaps in the histories of famous diamonds with mentions of unidentified large stones. Mir Jumla's 900-carat gift to Shah Jahan has been said by Victorian writers to have been either Babur's diamond, a famously lost huge diamond that belonged to the first Mughal emperor, or the Koh-i-Noor (or both at the same time).[113] The Koh-i-Noor, an Indian diamond of almost 109 carats that is part of the British Crown Jewels, is the best-known example of the difficulty to trace a diamond back to its origins.[114] It was given by the last maharaja of the Sikh kingdom in the Punjab to Queen Victoria in 1849; subsequently, a false history for the stone was fabricated, which gave it its mythical status.[115]

In the south, the *nizam* of Hyderabad controlled the Bijapur mines and some of Golconda's mines. In the meantime, the British East India Company (EIC) had beaten its rivals to become the dominant European presence in India, and a lively Indo-European diamond trade had developed through the EIC. Establishing a direct commercial presence at the mining sites remained, however, impossible. In early 1766, when Robert Clive was governor of Bengal, he sent Thomas Motte to the diamond mines at Sambalpur in Odisha, near the junction of the Hebe and Mahanadi rivers, hoping he could set up a commercial arrangement with local vassals of the Marathas. Clive, who was also commander-in-chief of the EIC's own army, was probably inspired by the establishment of mining and trading monopolies designed to manage the Brazilian diamond supplies, as his friend Joseph Salvador, one of the foremost Jewish diamond merchants of his time, was at one time involved in the commercial monopoly for Brazilian diamonds.[116] Not much came of Clive's plain in Odisha: 'mountains abound with gold and diamonds but the natives are deterred from working the mines by their indolence and fear of the Mahrattas, to whom their riches would only point them out as a more desirable prey.'[117]

The Anglo-Indian Diamond Trade

Thomas Motte's failed mission marked the endpoint of a century of English domination in the Indo-European diamond trade, exemplified by the East India Company's control over the maritime trade and transport of rough Indian diamonds. While individual European traders always remained active in India, their importance was quickly overshadowed by the rise of the several East India companies. The Portuguese had been the first European maritime power to establish commerce with the Indian subcontinent, developing an interest in diamonds that led to the establishment of Lisbon as a diamond centre, from where diamonds were exported to Antwerp. The Portuguese *Carreira da Índia* ('India run') was dominant during the sixteenth century, and often the European travellers, merchants and diamond workers who went to India did so on a Portuguese ship. The Portuguese managed to develop their trading networks through the diaspora that followed the mass conversion and expulsions of Jews from Spain, and later Portugal, after 1492. James Boyajian has shown that the New Christians – Jews who had been forced to convert but often still adhered to their old religion – were not only active in trade routes linking Lisbon with diamond centres further north in Europe, but had established themselves in India, where they developed further trade connections.[118] Balthasar da Vega, for instance, was a Portuguese merchant in Goa from 1618. He supplied diamonds to business correspondents in Lisbon and Antwerp, but was arrested in 1644 by the Inquisition on the grounds of being a 'Judaizer'.[119] Networks like these were the backbone of the commercial axis between Goa, Lisbon and Antwerp, but with the persecution by the Inquisition, and the expansion of the Dutch and English East India companies, these networks were gradually destroyed.[120]

The Dutch East India Company (voc) had been established in 1602 and monopolized trade between Asia and the United Provinces.[121] While these early Dutch efforts threatened the Portuguese, the voc was never able to take Portugal's place in the Asian diamond trade. They did manage to establish a monopoly in spice trade, brutally slaughtering and enslaving local populations on the way. In 1608 the Dutch set up a trading factory in Masulipatnam (now known as Machilipatnam), wresting the Portuguese out of trade there. The city was the main port of the Golconda kingdom, and served as a trading centre for textiles, indigo and diamonds, coming straight from the Golconda mines.[122] The English followed suit a decade later, and Machilipatnam became an important outlet for English private trade in India, including the shipment of diamonds.[123] Both the English and Dutch East India companies quickly tried to put a stop to private trade. Efforts by the voc to negotiate sales directly at the mines mostly

failed, and in 1631 all private trade by the company's servants was forbidden, 22 years after the EIC had issued similar prohibitions.[124] In 1643
the Dutch were able to secure a contract with the king of Karnataka,
guaranteeing direct trade with the diamond mines near Gingi, a town
in present-day Tamil Nadu. It was agreed that the English, Portuguese
and Danes could not trade there, and that the local inhabitants were to
sell diamonds only to the VOC. In return for this favour, the Dutch had
to limit their sales of elephants and horses to the king alone.[125] Despite
these Dutch endeavours, the VOC never managed to replace the supply
channel through Goa and Lisbon, and most rough diamonds that arrived
in the Low Countries had come that way.[126]

By the 1660s it had become clear that neither the Portuguese *Carreira*
nor the Dutch VOC were able to resist the expansion of the EIC.[127]
Portuguese diamond exports through Goa had fallen from 2 million cruzados to 3,000 cruzados, while Dutch diamond exports out of India had
become insignificant.[128] Since Portugal's independence from Spain in
1640, the English had forged a strong commercial relationship with the
Iberian kingdom, solidified by the marriage between Catarina, daughter
of the Portuguese king D. João IV and King Charles II of England in 1661.
When Catarina arrived in London the next year, a New Christian trader
named Duarte Silva accompanied her, soon followed by groups of other
converted Jews, all escaping the Catholic Inquisition.[129] Portuguese Jews
and New Christians had been instrumental in Portugal's diamond trade
out of Goa, but their insertion in Portugal-oriented trade networks was
rendered difficult by the Inquisition. When Oliver Cromwell decided
to allow for the resettlement of Jews in England in 1655, several Jewish
and New Christian diamond traders took the opportunity to incorporate
their activities into the developing structures of the Anglo-Indian diamond trade. It was a move that generally pleased the government, as the
resettlement decision was partially driven by commercial motives.[130] One
of the main reasons why Sephardic Jews played such an important role
in the diamond trade from a very early stage onwards might be that they
were lucky enough to be in the right place at the right time twice; first
in Portugal when that country held a grip over European imports with
India, but forced out of that country later and re-emerging in London
(and Amsterdam) around the time that the East India Company's trade
policies opened up great possibilities for diamond traders.

The huge decline in Portuguese diamond exports through Goa can largely be attributed to the growing reluctance of New Christians to use a Portuguese channel, and the English used this to their advantage by providing this group of traders with an alternative commercial channel. While the EIC's general policies were often directed at monopolizing the trade between Europe and India, the commerce in Asian diamonds was gradually opened for private traders, who were directed to ship diamonds on the Company's ships. Even foreigners could participate in the trade, but they were subjected to higher duty tariffs.[131] In 1664 the Company allowed Jewish merchants to ship bullion from London to Goa to get a return in diamonds.[132] These efforts led to a rapid expansion of England's diamond trade. In 1669 rough diamonds that had been purchased for £17,082 were sent from India to London, 40 per cent of which were consigned to Jewish merchants. In 1677, 88 merchants in London received rough diamonds that had cost £83,829. Almost half of that value had been spent by six businesses who spent over £2,000 each, two of these being Jewish firms.[133]

The abolition of the obligation that all diamond transactions in India had to be executed by EIC officials led to a growing practice in which London-based firms, or firms with good connections in the capital, sent agents to India to participate in the diamond trade there on their behalf.[134] Two of the most famous merchants who spent time in India were the brothers Jean (1643–1713) and Daniel (1649–1709) Chardin. Born to a successful Parisian jeweller, the Chardin brothers became jewellers themselves, and both men travelled to Asia for professional reasons. In 1664 Jean went for the first time to Persia, selling jewels at the Safavid court. Three years later he visited diamond mines in Mughal India. He went back to Paris in 1670, but left again the following year in the company of a fellow jeweller from Lyon named Antoine Raisin, an acquaintance of Jean-Baptiste Tavernier. The two men stayed in India for four years, and Chardin learnt the Persian language. One of the reasons Chardin had decided to leave Catholic France was that, as a Huguenot, he risked religious persecution from the Catholics.[135] When he decided to return to Europe in 1679, he retired from being an itinerant merchant and settled in London, devoting himself to writing a manuscript about his travels in Persia and India. Eventually he was knighted (as Sir John Chardin) and became a member of the Royal Society.[136] It was now his brother

Daniel's turn to live in India and continue the family business from Fort St George, the English trade settlement now part of present-day Chennai, formerly known as Madras (illus. 9). Even though Jean had retired from the life of an itinerant jeweller, he had not quit business entirely, and with Jean in London and Daniel in Fort St George, the two brothers entered a partnership with Sephardic Jewish brothers Salvador Rodrigues (also known as Isaac Salvador) and Francis Salvador the elder, the former joining Daniel in India and the latter staying in London. The partnership lasted until Salvador Rodrigues decamped with the partnership's money to begin a new life near a diamond mine, where he learnt the local Telugu language, married a local woman and dressed in the local fashion.[137]

One of the first English private merchants to settle in India was Nathaniel Cholmley, a London diamond trader. In 1667 he went to diamond mines in the Golconda sultanate to purchase diamonds for himself and his brother John. He resided in Machilipatnam between 1662 and 1675 and spent five years at Fort St George, which had replaced Surat as England's most important trading post, before returning to England in 1682. The Cholmley brothers worked with the official EIC regulations and sold precious stones in Europe through an extensive network that reached buyers in England, Flanders, the United Provinces and France.[138] Other merchants followed in the footsteps of the Chardin and Cholmley brothers, leading to the establishment of the English corporation of Chennai in 1687, ruled by a mayor and twelve aldermen. Amidst their ranks, one could find several Jews, but also two Portuguese Roman Catholics and three Hindu traders.[139]

In the last decades of the seventeenth century, it was clear that the permissiveness of the EIC towards private merchants dealing in Indian diamonds had greatly contributed to the success of a number of Christian and Jewish London-based diamond firms. With expanding private profits came a renewed Company interest in monopolization, and in 1679 the Company directorate discussed the possibilities of reinstating restrictions on private diamond trade.[140] It was concluded that such an overhaul of the regulations was neither feasible nor desirable, and subsequently, private trade efforts were encouraged rather than restricted. A resolution published in 1682 set import duties of 4 per cent for English traders bringing rough diamonds on EIC ships from India, and 8 per cent for foreigners. These rates were almost immediately changed to 3 per cent for Company stockholders and 6 per cent for other traders, a measure that not only lowered import duties but abolished the difference between Englishmen and foreigners, a distinction that was a thorn in the side of the Jewish merchants, who were unable to become English subjects at the time.[141] The last differences between merchants holding EIC stock and those who did not were removed in 1687, when it was decided that the higher import rate for the latter was abolished. Additionally, the rate to be paid on the consignment of silver and gold to India, which was used there to purchase diamonds, was set at 2 per cent for stockholders and non-stockholders alike.[142]

One of the main architects of the open trade regime was one of the Company's foremost directors, Sir Josiah Child (1630–1699), a man who favoured the foundation of 'a Dutch government amongst the English in India', by which he meant an administration based on religious tolerance to foster trade.[143] The advance of English trade had also been one of the motives for the resettlement of Jews in 1655, as described by Child in his *New Discourse on Trade*, originally published in 1693: 'they are like to encrease trade, and the more they do that, the better it is for the Kingdom in general.'[144] While the evolution of rules regulating the Anglo-Indian diamond trade seemed to have reached an endpoint in 1687, the Glorious Revolution that occurred the following year was the start of three decades of difficult relationships between the government, the EIC and private traders, a period that also saw the temporary establishment of a second East India Company, challenging the EIC's Indian monopoly.[145]

The situation finally stabilized in 1718, with the establishment of a system of licensed private trade. Merchants who wished to purchase rough diamonds sent silver, jewels, ostrich feathers, polished precious stones and Mediterranean coral to India, and their agents or correspondents there sent the required commodity back in return.[146] Following seventeenth-century mercantilist ideas, it was forbidden to export domestic bullion out of England, so the silver sent to India could not be English. The export of foreign coin, however, was allowed, leading to a transnational currency trade in which the Jewish diaspora played an important role.[147] Coral was fished in Mediterranean waters, and the trade in it was controlled by diaspora merchants, often Jews but also Armenians, who had established themselves in Livorno.[148] The city was declared a free port by the Grand Duke of Tuscany at the end of the sixteenth century in an

9 Fort St George, India, 1754.

effort to attract foreign merchants and make commerce flourish.[149] After 1725 the volume of coral outweighed the amount of silver that diamond merchants sent on EIC ships to Fort St George.[150]

While the particular exchange between Indian diamonds and European coral, jewellery and silver only came to full fruition in the context of the eighteenth-century Anglo-Indian diamond trade, barter was already a well-established manner by which Europeans obtained Indian diamonds. Diamond trader Jacques de Coutre, for instance, wrote in his journal that during the late sixteenth and early seventeenth centuries Portuguese ships arriving in Goa brought jewels, rubies, emeralds and pearls from New Spain and coral from the Mediterranean, commodities used to purchase rough diamonds.[151] Throughout the eighteenth century the English settlement of Fort St George was the central point in this trade, although diamond barter trade also took place in Bengal, Mumbai, Kolkata and Surat.[152]

It was at these places that the two flows necessary for business met: European commodities arrived on EIC ships, while rough diamonds came from the mines further inland through local trade networks. Once European traders or their agents obtained the rough diamonds they could exchange for their silver, coral and jewels; these were registered at Fort St George and put in purses made of leather ('bulses'), then transported aboard EIC ships and placed in the care of a captain for a fee of 1.4 per cent of the diamonds' worth. In London these purses were transported to India House, and the law prescribed that they were to be sold at a public sale. Gedalia Yogev has shown that the public auction of privately obtained diamonds was 'nothing but a farce', in order to ensure formal compliance with the law. In reality, they were given to the traders they had been consigned to.[153] After the rough diamonds made their way to their rightful owners, they could be sold to wholesale traders in London or abroad, after which the diamonds were cut and polished. Polished stones could be set in jewellery that had been commissioned by the consumer, or they could be put up for sale by jewellers specializing in finished gemstones.[154]

The establishment of the EIC-dominated maritime route, the involvement of the Sephardic diaspora and the reliance on barter were perhaps the three most important characteristics of the officially regulated Indo-European diamond trade between the end of the seventeenth century and the middle of the eighteenth. It ensured the growing importance of London and Amsterdam as diamond centres at the expense of Lisbon and Antwerp, but it also resulted in a higher interconnectedness of different international networks of trade, resulting in a growing cross-cultural trade environment that connected the Indian Ocean with the Mediterranean and the northwest European commercial cities, and later even with the Atlantic system, after the discovery of diamonds in Brazil. Several of these interconnecting networks had been based on shared kinship or religion and were often part of a diaspora, with Jewish traders as the prime example of this. Because of the historical involvement of Portugal in India and the expulsion of Jews from Portugal after 1492, the Jewish merchants involved in the diamond trade were Sephardim, meaning they had Iberian roots, but over time, more and more Eastern European Jews (Ashkenazim) came to be involved in the diamond trade as well, which sometimes sparked fierce competition between traders belonging to these different groups.[155] The reliance on kinship and religious connections was not strange in an early modern business world that operated to an important degree on the basis of trust, but this does not mean that intercultural partnerships involving Protestants, Jews, Huguenots, Catholics and Armenians were rare. In recent decades, historians have come to look at the mechanisms that rendered such intercultural business possible in the absence of an international legal framework that could punish cheaters.[156]

A good example is the relationship between the Jewish diamond trader Marcus Moses, whose son Levy went to India to act as his agent, and Richard Hoare, the founder of C. Hoare & Co., the oldest privately owned British bank that still exists today.[157] In the early eighteenth century both men did regular diamond business together as partners, selling Indian gems in Amsterdam and Hamburg.[158] They acquired at least part of these stones through Levy Moses, who had associated himself in Fort St George with a Christian trader named George Jones, and both men not only supplied Marcus Moses but worked on commission for others.[159] In the second half of the eighteenth century the Hoare firm was involved in diamond transactions on behalf of a partnership between the Christian firm of William and Charles Turner and the Indian merchant Gocaul Tervady, who sent rough diamonds to London to be sold for their joint account.[160] The traces we have of such partnerships are mostly found in bills of lading, accounts or merchant letters. Only on occasion were such cross-cultural partnerships solidified in written contracts, as happened in 1721, when a contract was drafted between Robert Nightingale and George Drake on the one side and Anthony da Costa and Joseph Osorio on the other. Osorio and da Costa were Sephardic Jews, the former living in Amsterdam and the latter in London, and all parties agreed to begin a partnership in the trade in diamonds, for which Nightingale and da Costa were to move to Fort St George.[161]

The historical trajectory of the famous Orlov Diamond (illus. 10) is a good example of the cross-cultural nature of many diamond transactions. The stone, cut in the typically asymmetrical Indian way to avoid loss of mass, weighs 194.75 carats and is preserved in the Diamond Fund in Moscow.[162] It was mined in Golconda and possibly stolen by a French military deserter in the middle of the eighteenth century. It passed through the hands of an English captain and Jewish, Armenian and Iranian traders before the Russian Count Grigory Orlov bought it in Amsterdam and gifted it to the woman who had taken him as her lover, Tsarina Catharine the Great. In 1774 it was set in a sceptre that belonged to her.[163]

The success of cross-cultural diamond partnerships connected to the EIC was reflected in the rise to prominence of several outsiders in London's high society. The aforementioned Jean Chardin became a well-known intellectual, but others rose in society's ranks as well. As a very successful Sephardic trader who came from a family of diamond

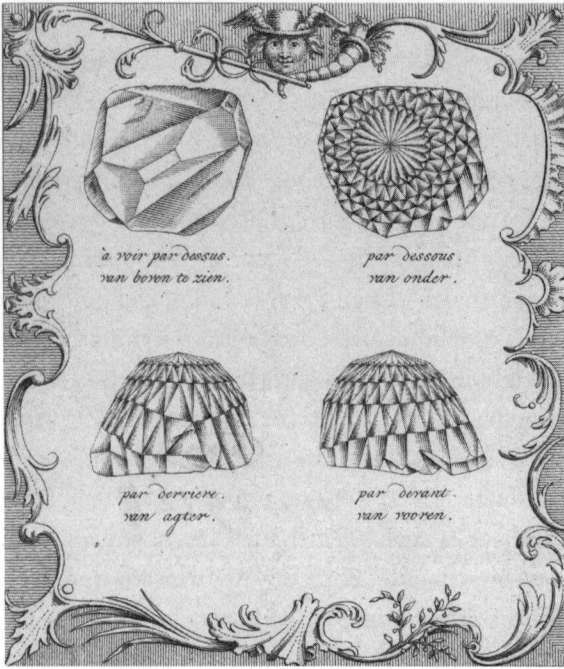

10 The Orlov
Diamond, 1767.

merchants, Joseph Salvador became quite well known in his time, advocating Jewish citizenship and adopting an elite lifestyle that brought him to the attention of the newspaper gossip columns for his affairs with such notorious women as Kitty Fisher, one of London's best-known courtesans.[164] This rise in society brought men such as Salvador powerful allies with concrete links to English policy-making and the EIC. Salvador was a personal friend of Robert Clive and had advised him on colonial policies when Clive was part of an internal power struggle within the Company.[165] Such friendships were not only beneficial to the merchants but advantageous in a reciprocal manner, an essential characteristic of the early modern notion of friendship, and it benefited the officials as much as the merchants.[166]

One consequence of Josiah Child's open policies was the growing involvement of EIC governors in private trade, first as intermediaries, but later also on their own account. Their success often depended on a successful association with well-established diamond merchants. Some of these governors became very wealthy through diamonds. A good example is Elihu Yale, who was president of the English settlement in Chennai from August 1684 to January 1685, and between July 1687 and October

1692. He traded in enslaved Africans and diamonds, and amassed a large fortune, part of which he used to become the first benefactor of Yale University.[167] Another famous official was Thomas 'Diamond' Pitt, president of Chennai between July 1698 and September 1709. Pitt became most famous for his purchase of a large uncut diamond of 426 carats found at the Kollur mine in 1698. It was cut in England, and the largest stone, the Regent, weighing 140 carats, was sold to the French regent Philippe d'Orléans in 1717.[168]

Over time, diamonds became popular as a means by which Indian nabobs such as Yale, Pitt and Robert Clive remitted the fortunes they amassed in India back to England, something that put an enormous strain on the Indo-European diamond trade.[169] The activities of the nabobs who had returned, their involvement in the diamond trade and the use they made of diamonds to buy a seat in Parliament were often negatively judged by English public opinion, a judgement extended to the higher echelons of government. Satirical prints such as 'The Diamond Eaters' (illus. 11) depicted this. Warren Hastings, the first governor-general, is seen pouring diamonds ('Indian plunder') into the mouths of Baron Thurlow, an ally of Hastings, shown with devilish hands, King George III and Queen Charlotte. This perception was further fuelled by existing negative stereotypes of Oriental luxury goods as decadent. Existing socio-cultural ideas at the time labelled this decadent consumption of riches as feminine, and it is probably not a coincidence that the only face that is fully visible on the satirical print is that of a woman, the queen, with her mouth wide open.[170]

The growing use made by the nabobs of diamonds, as well as a still expanding trade in spite of the competition from Brazilian diamonds, culminated in soaring diamond exports to England in 1767, when the total value of imported Indian diamonds equalled £300,000. It was to be a last high point of the Anglo-Indian diamond trade, which started to collapse that same decade to drop to a negligible volume by the 1790s.[171] This decline can also be observed by the diminishing participation of Jewish traders; before 1767 their share in diamond imports almost never fell below 50 per cent, but during the 1780s it fell to 10 per cent.[172] This decline was related to the emergence of Brazilian diamonds and the gradual exhaustion of several of India's diamond mines. While Brazilian diamonds increasingly replaced Indian stones in Europe, some European traders tried to diversify by attempting to cater for a growing Indian

THE DIAMOND EATERS,
HORRID MONSTERS!

11 'The Diamond
Eaters, Horrid
Monsters!', 1788,
satirical print.

consumer market, but these efforts failed. Others tried to set up business catering for the nabobs' needs. In 1777 a man named Jacob Barnet went to Fort St George as a representative of the Jewish diamond firm of Moses Franks. He quickly found that business worked better in the north, and between 1778 and 1785 he stayed in Benares, near the diamond mines of Patna. There he was offering to assist in remittances of either diamonds or diamond-backed bills of exchange to anyone interested in transferring their monies to England.[173] The year Barnet left Benares, a well-known Ashkenazi diamond trader named Israel Levin Salomons, who was also known as Yehiel Prager, attempted to establish a monopoly in Anglo-Indian diamond trade, but his project failed.[174] The golden era of Indian diamonds had come to an end.

The World Outside the East India Company

Before Brazilian competition changed the whole world of diamonds, the EIC-controlled commercial system was the main channel by which Indian diamonds reached Europe between the mid-seventeenth and mid-eighteenth centuries, but this should not obscure the fact that a great deal of the trade in precious stones took place within Asia, without any European interference, and overland, using routes that remained outside the colonial grip of the EIC. In addition, many merchants did at least part of their business outside legal frameworks. Smuggling and clandestine transactions are hard to trace, but sometimes we can find indications on the widespread nature of both, for instance in the substantial level of non-EIC trade that was taking place on the Coromandel Coast, which included business in diamonds.[175] The EIC and its European competitors always had to face alternative networks. They even needed them, as Europeans were officially not allowed to do business at the Indian mining sites. While some traders, such as Jean-Baptiste Tavernier, were allowed to visit, and might even have conducted some illicit business affairs, as a general rule Western traders had to buy their diamonds in Surat, Goa or other trading centres, often from Jain or Hindu *banyans* originating from the princely state of Gujarat, who acted as middlemen between Indian producers and European buyers.[176]

Indian traders were part of networks that connected the mines with the main trading centres, and some of the more powerful ones even extended abroad. Some of the more successful Indian merchants made a name of their own as wealthy entrepreneurs. Men such as Shantidas Zaveri (*c.* 1585–1659) and Virji Vora (*c.* 1590–*c.* 1670) became very wealthy and famous. The former was a Jain businessman who resided in the jeweller's quarter of Ahmedabad and relied on a commercial network extending to the sapphire and ruby mines in Pegu (present-day Myanmar). He designed his own jewellery, and the Mughal emperor was an important client. Vora dealt in spices, coral and diamonds, and his network connected Ahmedabad, Agra, the Deccan and Golconda. The English considered him to be one of the richest merchants in the world.[177] The direct connection of certain groups of Indian merchants with the mines made Europeans resort to ingenious ways in order to try to get rough diamonds without middlemen, attempting to evade trading restrictions.

French traveller Robert Challe, who was in Surat in January 1691, recorded stories about Jesuits involved in the diamond trade. He wrote that some of them 'dressed themselves as Banyans, spoke their language as well as them, live and eat with them, and like them, participate in their ceremonies. In a word, those who don't know, take them for true Banyans.'[178] Challe also described a method invented by Jesuits of smuggling diamonds by replacing the wooden heels of their Portuguese shoes with special hollow iron heels manufactured in Europe.[179]

In spite of the general prohibition for Europeans to go to the Indian diamond mines, a handful wrote about their visits to several of them. Some of the travel journals these men have left behind provide great insight into how locals traded diamonds at these sites. While Jean-Baptiste Tavernier is without doubt the most famous of these European eyewitnesses, he was not alone. The Dutch VOC merchant Willem den Dorst, for instance, described diamond trade taking place at a mine in Karnataka at the end of 1615. Merchants from Visapur, Goa and other cities sent their agents there to buy rough stones, some weighing as much as 400 carats, partially in exchange for jewellery and pearls.[180] Henry Howard, author of a report on Indian diamond mines sixty years later, observed that miners and merchants in Visapur were Indian non-Muslims. Miners often belonged to the local Telugu, while the merchants were Gujarati, 'who for some generations have forsaken their own country to take up the trade', maintaining commercial networks that connected Goa, Surat and Agra with the Golconda and Visapur sultanates.[181] European presence at the mining sites might have remained anecdotal, but an impressive number of Indian traders migrated to diamondiferous regions. A Dutch description from 1663 observed that *banyans* lived in four of the fourteen villages surrounding the Kollur mine, and stated that between three and four thousand *banyan* families, or 90 per cent of the total population, left due to mismanagement of the mine, but returned after a *Brahmin* was made head of the mine.[182]

One of the best descriptions of diamond trading comes from Tavernier, who witnessed transactions at the Raolconda mine in Karnataka. The masters of the mine showed diamonds for sale to merchants every morning between ten and eleven o'clock. An interested trader had to conclude the deal quickly and issue some sort of promissory note, against which the seller could then collect a bill of exchange payable in Surat, Agra or somewhere else from the *sharaf* (moneylender). Children of merchants, fifteen or sixteen years old, gathered in the morning under a big tree, all carrying a little bag of weights and a purse with golden pagodas, while they waited for sellers. At the end of the day, the children put all their purchases together, sorted the stones and sold them to merchants.[183] Hindus and Muslims had a specific manner of concluding their diamond deals. Buyer and seller squatted opposite one another. One of the two unbuckled his belt, then the seller took the right hand of the buyer, and covered it with his own hand and the end of the belt. If he covered the whole hand, he indicated the number 1,000. Handshakes and gestures with fingers further led to a final price, which was thus negotiated without talking or making eye contact (illus. 12). According to Tavernier, no one witnessing the deal could tell the final price, except buyer and seller.[184] Physical gestures, rather than written or spoken words, remain an essential part of the trade in diamonds (illus. 13). They are testimony to the nature of diamond trade, often perceived as informal, secretive and in a world of its own.

After business was concluded at the mines, *banyan* networks ensured that part of the rough diamonds became available to outside buyers in the main commercial centres of Surat, Goa and Chennai. Europeans were never able to control the flow of rough diamonds that came out of the mines. Some went to the Mughal rulers, others to local princes and maharajahs, who were entitled to the best stones found on their territories. Others were sold within Asian networks, finding Asian buyers. Of those diamonds that did eventually end up on European markets, not all were transported aboard EIC ships. The Company's maritime route and surrounding regulations had effectively beaten the competition of other European India companies, but several of the ancient and medieval land routes connecting India with Europe still remained active, and different trading networks flourished because of it.[185] On several occasions, officials of the European East India trading companies wrote about the difficulty in overcoming the competition from traditional overland trade circuits. In a letter written in 1626, for instance, a Dutch official complained of the traders coming from Aceh, Gujarat and other Asian localities who bought almost all the diamonds.[186]

Perhaps the most important overland network that persisted, in spite of growing European maritime competition, was that of the Armenian trading families established in New Julfa, near Isfahan.[187] An Armenian trading community had been resettled there by the Persian shah Abbas the Great in 1606, after he had defeated the Ottomans in a battle for hegemony of parts of Armenia. The shah was hoping the Armenians' business experience would benefit the trade in Persian raw silk.[188] While the full extent of the Armenian diamond trading networks remains unknown, it was clear to their European competitors that they were a commercial force to be reckoned with. Following the establishment of New Julfa, the Armenian diaspora had established itself in Izmir, Livorno, Venice, Marseilles and later also Amsterdam and London.[189] These networks also managed to build up an influential commercial presence in Mughal India. Even though some Armenians had been established there prior to the seventeenth century, it was during the arrival of the European East India companies that larger groups of Armenian traders settled in Surat and Chennai.[190] The extent of these networks enabled them to play an important role in the barter trade in diamonds and coral that was becoming increasingly important as a consequence of the rising influence of the EIC.[191]

The networks that had originated in New Julfa relied strongly on kinship, perhaps even more so than comparable diaspora networks such as that of the Sephardic diamond traders. Jean Chardin found that the Armenians were particularly difficult to get into commerce with, as he wrote to his brother: 'the defiant spirit of the Armenians does not allow them to put their affairs into the hands of anyone.'[192] As this came from the pen of a man who was personally acquainted with several Armenian traders and had engaged in business with them, this statement must be

12 Eastern diamond merchants bargaining, 1859.

13 A diamond transaction confirmed by a handshake, Antwerp.

taken seriously, but on the other hand, a reliance on kinship and shared religious ties was by no means an Armenian exclusivity. Additionally, Armenian merchants, like many others, did engage in cross-cultural relationships with Jewish, Christian and Mughal traders. At the same time that Daniel Chardin was active in Asia, an Armenian trader referred to as Rupli set up a business in precious stones together with Tavernier. Business went well to the extent that Rupli wished to travel to France to sell his precious stones there. In 1671 he arrived in Nîmes, where he was duped by the customs officer who also worked for the tax collectors there. The man confiscated Rupli's diamonds and, in spite of a trial in Montpellier, the tax collectors refused to address Rupli's complaints. The case was only resolved after Rupli managed to obtain an audience with King Louis xiv at Versailles. There the Armenian was assisted by a member of the old gentry who explained the case in such a clownesque manner that the king had to laugh. The discourse convinced him, though, and after a trial the tax collector was sent to prison for life. Rupli also received reimbursement for the confiscated diamonds to the value of 450,000 livres, and an additional 120,000 livres for expenses.[193] Experiences such as Rupli's must not have encouraged the Armenian trading families to associate themselves more often with European traders, and Challe described Rupli as 'tired and repelled of so much manoeuvring, unknown in his country'.[194]

Rupli's ability to meet in person with Louis xiv is telling of the success enjoyed by Armenian diamond merchants. In the middle of the seventeenth century, with the battle for control over diamond supply routes into Europe still open, in spite of the growing dominance of the eic, the Armenians were doing well. In 1658 representatives of the voc had stopped buying diamonds altogether, because large purchases by Armenian traders had raised the price by 40 per cent.[195] Thirty-five years later, Jean Chardin wrote to his brother in India that Armenian traders sending their goods from Surat to London had obtained very good profits, with a return of 90 to 100 per cent on diamonds they remitted. It made Chardin write in admiration to his brother that 'in comparison to them, we are not merchants.'[196]

The importance of the Armenian trade networks was such that the emerging eic was not able to put them out of competition. Even more, the eic's agents in India were often in need of loans, which were at times granted by Armenian traders. In 1690 Jean Chardin, who acted as a go-between in dealings between Armenian merchants and the eic, informed the Company that the Armenian community of Venice was willing to provide the eic's office in Surat with letters of credit amounting to a total of 400,000 rupees.[197] Commercial friction between the two parties had started to grow ever since the eic began attempting to trade in Safavid Persia in 1615 and was only settled with the signing of an agreement between the Armenian nation and the eic in 1688. A man named Coja Panous Calendar signed the agreement on the Armenians' behalf. This specified that the Armenians would be allowed to settle in India and ship their merchandise by means of the eic, in exchange for which they had to abandon the overland route from India to Europe.[198]

Sure enough, Armenian names started to appear more often in the lists of requests for trade and settlement that were registered in the Company's books from that moment on. Calendar himself figures among them, and several transactions involving him were registered in the Company's books, but never in diamonds.[199] In 1695 Coja Israel Sarhad and Baugher Aghamell were permitted to go to the Bay of Bengal on board a Company frigate, carrying two chests with 'wearing apparell, cheese and other eatable provisions'.[200] Armenian names hardly ever appear in the eic books registering merchants' official requests to participate in the Company-regulated diamond trade. Part of this absence can be explained by the fact that sometimes the Company's books refer to commercial requests without specifying the commodities. A 1691 entry mentioned '£4000 to be paid to the Armenians under account of their goods sold at the Company's Candle'.[201] A rare exception of an Armenian trader transporting gemstones on an EIC ship was a certain Coja Sukia D'Oulat, who brought £1,161 worth of rubies from the Bay of Bengal in 1733, but specific indications of diamond transactions are nowhere to be found.[202] The absence of Armenian requests to ship diamonds on EIC ships did not mean that they had given up on trading diamonds, but rather that they were not adhering to the agreement made with the EIC.

Historical evidence shows that during the eighteenth century Armenians continued to do business in diamonds and coral using the overland route. One of the foremost interests involved in this trade was the Sceriman family, with roots in Old Julfa but among those who settled in New Julfa in 1604.[203] Later family members settled in Venice and Livorno, from where they dealt in gemstones and coral, but were also active in banking.[204] In the first decades of the eighteenth century, David Sceriman was considered the richest Armenian in Livorno.[205] Part of this wealth derived from clandestine diamond trading, and to that purpose Sceriman sometimes sent agents working for him to India. We know of one such particular enterprise because it took a wrong turn. In 1725 David Sceriman employed three Armenians to travel from London to Surat and Fort St George (illus. 9), where they were to purchase rough diamonds coming from the Golconda mines. They were given cash and pearls to pay for the merchandise, and they were supposed to travel from Italy to London by way of Marseilles, Lyon and Paris.[206] Two of the men came from Venice and were known to the family there, while the third, Giovan Battista Giamal, was part of Livorno's Armenian community and a personal acquaintance of David Sceriman. And yet it was Giamal who took the initiative to deceive his employer, when he decided to buy silk in London, for which he paid by drawing a bill of exchange on Sceriman. The latter, who had not authorized such a move, fired Giamal from the job and the two other men embarked for Surat without him, with the help of the Sephardic firm of Jacob and Abraham Franco.[207] Apart from Giamal's actions, the voyage seems to have been a success and the two agents returned with rough diamonds that were to be cut in workshops with which Sceriman had made special arrangements.[208]

One of the agents, Pietro di Saffar Nuri, travelled more often to India on Sceriman's behalf, on one occasion even bringing back diamonds leading to a 600 per cent profit, but Giamal was no longer considered.[209] The relationship between him and Sceriman had turned sour, and because the latter refused to pay Giamal for any services, let alone the bill of exchange used for the silk, the agent decided to take his employer to the maritime court in Pisa. Sceriman was eventually condemned to pay a sum to Giamal, but insisted he would appeal, and at the same time wrote to the Francos in London to ask them not to furnish Giamal with any money.[210]

This was not the first time that David Sceriman and his affairs had come under legal scrutiny. Several years earlier, in 1719, David and Peter Sceriman had to defend themselves against claims made by an Indian merchant named Zorab di Alucan on a transaction made ten years earlier, in which Alucan had brought merchandise belonging to the Scerimans with him from Goa to Lisbon.[211] Alucan claimed he was still owed money by the Armenians, and the affair was also settled in court.[212]

Armenian involvement in the diamond trade with India shows a few things. First, even though there was a tendency to engage in business with fellow Armenians, a characteristic shared by other groups in the diamond trade such as Jews, Christians or Gujarati, there were cross-cultural partnerships as well, and they were important. Second, these partnerships and networks made use of the institutions put in place by the EIC to transport their merchandise to India and to get rough gemstones in return. But at the same time, legal, semi-legal and illegal trade in which these networks were involved also challenged the business operations of the EIC, something of which the Company was well aware, but was only able to react against in a limited manner.

Gems on an Island

While India was for a long time the world's best-known and largest supplier of Asian diamonds, it was not the only source. Diamonds were also found on the Indonesian island of Borneo, although it remains unclear from what time onwards knowledge of these diamond fields existed. The idea of a diamondiferous island in Asia goes back at least to the Middle Ages and can be found in both Arab and European sources. Al-Masudi, who wrote about gems in the first decades of the tenth century, thought that diamonds came from more places than India alone, and he referred to precious stones sparkling inside a mountain on 'Serandib' (Sri Lanka).[213] The mountain on Sri Lanka that Al-Masudi referred to can be identified as Sri Pada, located in the southwestern part of Sri Lanka, which plays an important role in Buddhism, Hinduism, Islam and Christianity. For Christians and Muslims, the mountain's name is Adam's Peak, as some considered it to be the place where Adam and Eve retreated to after they had been expelled from the Garden of Eden.[214] The Italian Franciscan friar Odoric of Pordenone (1286–1331) compiled various manuscripts in which he narrated his travels in Asia. He seems to have visited Sri Lanka personally and confirmed the existence of diamonds there. While he dispelled the myth of a lake on the mountain that was said to contain the tears of Adam and Eve, he did claim to have seen diamonds and leeches, which he identified as snakes, in the water. Allegedly, these diamonds had grown in Adam's footsteps.[215]

It has been known for a long time that the stories about diamonds near or on Adam's Peak contain no truth, although room for doubt remained as late as the nineteenth century. In 1860, however, James Emerson Tennent, former British colonial secretary on what was then called Ceylon, remarked in his account of the island that:

> Caswini and some of the Arabian geographers assert that the diamond is found at Adam's Peak; but this is improbable, as there is no formation here resembling the *cascalho* [diamondiferous earth] of Brazil or the diamond conglomerate of Golconda. If diamonds were offered for sale in Ceylon, in the time of the Arab navigators, they must have been brought thither from India.[216]

Tennent's comment confirms that ill-informed stories about mythical and ancient sites that contain diamonds might indeed have spread through the trade networks that brought rough diamonds from faraway lands.

Even though Sri Lanka does not contain diamonds, the stories of an Asian island that did are relevant for two reasons. First, it is interesting to see how the island discourse became conflated with the narrative of the Diamond Valley discussed earlier. As early as the tenth century, a Persian sea captain named Ibn Shahriyar made mention of the existence of a snake-infested diamondiferous valley near Adam's Peak. Odoric narrated how adventurers threw meat down in the valley, to which diamonds as large as chickpeas stuck. The meat was then picked up by vultures, who carried the diamonds to higher ground, where they were left for picking, a narrative identical to the story of the Diamond Valley.[217] The story of Sinbad the Sailor describes that, when Sinbad was stranded on the island, he met with the king of Serandib (Sri Lanka) and even visited Adam's Peak.[218] Al-Biruni, who falsely believed in the presence of diamonds on Sri Lanka, wrote explicitly that stories about the Diamond Valley were false, wherever they were located.[219] Second, old island stories are relevant because they got one thing right: the idea that there was an Asian island that contained rich diamond deposits. But that island was not located off the coast of India, and it was not Sri Lanka. The only known island where diamonds are found is Borneo, located a bit less than 4,000 km to the east of Sri Lanka, in the Indonesian archipelago.

It is not known when diamonds started to be extracted from Borneo. Some evidence suggests that it might have begun as early as 600 CE, but certain scholars claim that diamond mining in Borneo only started as late as the sixteenth century, which makes all historical narratives about diamonds on an island harder to explain.[220] Their assessment cannot be correct, as a long historical connection between Bornean diamonds and China can be traced back to at least the Sung period (960–1279). Chinese pottery from that period has been found in Borneo's diamond region. Tavernier reported that Borneo's local rulers were paying part of their tribute to the Chinese emperor in diamonds.[221] The chronology becomes clearer when European colonizers started to become interested in the wealth that several of the Indonesian islands had to offer. The Dutch started to trade in Bornean diamonds from the early seventeenth century onwards, but by that time their existence had already been known to Portuguese chroniclers for almost a hundred years. In his history of the Portuguese discovery and conquest of the East Indies, Fernão Lopes de Castanheda (c. 1500–1559) wrote about diamonds coming from Taniampuro in the Sukadana area, which was a reference to the old capital of Matan, Tanjung Pura, on the west coast of the island, not far from Sukadana. It is perhaps this first occurrence of Bornean diamonds in European sources that made scholars mistakenly think that diamond mining on the island only started at that time.

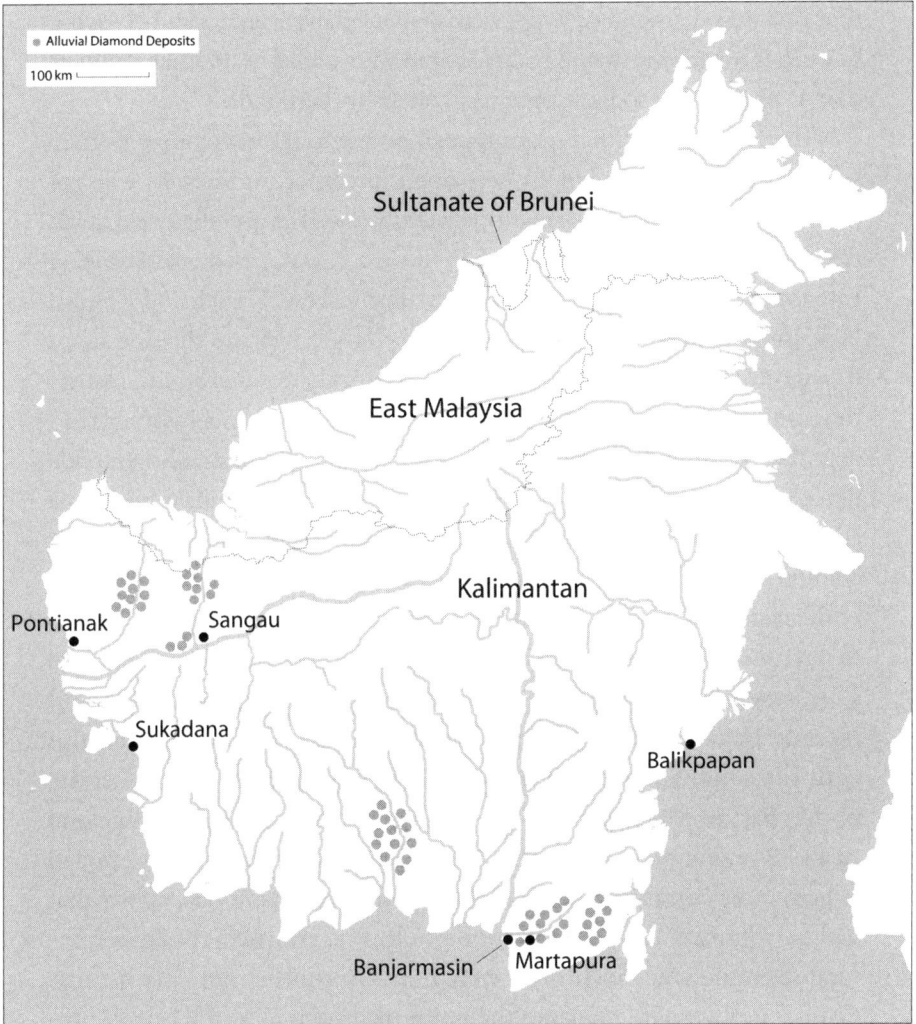

14 Diamond deposits in Borneo.

The famous Dutch explorer Linschoten wrote about large diamond finds at Tanjung Pura, which appeared as 'Tamia baiao' on a map drawn by Theodore de Bry in 1602.[222] Unlike European descriptions of India, most of the early modern European sources concerned with Borneo discussed aspects of trade, but were not much concerned with observations on mining. This was related to a lack of prior knowledge but also to the concrete European interest in establishing commercial relations with the rulers on the island. It did not take long, however, before a European power was interested in more than trade. Europeans quickly found out that Borneo's diamond deposits were dispersed over territories belonging to various kingdoms that regularly waged wars with one another, conflicts that at times seem to have been motivated by diamonds.[223]

The Dutch were the first European power to try to colonize Borneo and they strived to establish a permanent presence on the west coast of the island, even though their initial involvement in the diamond trade remained limited. Since its inception in 1602, the voc had been active in India, where it had to compete with the Portuguese, French and English East India companies. As it turned out, the eic became the dominant European factor in India, and the Dutch quickly decided not to restrict the voc's activities to India alone. In 1609 an envoy was instructed to negotiate trading deals for the voc with several of the small diamond-iferous Muslim sultanates in western Borneo, such as Landak, Sukadana and Sambas.[224] An agreement was reached with the last of these, by which diamonds mined 'in the land of the wild' were to be brought to the market of the capital of Sambas, where the Dutch would be the only Europeans to have the right of purchase. Additionally, the voc was allowed to build a settlement, in exchange for which they were to provide military assistance to Sambas when asked.[225] The Dutch also fostered relationships with the sultanate of Banjarmasin, the most powerful political entity in that part of the island, but it would take until 1750, when a diamond cleaver was sent there at the sultan's request, before the Dutch attempted to gain more complete control over Banjarmasin's diamonds, efforts that had only limited success.[226] On the whole, voc efforts to set up a structural diamond trade in Borneo were not very fruitful, not only because regular local warfare rendered the political situation on the island difficult, but because there was powerful competition from Chinese traders. In 1610 the Dutch settlement in Sambas was destroyed. Thirteen years later, the Dutch *comptoir* in Sukadana was closed.

Despite this failure, the voc's endeavours in Borneo sparked English interest, and a report sent to London in December 1608 stated that 'I have many times certified your worships of the trade the Flemmings follow to Soocadanna which place yieldeth great store of diamonds, and their manner of dealing for them for gold principally which comes from Baniermassen and blue glass beads which the Chinese make and sell.'[227] A jeweller named Hugh Greete was sent to Sukadana to collect rough diamonds. He arrived in 1613, accompanied by a young Russian, and soon they ventured into Sambas and Landak, but their efforts to establish a durable relationship failed, leaving the island's diamond trade in local, Dutch and Chinese hands.[228] Chinese and Dutch traders set up trade routes connecting Borneo with the Dutch capital of the East Indies, Batavia.[229]

Dutch efforts received a boost in 1698 when the sultan of Landak requested and received support from both the Dutch and the Bantam sultanate on Java to attack Sukadana. The Bantam sultan, who had just succeeded to the throne and was eager to expand his power, was drawn to Borneo by a large diamond in the possession of the Sukadana ruler. Both kingdoms became vassals of Bantam, and all diamonds found in Landak had to be offered to the Bantam sultan for half of their estimated value.[230] This situation continued for the remainder of the early modern period, with European powers unable to break the sovereignty of the Bantam sultanate and its control of the diamondiferous areas of Borneo until 1778. That year, both the Sukadana and Landak kingdoms were handed over to the Dutch East India Company by the Bantam sultan, an action that led to the establishment of a Dutch colonial state on the west coast of Borneo.[231] In the century that followed, the Dutch would try, without much success, to further diamond mining on the island. It never ceased altogether, but the zenith of Borneo's diamond production must be situated in the early modern period. The story of the Matan diamond, found near the Landak river in 1789 and weighing 369 carats, is perhaps symptomatic of the lack of knowledge about Bornean diamonds. It was owned by the raja of Matan, and in the nineteenth century some thought it was the largest existing diamond in the world, while others were of the opinion that it was made of quartz. An engineer named Tivadar Posewitz wrote in 1892 that careful examination in 1868 had unmasked the diamond as a rock crystal.[232] But Edward Balfour (1813–1889), a Scottish scientist who wrote an extensive work on India, eastern and southern Asia, insisted that the Matan diamond was real, and that the confusion had arisen because the raja only showed a fake crystal to strangers.[233] Today it is commonly accepted that the stone was made of quartz.[234]

The Early Development of Diamond Cuts

Tales of frauds and forgers selling fake stones, news of thefts and exotic stories of well-known diamonds with illustrious names such as the Sancy, the Koh-i-Noor, the Orlov and others have fascinated consumers for centuries. The Hope Diamond, originally the French Blue, was a blue stone of 45.52 carats found in the Kollur mine. It was one of the diamonds that Tavernier brought back with him to Paris, where he sold it to Louis XIV. It was stolen in the turmoil of the French Revolution and reappeared in a recut form in London in 1839. A century later, in 1949, it was bought by famous New York-based jeweller Harry Winston, who donated it to the National Museum of Natural History in Washington, DC, where it is still exhibited.[235] In the late nineteenth and early twentieth centuries the myth of a curse was introduced, according to which everyone who had possessed the Hope Diamond would suffer misfortune. The curse fitted well within orientalist discourse, and still appeals to audiences today, but it can be categorized as a myth, a marketing tool.[236]

Stories of famous diamonds work well to entice consumers, even when precious stones were only available to kings and queens, but they only refer to a handful of almost mythical stones that can be recognized from the appearance into which they have been fashioned. And while the consumption history of the bulk of diamonds, whether qualifying as gemstones or not, is perhaps a bit more prosaic, looks remain crucial. Any history of the use of diamonds is therefore a history of appearances. While the colour, size, shape and cut of some of these diamonds make them qualify as diamonds in the eyes of the consumer, they also determine a stone's value. Colour is a natural characteristic, while the cut depends on human expertise. Size and shape depend on both. Rough diamonds that come straight from the mines do not have an immediate appeal as objects of beauty, whether they were found encapsulated in rocks (illus. 2) or as loose stones in riverbeds (the three uncut diamonds at the bottom of illus. 18, for example). Before the discovery of cutting and polishing techniques able to make diamonds shine, these stones were not so much appreciated for their qualities as a jewel but rather for their outstanding hardness. Godehard Lenzen asserted that Indian historical sources on gemstones generally valued diamonds on the basis of mythical properties related to their exceptional hardness. The rarity of diamonds also played a role in their valuation. Wearing a diamond as an amulet was linked to invincibility, and the rough stone was often also claimed to have magical powers.[237] For Lenzen, these 'religious-magic ideas' that became linked to the diamond made them a valuable commodity not only in India, where they were found, but further away, in Roman Europe and China.[238]

In India, different colours of diamonds became associated with different Hindu deities. White diamonds became a symbol of Indra, god of war, thunder and lightning. In Hindu mythology, Indra was the source behind thunderbolts, which were made of diamonds and referred to as *vajra*. In Sanskrit, the word 'diamonds' is translated as *vajra* and as *indrayudha*, meaning Indra's weapon.[239] An alternative story has it that Indra, one of the most powerful gods in the Hindu mythology, battled a demon named Bali. After the latter's defeat, sapphires sprang from his eyes, rubies came from his blood and diamonds from his bones – not coincidentally the hardest part of the human body.[240] Black diamonds were linked to Yama, god of death, and another variety was associated with Vishnu, god of heaven.[241] The relationship between diamonds and deities in India was complemented by more earthly magical powers as protection against 'snakes, fire, poison, disease, thieves, water, and black magic'.[242]

According to Lenzen, one of the few authors to elaborate on the link between the religious-magical significance of diamonds in India and the ability of Indian traders to create a market in the Roman Empire, it is precisely this symbolic value of diamonds that established a demand there.[243] The connection is confirmed by the observation that, with the advance of Christianity, the demand for diamonds declined: 'as the religious basis of valuation changed, the diamond necessarily lost its eminence. Only as the result of the spread and perfection of cutting techniques in Europe was it able to reclaim the first place in the value scale of gems.'[244] This observation, of course, does not apply to regions where Christianity did not spread. Asian trade, with diamonds going to regions where the dominant religion was Islam, Buddhism or Hinduism, was not affected by this and must have continued or even expanded. A lack of source material complicates the assessment of the nature of consumer demand in Asia and Europe before cutting was invented, but references to diamonds in Arab manuals on gemstones at least confirm a continued interest in the hardest of all gemstones, while in medieval European writings diamonds had ceded their place to other gemstones. When Garcia da Orta published his *Coloquios dos Simples e Drogas da India* in 1563, cutting and polishing had been invented, but he observed that 'here and everywhere in the world', lapidaries considered the diamond as the third-most important of gemstones, behind emeralds and rubies.[245] Their valuation, da Orta continued, stemmed from the demand of the people and their scarcity, as even a lodestone (a magnetized mineral) possessed more 'virtuous' powers than diamonds.[246]

While the advent of Christianity greatly impacted the diamond trade between Europe and India, it should never be forgotten that before the invention of cutting techniques, it was always a relatively small trade. In addition, the best diamonds – those that were the largest or had the best natural shape – never made it to Europe. At the Indian mines, the biggest diamonds were preserved for the local rulers and hardly ever entered into the commercial chain.[247] In Roman and medieval times, all trade routes between Europe and India were overland routes, dominated by Arab and Persian middlemen. While they were a crucial element in the commodity chain between India and Europe, they also sold diamonds in their home markets. It should be concluded that the European demand was but one element of the pre-early modern diamond trade, and perhaps not even the most important element.[248]

Nevertheless, Indian mines were producing a great deal of diamonds and this growing supply contributed to the expansion of European consumer demand for precious stones in the early fourteenth century, particularly at the courts. In Paris in 1369 the Duke of Burgundy bought an ornament for his mother set with four pearls, four diamonds and a ruby in the middle.[249] This setting still shows the pre-eminence of other gemstones over diamonds in Europe, but also demonstrates a growing interest by rulers and their courts in the consumption of diamonds. According to Karin Hofmeester, monarchs, irrespective of gender, started to incorporate diamonds in their crowns and sceptres on the basis of the old symbolic link between hardness, invincibility and power.[250] From the courts of first Burgundy and France, but later also England and other European monarchical states, the use of diamonds further spread to the nobility. The gift of a diamond from Charles VII of France to his mistress Agnès Sorel, who died in 1450, is generally considered to be the first time when a woman of common descent obtained and wore a diamond as jewellery.[251] Apparently, Sorel appreciated a jewellery piece known as a 'parure', a set of different jewels such as earrings, necklaces and so on, carefully crafted to fit together. In 1477 the Holy Roman Emperor Maximilian i married Mary of Burgundy in Vienna. She is recorded as the first bride-to-be – but far from the last – to receive an engagement ring with a diamond set in it.[252]

It is not a coincidence that instances in which diamonds are used at European courts become more numerous in the second half of the fifteenth century. It is in this period that diamond cutting becomes a known technique mastered by European artisans. It is not exactly known where, when and by whom the process was invented that allowed rough diamonds to be cut into facets. For a long time they were used in their natural form as rough diamonds, although some rudimentary forms of transforming a diamond were in use. Historically, diamonds naturally shaped as an octahedron were most in demand, and their surfaces were polished to enhance their brilliance. Old Sanskrit texts such as the *Ratnapariska of Buddhabhatta*, which dates from the fifth or sixth century, are not only ancient examples of diamond valuations, they confirm the symbolic protective qualities of the diamond and refer to a form of polishing the outer shape of the stone: 'wise men should not use a diamond with visible flaws as a gem; it can be used only for polishing of gems, and it is of little value.'[253] A thirteenth-century Indian lapidary confirms that diamonds can only be polished by other diamonds.[254] Another Indian lapidary published an undated manuscript before the end of the fourteenth century in which he mentions the use of diamonds to work other diamonds on a wheel.[255] Polishing, however, is not the same as cutting, a process in which a diamond is reshaped into a symmetrical object with a number of facets, intended to make the diamond shine.

The developing practice of reshaping diamonds led to higher prices for more finished products. As early as 1403 a Venetian jeweller observed a price difference between rough and finished diamonds.[256] An early and rudimentary cut was the pointed cut, which made a diamond look like two pyramid shapes glued together at their respective bases (illus. 15). This form, which was known by polishers in Nuremberg in 1375, served as the basis for the table cut, which was invented in the fifteenth century, possibly in India, from where it must have reached Europe through Venice. In a table cut, the upper half of a diamond was flattened.[257] Soon after, a second cut, the 'lozenge', was used on octahedrons, such as the central diamond in illus. 16.

15 Illustrations of older diamond cuts.

Although this type of finishing led to a huge loss of weight, it was attractive due to the use of the form in heraldry.[258] In 1467 Charles the Bold (1433–1477), Duke of Burgundy, possessed an ornament set with table diamonds.[259] In 1669 Robert van Berken wrote a treatise on precious stones in which he argued that his grandfather Lodewijk was the first to polish diamonds with diamond powder.[260] It gave way to the idea that Lodewijk van Berken, a Flemish jeweller from Bruges, accidentally discovered diamond cutting while working for Charles the Bold. It's a claim that is still being used to demonstrate the long involvement of Flanders in the diamond industry, but the process was known elsewhere before this period. It is possible, however, that van Berken contributed to the technical development of the rotating wheel, a so-called scaif.[261] This more realistic claim was also made by Robert van Berken, who wrote about his grandfather polishing diamonds 'on a mill and certain iron wheels of his invention'.[262]

Following the spread of cutting techniques in Europe, diamond-cutting industries developed in a few places, perhaps first and foremost in Venice. There the guild of goldsmiths forbade its members from passing on knowledge about working precious stones to Jews in 1434.[263] The city's artisans became a prime example of craftsmanship. Benvenuto Cellini, a Renaissance goldsmith and sculptor living between 1500 and 1571, mentioned diamonds on several occasions in his autobiography. One episode refers to him working on a diamond ring for the pope, the diamond of which had been set by what Cellini called 'the most famous jeweller in the world, a Venetian called Miliano Targhetta'.[264] In 1503 Bartholomeo di Pasi, a Venetian, published an overview of trade relationships between Italian cities and other places, in which 'diamanti di punta', diamonds with a natural pointed shape or a point cut, were sent from Venice to Lisbon and Paris, while 'diamanti', stones that needed to be cut, were sent from Venice to Antwerp, and from Aleppo to Milan.[265] The deepening of trade relationships between different cities also led to the dispersion of knowledge on diamond cutting. Venice had established a cutting industry very early, and mentions of the practice are recorded for Nuremberg (1373), Paris (1407) and Augsburg (1538).[266] In Antwerp, a city ordinance of 1447 warned against the practice of selling fake diamonds, which must have meant that there were workshops in the city.[267] The first reference of the profession can be found in 1491, when the diamond cutter Peter van der Hoodonk made a marriage contract.[268] The establishment of a cutters' guild took longer: in 1580, after complaints about cutters who were active in spite of their lack of training, diamond cutters consulted with the

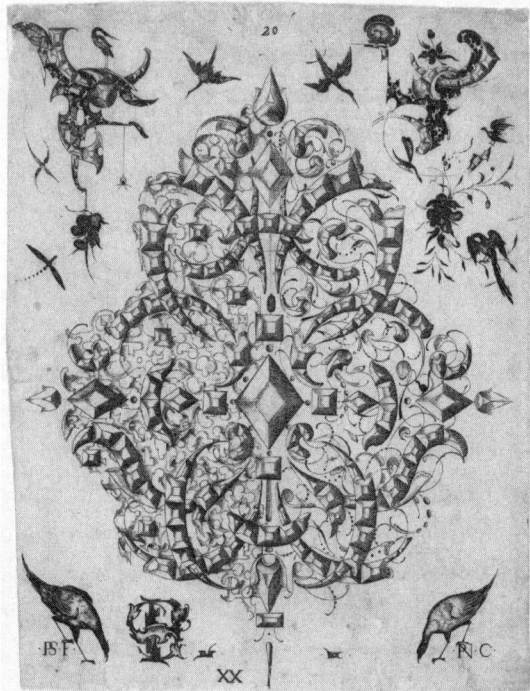

16 Jewel in the shape of a goldsmith's bouquet, 1621.

goldsmiths about the privileges they had managed to obtain. Two years later an ordinance that confirmed the foundation of the diamond cutters' guild was published.[269] The guild organization was immediately appealing, as later that year several foreign diamond cutters tried to become freemen of the city of Antwerp so they could join the guild.[270]

The year 1586 is often considered as the starting point for Amsterdam, which was to develop one of the most important diamond-cutting industries of the early modern period. The city's marriage registries for that year contain the first mention of the profession, when an immigrant from Antwerp named Willem Vermaat married and declared himself to be a diamond cutter.[271] It is not a coincidence that diamond cutters had started to leave Antwerp. The spread of Protestantism and the Dutch Revolt led to an exodus of many Protestants, particularly after Antwerp was taken by Spanish troops in 1585.[272] Karin Hofmeester has shown that Antwerp diamond cutters were not only instrumental in the establishment of a cutting industry in Amsterdam, but that in the early seventeenth century they transferred their knowledge through learning contracts with aspiring craftsmen in London and Lisbon.[273] These cities, though, did not establish a separate guild for diamond cutters, which made it easier for foreigners to become active in the profession.

During the sixteenth century the process of working diamonds became more complex and the cutting workshops employed different types of personnel. Cleavers split a diamond into smaller stones and worked the stone into a better-suited shape, the first of a three-stage process.[274] This step was so important for the final outcome that cleavers earned the highest salaries.[275] Sawers used thread with diamond powder to better shape the diamond for cutting in case cleaving was not possible. It was a lengthy and trying process that could take as long as ten months to complete.[276] A second stage was called bruting, a process in which two diamonds were rubbed against each other to round off the edges. This was the last step in preparing the stone before polishing. In the third and last stage, polishers gave the stone its final faceted shape by holding it against a greasy disc with diamond powder.[277] Several authors have remarked that cleaving was a later invention, made when the lower quality of Brazilian diamonds necessitated new forms of working diamonds, but the profession of cleaver is clearly mentioned in the seventeenth century.[278]

The cut that was adopted for a particular diamond depended on the form of the rough diamond and on fashion. Not all rough stones were shaped as octahedrons, suited to be cut as lozenges and table diamonds. In his seventeenth-century history of precious stones, Thomas Nicols mentioned that diamonds were also cut in pyramidal form, although these were valued lower than table diamonds.[279] Around 1520 the rose cut was invented and quickly became popular. Until the breakthrough of the brilliant cut at the end of the seventeenth century, the rose, table and lozenge cuts existed next to each other (illus. 15 and 16).[280]

Developing techniques went hand in hand with the consumers' appreciation for diamonds. In Europe the diamond became more and more a luxury item, a symbol of status and power, worn by the rich.[281] By the second half of the sixteenth century, the clientele for diamonds had expanded beyond the courts, but their use in jewellery became increasingly a matter of gender, with women now the dominant wearers of these precious stones in necklaces, brooches and earrings.[282] For Joan Evans, the jewels of that time 'are the products of the courts of kings and queens who were seeking power and wealth rather than the cultivation of the things of the spirit'.[283] In the late sixteenth and early seventeenth centuries the interest in gems 'for their own sakes' was revived, leading to more simplified jewellery designs.[284] The century ended with the publication of works by jewellers such as Tavernier, and his descriptions of diamond mines in India went well with the growing tendency to appreciate diamonds as objects of beauty. This idea went together with the development of techniques that were designed to bring out that beauty – or the European perception of it – as clearly as possible, a quest that culminated in the invention of the late seventeenth-century brilliant cut (the 'old European cut', illus. 17).[285]

In India, both consumption and cutting took a different trajectory. Indian appreciation for finished diamonds relied on weight and clarity alone, which explains the asymmetrical nature of many diamonds cut in Indian workshops. The point was not so much to create light and symmetry, but to preserve weight and size (see illus. 10). While the Mughals certainly appreciated diamonds, they were accustomed to possessing a great deal of jewellery and rated both rubies and spinels as more valuable stones than diamonds.[286] Unlike European monarchs, who had to get their diamonds through international trade networks, Indian rulers were able to obtain diamonds directly from the mines. Additionally, Mughal emperors were part of a complex tributary web of gift-giving, of which jewellery was an important part. In India the wearing of precious stones did not become feminized and Mughal rulers were often depicted wearing extensive jewellery.[287] This different appreciation, however, did not mean that Mughal emperors or other Indian local rulers had no interest in European-shaped jewellery, and exotic curiosity from the Mughal courts was perhaps the main reason why jewellers such as the Chardin brothers and Tavernier were able to conduct business in India. The picture of diamonds Tavernier brought back to France for Louis XIV contains several irregularly cut diamonds (illus. 18).

The growing interest in European jewels was also exemplified by the presence of European artisans in India. While European merchants tried

OLD EUROPEAN CUT   MODERN BRILLIANT CUT

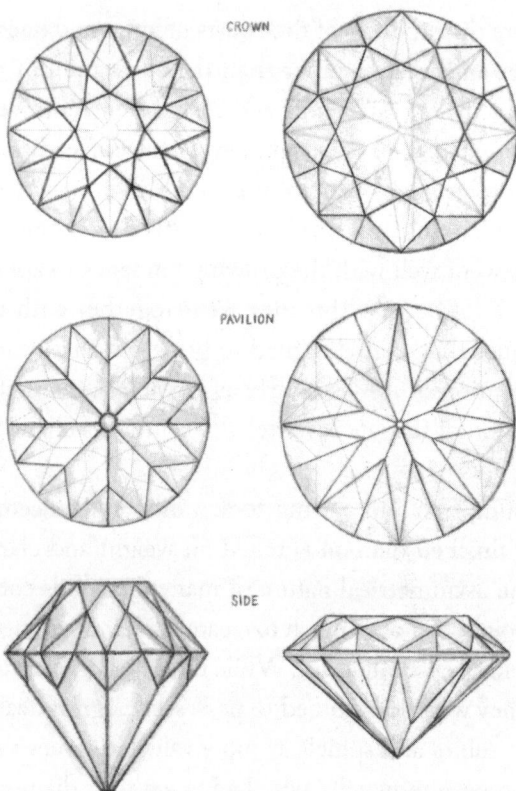

CROWN

PAVILION

SIDE

17 Old and modern brilliant cuts.

18 Tavernier's
diamonds, 1676.
Original engraving
by Abraham Bosse.

to do business by buying and selling both Indian- and European-style jewellery, European cutters and polishers sometimes gained employment to satisfy Mughal curiosity about diamonds that looked exotic to them.[288] A well-known story, told by van Linschoten in his travel account, is that of the Antwerp diamond cutter Frans Coningh, who spent most of his youth in London but was sent to his uncle in Venice around 1580. A year later he left for Aleppo to gain experience in the diamond trade, but he lost all his money due to his spendthrift lifestyle. He started to work as a diamond cutter in Goa, where he married. In 1588 he was murdered by his wife and her lover.[289]

With the employment of European artisans in the Mughal Empire as diamond cutters, the number of diamond workshops grew. It is likely that we know of some stories about European craftsmen in India because their presence drew the attention of European travellers, but most diamond cutters in Mughal workshops must have been local, or at least non-European. When French traveller Jean de Thévenot visited the fortress of Golconda in 1666, he observed that

the king [meaning the sultan of Golconda] wants the good workers to stay there . . . he makes jewellers even stay at his palace . . .

the workers of the palace are so busy with the common jewels of the king, who has such a great quantity of them that these people can hardly work for another person.[290]

Tavernier also informed us about cutting workshops established near the mines. As in Europe, diamonds were set in a dop to keep them steady and fixed, after which they were exposed to the force of mill-driven discs, greased with oil, and diamond powder was used on the discs for polishing. The French jeweller noticed that the process in Europe was facilitated by using wooden discs, while in India slower steel discs were used.[291] He also observed that the diamond mills at Raolconda were driven by black people, 'nègres'.[292] While we do have some information on diamond workshops in India, nothing is known about the practice of diamond cutting in Borneo in early modern times: 'there seems no evidence that diamonds were being cut in Borneo or elsewhere in southeast Asia in the seventeenth century.'[293]

European diamond cutters working in Asia were probably among the highest-paid workers there, so their experiences do not say all that much about the wages and working circumstances of the ordinary workers. The same can be said about differentials in remuneration in the diamond workshops in Europe. A declaration drafted before a notary in Amsterdam in March 1670 by five diamond cutters and cleavers is specific that work on diamonds is not paid by the hour, but according to 'the subtlety and craft of the work'.[294] They declared that a good cutter could earn between 20 and 30 guilders a day, working five hours. Thobias Delbeck, a diamond cleaver who had earlier been working in Antwerp, declared that he was even able to make 40 guilders per day.[295] They declared further that cutting and cleaving was considered a particular craft and science, and experienced workers could prosper as much as a talented painter could.[296] This means that talented diamond workers earned high wages, as specialized workers such as master carpenters earned about 1.5 guilders a day. Painters working in a Dutch city could earn up to 3 guilders a day, but only if they produced up to two paintings a week.[297] The wages surely also reflected the risk of legal persecution should a diamond cutter produce poor work. In 1685, for instance, a jeweller demanded compensation from an Amsterdam cutter who had cut away the lustre of a diamond.[298]

While the high wages for expert cutters and cleavers are very believable, they did not apply for workers lower on the ladder, those working

19 Diamond cutter, 1694.

low-quality diamonds or those driving the mills. In Amsterdam, women often drove the wheels of the diamond mills (illus. 19), a practice that even led to Christian complaints about Jewish competition, as the latter were accused of employing their whole families, which allowed them to lower their costs.[299] In spite of these complaints, Jewish and Christian diamond cutters worked in the same workshops as early as 1615, and entered each other's service as personnel or apprentices, and Christian women worked the wheels driving the mills as well. In 1735 a declaration made before an Amsterdam notary described the bad behaviour of diamond polisher Juriaan Hupker, who pressed his disc so hard that Antje Hendriks could hardly turn the mill. She also complained that Hupker was smoking and singing indecent songs.[300] Perhaps he was singing about his troubles. A Dutch song manual from 1774 contains a conversation in song between two diamond cutters lamenting their dire state of affairs. They had debts, no money and no work. One even considered employment as a sailor to go to the East Indies, a notoriously difficult and dangerous navigation.[301] Such songs show that, even though diamond cutting required skill, for many cutters, labour was hard and precarious – and it would remain so until far into the twentieth century. But by the time Amsterdam's diamond workers were complaining about the hardships of their lives, the diamond world had been shaken by the discovery of new and very rich deposits of diamonds on the other side of the world – in Portuguese Brazil – and the classic world of Asian diamonds had come to an end.

2

Slavery and Monopolies: Diamonds in Colonial Brazil, 1720–1821

We take the Liberty to Inform you that in Company with one or
two more we have Contracted for all the Brazil Diamonds that will
be sold in some years in Europe we hope to pass many thro' your
Hands & when this Affair is fully Settled Shall write you more
fully thereon.[1]

This excerpt comes from a letter written by the Jewish diamond merchants Francis and Joseph Salvador to one of their foremost business partners, the Catholic Englishman James Dormer, who lived in Antwerp.[2] It is telling for a number of reasons. First of all, it confirms the role played by Jewish merchants and their international networks in the diamond trade. The discovery of diamonds in Brazil challenged that role, but some, such as the Salvador firm, attempted to adapt to these new circumstances. Second, it shows that the desire to monopolize the flow of rough diamonds is not a modern prerogative but has been attempted by different parties in earlier times as well, with mixed success. Salvador and Dormer would never obtain a monopoly in Brazilian diamonds, at least not for long.

During the 1720s gold miners active in several riverbeds of the Minas Gerais province fortuitously discovered that the same rivers yielded diamonds. After reports about these finds reached the Portuguese court, efforts were made to prevent the increased supply harming European prices. First, a mining monopoly that was established in 1739 ensured control over production. The area in which diamonds were mined became known as the diamond district (illus. 21) and was guarded by colonial troops. Second, a commercial monopoly was introduced in the 1750s, ensuring control over the trade in rough diamonds. The establishment of these two monopolies was the first serious effort to control the flow of all rough diamonds coming from a specific region. Francis Salvador

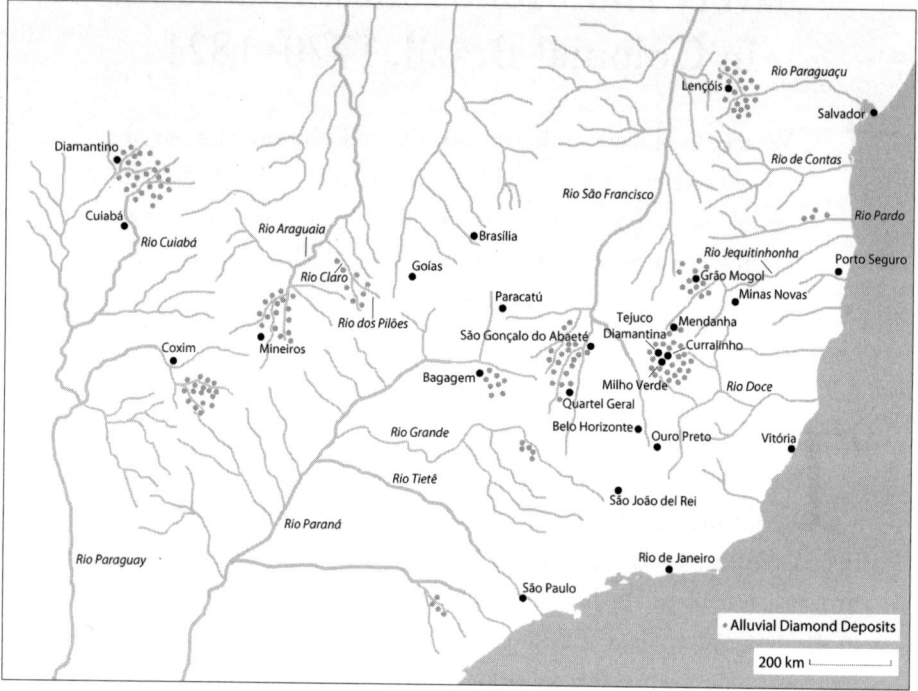

Diamantino

Cuiabá

Rio Cuiabá

Rio Araguaia

Rio Cláro

Rio dos Pilões

Coxim

Mineiros

Goías

Brasília

Paracatú

São Gonçalo do Abaeté

Bagagem

Quartel Geral

Rio Grande

Rio Tietê

Rio Paraná

Rio Paraguay

São Paulo

Rio de Janeiro

São João del Rei

Belo Horizonte

Ouro Preto

Vitória

Rio Doce

Milho Verde

Tejuco
Diamantina

Mendanha

Curralinho

Rio São Francisco

Rio Jequitinhonha

Grão Mogol

Minas Novas

Porto Seguro

Rio de Contas

Rio Pardo

Salvador

Lençóis

Rio Paraguaçu

Alluvial Diamond Deposits

200 km

20 Diamond deposits in Brazil.

was briefly involved in the trading monopoly, but when his involvement, which was secret, was discovered by the Portuguese prime minister, the contract was cancelled and sold to new parties.

Between the 1720s and the 1870s Brazil was to be the prime source for diamonds, and both the colonial and independent governments attempted to control mining through different regimes, ranging from free but heavily taxed mining to monopolization, a form of royal extraction, and a return to free mining. In spite of these efforts, clandestine mining, the so-called *garimpo*, always remained a crucial aspect of Brazilian diamond mining, next to the slave labour used to extract diamonds.

Finding Diamonds in the Brazilian Highlands

Ever since Portuguese navigator Pedro Álvares Cabral accidentally stumbled upon Brazil while sailing to India in 1500, the Portuguese monarchs had attempted to benefit from the natural resources Brazil had to offer.[3] Initially, Portugal's colonization of Brazil was limited to the coastal region, which was divided into administrative areas called 'captaincies'. These areas either fell under the colonial government of the Estado do Maranhão in the northeast, or the Estado do Brasil in the rest of the colony. Colonial products that were exported to Lisbon were brazil wood and sugar, and later tobacco. The plantation system was to remain fundamental to the colony's economy but was soon to be complemented by the development of the gold and diamond mining towns of the captaincy called Minas Gerais ('General Mines' in Portuguese). From the middle of the sixteenth century onwards, groups of adventurers called *bandeirantes* set out to discover the country's wild interior, motivated by tales of riches and the myth of Eldorado. These groups, which could be as small as a few dozen lawless men and women but sometimes grew to several hundred people, reached the area that was to be known as Minas Gerais before the end of the century. A lack of provisions, belligerent locals and epidemics prevented their permanent settlement, and initially they were more successful in capturing locals than they were in digging up precious stones or gold from the earth. It has been estimated that during the first three decades of the seventeenth century they might have captured as many as 40,000 indigenous people.[4]

The quest for mineral riches, however, remained an important motivation. In 1550 the Portuguese king received a letter from a man who intended to explore riverbeds near Porto Seguro, in the south of Bahia, hoping to dig up emeralds and other precious stones.[5] According to Wilhelm Ludwig von Eschwege, a German geologist who was working in Rio de Janeiro in the first half of the nineteenth century, emeralds were found in Brazilian river valleys as early as 1573.[6] Eventually, in the last decade of the seventeenth century, the *bandeirantes* struck gold in the same riverbeds that were said to contain emeralds. According to a Jesuit who published an account of Brazilian riches, it was a man of mixed descent who first found gold, near the later capital of the gold region Vila Rica de Ouro Preto.[7] This led very quickly to a gold rush, with an estimated eight to ten thousand people migrating to the gold areas in Minas Gerais during the first half of the eighteenth century, many from the Minho region in northern Portugal.[8] In the slipstream of this migration, a great number of enslaved Africans, who were forced to do most of the actual digging, were sent to Minas Gerais. In 1698 the registration lists for the payment of the royal fifths – a tax of 20 per cent on different goods, including precious metals and slaves – did not mention any slaves in the whole captaincy. Twenty years later, however, the names of 35,094 enslaved Africans were registered for payment.[9]

For the fifty years after the discovery of gold in Brazil, the Portuguese colony was producing as much as 85 per cent of the world's supply.[10] At some point during the 1720s, but perhaps earlier, gold diggers accidentally found diamonds in riverbeds located in the cold, windy and mountainous region of Serro do Frio. The person most commonly referred to as the first to realize he had found diamonds was Bernardo Fonseca Lobo. In an undated petition to the local authorities, he claimed to have found diamonds in 1723 but only showed them to the governor, D. Lourenço de Almeida, five years later.[11] The king rewarded Lobo for the discovery, and he was made an army captain, but soon his story was challenged. In 1732 a dying man named Sylvestre Garcia do Amaral was visited by a Portuguese official, who recorded his narrative. Amaral claimed to be a lapidary who had been sent to Minas Gerais, where he had discovered diamonds in 1727. It was only in 1728, after hearing of Amaral's discovery, that Lobo realized that what he had found in 1723 were also diamonds.[12] As Amaral was too ill to embark for Europe himself, it was the official who went to Lisbon to announce the discovery to the king, who now reserved a reward for Amaral, whose claims seem to have been more believable, not in the least because he was a lapidary.[13] A government official who was sent to the diamond fields in 1734 wrote in his memoirs about even earlier discoveries in 1714, 1721 and 1722.[14]

One of the most interesting stories about those initial years was that of a partnership between four men, including an Italian cleric, who sold Brazilian diamonds as Indian stones.[15] The memoirs of the official did include a slightly different version of Lobo's story. In 1726 Lobo was said to have travelled to Ouro Preto, where he gave sixteen diamonds to the governor, who was rumoured to have hidden the presence of diamonds from the Portuguese king by sending crystals to Lisbon instead. The same governor was accused of being secretly involved in the partnership of the four men mentioned earlier and was later expelled for disturbing public order. By 1728 Lobo, originally a gold digger, had left the region where he had found diamonds to go to the newly discovered gold deposits at Minas Novas (see illus. 20). He was one of many adventurers exchanging Serro do Frio for Minas Novas. Everyone knew of gold, but what Brazilian diamonds were to become still remained very uncertain. Those who stayed behind, however, believed in the opportunities that were suggested by these first finds. The memoirs of Martinho de Mendonça de Pina e Proença, sent to Serro do Frio in 1734, provide interesting details of these first years. He told the story of a priest who employed fifteen slaves in his search for diamonds.[16] These early references to clerics are interesting and help to explain the later legal restrictions on men of God entering the diamond region. The secrecy surrounding some of these early stories, and the involvement of the governor, point to the possibility that a trade in Brazilian diamonds existed well before the Portuguese king was officially informed about their discovery, something that happened only in December 1729.[17] This can be confirmed by further evidence, such as the letter that had been sent five months earlier from Brazil to a merchant in Lisbon, discussing prices and the cutting of diamonds coming from the colony.[18]

In a response to the official news of discovery, the Portuguese king demanded that the governor of Minas Gerais come up with a set of regulations. Specific tracts of land were allocated to miners at 12 square metres (130 sq. ft) per employed slave. For each each of them, a yearly head tax of 5,000 reis had to be paid, equivalent to £3 6s at the time.[19] Gold mining was forbidden and free movement restricted, particularly for itinerant traders and clerics. The king received a tract of land that was to be mined for him, and a specially designated government official, the *intendente*, was made responsible for overseeing diamond mining and for settling mining disputes. When being informed of these plans, the king desired to introduce more severe forms of punishment for those acting against laws aimed at regulating diamond mining. These included the confiscation of goods and banishment to Angola.[20] Information about the diamond deposits spread to other parts of the colony, and as early as 1730 colonial officials complained about slaves employed in gold mines in nearby Bahia running away to join the ranks of adventurers looking for diamonds in Minas Gerais.[21] The desire to exercise a larger control over the expanding diamond fields led to the announcement of stricter regulations in 1732. The fear that diamond mining would be subjected to much more rigorous colonial supervision led to a lot of local unrest, and a group of miners gathered before the city hall at Vila do Príncipe (present-day Serro) bringing a list of all their grievances.[22] They wished mining to be entirely unrestricted and substantially cheaper, and did not want to accept the curtailing of the free movement of persons of mixed descent and free black individuals.[23] A counterproposal made by the miners was rejected, but the governor, keen to maintain a good relationship with the diamond miners for personal gain, was sympathetic to their protests.[24] Consensus was found in a head tax of 20,000 reis per slave (£13.20), and the right to 'mine diamonds in all the rivers, and lands of Serro do Frio, as is being done until now'.[25]

In September that year a new governor arrived, and within a year he had doubled the head tax, which was also expanded to free black and mixed-race men working on the fields. Official trade was restricted to the diamond region's capital Tejuco (present-day Diamantina).[26] It is not hard to guess why the Portuguese king instructed the new governor to implement more severe measures. The Brazilian discoveries had led to a dramatic fall in prices paid for diamonds on the European market, and several well-known diamond traders in Antwerp and London had begun to voice their concerns in letters to the Portuguese government, particularly after the opening of new deposits at Guapiara and Curralinho raised Brazilian production even more. In June 1734 a new *intendente*, Rafael Pires Pardinho, arrived in Tejuco, accompanied by de Pina e Proença, author of perhaps the first memoir on Brazilian diamonds. Pardinho carried orders with him to expel all 'useless and pernicious people' and to establish an official demarcation for the diamond district, which was isolated from the rest of the Brazilian colony and subject to a separate colonial administration.[27] The first cause of action, when the borders of the diamond district were delineated (illus. 21), was a complete closure of the diamond fields, on the advice of Francis Salvador, who held a considerable interest in the diamond trade with India.[28] Anyone within the diamond region was forbidden to carry mining instruments or participate in public gatherings.[29] The miners' desperate petition asking for permission to mine for gold as a livelihood was denied, but in 1738 they were allowed to look for gold at a number of sites that were already considered to have been exhausted.[30]

The Mining Monopoly of João Fernandes de Oliveira

The authorities used the years of closure to evaluate different solutions to better control Brazil's diamond production. In 1734 several foreign merchants based in Lisbon had offered to buy exclusive mining rights, but their proposals were rejected in favour of total closure. Four and a half years later, in January 1739, the idea of a monopoly had been revived and posters encouraging interested parties to come forward were circulating in the diamond district.[31] Several meetings with locals took place, but it was a Portuguese immigrant named João Fernandes de Oliveira who made the best offer. He lived in Ouro Preto and had already obtained a contract to collect royal taxes in Mariana, a nearby gold-mining town. In June 1739 a contract was signed giving de Oliveira the exclusive right to mine diamonds in a demarcated area.[32] It was to last four years, and de Oliveira was allowed to employ six hundred slaves, for which he had to pay a yearly amount of 230,000 reis each as a head tax. The contract contained clauses that dealt with illegal mining and smuggling, and transferred a great deal of power to de Oliveira, as his suspicion about someone was sufficient grounds for punishment. The penalties for infractions varied from fines payable in gold to banishment to the Rio Plate or the island of Santa Catarina, both in the south of Brazil. Three companies of dragoons, each counting sixty men, were responsible for maintaining order, with a fourth one added in 1746. All merchants were denied access to the diamond district, shopkeepers had to abide by strict rules, and people without official employment were instructed to leave the area. All diamonds that were found had to be kept in a special box, to which the contract holder

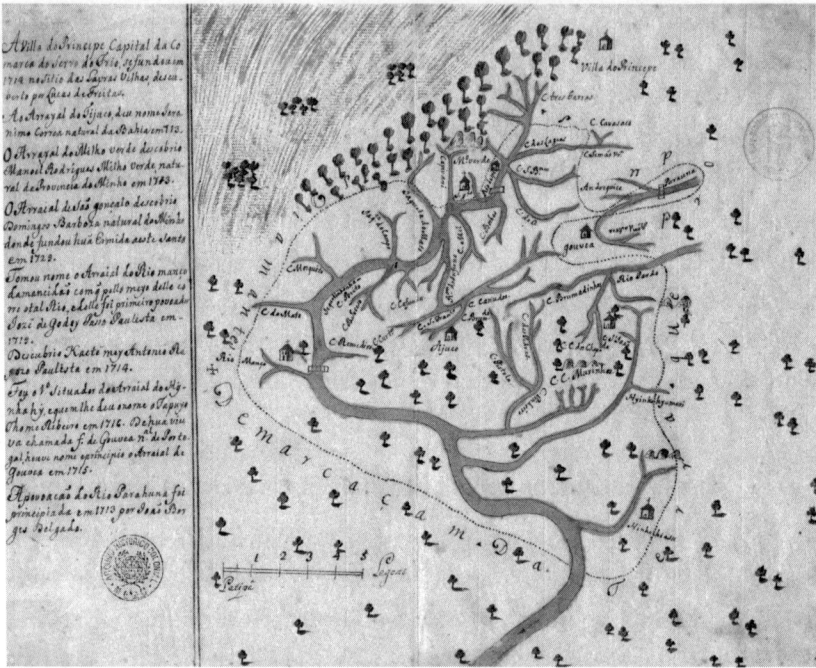

21 Map of the diamond district, Brazil, *c.* 1734.

and the *intendente* possessed a key. At designated times, diamonds were transported to Rio de Janeiro, and from there to Lisbon. In the Portuguese capital, representatives acting on de Oliveira's behalf could sell the diamonds, but always in the presence of a Portuguese minister. Additionally, the king had the first choice of purchase.[33]

De Oliveira did not have great financial means and he relied on a partner, Francisco Ferreira Silva, to bring in most of the necessary capital. Silva had sailed to Brazil on the same ship as de Pina e Proença and António Gomes Freire de Andrade, who was governor of Rio de Janeiro between 1733 and 1763, and of Minas Gerais three times, the second time between 1737 and 1752. De Andrade was a powerful man, and supported the contract holders to the extent that rumours circulated about de Oliveira and Silva acting only as middlemen, with the governor being the real contract holder, although official sources cannot prove the latter's involvement.[34] When a conflict arose between de Oliveira and Pardinho about the number of slaves employed, de Andrade sided with the monopolist, requesting Lisbon to lift the limitation of six hundred slaves.[35] The request was officially turned down, but Pardinho resigned. With the disappearance of Pardinho, de Oliveira and de Andrade had eliminated their biggest opponent and mining operations flourished. After four years the contract was extended for another four, under the same conditions.

The mining monopoly, however, needed substantial financial investment. The head tax was a large expense and the enslaved workforce needed lodging and food provisions. Additionally, diamonds were alluvial, located mainly in riverbeds, which needed to be drained. For this purpose, dykes were built, water was pumped and some streams were diverted. These construction works could be costly and it could take a long time for the proceeds from diamond sales in Lisbon to get to Brazil. In order to cover expenses, de Oliveira relied on investors in the Portuguese capital, but also in Rio de Janeiro. When the second contract expired at the end of 1747, the contract holder had accumulated so much debt that he was unable to compete for a third contract, which was given to the brothers Felisberto and Joaquim Caldeira Brant. Born in the São Paulo captaincy, they were miners with a penchant for violence; in 1730, had been accused of shooting at an official in the Rio das Mortes area, an old gold-mining region close to São João del Rei.[36] They could, however, count on a great deal of local support: rather than relying on investors in Rio or overseas, they involved nineteen partners in the contract, almost all people living in Tejuco, including a priest.[37] Nothing fundamental changed in the conditions, although new diamond deposits located in Goiás, where the Caldeira Brant brothers had been active as miners since 1735, were now officially included. A new clause stipulated the relocation of two hundred slaves to these deposits.[38] The diamond district was now under the control of people who were miners themselves, and who won further sympathy for their operations by turning a blind eye to diamond smuggling and clandestine mining operations. They also forged a good relationship with the colonial authorities. The *intendente* had made Felisberto Caldeira Brant a testamentary, and the governor was godfather to two of the children of Luís Alberto Pereira, one of the partners based in Tejuco. He was also present at the baptism of Felisberto's daughter Tereza.[39]

It was hardly surprising that the official production during the years of the Caldeira Brant management dropped by about 13 per cent (see illus. 30). The arrival of a new *intendente* who wanted to eradicate the illegal employment of too many slaves and the clandestine diamond trading would soon bring about the downfall of the Caldeira Brant brothers and their partners. In February 1752 Gomes Freire de Andrade had gone to Rio de Janeiro, leaving Minas Gerais to be governed by his brother José. In June the conflict escalated when the *intendente* and Felisberto Caldeira Brant accused each other of diamond theft. Threatened by an armed mob, including Felisberto Caldeira Brant and Luís Pereira, the *intendente* ordered Felisberto's arrest, but he was relieved of his position instead.[40] It seemed that, much like de Oliveira against Pardinho earlier, Felisberto and his partners had managed to have it their own way, again with the support of the governor. They did not expect, however, that their downfall would come so quickly the following year. In January 1753 the contract holders were unable to repay a series of bills of exchange and promissory notes covering investments in the diamond district. Two months later the discovery of a large amount of clandestine diamonds aboard a ship that had arrived in Lisbon from Brazil sealed the contractors' fate. The amount of diamonds found was so large that the authorities were of the opinion that such a smuggling operation could only have taken place with the Brazilian monopolists' knowledge, and both Felisberto Caldeira Brant and Luís Pereira disappeared behind the bars of the notorious Limoeiro prison in Lisbon. Felisberto was said to have been a witness to the 1755 earthquake that ravaged the Portuguese capital. According to some sources, the marquês de Pombal granted him his freedom afterwards and allowed him to spend the last year of his life in Caldas da Rainha, a little coastal town north of Lisbon. Others have claimed that he died of a stroke in prison in 1769.[41]

The period of Caldeira Brant's downfall was a turbulent moment in Portugal's history. King João v had died in June 1750, and his successor D. José had made Sebastião José de Carvalho e Melo, the later marquês de Pombal, secretary of war and foreign commerce. De Carvalho e Melo had been ambassador in London and Vienna and was to become Portugal's most important political figure after the earthquake. De Oliveira had returned to Lisbon in 1751 with the aim of winning the fourth diamond mining contract. In early 1752, when Felisberto and his partners were winning their conflict with the *intendente* in Tejuco, de Oliveira was taken to court by several of his creditors. In growing desperation, he requested an audience with the new king, at which Pombal would also be present. The secretary remarked that de Oliveira was 'a very vulgar man, very simple and so insane that ... he had rented a contract that he could not fulfil'.[42] In spite of a personal dislike, the events of early 1753 made the Crown accept de Oliveira's bid for a new diamond contract. Pombal decided to take care of things personally, as the inability to repay debts incurred under the third contract had led to a total breakdown of all diamond trade in the Portuguese capital.[43] De Oliveira's debts were paid and he received the full support of the authorities, who at the same time decided to arrange Brazilian diamond trading on the basis of a monopoly.[44] A new and very severe law, issued on 11 August 1753, formed the new legal framework within which both monopolies had to operate. It forbade anyone in the diamond district from trading, mining or transporting rough diamonds without de Oliveira's permission, and confirmed several existing punishments such as banishment, confiscation of goods and slaves, and monetary fines. The exact punishment depended on the colour of one's skin. While free whites living in Brazil were sent to Angola, enslaved Africans who were caught in illegal activities had to continue their mining labour in shackles. Free persons of African descent found guilty of crimes were also condemned to a period of forced mining, but without shackles. Rewards were given to informers, and entry to the diamond district was strictly controlled. Shopkeepers had to register and be of impeccable background, while soldiers were alternated every six months to prevent their involvement in smuggling.[45] The diamond district had become 'a colony within a colony'.[46]

During the fourth contract, a vast amount of diamonds was mined. Two more contracts were signed with João Fernandes de Oliveira and his son, who bore the same name. The son was best known for his illustrious mistress, the famous enslaved woman Chica da Silva. She has become part of Brazil's cultural heritage and as such she figures prominently in soap operas, movies and even modern music.[47] The younger Fernandes de Oliveira remained in charge until 1771, when the Crown decided to take the exploitation of the Brazilian diamond fields into its own hands.

Enslaved Workers and Persecuted Miners

In the Indian mines, labour was secured by using local workers who operated in circumstances that were close to slavery. The workers, however, were often locals and their insertion into mining was not all that different from the generally low positions they occupied in local societies. In Brazil, on the other hand, the workforce came from overseas. The diamond fields in Minas Gerais, Bahia and Goías were often the theatre

for illegal miners and adventurers, but they were not part of the structural workforce. Instead, mining authorities – first individuals, later the
private enterprise of the de Oliveiras and the Caldeira Brant brothers,
and ultimately the Portuguese colonial authorities – all relied on the
manpower of enslaved Africans who had been taken from across the
Atlantic, mainly from regions in the present-day countries of Angola and
the Democratic Republic of the Congo.[48] Academics behind the online
transatlantic slave trade database estimated that, out of more than 10 million
enslaved Africans forced to make the middle passage, 3.5 million, over
a third of the total, were transported to Brazil between 1551 and 1875.[49]
Most of these women and men ended up on one of the numerous coastal
sugar plantations, but a significant portion of them was taken along the
specially constructed Estrada Real, or Royal Road, from Rio de Janeiro
into the mining areas of Minas Gerais. In 1742, 54 per cent of the population of the captaincy of Minas Gerais consisted of enslaved Africans, a
proportion that remained stable until a slight drop to 52 per cent in 1776.[50]

The percentage of enslaved Africans in the mining areas was, of course,
much higher. It is, however, not so easy to find out how many enslaved
Africans lived and worked in the diamond district. There is only scant
historical evidence before the introduction of the mining monopoly in
1739. A list of slaves for whom the head tax was paid in 1734 shows that in
that year, just before the five-year closure of the diamond mines, tax was
paid for 1,100 enslaved Africans.[51] Stipulations in the monopoly contracts
between 1739 and 1771 always limited the official enslaved workforce to
six hundred miners, but estimates based on productivity numbers suggest
that the real number was always higher than 2,000, and in certain years
even surpassed 5,000 (see illus. 22). These estimates can be corroborated
by references in historical sources to numbers of 4,000–6,000 enslaved
Africans regularly employed during the colonial period.[52]

There are some clues about the origins of the enslaved Africans, and
although more research is needed, studies have shown that the majority in the captaincy of Minas Gerais came from Angola, Benguela and
Costa da Mina, a region in the Gulf of Guinea. Until 1760, 40 per cent
of the enslaved Africans in Minas Gerais came from Mina, and for the
remainder of the century this fell to 26 per cent.[53] There was a reason for
the high presence of persons from the Costa da Mina. It was commonly
believed that the people taken from that region had a special talent for

locating gold and diamond deposits.[54] Gold had been mined in parts of West Africa near the Costa da Mina since the Middle Ages, and in the twentieth century, rich alluvial diamonds deposits were to be discovered there as well.[55] Brazilian historians have demonstrated that enslaved women and men transported from the Costa da Mina indeed possessed knowledge on mining techniques, and that this knowledge proved itself useful in the diamondiferous rivers in Serro do Frio.[56]

The total number of enslaved Africans was still significantly higher, because the main columns in illus. 22 only show those employed on the diamond fields. The column showing the average number of female slaves per year has to be added to it, as well as the unknown number of slaves working in agriculture, food provision and other service industries for the mining operations. Women were an important part of the mining economy. They were in a strict minority in the mining settlements, and some were hired for domestic service, while others had to try to survive living off prostitution or concubinage. A few were house owners and a very small number of them owned slaves.[57] The economic agency that was most common among women in the diamond district was exercised by enslaved women active as street peddlers, the so-called *negras de tabuleiro*.[58] Slaves were paid small daily allowances that they could save while trying to purchase their freedom, the *alforria*, but they could also spend these small sums to complement their scant diet. Both enslaved and free women of African descent catered for those who wanted to buy food by visiting the mining sites with fish, *cachaça* (a fermented sugarcane juice typical of Brazil), tobacco and other consumer goods. As movement, particularly that of the black population, was severely restricted in the diamond district, these women, thanks to their mobility, became part of clandestine networks that linked the illegal settlements of runaway slaves, the so-called *quilombos*, with local inhabitants of Tejuco and with slaves. These networks exchanged information and were instrumental in the smuggling of diamonds.[59] The authorities were aware of this and attempted to curtail their movements by trying to force the women to set up shop at fixed sites, and sometimes by properly outlawing them, but they were never able to put a stop to the women's activities and their connections with illegal operations.[60]

While it has proven possible to provide estimates on the number of slaves employed in the diamond mines, it is more complicated to describe

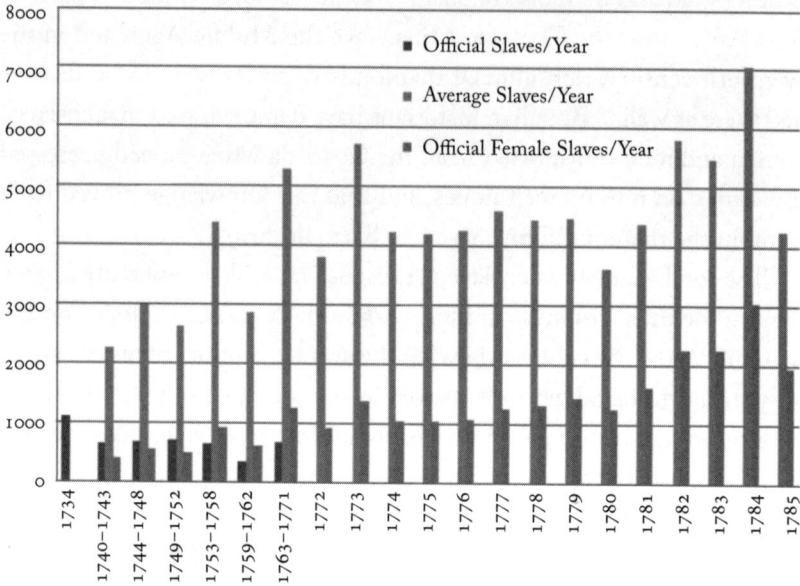

22 Estimated enslaved workforce in Brazil's diamond district
per year, 1734–85.[61]

their daily life on the basis of eighteenth-century material. From 1739 onwards these slaves were employed by the contract holders of the mining monopoly, and after 1771 their labour was exploited by the Portuguese colonial government, as Brazilian diamond mining was taken under direct royal supervision. While both these mining enterprises were large slave owners, they also hired additional slaves from the local population. Before diamond mining in Minas Gerais became a monopoly, it was free and attracted adventurers, including miners who had already amassed small fortunes as gold diggers. This enabled them to invest in the purchase of enslaved Africans, who were made to work for them, or were rented out to work for others. At times, local miners joined forces: in 1730, for instance, a group of well-off inhabitants from Ouro Preto, the main gold-mining town, founded a diamond mining company, which was able to employ forty slaves.[62]

During the colonial period, the diamond district was isolated, geographically as well as administratively, and no travellers who could record their observations were allowed to visit. Virtually all of the early modern material comes from sources officially tied to the colonial authorities.

These include two late eighteenth-century drawings that originally had been incorporated in a letter sent to Portugal by the *intendente* to relate the state of affairs to the government.[63] One shows how mining was done, including a mechanism to remove water (illus. 23), while the second shows the manner in which enslaved men were forced, under constant white supervision, to search the diamondiferous earth for diamonds (illus. 24).

The most famous imagery of Brazil's colonial diamond exploitation comes from Carlos Julião (1740–1811), an Italian engineer who worked for the Portuguese authorities in Brazil during the second half of the eighteenth century. His watercolour drawings provide a good visual depiction of the life and work of the enslaved Africans in the mining regions (illus. 25 and 26).[64] Julião's illustrations of diamond mining were made around the same time as the drawings and, in particular, the pictures showing the washing of diamondiferous earth are very similar. An almost identical variant of Julião's illustration can be found in the work of John Mawe (1764–1829), a British mineralogist who visited the diamond district in 1809 and 1810, when Brazilian diamond production had fallen into decline.

The distorted effect caused by the one-sided source material is very clear in the colonial drawings. The work is romanticized and depicted as a tranquil and harmonious outdoors activity. None of the illustrations come close to revealing the true nature of slave labour, which was harsh, oppressive and dangerous. Furthermore, the depictions that show enslaved Africans with clothes are false – they were forced to work naked, wearing nothing but a loincloth, to prevent smuggling. Julião's illustration of a man subjected to a bodily search (illus. 26) comes closest but is still far removed from the more realistic and very disturbing photographs taken in South Africa's diamond mines more than a century later (illus. 60 and 61).

The mining labour these enslaved men were involved in did not change much between the eighteenth century and today, as it remained a matter of manually going through river soil trying to find diamonds, so observations made in the early nineteenth century on the working circumstances of the enslaved miners are relevant for earlier periods as well; it must be remembered, however, that by the early nineteenth century the Brazilian diamond mines had entered a phase of decline from which they never recovered. This decline had already begun during the fourth and last monopoly contract, prompting the Portuguese king to alter policy. After the contract of the younger João Fernandes de Oliveira ended in 1771, it was decided to no longer award a mining monopoly to a private enterprise. Instead, an additional colonial apparatus was introduced to supervise all diamond mining in Brazil. This period is known as the *Extracção Real* (Royal Extraction) and lasted until 1832. A new body of law drafted under the supervision of Pombal on 2 August 1771 became known as the *Livro da Capa Verde*, the book with the green cover. It maintained or hardened most existing regulations against smuggling and illegal mining. These were particularly harsh on people of colour. Even free persons of African descent, men and women alike, were not allowed to visit stores or sell products themselves. They were forbidden to carry weapons. The enslaved population was still mostly hired from locals, and overseers were explicitly permitted to use the whip against them at will. Denouncing a crime was rewarded, but testimonies from enslaved Africans were only accepted if there was no other evidence available.[65] In 1798 the *Extracção Real* employed 505 free persons. Most of them, 351 men in total, were employed to supervise the slave labour.[66] The law from 1753 was already very severe, but in some aspects the 1771 regulations were even stricter. Merchants were no longer allowed in the diamond district, and shopkeepers had to find their provisions outside

23 Diamond mining in Brazil, 1775.

24 Diamond washing in Brazil, 1775.

of the diamond district. This led to the development of commercial networks that brought tobacco, brandy, corn and beans from farms in Minas Gerais, Rio de Janeiro, São Paulo and Bahia into the diamond district. With gold profits declining, provisioning the diamond district became an alternative means of subsistence for many *mineiros*.[67] To that purpose, a limited number of people were eligible for a yearly licence allowing the importation of foodstuff.[68]

All men holding office under the Royal Extraction were free, and either white or *pardo*, a term referring to people of mixed European, indigenous and African descent. But this group was only a tiny fraction compared to the large slave population. The diamond capital Tejuco counted 4,600 inhabitants in 1772, of which 3,610 were slaves.[69] In 1781 the diamond administration employed 340 free men and 4,383 slaves.[70] As in earlier periods, the great majority of slaves employed in the diamond district were looking for diamonds, and sometimes slaves from certain regions were considered better at it than others. Over time, the number of slaves declined. When the German travellers Johann Baptist Ritter von Spix (1781–1826) and Carl Friedrich Philipp von Martius (1794–1868) visited the region in 1818, they estimated only 1,020 enslaved Africans were employed on the diamond

25 Diamond mining, Brazil, 1770s. Illustration by Carlos Julião.

fields.[71] Next to the unfree people of African descent, the diamond district also counted various clandestine settlements inhabited by runaway slaves, the *quilombos*. Sources mention the existence of at least twelve such settlements, each inhabited by fifteen to sixty people.[72] These were unpopular with the white population and many *quilombos* were violently raided.[73] It comes as no surprise that the colonial government issued a series of laws trying to keep the mass of black people subdued, and as a general rule they were not allowed to carry weapons within the diamond district.[74]

Most of the slaves lived in small huts near the fields they were mining. The only social organization that they were allowed to be part of was the religious brotherhood, the so-called *irmandade*. After the law of 1753, clerics were officially no longer allowed in the diamond district, although late eighteenth-century inventories show that six priests lived in Tejuco.[75] The formal absence of the Church necessitated other forms of religious organization, and these were the brotherhoods. There were several in the diamond district and membership often depended on free status, wealth and skin colour.[76] Slaves had their brotherhoods, the main one being the Nossa Senhora do Rosário, but João Fernandes de Oliveira the younger, for instance, was also member of a brotherhood, the Irmandade de Nossa Senhora do Carmo.[77] Most of these brotherhoods built their own churches, several of which are still standing in Diamantina (the present name of Tejuco).[78] The brotherhoods played an important religious role and their practices were clearly syncretic in nature. They organized masses, religious feasts and processions. The brotherhoods also fulfilled important charitable and social roles, taking care of the sick and the poor.[79] Some of the white brotherhoods rented out houses and slaves to finance their activities: in 1792 more than 90 per cent of the income of the Irmandade do Santíssimo Sacramento came from renting out enslaved men and women.[80] Julita Scarano argued that, throughout the early modern period, racial distinctions and the abuse that followed from it were commonplace and accepted by most of the black brotherhoods.[81] This gradually faded away, and by 1794 several brotherhoods had abolished racial restrictions to membership.[82]

26 Enslaved man checked for hidden diamonds, 1770s. Illustration by Carlos Julião.

While this was an important step forwards, it should not be forgotten that slavery lasted particularly long in Brazil, until the so-called Lei Áurea ('Golden Law'). Even if the large organizations such as the brotherhoods complied with a colonial system of abuse, many individuals, such as clandestine miners and runaway slaves, challenged the authorities by setting up their own settlements, particularly the *quilombos*.[83]

As access to the diamond district was highly restricted during the eighteenth century, we do not have much source material describing the mining society in detail, with the exception of colonial archives and two anonymous eighteenth-century manuscripts, the *Deducçaó Compendiosa* and the *História Chronológica*.[84] There is more material for the nineteenth century, as the government allowed visits by a number of travellers. The most famous was probably John Mawe. In his travel journal he described the Mendanha mining site, where 1,000 enslaved Africans were living in 100 huts made of clay and tree branches (illus. 27).[85] They were fed with rice and beans, the famous *feijão*, and also received bacon and *cachaça*, Brazilian rum.[86] Part of their daily allowance was spent on food sold by the *negras de tabuleiro*. Work there was hard, and the enslaved men and women worked from 'a little before sunrise' until 'sun-set', with four to five breaks per day, two hours at noon.[87] Auguste de Saint-Hilaire, another European traveller, wrote that the enslaved Africans often sang about their regions of origin.[88]

Brazilian diamonds were alluvial, and mining sites were located in the riverbeds of the Jequitinhonha, the Rio das Pedras and the Ribeirão do Inferno in the diamond district. Operations later expanded to the Abaeté and Indaiá rivers, and to Bahia, with the establishment of diamond mining in the Paraguaçu, Mucugê and Rio de Contas rivers (see illus. 20). To a lesser extent, diamonds were found on dry land, even on the slopes of mountain ranges. The manual labour required was very similar to what happened on the mining sites in India. Slaves had to go through several layers of mud to find the *cascalho*, the diamondiferous gravel, which was made out of pebbles and earth, sometimes yellow, other times black or white. To access this gravel, walls and dams were built and water was pumped away by engines with wooden wheels (see illus. 23 and 27). This was not without danger, and in 1768 seventy enslaved men drowned in the Jequitinhonha.[89] Additionally, work in wet circumstances led to many suffering from hernias and frequent occurrences of pneumonia. Care for the sick was limited, as the first hospital in the diamond district was only built in 1790.[90]

27 Diamond mining in a riverbed, Brazil, 1825.

The *cascalho* was transported to washing sites, where slaves stood in wooden trays as water was constantly circulated to get rid of the muddy earth through holes, leaving diamonds behind. During the wet season, between October and April, river mining was often halted and washing earth that had been extracted earlier became the most important activity. The work was supervised by the *feitores*, who watched comfortably from an elevated position (see illus. 24).[91] Enslaved miners signalled a discovery by clapping their hands, and by holding the stones between thumb and index finger before handing it to the overseers (illus. 28).

In spite of surviving illustrations suggesting otherwise, slaves had to work semi-nude to prevent them hiding diamonds, and all their body cavities were regularly examined, a humiliating practice. It was said that slaves who found diamonds of more than 17.5 carats in size received their freedom, while smaller rewards were given for smaller discoveries.[92] The work method remained essentially the same in the nineteenth century, although John Mawe observed the use of waterwheel-driven carts to transport diamondiferous earth away and cylinders washing the *cascalho*, instead of enslaved women and men (illus. 29).[93] After the Golden Law of 1888 abolished slavery, mining was done by wage labourers or miners paid from a share of the profits.

Not all mining was done by enslaved Africans working either for the monopolists or the Royal Extraction, and many adventurers decided to risk their lives by mining illegally. These men, sometimes joined by run-away slaves or other outcasts, were named *garimpeiros*. The number of people opting for a life of clandestine mining is unknown but must have been substantial. Life for the *garimpeiros* was hard, as they were always on the move, strongly persecuted by the authorities. Colonial mining society was characterized by violence, as was demonstrated by remarks made by the governor of Minas Gerais in 1782, expressing his desire to 'extinguish the *garimpeiros*'.[94] The governor was replying to a letter sent by an envoy a few months earlier. In it he explained that diamonds had been found at the beginning of 1782 in a mountain range known as the Serra do Santo Antônio de Itacambiruçu, not far from Tejuco. He added that so many adventurers had gone to the site that, as a consequence, the streets of Vila do Príncipe and Tejuco were largely abandoned. The envoy might have been the first official to use the term *garimpeiros*, and he qualified them as *ladrões*, thieves.[95]

The diamond district had many remote parts that were difficult to control, and the government was never able to eradicate clandestine mining. Indeed, it seems that these miners were often quite poor, and the prospect of finding diamonds was one of the few hopes they had left. They could frequently count on the support of the local population as for many, such as the chronicler Joaquim Félicio dos Santos, the *garimpeiros* were not criminals but heroes, as they stood up to an unjust colonial government. Some even saw in them the embodiment of proto-Brazilian nationalist sentiment.[96] Travellers also noticed the presence of the *garimpeiros*. Spix and Martius, who wandered through the diamond region in 1818, described abandoned campsites that had been used by illegal miners.[97] Some of these sites became permanent, such as Grão Mogol ('Grand Mughal'), founded by clandestine miners in 1781. Today, it is a little town of about 25,000 inhabitants in the north of Minas Gerais.[98]

Although illegal miners were often described as belonging to the lower classes, higher strata of Tejuco's mining society were involved in diamond smuggling, and the involvement of various governors throughout the eighteenth century was a public secret. By the end of the century, diamond smuggling by families whose members held offices in the Royal Extraction and the army became connected to anti-colonial resistance, embodied in several famous figures, such as Father Rolim, whose father was a treasurer in the diamond administration.[99] The well-known *Inconfidência Mineira*, a revolt that occurred in Tejuco on 15 March 1789, counted several revolutionaries who were active in the Royal Extraction of diamonds and the army. Several of these men and some of their family members were holding official positions in the diamond administration, but they were also accused of smuggling, an activity that seems to have united rich and poor. The anti-Portuguese revolt failed, and several men were executed, but the seed for Brazilian independence was irrevocably sown.[100]

There was a cohesion in the diamond district that surpassed classes, also because everything was so much focused on mining. Clerics were officially not admitted, and there was only a very small nobility class. When the governor of Minas Gerais wanted to reform the local army, he was surprised to find that only a very limited number of nobles were able to participate.[101] This was also due to the regulations on land ownership within the diamond district, which was rendered difficult. Since the law of D. Fernando 1 from 1375 stipulated that land had to be productive, virtually all land in the diamond district was used for mining, because agricultural activities were restricted.[102] João Fernandes de Oliveira, who controlled much of the land

28 Diamond washing in Curralinho, Brazil, 1824.

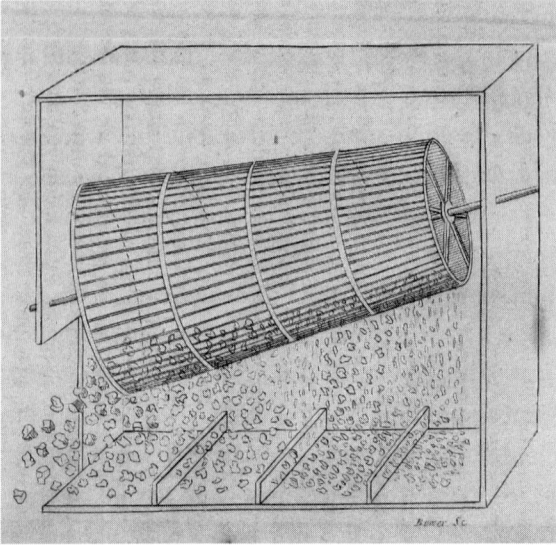

29 Cylinder for washing the *cascalho*, Brazil, 1812.

in the diamond district, used some of it for agriculture, and several of the men working for him, or later for the Royal Extraction, used some land to cultivate crops, tended to by slaves.[103] All of this meant there was a small elite of miners or mining investors who owned slaves and who were well connected to the powers that be, first de Oliveira and then the Royal Extraction. They sent their children to universities in Portugal, particularly Coimbra, and often came to be employed in the colonial apparatus.[104] While they exploited slave labour and tried to suppress all uncontrolled mining activities of the lower classes, some of them were also involved in smuggling with members of other classes, and a few even stood up against colonial domination in the tumultuous times of the late eighteenth century.

Beyond the Diamond District

The diamond district around Tejuco was relatively small, even when more remote deposits came to be included in the following decades. The captaincy of Minas Gerais was a vast territory with large unpopulated areas, the *sertões*, areas of forest and mountains crossed by rivers. Adventurers, illegal miners and agents working for the monopoly companies had been prospecting some of these lands, looking for gold, diamonds and other gemstones, and had also ventured into the neighbouring captaincies of Bahia and Goiás. In the latter, diamonds were found in the riverbeds of the Rio Claro and Rio dos Pilões as early as 1734, on territory inhabited by the Caiapó (see illus. 20). Miners clashed with locals, and it was rumoured that the Caldeira Brant brothers had worked on these diamond fields.[105] After military expeditions wiped out various *garimpo* sites in the region, an officially demarcated diamond area was designated and left in charge of an *intendente*. From Felisberto Caldeira Brant's diamond contract onwards, the monopolists were allowed to send two hundred men of their official workforce of six hundred slaves there.[106] Diamond mining in Goías remained a somewhat secretive enterprise, in part due to the remoteness of the area, and the quantity of diamonds mined there remains up for debate. One historian even went as far as to dispute the idea that diamonds were ever mined there.[107] While organized attempts at diamond digging may have been much smaller than hitherto assumed, sufficient evidence exists to at least support the historical existence of small-scale individual *garimpo* in the frontier captaincy. Francis de Castelnau visited Goiás in 1844 and observed that many local inhabitants had established themselves in camps next to riversides, extracting gold and diamonds, with some villagers venturing deeper inland, risking conflict with local Caiapó, trying to turn their *pénibles recherches* ('arduous pursuits') into great profit.[108]

The incorporation of the diamondiferous lands of Goiás into the monopoly system forced adventurers to look for precious stones elsewhere, and by the middle of the eighteenth century, miners were active along the banks of the Abaeté river, a big stream with various waterfalls, and the Indaiá river. This was a wild and extensive region with no official settlements, roamed by *garimpeiros* and runaway slaves, who clashed violently with colonial forces. In 1791 the authorities decided to send two hundred workers to the banks of the Abaeté in an effort to control mining, but profits were hardly higher than expenses and the project was abandoned four years later. Several stories emerged about miners digging up large diamonds, such as the legend of three banned convicts who were looking for gold in the Abaeté river. After six years of mining, 'braving cannibals and wild beasts', they came across a 144-carat diamond, but Richard Francis Burton (1821–1890), a well-known traveller who spent seven years in India, translated the *Arabian Nights* and the *Kama Sutra* into English, and travelled extensively in Africa and the Americas, including Brazil, concluded it was a false story. The tale of a diamond found in 1791 or 1792 by a fifteen-year-old boy in the Indaía river, on the other hand, was considered to be true.[109] Such stories attracted many adventurers, and some of their settlements developed into towns such as São Gonçalo do Abaeté, about 300 kilometres (186 mi.) from Diamantina (see illus. 20).[110]

The government was not always sure how to deal with the situation. In 1791 colonial officials in Tejuco reported that these deposits were of no importance, while others claimed the region was rich in diamonds. When a certain Captain Isidoro, leader of a group of *garimpeiros*, informed Governor Bernardo José de Lorena about their find of diamonds on the Abaeté, the latter decided to send an expedition there, headed by mineralogist José Vieira Couto, whose family came from Tejuco.[111] Couto concluded that the region was not only very fertile and suited for agriculture, but that it was also rich in platinum, lead, copper, silver, gold and especially diamonds. Couto excused the earlier mistake made by Tejuco's officials by stating that their expertise was with river mining, and not with the dry diggings that characterized Nova Lorena, as the area was named. Lorena was promoted to the position of viceroy of Portuguese India, and in 1807 the new governor was instructed to establish a government-controlled diamond extraction operation in Nova Lorena. Personnel and slaves were sent there from Tejuco, but lack of results ended state-controlled mining in the area the following year, leaving it again in the hands of the *garimpeiros*. Renamed Quartel Geral, the area continued to attract adventurers, and the local army commander wrote in August 1823 about more than three hundred people who arrived in every way, by trail and in canoes.[112]

The Two Brazilian Monopolies

Efforts at monopoly had more success in Brazil. When diamonds from Minas Gerais started to reach Europe, prices for rough diamonds fell and many panicked, thinking that diamonds might become so abundant that interest would disappear.[113] It was said that in 1732 the quantity of imported Brazilian diamonds was four times higher than Indian import figures.[114] That year the English consul in Lisbon, Lord Tyrawley, wrote a letter to the Secretary of State for the Southern Department in which he voiced his concern:

> The discovery of the Diamonds in the mines of the Brasils, has put a stop for the present to that Trade from East India, thô not to

the London market, on accompt of the advantage which England has over its neighbours in the Trade with Lisbon . . . so that the much greater part of the Diamonds that come from the Brasils have hitherto gone to London, from whence they are distributed to the rest of Europe.[115]

Diamond traders and jewellers in Amsterdam and Antwerp started to panic. The renowned trading and banking house of Andries Pels & Sons, established in Amsterdam, sent a letter to Lisbon in which they insisted that measures should be taken. The diamond trading firm of Meulenaer, from Antwerp, also wrote to the authorities in Portugal, complaining that they had a hard time to find buyers for their diamonds and had felt forced to lower their selling prices.[116] Diamond merchants in London petitioned the East India Company to act, and the EIC tried to improve Indian trade by dropping duties on coral and diamonds.[117]

One of the ways in which the established diamond traders attempted to preserve their Indian business was to spread the rumour that Brazilian stones were nothing more than uncut diamonds secretly imported from the Indian mines.[118] According to the nineteenth-century traveller Richard Burton, certain Brazilian miners used such false rumours to their advantage, by 'sending their stones to Goa, whence they were forwarded as true East Indian to Europe'.[119] Such a practice allowed clever miners to make a profit of the conservative story that Indian diamonds were superior in quality, but these unchecked networks would soon enough be the target of an effort made by European wholesale diamond traders and the Portuguese king to fully control the flow of Brazilian diamonds. Quickly, several merchants expressed their interest in buying a commercial monopoly for Brazilian diamonds, and the Portuguese authorities received offers from traders in Lisbon and the Low Countries, all of which they turned down.[120] They opted for a mining prohibition instead, as advised by Francis Salvador. In 1739, when it was decided that mining management needed to be organized on the basis of a monopoly, it was also agreed that the trade in rough diamonds was, to a large extent, to remain free. A few times a year diamonds were shipped to Lisbon, where they ended up in iron boxes at the seat of the overseas council, the Conselho Ultramarino. Representatives of the government and the monopolists, named *caixas*, were appointed to manage sales. Representatives of the king had the first right of purchase, after which the *caixas* were free to sell to any buyer, but always in the presence of a government official.[121] Profits of these sales went to the monopolists, and they served to reimburse bills of exchange issued by the contract holders to keep the mining operations afloat and bought by investors in Lisbon and Rio de Janeiro.[122]

Fraud and diamond smuggling by the third contract holder, Felisberto Caldeira Brant, caused a collapse of the financial system supporting the mining privilege in the early 1750s. The crisis was worsened when the Lisbon *caixas* of João Fernandes de Oliveira, who had won the fourth contract, refused to reimburse bills of exchange still payable under the third contract.[123] Additionally, one of Felisberto Caldeira Brant's privileged trading partners in Lisbon, the firm of Sebastian and Manoel Vanderton, had bought diamonds on credit and then used them as security. Suggestions that the Vanderton firm was the first to hold a commercial monopoly are wrong, but a French diplomat's report written later in the eighteenth century confirmed the dominant position of the firm: 'one of those buying all rough diamonds was Sebastian Vanderton, son of Ernest Vanderton, Antwerp native, lapidary of profession and very experienced in this trade.'[124] The actions of the Caldeira Brants and the Vandertons caused a complete standstill of the diamond trade in Lisbon.[125] One man, however, thought he could use this crisis to alter the existing structures of global diamond trading: the powerful first minister, the marquês de Pombal. He was of the antisemitic opinion that the Jews controlled the diamond trade, that they shared knowledge with each other, and that they set up secret partnerships, with which they purchased all diamonds sold in London, Amsterdam, Livorno and Venice. For the prime minister, diamond trade was de facto a Jewish monopoly, and Francis Salvador was one of its main protectors.[126] While many Jewish merchants indeed participated in the diamond trade, Pombal's opinion of the Jews was extremely negative and partially motivated by his earlier encounters with Salvador. When Pombal was Portuguese ambassador in London, Salvador had lent him money for reconstruction work at the Portuguese embassy, and this had caused a rift between the men.[127] Salvador had also been actively involved with several petitions asking the EIC to reduce duties on Indian diamonds, in order to be able to compete better with Brazil.[128] Pombal wrote in a memoir that Salvador had provided 'sinister counsel' to Portuguese officials, and that the closure of Brazil's diamond mines had 'caused great joy to the famous Hebrew'.[129]

The crisis of 1753 provided Pombal with an instrument to build a Christian trade network that would be able to compete with Jewish merchants. At least, that is how Pombal described it in his memoir.[130] He realized that the diamond trade needed foreign capital and people with connections in Amsterdam and London, where he had been ambassador. The name of Herman Joseph Braamcamp (1709–1775) was suggested, a Dutch merchant who had been Prussian consul in Lisbon, and who had already tried to obtain a mining monopoly in Brazil together with his brother.[131] Braamcamp was given the commercial monopoly in partnership with John Bristow, an English trader and partner of Bristow, Warde & Co., a firm that had been based in Lisbon since 1711. He had been involved in smuggling bullion out of Lisbon in the 1730s and '50s, but had been saved through Pombal's personal intervention.[132] Braamcamp and Bristow signed an agreement with the Portuguese government on 10 August 1753, agreeing to purchase 45,000 carats of rough Brazilian diamonds each year, at 8,000 reis per carat (equivalent to £5.28 then, or a purchasing power between £1,056 and £1,584). The date was not a coincidence, as it was the day before the new law that dealt with Brazilian diamond mining was published. Only the joint venture between Bristow and Braamcamp could sell rough Brazilian diamonds within the Portuguese Empire, but outside the reach of the colonial authorities trade remained free. The contract was signed for an initial period of six years, and its execution would be supervised by Pombal himself. One clause stipulated that Bristow and Braamcamp were to enjoy a discount in case the discovery of new diamond mines in Brazil led to a decline of prices in Europe. Two of the wealthiest Portuguese merchants, Domingos de Bastos Viana and Antonio dos Santos Pinto, were given the function of *caixas*, acting as intermediaries between the different monopolists, a first step in Pombal's plans to draw the Portuguese commercial bourgeoisie closer to colonial trade.[133]

Not long after calm had returned to Lisbon, it was discovered that Francis Salvador and his son Joseph had been secret partners in the contract, as confirmed by Joseph Salvador in 1757: 'the Brazil diamonds in which contract I was formerly concern'd but which I had given up for about a twelve month past now has been taken from Mr. Bristow and his society.'[134] It proved a fatal blow for the two contractors, who were already in difficulties fulfilling their required quota of purchases. Bristow had lost a lot of money in the earthquake that shook Lisbon in 1755, and Bristow, Warde & Co. went bankrupt in 1756.[135] Orders were given to Portuguese officials in London to look for a replacement, and in December 1756 a contract was signed with Anglo-Dutch trader Joshua van Neck and Englishman John Gore, an MP, trader, former South Sea Company director and army contractor.[136] Even though the initial term agreed was three years, history repeated itself and the contract ended prematurely.[137] In 1758 Gore and van Neck wanted to get out of their obligations. The Portuguese ambassador in London received a letter from Joshua van Neck in which he declared that the arrival of ships carrying Indian diamonds worth more than van Neck's Brazilian stones made it impossible for him to sell Brazilian diamonds.[138] A furious Pombal saw in this the hand of the 'Corporation of Jews', whose anger over being left out had made them try to destroy the reputation of the Christian merchants involved.[139]

This time Pombal had had enough of the English. He already considered their participation in Portugal's colonial trade detrimental to the country, and his economic policies had been directed towards excluding foreign traders from Portugal's overseas trade, to which purpose he had established a trade council in 1755 and two Brazilian trading companies, in 1756 and 1760. Yet the third monopoly was still given to a foreigner, this time the Dutchman Daniel Gildemeester. His older brother Jan had come to Lisbon at the age of sixteen and established his own firm in which Daniel became a partner. Later he was named Dutch consul in Lisbon. When Jan returned to Amsterdam, Daniel took over the position, which he still held when he obtained the commercial diamond monopoly in 1761.[140] Gildemeester was given more favourable conditions than his predecessors. He committed to purchasing 40,000 carats of diamonds per year, for 8,600 reis per carat. The contract was to last for three years, but should it be extended, the price would be raised to 9,200 reis. He was explicitly forbidden from trading in Indian diamonds.[141] Gildemeester, and later his son Daniel, secured the commercial monopoly until 1787. It made them very wealthy, and Daniel built the Seteais Palace in the town of Sintra, near Lisbon.

The Gildemeesters were still connected to Amsterdam, and their success in Lisbon ensured Amsterdam a larger supply of rough diamonds than before, which also benefited the cutting industry, already the biggest in Europe, with six hundred families depending on diamond cutting in 1750.[142] During the Gildemeester period, Pombal executed his plans to tie the local commercial bourgeoisie closer to colonial trade. Members of the Bandeira, da Cruz-Sobral and Quintela families were given import-ant posts in commercial organizations and government structures such as the Royal Treasury.[143] Two additional posts as *caixas* in the diamond administration were given to José Francisco da Cruz and José Rodrigues Bandeira, and their families were to occupy these offices for decades to come.[144] Ties were further strengthened through several marriages, not only between the local families but also with notable foreign families such as the Braamcamps. From the diaries of the French ambassador at the time, it is known that the Quintela family, at least, maintained social contacts with the Gildemeesters.[145] The growing involvement of Portuguese merchants can be illustrated by the presence of these families among the investors in the mining contract. A list of bills of exchange covering expenses in the diamond district that were still unpaid in 1770 shows that 29 per cent was in the hands of the Quintela, Bandeira and da Cruz-Sobal families.[146]

Initially, business under Gildemeester went very well, with the Dutch consul buying more diamonds than the minimum he had committed to, with a peak of 91,380 carats in 1767. In 1776 Gildemeester still bought 66,000 carats, but his purchases declined rapidly from 1780 onwards, with 37,000 carats bought that year, 20,000 in both 1781 and 1782 and only 12,000 in 1787.[147] At that time, production in Brazil was dwindling, and the monopoly in mining had already been replaced with the Royal Extraction system. It would take longer before the commercial monopoly also came to an end. Gildemeester's involvement was terminated in 1787, ending a period of 26 years. For a short time he was replaced by two Portuguese traders, Paulo Jorge and João Ferreira, but they quit after wars in Europe and the Ottoman Empire had caused a decline in prices for rough dia-monds.[148] In 1788, six years after Pombal's death, three merchants from Hamburg negotiated a deal with the Portuguese government on behalf of the brothers Benjamin and Abraham Cohen of Amsterdam, and until 1790 the Cohens bought 95,000 carats of diamonds, for 840,800,000 reis. After that, the commercial privilege came into the hands of Pedro Quintela, who purchased 158,168 carats of diamonds between 1791 and 1800.[149] The number equals an average purchase of 15,817 carats per year, while during those years, Brazil produced an average of 20,423 carats of diamonds, meaning Quintela bought 77 per cent of annual production.

By that time Europe had caught revolutionary fever. Neutral Portugal was pressured into abandoning its long-standing alliance with the English, while it also had to borrow money from merchants in 1796 and 1801.[150] Part of the money was paid to France to avert the threat of war, but the short Guerra das Laranjas (War of the Oranges) in 1801, which saw a French-supported Spanish invasion of Portugal, forced the latter into additional monetary payments and the ceding of the town of Olivença to Spain. With French pressure growing, Portugal decided to borrow 13 million florins from two banks, Baring Brothers & Co. in London, and Hope & Co. in Amsterdam. The latter had a history with Brazilian diamonds, at least since the 1740s, selling diamonds in Russia and Turkey. In Lisbon, they maintained contacts with the Vanderton firm, and they also sold Pedro Quintela's diamonds in Amsterdam.[151] It was Quintela who convinced the banks to issue the loan, which was to be repaid in rough Brazilian diamonds between 1802 and 1811.[152] Between 1802 and 1810, Baring received 243,500 carats and Hope 258,000, an amount substantially higher than Brazilian production for those years, causing Portugal to delve into its reserves.[153] A large part of the money was used to sweeten Napoleon, but ultimately it proved insufficient to stop Junot's invasion in 1807. The country went into disarray, and many rough diamonds still stored in the capital were plundered and taken to Paris. Thirty-six ships carrying 15,000 men, including the Portuguese court, were escorted out of Lisbon harbour by English ships, destined for Brazil. The fleet reached Rio de Janeiro in March 1808, where the Portuguese court remained until 1821.[154] Two years earlier, all accounts with the Hope bank had been settled. Between the beginning of the Royal Extraction and 1819, no less than 40 per cent of official Brazilian diamond production was used to repay the loan made with the banks in 1801.[155]

When the court moved to Rio de Janeiro, however, the loan was still open, and the government tried to strengthen its grasp on diamonds. A partially successful attempt was made to control sales through the Banco do Brasil, founded in 1808.[156] But the door had swung open, and several British firms interested in Brazil's riches established branches in Rio de Janeiro. The firm of Samuel, Phillips & Co., related to Nathan Mayer Rothschild through marriage, started to purchase Brazilian gold and diamonds on his behalf, helped by their good connections with the Portuguese royal family. They continued to do so until the mid-nineteenth century.[157] The world of diamonds was not all that big, and Rothschild was married to a daughter of Levi Barent Cohen, an Amsterdam-born Jew who had migrated to England in the 1770s. Cohen traded in various commodities, including Brazilian diamonds, which he consigned to Hope & Co., and was described as a leading diamond trader in London between 1781 and 1794. He joined forces with other Jewish merchants to outbid both Baring and Hope for the purchase of a large amount of Brazilian diamonds in Paris in 1802.[158] Levi Cohen had a cousin in Holland named Benjamin, a trader in tobacco, silver, grain and Brazilian diamonds. It seems plausible that this was the same Benjamin Cohen who held the Brazilian diamond monopoly with his brother between 1788 and 1790.[159]

In March 1821, not long before the return of the court to Lisbon, the king ordered that, in order to repay the debts of his Royal Treasury, all rough and polished diamonds in possession of the diamond administration should be handed over to the Banco do Brasil, which could sell them in Brazil or Europe.[160] Later that year the role of the bank came under scrutiny when a revolutionary council decided in Lisbon that all Brazilian diamonds were to be nationalized, sparking political controversy about the ownership of these precious stones. When Brazil declared itself independent in 1822, the government assumed full possession of all Brazilian diamonds, which in turn led to local protests in Minas Gerais.[161] When the Banco do Brasil went into liquidation in 1829, the commerce in Brazilian diamonds became a free enterprise once more, but by that time production in Minas Gerais had declined a great deal. Trade in Brazilian diamonds was only revived with the discovery of mines in Bahia. Dreams of state-supported monopolies were resurrected sixty years later, in South Africa.

European Consumption in the Eighteenth Century

Methods of alluvial mining did not change much over time, and hardly any new technology was introduced during the nineteenth century. Fluctuations in the quantity of rough diamonds that were being mined depended mostly on the gradual exhaustion of the alluvial diamond fields and the search for new deposits. In the years between 1740 and 1806,

2.7 million carats of diamonds were officially mined: 61 per cent of that quantity was taken from the earth by the monopolists during their 32-year reign, the remainder during the first 35 years of the Royal Extraction.[162] The yearly average of 40,872 carats was frequently surpassed during the contract period and in the first ten years of the Royal Extraction, but 1784 was the last year this average was surpassed.[163] The rise of production during the fourth contract is not surprising as the period was longer, and it was during those years that the deposits at Minas Novas, disputed territory between Bahia and Minas Gerais, came to be included in the diamond district and the official numbers.

The available data for diamond sales in Lisbon show that prices per carat were, with some exceptions, declining, which can be explained by various factors, of which the declining quality of stones was an important element. We also have some information on the costs needed for mining. For the contract period, the known expenses were limited to the head tax on slaves paid to the Crown. For the Royal Extraction period, the sums of money represent the entire cost, including the hiring of slaves, for a given year. Comparing costs to sale prices, the large proportion of the former is very visible. During the contract period, the head tax could amount to more than 40 per cent of the value of sales, while for the period between 1775 and 1790, 85 per cent of sale proceeds was necessary to cover expenses, a large share. There were, however, two caveats. First of all, the king could claim a number of high-quality diamonds. Second, sales numbers did not include all diamonds that were extracted officially, as there was always an amount of unsold diamonds hoarded either in Brazil or Lisbon. In 1790, for instance, a total of 137,622 carats of rough diamonds remained unsold. Still, these ratios show how ineffective the colonial enterprise of diamond mining had become, not least due to a high level of illegal activities.

Yearly averages peaked in the middle of the eighteenth century, and by then it had become clear that the steady mining of diamonds in Brazil disrupted the European market, which was undoubtedly one of the reasons behind the establishment of a monopoly in trade. Contrary to the complaints listed by Pels, Meulenaer and other European houses trading in diamonds, however, it has been asserted that the price in polished diamonds was not influenced by the growing numbers of rough diamonds imported from Brazil. First, it compensated for a declining Indian production, but, more importantly for the European consumer markets, the

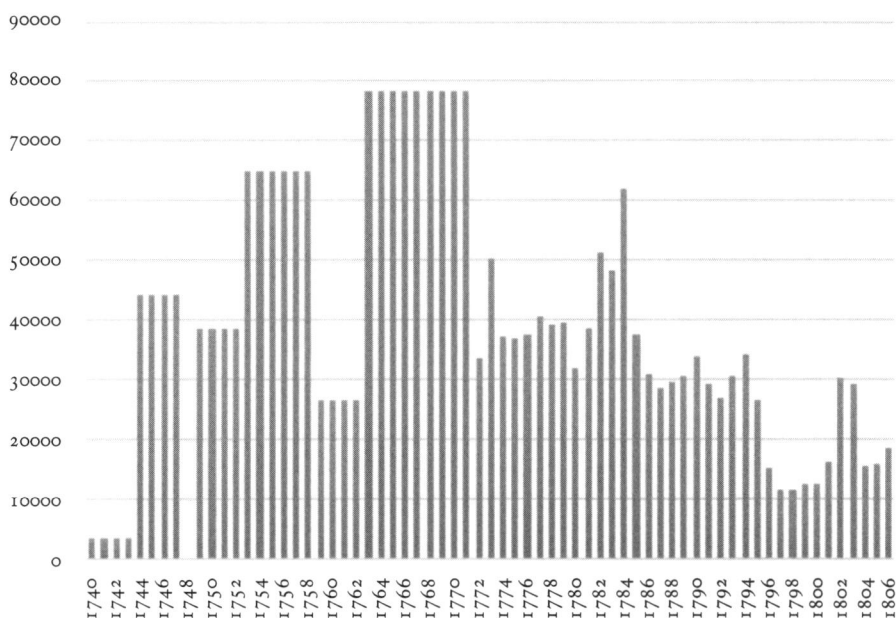

30 Official diamond production in Brazil in carats, 1734–1806.[164]

prices for rough and polished diamonds were not connected. On the basis of price quotations given in early modern accounts, such as the writings of Jean-Baptiste Tavernier and David Jeffries, Godehard Lenzen asserted that the price for 1 carat of polished diamonds with a brilliant cut remained steady: Tavernier quoted it to be 200 gold francs in 1665, while an anonymous manuscript on jewels from 1672 provided the same price. David Jeffries claimed it to be £8 in 1750, the equivalent, according to Lenzen, of 200 gold francs.[165] Lenzen sees an explanation for this remarkable price stability in the fact that the trades in rough and polished diamonds were separated in the early eighteenth century.[166]

In earlier times the European jewellers who travelled in person to India, often through the Portuguese *Carreira da Índia*, went to trade in both the finished and unfinished product. When the Dutch and, in particular, the English East India companies began to control imports of rough diamonds into Europe, a group of merchants in London came to specialize in dealing in rough diamonds alone. Through the EIC they imported rough diamonds that were sold on to jewellers, or to merchants abroad. The EIC also held public sales of rough diamonds, which attracted jewellers who might not have had concrete commercial connections with

India.[167] Public sales allowed for a control of the supply that made it on to the market, and the Brazilian diamond monopoly, with the Portuguese king able to select stones for himself, achieved the same purpose. When the diamond contract system was superseded by the Royal Extraction, it became clear that a significant amount of diamonds had been hoarded. Some accounts pertaining to the second, third and fourth mining contracts were still open, and it was registered that about 33 per cent of all rough diamonds transported by the holders of these contracts to Lisbon had been hoarded. They were transferred to the Royal Treasury after settlement of the accounts.[168] The ability to control supply through hoarding was an essential part of the monopolization of diamond mining and trading. It had been part of the strategy of the East India Company, but they could not control mining. The Portuguese double monopoly was the first time a successful effort was made to control the world's rough diamond supply, and as such the mechanisms that Pombal introduced were direct predecessors of the later successful attempts by De Beers to control the world's diamond production in the twentieth century.

Karin Hofmeester remarked that it was during the eighteenth century that 'a growing circle of bourgeois customers started buying jewellery, and a special taste for diamonds developed as a consequence of the fashionable brilliant cut. Its relative cheapness helped to bring the brilliant within the reach of a wider circle.'[169] Indeed, the eighteenth century was the time of the brilliant. In the second half of the seventeenth century, the French word *brillant* started to be used for diamonds cut with multiple facets. Cardinal Jules Mazarin (1601–1661), chief minister for both Louis XIII and Louis XIV, can be credited as the man who made an early form of the brilliant popular. Mazarin greatly appreciated diamonds and possessed an impressive collection: an early cut of diamonds into brilliants with sixteen facets became known as the 'Mazarin cut' (see illus. 15).[170] According to Marcel Tolkowsky, the Mazarin cut was further improved by a Venetian named Vincenzo Peruzzi, who managed to double the number of facets from 16 to 32 at the very end of the seventeenth century.[171] This cut quickly became very fashionable, and knowledge of it spread so fast that by the turn of the century English cutters had already made themselves a name as specialists in the technique, leading some to consider that the 32-facet brilliant cut had actually been invented in England.[172] It maximized dispersion of light by making its path travelling within the stone as long as possible and remained the standard until the twentieth century. In 1751 the English jeweller David Jeffries wrote about the different ways to polish diamonds, and remarked that

> nothing can more perpetuate rose diamonds on the esteem they have hitherto had in the world, than maintaining the truth of their manufacture. Nor was it ever more fit to be recommended than at present, on account of the corrupt taste that has of late prevailed, in converting rose diamonds into brilliants, under pretence of rendering them, by that means, a more beautiful, and excellent jewel.[173]

The brilliant cut dominated the eighteenth century, characterized by the consumers' 'passion for light and lightness'.[174] Its symmetry and ability to disperse light has made it the dominant form of diamond today, even though much less popular alternative shapes, often labelled as 'fancy cuts', continued to exist.[175]

The same can be said of variations in colour. The French royal tradition in jewellery shifted to an interest in simplicity, to the extent that coloured gemstones were declared out of fashion in 1722.[176] This shift continued into the French Revolution, which further undermined old taste based on class: 'the model of aristocratic fashion and artifice was firmly replaced by a moral model that stressed natural beauty and simplicity . . . simplicity and visibility were powerful concepts because they allowed the new order to justify its ascendancy over the old aristocratic heritage without overthrowing the members of that coterie.'[177]

It is perhaps not a coincidence that a jeweller from Alsace named Georg Friedrich Strass developed a technique in the 1730s to produce fake diamonds by coating lead glass, such as rhinestones, with metal powder. Strass had not come up with his process from nowhere, and there are indications of efforts to produce fake precious stones in Paris since at least 1657, but his improved techniques seem to have been particularly successful; by 1734 Strass had become French royal jeweller and his last name became synonymous with paste jewellery in France. Thirty years later, 314 *joailliers-faussetiers*, or jeweller-counterfeiters, were working in the French capital.[178] The changing European consumer pattern according to gender, which had begun in the seventeenth century, continued during the eighteenth. Women wore jewellery more than men, but it should not be forgotten that 'while the fashion for men's diamonds has fluctuated, it is clear that through long periods of history, men have worn diamonds in rings and hat jewels, on pins attached to cravats, on ceremonial sword hilts, in accessories like snuff boxes and most extensively on shoe buckles.'[179] Historian Marcia Pointon saw in the importance of diamond-laced shoe buckles a reason behind the development of the kind of fake diamonds perfected by Strass, because if a fake diamond were lost from a shoe buckle, the financial loss would be minimal.[180]

The advance of fake diamonds during the eighteenth century is a strong indication of the developing consumer interest in the product. An Amsterdam newspaper published an announcement in 1730 that a considerably large diamond was to be shown to the public in The Hague on a Wednesday morning between 9 and 12. A day before the public viewing, interested parties could go to the house of a certain Mr da Gama, where they could get notes signed by the diamond's owner that were to serve as admission tickets.[181] Five days later, news was published that the public viewing had been cancelled following the discovery that the diamond was a fake.[182] Stories like this confirm the expanding importance of diamonds as luxury products that were coming within reach of an ever-expanding clientele. Specialization of markets, the separation of the commodity chains of rough and polished diamonds, and the growth in supply were all related to the changes that occurred in the world of diamonds after the discovery of the Brazilian deposits. Some of these changes were to remain dominant in the functioning of the mining and trade in rough diamonds for centuries to come. But however disruptive the discovery of diamonds in Brazil, it was dwarfed by the changes that were to come 150 years later in the southern tip of the African continent.

While the discovery of diamonds in Africa at the end of the nineteenth century was to shake the diamond industry to its core, it was in the eighteenth century that the positions of Europe's main diamond centres were solidified.[183] Directly connected to the trade in both Indian and Brazilian rough diamonds, London was the main centre of import, while Amsterdam had become Europe's foremost diamondcutting centre. In 1748 there were more than three hundred polishers active there.[184] Antwerp, which had established a cutting industry before Amsterdam, was struggling to retain a role in the diamond industry, and managed to do so only by specializing in cutting smaller and lower-quality diamonds into roses.[185] In 1739, the year when Brazilian mining was organized as a monopoly, the number of apprentices in the Antwerp Diamond Cutters' Guild peaked at almost 80. In 1754 there were 180 master cutters active in Antwerp, and as many as 1,500 persons (merchants, cleavers, cutters and polishers) earned their income from diamonds.[186] London had a small cutting industry as well, which was said to have produced some of the highest-quality brilliant cuts in the early eighteenth century, such as the Regent diamond.[187]

David Jeffries remarked in his treatise on diamonds that English workers were as good as any other in cutting diamonds. He continued, a tad arrogantly perhaps, that they might be the most skilled in the world, but that the higher wages they earned in comparison to neighbouring countries prevented the establishment of a larger cutting industry.[188] London's cutting industry all but disappeared in the second half of the eighteenth century, while only 26 polishers remained active in Venice in 1773.[189] The French tried to set up a Royal Cutting Factory in Paris in the 1780s, managed by a Jewish cutter from Amsterdam, Isaac Schabracq, who hoped to obtain Brazilian diamonds directly through Gildemeester, holder of the commercial monopoly at the time, but the enterprise came to nothing.[190] Paris, just like Moscow, Istanbul and several Italian cities, had to content itself with remaining a consumer market that was important for the trade in and fabrication of jewellery.

This specialization remained essentially unchanged until the late nineteenth century, although it was contested on several occasions. At times, religion was an important motivation behind such challenges. The Brazilian trade monopoly was explicitly established on the grounds of providing an alternative to Jewish trade networks extending into India. Christian merchants in Antwerp and Amsterdam complained about the Jewish competition and 'our friends who broker or clandestinely trade here [Amsterdam] with smouses or Jews instead of sending their goods to honest Christians'.[191] In 1753 Antwerp traders complained about Jews and other foreign merchants.[192] Four years earlier, about a hundred non-Jewish diamond workers had petitioned the government of Amsterdam for the establishment of a guild in order to deal with Jewish competition. They threatened to leave if their wishes were not granted.[193]

Some of the antisemitic comments made by Christian diamond cutters in their petition are very telling about the shift towards Jewish dominance of the cutting industry. In an attempt to explain why they needed more means of subsistence than the Jews, a number of Christians wrote that 'it is impossible for us, because of our innate nature, to do as the Jews do, and make a living by cleaning shoes, or by buying up combs, glasses and old rags and to help ourselves like swines do, 10 or 12 in a pen.'[194] This comment refers to the old idea that many Ashkenazi Jews were active as pedlars, and that they lived with larger families under one roof. Such virulent antisemitism could not prevent the evolution towards a diamond industry that was dominated by Jewish workers.

Lisbon's role in the Indian diamond trade had already ended in the seventeenth century, but the city managed to become important again thanks to Brazilian diamonds. It did not manage, however, to play a substantial role beyond that of a political decision-making centre. While there were diamond traders active in the Portuguese capital, the issuing of a commercial monopoly avoided the development of Lisbon as a commercial diamond centre itself, in spite of efforts to sell the commercial monopoly to Portuguese businessmen at the end of the eighteenth century and the beginning of the nineteenth. The city also never managed to challenge the position of the cutting industry in the Low Countries, even though it tried. From scant archival material, we know that in the early nineteenth century an attempt was made to develop a diamond-cutting factory near the site of Campo Pequeno in Lisbon. At a time when the Royal Extraction was controlling mining in Brazil, and a Portuguese businessman, Pedro Quintela, held the trading monopoly, it might have been an attempt to keep all three branches of the rough diamond business in Portuguese hands. It was short-lived, however, and there are only receipts for diamond cutters employed in the factory for 1806 and 1807.[195] In 1808 the Portuguese court fled to Rio de Janeiro following the Napoleonic invasion, halting all further attempts to concentrate control over the Brazilian diamond industry in Portuguese hands in Lisbon. When hostilities with France were over, Brazil was already well on its way to independence, and Portugal had to wait until the twentieth century before another of its colonies, this time in Angola, provided them with a new shining treasure.

3

The Rollercoaster towards Industrial Modernity, 1785–1884

And whilst Golconda and Visapur have failed, and the Cape of Good
Hope, Australia, and California are but beginning, and whilst men
sink capital in the trash manufactured in Paris and Birmingham, the
Brazil [*sic*] may still hope to do great things in the 'diamond line'.[1]

T he explorer Richard Burton had already travelled to India, the
Middle East and Africa before a diplomatic posting brought him
to Santos, Brazil, in 1865. He was one of a number of European
travellers who visited the country's diamond fields in person in the nineteenth century. The above quotation exemplifies the optimism many had
in Brazilian diamonds, a feeling that had begun soon after these precious
stones were discovered in Minas Gerais in the early eighteenth century.
The uncertain hopes that Richard Burton still cultivated, however, would
not become reality: by the time he wrote his observations, Brazilian diamond fields had entered a decline from which they would never recover.
And even though he already understood that diamonds had been found in
the Cape Colony, he clearly did not have the foresight that other observers
had about South Africa at around the same time.

In 1870 a Scottish geologist from Glasgow named John Shaw, who
had moved to Colesberg in South Africa to become a school headmaster,
remarked that 'from all I saw and for the reason I have now advanced,
the present diamond digging of South Africa is only trifling in comparison to what it should and will ultimately be.'[2] Three years earlier, the
chance discovery of diamonds by a farm boy had turned the diamond
world upside down. By the middle of the nineteenth century, mining at
the traditional diamond deposits of Borneo, Brazil and India had severely
declined, and the discovery of diamonds in Bahia did not suffice to rescue
Europe's diamond centres in the long run. The basic problem, people grew

to realize, was scientific ignorance about where diamonds came from. So far, throughout history, all diamond findings had been alluvial, keeping mining a relatively primitive and labour-intensive affair. When one area was depleted, miners just moved on to the next. Initially this modus operandi stayed the same when precious stones were found in South Africa, but soon enough the fields of South Africa proved to be rich beyond comparison. Eventually the discovery of diamonds deep in the ground led to the development of pit mining, first in the open air, but later also underground. A new era had been born, and nothing would remain the same. The transition from old to modern, from artisanal to industrial, that took place during the nineteenth century is the subject of this chapter.[3]

An Image of Oriental Decline

Even though there is hardly any information about the quantity of diamonds mined in India and Borneo before modernity, by the mid-eighteenth century it was clear that Asian diamond mining was past its prime, and that existing mining and commercial arrangements could no longer compete with the colonial machinery established in Brazil. At the same time, political rule over the Indian subcontinent was being overturned after the defeat of Siraj ud-Daulah, the last nawab of an independent Bengal, by an EIC army commanded by Robert Clive at the Battle of Plassey in 1757.[4] The well-known battle, dubbed the 'Plassey plunder' by historian Sekhar Bandyopadhyay, initiated British political dominance over the Indian people.[5] Initially the expansionist effort was an EIC project and led to control over eastern India by 1765.[6] Further south, the English were fighting for dominance with the French, who controlled the area around Pondicherry (present-day Puducherry). In 1746 a French naval force led by Bertrand-François Mahé de La Bourdonnais attacked and plundered Fort St George (illus. 9), and many diamonds fell into his hands. La Bourdonnais remained a threat to the trade in diamonds carried by EIC ships in the following year, and in November 1747 the Salvador firm wrote to their correspondent in Antwerp, James Dormer, that:

> The moutfort from Bengall is also arrived this Ship in June was going in to St Paul on the Coast of Africa but notice was given that La Bourdonnaye was in Port on which she tack'd however

La Bourdonnaye Came out x Chased 3 hours 'till it was dark this makes me think that our first Ship from Fort St Davids [near Chennai] runs some risk in Case she should be taken by La Bourdonnaye the whole quantity of Diamonds from India will Center there x the Coup in buying 'tho the larger will be the Surer as we shall be intirely masters of that branch for the present untill a fresh supply Comes to Europe which Cannot be 'till next year.[7]

The Salvador firm obtained most of its diamonds from India, but they saw in the Anglo-French hostilities an opportunity to dominate the global diamond trade, at least for a while. When La Bourdonnais fell out of favour with the French government, which led to his arrest and imprisonment in the Bastille until his release in 1751, Salvador and Dormer tried to locate his wife. She was rumoured to be travelling across Europe trying to sell parcels of diamonds her husband had obtained in the siege of Fort St George.[8] These incidental French successes did not prevent the loss of France's Indian possessions during the Seven Years War.

Although the French regained their Indian settlements by the terms of the 1763 Treaty of Paris, they never managed to play any further role in the European oppression of India and the French East India Company was dissolved in 1769, leaving the English as the dominant European colonial force on the Indian subcontinent.[9] Several India Acts published by the British government at the end of the eighteenth century and beginning of the nineteenth first led to the establishment of joint control by the Company and the government, represented by the governor-general, over India. This period also included further expansion at the expense of several local rulers, particularly the Marathas.[10] In the northwest, the Anglo-Sikh wars of the 1840s resulted in British victory and the annexation of the Punjab to British colonial India. Ten-year-old Duleep Singh, son of Ranjit Singh and the last maharajah of the Sikh Empire, was forced to hand over the Koh-i-Noor diamond to Queen Victoria as stipulated in a treaty of surrender the young maharajah signed in March 1849.[11] The British had made some requests in the treaty of surrender and the handover of what was perhaps the world's most famous diamond figured high on the list, an indication of both the symbolic and financial value that was attached to the ownership of the Koh-i-Noor, which had passed from the Mughals to Ranjit Singh to the British. In 1851 it was shown for the first time to the public in the Crystal Palace built in Hyde Park for the Great Exhibition of the Works of Industry of All Nations in London.[12] The government of India has demanded the return of the Koh-i-Noor on various occasions since independence, and as recently as 2019 a similar request was made by the minister of information of the Pakistani government, Fawad Chaudhry. He expressed the hope that the British would give the diamond to the Lahore Museum. In spite of these requests, which are part of a growing demand of governments of formerly colonized territories to return plundered cultural artefacts, neither the British Crown nor the British government has complied.[13]

In 1857 an event sometimes referred to as the First Indian War of Independence but often still known as the Sepoy or Indian Mutiny led to uprisings throughout Company-controlled territories. Sepoys were Indian soldiers originally in Mughal service, but in this context they were infantrymen in British service. They protested against British colonial regulation and the unrest that followed was met with bloody reprisals, leading to the deaths of hundreds of thousands of Indians, possibly even many more.[14] In 1858 the British government abolished Company rule and British India became a colony under full and direct rule by the British government.[15] India's political evolution from Mughal rule to Mughal decline and the rise of the Marathas, the Sikhs and other local rulers, ending with territorial occupation by the East India Company and the British government, created long periods of chaos and warfare in several parts of the immense country, adding to the general decline of diamond exploitation.

This image of decline is confirmed by travel accounts and contemporary scientific publications. We know a great deal about the state of India's diamond mines in the late nineteenth century thanks to the work of Valentine Ball (1843–1895), an Irish geologist who worked for the Geological Survey of India, established by the EIC in 1851 to explore the possibilities to extract coal to be used for the railways. It still exists as part of India's Ministry of Mines.[16] In 1881, the year he left the Geological Survey, Ball published a report on the mining of coal, gold and diamonds in India, which contains ample information on the state of India's diamond affairs at the time. A number of diamondiferous areas belonging to Ritter's Kedapa group were still being worked (see illus. 5). Near the town of Condapetta miners were 'digging out' pebbles and gravel, which they transported to small reservoirs on mounds, in which the gravel was washed to collect diamonds under the supervision of local diamond contractors who paid 250 rupees for the exclusive right to mine diamonds in a zone stretching 100 yards long and 50 yards wide for four months. The contractors, who were personally interviewed by Ball, claimed to have made a profit in 1834, but to have suffered a loss a year later.[17] In Chennur, near Kedapa, a certain gentleman from Chennai named Richardson had obtained permission to work at the reopened mines there for 100 rupees per year. Although the works were said to have yielded two diamonds, sold for 5,000 and 3,000 rupees respectively, the operation did not prove to be profitable.[18]

On the basis of earlier reports, Ball asserted that most of the fourteen diamond localities in the Karnool district, which corresponds largely with Ritter's Kedapa and Nandial groups, were deserted. Banaganpilly, located 60 kilometres (37 mi.) from the city of Karnool in present-day Andhra Pradesh, was one of the few places in the region where miners were still active.[19] The mines at Banaganpilly were not alluvial, but rock workings. Local labourers extracted diamondiferous rock, then transported it to a washing site where women and children looked for diamonds. When Ball visited the mines, he did not see any diamonds being found, although several stones that were brought to him were said to originate from there. Ball felt, however, they were 'most disappointing in their minuteness, flaws, and dirty colours'.[20] His description suggests a dire state of affairs. They were not much better at Ramulkota, where the rock workings had been deserted, but three hundred locals were still working the riverbeds during the wet season. Contractors leased the area from the nawab of Karnool and sublet it to third parties. The labourers were hired for only three half-pence and a meal of rice per day.[21] The diamondiferous zone that Ritter had named the Ellore or Golconda group, and which contained some of India's most famous mines, was hardly producing better results. At the time of a British visit in 1871, the Golapilly mine 'had the appearance of having been long abandoned, being covered with bush jungle'.[22]

Up north, the various riverside fields in the Chota Nagpur area were still being worked in the first half of the nineteenth century, witnessed by several European travellers who visited alluvial sites in the Mahanadi river during that period.[23] When Ball was writing about these areas, however, mining activities had almost stopped completely, and the Irish geologist mentioned several spots that locals pointed out as places where diamonds had been mined. The descendants of the raja of Chota Nagpur were said to still own several large diamonds mined in the area.[24] The most famous mine in central India, to the east of Chota Nagpur, was Sambalpur, which, together with the rest of Odisha, had come under British control in the early nineteenth century. Until 1833 an EIC agent, who was stationed near Sambalpur, went to the mines once a year to collect, sort and class diamonds. He was responsible for sending the diamonds found there to Kolkata, but results were so disappointing that the Company put a stop to it. Sambalpur was well known and regularly visited, so Ball spent several pages tracing the known history of the locality, already described by Jean-Baptiste Tavernier in the seventeenth century. In spite of several efforts to install a mining lease in Sambalpur during British occupation, it seems that Sambalpur's productive history had come to an end in Ball's time:

> Within the past few years statements have gone the round of the Indian papers to the effect that diamonds are now occasionally found by the gold-washers of Sambalpur. All my inquiries failed to elicit a single authentic case, and the gold-washers I spoke to and saw at work assured me that the statements were incorrect.[25]

Next to failed efforts by the EIC, it seems the dire state of the country's diamond mines as well as the growing control of the British attracted adventurers hoping to make a fortune. In the early 1840s the EIC declined an offer made by a gentleman of the Bengal army who had come to England to convince the Company's directors to allow him to manage the diamond mines at Sambalpur and Bundelkhand in person.[26]

The most famous mines in Bundelkhand, Ritter's fifth and final group, were located in Panna (see illus. 5). Bundelkhand had been under Maratha control since the early eighteenth century, but it was ceded to the British in the first decade of the nineteenth century when its maharajah became a British vassal.[27] The maharajah was still able to grant local people licences for diamond mining on his lands. Sometimes, outsiders obtained such permissions, as the list for 1833 contains one European. Ball noted that about three-quarters of the population of Panna and the nearby villages earned their livelihood from diamond mining, either as hired labourers or working for themselves.[28] During his travels in India during the 1860s,

French writer and photographer Louis Rousselet (1845–1929) met Panna's maharajah, who was wearing not only the costume of the 'réformateurs du Bengale [reformers from Bengal]' but a 'magnifique collier de diamants de ses mines [a magnificent necklace made of diamonds coming from his own mines]'.[29] Rousselet's assertion that the Panna mines may be the oldest diamond mines in India confirms how difficult it is at times to identify ancient mentions of diamond localities with present-day names. The Frenchman substantiated his claim about Panna by referring to Ptolemy's 'Panassa', but recent GIS-based research has identified Panassa with present-day Bhagsar in the Punjab, more than 1,000 kilometres (620 mi.) northwest of Panna.[30]

Panna's mines were certainly old, though, and the maharajah's promise to allow Rousselet to visit the mines must have made the Frenchman quite excited, but he could not hide his disappointment when he arrived at a hole near an elevated hill, guarded by a few ragged soldiers, where the only activity was a wheel worked by four oxen to pump the water out, and the movement of a few naked workers transporting diamondiferous

31 Diamond mine, Panna, India, 1875.

gravel to a washing site. The hole had a diameter of about 12 to 15 metres (40–50 ft) and a depth of 20 metres (65 ft). Inside, labourers were working almost naked, knee-deep in the water (illus. 31). Operations were primitive and costly: in order to get 1 cubic metre (35 cu. ft) of diamondiferous earth, 100 cubic metres needed to be displaced by the miners. Rousselet had no doubt that modern mining techniques, such as the construction of underground galleries, would yield much better results.[31]

Panna diamonds were generally of good quality, with all shades of colour found there, and measured on average five to six carats. He claimed a produce of 1.5 to 2 million francs was extracted out of the mines every year but had no doubts that real revenues were twice as high. Rousselet further remarked that the maharajah sold the diamonds in Allahabad and Benares. Originally, only rough diamonds were sold, but Rousselet stated that in recent years a few cutting workshops had been established near the mines. The Frenchman felt that theft and smuggling were incurable in a country rife with corruption among all classes. The maharajah's solution was the establishment of approximative revenues; if the mine's production did not yield a certain amount, one of the supervisors was decapitated.[32] While Rousselet was disappointed when he actually saw the mines, he did not express any opinion on the nature of the labour. Similar to the treatment of workers and slaves in India and Brazil during the early modern period, the men Rousselet watched at work were operating in unrelenting and unhealthy circumstances. Working underground, with both feet in water, made these men susceptible to disease and to accidents.[33] Ball's description of the different mines in Panna contains a few more references to the nature of labour. He felt that miners 'go to the immense labour of excavating deep pits . . . for the sake of the small patch of diamond conglomerate thus uncovered'.[34] This observation confirmed the growing exhaustion of India's diamond deposits, leading to a need to always dig deeper, at the expense of the labourers. Ball included a text from an article that had appeared in an Indian newspaper, providing more detail on the working circumstances:

> manual labour being cheap, as the poorest subjects of the State work them [the mines]. From the commencement of the rains to the beginning of the cold season the mining goes on, since a plentiful supply of water can be had in all parts of the State – an article highly necessary to facilitate the search . . . Almost

three-fourths of the people of Panna and the adjacent villages derive their living by working either for themselves or as hired labourers for others. When employed on their own account, it is not unusual to hear them complain of 'no luck for months and months'. Indeed, I never knew a native, during the short time I was in the State, who said he had found a diamond.[35]

Next to cheap wages and the difficulty of finding diamonds, the article also described that the previous maharajah had been a very avaricious ruler, whose revenues relied mainly on diamonds. He had taxed mining unreasonably high and decided that diamonds above a certain weight automatically became his property – a common practice for rulers. All of this created a vindictive spirit among the workers and contractors.[36]

The dire state of Indian diamond mining in the late nineteenth century is also reflected in the functioning of local workshops. These always existed side by side with the European workshops, as a great deal of diamonds remained in India to suit the ruling elites. Diamond cutters had operated for centuries near famous diamond mines in Golconda, Ramulkota and elsewhere, as described by Tavernier and others. Karin Hofmeester used the example of the cutting industry near Ramulkota to demonstrate that the cutters' activities were disturbed by the political violence of the time, as they fled from the invading Marathas at the end of the second decade of the nineteenth century.[37] Such displacements, as well as the establishment of workshops in trading centres such as Allahabad and Benares, led to a dispersed cutting industry that was able to cater for the local market, but that could not compete with the European diamond industry, although that would change in the twentieth century. Ball concluded his chapter on Indian diamonds on a rather pessimistic note. He believed that, even with scientific support and extensive prospecting, it would be difficult to set up a viable operation and would only be tempting for those 'content with a slowly-paying occupation and a hard life'.[38]

The Failure of Colonial Extraction Schemes in Borneo

The situation in Borneo was not that different from what was happening in India. After the Bantam sultan had taken over Sukadana and Landak, the western states came increasingly under Dutch control. In 1818 the

Dutch concluded treaties with the sultanates of Sambas, Pontianak and Mempawah. Six years later an Anglo-Dutch treaty effectively divided the island into two parts, based on a fairly random drawing of borders, ending colonial competition over the island. In 1849 Pontianak became the capital of the Dutch Western Division of Borneo.[39] Next to this Division, the Dutch also had a second colonial administrative unit, the Southern and Eastern Division, which included the former sultanate of Banjarmasin and its diamond mines.[40]

The Western Division contained the bulk of Borneo's diamond deposits, particularly the region around the town of Martapura, which became an important diamond centre (see illus. 14). Systematic exploitation of the island's diamond deposits in the nineteenth century was done mainly by the Dutch. Since the eighteenth century there had been an important Chinese presence in Borneo, but Chinese workers and businessmen focused more on gold extraction than on diamonds, while the Dutch colonial government made various attempts to expand its diamond mining operations.[41] From the 1850s onwards, engineers were exploring the mineral possibilities of Borneo in a more systematic manner, investigating deposits of gold, tin, platinum, copper and coal.[42] Several studies were published discussing new diamond prospecting in known regions of Borneo. One of the most extensive reports was compiled by Tivadar Posewitz, an engineer who had spent three years on the island. He was aware of the island's diamond-rich history, and wrote that diamond exports in 1738 had been valued somewhere between 8 and 12 million guilders, but that these numbers had fallen to a million in the early nineteenth century, 117,000 in 1838 and 339,000 in 1843.[43]

In 1833 all monopoly rights on diamond mining in Borneo were abolished to make way for freedom of enterprise, at around the same time it happened in Brazil.[44] Interested parties in Borneo were not subject to many rules: they only had to register and pay a licence fee of 1 guilder per month.[45] This was raised to 3 guilders in 1875.[46] The higher fee, though, came at a very bad time for Borneo's diamond miners. Prices for rough diamonds on the world market had fallen after the understanding that South Africa's diamond deposits, discovered about a decade earlier, had enormous potential. Dutch records of imports of Bornean diamonds arriving on Java show a steady decline, from 5,473 carats in 1836 to 1,315 carats in 1843, a number that is compatible with Posewitz's observations mentioned above. The licence system did manage to introduce a small rise, even at the increased prices. In 1876 toll registers indicate the import of 4,062 carats from Borneo into Java, a number that rose to 6,673 carats in 1879, the apogee. A year later imports had fallen to 3,013 carats,[47] while only 235 licences were issued.[48]

In 1880 the French mining engineers F. E. and L.C.J. Simonar went on a prospecting trip to the southeastern corner of the island and managed to obtain a 75-year concession to exploit different gold and diamond deposits in an area of 2,100 hectares (5,200 ac), against payment of 6 per cent of net proceeds. The enterprise was financially backed by the Rothschild bank in Paris, and later by the De Beers DMC.[49] Despite this support and the arrival of modern machinery, results were disappointing and mining was suspended in 1883. The operation was sold to the Borneo Mining Company, which also did not achieve any results.[50] Further efforts by companies based in Amsterdam and London, with long-forgotten names such as the Pontianak Diamond Syndicate and the Sambas Exploration Company, demonstrated a continued European interest in directly exploiting diamond mines in Asia, without much success. The failure of industrialization in Borneo was strongly reminiscent of Western efforts in South America, and very different from the developments in South Africa.[51]

Borneo's diamond production remained small and based on traditional methods, and licence-based digging remained in place. Between 1876 and 1884 a total weight of 36,546 carats of diamonds was exported from Landak, a number that could not compare with Brazilian exports of the eighteenth century or South African profits in the late nineteenth century.[52] These numbers dropped to a low point at the turn of the century, with a production of 859 carats in 1904 and 710 a year later.[53] In 1906 the total produce of diamonds in Borneo was 3,800 carats, obtained by 10,450 licences. A year later, these numbers had risen to 4,100 carats and 12,073 licences, but they gradually diminished again to 1,590 carats and 8,120 licences in 1913.[54] A licensed area was worked by twelve men, meaning that, between 1906 and 1913, a yearly average of 740 men was working in the diamond mines of Borneo, still a substantial number, but tiny in comparison to the more than 11,000 labourers employed at Kimberley in South Africa in 1914.[55]

Posewitz saw different reasons for the poor state of Borneo's diamond mining industry. First, the most accessible deposits had been mined extensively. In spite of his conviction that rich deposits remained present in Borneo, Posewitz felt a lack of investment hindered mining. Second, Borneo's diamonds had difficulty competing with the cheaper South African diamonds that were imported onto the island to be worked in the local workshops.[56] A third reason was the local rulers' oppressive treatment of the workers, both local and Chinese. Even though the monopoly system had been abandoned by the Dutch, the control of several mines remained in the hands of the local ruling families, who paid very low wages and forced workers to hand over diamonds of a certain size. According to Posewitz, such discouraging mining regimes led miners to abandon their work. Posewitz gave the example of Landak, where 'before the eighties [1880s], the natives dug diamonds in the mines for the Sultan, receiving in exchange rice, tobacco, and one dollar per carat.'[57] The number of workers looking for gold and diamonds there decreased from 344 in 1881 to 87 in 1884.[58] In Sangau, where 462 miners were working in 1857, 'the diamond mines were worked by means of forced labour, the slaves of the Sultan being during the twenties put to work there.'[59] Even in an environment in which slavery officially did not exist and mining might have been technically free, concentration of political power into the hands of a few ruling families and the uncertain state of mining allowed for the continuing abuse of the workforce.

As was the case in India, local cutting industries had developed near the diamondiferous areas of Borneo. According to Posewitz, one of the local sultans decided to employ diamond cutters from nearby Java, where the Dutch capital Batavia was located. The sultan apparently had decided to establish his own cutting factory because Chinese merchants had pointed out to him that finished diamonds were worth more than rough ones.[60] Posewitz, one of the few authors who has provided some numbers on the matter, claimed that in Ngabong, Landak's main town, sixteen diamond workshops existed in 1838, a number that had dropped to seven in 1858.[61] It seems that next to European-style cuts, local cuts also existed. Posewitz wrote that Landak's workshops cut diamonds either as a brilliant or as a *belahan*, an Indonesian word that means cleavage, and that according to Posewitz was a cut that turned the diamond into a flat stone. Diamonds were also cut as rosettes, but in spite of this local industry, most cutting was still done in Europe.[62] John Crawfurd (1783–1868), a Scottish diplomat who had been resident in Singapore and Java and who wrote extensively about the history of the Indonesian archipelago, observed that local populations on the different islands all appreciated diamonds, and that it was the only gemstone that was cut by them. He thought that the art of cutting was a local skill, and not an imported one, but he also remarked that 'if ever the principal tribes, the Javanese, Malays, and people of Celebes, understood the art of cutting the diamond, they have now lost it, but diamond-cutters are still found in Banjarmasin, near the seat of the mines.'[63] Crawfurd also saw that local taste differed from than that of Europeans, as he argued that local consumers preferred 'a kind of table cut', which might be the same as Posewitz's *belahan*, while they did not appreciate the brilliant or rose cuts.[64]

The Return of Free Mining in Brazil

It is tempting to reduce the history of diamond mining in the nineteenth century to a story of Asian decline and African success. Although a simplification, this narrative still contains a great deal of truth. It fails, however, to look at events in South America. Brazil's diamond production was very much rooted in Portuguese colonialism. Trade networks developed following a state-issued monopoly on the diamond trade, and mining in Brazil took place in well-defined areas, first by a Portuguese enterprise supervised by colonial officials, and later by the colonial government itself on behalf of the Portuguese Crown. Work in the mines was done by enslaved Africans, who were brought to Brazil in enormous numbers. Although most of these abused men and women were forced to work on plantations, the *Estrada Real* (Royal Road) connected the diamond region with Rio de Janeiro, ensuring the transport of rough diamonds to the port city (illus. 32) and from there to Lisbon and bringing in thousands of African slaves to labour in the mines.

A focus on the colonial period of Brazilian diamond mining has created a lacuna in most historiographies on Brazilian diamonds, which often stop at the time of the French invasion of Portugal and the financial arrangements involving diamonds made with Britain and France. While diamond mining in Brazil plunged in productivity as it did on the other side of the globe in Asia, it never came to a halt.[65] By the time D. Pedro declared himself emperor of an independent Brazil in September 1822, it was clear that the colonial extraction of diamonds was in a dire state.

32 Diamond convoy passing through Caeté, Brazil, 1835.

The debts of the diamond administration had risen to a million cruzados, a huge amount.[66] Ten years later, in October 1832, a year after Pedro II had come to the Brazilian throne at the age of five, the Royal Extraction system was abolished. It was decided that lands were to be rented out to individual miners, who had to be Brazilian. The system was to be overseen by a specially appointed inspector.[67] While this plan offered a legitimization of the *garimpo* and was a way out for those miners who had been working illegally, the proposed abolition of the colonial structure was not turned into practice, although it was no longer officially 'colonial'. Governmental mining continued, but at a very low level. A well-known local chronicler of the area, Joaquim Félicio dos Santos, wrote that in 1841 operations were limited to Curralinho, with one 'gloomy and melancholic' overseer and ten hired slaves (see illus. 20). Illus. 28, from twenty years earlier, shows the same site, but does not really reveal to what extent the situation had improved since colonial times, only that black enslaved men had to work under the supervision of three white overseers.[68] Several terrains in the area were worked by individual miners for their own account, but it was not entirely clear how they related to extraction by the state. Finally, amidst chaos and uncertainty, the government abolished the Royal Extraction system for good, by a decree issued in September 1845. The special administrative status of the diamond district disappeared, and mining was to be supervised by the provincial government of Minas Gerais. For diamonds, this was done through the Administração-Geral (or Inspetoria-Geral) dos Terrenos Diamantinos, established in Tejuco, which had been renamed as Diamantina in 1832. Tracts of land were rented to miners for varying prices, allocated through pubic auctions for periods of four to ten years. In 1864, 1,000 reis were asked for each 3.7 square metres (40 sq. ft) of land that had been mined before, while 5,000 reis were asked for yet unexplored territory. Gold miners were restricted to work in designated areas so they would not interfere with diamond extraction.[69] Certain difficulties remained, and many people illegally continued to look for diamonds, leading the government to abandon the public auction system and regularize land rents to accommodate the existing situation. Rental sums were lowered, and the system was accepted by the miners, leading dos Santos to write that 'it was a law we judged to be excellent.'[70]

Around the middle of the nineteenth century, two types of diamond mining existed. There was a lot of small-scale activity by individual *garimpeiros*, itinerant workers who sometimes joined forces to prospect and work an area together. There were also a number of partnerships and small companies that continued to employ slaves. Brazil was one of the last countries to abolish slavery, with the Golden Law of 1888, a law that liberated about 700,000 enslaved women and men. By that time most people of African descent had been manumitted or were born free, but substantial numbers were still held captive in slavery.[71] In colonial times, the diamond district was difficult to access because of legal impediments, something that changed during the nineteenth century. Most of the foreign travellers who visited the diamond fields at that time, such as Richard Burton, John Mawe, Auguste de Saint-Hilaire, Spix and Martius, Francis de Castelnau, George Gardner, Johann Jakob von Tschudi, Maria Graham and Johann Pohl, focused on descriptions of the larger mining operations done by firms, and dealt only in a limited manner with individual mining. Von Tschudi, for instance, visited a washing site (*lavra*) in 1858, where a company forced 120 enslaved Africans to mine at a depth of 18 metres (60 ft). Here they were digging up about 35 to 70 carats per week, which would amount to a very low production totalling between 1,820 and 3,640 carats per year. Von Tschudi confirmed that mining activities were not very lucrative. On the *garimpeiros*, he only wrote that they were poor people, that their numbers were in the thousands, and that they sometimes joined forces to pay the necessary taxes.[72] A decade later, Burton described his visit to a mine supervised by a descendant of the Brant family (illus. 33).[73] Another mine Burton visited had a pit that was 25 metres (80 ft) deep and approximately 6 metres (19–20 ft) wide, in which 'black and whitey-brown labourers, free as well as servile' were extracting diamondiferous earth, using an oval-shaped iron tool called an *almocafre*, which was then brought to the surface for sieving and washing, in a manner similar to practices in India (see illus. 8). As methods had changed so little, Burton quickly recognized them from the images he had seen in John Mawe's book as a child. He did not see any machinery in use, only water pumps, remarking that he saw 'no trace of kibble, crane and pulley, or rail ... the negro was the only implement'.[74]

Burton observed that the need to dig deeper, which had to do with gradual exhaustion of the diamond areas (illus. 33), had restricted mining operations to capitalists, at times employing hundreds of slaves, a remark that shows the foreign travellers' general lack of knowledge about the widespread practice of the *garimpo*.[75] Official sources show that illegal individual mining was still rampant. In 1860 the arrival of between 3,000 and 4,000 adventurers along the Ribeirão das Canôas led to the establishment of a town with brick houses and a church.[76] In May 1863 the city council of Lagoa Seca, not far from Diamantina, reported the arrival of more than two hundred *garimpeiros*, 'people in a poor condition' with nothing to lose. When a police force of more than a hundred strong tried to expel them, fights broke out, leading to several deaths.[77] A similar letter sent two years later mentioned an invasion of four hundred illegal miners and labelled them as 'persons who for the most part belong to the lowest class of society'.[78]

Not all small-scale mining was illegal, however, and the majority of lands were rented by individual miners. In the municipality of Diamantina, 74.6 per cent of the land rented out between 1875 and 1890 was given to individuals, who were all male, with very few exceptions.[79] One of them was the son of a carpenter who had come to Brazil from Bohemia in 1831. His name was Augusto Elias Kubitschek, and he was the grandfather of Juscelino Kubitschek, who was president of Brazil between 1956 and 1961. Born in Diamantina and affectionately known as 'JK', President Kubitschek constructed the nation's current capital of Brasília, in the heart of Brazil.[80] Originally the legislation of 1832 had preserved the right of mining for Brazilians, but as the example of Kubitschek shows, half a century later, foreign adventurers had found their way to the Brazilian diamond fields. Burton himself had heard of an Irishman working for the Diamond Administration, and encountered Cornish miners in the diamond region, but also other Englishmen, a Prussian and a Frenchman.[81]

33 Mining the diamonds of Felisberto d'Andrade Brant,
São João da Chapada, 1869. Photograph by Augusto Riedel.

The participation of the city of Diamantina in several world fairs from the 1850s onwards and the establishment of a mining school in Ouro Preto contributed to the attraction of foreign capital to the diamond fields.[82] Following the rapid development of industrial diamond mining in Africa at the end of the nineteenth century, these foreign investors hoped to mechanize diamond washing and dredging in Brazil. The first company to implement modern mining methods was the Companhia de Boa Vista, founded with French, Belgian and Brazilian capital to purchase modern machinery such as hydraulic pumps. Its mining operations in Curralinho were abandoned by 1907. Twelve years later, fifteen foreign companies were operating around Diamantina.[83] None of these foreign mining companies, with names such as Serrinha Limitada, the Pittsburgh-Brazilian Dredging Company and the Diamond Mining Company, managed to set up long-lasting and profitable operations, and they all disappeared. A similar fate awaited most of the foreign adventurers who were attracted to the promise of riches. Most of their names have vanished in history, leaving little trace beyond an occasional nameless mention in a travel journal. A notable exception was the Dutchman Nicolaas Verschuur, who travelled in the wild *sertões* of Bahia and Minas Gerais looking for diamonds and other precious stones. He sent letters to the Netherlands that were published in the newspaper *Het Nieuws van de Dag* between 1897 and 1902.[84]

A Diamond Rush in Bahia

So far it is clear that the historical diamond mining sites in Brazil, Borneo and India were all in a state of decay during the nineteenth century. Until the discovery of diamond deposits in South Africa turned the world upside down, hardly any new areas were being mined, adding to the general image of decline. There was, however, one major, but short-lived, exception: the diamond rush in Bahia. In colonial times diamonds had been found in the border region between Bahia and Minas Gerais, and as early as October 1734, even before the diamond mines around Tejuco were closed following the European price crisis, the viceroy of Brazil had given orders forbidding diamond mining in Bahia.[85] Miners defied these laws, but in spite of their growing activities, the colonial authorities did not see enough potential in the area to establish a Bahian diamond administration. Perhaps the government felt that by allowing miners to work uncontrolled in Bahia, the diamond district around Tejuco, deemed to be much richer, would be easier to control. During colonial times, diamondiferous areas in Bahia were never put under any official regime and unorganized diamond mining continued.

When the German explorers Spix and Martius visited the valley of the diamondiferous Serra do Sincorá mountain range in the autumn of 1818, they described it as an idyllic alpine landscape, complete with a clear mountain stream and purple-red flowers. Everything reminded them of the old diamond capital of Tejuco, they wrote, and they expressed regret at not being able to stay there longer.[86] Had they indeed decided to remain in such pleasant surroundings, their enjoyment would surely have been disrupted a few decades later. In the early 1840s the story of an enslaved man who collected 700 carats of diamonds in twenty days led to a diamond rush that brought between 8,000 and 9,000 criminals, speculators, adventurers and sugar planters, accompanied by their slaves, to the Serra do Sincorá, even though the story of the discovery was exaggerated and quite possibly false.[87] In July 1845 newspapers reported that the number of miners had grown to 30,000, spread over seven towns, the most important of which became Lençóis, its name deriving from the miners' white tents (*lençóis* is Portuguese for sheets) (see illus. 20).[88] European companies rushed to Bahia as well, and it was reported that during a few months in 1845 English vessels had shipped more than 1.5 million French francs worth of diamonds, with one English company gaining as much as £200,000. The Bahian fields were estimated to produce about 1,450 carats per day, which would be equivalent to about half a million carats per year, a number that the diamond district did not reach even during its colonial heyday, and which might have been an exaggeration or only applicable for a short period of time.[89]

These numbers were so promising that the authorities decided to establish a General Administration, much like the one in Minas Gerais, and the first official report on Bahia's diamond fields came from the general inspector, Benedicto da Silva Acauã, in 1847. His comments, published in 1869, provided more insight into the story of the diamond rush in 1844. According to Acauã, a man named José Pereira do Prado found several diamonds in the Paraguaçu river and a few smaller streams nearby, all reachable within four days' travel from the provincial capital Salvador.[90] All of these sites were alluvial, and mining was very similar to operations in the diamond district in Minas Gerais. Acauã described one important novelty, the practice of installing poles in the middle of rivers, which were used by divers who collected the *cascalho* from the bottom of the river.[91] Bahian diamond production soon surpassed that of Minas Gerais. Between 1850 and 1885, digging at the Serra do Sincorá produced an estimated 1.5 million carats, an average of about 42,000 carats per year, with peaks of 300,000 in 1850 and 1851, or about 822 carats per day, a number still far from the 1,450 carats reported earlier. Averages for Diamantina between 1843 and 1885 were about 35,000 carats per year, and the same number applied to the combined production of other regions in Minas Gerais, Goiás and Mato Grosso, which had mining deposits near the towns of Diamantino and Cuiabá.[92] If these numbers were correct, it meant that total Brazilian diamond production for the second half of the nineteenth century increased by a third because of the Bahian diamond fields. As they do not include clandestine mining, these numbers have to be taken with a pinch of salt, but they are still indicative of the importance of the Bahian diamond rush, especially at a time when most diamond fields were becoming depleted. Harry Emanuel (1831–1898), a well-known British jeweller who wrote a book on diamonds and other precious stones, asserted that the early years of the Bahian diamond rush led to a 50 per cent fall in prices for rough diamonds in Europe. He also remarked that Bahian production numbers lowered rapidly, which brought the price level back to normal.[93] Even though the rush was spectacular, events in Bahia soon vanished against the developments in South Africa. While at least 20,000 miners were active in Bahia in 1845, their numbers had fallen to 5,000 by 1901.[94]

The rapid decline of the Bahian diamond fields did not signify the end of the region's involvement in diamond mining. From an early stage, it was clear that Bahian rivers contained more than diamonds. The rivers contained dark-coloured masses that were made up of very small diamond crystals mixed with other minerals such as graphite. Originally discarded as worthless, these masses became known as *carbonados*, or black diamonds (illus. 34). Their origins in geological terms have not yet been explained to full satisfaction, and it is possible that they were originally created in space.[95] When the Genevan engineer J. R. Leschot came up with his idea for diamond drill bits in 1862, he found that *carbonados*, with a hardness approaching that of the diamond, were very suited for that purpose (illus. 35).[96] Subsequently, the price of Bahian black diamonds increased fifty-fold between 1870 and 1906, and during the early years of the twentieth century black diamonds worth about $4 million left the port of Salvador each year, exported to Paris, London, Amsterdam and New York. The First World War led to higher u.s. investment in Brazil, at the expense of France, Britain and Germany. In 1919 more than 50 per cent of Bahia's black diamonds were exported to the usa, and American firms such as the Bandler Corporation, established in 1927, leased large parts of Bahia's diamond fields, where 98 per cent of the world's *carbonados* came from.[97]

34 *Carbonados*, or black diamonds, Bangui, Central African Republic.

35 Leschot drilling machine, *c.* 1883.

The corporation's stock fell drastically in 1931, after which they continued mining in the Paraguaçu for two more years, giving way to individual miners once more.[98] With the price rise for *carbonados* and a growing demand for industrial diamonds, other substitutes were developed.[99]

Eureka! The Discovery of the River Diggings

In the second half of the nineteenth century, much of what would later be South Africa was a British colony, the Cape Colony. In 1814 the Dutch, who had been the first European colonizers in the region, had ceded control to the British at the Convention of London. Many Boers, descendants of Dutch settlers and farmers, were unhappy with British rule, particularly after the colonial government officially put free people who were not white on equal footing with whites in 1828 and the abolition of slavery in 1834. Many moved north, in a movement called the Great Trek, which led to the establishment of two independent Afrikaner republics, the Transvaal (recognized by the British in 1852) and the Orange Free State (1854).[100]

Violent clashes between colonists, adventurers and African people were a common feature of frontier life, aggravated by the Boers' practice of kidnapping local children to fill the need for labourers.[101]

In the early days of colonization, there was a clear separation between the different ethnic communities. White colonists and Boers were a minority in South Africa, which was home to the pastoral Khoi, the San and various peoples such as the Xhosa, Basotho, Tswana and Ndebele.[102] Later, interracial sexual relationships, many of them undoubtedly forced by the newcomers upon the original inhabitants, led to the development of a heterogeneous group of people of mixed background.[103] One of the oldest of such groups were the Griqua, who descended from Khoisan and Boers.[104] It has been asserted that 'many Griquas were born out of sexual abuse of Khoi-Khoi female slaves by Dutch settlers. And the Khoisan people in general were not well equipped to defend themselves against western colonisation.'[105]

In spite of the violence brought about by colonialism, the Griqua managed to maintain their independence and were organized around the leadership of so-called 'captains'. Under the influence of missionaries who wished to keep the Christian Griqua people separated from non-Christian peoples, they settled around a place called Griquatown, but remained autonomous and would sometimes move away to establish new settlements. In 1820 a man named Andries Waterboer (c. 1789–1852) was elected captain, which estranged several factions within the Griqua community who went on to establish their own separate communities. Waterboer's rule extended over a territory now dubbed Griqualand West, with Griquatown as its capital.[106] The British, wanting to protect the unstable northern border and the road through Griqualand West, which was used for the colony's barter trade, signed a treaty with Griqualand West in 1834. In return for his assistance to the Cape Colony, Waterboer received money, weapons and ammunition.[107]

While the struggle between locals, British and Boers for territorial control of the South African frontier zones never ceased, the stakes were raised in 1867 when a farm boy named Erasmus Jacobs, whose father owned 'De Kalk' farm, was playing a game called 'five stones'.[108] An observant neighbour named Schalk van Niekerk became interested in a pretty white stone Erasmus was using. The boy's mother gave van Niekerk the stone for free, and it was brought to Jack O'Reilly, an itinerant trader in

Colesberg, who gave it to William Buchanan Chalmers, civil commissioner and magistrate of Hopetown, the nearest frontier town, situated on the Orange river near where Griqualand West, the Orange Free State and part of the Cape Colony met (see illus. 36). Chalmers advised sending it to Dr William Atherstone in Grahamstown, an amateur mineralogist, who had received it by April 1867 and confirmed it was a genuine diamond. It was sent to Cape Town, where the French consul, Ernest Héritte, who had prior knowledge of precious stones, and a Dutch diamond cutter named Louis Hond confirmed that the stone was indeed a diamond.[109] Colonial secretary Richard Southey had the stone shipped to Britain, where it was cut to the weight of 10.73 carats and named the Eureka.[110]

Although the Eureka is generally recognized as the first diamond found in South Africa, there are signs that a government surveyor named W.F.J. von Ludwig, who was inspecting farms along the Orange river in 1859, including 'De Kalk', was already aware of the diamondiferous character of the region.[111] This could also help explain the presence of Louis Hond in South Africa prior to the discovery of the first diamond. It was quickly realized that, although this first discovery was an accidental surprise, much more was to be found; W. B. Chalmers remarked in the Cape Colony Blue Book for 1867 that, although van Niekerk was a 'Boer farmer without any education . . . we have to thank this very natural shrewdness and enquiring turn of mind of Mr Niekerk's for bringing into light the existence of Diamonds along the Orange River'.[112] More diamonds turned up, but no one really knew how great the potential was. In July 1867 it was decided after a parliamentary debate in Cape Town that the colonial authorities would wait and see, as the stones had turned up on private property. Debate only resumed two years later.[113] Colonial secretary Richard Southey, however, remained interested in diamonds, and maintained a lengthy correspondence on the matter with Chalmers in Hopetown and a clerk in Colesberg, a nearby frontier settlement. In June 1868 he asked Chalmers, in whose jurisdiction most of the stones had turned up, to send a detailed report about all the diamonds thus far discovered.[114]

In those early days, some in the Cape government took a personal interest in diamonds. Governor Philip Wodehouse bought several of the first diamonds and took them with him when he returned to England in 1870. Richard Southey kept a close eye on the increasing numbers of

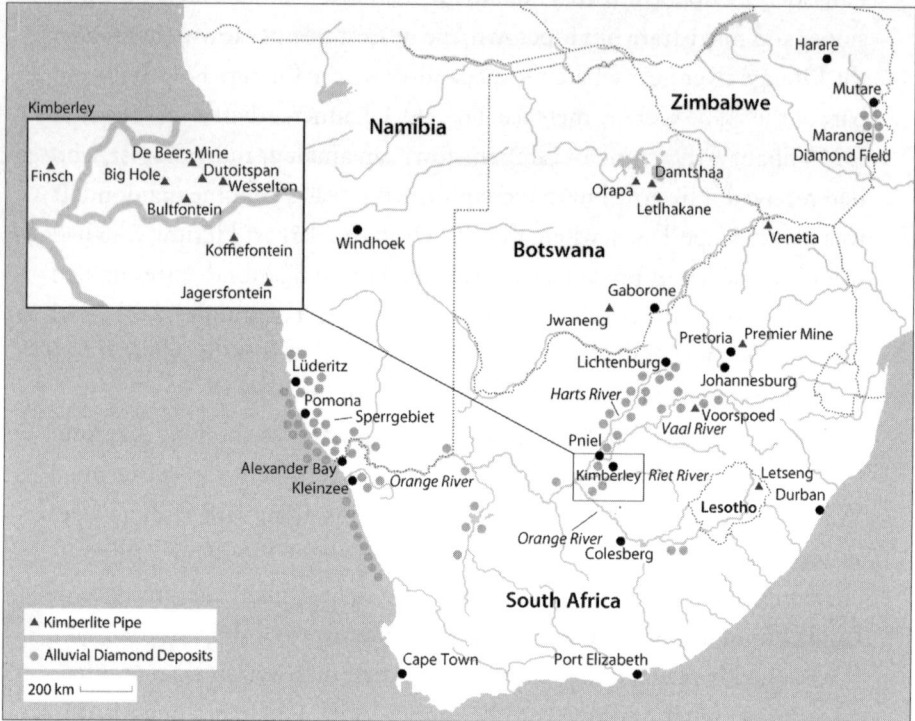

36 Diamond deposits in southern Africa.

diamonds that arrived in Cape Town, although some were identified as worthless quartz crystals. It was a chaotic period, but more and more South African diamonds made it, via merchants in Port Elizabeth, to London, where interest was growing alongside the familiar worries about a possible decline in prices. This led an important jeweller, Harry Emanuel of Bond Street, to send a geologist named James Gregory to South Africa to investigate the diamond fields. Emanuel was no stranger to the world of diamonds; he had published a treatise on precious stones in 1865 and had seen the Eureka diamond in person.[115] Gregory was instructed to proceed discreetly and his itinerary was clouded with mystery. When he returned to England rather abruptly, William Atherstone attributed his departure to Gregory's ability to locate the origins of the diamonds found thus far, all alluvial: 'I believe Gregory has found the true diamond formation . . . the Ilacolumite in which Diamonds are found in other Countries, exists near Hope Town.'[116] It was the beginning of a fierce debate among scientists. James Tennant, a professor of mineralogy at

King's College who considered Gregory 'a first rate mineralogist', held the opinion that the diamonds came from the Drakensberg range, which had been British territory since the annexation of Basutoland (present-day Lesotho). Sir Roderick Murchison, a geologist at the Museum of Practical Geology, was altogether sceptical about the existence of a diamond matrix in South Africa.[117] Gregory was of the same mind, much to the outrage of Chalmers in Hopetown:

> Mr. Gregory tried to cry down the diamonds; and even went so far as to say there are no indications of the existence of diamonds in this part; and that these which have been found must have been brought here by birds (!). This is simply ridiculous ... I think however that he merely said this to blind people.[118]

Gregory's comment about birds is interesting, as it is reminiscent of the old Diamond Valley myth discussed in Chapter One. When he returned to England, he published an account in the *Geological Magazine* that became famous for missing the historical moment, and that he concluded by writing that 'I can now only conclude by expressing my conviction that the whole diamond discovery in S. Africa is an imposture – A Bubble.'[119] Atherstone considered Gregory's article a personal attack, particularly when Gregory pointed out that:

> All Dr. Atherstone's information ... is obtained from the statements made by Dutch Boers, natives, farm-labourers, women, and children; and he does not appear in any single instance to have visited any reputed diamond region, so that at present we are no nearer than we were last year to the *actual locality* whence the diamonds announced were derived.[120]

In November 1868, between Gregory's two contributions to the *Geological Magazine*, Emanuel published a letter in which he defended Gregory and concluded by stating that neither the discovery of diamonds, nor that of gold, was genuine, while also refuting Tennant's mineralogical claims on the origins of South African diamonds.[121] The two men were very wrong and we can only speculate as to Emanuel's motives. Maybe he truly believed there were no diamonds in South Africa. Maybe he was worried about a decline in prices and tried to protect his commercial interests. Perhaps he had even concluded secret deals to receive South African diamonds and wanted to discourage the competition. The fact is that only two months later he was much more enthusiastic about diamond prospects elsewhere, when he stated that 'the examination I have made has confirmed me in the opinion long entertained that Australia must soon rank among the diamond-producing countries.'[122] In the same article he mentioned diamond fields in Brazil and India, but not a word on South Africa. Today, in South African slang, a 'Gregory' still means 'a major blunder'.[123]

An important discovery made in March 1869 finally put to rest any existing doubts about the genuine occurrence of diamonds in South Africa, and again Schalk van Niekerk was involved. A Griqua named Swartboy had found a large diamond of 83.5 carats, which he used as a talisman. Van Niekerk managed to buy the stone, and Louis Hond was among those who confirmed it as a diamond.[124] Soon after it was sold to the Lilienfeld business firm in Hopetown for the sum of £11,200, which would amount to almost £400,000 today. Gustave and Leopold Lilienfeld, German Jews, named it the Star of South Africa.[125] (In 1974, it was put up for auction in Geneva by Christie's.) A local newspaper, the *Graaff-Reinet Herald*, asked its readers, quite vindictively, 'what will Mr. Gregory and Emanuel say now about the South African Diamonds, eh?'[126] Two months after the discovery of the Star of South Africa, Harry Emanuel wrote a letter to Richard Southey, in which he tried to correct his earlier mistake by stating that it was his firm belief in African diamonds that had led him to send Gregory there in the first place.[127] Emanuel remained doubtful about the potential, though, and when he was confronted in 1871 with news that £220,000 worth of diamonds were shipped out of the Cape Colony in the previous year, he stated that 'American demand is far in excess of the supply, that the Cape diamonds are very poor, and that the value will not decline perceptibly.'[128]

It was no coincidence that many of South Africa's first known diamonds were discovered by locals: 'the natives had long used the diamond mechanically for boring other stones, and made periodical visits hither [Orange Free State] to procure their supply,' a fact known to missionaries in the region.[129] Miners, merchants and adventurers often speculated on the know-how of locals, offering them barter in exchange, 'because the success of the surface searching of indigenous inhabitants was a good indication of where the diamonds could be found'.[130] In August 1869 the Griqua chief of Dikgatlong, near the junction of the Harts and Vaal rivers, had received an offer by a group of 'Bay merchants' to buy all diamonds found on his lands for some years, but he declined, insisting he could not stop his subjects from selling to whomever they wanted.[131] With news on the Star of South Africa spreading, January 1870 saw the beginning of a diamond rush that led many to the river diggings in the Vaal and Orange rivers (see illus. 36). An English newspaper published in Exeter received information from the Cape that 'sailors are deserting the ships in the harbour, police their corps, apprentices are absconding from service and youths from school, and all bending to the same great point of attraction, the banks of the Vaal'.[132]

Frederick Boyle, who visited the area two years later, mentioned that 5,000 people were digging near the missionary station at Pniel, many living in tents (illus. 37).[133] The diggers' ranks grew with Australians who had come back with nothing from the 1868 gold rush further north.[134] Forms of organized prospecting developed as well, and Jerome Babe described the adventures of two parties, one from King William's Town at the Eastern Cape and the other from Natal. They met at Hebron, where they ran into conflict with the local population, afraid that white diggers would take away their lands. Both parties moved downstream, north of the Vaal, and in little more than a month they found three hundred diamonds, with an estimated value of £80,000.[135] The arrival of a man named Stafford Parker led to a short-lived independent diggers' republic at Klipdrift, with Parker as its eccentric president.[136] By the time Babe visited the place, it had been renamed Parkerton, and counted 2,000 souls, mostly men. At nearby Town Kopje, a music hall had been built in brick, and there were photographers, butchers, doctors, bakers, grocery stores, diamond merchants, jewellers' shops and 'drinking saloons, till you can't rest'. Diggers were also contemplating building a church, as religious services were taking place at the billiard-saloon.[137]

Klipdrift was quickly brought back under the British flag, but other places remained contested. Pniel, for instance, had been under Orange Free State jurisdiction, while Transvaal and Griqualand West also laid claims on the river diggings. Nicolaas Waterboer, Andries's eldest son and his successor as Griqualand West's ruler, went through lengthy litigation trying to demonstrate that the Star of South Africa had been found on his territory, and was thus rightfully his, but he lost against the Lilienfeld firm.[138] The presidents of the Afrikaner republics took a different approach and sent officials and police to the river diggings, trying to assert their jurisdiction. Some miners preferred joining the Transvaal, while others, such as Stafford Parker's diggers, wished for independence, but many shared an antipathy towards the Griqua and the British government, which aimed to expand its territory. Basutoland had already been annexed in 1868, and the authorities were thinking about the possibility of incorporating the diamond region into the Cape Colony, while at the same time securing their northern frontier. After a visit to the diamond fields, the governor, Sir Henry Barkly, decided to appropriate Griqualand West for the British, to the dismay of the Earl of Kimberley, secretary of state for the colonies, who felt the government was not ready to incorporate the diamond fields.[139]

The annexation did not end the territorial disputes, or the occasional violence that came with it. A great deal of autonomy existed in mining settlements, as the new administrator of Griqualand West, Richard Southey, allowed mining boards to establish sets of rules against infractions and to collect income from licence fees.[140] The Afrikaner Orange Free State police, considered by one observer as 'seedy-looking raggamuffins', also kept crossing the border to make occasional arrests of British subjects, before British officials forced their release.[141] Violence was often directed at local people. In 1870 a Dutchman accused a local man of theft in Hebron and shot him in the leg. In response, the accuser was beaten

37 Kimberley, late 19th century.

up and taken to a local Bechuana chief. A group of miners, including eight hundred armed men, found the Dutchman in the hands of the chief's son, who was arrested and sent for trial. The chief had to pay for the stolen goods, worth £75, while the Dutchman was only fined £25 for shooting the tribesman.[142]

Digging the Big Hole on Colesberg Kopje

The river diggings were alluvial, just like all diamond deposits known in the world at that point, and miners quickly moved on from one area to the next, testing their fortune within the limits of what was known about diamond mining at the time. Several discoveries made at the end of 1869, however, slightly further away from the riverbanks, challenged everything known about diamond mining. Two owners of farms located about 30 kilometres (18 mi.) southeast of Klipdrift and Pniel had been renting out parcels to diamond miners, before they sold their farms to merchants, as the diamondiferous potential so far from the river diggings was considered modest at best. Between 1869 and 1871 Cornelis du Plooy sold Bultfontein for £2,000 to the Hopetown Company, predecessors of the London and South African Exploration Company (LSAEC), in which Gustave and Leopold Lilienfeld were partners with Louis Hond. The same company also bought Dutoitspan (or Dorstfontein) for £2,600. The sale of Bultfontein was contested in court by a previous candidate, a case that was settled in 1872.[143] Different sources mention different years for the sales, and also disagree on how aware the selling farmers were of the diamondiferous nature of their terrain, but the result, ownership by the Hopetown Company by the end of 1871, is undisputed.[144] Sources also suggest that some prospecting had taken place in the area at least since the end of 1869, without leading to a rush, and that the first initiative to buy the Bultfontein farm was taken in November that same year.[145] The new owners tried to fence off clandestine miners by putting up signs warning against punishment by the Orange Free State, but to no avail, as the miners simply took the signs away to use the wood for sieves and sorting tables.[146]

Many miners active at the riverside diggings had turned their eyes to the new dry diggings at Bultfontein (illus. 38) and Dutoitspan (illus. 39), to which the Vooruitzigt farm, owned by the De Beer brothers, was added in May 1871. Two months later, a second deposit was discovered on Vooruitzigt, on a hill named Colesberg Kopje, quickly renamed 'New Rush' (illus. 40 and 41).[147] Before the end of the year, the farm was bought by Dunell, Ebden & Co. of Port Elizabeth, for £6,000.[148] Newspapers started to print itineraries to the dry diggings, and by September 1871, 20,000 people were reported to dig for diamonds at Dutoitspan, Bultfontein and Vooruitzigt, all located in Griqualand West. A whole town was built 'round the public or market square. Bowling-alleys, billiard-saloons, hotels, restaurants, and stores without end'.[149] By December 1871, the miners' numbers had grown to 50,000, and 30,000 of them were black, a huge number compared to the 5,000 riverside diggers active in 1870.[150] They came from everywhere: there were Boer diggers from the Afrikaner republics; Griquas; colonists; men from Australia and the USA, often with prior mining experience; Germans, although these were more numerous as diamond buyers; and also Italians, Spaniards and Frenchmen.[151] Several contemporary observers were very outspoken about the presence of the Dutch Boers. Jerome Babe wrote that they thought they were going on a family picnic, and would return to their coffee carrying a fortune without having done any hard work.[152] Charles Payton, an adventurer who spent time digging for diamonds in Kimberley, was even

38 Bultfontein mine, *c.* 1870.

39 Dutoitspan mine, *c.* 1877.

more outspoken. According to Payton's description of the diggings, the Boers were detested by the English and the Americans, unrefined and uncivilized as they were. He seemed to have contempt for them when they tried to become diggers:

> Moreover, he has with him not only his 'vrouw' and 'kinders', *i.e.*, wife and children, but a lot of Kafirs, whom he has obtained in the interior at about the wages of *a cow*, or *3l.* per year. So he comes for the Fields, lives in his waggon, or in a tent which his Kafirs and his 'kinders' make for him, spends no money at all on the Fields, living on the stores he has brought with him. See him dig – well, you can hardly call it digging; the brutal old patriarch will sit at the sorting-table all day with his pipe . . . while half-naked Kafir boys (aye, and young girls, too) and his own children . . . are all toiling hard under the broiling sun, picking, shovelling, hauling, breaking, and sifting.[153]

One contemporary observer witnessed a 'sturdy, brown-faced, bearded, very thick-set digger' dancing in one of the billiard rooms after finding a 20-carat diamond, singing the chorus of the 'Marseillaise'.[154] The area became so crowded that a correspondent for the *Natal Mercury* remarked that 'standing between De Beer's and the Colesberg, at night, with lights

40 Kimberley's Big Hole, 1870s.

41 Kimberley's Big Hole, *c*. 1870.

on either side, the scene is exactly like that observed at a certain point in Hyde Park, where the long line of lights on the Bayswater road can be seen at the same time as those at Knightsbridge.'[155]

What was different about these discoveries was their non-alluvial nature. In a letter sent from Dutoitspan dated 20 September 1872, German geologist Ernest Cohen argued that the South African dry diggings were at the centre of ancient volcanic craters.[156] Finally, the world had stumbled upon the deeper origins of diamonds in what would become known as kimberlite pipes:

> The diamond-bearing material at first excavated was a crumbling yellowish earth, which, at a depth of about fifty feet, became harder and darker, finally acquiring a slaty blue or dark green color and a greasy feel, resembling certain varieties of serpentine. This is the well-known 'blue ground' of the diamond miners.[157]

The expanding South African production quickly led to territorial disputes. The Orange Free State, where the smaller mines of Koffiefontein and Jagersfontein had been discovered, claimed authority, and tried to enforce it by coming to the aid of several farm owners who wanted to keep groups of individual miners away. But there were too many miners working on a small surface, and owners were forced to cede and permit a system of mining licences. In May 1871 the proprietors of Dutoitspan agreed on a set of rules. Miners could work no more than two claims (a measure taken to keep bigger companies out) against 10 shillings and sixpence sterling per month. A Diggers' Committee oversaw mining, settled disputes and appointed personnel to supervise the development of streets and squares.[158] Kimberley in Griqualand West proved the richest mine, while Bultfontein became known as 'the poor man's diggings'.[159] Quarters of claims were regularly sold, and in 1872 an area of around 2 × 10 metres (7 × 30 ft) could reach £1,500.[160]

Territorial disputes were settled when the British annexed Griqualand West in October 1871. The territory was divided in three units – Klipdrift, Pniel and Griquatown – all governed at a distance by Sir Henry Barkly in Cape Town.[161] Local committees had been developing rules for the miners to abide by. The British did not overthrow that system, but it became clear that there was a new sheriff in town: 'and the flag of old England waves proudly over the busy camps, and the imperturbable British "bobby" is there too'.[162] The Earl of Kimberley, already unhappy about what he considered to be a hasty and underprepared annexation, felt that 'New Rush', or Colesberg Kopje, was not a good name for one of the richest diamond spots in the British Empire. The town and mine were renamed Kimberley, and the diamondiferous blue earth became

42 Kimberley's Big Hole, 1873.

43 Racial division of labour, Kimberley, *c.* 1870.

known as kimberlite.[163] Mining communities, however, struggled to recognize the new authority, and in early 1872 an anonymous miner at Kimberley voiced his discontentment with British police in *The Times*, stating the diggers were 'infinitely worse off' than they had been under Free State government. He complained that there was no magistrate to whom the 20,000 inhabitants of Kimberley could turn, that all the infrastructure of the Orange Free State, such as the post office, had disappeared, and he protested about heavy and arbitrary taxation.[164] He must have forgotten about the 15,000–35,000 black residents that were said to be in Kimberley the same year.[165] Only three things were appreciated: that 'no native can legally have diamonds in his possession', that 'any person buying diamonds from natives can be severely punished', and that 'no liquor may be supplied to them'. But unfortunately, the writer continued, the first rule was broken at Dutoitspan, where 'natives were free to mine for themselves, [a fact] not generally known among the diggers'.[166] Official British policy did allow for free black people to engage in mining, and in 1874, 120 of the 135 claimholders at Bultfontein, for instance, were non-white.[167]

The objections uttered by white diggers against their colleagues were frequent, racist and representative of South African society for many years to come. Many white people, the Boers in particular, were not happy about the racial equality law of 1828 and the abolition of slavery in 1834, and black South Africans, by far the most numerous group, were treated in an unrelenting manner by the white population, who often employed them on the diamond fields.

Initially, diamond mining in South Africa was similar in execution to the way it was done traditionally in Brazil and India. It was a matter of collecting diamondiferous earth, mainly extracted from rivers but also from rocks, and transporting it to a place where the collected earth could be washed and searched for diamonds (illus. 43, 44 and 45). Work relied on unskilled labourers who used picks, shovels, sieves and other hand tools. Diamond mining was labour intensive, and not without danger. In the first years there was a yearly replacement rate of 30 per cent among the labourers.[168] Unsurprisingly, many of the white adventurers employed black workers for the more labour-intensive work. This, and the growing backlash against the claims of ownership by black miners was the beginning of a labour division along racial lines: a division that was to grow in the following period, and that came to be synonymous with a divide between skilled and unskilled labour (illus. 43, 45 and 46). In Payton's words:

> Two Kafirs, if they understand the work, ought to be able to keep two white men constantly employed in sorting, and this is a very

44 Diamond washing, Kimberley, *c.* 1870.

45 Working and sorting diamonds, Kimberley, late 19th century.

good division of labour for the hot weather, while in the winter the 'baas' [boss] will often find it pleasant and warming to take a hand at pick, shovel, or sieve himself.[169]

Many workers came from Pediland, Tsongaland and Basutoland, often on foot, as part of a labour migration that already existed before diamonds were discovered, but which now reached an unprecedented scale. The temporary migration of men in the northern parts of future South Africa to the south was down to several reasons, and the ones cited most often were regional conflict, diminished productivity in agriculture and cattle breeding, and a decline in the profits made by hunting. These labour migrants stayed between four and eight months, according to historian Todd Cleveland, 'not coincidentally, roughly the amount of time it took them to earn enough to purchase a rifle'.[170] Sending male members of their tribes to the diamond mines, where wages were higher than what was offered elsewhere in the Cape Colony, became a recurrent strategy for local leaders in order to arm their tribes with rifles, but it was often at odds with the growing practice of these labourers to settle near the mines instead of returning.[171] From a very early stage the colonial administration attempted to force black Africans of various ethnicities into labouring at the diamond mines by imposing a 'hut tax' on their housing. In 1870, for instance, a tax of 10 shillings was introduced in Basutoland with the purpose of forcing non-whites into mining labour in order to pay for the tax.[172] In 1872 there were 10,000

Africans working at the Kimberley mine, a number that tripled during the boom years of 1878–81 (illus. 46).[173] Oswald Doughty, author of a history of the South African diamond fields published in 1963, praised the 'amazing endurance' of the migrating workers, arriving at the diamond mines after a trip of more than 1,600 kilometres (995 mi.) welcomed by their 'brother natives already installed at Kimberley'.[174] Although many of these migratory workers decided to relocate to the mines more permanently, they often only engaged in short-term contracts of one to two months, which enabled them to benefit from the rising demand, leading to a fivefold increase in wages between 1871 and 1875.[175] At the end of the 1870s it was estimated that about 9,000 black workers had relocated permanently to Kimberley, a number complemented by the continuing migratory labour.[176]

Sometimes members of different tribes clashed with one another. Payton remarked that the Zulu and the Basuto had a long-standing rivalry, and that single combat was encouraged for other people's amusement.[177] In general, however, such tribal tension paled in comparison to the racist feelings that were reigning amongst a great deal of the white population. These feelings were worsened by the realization that the local population was far more numerous than the whites, and further fuelled by the perceived connection between black labour, desertion and diamond theft (Illicit Diamond Buying, or IDB), the most serious crime on the diamond fields.[178] Doughty went as far as to think that the employment of black Africans by whites was part of a 'civilizing mission', the classic colonial racist trope, and he saw evidence for his thesis in the lowering of crime over time, with the appearance of 'more "civilized" and "educated" natives'.[179]

Several opportunistic whites established eating-houses and canteens for black workers, where soup, meat and bread were free, but where it was expected that clients would discreetly leave a 'soup diamond' behind in their bowls.[180] These were places where stolen diamonds turned up, and white miners sometimes took the law into their own hands: 'the diggers are irritated at the conduct of some canteen-keepers, who are accused of purchasing stolen diamonds from the natives, and have burned down five canteens . . . additional police are ordered to the diggings.'[181] In 1872 the government introduced a pass system that was designed to control black labourers. It obliged them to carry a document stating who their master was. Without it, they could get arrested. While the official legislation was

46 Racial division of labour, Kimberley, 1873.

not explicit on racial division, and merely used the terms 'servant' and 'master', it cleary intended to curtail the free movement of black workers, and the pass laws became the basis for the treatment of black African labourers for a long time to come, leading to closed labour camps and apartheid.[182] To add insult to injury, in 1879 the colonial administration used this system to create further distinctions among black workers on the basis of how 'civilized' they were perceived to be, and of the ethnicity of the masters they served.[183]

Still, white grievances against black people continued to exist and were made worse by racism against black and Asian claimholders. The environment in which diamond mining in South Africa was taking place was very much conditioned by imperialist, racist and colonial features.[184] Paternalism was one of the milder expressions of this context, and men such as Payton lamented the harsh treatment the Boers gave their black workers, but at the same time felt that the English treated the black population too kindly, causing a loss of respect for the masters. Payton, a diamond adventurer himself, did not limit himself to expressing his opinion on paper. He also wrote about his own actions and described how he employed a black man who he considered lazy, so every time he saw that worker leaning on his spade, Payton would throw stones at him.[185] He further stated that 'a nigger is all very well as long as he is kept in his proper place, that is "kept down"; to treat him in the "man and a brother" style of the Exeter Hall philanthropists, is only to spoil him and injure yourself.'[186] Racism, the development of the pass system and the growing need to unify mining efforts led to a 'white purge', or the gradual disappearance of black, Indian and Malay claimholders after 1872, and those Africans and Asians who owned successful claims were often considered as suspect, with white diggers believing they had gathered their fortunes through IDB.[187]

Growing racial tensions added to what already had become an explosive cocktail. The most popular form of employment was share-working, in which diggers worked the mines on behalf of claimholders, who only paid for licence fees and mining taxes. Diggers, against a percentage of the profits that ranged between 50 and 90 per cent, employed labourers, arranged the work and sold the diamonds. The enormous rise in the price for claims led to a reduction of claimholders. In 1875 only 757 men, of which 120 were not white, held the total of 1,243 claims in De Beers' mine (formerly known as 'Old Rush'), Kimberley (the Big Hole, initially known as 'New Rush'), Bultfontein and Dutoitspan.[188] Earlier, in 1871, the total number of claims at the dry diggings had been more than 3,200, some of them further divided into smaller claims.[189] Many more men were active as share-workers, and they started to voice their grievances.

Mining was becoming technically more difficult at the open-pit mines because of the need to dig deeper. Not only did this bring about higher risks, but the mines were becoming increasingly unworkable. The walls of the open mine were called a reef, and the deeper miners dug, the more reef collapses occurred. Sometimes this worthless earth fell on yet unworked claims, which burdened production. The dividing walls between the hundreds of claims in the open pits also caved in regularly, particularly because not all claims were being worked at the same depth. Periodic rainfall rendered parts of the mine unworkable at times. Many of these problems were caused by lack of uniformity. Diggers were not all working at the same depths, which raised the risk of collapses (illus. 42 and 47).

Additionally, complaints about the 'jumping' system, which allowed adventurers to take possession of claims that had remained unworked for three days, were growing.[190] Tensions rose between individual diggers and their sense of freedom, exemplified by ideas about diggers' democracies, on the one hand, and those with a desire to establish some form of monopolization on the other. In 1873 it was decided that a new administrative

47 Kimberley's Big Hole, *c.* 1875.

regime was necessary, and Griqualand West was pronounced a province of the Cape Colony. Richard Southey, a man with experience in the colonial administration at the river diggings, was appointed administrator and lieutenant-general of the new province.[191] Southey immediately suspended the 'jumping' system but operated in a legal vacuum as no new constitution had been drawn up for the province. Diggers kept on asking for a representative local government, but a new Mining Ordinance issued in 1874 replaced their committees with mining boards that were less powerful. Their competence was limited to mining affairs, and the Ordinance also proposed the appointment of an inspector, 'with responsibility for the safety of life and limb'.[192]

The introduction of an inspector answered a pressing need. By the end of 1874 the situation at the open mines was so bad that many share--workers were out of work, restless and angry. Following the Mining Ordinance, things improved greatly, even though political turmoil continued. By March 1875 the mining tempo had picked up to the extent that there was a sudden shortage of labour. The pit at Kimberley was now 49 metres (160 ft) deep (illus. 47), and claimholders had introduced a better haulage system based on horse whims or windlasses, which drove the 'cobweb' of aerial tramways that had been introduced to replace the dangerous partition walls (illus. 42, 48 and 49) and again allowed more

48 Reef-hauling system and rotary washing machine, Kimberley, *c.* 1875.

intensified mining.[193] A year later, steam engine-based transport machinery was introduced, but the difficulty of getting fuel and the uncertain potential of the diamond deposits prevented large-scale implementation of these machines, a problem that would only be solved with the entry of the mining capitalists a decade later.[194] A few years earlier a miner named William Hall had developed an inclined tramway system to transport gravel out of the pit, driven by the first steam engine at Kimberley, and he offered to provide the same service to other diggers for a fee. Hall, an advocate of monopolization, was turned down by his peers, who preferred their own individual haulage system, leading to the 'cobweb' imagery of the aerial ropes.[195] Technical innovation influenced the transportation methods, and the introduction of rotary washing machines (illus. 43, 44 and 48) created an additional demand for labour in washing the debris. The black workers, aware of the risks of mining near the edges of the pit, used these changes as an opportunity to demand higher wages and a lower degree of white supervision over their encampments. This, of course, was to the dislike of the white diggers, who felt the situation increased the threat of theft, while it also challenged their position of power.[196]

While white diggers and share-workers faced increasing difficulties in imposing themselves on the black population, they also came under growing pressure from claimholders and farm proprietors such as the LSAEC, which owned Bultfontein and Dutoitspan. They considered the future of mining at the dry diggings to be based on outside international capital and the arrival of bigger companies. Share-workers and diggers were opposed, as was Richard Southey, who believed British colonial interests would be harmed if mining was to be monopolized by foreign capital. He also did not want mining profits to be siphoned off into private hands.[197] It was this concern with the colonial economy that made Southey fight for the inclusion of a restriction of claims clause in the Mining Ordinance of 1874.[198] But with this policy the lieutenant-general alienated both the diggers and the proprietors. Resentment grew, and finally the cocktail exploded in 1875. Southey had refused to recognize mineral ownership by the farm owners, who wanted to collect as much rent as they could from miners. When Dunell, Ebden & Company, owners of the Vooruitzigt farm, where the Kimberley mine was located, raised rents in February that year, a Diggers' Protection Association was formed, vouching to protect white diggers' interests. In April a hotel keeper was arrested for selling weapons to one of the association's leaders, and an armed revolt broke out. The government had to intervene to restore order, but this so-called Black Flag Revolt proved the end of Southey's tenure, as his policies and response to

49 Kimberley's Big Hole, 1870s.

the revolt had angered too many parties, not least some of the land-owning companies, such as the LSAEC, who had good connections in London.[199]

This period marked the end of the diggers' democracy in which smaller groups of individual miners were setting the tone in the mining region. They had to give way to a new class that had already been present at the mines, and which seized the moment to turn the dry diggings into a venture for mining capitalists. The aftermath of the Black Flag Revolt also ended the colonial autonomy enjoyed by Griqualand West, where the dry diggings were situated.[200] The late 1870s saw a series of revolts against white colonists, including a rebellion in Griqualand East that spread to Griqualand West. Ultimately the movements of Griqua, Thlaping, Korana and San people were unsuccessful, and Griqualand West was annexed to the Cape Colony in 1880, including its diamond fields.[201]

English novelist Anthony Trollope (1815–1882) visited Kimberley in 1877 and used some of his impressions for his last novel, *An Old Man's Love*, published posthumously in 1884:

> If there be a place on God's earth in which a man can thoroughly make or mar himself within that space of time, it is the town of Kimberley. I know no spot more odious in every way to a man who has learned to love the ordinary modes of English life. It is foul with dust and flies; it reeks with bad brandy; it is fed upon potted meats; it has not a tree near it. It is inhabited in part by tribes of South Africans, who have lost all the picturesqueness of niggerdom in working for the white man's wages. The white man himself is insolent, ill-dressed, and ugly. The weather is very hot, and from morning till night there is no occupation other than that of looking for diamonds, and the works attending it.[202]

The Energetic Days of the Cape, 1870–76

The discoveries at the dry diggings revived the whole diamond industry in Europe. Following the rollercoaster of diminishing and expanding production, the size of Europe's most important diamond-cutting industry, located in Amsterdam, fluctuated greatly throughout the nineteenth century, with the nadir around 1820.[203] Over the following decades the cutting industry shifted in scale and evolved from small workshops, often set up in the houses where the cutters lived, towards larger factories.[204] This shift was accompanied by growing mechanization. During the early modern period, the diamond mills were often powered by the physical labour of women (see illus. 19), but in 1822 horses were introduced to drive the mills, and in 1840 the first cutting factory operating on steam opened.[205] Between 1822 and 1855 nine horse-driven cutting factories were established in eastern Amsterdam, where most Jews lived, employing up to four hundred workmen.[206] This growing industrialization had severe consequences for the workers, and a Jewish doctor who wrote about labour conditions in the cutting factories of Amsterdam reported cramped spaces, with a lack of fresh air and an abundance of dust. Workers suffered from nose bleeds, diarrhoea, a tight chest, eye infections and tuberculosis. They worked long twelve-hour days, five and a half days a week.[207]

The expansion after 1820 was largely fuelled by the import of diamonds from Bahia and was used by the Diamantslijperij Maatschappij (Diamond Cutting Company) to obtain a monopolistic position, owning 520 of the 560 polishing tables in Amsterdam by 1850. These circumstances amplified the call for a union of diamond workers to protect their interests. The first workers' organization, the Diamantslijpers-Vereeniging (Diamond Cutters' Association), was eventually founded in 1866.[208] It came at the right time because the industry again went into decline, particularly after reduced consumption following the outbreak of the Franco-Prussian war in 1870, which led to a great deal of unemployment.[209] The discovery of diamonds at the Cape, the end of the war and rising demand in the United States and Russia were all welcome ingredients in the revival of Amsterdam's diamond industry for the second time in half a century. This revival became known as the *Kaapse Tijd* (Period of the Cape) and lasted from 1870 to 1876. The Jewish population grew from 18,000 in 1815 to 40,000 in 1879, and many worked in an industry that now employed thousands of workers, instead of hundreds, often in newly constructed factory buildings (illus. 50).[210] Antwerp also benefited from the revival, while the introduction of steam engines to drive the diamond mills in 1865 made the city more competitive. It attracted new Jewish migration from eastern Europe after 1870, and many were employed in the cutting industry, which still lagged behind that of Amsterdam.[211]

The changes that occurred in mining and cutting were accompanied by a change in consumption. The era of classic aristocratic consumption had ended, making way for industrialization. This, as well as the rising supply, which now included also stones of lower quality, led to a late nineteenth-century appreciation of diamonds as a relatively common good. Joan Evans concluded her historical study on jewellery in the year 1870, remarking that 'beauty which has departed from things may live on in words; and so it was with jewels in the last third of the nineteenth century.'[212]

This imagery of melancholy Victorian austerity and dark industrialization can also be found in the cutting factories. While the revival made the fortune of many factory owners and traders, and gave employment to many new Jewish immigrants, the work in the diamond factories remained hard and relatively unrewarding. An American who visited Amsterdam published an article in *Harper's New Monthly Magazine* in 1872, in which he described the city's predominantly Jewish cutting industry, and he observed a great socio-economic gap: 'nearly all the owners of the Amsterdam diamond-mills are wealthy; but the operatives, though they have what is regarded as very good wages in Holland, are quite poor.'[213] It is true that the economic boom that followed the discovery of South African diamonds did not mean that the diamond workers suddenly improved their socio-economic position. Amsterdam's Jewish population indeed had a sizeable underclass, in spite of them obtaining full citizenship rights in 1796.[214] Nevertheless, the changing political context following Jewish emancipation and the economic growth did create opportunities, and, as the workforce expanded, some families were able to leave the Jewish quarter of the city to move to more upmarket neighbourhoods.[215] But many of the workers continued to live a harsh life, described in detail in *Harper's* article of 1872:

> Diamond-cutting seems to me a most dismal trade. The hundreds of men I have seen engaged in the mills appeared wan and worn and melancholy, as well they might, with their perpetual and monotonous round of cheerless and consuming toil. To them, each day is like every other day. The seasons and the years come and go, and go and come, without chance or change. Their world is but a revolving disk; the straining of the eye, the tension of the nerves, a painful pressure of the hand against the little gem

50 Diamond factories bordering the Amstel river, Amsterdam, 1860–75.

which mocks them with its brightness, and defies them with its impossibility of possession. So, in one unbroken repetition of wistful work, their life creeps darkly on, and only when the end comes does their rest seem to begin.[216]

This observation of Amsterdam's diamond mills in 1872 could equally be applied to many factory settings in different places throughout time. Repetitive and physically painful work had become a staple of the European nineteenth-century industrial system. What made the particular context of diamonds so bitter, for workers and miners alike, in all places and throughout all of history, was the fact that they were involved in creating a luxury product that was reserved for a small elite. Workers were never part of the promise that diamonds brought to miners, both free and unfree: the promise that by finding an extraordinary diamond, a miner could be rewarded to the extent that he might escape the harsh working circumstances he had to endure. A slave could obtain freedom, an adventurer could win the lottery and a wage-labourer could be paid a reward, but a diamond worker had little hope for improvement.[217] Following the establishment of the first diamond workers' organization in Amsterdam in 1866, several smaller unions were established in the following years, but it would take a couple of decades until an organization was founded that managed to unite workers to the extent that they were able to exercise pressure on the factory bosses. In 1894 the Algemene Nederlandse Diamantbewerkersbond (General Diamond Workers' Union of the Netherlands, or ANDB) was established through the efforts of the social democrat Henri Polak (1868–1943) and socialist diamond cutter Jan van Zutphen (1863–1958).[218] A year later a similar union was founded in Antwerp, the Algemene Diamantbewerkersbond (General Diamond Workers' Association of Belgium, or ADB). While the two cities were competitors, there was also solidarity between the workers, in their joint efforts to improve their labour conditions, which culminated in the establishment of the Wereldverbond van Diamantbewerkers (Worldwide Union of Diamond Workers) in 1905.[219]

This worldwide union connected more remote and small cutting industries to the main centre of cutting, which was still in Amsterdam. At the end of the nineteenth century there were small industries in the United States and France, fuelled by migrating workers from the Low Countries. It seems that the first successful diamond-cutting factory in the USA was set up in Boston by Henry Morse (1826–1888).[220] While migrants had built up a small cutting industry in Paris, it was further away from the French capital that a fully fledged diamond economy was to develop in the Jura, a region south of Dijon and Besançon and bordering Switzerland. The cutting industry that sprang up here after 1870, particularly in and around the town of Saint-Claude, employed about 1,500 workers on the eve of the First World War.[221] Delegations of workers' unions established in these different sites met at regular international congresses held in the last decade of the nineteenth century and the first decade of the twentieth, and efforts were made to regularize labour at the sites on a similar basis. One of the biggest successes was perhaps the introduction of the eight-hour working day in 1910.[222] The shared fight to improve the lives of diamond workers created a temporary unity within the global diamond industry, but it also had a negative effect on Amsterdam. With its strong union, workers were able to improve their lives in a manner that their colleagues in Antwerp and New York, working for lower wages, could not. Not surprisingly, employers started to leave Amsterdam in favour of these other cities.[223] At the same time, a fierce struggle was happening at the mining sites in South Africa. The fight was for unification, but it was not motivated by demands to improve social circumstances. Miners and mining companies were fighting for control over the mines and over labour, a struggle that would result in the creation of the biggest mining monopolist that the world had ever seen: De Beers.

51 Ernest Oppenheimer visiting an Amsterdam diamond factory, 3 December 1945.

4

Building a Worldwide Empire:
The Century of De Beers, 1884–1990

It is alleged that, beginning in 1890 . . . De Beers coordinated the
worldwide sales of diamonds by, *inter alia*, executing output-purchase
agreements with competitors, synchronizing and setting production
limits, restricting the resale of diamonds within certain geographic
regions, and directing marketing and advertising.[1]

This extract from a court case against De Beers in 2011 is very telling
of the monopoly the company managed to obtain in the decades
after the amalgamation of the mines at Kimberley (Big Hole) and
De Beers (formerly known as 'Old Rush'). The company followed a policy
of purchasing as many of the new African discoveries as possible, to control production and construct a selling organization in London through
which its diamonds passed. During the twentieth century De Beers had
become the almighty spider in the web spun by the extraction of rough
diamonds. It was involved in all aspects of the commodity chain, everywhere. The main architect for constructing this diamond empire was Ernest
Oppenheimer (1880–1957) (illus. 51). Oppenheimer was born in Germany,
but when he turned seventeen, he was sent to London to work for Anton
Dunkelsbühler's diamond firm. After the end of the Second Boer War in
1902, Dunkelsbühler needed a new agent in Kimberley and he chose young
Ernest, now a naturalized British subject whose older brothers were already
active diamond traders in London and Kimberley. Ernest married in 1906,
became mayor of Kimberley in 1912 and soon thereafter joined the board
of directors of the company that was running Jagersfontein.[2] It was the
beginning of the involvement of the Oppenheimer family with De Beers,
and the family remained at the helm of the company until it sold its stake
to Anglo-American in 2011.

This chapter focuses on the construction of the De Beers empire, from
the amalgamation of the various mining companies active in Kimberley

during the 1880s, to the introduction of underground mining and African compound labour, and the establishment of a commercial infrastructure that extended De Beers' control over mining to trading rough diamonds. The chapter discusses emerging competition and the incorporation of most of it into the empire, and how the company, and the diamond industry in general, dealt with two World Wars and the atrocious political regime in South Africa to show that De Beers, during the twentieth century, was resilient enough to weather these challenges and even managed to use them to their advantage.

Compounds, or the Invention of Racial Segregation at Work

After the Black Flag Revolt was tamed, other problems persisted. Land ownership remained a worry for the colonial government. Certainly, one of Southey's last decisions had been to buy the Vooruitzigt farm for £100,000 in an effort to end the disagreements between diggers and proprietors, but the farms at Dutoitspan and Bultfontein were still in the private hands of the LSAEC.[3] Other major issues were the high price of black labour following the wage rises of the first half of the 1870s, and the lack of investments brought about by restrictions on the use of foreign capital. But perhaps the biggest problem was the decline of prices paid for rough diamonds on the European market, as the almost unchecked growth of individual mining led to oversupply. The number of claims one could own was still limited to ten, which meant that it was difficult to keep production under control. Furthermore, £100,000 was still owed to the Orange Free State in compensation for territorial claims on the diamond fields. A crisis ensued and the new administrator decided to remove the claim restriction and hand over power to the reinstated mining boards, who represented the claimholders.[4] This paved the way for the bigger companies, an evolution that had been feared for years:

> The great bugbear of the digger is the word 'company', but even now small proprietorships are becoming merged in large aggregations of claims, and the next phase of mining operations must undoubtedly be that of several large and competing companies, or perhaps a single one controlling the whole mine. Then the romance of individual diamond hunting will be over.[5]

These words, published in 1877, turned out to be prophetic, and soon after they were put to paper several men started to buy up claims in Kimberley, either for themselves or for firms in Europe and Port Elizabeth in the Cape Colony. By the end of 1879 twelve companies owned 75 per cent of the Kimberley mine, with similar concentrations of ownership occurring at the De Beers, Bultfontein and Dutoitspan mines. At the same time, the value of the Kimberley mine tripled between 1876 and 1881, De Beers increased fivefold, Bultfontein's value was multiplied by fifty and Dutoitspan increased sixty times in value.[6] Many of the white diggers and share-workers became overseers and managers in the employ of these companies, supervising a growing black labour force. Although production increased, further investments were needed to address the rising costs of reef removal and workers' wages.[7] After 1879, following the firm of Martin Lilienfeld & Co. in Port Elizabeth, most mining firms decided to go public, and by April 1881 a total of 66 had become joint-stock companies, creating a 'share mania'.[8]

Two groups of claimholders emerged as dominant players. The first was the Compagnie Française des Mines de Diamants du Cap (referred to as the French Diamond Mining Company in illus. 52), headquartered in Paris and founded in 1880 as a merger between the company of Jules Porges, a Jewish immigrant from Prague who had become the largest importer of Cape diamonds in London, and the venture of Lewis & Marks, two men who had migrated from Lithuania to the Cape. Their most important agents in Kimberley were Alfred Beit and Julius Wernher, names that were to be associated later with the formation of De Beers. A second group of entrepreneurs centred around the figure of Charles J. Posno, whose family had roots in the diamond-cutting industry of Amsterdam.[9]

Most of the European-based firms concentrated on Dutoitspan and Bultfontein, still located on LSAEC territory, and companies active on these mining sites were built on connections between local businessmen and European investors. Posno, for instance, was involved in nine companies that were active there. Harry Mosenthal, son of a Port Elizabeth merchant named Adolph Mosenthal, was a director of five.[10] Adolph, related to the Lilienfeld brothers, exported diamonds to London from the South African port and had sent several of his sons, including Harry, to the British capital to make business easier.[11] Out of all these men, three major local magnates in Kimberley, spurred on by enormous ambition, were jockeying for a place at the front. Two of them had been miners: Cecil Rhodes (1853–1902), who had moved to the diamond fields in 1870, and the ill-tempered J. B. Robinson (1840–1929). The third was the eccentric Barney Barnato, a Jew from London's East End who had long struggled to make ends meet, even including a stint as an actor, but who finally made it as a diamond broker (*kopje-walloper*) in the town of Kimberley.[12]

Not all of the three competitors fared equally well at the diamond mines. J. B. Robinson, one of the directors of the Compagnie Française, went bankrupt in 1886 and decided to exchange the diamond fields for Witwatersrand when gold was discovered there. The other two men were to play a crucial role in the further development of diamond monopolization in South Africa.[13] Rhodes quickly decided to concentrate his mining efforts on the De Beers mine, where he established the De Beers Diamond Mining Company (De Beers DMC), which soon became the controlling entity there.[14] Barnato's firm, Barnato Bros., held very valuable claims at the Kimberley mine, and he became a highly influential man when his company merged with Kimberley Central Diamond Mining Company in 1887, a company that had come into existence six years earlier and was centrally established in the Big Hole (illus. 52). Barnato held a controlling share of the new enterprise, dominating Kimberley's first mine.[15]

The amalgamation of mining companies and the further development of mining capitalism in the diamond region had brutal consequences for the black workforce. Obsessed with a perceived relationship between skin colour and diamond theft, and fully in sync with the colonial desire to regulate, shape and restrict the patterns of black labour migration as much as possible, white men had long been thinking of a way to control black labourers through housing. In the early 1870s Charles Payton wrote that

> with regard to sleeping accommodation for the Kafirs, some generous diggers provide them with a rough tent; but if the 'boys' are smart and active they will soon make a comfortable little hut for themselves with branches, bushes, &c., which they can go into the country to fetch on Saturday afternoons and Sundays.[16]

Initially the miners and diggers were responsible for their own housing, and that of their employees. But in 1876 the colonial administration of

Griqualand West had begun to think of introducing the location system, an early form of racial segregation in which black Africans were forced to live in areas specifically allocated for that purpose – areas that 'featured little or no fertile soil'.[17] The system existed in the Cape Colony but would only find its way to Griqualand West after the tumultuous period of the late 1870s.[18] The informal segregation that already existed at the mining sites was replaced by a formal colonial location system in 1879 through the Native Locations Act. Colonial administrators felt it would be easier to control theft and labour efforts, while the system also ensured a stable flow of workers. Land for use by non-whites was less fertile and allocated in areas too small to be self-sufficient, which created a push for black men to work at the mines. It was, in other words, an ingenious system designed not only to better control the workers but to force them into mining labour.[19]

T. C. Kitto, a Cornish mining engineer who had compiled several reports on the state of mining in the Cape Colony and Griqualand West in 1879, was one of the first to suggest practical ways of taking the colonial system of segregation and exploitation one step further. He had drawn the comparison with the situation in Brazil, where work on the diamond fields was still done by slave labour, which was only abolished in 1888. He described the barracks used by English companies to lodge the enslaved Africans, and thought it would be fruitful to introduce a similar system in South Africa: 'I believe the natives of South Africa, under European supervision, are capable of being made almost – if not quite – as good as the blacks of Brazil, provided they are dealt with in the same manner.'[20] The first organized compounds were open, in the sense that the workers lodged there still had the ability to move around freely, but later, following the Brazilian model of slave barracks, the compounds were closed, a change that did not come about without protest: white liquor sellers protested that black customers could no longer make it to their businesses, while black workers periodically went on strike to complain about the confined living conditions, although in the end these strikes were unsuccessful.[21]

The first company to act on Kitto's suggestions was the Compagnie Française, which set up a compound for 110 African workers from Natal in January 1885. A few months later, Kimberley Central followed with the construction of a compound to house four hundred black workers, while De Beers DMC built closed barracks for their 1,500 African workers

52 Map of the claimholders at Kimberley's Big Hole, 1883.

in July.[22] The architectural set-up of these first closed compounds, which fully segregated black workers, separated them from their families and penalized them by treating them as criminals, was repeated in other industrial areas of South Africa, and later, in wartime, used for building concentration camps (illus. 53, 54, 55, 63 and 64). By 1889 the whole non-white labour force of 10,000 miners working in Kimberley, De Beers, Dutoitspan and Bultfontein was living in closed compounds, the biggest of which, the West End, housed as many as 3,000 workers.[23] After a visit to Kimberley around that time, Zélie Colvile, the aristocratic wife of a British major-general, referred to these compounds as the 'kaffirs' quarters'.[24] She described them as surrounding a 'large square, with an asphalt floor, surrounded by a fence of corrugated iron ten feet high' (illus. 53).[25] The black miners inside were 'engaged for three months, during which time they cannot leave the "Compound". At the end of this period, if they like to re-engage themselves, they can; and some of them were pointed out to us as never having been outside the place since it was started two years ago.'[26] Several photographs taken at the same time as Colvile's visit, or not much later, show similar scenes to those described by her (illus. 54 and 55).

Gardner F. Williams, an American mining engineer brought in by Rhodes as a manager at De Beers DMC in 1887, stated that when the claim-owners combined in companies, their workmen were frequently kept together in enclosures called 'compounds', where they were furnished with food and shelter at moderate charges deducted from their pay. This separation and partial restriction was of undoubted service, not only in diminishing the opportunities for successful theft and disposal of stolen diamonds, but in checking the drunkenness of the black workmen and the outbreaks in the canteens and streets.[27]

The compound system put checks on the practice of temporary migratory labour and adapted it into a form of semi-forced employment much more suited to the needs of the mining companies.[28] The human toll was enormous, as tens of thousands of black men died in these camps and compounds.[29] It also made the racial division of the workforce very tangible. With black miners confined to compounds and the underground mines (illus. 57), white people circulated freely in the town of Kimberley and its surroundings, and were employed in the offices of De Beers and the other companies that required more skilled labour (illus. 58).

The need to exercise larger control over the African workforce was directly related to the development of underground mining. Diamondiferous kimberlite extended well beyond the technical limit of open-pit mining at about 120 metres (395 ft; see illus. 1).[30] Small shafts and

53 Zélie Colvile's compound, Kimberley, 1893.

54 Compound, Kimberley, c. 1890.

tunnels had been constructed to prevent reef collapse, but this was costly, dangerous and not a structural solution. Water drainage had become a serious problem as well, particularly at the Big Hole in Kimberley. Gardner Williams observed that, in 1878, more than a quarter of all claims were covered in fallen reef, and that drainage and reef hauling cost £150,000 a year in 1879 and 1880, and more than £200,000 in 1881. These expenses drove the Kimberley Mining Board to bankruptcy in 1883, at a time when the open pit at Kimberley had reached its limits.[31] The Big Hole had become deep, and the older aerial tramways were now also used to bring miners to the bottom of the pit (illus. 56 and 59).

The concentration of mining in the hands of only a few companies helped to face these rising costs, and between 1883 and 1885 the Kimberley mine went underground. De Beers DMC, adapting early, gained a competitive advantage over its competitors.[32] Underground mining relied on unskilled labourers, but it also needed skilled miners, who were recruited from traditional British mining areas such as Cumberland and Cornwall. Fatal accidents increased, and although several could be attributed to underground mining, such as the explosion of dynamite magazines in 1884, or the fire at a De Beers DMC mining shaft in 1888, most deaths were still related to reef collapses, with a reduction only visible after underground

176

55 Workers taking a break in a compound, Kimberley, 1901.

mining had been generally implemented by 1889.[33] There were hospitals in the compounds to take care of those injured during work. Zélie Colvile visited one and saw 'forty wounded men, laid up mostly with broken arms and legs – casualties that had happened in the mine'.[34] Historian Robert Turrell asserted that in the underground gold mines on Witwatersrand the death rate was about 4 per 1,000. It was higher in Kimberley, particularly during the transition to underground mining, but in the last decade of the nineteenth century the Kimberley death rate stabilized at about 6 per 1,000, which was twice as high as what was deemed the acceptable limit in Great Britain at that time.[35] Recent research of the skeletons of miners who had died in Kimberley at the end of the nineteenth century has shown that these men had suffered from unhealthy circumstances, both at the mines, causing damage to the spine and fractures to bones,

56 Rollercoaster, Kimberley, c. 1886.

as well as in the compounds, where a limited diet and lack of hygiene led to scurvy and tuberculosis. A high occurrence of skull fractures was considered indicative of the excessive use of racist violence against them.[36]

With black workers now mostly mining underground, white supervision at the mines was exchanged for the security of the closed compound system, where workers were also subjected to a regular 'strip and search' that was extremely humiliating (illus. 60 and 61).[37]

The need for unskilled white workers vanished, and as share-working had all but disappeared, a poor and unemployed white class emerged.[38] This development was but one ingredient of what was rapidly becoming

57 Miners working underground at the De Beers mine, 1896.

58 De Beers employee counting diamonds, Kimberley, 1896.

an explosive situation. A lowering of wages and the introduction of new search systems to prevent theft, both of which drawing the treatment of lower white class nearer to that of black workers, led to protests, and white miners went on strike in 1883. The turmoil was sparked by these measures, but it also had to do with the white miners' loss of status. Many had been diggers and claimholders themselves, and had now become employees who, in certain regards, were treated as badly as their black colleagues, which was difficult for many of them to accept, as colonial and racist ideas were still so deeply ingrained in society.[39] The mining companies quickly made a deal, partly out of fear that the African miners would return to their native regions, and within a week agreed to make adjustments to the new search system, but the outbreak of a smallpox epidemic, further wage cuts and a renewed effort to install the severe search system led to a second strike in 1884.[40]

The strike of 1884 did not bring about any positive development for the workforce and raised the question about the relationship between black and white workers. White strike leaders had made it clear they were not interested in representing black miners as well, and refused to stand at 'the head of a lot of niggers with the intention of smashing the property of the employers'.[41] Still, Cecil Rhodes foresaw a working solidarity that could harm his imperial project and he informed the Parliament of

59 Kimberley's Big Hole, 1888.

60 Checking for hidden diamonds, Kimberley, *c.* 1884.

61 Checking for hidden diamonds, Kimberley, *c.* 1884.

the Cape of Good Hope that the strike was something he 'hoped never to see in this colony again, white men supported by natives in a struggle against whites'.[42] The black miners were a much larger group than the white workers and counted for about 85 per cent of the total. It is therefore no surprise that, after violently ending the strike, mining companies focused on keeping the black miners in check, which resulted in the establishment of the closed compound system in 1885. Two years later, in 1887, De Beers DMC and Kimberley Central advocated the idea of compounds for white workers, although it never took root.[43] In addition to the black workers and a small percentage of white miners and overseers forced to live in compounds, De Beers had also struck a deal with the government to use convict labour. Kimberley's jail was the highest populated prison in the colony, with a daily average of 658 prisoners in the 1880s. The jail was turned into the De Beers Company Branch Convict Station, and the company paid the colonial government per prisoner employed in the mines, a practice that led to the transfer of prisoners from elsewhere to Kimberley. This was another labour force whose efforts could be bent to the will of De Beers; Gardner Williams remarked that convict labour would always be at hand, and that theft and escape could be better managed, as convicts could be shot.[44]

The International Grasp of De Beers Consolidated Mines

In 1885 the colony's diamond mining operations were in a state of crisis. Many companies were in financial difficulties and competed evermore fiercely with one another. Production was expanding, but so were the costs, and parliamentary elections at the Cape in 1884 had led to a defeat for those representing the mining capitalists. Cecil Rhodes was one of the few who did not lose; he managed to keep his seat in Parliament, and his De Beers DMC was one of the few companies with a good business balance. This had to do with Rhodes's ability to keep labour costs lower than the competition. De Beers DMC did not mine as deep as the other companies and Rhodes regularly ignored safety restrictions. On 11 July 1888 one of the shafts of the De Beers mine caught fire and 24 white miners and 178 black miners, all working underground, were killed, although more than five hundred were rescued.[45] The *Daily Telegraph* reported that it was 'feared that 500 have perished, including Mr. Lindsay, the manager, and a number of other white men'.[46] The article lamented the human sacrifice of 'some of our fellows' in this 'terrible race for wealth in which all the world engages'.[47] No word, though, on the fate of the 178 black miners who perished in the same incident.

Accidents such as these did not harm Rhodes, who was doing well both in business and politics, and his political victories enabled him to take on his competitors in the mines. Rhodes turned out to be the man who was able to amalgamate the different mining companies into one operation, but the idea of amalgamating the four mines – Kimberley, De Beers, Dutoitspan and Bultfontein – as a solution to problems of labour and capital was not new. Nathan Rothschild had already investigated such an option at Dutoitspan in 1883, and C. J. Posno had failed with his Unified Diamond Mines Company in 1885.[48] When manoeuvring towards amalgamation began, De Beers DMC was in control of the De Beers mine and Kimberley Central owned almost all of Kimberley. In 1887 Rhodes made his big move and purchased the Compagnie Française, the only remaining competitor to Barnato Bros' Kimberley Central at the Kimberley mine. A struggle began between Rhodes's De Beers DMC and Kimberley Central, controlled by Barney Barnato. Eventually Rhodes was forced to sell the Compagnie Française to Central, in exchange for £300,000 and shares in Central to the value of £356,000, giving Rhodes entry into Kimberley and Central. This started a process of buying up shares on both sides that ended with Rhodes gaining a dominant holding in Central after Barnato agreed to sell his shares, for which he was rewarded a life directorship at the new company.

The new company, set up to control Kimberley and De Beers, was founded in Kimberley in March 1888 as De Beers Consolidated Mines Ltd (DBCM), with a board of directors in London and Kimberley. Several Central men, including its chairman, objected and tried to stop amalgamation through litigation, but to no avail. By October 1888 resistance had ceased and DBCM bought the Kimberley mine.[49] It is commonly held that Barnato lost against Rhodes, but financially Barnato and Central's shareholders got the better deal. Barnato also remained involved in DBCM, making a handsome profit, until his mysterious death at sea in 1897.[50] Rhodes did get the control he wanted, though, and he dreamt of using the diamond monopoly as a foundation on which to build an imperialist project that would expand Britain's political and economic control over the African continent. In his mind, this project would be financed by Rothschild capital and the income from South African diamonds. Rhodes himself would, of course, be the main political actor, and he became prime minister of the Cape between 1890 and 1896.[51]

The amalgamation of Kimberley and De Beers had been successful, but Dutoitspan and Bultfontein, where De Beers had several claims, were still on lands that belonged to the LSAEC. River digging continued but yielded few results. All the same, declining prices motivated Rhodes, now prime minister, to continue his attempts to fully control South Africa's diamond deposits. DBCM had some influence in the Jagersfontein and Koffiefontein mines in Orange Free State through the interest held in the mining companies there by Barnato Bros.[52] These were not part of the amalgamation that was taking place at Kimberley, but the two mining companies that had been able to buy up the diggers' claims at Jagersfontein merged to form the New Jagersfontein Mining and Exploration Company in 1889.[53] The threatening new discovery of the Wesselton (Premier) mine in 1890 quickly caught the eye of Rhodes, who manoeuvred rapidly to incorporate the mine into his business empire in 1891.[54] In 1898, thanks to heavy borrowing, including a million pounds from the Rothschild bank in London, De Beers finally purchased the land titles of the LSAEC.[55]

In 1887 Rhodes hired Gardner Williams, who had been working for the Rothschild-supported Exploration Company, an enterprise that was involved in gold mining, and appointed him general manager of De Beers.[56] Under Williams's supervision, Kimberley's infrastructure improved a great deal and the four mines of De Beers were connected through railways. The whole area around Kimberley was turned into an industrial city, with interconnected pits, mining shafts, floors where the diamondiferous blue ground was exposed to the elements for periods of up to six months, and fenced-off compounds.[57] The population of the city reached 20,000 in 1905, when the Kimberley mine reached a depth of 914 metres (3,000 ft). Williams oversaw several technical improvements, such as a new plant to pulverize hard earth and the 'greasing' table that made sorting automatic. There was a strong increase in the loads that could be processed, but mechanization did not reduce the labour force, which tripled between 1890 and 1914. That year, a daily average of 11,377 labourers, of which 80 per cent were black, worked in the underground and surface operations of the De Beers enterprise.

The hardest task remained the underground drilling in groups of up to thirty men, but overall, mortality rates declined over time. Labour was still organized on the basis of short-term contracts, with high replacement rates and based on seasonal migration, which made it very well suited for the demands of the diamond industry, since fluctuations in prices on the world market sometimes necessitated temporary shutdowns, as had been the case for Dutoitspan and Bultfontein in 1890.[58] The ruthless living circumstances of the closed compounds, arbitrary punishment and the low wages paid to black workers incited strikes, which were often broken by violence.[59] The compound system did not abolish the tendency to draw labour from communities at a great distance from Kimberley. Archaeological research on the remains of labourers who died at Kimberley between 1897 and 1900 confirms that the black workforce relied extensively on migration from regions further away in South Africa, while local Griqua, Kora and Thlaping managed, at the time, to stay out of the mines by gaining an income by selling wood and food to the mining towns.[60] The Dundee-based *Evening Telegraph* published an extensive article on the diamond mines at Kimberley in 1900, and concluded with a telling passage on the involvement of 'natives':

> The black men who work in the mines come from many tribes in South and East Africa, and they are watched with more than fatherly consideration . . . When they come to look for work they have to contract to remain at least six months. During that period they are never permitted to go outside the walls. They are kept in what is known as a compound, and inside that they can buy all they require, or at least all that is good for them. De Beers sees to that; De Beers is the dealer. The compound is a subject of vexed controversy, so I shall say no more about it.[61]

Indeed, it is not difficult to find articles in British newspapers defending the compound system around the turn of the century. The *Daily Telegraph* included a report by an eyewitness who stated that 'the compound system, as organised at Kimberley, combines all the privileges of freedom – save that of getting drunk – with that absence of responsibility, which is the compensation of the slave.'[62] The choice of the term 'slave' is particularly revealing as slavery was abolished by that time, but even defenders of the compound system seemed to realize that it advocated a form of slavery – and they saw no harm in it. An article in *The Times* indicates that there were several organizations active that rallied against the compound system, as the article's author decided to write against a pamphlet issued by 'one of the London labour leagues' that denounced the compound system in which black workers were whipped, underpaid and imprisoned.[63]

In spite of some voices speaking out against the compound system, nearly all the newspapers that covered it were defending a colonial, abusive and racist system as something good.[64] The compound system in Kimberley became an example for mining companies elsewhere in British African colonies, which sent observers to De Beers to implement the system at their own mining sites. Following De Beers' example, mining firms in Witwatersrand and Rhodesia installed compound systems of their own, and 60,000 Chinese indentured workers were lodged in close compounds at the Rand in 1904. Six years later, after the Chinese labourers had departed again, closed compounds in the Rand housed 200,000 black labourers.[65] In 1923 a new Natives Act obliged municipalities to lodge black migrant labourers in specific areas, preferably in separate buildings called hostels.[66] By that time, De Beers had also taken various measures to ensure no one could enter the mines unseen: searchlights kept the pits lit during the night and barbed wire fences were built around them, with openings to take away the diamondiferous blue earth (illus. 62).[67] The mines were directly connected to some of the compounds through tunnels and underground passages, meaning workers were sent from one sealed-off environment to another (illus. 63 shows one of those connected compounds).

The lack of critical voices when the compound system came into being continued throughout the twentieth century. A two-page photospread in the *London Illustrated News* published in February 1932 showed, next to photos of the security measures that were taken, a variety of pictures of mineworkers who (according to the accompanying comments) were happy. They were photographed dancing, strolling and cultivating roses. One picture is particularly telling in the disceprancy between what is seen and how it is described: 'a care-free life, despite the restrictions: native mine-workers content in their quarters, knowing that they will earn enough to buy cattle for wife-purchasing' (illus. 64).[68] The comment, to be read by a predominantly white audience back home, leaves nothing to the imagination as to how black workers were perceived at the time, and how easy it seemed to be to disguise the horrible circumstances they were forced into.

The establishment of the compound system was facilitated by the fact that, by the end of the nineteenth century, DBCM had successfully monopolized non-alluvial South African diamond mining, and the company controlled 90 per cent of global diamond production.[69] With the industrial organization of mining falling into place at Kimberley, Rhodes and De Beers shifted their attention to how to put the diamonds on the market. Since early modern times, diamond traders had realized that new production greatly altered prices and that controlling supply was a crucial aspect of keeping the price level up: both the Indo-European and Brazilian diamond trades had been subjected to monopolization at different stages throughout their history. During the 1870s, the trade in rough diamonds in Kimberley had become hierarchically structured. At the top of the pyramid were merchants involved in international transactions, exporting diamonds to Europe and bringing capital to the Cape Colony. Several of these men were partners in larger mining

62 Barbed wire around a diamond mine, Kimberley, 1932.

63 Compound, Kimberley, late 19th–early 20th century.

firms. One step lower were the agents who represented large enterprises in Europe or in the Cape Colony. A third group were the diamond brokers, acting as intermediaries in transactions between buyers and sellers. While there were rules for this third group, including an official registration, there were also so-called *kopje-wallopers*, brokers who refused to submit to these regulations, opting for a life of clandestine business instead.[70]

Growth in the number of mining companies in the 1880s came at the expense of local traders and brokers, and the trade with London came into the hands of a small number of companies, of which the most important were Jules Porges & Co., A. Mosenthal & Sons, Anton Dunkelsbühler, Barnato Bros., Joseph Bros., Lewis & Marks, Ochs Bros. and Julius Pam & Co. Half of these 'big eight' had been active in diamond trade before the discoveries in South Africa. Both the Mosenthal and Dunkelsbühler enterprises were associated with the Salomons family, Ashkenazi Jews with family members installed in Amsterdam and London, who had been involved in the diamond trade since the eighteenth century.[71] Now that production was firmly monopolized by the DBCM, which had grown thanks to the financial input of a number of merchants established in Kimberley and London, voices grew louder advocating some sort of agreement that would enable those who were buying De Beers' production to align their

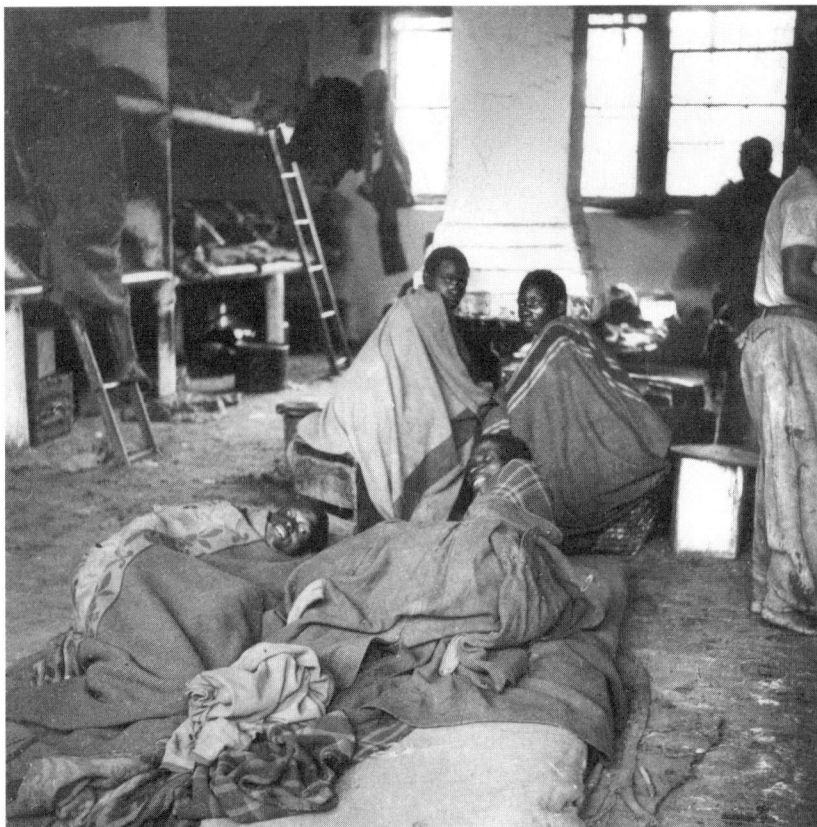

64 Inside a compound, Kimberley, 1932.

actions in order to protect the prices of rough diamonds. The trade in South African diamonds was already in the hands of a relatively select number of firms, although De Beers also sold directly to smaller traders in Kimberley.[72] Most of the London-based firms that bought rough diamonds from De Beers held shares in DBCM and had been connected to Kimberley since the days of the share mania. At the end of 1889, 60 per cent of the company's capital was in the hands of eighteen merchants, several of whom had played a role in Rhodes's amalgamation scheme through financial investment.[73]

Thoughts on commercial monopolization led to a deal in 1889, in which it was stipulated that the total production of the De Beers diamond mines was to be sold through a diamond syndicate that consisted of four firms, all based in London and part of the 'big eight': Wernher, Beit & Co.; Anton Dunkelsbühler; Mosenthal Sons & Co.; and Barnato

Bros.[74] Wernher, Beit & Co. was the successor of Jules Porges & Co., and Alfred Beit had been one of Rhodes's closest associates during the amalgamation and the firm had lent a substantial amount of money to DBCM.[75] Anton Dunkelsbühler had been sent to Kimberley as agent for the Mosenthals, but set up his own company in London in 1875. The composition of the syndicate changed in the following years, with the inclusion of six more firms, including Martin Lilienfeld & Co. and Joseph Bros. Most of these firms disappeared from the syndicate's con-stellation again the next year, and between 1892 and 1906 the syndicate was formed by the four initial firms and Joseph Bros.[76] In 1909 the syndicate was joined by Central Mining & Investment Corporation, a firm established by Wernher and Beit, and in 1914, just before the out-break of the First World War, the syndicate's composition was back to its four original members plus the Central Mining & Investment Corporation.[77]

The majority of the production from the mines of DBCM was sold to this syndicate, although small sales continued to be made to outside traders, at times with the specific purpose of getting rid of reserves that were secretly being built up by Rhodes.[78] In spite of the changes in the syndicate's membership in the years following its inception, and the ad hoc nature of commercial agreements between the syndicate partners in London and DBCM's Kimberley Diamond Committee, the commercial arm of the company, the creation of the syndicate meant the establish-ment of a unified selling process that was called 'single channel selling'. While this method would be further refined during the next half-century, its essentials remained the same, and single selling was the commercial component of the mining monopoly, both of which enabled De Beers to almost completely control the diamond industry until the end of the twentieth century.[79] Single selling required a smooth process of getting rough diamonds from South Africa to Great Britain. In Kimberley, the diamonds that came out of the mines were sorted and classified according to weight and quality, after which they were valuated. Following valu-ation, rough diamonds were either placed in the reserve stock or sent to London, where they were resold to dealers by members of the syndicate. These participating firms received a discount but had to buy on the basis of the sometimes-contested valuation and in bulk. Syndicate firms then reassorted the parcels they bought and offered them at weekly 'sights' to dealers who could have the stones polished and set in jewellery, or sell them on further.[80]

Gradually other buyers at Kimberley were eliminated from the process, while buyers not related to the syndicate were at times allowed to purchase rough diamonds from De Beers, albeit at higher prices, particularly to offload reserve stock. In the early years the syndicate members were not always in full agreement on how to proceed, and producers and buyers quarrelled over valuation, particularly as the quality of parcels went down when the produce at the older mines deteriorated. Rhodes and the syndicate were also at odds over the issue of profit-sharing, the entry of reserve stocks on the market, and setting prices for the lower-quality diamonds that were produced by the Wesselton mine. Additionally, there were disagreements between De Beers' directors, some of them also representing syndicate members, on the level of reinvestment of profits into the company and the involvement of Rhodes and De Beers in the economy, infrastructure and finances of the Cape Colony.[81] An agreement was reached in 1901, when a new contract was signed with a syndicate that now counted seven members.[82] The new contract guaranteed De Beers a share of the profit of resales, and it introduced six-month periods for checking up on the valuation of parcels.[83] The total value of sales rose 140 per cent between 1890 and 1907. Between 1901 and 1909, sales profits amounted to £3.3 million to the syndicate and £1.5 million to De Beers, with about 5 million carats of diamonds sold every year, practically all that was available on the world market.[84]

The expansion of De Beers during those years had everything to do with the development of a consumer market in the United States. The American economy was doing well in the decades between 1890 and 1910, leading to higher consumption, including that of luxury products. In Europe, the consumer market had undergone important changes as well. Luxury items came to be more accessible, and the development of advertising played an important role in igniting consumer interest amid the developing industrial bourgeoisie.[85]

The growing dominance of De Beers, the further development of a popular written press and the American economic success all contributed to the establishment of an American market for jewellery. The tendency to render the wearing of jewellery an exclusively female activity, which had already begun in Europe in the seventeenth century, culminated in the practice of men giving engagement rings to their fiancées. The concept of a diamond engagement ring is so ingrained in traditional bourgeois Western culture that it is almost hard to imagine that it had a beginning, which can be situated around 1900 in Birmingham.[86] Advertisements published in American newspapers at the turn of the century clearly demonstrate the growth of the American market for diamonds and the role played by constructed femininity. One that appeared on behalf of the jeweller R. Harris and Company, published in the Washington, DC-based *Evening Star* on 15 December 1898, says it all (illus. 65). First, the firm called itself 'the Jewelers of the People'.[87] Second, it clearly sold the idea of male buyers and female consumers by calling diamonds 'the most exquisite gems that ever beguiled the heart or lost the soul of woman, with their dangerous, lurking glitter and irresistibility'.[88] The advertisement tried to tempt men to buy diamond jewellery, as it as 'a fit gift for the American Queen – your sweetheart – your wife – your daughter'.[89]

An article in the *San Francisco Sunday Call* from 21 March 1909 is a bit more explicit on the developing economic connection in diamonds between the USA and South Africa. The article starts with the observation that 'it seems hard to realize that the business depression which passed over the United States in the fall of 1907 had the effect of throwing great numbers of semicivilized natives out of employment in South Africa.'[90] The author asserted that the events of 1907 caused a drop in the number of labourers from 36,000 to less than 3,000. The American consumer market had become so important that 75 per cent of South Africa's rough diamonds were sold in the USA, largely to be explained by the fact that 'probably in America a million girls become engaged each year. Every one of them requires, as her unquestionable right, that she be presented with a diamond engagement ring.'[91] De Beers was, of course, well aware of the growth of consumer interest, at a time in which the company controlled 80 per cent of the world's production. In 1904, for instance, the *New York Tribune* wrote that the company raised prices for diamonds by five cents on the dollar, so 'whoever has been planning to buy diamonds as Christmas presents must now go deeper into his pocket.'[92] The article continued by writing that the higher price would please not only the directors of De Beers but 'many a European nobleman'. The newspaper quoted a jeweller from London's Maiden Lane who explained the practice of dismantling jewels from poverty-stricken nobility, and asserted that 'on any opera night one

65 Advertisement for R. Harris & Co., 'the Jewelers of the People', Washington, DC, 1898.

"R. HARRIS & CO., for 22 Years the Jewelers of the People."

Incomparable Display of Diamonds!

Princely! Royal! Imperial!

The most exquisite gems that ever beguiled the heart or lost the soul of woman, with their dangerous, lurking glitter and irresistibility! Not often can one feast the eyes on such marvelous wealth of beauty--rich and rare. Seize the opportunity--come and see this magnificent array of mounted Diamonds--the work of our own factory--and then you will decide that after all it is Diamonds--and Diamonds only--that are a fit gift for the American Queen-- your sweetheart--your wife--your daughter. Diamonds are her heart's desire--ask her--Diamonds alone are worthy of her. And soberly speaking, you save 20 to 30 per cent by selecting them here. We have no credit, losses--hence, no high prices. Beware the danger of paying too much--unscrupulousness abounds in gaudy disguise.

R. HARRIS & CO., Jewelers, Diamond Importers, 7th & D Sts.

may see glittering about the necks and arms of any number of New-York women jewels that once adorned the courts of kings and emperors.'[93] The glamour that was mainly worn by white consumers stood in stark contrast to the evermore brutal attempts to exercise full control over black bodies toiling in South Africa's mining pits, as shown in illus. 66. This image, part of a book published in the first decade of the twentieth century, shows the hands of workers being manacled during a rare break from work; a measure intended to prevent theft.

The arrival of the twentieth century meant the definitive shift from a consumer market in Europe and Asia that had been dominated by an elite, first the nobility but later also the bourgeoisie, to a consumer market that started to look to the middle class in the United States. It was a relatively sudden but profound change. The article in the *New York Tribune* suggested that forty years earlier, right before the discovery of South African diamonds, American consumers spent one-twentieth as much on diamonds as they were to spend in 1904.[94] It remained silent on the oppressive methods designed to build a more efficient mining environment without much consideration for the black workers, who were so necessary to support this enormous increase in consumption.

African Threats: The First Challenge to Monopoly

De Beers and the syndicate now controlled the world's diamond supplies, but they could not foresee that Africa had not yet shown all its diamond treasures. In 1903 a new diamond deposit was discovered about 40 kilometres (25 mi.) from Pretoria in the Transvaal, which had lost its independence a year earlier after British victory in the Second Boer War turned the Transvaal into a colony (see illus. 36).[95] Just before the end of the conflict, Cecil Rhodes, who normally stayed in Cape Town but had come to Kimberley to force the British colonial army to break the Boer siege of the diamond city, died at the age of 48. Rhodes's ideas were already controversial in his own time, and his legacy in colonial expansion and imperialist projects is very much contested to this day, as is his involvement in South African segregation and the abuse of African labourers through the compound system.[96] Mark Twain wrote about him in 1898 that 'I admire him, I frankly confess it; and when his time comes I shall buy a piece of the rope for a keepsake.'[97]

The deposit discovered in 1903 was named the Premier mine (not to be confused with the Wesselton mine) and proved to be the largest kimberlite pipe yet discovered (illus. 67). Its owner, Cape-born Thomas Cullinan, however, refused to join the group of De Beers and the syndicate. Instead, Cullinan struck a deal with the colonial authorities in Transvaal, where legislation preserved only one-eighth of the area for the owner, with the state allowed to manage the rest as licensed public diggings.[98] It was an arrangement that was only beneficial for the state in the case of alluvial diggings, which were spread out over a larger area. In the case of pit mining, however, it preserved the best area for the owner, leaving hardly anything for the state. In the end, the Transvaal authorities, looking for ways to relieve their gold mines of repaying standing debts that had resulted from the Boer wars, accepted a situation in which they received 60 per cent of the profits, but no ownership. The arrangement led to the formation of the Premier Diamond Mining Company (Premier DMC). One of its black labourers discovered the world's largest rough diamond there in January 1905. The stone weighed 3,106.75 carats and was named the Cullinan Diamond. Louis Botha, commander of the Boer army during the second war with Britain, was made first prime minister of an autonomous Transvaal colony in 1907, and to express his gratitude and loyalty to the Crown, he arranged for the Cullinan Diamond to be given to King Edward VII, a decision that stirred some controversy in London, where voices felt that British subjects in the Cape Colony should be catered for before such luxurious gifts were given.[99]

When the Cullinan Diamond arrived in London, it still needed to be cut. The Amsterdam cutting industry was considered superior to the one established in London, and the decision to send the diamond to the Dutch capital was met with discontent by London cutters who felt they were also able to do the job. A London-based jeweller interviewed on the subject was of the opinion that London's cutting industry was decent, but focused on polishing and the setting of small diamonds into jewellery, and only rarely actually cut diamonds. The London-based Garrard firm, for instance, employed to cut the Koh-i-Noor, had received assistance from Amsterdam.[100] In the end the Cullinian Diamond was sent to Amsterdam, where a group of cutters from the world-famous Asscher

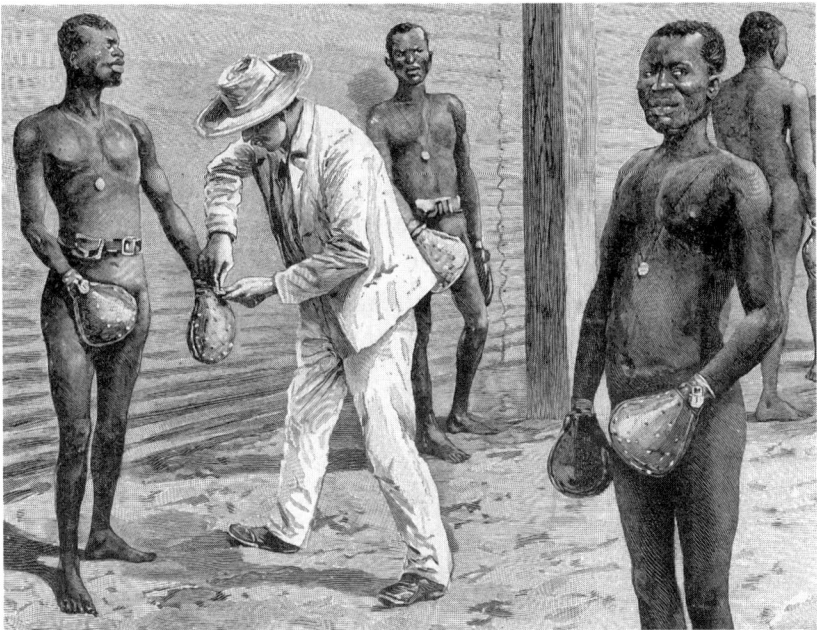

66 Restriction of black workers' hands during a break, Cape Colony, 1910.

67 Thomas Cullinan's Premier mine, 2011.

firm cut the enormous diamond into smaller stones. The Cullinan I and II diamonds are now part of the Crown Jewels of the United Kingdom, kept in the Tower of London (illus. 68).[101] The Cullinan was an exceptional diamond, as generally the Premier mine yielded diamonds that were smaller and of lesser quality than those offered by De Beers. When the American economy went through a depression in the autumn of 1907, Premier DMC was better equipped to deal with it than De Beers because of this difference in quality.[102]

Premier DMC was doing so well that in 1908 the mine produced 40 per cent more carats than the mines of De Beers (see illus. 69). Instead of selling its production through the London-based syndicate, Premier DMC opted to sell directly to merchants and jewellers in Amsterdam and Antwerp, providing a serious threat to the monopoly designed by Rhodes. De Beers and the syndicate were unable to convince Cullinan and Premier DMC to reach an agreement, so affiliated firms under the leadership of Barnato Bros. started to buy up shares of the Premier mine whenever they became available. In 1917, when Ernest Oppenheimer became the head of De Beers, DBCM managed to acquire a controlling interest in Premier DMC. The remaining shares were bought up in 1977. In 1995, the Premier mine was still among the world's top ten diamond mines in terms of production numbers (illus. 67).[103]

The Premier mine was not the only operation threatening the De Beers monopoly. Prospectors in the employ of De Beers, but also adventurers working for themselves, were looking for new diamondiferous areas in the basin of the Orange river. As early as 1900 there were newspaper reports about the discovery of the diamond-rich blue ground near Gibeon, still within the Orange river basin but part of German South West Africa.[104] *The Times* reported that a deal had been made between the South West Africa Company (SWAC), which was dominated by British shareholders, and De Beers.[105] The SWAC had obtained a concession in the German colony in exchange for the construction of a railway between Swakopmund and Otavi and was interested in mining activities. The involvement with Rhodes and De Beers was met with disapproval in Germany, particularly by the Deutsche Kolonialgesellschaft (German Colonial Society, or DKG).[106] In 1906 reports mentioned the discovery of blue ground on the Caprivi Strip, part of German South West Africa between Angola and northern Rhodesia (now Zambia) in the north and Bechuanaland (now Botswana) in the south.[107]

Finally, large diamond deposits were discovered in German South West Africa in 1908 by a black worker named Zacharius Lewala, who had gone from the Cape to German South West Africa to work for a German railway pioneer named August Stauch (see illus. 36).[108] The original location was photographed and published in London the following year, in an

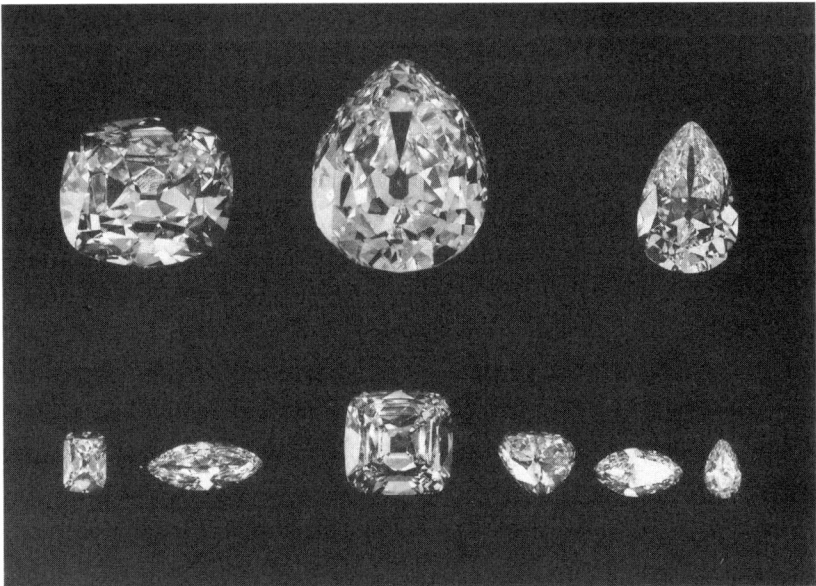

68 The Cullinan diamonds, 1908–11.

	De Beers	Premier (Transvaal)	German South West Africa	Total World	% De Beers	% rise annual rise world production
1902	2,025,132			2,025,132	100	0
1903	2,205,652	99,208		2,304,860	95.7	14
1904	2,060,017	749,635		2,809,652	73	22
1905	1,953,255	845,652		2,798,907	69.8	0
1906	1,936,788	899,746		2,836,534	68.3	1
1907	2,061,973	1,899,986		3,961,959	52	40
1908	1,473,272	2,078,825	2,083	3,554,180	41.5	-10
1909			495,536	495,536		
1910			891,307	891,307		
1911	2,514,688	1,774,206	816,296	5,105,190	49.3	
1912	2,432,027	1,992,474	1,003,265	5,427,766	44.8	6
1913	2,656,866	2,107,983	1,284,727	6,049,576	43.9	11

69 Official world diamond production in carats, 1902–13.[109]

article that alluded to India's riches: 'Germany's diamond-studded sands: a Golconda in the desert' (illus. 70).[110] Stauch had obtained a prospecting licence from the DKG, the Berlin-based organization that had come into being in 1885, just after Bismarck's Congo Conference in Berlin had ignited Germany's imperial project.[111] The diamonds were discovered on territories owned by the DKG. Following the discovery, Stauch and two of his partners promptly departed further south to an area named Pomona, setting off a diamond rush that quickly began to greatly concern De Beers.[112] In November 1908 it was reported that sales were being made to South African merchants of up to £7,500 in total. According to the *Financial Times*, the diamond areas were closed to the general public and mining was organized on the basis of licences sold to several companies for a period of fifty years. The lucky miners included August Stauch, the 'Colmanskopf Diamond Prospecting and Mines Company' and two Germans who resided in Lüderitz.[113] Additionally, the German colonial office instructed the governor in German South West Africa to introduce a registration obligation and export duties for diamonds. Diamond trade was to be a licensed business and prospectors who found new diamond fields in the colony were under the obligation to report their findings to the authorities in Windhoek. At the same time, the government was negotiating with interested parties, including banks such as the Berliner Handelsgesellschaft and the Darmstadter Bank, to establish a mining company that could take charge.[114]

GERMANY'S DIAMOND - STUDDED SANDS: A GOLCONDA IN A DESERT.

70 Discovery of diamonds in German South West Africa, 1909.

In the end, the Germans placed management of their Golconda in the desert in the hands of the Diamanten-Regie des Südwestafrikanischen Schutzgebietes (Diamond Management of the South West African Protected Areas), an organization composed of representatives of the DKG and the German government.[115] The Regie was to be responsible for selling German diamonds that were being mined by concession holders and the Regie or DKG itself. As far as mining was concerned, the problem was that several areas within the German colony had been given in concession to companies, several of them foreign. The terms of agreement often included mining rights, easily given at a time when the area was being prospected, but before any diamonds had actually been found. In addition, men such as Stauch and firms such as the Colmanskopf Company had been given mining rights along the coast after the discovery of diamonds. While these arrangements were respected by colonial authorities, the DKG was given a *Sperrgebiet* (prohibited area), where it was the only company that was allowed to mine, under the name Deutsche Diamanten Gesellschaft (German Diamond Society, illus. 71).[116] A major problem was that the richest diamond deposits were in an area called Pomona, which fell into this *Sperrgebiet*. Pomona had been given as a concession to the Cape Town firm of De Pass, Spence & Co., which obtained perpetual rights of exploitation there in 1886, following an agreement with the German colonial authorities.[117] De Pass decided to sell diamond mining rights to the Pomona Mining Company (PMC) in 1909, leading to an arrangement in which the PMC received 42⅔ per cent of the financial value of the diamonds they dug up, the Regie 48⅓ per cent in taxes and charges, and De Pass 9 per cent.[118]

The Regie wanted to get the mining rights of De Pass, and a legal battle ensued in which one of the Regie's arguments was that De Pass only possessed the rights to mine for silver and lead, but not for diamonds. The Regie pressured De Pass to reach an agreement, while the Cape Town-based firm urged the British government to intervene on their behalf. When a deal was on the brink of being concluded in 1910, the individual prospectors voiced their concern about the 15 per cent they were to receive from the Regie in exchange for the rough diamonds they mined. An agreement was finally reached in 1912, with de Pass receiving 8 per cent of the value of the production in Pomona, now firmly in German hands through the PMC. Prospectors accepted the percentage given to them by the Regie, which was in control of the whole diamond mining industry in the area. British companies and investors were still lured to German colonial diamonds, but as a rule were only active in the business as partners of German investors.[119]

Production quickly rose to a level that sparked De Beers' interest. In 1909 the newly elected chairman of the board of directors of De Beers,

71 Diamonds in the desert, a postcard from German South West Africa, 1910.

Francis Oats, met with the German colonial secretary in Berlin to discuss possibilities of cooperation in the mining process. The *Financial Times* reported that rumours of Oats's mission being intended to establish a 'diamond trust', which would bring German production into line with De Beers' single-selling channel, were a misunderstanding, although such possibilities certainly must have been on British minds.[120] In 1911 De Beers was controlling less than half of the world's diamond production (see illus. 69). Production in German South West Africa was steadily rising and 816,296 carats of alluvial diamonds were mined in 1911, about a third of De Beers' production for that year. Two years later, production had risen to 1,284,727 carats, or almost half of South African production through De Beers.[121] Germany did not possess a diamond-cutting industry, which made it necessary for the Regie, in control of selling German diamonds, to look for international partners with experience. It would be of no use to build up large stocks of rough diamonds in Germany without attempting to arrange a good selling mechanism that could compete with De Beers and the syndicate. Diamond merchants outside of London saw this as an excellent opportunity to challenge single selling, and it did not take the Regie long to reach an agreement with an important firm of Antwerp traders, the Syndicat Anversois des Diamants (Antwerp Diamond Syndicate), owned by two of the city's foremost diamond traders, Louis Coetermans and Jacques Krijn.[122]

At the time Antwerp was Europe's second diamond-cutting centre, after Amsterdam. Much of what applied to Amsterdam during the nineteenth century was equally valid for Antwerp, although the latter's cutting industry and Jewish population were both considerably smaller. In order to defend the diamond workers' interests, both cities established a diamond workers' union in 1894. In that year Antwerp's diamond industry accounted for 2,500 polishing tables, about one-third the size of Amsterdam's industry.[123] Around the turn of the century the Belgian city started to catch up on Amsterdam. Part of Antwerp's renewed success can be explained by the arrival of Jews fleeing pogroms in Eastern Europe. It created a workforce that was able to deal with the higher import numbers due to the arrival of diamonds from Germany's African colonies. In 1897 Antwerp's cutting industry relied on four hundred Jewish workers, a number that grew to 1,000 in 1914, 15 per cent of the diamond labour force.[124] The quantity of diamonds imported from German South West Africa became so large that it could not be absorbed by existing factories in Antwerp and Amsterdam, leading to the development of an outlying industry in the Kempen ('Campine' in English), a Catholic rural region near Antwerp (illus. 72).[125] In 1913, 6,700 diamond workers operated in 170 factories, often small and unorganized, at lower wages.[126] By the time war broke out in 1914, Antwerp had beaten Amsterdam in terms of trade volume and number of diamond workers.[127]

Even though German colonial diamonds provided an enormous boost to Antwerp's status as a diamond centre, the commercial arrangement with

72 Diamond factory Charel Roevens and Mit Nicasi, Nijlen, 1938.

73 Kimberley's Big
Hole, 2007.

the Syndicat Anversois did not last long, as De Beers was still looking
for a way to control the sales of the diamonds mined in German South
West Africa. Additionally, the Germans were developing their own cutting industry in Idar-Oberstein and Hanau, near Frankfurt. A party led by
Ernest Oppenheimer and Gardner Williams's son and successor, Alpheus,
went to Pomona to observe the situation in person. Upon their return they
compiled a report on the diamond mines in German South West Africa
that was meant for the eyes of the De Beers directors only.[128] Williams
and Oppenheimer concluded that the companies active in German South
West Africa's alluvial mining operations would be hard-pressed to accept
limiting their production. Alluvial mining was much harder to control,
and the relative freedom given to it in Germany's colony added to similar problems that De Beers faced in South Africa, where uncontrolled

alluvial production employed as much as between 7,000 and 8,000 black workers in the riverbeds around the Vaal.[129]

Two conferences were held in 1914 to settle these issues. In Johannesburg, board members of De Beers conferred with the directors of the independent companies managing the Premier mine, Jagersfontein and Koffiefontein. Although they did not manage to fully unify their strategy, they did meet later that year in London to negotiate with the Regie and the syndicate. Negotiators agreed on a fixed amount of diamonds that was to be put on the market, with each producer allocated a specific share.[130] The selling itself was to take place on the lines of the single-selling channel as it had been developed by De Beers and the old syndicate, which meant the organization of 'sights' for diamond dealers interested in buying rough diamonds. While this was accepted by all the involved parties, the agreement never came into practice as, shortly after it was concluded, the First World War broke out. It still, however, served as the blueprint for the development of the diamond industry after the war.[131] This arrangement did not include production at Kimberley's Big Hole, the first kimberlite pipe mine in the world, as it was closed down in 1914. Today it remains a popular site that is visited by many tourists (illus. 73).

The Challenges between Two World Wars

The war had alienated several of the German diamond merchants working in South Africa from the rest of the population, and none more so than Kimberley's mayor, Ernest Oppenheimer. In May 1915 everything changed: a German U-boat sank the RMS *Lusitania*, killing nearly 1,200 passengers and crew. Anti-German riots broke out in many places, including Johannesburg and Kimberley. Oppenheimer had no choice but to resign and leave, but Kimberley had not seen the last of Ernest Oppenheimer.

He returned to London, where he became interested in African gold. In 1917 he founded Anglo-American, with financial help from J. P. Morgan. The company was a gold-mining enterprise and established its headquarters in Johannesburg, near the gold mines of the East Rand. While operations were successful, Oppenheimer had not forgotten about diamonds, and the end of the same war that had seen him chased out of Kimberley now provided a new opportunity. German South

West Africa had fallen under the tutelage of British South Africa, which retained control over the territory until the declaration of an independent Namibia in 1990. With the future ahead uncertain, British control made German mining companies very willing to sell. De Beers, however, seemed convinced the Germans did not want to sell, and it was Oppenheimer's Anglo-American that snatched the big prize in 1919, for £3.5 million, to the consternation of De Beers. A new company, Consolidated Diamond Mines of South West Africa (CDM), was to take care of mining, and the syndicate, in which Oppenheimer had a direct connection through Dunkelsbühler, agreed to buy CDM's production. Ernest was back in the diamond business.[132] The war had caused a rise in prices, and the successful manoeuvre to distribute diamonds during the war exclusively through London had contributed greatly to the consolidation of De Beers and the syndicate, which contained five members in 1919: Ludwig Breitmeyer & Co., Barnato Bros., Dunkelsbühler & Co., Mosenthal & Sons, and Central Mining and Investments (the former Wernher and Beit company).[133]

Exports to the United States, the most important consumer market for diamonds in the world, went up in the first years of the war, to reach a high point in 1916, but declined somewhat the two following years. In 1919, however, diamond imports to the United States reached a value of $84 million, a number that would be reached again only in 1955 (the Great Depression and the Second World War both having an enormous impact). The period immediately after the First World War, however, turned out to be a good time to ensure market stability and high prices; also in 1919 the South African producers, the syndicate and the Union of South Africa came to an understanding that became known as the Convention of Pretoria. Non-alluvial producers agreed on quotas inspired by the agreement that had been reached at the conferences of 1914. The syndicate agreed to buy a yearly amount of about £13 million worth of rough diamonds, and De Beers was to deliver 51 per cent of the supply. Other producers agreed on 18 per cent (Premier DMC), 10 per cent (New Jagersfontein Mining and Exploration Company) and 21 per cent (Oppenheimer's CDM).[134] The convention was approved by the Union of South Africa and its Department of Mines, which had everything to win by a South African monopoly, as the Union's policy towards diamonds was based on the Precious Stones Act of 1899, which gave the state 60 per cent of the profits of diamond deposits that were discovered after the Act had come into practice.[135] In spite of the harmony that was established by the agreements concluded between producers, the syndicate and the Union, the situation quickly turned sour.

The year 1919 was also when a young man of Jewish-Polish descent from Antwerp published a very important book on diamond cutting, the tailpiece of a series of technological innovations in the context of the Industrial Revolution that modernized the cutting process. The late nineteenth-century invention of the mechanical bruting machine, operated using steam power, enabled diamonds to be perfectly round. Bruting was the process in which a diamond's edges were rounded off. Before then it was done by rubbing two diamonds against each other, resulting in a less perfect shape.[136] A second innovation was made around 1900, when sawing became mechanized. Sawing was an important but laborious step, and the shift to machines greatly reduced the time needed to prepare the diamond for cutting.[137] The third and most visible change to diamond processing came from altering the brilliant cut itself. Bruting allowed for a rounder shape, and as such enabled the modern round brilliant cut. It was this cut that was the object of a crucial study by a young engineer named Marcel Tolkowsky, who wanted to establish the perfect cut on the basis of scientific criteria, allowing for a maximal reflection of light within the stone. Born in 1899, Tolkowsky was a descendant from a Jewish family that had migrated from Poland to Belgium in the early nineteenth century, where they became active in the diamond industry. Tolkowsky went to the University of London, where he wrote a doctoral dissertation on the grinding and polishing of diamonds. Although the doctorate in engineering was formally awarded to him in 1920, his thesis was finished earlier, and in 1919 he had obtained a patent for a new dop for holding precious stones that needed to be ground or polished.[138] That same year he published his book on diamond designs, an extension of his PhD research, where he studied the perfect brilliant cut using algebra, trigonometry, geometry and optics to arrive at the ideal shape.[139] Tolkowsky is now recognized as the father of the modern, or round brilliant cut, which contains 57 facets, or 58 if one includes the culet, the point at the bottom of the stone (see illus. 17).[140]

The modern brilliant cut remains the most popular today, but this does not stop inventors coming up with new designs for cuts with a higher number of facets. In 2004, for instance, the u.s. Patent Office granted a patent for a cut with either 116 or 122 facets.[141] Research on brilliant cuts still continues, as does the involvement of the Tolkowsky family in the diamond industry.[142] Marcel's nephew Gabriel, or 'Gabi', born in 1939, is one of the world's most famous diamond cutters. In 1988 he was asked by De Beers to cut the Centenary Diamond, found in the Premier mine (see illus. 67). It resulted in a heart-shaped diamond with 247 facets of 273.85 carats, still the world's largest modern-cut and colourless diamond.[143] Long before that would happen, and right after the German invasion of Belgium in 1940, Marcel migrated to New York, where he passed away in 1991.[144] The fact that the new cut quickly became known as American Standard or American Ideal Cut indicates that the consumer market for polished diamonds had definitively shifted to the United States, and fluctuations on the American market were influencing worldwide diamond prices to a great extent. The top position of the American consumer market for diamonds attracted smugglers, both individuals and organized networks. According to a Dutch newspaper, the port of New York had become a smugglers' paradise during the 1920s, receiving clandestine diamonds with a value of more than $100 million. The newspaper reported that more than four hundred smugglers had been arrested there in 1929, including 186 women, who were, according to the article, 'more cunning than the men'.[145]

It is hard to assess to what extent such newspaper articles were underestimating the true volume and value of smuggled diamonds, but smuggling was a huge problem for the American authorities, missing out on customs taxes, and for De Beers, particularly considering the changes brought about after 1920. From that year onwards, prices for diamonds had started to decline. The Great Depression had a huge impact on demand, the market was adapting to the peace after the First World War, and existing stocks from Russia and Germany were thrown on the market.[146] The availability of German diamonds was caused by the capture of German South West Africa by the Union of South Africa during war, after which the Union, a self-governing dominion within the British Empire, ruled it as a Mandate. Russia's diamonds had come from Bolshevik seizures of gold, silver and precious stones from the tsarist elite. Inexperience and a pressing need for money made the revolutionaries sell their diamonds for only a third of their value, but these Russian diamonds were still seen as a serious threat to the cartel, and the syndicate purchased as many of the Russian diamonds as they could.[147] In 1920 a Dutch newspaper published an extensive article on the matter, based on a letter it had received from Stockholm, where Soviet diamond agents had established their headquarters. The letter stated that 'the bolsheviks have socialized the Crown jewels, those of jewellers and individual persons, insofar as these weren't hidden. Lenin, Trotsky, Kamenev and Co. are now the largest jewellers in the world.'[148]

The post-war situation established the crucial role the syndicate was to play in the years to come: that of systematically buying up all diamonds from producers whose mines fell outside the De Beers empire. It was a practice that burdened both the syndicate and the producers, particularly in the light of expanding alluvial activities in South Africa, British Guiana and in the newly discovered deposits in the Congo and Angola. Most of these were hard to control, although in South Africa outsiders reduced their production, which was brought down from 3.9 million carats in 1920 to 1.4 million in 1922.[149] In 1924 the Convention of Pretoria that regulated all of South Africa's industrial production was up for renewal, and negotiations started between the various producers, including De Beers, and the syndicate, in which Anglo-American now held an 8 per cent participation.[150] No agreement was reached, and the Union of South Africa saw this as an opportunity for legal reform, hoping to offer a way out to an unemployed white class by constructing a domestic cutting industry and by exercising a much larger role in the diamond trade through a newly created government agency.

Even if the talks in Pretoria were to be successful, they offered no structural answer to the production of diamond mines outside of South Africa and De Beers. When Oppenheimer found out that a deal was being negotiated between the authorities in South West Africa and a number of diamond merchants in Antwerp, Anglo-American moved quickly, offering to buy South West Africa's quota and sell it outside the structure of the syndicate. Oppenheimer also reached an understanding with other mining companies: Diamang in Angola between 1922 and 1924, CAST in West Africa in 1925, and Forminière in the Belgian Congo in 1926.[151] Smaller deals were also made that year with the major independent non-alluvial producers in the Union of South Africa, and a new syndicate came into being, which consisted of Anglo-American, Dunkelsbühler, Barnato Bros. and Oppenheimer's Johannesburg Consolidate Investment Company. The system of a single-selling channel based in London stayed the same, even though only two members of the old syndicate remained (see illus. 74).[152] The biggest difference was that the reins of the new syndicate were firmly in the hands of Oppenheimer, and the *Financial Times* reported in January 1926 that 'while other people were talking, Ernest Oppenheimer was acting, and we gather that, owing mainly to his efforts, the new Diamond Syndicate controls directly and indirectly the sale of some 90 per cent of the world's output of the gems.'[153] Six months later Oppenheimer was elected as a director of De Beers.

The new syndicate soon had to deal with the discovery of alluvial deposits at Lichtenburg, around 190 kilometres (118 mi.) east of Johannesburg, in 1925. The Department of Mines was somewhat taken aback by the diamond rushes that employed, in 1927, 50,000 whites and 90,000 black workers on the riverside diggings at 309 different sites.[154] In March 1927 there were 19,937 diggers active on the Lichtenburg fields, and claimholders employed 590 whites and 35,575 black workers.[155] Life on the alluvial fields was hard. Black workers were exploited and suffered a great deal of discrimination, while a substantial part of the whites came from an impoverished unemployed class that hoped to reverse its fortunes. In many ways it was a human disaster; the alluvial mining camps were overcrowded, disease spread and there was a lack of facilities. The main distinction was between those with access to capital and those without, who were forced to use a pick and a shovel to dig for diamondiferous gravel. In 1927 the Union of South Africa issued a Precious Stones Act intended to deal with the problems at the alluvial sites. The government's motives were twofold. First, it wanted to preserve riverside digging for the common man, providing opportunities for a rural impoverished class that was part of the electorate and needed relief, something diamonds could provide, at least in theory.[156] To that purpose, the presence of companies on the fields was restricted. Second, overproduction was a constant threat in the world of diamonds, and the government included a ban on further prospecting activities in the Act, which allowed for a limit on mining. While politicians had ensured that the message of social relief was emphasized, the Act was not well received by all. Black workers went on strike when white claimholders cut their wages, while the complaints of disgruntled diggers also found their way to the newspapers:

> The unlucky one, the ignorant and the oppressed have only one
> conclusion to come to, and that is they have been beaten again

Old syndicate (1889)	Old syndicate (1914)	Old syndicate (1924)	New syndicate (1926)	DICORP (1930)
Wernher, Beit & Co.	Wernher, Beit & Co.	L. Breitmeyer & Co.	Anglo-American	Anglo-American
Barnato Bros.	Barnato Bros.	Barnato Bros.	Barnato Bros.	Barnato Bros.
A. Dunkelsbühler & Co.	A. Dunkelsbühler & Co.	A. Dunkelsbühler & Co.	A. Dunkelsbühler & Co.	A. Dunkelsbühler & Co.
Mosenthal, Sons & Co.	Mosenthal, Sons & Co.	Anglo-American	Johannesburg Consolidate Investment Co.	Johannesburg Consolidate Investment Co.
		Bernheim		De Beers Consolidated Mines
		Dreyfus & Co.		Consolidated Mines South West Africa
		Central Mining & Investment Corporation		New Jagersfontein

74 Composition of the diamond syndicate and DICORP, 1889–1930.[157]

... the poor digger ... has been beaten from forming small syndicates; he has been beaten from obtaining employment from small companies; he has been beaten from obtaining financial support from the buyers who are mostly on the spot almost daily; and last, but not least, he has been beaten from participating in one of the richest known alluvial fields in the world – namely Namaqualand – on the ground that to have a lot of poor diggers there would make conditions worse than before and cause greater starvation than at present exists.[158]

Large alluvial deposits had been discovered at the mouth of the Orange river near Kleinzee in Namaqualand in 1926, and in 1928 the government decided to make these State Diggings, with a state-employed workforce.[159] Alluvial production was expanding rapidly: in 1927 the Union produced 2.4 million carats through its kimberlite mines, and 2.3 million carats of alluvial diamonds. The following year the rate was 2.3 million versus 2.1 million (of which 906,000 carats came from Namaqualand). In 1929 the gap had widened again, with 2.3 million carats of kimberlitic diamonds and 1.4 million alluvial.[160] By that year, independent digging had been tamed through the new legislation, although alluvial mining remained an important source of production.[161] Between 1932 and 1935 the weight in carats taken from alluvial mining was higher than that of diamonds extracted from kimberlite.[162]

The lower share of kimberlite-mined diamonds was partially due to reduced production from the Union of South Africa's non-alluvial producers. But the constant efforts to buy up outside production, that of Angola and Congo in particular, not only strained the syndicate's finances, it left them with a reserve stock of rough diamonds estimated at £10 million in 1929.[163] Rough diamond prices were very much linked to the u.s. market, which was greatly affected by the Great Depression. The value of American imports of rough diamonds dropped from $9.9 million in 1929 to $5.6 million in 1930.[164] It became clear that the syndicate needed to change its financial structure if it were to continue to absorb outside production, even in times of crisis. Oppenheimer wanted the producers themselves to become involved in the selling structure, leading to the creation of the Diamond Corporation (DICORP) in 1930, the year in which Ernest Oppenheimer became chairman of De Beers (see the first two columns of illus. 75). DICORP replaced the syndicate as the single-selling structure, and half of its capital was provided by three of the biggest producers (initially, the Premier DMC did not join), while the other half was furnished by the four members of the London-based Oppenheimer syndicate (see illus. 74). A sales ratio of 5:3 between South African and outside producers was agreed upon.[165]

This new structure had access to more capital, and it was also able to act with more unity as producers and sellers were tied closer together. This was further solidified by the general meeting of De Beers' directors held in December 1930, when it was decided to make a move to obtain large interests in the New Jagersfontein Mining and Exploration Company, the Consolidated Diamond Mines of South West Africa and Cape Coast Exploration from Anglo-American and Barnato Bros.[166] But still, not all of the producers were part of the new structure. The Premier DMC had not joined, and the Union of South Africa, still dreaming of its own cutting industry, was a producer itself, controlling the alluvial deposits in Namaqualand. The quota agreements that existed were not enough for De Beers to control the Union's actions.[167] DICORP also could not battle the effects of the Great Depression, and American imports of rough diamonds stood at a historic low of $1.5 million in 1932.[168] That year, both

New Jagersfontein Mining and Exploration Company and Premier DMC ceased all production. De Beers followed by closing the plants where they mechanically crushed and washed the kimberlite to select the rough diamonds.[169]

In 1933 the questions of how to deal with the crisis and how to ease the complicated relationship with the Union of South Africa led to an answer in the creation of a second structure, alongside DICORP: the Diamond Producers' Association (DPA) (columns 3 and 4 of illus. 75).[170] It replaced older quota agreements between De Beers and the outside producers, and its main tasks were to oversee policy that benefited the producers and to allocate quotas to each member – in short, to control the flow of rough diamonds onto the market, and thus the price level. The Union was a full member of the DPA, with a 10 per cent quota for the State Diggings of Namaqualand. A 2 per cent quota was given to Cape Coast Exploration, which held lands where alluvial deposits were suspected, and in which De Beers was the most important stakeholder.[171] Sixteen per cent of DICORP's quota was allocated to cover the purchases of outside producers in Congo, Angola, Sierra Leone and the Gold Coast.[172]

DICORP (1930)	Share (%)	DPA (1933)	Quota (%)	DICORP (1939)	Share (%)	DPA (1950)	Quota (%)	DPA (1955)	Quota (%)
De Beers Consolidated Mines Ltd. (producer)	32.5	De Beers Consolidated Mines Ltd.	30	De Beers	60	De Beers	53.5	De Beers	25
Barnato Brothers	22.5	DICORP for purchases outside production	16	Consolidated Diamond Mines SWA	23.1	CDM SWA	23.5	DICORP	35
Anglo-American	12.5	DICORP for stock	15	Anglo-American	16.9	South Africa	16	South Africa	10
Consolidated Diamond Mines South West Africa (producer)	12.5	Consolidated Diamond Mines SWA	14			Premier DMC	7	Premier DMC	4
A. Dunkelsbühler & Co.	12.5	Union of South Africa	10					Mandatory Administration SWA	26
Johannesburg Consolidated Investment	2.5	Premier Diamond Mining Co. Ltd.	6						
New Jagersfontein (producer)	5.0	New Jagersfontein	6						
		Cape Coast Exploration Ltd	2						
		Koffyfontein Mines Ltd	1						

75 Composition of DICORP and DPA, 1930–55.

DPA centralized production as DICORP had centralized marketing and selling, and both structures were legally overlapping entities. The DPA was the larger association that could be expanded to include any major diamond producer, while DICORP, as the marketing agency, was responsible for buying up outside production and for selling all rough diamonds. In 1934 the decision was taken to transfer the marketing part to a new entity, the Diamond Trading Company (DTC), whose shares were owned by DICORP. DICORP's sole responsibility was now the purchase of outside production. In 1935 U.S. imports of rough diamonds had risen again to $4.3 million.[173] The system of direct sales to a selective group of buyers, which had existed since the days of the old syndicate, was slightly altered. Mixed parcels of specific assortments, compiled by a Central Sorting Office in Kimberley, were offered at fixed prices to the buyers, who were given the choice to 'take it or leave it'. Participation in these 'sights' was a privilege, and in 1938 there were only 175 'sightholders'.[174] To become one, a candidate needed experience, sufficient capital to handle purchases of at least £5,000, commercial connections for further reselling, and the ability to pile up stock in times of need. Sights were organized every three months, and the best stones were reserved for the American market. Between 1921 and 1939 separate sights were organized for merchants specializing in industrial diamonds, although that market would only take off after the Second World War.[175]

In the public eye, DTC, DICORP and DPA all became synonyms for De Beers, the largest shareholder in these companies, and De Beers became synonymous with diamonds. De Beers further confirmed this image by buying up the holdings of the smaller shareholders, resulting in a much simpler structure for DICORP (columns 5 and 6 of illus. 75), and, as a consequence, also for DTC. Control of the world's diamond supply was now firmly in the hands of Ernest Oppenheimer, who stood at the helm of a leviathan.

Old Alluvial Fields and the Failure of Mechanization

The surprisingly large share of alluvial mining in the early 1930s can mostly be explained by the development of mining in West and Central Africa, but is also related to the failure to adopt mechanization on some of the old diamond fields in Asia and South America. Hardly any diamond mining activity was recorded in India during the first half of the twentieth century.[176] With regards to Borneo, still part of the Dutch colonial empire, a Dutch minister described artisanal diamond mining there as searching for needles in a haystack.[177] The end of the First World War caused an increase in demand for diamonds, particularly in the United States, and jewellers from Amsterdam started sending personnel to Borneo in 1918 and 1919 to procure a better and more independent supply.[178] Senator Henri Polak, one of Amsterdam's best-known diamond cutters, was one of the strongest advocates for the revitalization of Dutch mining activities in Borneo (see illus. 14). Fully aware that global developments in the diamond industry had weakened the position of Amsterdam in comparison to London and Antwerp, Polak attempted to gather support in the government for the establishment of a mining company that could guarantee a supply of rough diamonds for Amsterdam outside of the De Beers' sales cartel in London. Polak thought this could save the city's position, particularly as plans were taking shape across the North Sea to establish a more significant cutting industry in London.[179]

The Dutch sent new machinery to the island, where geologists were still hoping to discover the island's primary deposits – even though there were doubts about that possibility considering the lack of scientific knowledge about such deposits.[180] Polak, however, was soon accused of exploiting Borneo's fields for personal gain, and the employment of unskilled indigenous labourers at low wages even earned him the nickname 'Coolie Polak'. Others saw in Polak's efforts an attempt to redeem himself after an earlier mishap when, as president of the ANDB, he had refused to buy a tract of land in South Africa that turned out to be immensely rich in diamonds. Polak defended himself by arguing that he only tried to save the diamond cutters from 'chronic unemployment and permanent misery'.[181] Whatever Polak's motivations might have been, the industrialization of Borneo's diamond mining was to fail once more. This let-down stood in contrast to the development of the cutting industry in Martapura (illus. 79). Factories had come to rely heavily on South African rough diamonds imported through Singapore, although they were not of the best quality. In its prime Martapura's diamond factories, often owned by Muslims, rented out as many as 1,100 working places to individual cutters, but when the First World War stopped imports of rough diamonds, several factories had to close until the war was over.[182]

In the 1930s only five hundred diamond cutters were registered in Martapura, but their work was considered of high quality.[183] In spite of their reputation, the wages Martapura's cutters earned were lower than what was paid at Europe's established cutting centres, and one Muslim owner regularly travelled to Paris to buy rough diamonds to be cut in Martapura, after which they were exported to Europe again or sold in Asia.[184] In July that year, only two mining concessions remained, the one held by Polak, and one that had been given to a Mr Christoffel, a retired army officer. The remainder of the diamond deposits were mined under direct management of the Dutch colonial government, as was also the case for gold, platinum and mercury ore. The Dutch operations were not the only ones affected. The last English diamond mining company on the island, rumoured to be backed by De Beers, ended business in 1921.[185]

Following another failure, the Dutch government returned to the system of licences. It accepted that diamond mining on its colonial territory was never going to develop as a modern industry, and decided to use artisanal alluvial mining as a means of income for the local population.[186] Although foreign mining companies remained welcome, legislation ensured that they had to employ at least twenty locals at all times.[187] It was also a means to keep governmental checks on the local population, and licence fees were lowered in times of poverty, and sometimes, part of the revenue was given to indigenous groups in order to avoid social unrest.[188] It was now a means of support for locals rather than a business opportunity for foreigners. Official production figures kept dropping: in 1925 Henri Polak remarked that production was so low that numbers had not been included in official colonial reports for the last twenty years.[189] They were insignificant in comparison to African production. Between 1929 and 1937 Borneo's share of rough diamonds in world production amounted to 0.01 per cent. In total, 29,375 carats of diamonds were mined between 1913 and 1939, worth 1.5 million guilders, which was a steep decline in comparison to the value of the island's production at the end of the nineteenth century.[190] The diamonds that were found were quite small, between 0.5 and 1.5 carats, and often quite clear, although with a yellowish tint.[191] Despite these disappointing results, the Dutch had not yet given up on diamond prospecting. In the 1930s newspapers reported at various times about new discoveries, but most turned out to be disappointing. One journalist visited excavations near Martapura, where diggers found one or two diamonds every half hour, but these were small, never more than a tenth of a carat.[192]

In 1932 several newspapers wrote that Dutch researchers had managed to locate the primary deposits of Borneo's diamonds, based on existing knowledge on the occurrence of diamonds in South Africa's kimberlite pipes. Unfortunately, the hard ground turned out to be unworkable.[193] These finds, however, did lead to the discovery of new alluvial fields at Cempaka near Martapura, and 1935 was a peak year, with a new mine at Rantjah Sirang alone producing 3,273 carats. It was exploited by a Shanghai-based enterprise founded by George McBain, a Scotsman deemed the richest man in that city and referred to as 'the Shanghai Croesus'.[194] In spite of such a promising nickname, McBain suffered the same fate as so many foreign companies and failed to turn his enterprise into a profitable asset. According to the Dutch press, which continued to hope that the government might give a concession to a modern mining company, 'no one becomes richer by the tinkering that now passes for diamond extraction, except the few Hajjis controlling the whole affair.'[195] It was common for Dutch newspapers to refer to Muslim merchants and cutting factory owners as Hajji, an honourable title for those who had completed the pilgrimage to Mecca.[196]

In Brazil the alluvial fields became harder to exploit, making investments in modern technology risky. Late nineteenth-century initiatives to mechanize diamond production in Brazil all failed, and mining continued to exist in the same traditional manner. And although slavery had officially been abolished in Brazil in 1888, photographical evidence is still clearly showing the persistent racial division of labour, with black people mining and white men supervising (illus. 76 and 77).

Following the discovery of new diamond deposits at various sites in Africa in the early decades of the twentieth century, some mining companies with an international portfolio attempted new investments in the old diamond district. The British Sopa Diamond Company, for instance, which had business connections with De Beers, mined for diamonds in West and South Africa, Angola and the Congo, and they decided to become active at a mining site about 15 kilometres (10 mi.) way from Diamantina. By 1922, however, not much had come of it and the company was sold to Brazilians, a fate awaiting most of these foreign businesses.[197] During those years efforts were made to establish a cutting industry in Brazil. Historically, some small workshops, the traces of which have vanished, must have existed in Brazil, but they were never in any way competitive with European workshops. When Belgian journalist S. Hartveld visited Lençóis in 1920, he witnessed the presence of a number of cutting workshops with diamond mills that had been fabricated in Belgium, and which were driven by hydraulic power from a nearby waterfall.[198] According to Hartveld, 'the finished diamonds had been cut relatively well', but the cutters had paid too much attention to weight, leading to somewhat asymmetrical stones that could not be sold in Europe.[199] In spite of the limited success mining companies enjoyed in Brazil, the country was still promoted in Europe as a notable diamond producer. In 1923 the city of Antwerp organized a Jewels Pageant, and Brazil was represented by a float with a woman holding a diamond in one hand. The float was carried by miners in their working suits.[200]

Dressing these workers in special mining suits seemed overly optimistic, as the failure of mechanization meant that Brazil's diamond fields

76 Mr Vidigal's diamond mine on the Rio Jequitinhonha, 1868.
Photograph by Augusto Riedel.

77 Diamond mining in Brazil, 1910.

were dominated by individual fortune-seekers, *garimpeiros* and adventurers, who were responsible for well-known twentieth-century finds of Brazilian diamonds such as the Getúlio Vargas in 1938.[201] Rough, the Vargas diamond weighed about 727 carats. After it was found in Patrocinio in Minas Gerais, about 120 kilometres (75 mi.) from the southeastern tip of Goiás, it was sent to Belo Horizonte, the provincial capital, where it came into the hands of a Dutch group. They sold it to New York-based jeweller Harry Winston, who had it cut into various smaller stones in his workshop.[202] When the Vargas diamond passed through Belo Horizonte, the brother of one of the Brazilian men involved in selling it met with a French Jewish war refugee. Jules Sauer had fled Antwerp in May 1940 and, after a period in Lisbon, had ended up in Brazil where he worked as a language teacher. His linguistic skills landed him a job with the Brazilian who had briefly owned the Vargas diamond and who had a workshop in Belo Horizonte where he employed 75 gemstone cutters.[203] Sauer began as a secretary, but became an expert in jewellery and learnt the skills of diamond cutting. He discovered the first emerald mine in Brazil, during the 1960s, wrote several books on diamonds and emeralds, and taught the art of faceting to others. When he passed away in 2017, aged 95, he had become known as 'the gemstone hunter' and the museum in Rio de Janeiro that houses his collection of precious stones is the largest of its kind in Brazil.[204]

Strategic Diamonds and the Tragedy of the Holocaust

Just when Ernest Oppenheimer's efforts had again solidified De Beers' monopolistic position in the diamond industry, larger events interfered, as war once again shook the diamond industry, this time harder than it had ever been shaken before. The Nazis' antisemitic agenda to murder the entire Jewish population of Europe made the war a personal affair for many of the families working in the diamond industry as traders, wholesalers, cutters or jewellers.[205] The outbreak of the Second World War greatly upset the market for diamonds. Demand for jewellery went down, but the range of uses for industrial diamonds in the weapons and aircraft industries expanded, causing them to be branded as a strategic mineral by Axis forces and Allies alike. When the Nazis invaded the Low Countries in May 1940, they hoped not only to use the diamond stocks they confiscated in the war industry, but to further finance the war effort. The export of diamonds was forbidden and a special unit was established to systematically buy up diamonds at a fraction of their value. Later, diamonds became subject to forced deposition and confiscation. Jewellers tried to smuggle their stocks into neutral or Allied territories, but it has been estimated that in Belgium the Germans got their hands on 13,000 carats of polished diamonds and 79,000 carats of rough and industrial stones, while in the Netherlands, the weight of stolen diamonds was assessed to be 60,000 carats, of which 36,700 were recovered after the war.[206] These seem relatively low numbers: in 1942 the U.S. Board of Economic Warfare shared an intelligence report with the Dutch embassy about the German seizure of a ship anchored in the Gironde estuary near Bordeaux, on which Dutch diamond cutters had collected 1 million carats of industrial diamonds, 'one swoop ... which assured German war factories of all their needs for the whole war'.[207] The event could not be confirmed by Dutch officials, but it was known that several Belgian diamond dealers organized diamond markets in Royan, a seaside resort at the mouth of the Gironde.[208]

These men had fled Nazi occupation, and their presence there was part of an attempt to relocate Antwerp's diamond industry. Romi Goldmuntz, a Kraków-born Jewish businessman who became one of

Antwerp's most prominent diamond dealers, went to London to negotiate a deal for Antwerp's Jewish diamond personnel, and the British government responded by inviting Antwerp craftsmen to the capital. In Belgium, however, there was not much enthusiasm for this proposal out of fear that the diamond-cutting industry would never relocate back to Antwerp after the war. The Belgian city was still the world's most important diamond centre, but competition had been growing in the years building up to the war, particularly from Germany's diamond industry. In 1939, the year before the German invasion of Belgium and the Netherlands, Antwerp employed 25,000 diamond workers. Dutch competition had been reduced to 8,000, the same size as the total number of workers in Germany's diamond factories in Idar-Oberstein and Hanau, which had been expanding in size.[209] This rise of the German cutting industry, combined with the growing ability of the Germans to gain access to industrial diamond deposits, created a situation in which the Belgian position in the world of diamonds was threatened, but the Belgian government still held a strong hand when it came to avoiding the possible decline of Antwerp as diamond centre. Its African colony, the Congo, possessed the world's largest known deposits of industrial diamonds, which were still controlled by Forminière, a company that had managed, through political manoeuvring, to take a semi-independent position vis-à-vis De Beers. Britain, like the other Allies and Nazi Germany, was greatly interested in the Congo's deposits. The British invitation was declined and instead the decision was made to move to Cognac, north of Bordeaux, with the idea that the Germans would never make it that far.[210] In May 1940 some 3,000 diamond traders and 2,000 diamond workers, mostly Jewish and half of them Belgian, left for Cognac, where they were informed that they should continue to Royan, as the French government had decided to make the seaside town the centre for the diamond trade in France.[211]

When the mayor of Royan made it clear he did not want such a large group in his town, a new plan was negotiated between the three big players in the matter – De Beers and the Belgian and British governments. Several diamond traders and workers went to the UK, others went back to Antwerp, while yet another group decided to stay in the Gironde region. With the advance of German troops, the diamond families who had stayed in France tried to send their merchandise to Vichy France or to Switzerland. The demand for visas to go abroad increased.

Efforts to obtain visas to go to the Congo, however, largely failed, even though Forminière had made provisions to sit out the war in the Belgian African colony.[212] Several of the Antwerp diamond merchants attempted to cross the Atlantic and hoped to reach New York, where a diamond industry had been established since 1890. An exclusive Diamond Dealers Club was established in 1931 and several Jewish refugees from Antwerp hoped to find a safe haven there.[213] New York was a logical destination for Jewish diamond refugees from Antwerp, but groups of them also ended up in Cuba, Brazil, Argentina, South Africa and even India, Palestine and Ceylon.[214] In all of these places they were joined by Jewish diamond personnel from Amsterdam, and by Jews who were not active in the world of diamonds.[215]

Amsterdam faced similar troubles to Antwerp, but the city was subject to special attention.[216] The Nazis hoped to establish a German-controlled diamond-cutting industry in the Netherlands, perhaps because the cutting industry of Amsterdam was smaller and easier to control than its counterpart in Antwerp. The Dutch city accounted for about 1,000 diamond workers in 1940, and 70 per cent of them belonged to the ANDB, the diamond union.[217] Initially the Jewish diamond personnel in Amsterdam were among those who were able to obtain a stamp that prevented their deportation to the concentration camps.[218] Gradually, however, their situation worsened. The ANDB was dissolved in the winter of 1941, and mass deportations started in the summer of 1942. From 1943 onwards half of the privileged diamond personnel were deported, and by mid-1944 only 44 Jewish diamond workers were left in Amsterdam.[219] It seems that plans to establish a Nazi diamond industry in the Netherlands were abandoned in favour of a project that intended to use Dutch diamond personnel to create a diamond-cutting factory in the concentration camp of Bergen-Belsen.

In May 1944 a letter was sent between ss officials confirming that an existing arrangement in the Dutch concentration camp at Vught, where Heinrich Himmler had equipment necessary for working diamonds sent to, was countermanded to pave the way for the plans in Bergen-Belsen. The Nazis wanted to establish a 'European diamond-cutting monopoly' and felt that 'the urgency of the decision [the Bergen-Belsen project] is based on the fact that the diamond industry in Amsterdam practically came to a standstill by the deportation of the Jews on 18 May [1944].'[220]

ss officials felt that a factory should be established in Bergen-Belsen for about 150 to 200 skilled workers.[221] To achieve these plans, the Dutch 'Diamond Jews' who had not yet been killed in the camps were transported to Bergen-Belsen, where they stayed until the plan was dissolved at the end of 1944. After that, many of them were sent to other camps, where they were murdered.[222]

The German occupiers had given Amsterdam's 'Diamond Jews' exemption from deportation, at least for a while, but their lives remained harsh and their futures uncertain. Some stayed, but others decided to leave, and the Dutch government in exile in the UK had to deal with many visa applications for diamond workers to come to London, or to go to the USA, Canada, Venezuela, Brazil or Suriname. The British refused several applications, claiming there was no need for additional personnel, but the Dutch also stopped them, fearing that it would lead to the permanent establishment of cutting centres elsewhere. Several countries, however, were happy to welcome skilled refugees, and in 1941 the Dutch Ministry of Foreign Affairs in London received a letter from Caracas containing the news that the 'Venezuelan government fosters the immigration of experts in the diamond business, as it hopes to develop the Venezuelan diamond mines. It has therefore demanded the Venezuelan consul in Marseilles to issue passports.'[223] While several Jewish families active in the diamond industry managed to escape through one of these routes, many, particularly in the Netherlands, died in the Holocaust.

The Allied forces were not only concerned about the mass murder of diamond workers and traders.[224] They were especially interested in the diamonds themselves, both to keep them out of the hands of the Germans and to use them in their own war industries.[225] With DICORP controlling 97 per cent of global diamond sales in London, the United Kingdom and the United States had to deal with Oppenheimer, who initially considered shifting De Beers' main centre of activities from London to South Africa, from where he might establish direct trade links with the United States. But neither the British government nor British diamond traders were very happy about the prospect of dislocating the trade's epicentre to South Africa, and the British sank Oppenheimer's early plans to set up direct trade links between South Africa and the United States.[226] Furthermore, there was no guarantee that malevolent diamond dealers in neutral countries such as Portugal, which was still receiving Angolan diamonds, or Switzerland, or even in the U.S. itself, would not re-export diamonds to the enemy. De Beers itself was later accused of such practices.[227] Claims were made that a smuggling route existed through British colonies, taking South African diamonds to Germany by way of Egypt to Palestine, where a small diamond industry had been established, and then to Lebanon, Syria and Turkey.[228]

In short, the war threatened traditional trading and cutting centres, and the governments concerned would go to any length to prevent this shift, while at the same time keeping up with the war effort. Refusing industrial exports to North America was not an option either. The U.S. received part of their requirements through re-exports from neutral countries and from areas not controlled by De Beers. A straight-out refusal to cooperate with the Americans would not be good for business. A plan was discussed to bypass New York merchants, in order not to upset existing trade links, but American manufacturers made it clear they would only support this plan if De Beers would deliver according to a specific demand on quality, as they did not want low-grade Congolese diamonds. This demand made it difficult to sell off existing stock.[229] And the United States wanted more than a supply that answered their immediate demand: they wanted to build up a reserve of their own, far away from any German threat and immune to De Beers' commercial decisions.

In a reaction to Oppenheimer's plans, the UK issued a trade embargo on diamonds, but had difficulties dealing with the export of industrial stones to the United States, a practice that undermined the system of single selling. Forminière, the colonial company that mined Congo's diamonds, had seen its production of industrial diamonds rise to 8.5 million carats in 1944, and was interested in setting up a direct trade partnership with the United States.[230] Even if an agreement could be reached between various producers to export to the United States through DICORP, the cartel was legally forbidden from operating within American jurisdiction. Pressure mounted when President Roosevelt ordered 6.5 million carats of industrial diamonds from DICORP, but was turned down by Oppenheimer.[231] A compromise was reached at the end of 1942, with the agreement to build up a reserve of 11.5 million carats of industrial diamonds in Canada, upon which the UK and the USA could draw in times of emergency only, preserving single selling through London. Supply came from DICORP, but also from producers in the Congo (Forminière),

Angola (Diamang) and the Gold Coast (CAST and SLST).[232] The demand for quality was solved by forcing the DTC to give up part of their reserve of almost gem-quality stones.[233]

In Europe the impact of the war on the diamond industry was enormous. First, it shook the Jewish diamond communities in Antwerp and Amsterdam to their core, by murdering and deporting many families with ties to the diamond industry. Second, it forced De Beers and several of the Allied governments to reconsider trade routes, cutting centres and the stocking of industrial diamonds. Several of the decisions that were taken during the war affected the diamond industry for long after the war had ended. More than ever before, national governments interfered and took measures to protect their country's interests in diamonds, from a strategic, political and economic point of view. It had become clear during the war that the Congo's abundant industrial diamond deposits would be an important asset for the future, particularly in the context of the emerging Cold War, considering the growing importance of industrial diamonds. The geopolitical conflict between the USA and the USSR was to play out differently in different diamondiferous African countries. Right after the war, Belgium was able to use the mineral riches of the Congo as an important tool for political pressure.[234] In 1942 all industrial diamonds were being kept in either the UK or the Congo, but the Canadian agreement had caused a shift of two-thirds of the world's supply across the Atlantic. This put the system of single selling through London under further pressure.

After the war had ended, the Belgian government needed assistance to revive its cutting industry in Antwerp and aligned its interests with the British, who wanted to preserve the centralization of sales in London. London's dreams of establishing its own cutting industry were abandoned, to the benefit of Antwerp.[235] It was, in a way, the Congo that saved Belgium's diamond interest. The Dutch had Borneo, but diamond production there was nowhere near that of the Belgian African colony. This resulted in the permanent loss of the diamond-cutting industry in Amsterdam. A substantial section of the Dutch Jewish population did not survive the war: it was reported that, of the 1,500 to 2,000 Jewish diamond cutters who had been deported to the concentration camps, only sixty returned.[236]

In spite of the Nazi persecution, several Jewish diamond entrepreneurs managed to escape, and important alternative wartime cutting and trading centres had been established in New York, where 6,000 workers were active, Palestine (5,000), Brazil (5,000), where a small cutting industry had existed for some time already, Cuba, South Africa and London.[237] Not all of these centres survived the war, but those that did either already had a history, such as New York, or remained harmlessly small, catering for local production, such as Brazil.[238] The main exception was Palestine. Particularly in Tel Aviv, a cutting industry was developing that became a threat to Antwerp. Plans to set up diamond activities in Palestine did not originate in the war. The Jewish connection, the interest of local businessmen, the fact that it was a British Mandate, and the growing focus on Palestine's economy being based on domestic and artisanal work through family traditions, made Palestine a logical territory to consider.[239] During the war Jewish and Zionist political forces, consulting with Jewish businessmen who saw the establishment of a cutting industry as an excellent opportunity to industrialize Palestine, managed to convince De Beers, the British and the Belgians to permit setting up a wartime diamond industry, mainly in Tel Aviv and Netanya. To mollify the Belgians, it was agreed that Palestine's industry should remain limited and specialize in working with small diamonds.[240]

After the war, however, the British and De Beers chose to help Antwerp recover its pre-war position. This had an immediate effect on Palestine and other diamond centres, particularly as it took a while for American consumption to recover fully. By 1947 employment in the diamond industry in Palestine was reduced to 1,600, working for lower wages than before, while it had been 4,592 one year earlier.[241] Employment in New York also took a blow, with only eight hundred cutters employed in 1947. In Brazil the 5,000 cutters active during the war were reduced to five hundred in 1947.[242] Antwerp, on the other hand, was on the way up again, with more than 10,000 diamond workers employed in 1946.[243] By 1948 Palestine's diamond industry had all but gone, but it was to be rescued. That year the state of Israel came into being, and preserving the diamond industry was part of their economic and political agenda, as historian David De Vries has described:

> the 1948 Arab-Jewish war made the Zionism of the diamond manufacturers, workers, and merchants more explicit and blatant

... The economic nationalism that was expressed in the competition with other diamond-cutting centers, the barring of Arabs from the industry that was greatly helped by the British, and the moral justification to inherit the German diamond industry were equally essential ingredients in this national vocabulary.[244]

The comparison with the German industry was one of the arguments to appease Antwerp's diamond sector and the Belgian government. Rather than a competitor, Israel's diamond industry was now to be seen as an ally, not taking Antwerp's place but that of Germany, which had ideas of its own to keep a diamond-cutting industry going after the war. Israeli pressure and a boycott managed to provide the final blow to the factories in Germany.[245] The agreement made between De Beers, Israel and Belgium allowed for a permanent Israeli cutting industry, now centred in Tel Aviv. Its survival was helped by the changing global economic context. American demand for jewellery was on the rise again, approaching pre-war levels, and production was growing. Antwerp's industry, now that the Dutch and German rivals were permanently gone, could live

78 Diamond mining, Martapura, 1951.

with an additional diamond centre in Israel.[246] The industry continued to grow, and by 1971 the share of Israel's trade on the international diamond market reached 30 per cent, mainly consisting of the export of polished stones.[247] Today Tel Aviv and Ramat-Gan remain important diamond centres, employing about 20,000 women and men.[248]

The outbreak of the Second World War did not affect the diamond industry in Asia so dramatically, although it led to temporary supply problems for the Martapura diamond factories in Borneo. Mining continued, but the Japanese who occupied the island confiscated diamonds and took them home. After the war, the Bureau for War Damages in Batavia received numerous letters from Borneo's inhabitants trying to reclaim stolen diamonds. In 1947, for example, Lim Kang Tjoean wrote that he had been arrested in 1944 by a man named Hirosaki, who ordered a spy to break into Tjoean's house and seize his valuables. In his claim, Tjoean observed that 37 brilliants weighing 305.75 carats and valued at 750,000 guilders had been taken from their hiding spot.[249] By 1948 only two of Martapura's original six cutting factories had survived, now not only polishing diamonds but producing discs used for polishing in

79 Diamond factory, Martapura, 1948.

Malacca, Burma, Shanghai and Hong Kong, further solidifying the role of Martapura as an Asian diamond centre (illus. 79).[250] The main change was a political one. After the war the Dutch colonies in Asia no longer wished to accept European rule, and the islands that were to become Indonesia fought a war of independence that was finally won in 1949, when the Dutch accepted Indonesian independence.[251] The former Dutch part of Borneo was renamed Kalimantan, with the diamond region around Martapura now part of the province of South Kalimantan. But even though Indonesian independence created a whole new political situation, it did not change the nature of local diamond mining, nor the Dutch involvement in it.[252] It also did not change the downward spiral of declining production. Diamond mining in Borneo, like in many other places with a long history of alluvial mining, stayed alluvial and continued to rely on traditional methods (illus. 78).

In India, still a British colony, the long struggle against British colonization equally led to a successful ousting of European rule in the years after the war, culminating in an independent India in 1947. This was immediately followed by the partition of the Islamic Republic of Pakistan and the Republic of India, leading to ongoing territorial conflicts in a number of regions, most famously the Punjab and Kashmir.[253] The independence of India led to a new protective diamond policy. Historically, the Indian elites had inspired a notable demand for jewellery and stones cut in a European fashion, and a portion of those stones were cut in Indian factories. The Indian cutting industry had always remained small, and it relied, after the decline of domestic production, on the import of South African diamonds.[254] Indian factories were not supplied with the highest quality stones, so the local cutting industry came to specialize in smaller stones, for low wages. Indian merchants bought the rough diamonds from representatives of Antwerp firms in Mumbai and Kolkata (see illus. 5). In the 1920s this became increasingly difficult and Indian merchants, mostly coming from interconnected Jain families from the city of Palanpur in Gujarat, started travelling to Antwerp in person. This was the beginning of the presence of an important and still-continuing Jain diamond diaspora in Antwerp.[255]

During the war the British colonizers forbade all diamond exports to India as part of the general attempt to control diamond flows. After independence, the Indian government continued this ban, trying to push businessmen to invest in local enterprises rather than in the purchase of foreign diamonds.[256] The ban was lifted in 1952, but 90 per cent of any individual imported consignment needed to consist of rough diamonds. In this way, the government was hoping to develop the cutting industry. The Jain networks that connected the industry with Antwerp were quickly revived, new technology was imported and India's cutting industry boomed, partially because Antwerp considered the Indian factories as a good and cheap way to dispose of low-quality diamonds.[257] In 1969 B. Arunkumar & Co., founded in Mumbai in 1960 by the Palanpuri businessman Arunkumar Mehta, became the first Indian sightholder of De Beers. During the 1970s the company moved its headquarters to Antwerp, and was eventually rebranded as Rosy Blue. Today it is active in various enterprises, including real estate and finance, and remains one of the biggest diamond firms. The Mehta family figures on the list of the one hundred richest Belgians. In 2016 Rosy Blue was acquitted of diamond fraud and smuggling in one of the largest trials of the type ever held in Belgium.[258] Rosy Blue's position as one of the wealthiest diamond trading companies today is the culmination of the growth of the Indian diamond sector that began with the measures taken by the Indian government in the 1960s. Alongside the rise in commerce, the Indian cutting industry also continued to expand. The post-war protective measures taken by the government helped, and 12 per cent of the financial value of India's exports came from the domestic cutting industry by 1979, whereas it had been only 2 per cent four years earlier.[259] Another, even bigger, spurt in growth came with the opening of the Argyle mine in Australia in 1985 (illus. 98).[260] Argyle produced very small pink diamonds, which were often cut in India's low-wage factories, substantially closer than Antwerp. The rise of India's cutting industry came at the expense of Antwerp: 15,000 diamond workers were active in Antwerp in 1965, only half as much as the number of diamond workers active in India. In 2004 there were over a million diamond workers active in India's cutting factories.[261]

Booming under Apartheid

The war had posed a challenge for governments' attempts to keep diamonds out of the hands of the enemy, while the years after were challenging in terms of dealing with new competition that had arisen. The new situation was equally testing for De Beers' carefully crafted monopoly. It was not out of charity that De Beers invited Arunkumar Mehta's company to become the first Indian sightholder in 1969, but because the Indian diamond merchants were selling their material outside of the established channels of De Beers.[262] It had always been a tactic of the South Africans to incorporate the best of the competition into their own system of single selling. The war and its immediate aftermath not only disrupted single selling, it exposed that the cartel's structure was ill-suited to deal with the separate market for industrial diamonds. To address the second problem, the DTC was split into two companies in 1946. The Diamond Purchasing and Trading Company Ltd (DPTC) became a marketing branch that dealt exclusively with gemstone diamonds, while Industrial Distributors (Sales) Ltd (IDS) handled trade in industrial diamonds in London.[263] Between 1946 and 1951 sales of polished diamonds by the renewed DTC doubled, suggesting De Beers swiftly landed on its feet, in spite of the 1947 crisis that had hit Palestine so hard.[264]

The reorganization was part of a strategy by Oppenheimer that aimed at a relocation of stocks in South Africa. Oppenheimer wanted more control over diamond supplies but was also happy to avoid the heavy company taxation in Great Britain. Sorting and grading activities were moved to a Central Sorting Office in Kimberley, which now received diamonds obtained from outside producers through DICORP, mostly Congolese industrial diamonds. Parcels of industrial diamonds were sent to IDS in Johannesburg, which held the stocks until they were ready for sale in London. In 1961, after the invention of synthetic diamonds, the role of IDS was restricted to only selling boart (which is a category that encompasses different sorts of low, non-gem-quality diamonds), synthetic diamonds and drillstones, while DICORP and DTC sold all other diamonds, including industrial stones. The ensemble of De Beers' marketing and producing companies (DTC, DICORP and IDS) became known as the Central Selling Organisation (CSO).[265] Oppenheimer's relocation strategy was clearly visible in the dramatic rise of South African diamond imports in the fifteen years after the end of the war. In 1964 some 20 million carats of diamonds were exported from South Africa, of which only 2 million carats had been mined there.[266]

It was customary for agreements between the DPA producers to be renewed every five years, and some important changes took place in 1950. The Premier mine (illus. 67) reopened and was allocated a quota, while

DICORP was no longer subject to one, but received the guarantee needed to fulfil its contractual obligations towards outside producers in West Africa, Congo, Angola and British Tanganyika (later Tanzania), and to some South African alluvial producers. In 1955 DICORP was given a quota again (see illus. 75).[267] De Beers remained by far the most important company in these structures. It now incorporated nine diamond mining and prospecting companies, DICORP and three enterprises established to cover investments in gold, coal, chemicals, textiles and engineering.[268] Diamonds, however, remained De Beers' core business, and the post-war years were prosperous, with sales numbers and production rising due to renewed consumer demand for polished goods and jewellery, and an expanding demand from industry for low-grade industrial diamonds. Between 1945 and the 1960s the global output of rough diamonds doubled to 27 million carats a year. The Congo, Angola and West Africa surpassed South Africa in production numbers due to their large deposits of industrial stones. Gemstone diamonds now accounted for only a quarter of the weight, but about three-quarters of the sales value.[269] It is no coincidence that De Beers employed an advertisement agency to market their diamonds worldwide, and Mary Frances Gerety, a copywriter at N. W. Ayer & Son, came up with the famous slogan 'A Diamond Is Forever' in 1947.[270] Expanding production necessitated a growing consumer market, and De Beers' post-war publicity campaigns proved to be a success. The glitter they sold to Western customers stood in stark contrast with the growing hardships endured by those employed in the diamond industry. De Beers, in particular, established a poor track record in its treatment of labourers, while others made attempts to create better, but paternalistic, conditions for the workforce, such as John Williamson in Tanzania.

Existing outside production elsewhere in Africa had been secured through contractual agreements, and every new discovery was considered a potential threat to the De Beers' monopoly. In 1942 Kleinzee's alluvial deposits came under the direct control of De Beers. A mining town developed, relying on migratory wage labour, particularly after the expansion of mining activities in 1956, and the town's 4,000 inhabitants at the end of the twentieth century all gained their livelihood through De Beers.[271] The most important challenge to De Beers in the immediate post-war years came from a discovery made in British Tanganyika. In 1940 the Canadian geologist John Williamson found the Mwadui kimberlite pipe (see illus. 82), about 160 kilometres (100 mi.) south of Mwanza, near Lake Victoria. The pipe, with a surface area of 146 hectares (360 ac), is still the world's largest exploitable diamond mine today. It turned out to be very rich in diamonds and De Beers quickly moved to buy the mine. In 1947 the decision was made to enter the DPA, and Williamson Diamonds Ltd was given a 9.17 per cent producers' quota; production rose to 195,000 carats in 1949. Before long, however, Williamson and DICORP quarrelled over prices, and Williamson withdrew. During the 1950s the production of the Williamson mine was higher than the combined output of the De Beers' mines in South Africa, and the diamonds were of gemstone quality. It was a dangerous situation for De Beers that was only resolved after Williamson died in 1958, enabling De Beers to buy the mine in a deal with Williamson's brother and the colonial authorities.[272] The people who most regretted De Beers' expansion were probably the labourers. Williamson had been responsible for the construction of schools and hospitals, and managed to create a model working environment for the thousands of black labourers he employed.[273]

According to Rosemarie Mwaipopo, who has extensively studied diamond mining in Tanzania, the story of how Williamson developed his mining site was remarkable. He had started out as a prospector, and when it became clear he had located a rich deposit, he negotiated with local leaders (after one of whom, Mwadui, the mine had originally been named) and obtained their permission to mine. Later he legally purchased the land on which the mine was located rather than resorting to the historically more common practice of simply stealing or appropriating land.[274] Williamson created a mining society in which retired workers went to live in nearby villages, which totalled about 20,000 inhabitants in the mid-2000s, including a number of active artisanal miners.[275] While Williamson's enterprise was certainly unlike South Africa's mining compounds, it was not a utopian workers' paradise either, and in 1946 the Williamson mine's 6,000 workers lived in a fenced encampment guarded by two hundred men.[276] While the establishment of a heavily guarded camp remained a classic solution by the mine owners to prevent theft and smuggling, the facilities Williamson built for his workers, and the way he negotiated in the creation of his mining enterprise, was very different from the situation in South Africa and South West Africa.[277]

De Beers had not only been treating its black workers very poorly ever since the nineteenth century, the company and Oppenheimer himself were now very much an integral part of South Africa's industry and politics, both characterized by an abundance of racism. As one of the country's most important economic forces, De Beers was not only a giant, it was a South African giant, and the Union of South Africa, nominally independent since 1910 and fully independent since 1931, was a country based on an official policy of segregation (apartheid) installed after the National Party won the elections in 1948. A white minority used racial laws and violent oppression as the means to control a black majority, and South Africa's turbulent history during the decades of apartheid was characterized by white violence, black resistance, international outcries and boycotts.[278] In March 1960 a large demonstration took place in the Transvaal township of Sharpeville against the pass laws, the internal passport system that underpinned apartheid. Police killed 67 demonstrators, leading the United Nations to take an official stance. Resolution 1761, passed in November 1962, condemned apartheid policies and called for a voluntary boycott. In August 1963 the UN Security Council signed another resolution aimed at putting a stop to weapons exports to South Africa, a resolution signed by all its members, including the USSR, with the exception of France and the UK.[279] The signature of the Soviets led to the temporary suspension of a secret agreement by which De Beers could purchase Russian diamonds.[280] International boycotts expanded, foreign investors stayed away, and South Africa's economy suffered.

Harry Oppenheimer, who had followed his father in 1957 as head of Anglo-American and De Beers, took a pragmatic stance. At the end of his life, Harry's father had become somewhat aware of the dire conditions in which many black workers lived and worked, but his efforts to improve his workers' lot can be considered as 'enlightened self-interest'.[281] There was no denying the Oppenheimers were part of a white elite, who lived in luxury and had made their fortunes on the back of black labour. The Oppenheimers also shared a common economic interest with the government, and the latter's practical implementation of apartheid had been based on regulations invented by mining enterprises, including De Beers.[282] On the other hand, Harry Oppenheimer realized that the political system of apartheid could not be sustained in the long run and that reform was necessary. When he met Nelson Mandela in 1961, he was struck by his 'sense of power'.[283] Harry thought the development of a black middle class would be a breakthrough and took some initiatives to

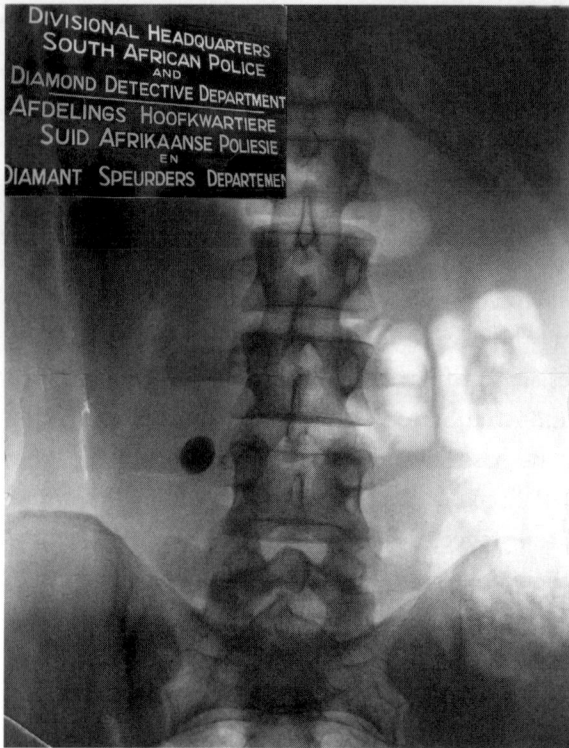

80 X-ray of a stolen diamond, Kimberley, 1932.

that purpose. On a visit to the United States, he was praised by President Johnson for his humane treatment of black labourers, but was also told that it was not enough.[284]

The American president was free to express his own views of De Beers' racist treatment of their black workers, but in South Africa opinions on the persistence of the oppressive system of compounds, discrimination and unequal wages were much more negative. A black worker employed by De Beers earned on average $97.5 a month, while a white worker was paid $480. Students at the University of Cape Town, where Oppenheimer was chancellor, protested against his inability to follow up his words with concrete action. In response, wages were raised, but not equally between black and white workers. In September 1973 a strike of gold-mine workers was violently broken up by the authorities, killing twelve men and demonstrating that apartheid, the oppression of black labour and violence still went hand in hand.[285] During the 1970s De Beers finally decided to abolish its closed compound system, although, in line with the general South African approach to black migrant labour, the 'hostel system', in which specific buildings were designed to house the black workforce in otherwise white-only areas, continued to exist.[286] In his monograph on the legacy of colonialism in Africa, first published in 1996, Ugandan scholar Mahmood Mamdani mentioned a study that concluded that the hostels for labourers provided 529,784 beds, almost 60 per cent of them located in the gold-mining region of the Rand. At the same time, Mamdani asserted that this number was not representative of the total of labourers housed in the hostels, as a person with a bed was considered privileged.[287] The environment was often difficult: beds were small, pedlars sold cigarettes, drugs and alcohol, and after the abolition of mechanisms to control arrivals in 1986, unemployed workers entered in numbers that were too large to sustain.[288]

In the diamond mines, the compound system had been defended for its ability to control black labourers and prevent diamond theft. One of the standard tools was the use of X-rays, and workers were confined to the closed compounds for periods of seven weeks, the safe period needed for individuals to be subjected to consecutive X-rays (illus. 80, in which a man's chest cavity with a swallowed diamond is shown).[289]

An article on labour at the diamond mines, which appeared in the *Sunday Times* in February 1976, confirmed that the official motive to introduce the closed compound system had always been the prevention of theft, and that it was a system 'by which mine workers from the tribal areas contracted to live a prison existence for seven months in exchange for a bed in a hostel and the basic needs of life (excluding wine and women)'.[290] The historical evidence, not in the least the illustrations, makes it abundantly clear that the main motivation behind the measures taken against theft was the attempt to fully control the black workforce, to be used, disposed of and curtailed in any way their white employers saw fit. The article continued that, while illicit diamond buying had declined, the system 'has been frequently criticised for its moral and social effects'.[291] It seems that protest against the system was continued in the 1970s by religious organizations, and the Dutch Reformed Church labelled it 'a cancer which rages in the life of the African population'.[292] The Church was not so much concerned with governmental wrongdoings in the context of apartheid, but complained about the ruinous effects the compounds had on family life, believing it bred prostitution and venereal disease. De Beers had already begun to substitute its housing and was constructing 250 houses in the township of Galeshewe, near

Kimberley. It was also hoped that a wage rise would attract more local labour to replace the migratory workforce.

The journalist concluded, though, that in spite of growing protest against the compound system, the real reason behind De Beers' readiness to phase out the 'closed hostels' was the improved security and the introduction of the 'honesty bonus'. The article started out with the story of Abel Maretela, a black miner who was rewarded £5,680 and a house 'in his tribal homeland' for unearthing the '10th biggest diamond ever found'.[293] Maretela, who earned £78 per month, had previously earned 'honesty bonuses' of £340, £470 and £11 for 'spotting stones that have fallen off the conveyor belt'.[294] These financial incentives were shown to reduce theft, and the author of the article was optimistic about the possible advancement of black workers following the gradual disappearance of the compounds, but also pointed out that a major problem remained with the white mineworkers' unions. Much like the unwillingness of the white strikers in 1883 and 1884 to unite with their black colleagues, the white unions refused to accept black workers for the better-paid and more skilled jobs.[295] In opposition to these forms of local and national white resistance against black labour emancipation stood the development of international protest. The Unites States restricted imports from South Africa through the Anti-Apartheid Act of 1986, which also foresaw additional sanctions in case segregation should continue. African American voices started to take a harsh tone with De Beers, and lamented the company's strategy of opposing both apartheid and the sanctions against it.[296] In 1987 Oppenheimer tried to loosen the ties between De Beers and South Africa by leaving the DPA, but this was no more than a cosmetic measure, as De Beers' share of global diamond production had fallen to 11 per cent, while the CSO, in which De Beers was the most important presence, handled 80 per cent of global sales.[297]

Others were to overthrow the South African political system, and a large role was played by the mineworkers. In 1982 the black National Union of Mineworkers (NUM) was founded. The fast-growing union played a major part in ending apartheid, through strikes but also through assistance to the African National Congress (ANC) and successful attempts to unify the various trade unions.[298] Their efforts were complemented in South West Africa, which became the independent nation of Namibia in 1990. The South West Africa People's Organization (SWAPO), which had fought for independence and became Namibia's ruling party, branded the country's mines as 'key sites of exploitation and wealth appropriation'.[299] Negotiations about nationalizing part of the mines owned by De Beers in Namibia did not result in the state owning the mines, but it did create better labour conditions for the black workforce, which ultimately also benefited their South African colleagues, who had been fighting for decades to improve their lot.[300] The election of Nelson Mandela as South African president in 1994 put an end to apartheid as a political system. The reputation of De Beers, synonymous with diamonds and South Africa, was tarnished for its reliance on exploited labour and its contribution to racial segregation, but the company nonetheless remained the dominant factor in the world of diamonds. In spite of its historical wrongdoings, the company turned out to be luckier than many of the colonial mining companies in other parts of Africa, most of which were dismantled after the independence movements of the late 1950s and the 1960s.

5

The Enduring Attraction of Alluvial Mining, 1884–2018

And Sierra Leone is littered with diamonds, mostly along the courses
of the rivers . . . hundreds of miles of streams and swamp. Even
with thousands of police and helicopters and God knows what, you
couldn't do much about illegal mining over that sort of area . . . If
you flew round in a small aircraft or hacked your way through the
bush, you could see the banks freshly pockmarked with diggings
every morning.[1]

The discovery of kimberlite pipes in South Africa and the development of underground mining turned the world of diamonds completely upside down. It reignited a declining mining industry, but also allowed for much higher production of rough diamonds. This, in turn, led to a revival of the old dream to control diamond prices through monopolies on production and trade. The development of South African diamond mining through De Beers Consolidated Mines and the links with a London-based syndicate ensured that the bulk of rough diamonds found their way to consumers through the very tightly controlled channel of single selling. In addition to fully controlling production and sales, De Beers also perfected the century-old system of enslaved labour to be used in the mines. Officially, slavery had been abolished everywhere, but in South Africa the closed compound system and racial segregation were the foundations on which De Beers was able to build its almost total control over the black mineworkers.

The industrial form of mining as it was developed in South Africa set the tone for the diamond industry until today, but it did not end the older practice of alluvial mining. Adventurers never stopped looking for diamonds, and mining rushes continued to occur in riverbeds in the old diamondiferous areas of Brazil, India and Borneo, but also in the heart of Africa. Parallel to the development of De Beers as a worldwide empire, prospectors discovered important alluvial deposits in West and Central Africa. During colonial times, large European companies established monopolistic rights over areas in the Congo, Angola, West Africa and Tanzania (see illus. 82), but after independence and nationalization of many domestic exploitation industries, African governments found it increasingly difficult to control the activities of the thousands of fortune-seekers active in remote and dispersed diamond fields. It was on these fields that the term 'blood diamonds' was born, a reference to the use of diamonds in the funding of violent civil wars. Africa's alluvial stones, which were often industrial diamonds, became a heavily smuggled commodity that placed an enormous burden on local economies and populations. Many suffered as they were coerced to work for powerful men or driven by hopes to escape poverty. And it all began under one of the most atrocious colonial regimes Africa has known, that of Belgium's King Leopold ii.

While the twentieth century saw the strong association between Africa and diamonds, both industrially and artisanally mined, it should not be forgotten that artisanal small-scale mining activities remained in the old mining fields in India, Borneo and Brazil. This chapter is about the persistence of alluvial mining in Africa as well as elsewhere. It runs parallel in time to the previous chapter, one being about De Beers' industrial operations and the other about the alluvial competition.

The Persistence of Traditional Methods in Borneo

The development of industrial mining had brought new techniques of mining, selling and controlling labour that had a major impact on the modern diamond world. However, it never fully replaced the old practice of alluvial diamond mining: the two different forms of mining were not mutually exclusive, but just demanded a different mining management. Industrial underground mining was much easier to control, as it took place in a smaller area, not in riverbeds but in underground mines. The workers active in African riverbeds in the twentieth century relied on the same techniques that had been used by miners all over the world's diamond deposits throughout all ages.

A 1786 account of a diamond mine above the Molucco river, near Banjarmasin (see illus. 14), described how local people living in the mountains were assisting diamond miners, as they were better able to discover the diamondiferous earth through its colour and the presence of certain small stones. They did not seem to be aware of the commercial value of stones extracted from the earth, and the observer noted that locals were willing to find a location, dig a hole and take out soil using iron pans, all for free. The soil was then transported, sieved and washed, and diamonds were collected by leaseholders, paying very mediocre prices to miners. Stones weighing over five carats had to be handed over to the local ruler, and the rest found their way to the market. The anonymous author of the description commented that it was a 'rule for the dumb', as diamonds over five carats would still be easy to swallow. The holes could be as deep as 17 metres (55 ft), sustained by wooden constructions to stop them collapsing.[2] This traditional way of alluvial mining was very much like mining at other places in the southern hemisphere and hardly changed over time.

An account written in Batavia in the nineteenth century described how locals in Landak's main settlement would dig holes to find diamonds. There were 250 houses, accomodating 4,000 Muslims who mainly lived from barter trade and diamond mining. Landak was a regional entity within Borneo. Its name, derived from a local word meaning 'porcupine', was given to it by Europeans who found it descriptive of the pockmarked terrain, so characteristic of diamond mining in Borneo.[3] The description of holes is also found in a travel report made by a government official in 1824. He described three mines at Soengi-Roentie, Banjarmasin, dug straight into the ground, half a metre square (6 sq. ft) and 4 metres (12 ft) deep. Scaffolding had been built at a depth of just over 1 metre (4 ft) from where men were hauling up buckets of water from the miners below, who were working shoulder-deep in water. They were looking for the diamondiferous earth, characterized by the presence of stone with a colour that resembled lead, the 'soedara intan' (brother of the diamond). At the surface it was sieved through bamboo baskets. The fine sand that remained was further washed in round wooden containers, until diamonds could be picked out by hand.[4]

The sultan of Banjarmasin carried a 77-carat diamond around his neck, found at Soengi-Roentie. When the Dutch gained control of the sultanate in 1859, the diamond found its way to Amsterdam, where it was cut into a stone weighing 36 carats and is currently preserved in the Rijksmuseum.[5] This size was exceptional for the island, although diamonds weighing between 24 and 40 carats were sometimes found there. In 1858 a Chinese miner handed over a 40-carat diamond to the Landak ruler.[6] Ten years later a 25-carat stone, found in one of the diamond mines, was cut down to 18.5 carats.[7] These methods hardly changed over time. An account from 1919 described how miners determined the depth of the diamond-iferous earth in shafts by sticking an iron pin in the ground. The rubbing sound it made when it touched quartz indicated to the miners whether the diamondiferous layer had been reached. The practice of sieving dia-mondiferous earth through different baskets, with one sieve picking up all diamonds weighing three carats and above, was 'a measure that was a remnant from the era of the sultan, when all stones of and above this weight had to be delivered to him'.[8]

According to Tivadar Posewitz, author of a survey of Borneo's mineral resources, those looking for diamonds were 'extraordinarily skilful', able to find even the smallest stones where the untrained eye saw nothing.[9] He also wrote that superstition was important in the mining for diamonds, and that certain people were attributed with the ability of 'determining the place where diamonds lie buried, by an occult perception of their lustre . . . If they do not succeed in finding the supposed precious stones, in spite of the statements of the magicians, they comfort themselves with the idea that the stones have been secretly removed by evil spirits.'[10]

Alluvial mining was not only carried out by collecting and washing soil dug from holes. Some miners also dived for the soil, without res-piratory aids, but using a wooden cage that generally measured about 3 square metres (32 sq. ft) and could hold three or four miners. The cage was there to protect the divers from crocodiles, although it could not always prevent accidents: between July 1927 and July 1928, eighty people were killed in the Martapura river.[11] Today local people, mainly in West Kalimantan, are still diving for diamonds and risking their lives in the process.[12] In the early twentieth century divers had been mostly Malay, sponsored by Chinese or local merchants. Although locals always played a great role in mining, they were never alone. In 1932 an engineer referred to diamondiferous river areas that had been worked by the Chinese, Malays, Dayaks, Japanese and Europeans. Traces of earlier diggings could be found in the jungle, often up the mountain slopes, and locals claimed that these had mainly been worked by the Chinese.[13] These traces could be holes that had been refilled, as was the usual practice once mining had ended. It was also permitted, however, to put a little flag on a hole to indicate to others that it was still being worked. This practice led to misunderstandings, particularly when another miner reworked an older hole and found diamonds, which regularly resulted in disputes over whether there had been a flag or not.[14] The Chinese were mining for gold and diamonds, but the Dayak people were more prone than the Chinese 'to accept the disappointments in the finding of gemstones, even though at times they poach the earth for days, in vain, with great effort'.[15] By the middle of the nineteenth century, most of Borneo's gold, diamonds and jewels, estimated at several millions of guilders per year, were exported to China.[16]

Miners organized themselves in *kongsi*, commercial partnerships based on clan-like attachments within the group, a social structure that was Chinese in origin.[17] *Kongsi* were formed on the diamond fields when the dry season began, financed by traders in Martapura. Some of these were based on kinship connections, as diamond digging had become a family tradition passed on through generations, particularly among the Malay. An investor paid an advance to the miners, who gained around 15 guilders per month. In return, he received 10 to 20 per cent of the profits.[18]

Philanthropist, pharmacist and entrepreneur Hendrik Tillema travelled to the interior of Borneo in 1928 and 1929, and again in 1931 and 1932 to visit the indigenous Dayak people. He recorded his travels in an illustrated book and in a film shown in Dutch cinemas.[19] Tillema was concerned with the consequences of European contact with locals and wanted to use this film as a way of documenting Dayak culture and lifestyle. The Dayak had a long involvement in diamond mining, and the subject was present in the film. The Dayak started their working day with a *selamatan*, festivities that included the sacrifice of a pig, dog or chicken.[20] After that, a first sample of soil was procured and carefully washed in a petroleum can or similar container. If a diamond was found, it was considered a token of good luck and offered to the Dutch colonial official, after which mining began in earnest.[21] As in many other historical contexts, it was not uncommon for women to do the hard physical work, such as transporting the diamondiferous earth (illus. 81, compare also with illus. 19). In recent times, some modern equipment has been introduced to assist with washing and sorting, but diamond digging at the alluvial sites remains artisanal. During the 1980s fewer than five hundred miners were active at Cempaka, where layers were becoming exhausted.[22]

Many of them were Muslim farmers, who took up diamond digging in the hope that a lucky discovery might pay for a pilgrimage to Mecca.[23]

Diamonds in the Heart of Africa

Twenty years before Tillema's journey to Borneo, important alluvial diamond deposits were located in the heart of Africa, following expeditions to the area brought about by the Berlin Conference of 1884–5, which had made this region the subject of a colonial race.[24] At the same time as the diamond magnates were emerging in South Africa, the vast territory of the continent's interior was being explored in the name of the European powers. The famous journalist Sir Henry Morton Stanley explored the Congo Basin for the Belgian King Leopold II, who wished to establish a colony in the middle of Africa, and Pietro Brazzà did the same for the French. Germany developed an interest in southwestern Africa as the British were hoping to expand influence all over the continent.[25] While the imperialist ambitions and the political and economic motives behind this 'scramble for Africa' are still scrutinized by historians, the destructive impact of the late nineteenth-century expansion of European power in sub-Saharan Africa stands beyond doubt. Relationships between the rival European colonizers were settled during the Berlin Conference, which fulfilled King Leopold's dream to own a private African colony, the Congo Free State.[26] Leopold ceded large parts of his colony to rubber companies, and the brutal rule on the rubber plantations that came into being was enforced through the colonial army of the *Force Publique*. Locals were violently exploited to the extent that historians now label Leopold's rule of the Congo a genocide, responsible for as many as 10 million deaths between 1880 and 1910.[27]

At the turn of the century, opposition to the brutal treatment of the Congolese was growing in Belgium, and also found expression in newspapers in the United Kingdom.[28] Literature also made a contribution, most famously with Joseph Conrad's *Heart of Darkness*, first published as a serial in 1899. Conrad's novella, although not free of furthering existing stereotypes about the African continent and its inhabitants, did offer some insights into the horrors of European exploitation of Africa: 'to tear treasure out of the bowels of the land was their desire, with no more moral purpose at the back of it than there is in burglars breaking into a

81 Women transporting diamondiferous earth, Borneo, 1928.

safe' is a quote immediately applicable to diamond mining efforts virtually everywhere.[29] In 1907 a Dutch-language newspaper reported that the Belgian government was considering annexing the Congo, particularly now that its reputation as a 'mine of gold' had generated British interest. The newspapers compared British manoeuvres to discredit Leopold's colonial rule with their strategy in obtaining the Transvaal and its diamond fields.[30] The growing international awareness of what was happening in the Congo increased pressure on the Belgian government to take over the colony, which it did in November 1908.[31] The change of rule came at a time when efforts were made to reduce the importance of rubber in

Congo's colonial economy by actively developing an interest in mineral exploration. Three Belgian mining companies had been set up in 1906, the Union Minière du Haut-Katanga (UMHK), the Compagnie du Chemin de Fer du Bas-Congo au Katanga (BCK) and the Société Internationale Forestière et Minière (Forminière), all recipients of huge land concessions.[32] The Société Générale de Belgique (SGB), which would later control most of the Congo's economy, was a shareholder in all of these companies, but there was also American involvement, particularly in Forminière, in which an important shareholder was the firm of Ryan & Guggenheim.[33]

Forminière started its mining operations in 1907. Its prospectors were hoping to find gold deposits, but instead they found a diamond in the Kasaï river in the southwest of the colony. After experts in Brussels confirmed the diamond was genuine, several prospecting teams ventured out to find more, leading to more substantial diamond discoveries in 1911.[34] All of the new finds had occurred in the Kasaï river and its tributaries. At the confluence of the Tshikapa and Kasaï rivers, Forminière established the town of Tshikapa as its administrative headquarters (see illus. 82). Initially Forminière had been given more than 1 million hectares (2.7 million ac) of land for mining and agriculture, but when the Belgian state annexed the Free State, it reconsidered Leopold's concession policies, which had put mining rights in the hands of a very small number of corporations. In 1912 Forminière's concession was reduced to 150,000 hectares (370,000 ac) but as compensation the company received the right to manage diamond deposits that belonged to other companies.[35]

In spite of this territorial reduction, the new arrangement led to an augmented production of rough diamonds, further enhanced by the discovery of new diamond fields in 1916 by BCK prospectors near the Lubilash river and the town of Bakwanga, later renamed Mbuji-Mayi (see illus. 82). In 1920 the Société Minière du Bécéka, a BCK subsidiary, handed the practical management of these deposits over to Forminière.[36]

The beginning of diamond mining in the Congo was difficult and only truly kicked off after the end of the First World War. In 1911 a total of 240 diamonds had been dug up, but the exploration of these alluvial deposits quickly expanded to 15,000 carats in 1913, 104,000 in 1917 and 250,000 in 1922, a production that was higher than South West Africa's output at the time, estimated at 200,000 carats, but still lower than the total South African production of 669,000 carats.[37] The discovery of kimberlite pipes had changed the perception of diamond mining, and entrepreneurs were not satisfied by exploring alluvial deposits. In 1919 Daniel Guggenheim, a shareholder in Forminière, arranged a meeting in Paris with Jean Jadot, who was a director of the SGB and had been one of the main architects behind the formation of the three mining companies in 1906. Guggenheim showed him a scale model of the Chuquicamata mine in Chile, which was owned by his family's firm and was the world's biggest open-pit copper mine. He hoped to use the same techniques to develop industrial mining in the Congo, but it quickly turned out to be an unrealistic operation, as no proper kimberlite pipe could be located.[38]

Alluvial mining did not require heavy investment in machinery at first, and Forminière's prime concern was the access to cheap labour. While Forminière offered low wages to its black workers, they tried to compensate for this with cheap shoes and clothes, and by offering housing that resembled local architecture:

> Apparently the only large company in the Congo which follows the casual labor system is the Forminière – the American-Belgian diamond concession. Labor willingly seeks employment with this Company because it houses its labor in villages resembling those to which they are accustomed at home, and because of other attractive labor conditions.[39]

In 1919 the diamond diggings in the Kasaï employed 7,000 Congolese labourers, but by 1925 Forminière had built a network of roads measuring more than 1,000 kilometres (620 mi.), connecting sixteen villages and employing a workforce of 155 whites and 18,000 black workers, with their *entrepôt* at Charlesville and their headquarters at Tshikapa.[40] Most workers came from the local Luba (Baluba), a Bantu-speaking people. Forminière's employment was based on casual labour, in which temporary labour was recruited on the basis of seasonal contracts. The question of whether this form of employment was free is highly debatable, given that the restructuring of the local economy towards mining eliminated choice, and considering the heavy burden of taxation that was imposed on the local population.[41] Strategies to reduce the work options of local inhabitants to force them into mining labour were not new and had been employed even more rigorously in South Africa. In the Congo,

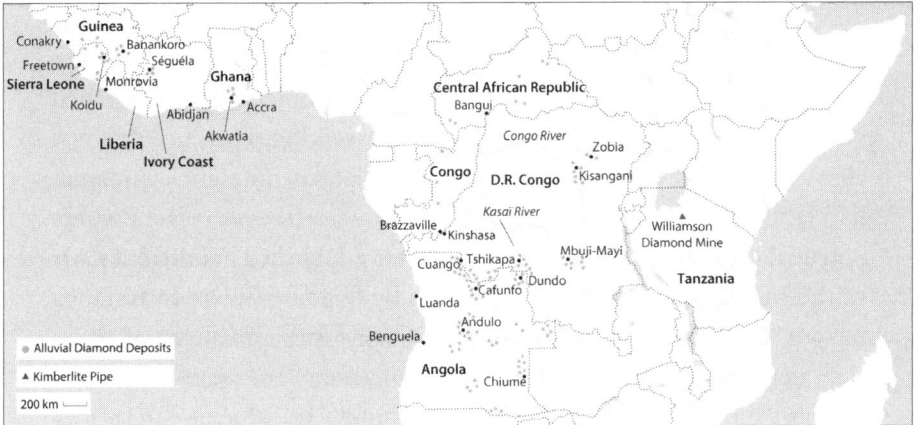

82 Diamond deposits in West and Central Africa.

closed compounds and migratory labour never became the rule, but the local economy was completely reshaped to play a subservient role to the mining interests.

The supply of food to the mining sites was particularly important. Since the early days of Forminière, the company had pursued a policy of buying up local produce, but when the labour force expanded this proved to be insufficient and part of the company's territory was used for agricultural production. Additional supplies came from the government, who had started to force locals into agricultural production, which was purchased by the state at a low price and sold to the mining companies.[42] Several zones in the Kasaï were incorporated within the colonial industry. Luiza, a region on the Angolan border between Tshikapa and Mbuji-Mayi, and a site where diamonds had been found since 1909, was made a restricted zone in 1915 and turned into a food supply zone for the mining towns (see illus. 82). Before mining took off, the region had been involved in long-distance trading, exporting ivory, raffia fabrics, palm oil, iron knives, enslaved Africans, millet, sorghum and rubber, and importing livestock, pearls and copper necklaces. All of these existing trade practices were forbidden and the local economy was adapted to the needs of Forminière, which also recruited workers from the area.[43] Forminière also cultivated its own crops on land given by the state; ten farms were operational in 1925, growing palm oil, manioc, corn, beans and sweet potatoes to feed the workers.[44]

The paternalistic effort made by Forminière to create a relatively attractive labour environment had to do with the amount of competition.

There was a high demand for labour among the mining companies active in Katanga. Union Minière alone employed 80,000 men in its gold, copper and tin mines.[45] Furthermore, several of the colonial enterprises relied on forced labour obtained through state intervention, a practice that was abandoned by the late 1920s.[46] To better regulate recruitment, companies had come up with the system of the *Bourses du Travail*, places where potential labourers were recruited. They were established in different parts of the colony, the first one being set up by Union Minière in Katanga in 1910.[47] Although these labour mechanisms were private enterprises, they were supported by the Belgian colonial state. The system managed to boost the exploitation of black employment in colonial enterprises, with the number of black workers rising from 45,702 in 1916 to 157,000 in 1922, and 409,665 in 1930.[48] A *Bourse* was established in the Kasaï in 1921: 40 per cent of it was owned by Forminière and 36 per cent by Bécéka. Recruitment agents operated opportunistically, obtaining help from village chiefs by promising a commission fee or using the threat of violence, and they found labour up to a few hundred kilometres away.[49] Forminière's workforce increased from 10,000 to 20,000 between 1921 and 1924, making the company the largest employer in the Belgian Congo.[50] In 1928 the government gave Forminière a recruitment monopsony within the Tshikapa region, which further reduced the labourers' remaining freedom of choice.[51] The same law introduced a division of the Tshikapa area into zones, accessible through a pass system, and granted the specially established mining police extensive powers to battle diamond theft. It hardened the company's approach towards its workers.[52]

The change in Forminière's behaviour towards its recruits, brought about by labour monopolization, was counterbalanced by the development of legislation aimed at improving the workers' conditions during the 1920s. Forced labour and the use of violence became illegal, and every worker would be able to sign a contract.[53] Forminière had to comply with certain standards regarding water supply, ventilation, sanitation and quality of construction in their labour camps.[54] Public hygiene and healthcare were improved, and a lazaretto to house those carrying an infectious disease was built in each mining site. A hospital was erected in Tshikapa as an increased workforce housed in labour camps led to outbreaks of tuberculosis. Forminière employed ten doctors, hired to treat tuberculosis and, particularly, sleeping sickness.[55] After all, healthy workers were good for profits: 'every day of sickness is a loss to production . . . Furthermore, a workforce in good health is the best of recruitment methods.'[56] In spite of these improvements to labour conditions, which made Forminière one of the more accommodating mining employers in comparison to others, it must never be forgotten that it remained a colonial system in which African labour and African minerals were being exploited by a European power. The Baluba and Congolese themselves had no say in the management of the mining area.

As in South Africa, racist colonial structures ensured that black labourers remained unskilled. The alluvial deposits found near the surface in the Kasaï did not need much expertise or mechanization. Mining methods were traditional and artisanal, with labourers shovelling, transporting gravel, washing and sieving until diamonds turned up. They were sorted by special personnel elsewhere. It was only when the richness of the deposits near Mbuji-Mayi became fully clear that technical investments became necessary. Mbuji-Mayi's diamonds came from enormous deposits of mostly industrial diamonds that were located deep underground, which made mechanization of mining necessary. Forminière invested accordingly during the 1930s, following the rise in demand for industrial stones.

In 1924 a value of 25.5 million Belgian francs of diamonds were exported from the Congo, against BFr223.5 million worth of copper, almost BFr43.5 million of gold, and BFr23 million of tin.[57] The existence of rich mineral deposits in the Congo makes the early American interest in mining there easy to understand, an interest that grew with the role played by industrial diamonds in warfare and the discovery of uranium.[58] American presence among the prospectors and engineers in Tshikapa was so prominent that the Fourth of July was the most important holiday in the Kasaï region during the 1920s.[59] Of the Congolese diamond production of 7,205,000 carats in 1942, 6,401,332 carats or 89 per cent were industrial stones, accounting for 61.5 per cent of global production.[60] Numbers rose from 106,000 carats of diamonds mined in 1917, to 7,205,000 in 1938, 10,147,000 in 1950 and 14,855,000 in 1959.[61] The shareholders of Forminière in 1948 were still largely the same as at the beginning: 55.5 per cent belonged to the Congolese colonial state, 25 per cent to the heirs of Ryan & Guggenheim, 4.1 per cent to the SGB and 15.4 per cent divided between smaller investors. SGB, however, was overrepresented in the company's management, an inheritance of Leopoldian times. Oppenheimer and Anglo-American did not have a direct share in Forminière, but held a 23 per cent stake in BCK, the Congo's other colonial diamond company. BCK, for its part, was an SGB vehicle and its mining concessions were exploited by Forminière.[62] By that time De Beers had already successfully negotiated for the Congo's diamonds to be sold through their single-selling system in London.

Crossing the Border from the Congo to Angola

The occurrence of diamond deposits was not contained by political borders, and it did not take long before prospectors working for European companies active in the Congo ventured into the Portuguese colony of Angola. The colonial economy there was based on rubber plantations, similar to the economy of the Congo, but that quickly changed when prospectors working for Forminière crossed the river into the region of Lunda, where diamonds were discovered in riverbeds in 1912 (see illus. 82). A prospecting company, Pesquisas Mineiras de Angola (Mining Research of Angola, PEMA), relying heavily on foreign investment, was founded in Lisbon, but the potential of Lunda's diamond deposits necessitated a more substantial mining company, which was the Companhia de Diamantes de Angola (Diamang), established in 1917. Many of PEMA's investors became shareholders in Diamang, such as Portugal's Banco Nacional Ultramarino and Henry Burnay & Co., and new investors included the SGB, Anglo-American and Ernest Oppenheimer, and Ryan & Guggenheim. Foreign investors held 80 per cent of the shares, while the Portuguese state owned 20 per cent. Forminière was brought in to take care of the technical management of the deposits themselves. Any rights PEMA still held on Lunda's diamond fields by 1918 were transferred to Diamang, which now held a monopoly on Angola's diamonds.[63] Diamang remained the sole company with diamond mining rights in Angola for seventy years (illus. 83). In 1988, the last remnants of the company were incorporated into its successor Endiama.

Diamang concluded a crucial agreement with the colonial authorities in 1921, which was to be the foundation for the relationship between Diamang and the government until the independence of Angola in 1975. Diamang received a large mining concession in Lunda, a monopoly status and a tax exemption in Angola, while the government also guaranteed its assistance in the recruitment of labourers and the maintenance of security in the mining zones. In exchange, Diamang handed 40 per cent of its profits to the state (later it would be nearer to 50 per cent), which also held a 5 per cent share in the company.[64] Diamang also made promises to the authorities for company loans in hard currency.[65] With financial backup secured, colonial high commissioner Norton de Matos crafted plans to invest £13 million in infrastructure, and he managed to double the total length of roads in Angola before he was forced to resign two years later.[66] The 1921 agreement gave Diamang a great deal of independence from the colonial authorities; the company developed its own health service, for instance, while it could rely on governmental assistance for a number of tasks.[67] Business went well for both sides, with 312,000 carats of diamonds sold between 1917 and 1929, for which the Portuguese state received almost £1 billion in profit and loans.[68] Additional prospecting unearthed new deposits in other areas of Lunda, mainly in the Cuango river valley, extending on both sides of the border, although the Congolese deposits would only be explored from 2005 onwards.[69]

Diamang not only relied on the state; particularly in its early years it received technical support from Forminière, which was active right across the border. Most management positions were held by Belgians or Americans; according to an American engineer who had worked for both companies during the 1920s and '30s, it was common practice for

83 Diamond mining on Diamang's concession, Angola, 1946.

Forminière personnel to be sent to Angola.[70] The close relationship between Forminière and Diamang also found expression in recruitment practices. Agents working for the *Bourses* in the Congo recruited workers from across a wide area, with help from locals. In Angola, colonial police visited village chiefs, the *sobas*, to demand the supply of a quota of workers. It was a form of forced labour in which the choice of recruits was shifted to locals, but in which the government played an enforcing role. Labourers were transported by trucks to the mines, accompanied by their families, and women regularly found employment within Diamang. The company also offered its workers housing and healthcare, and Diamang's paternalistic approach was one of the reasons why work at Angola's diamond fields took place in a relatively violence-free environment. Scholars also asserted that misbehaviour such as racist violence or sexual assaults on women was more due to individual misconduct than to structural wrongdoings by Diamang. The company was also helped by the isolation of the Lunda mining area, which reduced the need for closely monitored compounds, as well as by legal impediments to strikes and the formation of unions.[71]

In his analysis of Diamang's labour system, Todd Cleveland pointed out that the relatively peaceful atmosphere was not simply the result of a top-down creation by the company. He demonstrated that the miners played an active role as well. Most workers belonged to the same Chokwe ethnicity, which avoided ethnic tension, and they consciously adopted strategies to improve the social and professional context in which they were operating. It was their growing professionalism that was one of the pillars of stability in the region.[72] Still, despite this relative tranquillity, mining in Angola remained based on a colonial system of labour extracted by force from a local population, which was only abolished during the 1960s.[73]

A shortage in labour sometimes forced Diamang's health services to declare miners healthy when they were not,[74] or to resort to child labour in the mines or on the agricultural plantations, where risks of injury and physical abuse were never completely absent.[75] It leaves the question open as to what extent mining colonialism in Angola (and the Congo) was better than it was in South Africa. While there is substantial evidence demonstrating that workers in the colonial mining regions of Angola (and the Congo) were better off than their South African counterparts, who had to work under a more severe system of segregation and whose work environment was more dangerous because of the underground mines, there was no sense of equality in the mining regions of colonial Central Africa either. The discourse on the relatively mild oppression in Portuguese Africa fits within a larger, fictional, narrative of Portuguese exceptionalism, which depicts the Portuguese colonizers as less harsh than other Europeans. This has been explained largely by a broader tendency among Portuguese to miscegenate with the populations they oppressed, creating a mixed Lusophone empire free of racism and racial oppression. This myth, deconstructed by several historians, is still quite popular today.[76]

Initially Forminière and Diamang operated independently from the diamond syndicate in London, with diamonds being exported to Lisbon and Antwerp. Anglo-American, at the time a competitor to De Beers and the syndicate, held shares in Bécéka and Diamang, but had no interest in Forminière.[77] Oppenheimer realized that production in Central Africa was upsetting the market for rough diamonds, and in the early 1920s Anglo-American sent an engineer to the diamond fields in Central Africa. Soon thereafter, Oppenheimer himself went to Angola, and Barnato Bros. bought a share in Diamang.[78] This quickly led to the incorporation of Diamang within the cartel, facilitated by the absence of a diamond industry of note in Lisbon and the historically strong political and economic connections between Lisbon and London. In 1923 English newspapers reported on the deal, and the composition of the new board of directors of Diamang, as given by the *Financial Times*, was very international. Portuguese interests were represented by the president, who was a representative of the Banco Nacional Ultramarino, while the vice-president was an army general and the managing director was a Portuguese count related to Henry Burnay. One director represented British interests, and two others the interests of France. Three of the directors were American, two of whom had been nominated by Ryan & Guggenheim. One director represented Barnato Bros. Diamang had strong ties to Forminière, and Jean Jadot and Firmin van Brée were both on the board of Diamang, as was Ernest Oppenheimer.[79] Diamang had clearly become a colonial company that was not so much controlled by Portugal, but by the world's foremost diamond mining companies instead.

The situation in the Belgian Congo was more complicated. Forminière was selling its production in Antwerp, and in 1920 the company set up an office in the city, where diamonds were sorted, valuated and classi-fied before they were sold to merchants and cutters. One of De Beers' sightholders, the Krijn firm, was asked to organize Forminière's sales procedures in Antwerp, which started to look more and more like De Beers' single selling.[80] Congolese diamonds were mostly industrial, with only about 10 per cent of the rough diamonds exported from the Belgian colony being of gemstone quality, suited for being cut in Antwerp. The remainder was mostly sold in London. Ernest Oppenheimer travelled to Europe in 1922 in the hope of 'strengthening and cementing the relations between the Anglo-American Corporation and the Société Internationale Forestière et Minière du Congo, controlling the Congo and Portuguese diamond fields'.[81] His mission failed, but it was understood that a formal agreement with the diamond syndicate was best for all parties, and nego-tiations between Oppenheimer, Forminière and the Belgian government led to an understanding in 1926. In exchange for Forminière's inclusion and the acceptance of fixed prices, Oppenheimer promised to prioritize supplying the Antwerp cutting industry, which could not be satisfied by Congolese production alone. The strongest objection came from the cut-ting industry in the Kempen, in Antwerp's hinterland, whose supply lines were cut off. The fact that the diamond workers' union in Antwerp was socialist, while the cutters in the Kempen were Catholic, only aggravated the conflict.[82]

It is telling how secretive these deals were at the time, since no news-papers seem to have picked up on the deal concluded by Oppenheimer. The press paid much more attention in the 1930s when the deals were renego-tiated. In 1931 and 1932 several Dutch newspapers reported Oppenheimer's arrival in Brussels, where he was trying to renege on the structural obli-gation of having to buy up Congolese diamonds. In 1934 it was reported that Forminière was under pressure from the Antwerp diamond industry not to cave in to Oppenheimer's demands.[83] The negotiations of the 1920s and '30s had not been easy but, once concluded, they ensured De Beers' continued grip on the world's supply of rough diamonds and their prices. Because of the agreement and the importance of the Congo's industrial diamonds, Antwerp's prominence as a cutting centre grew, while the role of Amsterdam declined. It was reported in 1917 that 1,069 firms were active in the Amsterdam cutting industry, but in 1926 this had shrunk to 309. Illus. 84 shows a former diamond factory in the Dutch city. The cutting tables and the mechanical installation used to drive the mills are still visible, but in 1919, when the picture was taken, the building had been converted for use in the clothing industry.

Amsterdam's position was further weakened by the development of a cutting industry in South Africa, and the city's diamond industry never recovered.[84] Its place in the global world of diamonds continued to decline to the extent that, with the exception of a few museums linked to historically important cutting factories, such as Moppes Diamonds or Royal Coster Diamonds, Amsterdam's illustrious diamond history has been largely forgotten.[85] Antwerp, even though it never disappeared completely from the world of diamonds, became the world's foremost diamond centre of the twentieth century, a position it would later cede to other cities in the early twenty-first century.

The New Riches of the Old Gold Coast

In 1919, about a decade after the discovery of diamonds in the Belgian Congo and the same year as the Convention of Pretoria that settled diamond mining in South Africa, these precious stones were also found by a British geological survey near Abomosu in the Akyem Abuakwa region, located in the Eastern Province of the Gold Coast at a short distance from Akwatia (see illus. 82).[86] The Gold Coast, which became an independent Ghana in 1957, had been a British colony since 1901, after they had taken over earlier Dutch and Danish settlements and defeated the local Ashanti people.[87] The area was known as the Gold Coast because, by the time Europeans arrived, the area was already known for its gold deposits, and was incorporated in ancient trade routes that extended into the Arab world before the end of the eighth century.[88] When the British gained full control of the area, European companies had been prospecting for gold for more than a decade. These activities culminated in the 'jungle boom' of 1882 to 1901, in which over four hundred enterprises invested in gold mining, albeit with little success.[89] During the boom eight concessions were given in the Akyem Abuakwa region, and it was there that alluvial diamonds were found in 1919. The same year, additional discoveries were made further south, near Kade and Akim Oda in the Birim river valley. Diamonds were also unearthed in Bonsa riverbeds in the country's southwest in 1921.[90] Three companies held concessions: Gold Fields of Eastern Akim, Akim

84 Former diamond factory, Amsterdam, 1919.

Diamond Fields and Akim Alluvials. These merged to become Akim Ltd at the end of 1921. Akim held a concessionary area near Abomosu, which was explored until 1923, and at Akim Oda, near Akwatia.[91]

Early diamond digging was not very successful, and Akim continued to focus on gold, to which purpose Chester Beatty's Selection Trust (ST) was brought in. Charles Boise, a former engineer of Forminière, was asked by Beatty to assess the gold deposits, but he found that there was a rather good potential for diamonds, leading to fuller cooperation between Akim and ST under the flag of the African Selection Trust (AST) in 1922, in which Boise received a 5 per cent share as reward.[92] AST started digging south of Kade, at their Akwatia concession, an area of 10 square kilometres (4 sq. mi.).[93] Problems soon arose between the two main partners. Under financial pressure, Akim sold its diamond branch, leading to the formation of the West African Diamond Syndicate (WADS), a company that was reported to be listed on the London Stock Exchange in 1923.[94] In 1925 WADS informed its shareholders of a projected asset of 1 million carats of diamonds on their concession, which covered 15 square kilometres (6 sq. mi.). Although Akim had concessions in the Birim river valley near Akim Oda, which were incorporated by WADS, the only location mentioned by

WADS's chairman was near Manso, a village close to the Bonsa river deposits.[95] Disputes that had arisen within AST had not been resolved with the establishment of WADS, as the company still held a share in AST. Legal disputes in London ensued, until ST managed to find the necessary capital to buy WADS out of AST, leading to the establishment of a new company in 1925, CAST. Anglo-American and Barnato Bros. were approached to invest but turned the offer down.[96] Two major mining companies were now competing, and several other European enterprises also entered the fray, but most of them failed.[97]

To obtain a concession, a company had to deal with local chiefs under the hierarchical stool system. Akyem Abuakwa, a kingdom inhabited by the Akyan people and ruled by an elected king, the *okyenhene*, was divided into different stools, each under a sub-chief. Local tribes had been used to renting their lands for mining and agriculture to Europeans, and the system had been incorporated in British colonial structures through the Concessions Ordinance of 1900. This gave a specific Concession Court jurisdiction to assess the validity of a concession request, and to check whether the customary rights of the local stools were respected. Colonial government also acted as intermediary in the rent payments by the mining companies to the owners.[98] When diamonds were found in Akyem Abuakwa, its *okyenhene* was Nana Ofori Atta I (1881–1943).[99] He objected to the widespread alienation of stool land to the mining companies, and wanted to reduce it by imposing his authority on the sub-chiefs. These, particularly those of Asamankese and Akwatia, had been receiving substantial revenue through rents and royalties in diamond profits, and challenged Atta's authority, which led to a costly legal dispute.[100] Local tensions brought about by the growing commercialization of stool lands was not the only consequence of European diamond mining in the area. The mining companies attempted to curtail the free movement of all black persons within mining zones, and created a system of permits, which was contrary to established rights under the Concessions Ordinance. The focus on mining caused a decrease in agricultural activity and a reduction in the vegetation, and the companies were forced, following several food crises, to import provisions from neighbouring areas.[101]

Like elsewhere in Africa, the companies relied largely on migrant labour, which here came from the Northern Territories (Kingdom of Dagbon) and French West Africa. These men, mostly Muslim, arrived without their families, causing prostitution to increase. Although there were tensions due to religious differences, more generally a tolerant and heterogeneous society came into being. CAST built a mosque in Akwatia in 1930, and there was a tendency towards intermarriage between Muslim men and Abuakwa women. Mutual understanding between workers of different ethnicities and religions was also enhanced by a shortage in housing, which forced many workers to rent rooms from local landlords and share accommodation. To address this problem, CAST started to build accommodation for its labourers. Chester Beatty, a businessman first, wanted to improve housing and allow families to join the workers to create a better working environment, in an attempt to maximize productivity.[102] While the new buildings were an improvement, they were not much compared to the fancy housing given to the European labourers, the construction of which turned Akwatia into a model town.[103] The housing was dearly needed, as CAST's workforce expanded: between 1925 and 1930 790 Africans and 14 Europeans were employed; between 1955 and 1960 this had increased to 3,054 Africans and 80 Europeans.[104]

When diamonds were discovered near Kleinzee in 1926, CAST, now the largest of the Gold Coast companies, decided to invest there. It led to the establishment in Johannesburg of a joint enterprise in which Chester Beatty and Ernest Oppenheimer were both involved. It was in that period that CAST agreed to enter single selling through Oppenheimer's diamond syndicate.[105] Namaqualand was not the only area into which CAST expanded, and the company established diamond interests in Brazil, British Guiana, Venezuela, Ivory Coast, Sierra Leone and French Guinea.[106] Following the discoveries in the Gold Coast colony, other diamond deposits were found in West Africa (see illus. 82). In 1930 a geological survey had found diamonds in the Gboboro, near the village of Fotingaia in Sierra Leone. After negotiating with the authorities, CAST managed to obtain a prospecting monopoly over an area of 10,800 square kilometres (4,170 sq. mi.) in the east of the country, and additional investigations unearthed diamonds a bit farther away, in the Shongbo river near Tongoma, and in the Bafi and Sewa rivers, with deposits extending all the way to Sumbuya, a town in the south that was not included in CAST's concession.[107] It was very clear that diamond deposits containing high-quality gems existed in Sierra Leone, and in 1934 the colonial government granted CAST a mining monopoly. The Sierra Leone Selection

Trust (SLST) was founded to manage the diamond fields, entirely owned by CAST but with a representative of the state on the board of directors. The state was also entitled to a yearly rent and to 25.5 per cent of the profits. The monopoly was granted for 99 years, starting in 1933.[108]

Sierra Leone shares borders with Liberia, an independent nation since 1847, and French Guinea, and both countries were found to have diamond deposits as well. Diamonds were discovered in Liberia in 1910 in tributaries of the Junk river.[109] When the SLST was founded, research by CAST came to the conclusion that there were no commercially viable diamond deposits in Liberia. That did not stop efforts by alluvial diggers, however, and several concessions were granted to mining companies after 1959, but without any results. Liberia was to play an important role in diamond smuggling, but not as a producing country.[110]

The situation in French Guinea was different.[111] Charles Boise, who had inspected gold and diamond deposits in the Gold Coast at Chester Beatty's request, sent two Irish brothers named Ronald and George Dermody further into West Africa to find more diamond deposits.[112] In 1932 the Dermody brothers found diamonds near Banankoro, in the southeast of the French colony. Anglo-French companies developed mining activities, led by Minafro, largely owned by CAST, and later Soguinex, another CAST subsidiary. Production was initially modest, but 1.2 million carats were mined in 1957.[113] Soguinex adopted a labour system that bore a close resemblance to what Diamang was doing in Angola.[114] Minafro had also been active in Ivory Coast, also part of French West Africa, where a Forminière prospector had unearthed diamonds in 1928 near Séguéla. Forminière decided not to operate in the area, leaving the place to other companies that operated there until 1977, producing an annual amount of 10,000 to 20,000 carats. Near Tortiya, more than 200 kilometres (124 mi.) further east, Minafro personnel, which included George Dermody and Marcel Bardet, the future author of a major work on diamonds, located deposits that were deemed as unviable. After the war, companies returned to the area, mining 230,000 carats in 1972, but all activities stopped three years later.[115]

All diamond deposits in West Africa were alluvial, and all were explored by a handful of European mining companies, dominated by CAST and its subsidiaries. But alluvial mining was difficult to control, and none of the mining enterprises could avoid the arrival of groups of clandestine diggers drawn to the diverse diamond fields. In the area that was to become Ghana, groups of individual diggers, or *garimpeiros*, unearthed about 38 million carats between 1935 and 1974, more than three times as much as the total production of the active companies, which stood at 12 million for the same period (see illus. 85).[116] In Sierra Leone, diggers mined more than companies, but the difference between the two was substantially smaller than it was in Ghana. Large numbers of clandestine miners, often from French Guinea and Mali, had been arriving in Sierra Leone's Kono district since 1952.[117] In 1956 a diamond rush brought between 50,000 and 70,000 adventurers to Sierra Leone, and it was estimated that illegal production that year was twice as high as SLST's numbers.[118] Authorities introduced a system of licensed digging through the Alluvial Diamond Mining Scheme, and SLST gave up part of its concessionary area, but eight months after the introduction of the scheme, Governor Dorman of Sierra Leone ordered the expulsion of all foreign diggers.[119] French colonial authorities promised to help, but operations to evacuate French subjects were complicated and costly, while fear existed that the miners would invade diamond fields in French West Africa. The decision was made to close the border, but it could not stop the migration of 30,000–45,000 diggers. Some vanished in the frontier jungle area, others went to French Guinea, Liberia and Ivory Coast. Thousands ended up in the diamond fields at Séguéla, where an estimated 1.5 million carats were collected by clandestine miners between 1957 and 1960, eclipsing official production.[120]

Uncontrolled mining in West Africa not only attracted diggers, it led to the establishment of new illicit diamond buying networks. Part of the rise in the illegal diamond trade can be explained by increased demand from the Soviet Union for industrial diamonds, which it could not procure on the global market at that time because of the Cold War. According to the Dutch newspaper *Leeuwarder Courant*, 'many diamonds disappear via Beirut or Switzerland behind the Iron Curtain'.[121] In 1953 Sir Percy Sillitoe, newly retired as director general of MI5, formed the International Diamond Security Organization (IDSO), a private company that was paid for by De Beers and was trying to prevent smuggling from the diamond fields in South Africa, the Congo, Tanzania and West Africa to Antwerp, Tel Aviv, Beirut, New York, the USSR and China.[122] As part of his research for the fourth James Bond novel, *Diamonds Are*

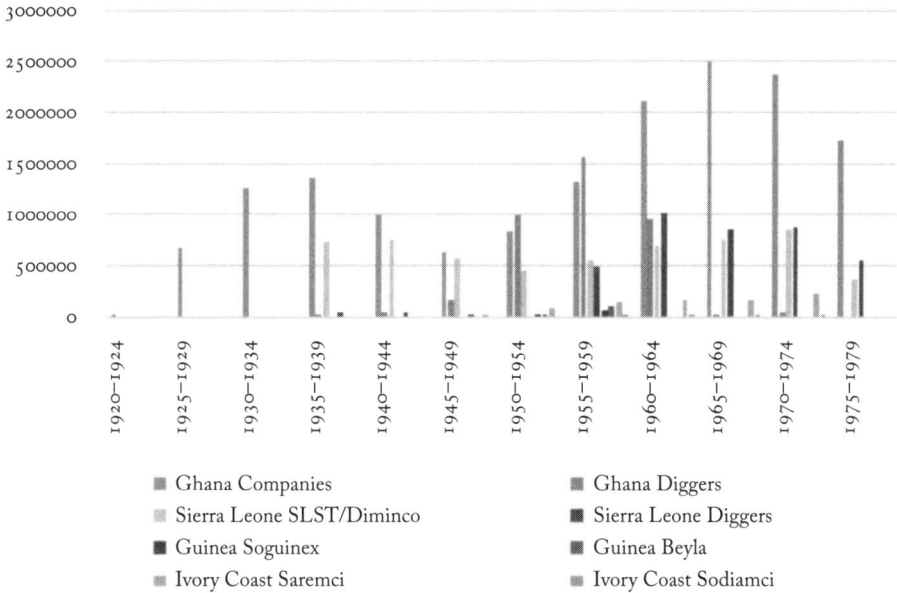

85 Official diamond production in West Africa in carats, 1920–79.[123]

Forever, Ian Fleming interviewed one of IDSO's employees in 1956, who claimed that in February of that year, diamonds worth nearly £500,000 were smuggled from West Germany across the Iron Curtain. Most were industrial diamonds from Africa, bought in Antwerp and sold in the USSR, China and other communist countries for use in the weapons industry.[124] Because Sierra Leone's deposits were spread over a wide area, and the country's diamonds were of high quality, battling smuggling networks out of Freetown and Monrovia became one of Sillitoe's main concerns, to which purpose he raised a private army of mercenaries through a Lebanese trader named Fred Kamil.[125]

The violent activities of these private forces never managed to extinguish clandestine activities, but soon it was up to independent governments in West Africa to curtail the illegal mining and trading activities, as the colonial era drew to an end. The independence movements of the 1950s and '60s affected the mining industries as much as other sectors of the economy. For many of those women and men involved in the daily labour of mining, however, a lot stayed the same. Colonial regimes controlling mining operations had always and everywhere relied extensively on slavery and the exploitation of both free and unfree labour. Additionally, labour systems always contained a strong racial component, particularly (but not exclusively) in Africa. Until the discovery of diamonds in Canada, Australia and Russia, the world's diamond deposits were all located in regions where the local population was subjected to colonial violence and enduring racism.[126] While hope must have been high that African exploitation could have ended with the creation of independent countries, the events that followed made it clear how hard it was to disentangle economic interests from Western manipulation. For many civilians the worst was still to come, and several authors have seen the twentieth-century history of alluvial diamond mining in places such as Sierra Leone as a consistent factor contributing to 'the development of underdevelopment'.[127]

Waves of Nationalization and Blood Diamonds

As a rule, the newly independent states attempted to gain control over their diamond production by creating new companies that were partially or fully owned by the government. The first of the diamond colonies to gain independence was the Gold Coast, or Ghana, in 1957, followed by French Guinea a year later. The Ghanaian government remained unstable for the next decades, but Sékou Touré ruled in Guinea until 1984. The state-owned Ghana Consolidated Diamonds exploited the Akwatia field, while alluvial digging has continued. The country produced 174,218 carats of low-quality gemstones in 2015, but only 53,573 in 2018.[128] Arédor, a company relying on foreign investment and a 50 per cent stake by the government, was created in 1981 to mine gem-quality stones at Banankoro, but activities ceased in 2004. The various mining enterprises currently at work in Guinea produced 208,307 carats in 1985, 166,881 carats in 2015 and 292,707 carats in 2018.[129]

While these countries did not escape some of the international conflicts fought out after independence, diamond mining remained relatively peaceful compared to what happened in neighbouring Sierra Leone, independent since 1961.[130] Immediately after independence, a diamond rush brought many of the expelled miners back to the Kono district and its capital Koidu Town. SLST still held two concessions and expanded its private security force from 662 in 1957 to more than 1,300 in 1971.[131] Siaka

Stevens, who held the presidency between 1971 and 1985, bought political cooperation by allocating mining rights to groups of diamond traders, who were often Lebanese. As many as 13,000 of them had fled civil war at home, and many became active in both legal and illegal diamond trading, sending part of their profits home to help finance Hezbollah.[132] Until he was deposed in 1992, his successor Joseph Momoh continued the practice of buying political loyalty through diamond concessions, which led to growing mismanagement by government officials in the mining zones. Production declined from 2 million carats in 1970, to 856,000 in 1973, 168,000 in 1980 and 88,000 in 1988.[133] The clandestine miners were considered an impediment to the deals made by the government, and violence in Kono grew.[134] In 1991 Foday Sankoh, one of Africa's most brutal warlords, started a civil war. His Revolutionary United Front (RUF) contained many child soldiers, trained to kill, and within four years of the outbreak of the war the RUF was in control of the diamond deposits of Kono. Diamonds were sold through existing smuggling routes via Liberia, where Charles Taylor, the future Liberian president and a supporter of the RUF, was also involved in a civil war.[135] Between 1991 and 1998, 31 million carats of diamonds were branded as Liberian, but most of them came from Sierra Leone.[136]

Another route took diamonds to Conakry, Guinea's capital, where they were exchanged for food, fuel and weapons by Mandinka men acting as middlemen between the RUF and Belgian and Lebanese diamond dealers.[137] Some of the world's most notorious arms dealers flourished during those conflicts, such as the Russian Viktor Bout, the 'merchant of death', who was sentenced to 25 years in prison by a U.S. court on terrorist charges in 2012.[138] The use of diamonds to fund civil war led to the adoption of the term 'blood diamonds', and in Sierra Leone money from the diamond trade fuelled a conflict that was becoming bloodier, with many men, women and children victims of atrocious violence on both sides. The government tried to hire a private mercenary force, Executive Outcomes, to fight the RUF over diamond concessions in Kono, but had to retrace its steps after international pressure.[139] The situation at the alluvial diggings was chaotic, and violence ruled as RUF retook control. One writer remarked: 'capturing a diamond mine is as easy as showing up with a rifle and ordering everyone in the pit to start handing their discoveries over to the new bosses.'[140]

On 6 January 1999 the RUF pillaged Freetown. The assault was so merciless it became known as 'Operation No Living Thing' and almost 6,000 people were killed. A West African army was sent to take back control of the city, but the damage had already been done.[141] Subsequent peace talks made Sankoh vice-president and minister for natural resources, a position he used to remain active in the clandestine diamond trade.[142] Finally arrested in 2000, Sankoh died of a stroke before he could appear in court. Charles Taylor, accused of aiding war crimes in Sierra Leone, fled but was arrested in 2006. Six years later he was found guilty at the International Court of Justice in The Hague, where he was sentenced to fifty years in prison for his role in the conflict.[143] Following the disappearance of Sankoh and Taylor, Sierra Leone slowly got used to peace. The civil war ended officially in 2002 and UN forces left the country three years later. Miners came back, and companies started to dig for diamonds again. Diamond exports went up from $1.5 million in 1999 to $11 million in 2000, and $142 million in 2005.[144] This boost was accompanied by institutional change. New legislation was implemented to battle clandestine diamond digging and trading, but the state is still having difficulties setting up an efficient revenue structure. In 2007 the government reported that 150,000 individual diggers were looking for diamonds at Sierra Leone's diamond fields, giving rise to a *comptoir* economy often dominated by merchants belonging to diasporic networks, such as the Lebanese entrepreneur Alhaji Shuman (illus. 86 and 87).[145] SLST no longer exists, but mining companies are still present. Koidu Holdings is currently exploring two small kimberlite pipes near Koidu Town, as well as diamond digging in Tongoma.[146]

It was in the aftermath of the war that the connection of blood diamonds to other international clandestine financial flows was exposed. *The Guardian* published an article in October 2002 that demonstrated a connection between Al-Qaeda and Lebanese diamond dealers, such as Aziz Nassour and Samih Ossailly, acting in coordination with the RUF and President Charles Taylor of Liberia. Diamonds smuggled out of Sierra Leone and the Democratic Republic of the Congo (DRC) might have financed Osama bin Laden's operations by some $20 million in the period leading up to 9/11.[147]

The civil war in Sierra Leone was not the only conflict that established the reputation of diamonds as a source of evil, with equally bloody conflicts being fought in Angola and the Congo. Internal factions in Angola started to challenge colonial power in 1961, but the Portuguese *Revolução dos Cravos* ('Carnation Revolution'), which overthrew Salazar's dictatorship, was the main catalyst for formal Angolan independence in 1975.[148] A civil war broke out and the warring factions found support from the opposing Cold War blocs, who were interested in controlling Central Africa's mineral sources, such as gold, tin, uranium, copper and diamonds. The main fighting parties were the MPLA of President Agostinho Neto, which was backed by the Soviet Union and Cuba, and Jonas Savimbi's UNITA, which received help from the USA and its later ally, South Africa.[149] When independence was declared, a great deal of Diamang's Western personnel had left the country. Production went down from 2.4 million carats in 1974 to less than 350,000 for the next two years combined.[150] In 1977 President Neto decided to nationalize the industrial companies, including Diamang.[151] After the state had taken an initial share of 69 per cent in Diamang, the company was abolished in 1988 and replaced by a state enterprise, the Empresa Nacional de Diamantes (Endiama).[152] While this reform successfully dealt with Angola's colonial past, it did not keep UNITA away from the diamond fields. In 1984 they invaded the Cuango valley and the next year Lunda's main diamond areas were attacked. Savimbi took control of the richest diamond areas, and the period between 1993 and 1997 was a golden age for UNITA diamonds. Savimbi brought in traders and

86 Alluvial diamond mining, Sierra Leone, 2011.

87 Alhaji Shuman's diamond dealing office, Sierra Leone.

sorters from South Africa, Belgium, Israel, Lebanon and the Congo. He also established control over the groups of individual miners, who could keep one-fifth of the diamondiferous earth they dug up. Luzamba airport served as a trading centre where foreign traders bought UNITA diamonds in public auctions, before they were flown out of the country or smuggled into neighbouring countries. *Comptoirs*, improvised business offices, were set up and Angolan diamonds were brought to Zaïre (the former Belgian Congo), the Democratic Republic of the Congo, Gabon, Zambia, Equatorial Guinea, Namibia, the Central African Republic, Burkina Faso and Rwanda, where agents working for foreign firms, often established in Antwerp or Tel Aviv, continued to buy diamonds from Angola. It has been estimated that diamonds worth as much as $600 million were sold by UNITA in 1997, perhaps as much as 10 per cent of the world's total production at the time.[153]

Diamonds were used to buy political allies in Africa and to acquire weapons. Aircraft from Europe and South Africa regularly arrived at UNITA's headquarters at Andulo, as well as Russian planes owned by Viktor Bout.[154] Violence in Lunda grew, leading to abuse and the murder of civilians and mining personnel, some working for foreign companies.[155] The UN issued an embargo on UNITA diamonds in 1998, but it was hard to control the origins of diamonds as stones from different countries were often mixed together, while inter-African smuggling routes hid the true origins of many of UNITA's diamonds.[156] In Antwerp, the final destination of many Angolan rough diamonds, trade was supervised by the Hoge Raad voor Diamant (Diamond High Council, or HRD) which could not explain the sudden rise in diamond imports from countries that had small or no diamond deposits. The UN estimated in 2000 that as many as 4,000 to 5,000 diamond dealers were breaking the embargo.[157] It has been estimated that between 1992 and 1998, UNITA was able to gain between $3 billion and $4 billion from selling rough diamonds.[158] De Beers, the final destination for a great deal of UNITA's diamonds, was reluctant to join the embargo. The company claimed it was almost impossible to determine the origins of a diamond after it had left its mining site, but eventually the company decided to stop all purchases from outside producers.[159]

Jonas Savimbi was killed in 2002 and President José Eduardo dos Santos, who had been in office since 1979, offered peace. UNITA's acceptance ended forty years of civil war. Diamonds were crucial to the country's economy. The government decided to control production as well as sales through the creation of Ascorp, half of which was owned by the state through Endiama, while the rest was sold to the controversial Israeli diamond trader Lev Leviev, a friend of Vladimir Putin. Leviev, a former De Beers sightholder, was considered one of the most important men in diamonds at the time, and he owned cutting factories in Israel, Russia, Armenia, China, India and South Africa. By 2005 his diamond sales were about two-thirds of what De Beers was selling through the CSO.[160] Ascorp ultimately failed, but the government remained in control of diamond production through Endiama, while enabling some foreign companies to join Endiama in several business partnerships. Endiama's production reached 7 million carats in 2005 and 8.4 million carats in 2018.[161] The company is now exploiting the nation's only viable kimberlite mine, the Catoca, which produces 35 per cent gem-quality diamonds, 15 per cent near-gem and 50 per cent industrial diamonds. Deposits in the Cuango valley contain 90 per cent diamonds of gem-quality.[162] Angola's diamonds are marketed by an Endiama subsidiary, Sodiam.

Alongside their industrial production, Endiama allows non-mechanized artisanal and semi-industrial production through a system of mining passes sold to a number of cooperatives by the Ministry of Geology and Mines. At their inception in 2019, the sixteen cooperatives were seen as a solution to illegal mining, while their existence should also increase revenues for the government and provide local workers with steady jobs and regular wages.[163] The cooperatives have recently come under scrutiny, as only ten of the 244 currently licensed cooperatives are operational, and both illegal mining and poverty are still rife.[164] Since the end of the war, the Angolan state and Endiama have also been investing in the region's infrastructure, mainly in the existing cities but also in some of the planned mining towns, several of which have continued to expand after the war. These investments are part of a conscious policy to reduce the relevance of illegal mining settlements, which are becoming increasingly unattractive through expanded government control and the consequences of the 2008 financial crisis. Only a few of the informal towns, such as Cuango, managed to turn into important urban centres.[165]

In spite of these efforts, Angola's government still has difficulties coming to terms with its past. Angolan journalist Rafael Marques de Morais published a book in 2011 on blood diamonds in Angola, based on his own fieldwork in Cuango. He collected oral testimonies between 2009 and 2011 to show the atrocities that were still taking place on the diamond fields there. Officially, the country adhered to the Kimberley Process (KP), but torture, murder and violations of human rights were still frequent on Angola's diamond fields, and the soldiers and security guards committing these crimes particularly targeted women and children. Marques recorded more than a hundred murders.[166] His accusation that several of the army's generals also owned their own private security company, which was responsible for some of the violence, led to a court case in which the journalist was accused, and found guilty, of defamation; in May 2015 he was sentenced to a provisional six months in prison.[167]

Bordering Angola, the Congo had its own demons to deal with, although it had a history of violence on the diamond fields that it shared with its neighbour. Until his government was overthrown in 1997, President Mobutu Sese Seko, who renamed his country Zaïre in 1974, had been one of Savimbi's most important allies, with his sons and allies controlling smuggling networks across the Angolan border. The young state was to suffer a great deal of bloodshed itself. The country was still the world's leading producer of industrial diamonds when it became independent in 1960. Belgian and American interests in its vast mineral deposits did not vanish with independence, and the young nation's first years were restless.

Immediately after independence, an army mutiny pulled the country deeper into chaos. Additionally, both the Kasaï region, where the diamond deposits of Tshikapa and Mbuji-Mayi were located, and the mineral-rich Katanga province seceded from the central government in Kinshasa. Both managed to obtain support from the Belgian government, which hoped to salvage its economic interests in the former colony. A mercenary force was installed in Katanga to protect mining interests.[168] A UN force arrived in July 1960 and was very critical of the approach taken by Belgium and the mining companies. In the capital Kinshasa, President Joseph Kasa-Vubu and Prime Minister Patrice Lumumba could not agree on how to deal with the situation. Lumumba was eventually stripped of his duties and placed under house arrest by the army commander, Joseph-Désiré Mobutu. In January 1961 he was taken to a prison in Katanga, where he was murdered.[169]

The Kasaï was brought back under the control of the central government in 1962, and the Katanga followed a year later. In 1965 Mobutu grabbed power and installed a political system based on buying loyalty through economic incentives and corruption.[170] Two years after the *coup d'état*, Mobutu nationalized Union Minière, the most important of the colonial mining companies. Forminière's successor Société Minière de Bakwanga (MIBA) was nationalized in 1973, but the sales agreements with De Beers continued until 1981, when selling rights were sold to a consortium of companies, one in London and two in Antwerp. Of course, none of this meant that Belgian corporate economic interest in the country disappeared.[171] Mobutu put a political ally in charge of MIBA and production declined, while various diamond fields were worked by individual alluvial miners, with no foreigners allowed.[172] It is hard to come up with trustworthy numbers, but official diamond production entered a downward spiral, with illegal mining networks and individual artisanal mining on both sides of the Angolan-Zaïrean border on the rise. Clandestine trade contributed to a large displacement of people. In the first half of 1994, between 25,000 and 30,000 diggers, mainly of the Lunda and Chokwe ethnic groups migrated to the UNITA-controlled Cafunfo fields near the border, and various diamond settlements arose in the frontier zone.[173] Zaïrean diggers, often young men, operated in groups called *écuries*, based on shared ethnic or regional background and led by a patron. Women were also part of these groups and were often recruited to transport gravel from the riverbeds, dug up by divers, to the sorting areas. These women ended up marrying UNITA men or successful diggers.[174] The development of digging activities in the frontier area led to the development of a *comptoir* economy, which brought about a dollarization of the economy in both countries and a devaluation of national currencies.[175]

A similar economy in which buyers, who were often foreigners, managed to drain all profit from a diamondiferous site had been developed elsewhere in the vast country. In 1986 diamonds were discovered near the city of Kisangani, an important commercial centre in the northeast of the country (see illus. 82).[176] Kisangani's production was soon more valuable than its southern counterpart, surpassing 1 million carats in the first quarter of 1994.[177] Foreign buyers from Mali, Senegal, Guinea and, particularly, Lebanon set up counters next to Congolese traders. The anarchy that came about was fuelled by steady streams of miners who migrated seasonally to the alluvial fields. In 1990 Kisangani was one of the theatres of war that brought government forces into conflict with rebel armies from Zaïre, Uganda and Rwanda. The struggle fought out in Kisangani was part of a larger war aimed at ousting the country's despotic president, Mobutu.

While Mobutu had been an important ally for the West during the Cold War, he had since become a growing nuisance and could not count on much support anymore. His reign came to an end in 1997, when a rebel commander named Laurent-Désiré Kabila, assisted by Uganda and Rwanda, took the most important towns in the diamond region before seizing the capital of Kinshasa. Zaïre was renamed the Democratic Republic of the Congo (DRC), and this change of power became known as the First Congo War (1995–7). Mobutu was flown out of the country in a plane arranged for him by Jonas Savimbi and died later that year.[178] Kabila had already sold diamond concessions to foreign companies to raise money for his army, but backed out when he took control of the country. Foreigners were not welcome on the diamond fields and he established a diamond exchange in Kinshasa where all diamond trading was to take place, against a high membership fee. At the same time, the country's political situation was far from stable, and Kabila's association with Rwanda and Uganda, whose troops remained in the Congo, became more problematic. The Second Congo War (1998–2003) ensued, ending with a transitional Congolese government and the troops of foreign governments in retreat.[179] During this second conflict Ugandan and Rwandan troops exercised control for short periods of time over Kisangani and its diamond deposits. Although neither Uganda nor Rwanda had any diamond deposits of their own, both nations exported $7.33 million in diamonds between 1997 and 2000, spoils of the Second Congo War.[180] Official sales and production numbers declined, and not even the old trick of a monopoly, given in 2000 to the Israeli company International Diamond Industries (IDI), could reverse the downward spiral. The clandestine diamond trade flourished, particularly through Brazzaville, the capital of the Republic of the Congo.

When Kabila was assassinated in 2001, he was succeeded by his son Joseph, who revoked IDI's monopoly, but soon another Israeli firm, with ties to IDI, managed to conclude a deal with Kabila, allowing them to purchase 88 per cent of MIBA's production.[181] While Joseph Kabila was constructing a business empire with the help of a number of foreign companies, individual artisanal digging continued, retaining some of the abuses and miserable living circumstances that characterized these operations everywhere on the continent. Brushing over the harsh aspects of alluvial mining, the government issued a bill of 500 Congolese francs in 2002 to honour alluvial miners (illus. 88). In 2015 a journalist writing for *Time* observed that child labour on the diamond fields persisted, despite an official ban issued by the Kabila government in January of that year.[182] Mbuji-Mayi, the most important diamond town in the Kasaï region and built on the illegal diamond trade, suffered the consequences of violent conflict and is now considered one of the least developed Congolese mineral towns, even though it contains Africa's richest industrial diamond deposits.[183] It makes Mbuji-Mayi an important place in a country in which only about 6 per cent of the mined diamonds are of gemstone quality, and 40 per cent of near-gem quality.[184]

The role played by diamonds in civil war and violence in Sierra Leone, Angola and the Congo led to the coining of the term 'blood diamonds'.[185] The media reported on it, and De Beers feared that it could destroy the romantic image they had so carefully crafted decades earlier. More and more voices arose holding De Beers accountable for the role diamonds played in the deaths of so many civilians in Sierra Leone, Angola, the Congo and other conflict areas. Statements such as 'the trade in conflict diamonds can be stopped, and could have been stopped years ago if De Beers had decided that human life was more important than profits' piled pressure on De Beers to act. Talks between producers and wholesalers in Kimberley led to the establishment of the Kimberley Process (KP) in 2003.[186] The KP stipulated that all diamonds needed a certificate that allowed them to be identified as conflict-free diamonds. The share of blood diamonds on the world market declined from 15 per cent in the 1990s to less than 1 per cent in 2010, but the KP did not manage to stop the abuses completely.[187] The official end of the conflicts in Sierra Leone and Angola, combined with the apparent success of the certificates, has lessened public interest. Countries could decide to leave the KP, and several ways remained that enabled traders to hide the true origins of diamonds. Additionally, the KP defined conflict diamonds narrowly as stones involved in civil war, which meant that the certification scheme was not well suited to deal with human rights violations in a country like Zimbabwe. The inability of the KP to stop abuses there has been considered one of the main failures of the KP.[188]

Compared to countries with enormous deposits, such as Angola or South Africa, and countries such as Sierra Leone that have suffered high-profile conflicts, Zimbabwe has remained below the radar. Diamonds had already been found there in 1903, and De Beers had claimed several territories, but failed to work them intensively. The promise of exploitation on a larger scale only started with the discovery of a kimberlite pipe by a Russian mining company in 1994.[189] Mining, particularly by foreign companies, was especially difficult in Zimbabwe because of the nationalizing policies of its president, Robert Mugabe.[190] Following his extensive nationalization of land and farms in the early 2000s, he announced the nationalization of 'all five hundred mines in the country'.[191] After his declaration, legal struggles for control over mining and mining rights ensued, and part of the country's mining industry remained in the hands of foreign investors.[192]

Viable alluvial diamond deposits were discovered in the eastern region of Marange in 2006 (see illus. 36). The government initially allowed individuals to dig freely, but when the Ministry of Mines awarded digging rights to the government-controlled Zimbabwe Mineral Development Corporation, the police and army were deployed to stop what had now become illegal mining. This led to the deaths of two hundred diggers in 2008, a military involvement in mining and smuggling, and finally an embargo on Zimbabwe's diamonds in 2009. Several parties circumvented this embargo, such as Surat Rough Diamonds Sourcing India

88 Congolese 500-franc note, 2002.

Ltd, which united the financial interests of the largest Indian diamond merchants and secured a deal with the government to export Marange diamonds to the Indian cutting industry.[193] Several rounds of negotiations involving the government, KP partners and NGOs led to the lifting of the embargo, despite reports of continuing abuse. Several mining companies with ties to the government are still active in the region.[194] One example is Anjin, a company that is half controlled by a Chinese construction and mining company and half by the Zimbabwean army and the Dubai-based Diamond Mining Corporation (DMC).[195] Zimbabwe's diamond deposits are considerable, and in 2013 the nation produced 8 per cent of the world's total output in weight (about 4 per cent in financial value). This share had fallen to 2.7 per cent in 2015, because of mismanagement and a struggle between the government and private companies.[196] In 2016 the country's all-powerful president Robert Mugabe declared that foreign companies had stolen the nation's diamonds, and that mining at the Marange diamond field was to be nationalized.[197] Since then the share has further fallen to 2.2 per cent of the total weight of global diamond production and 1.5 per cent of the total financial value.[198]

In several other nations, such as the Central African Republic (see illus. 82), currently suspended from the KP, violent conflict and abuse against diamond diggers continues, while in others, such as Namibia, compliance with the KP has benefited the industry, perhaps more than it has the local population.[199] This has contributed to renewed criticism of the KP, which is also considered inadequate to deal with several other challenges, such as child labour and environmental impact.[200] Many diamond traders involved in illegally exporting blood diamonds out of Africa have remained under the radar, but the Swiss Leaks scandal of 2015, which exposed fiscal fraud and money laundering at HSBC Private Bank (Suisse), has revealed the illegal activities of several diamond traders, including Rosy Blue.[201] The HSBC scandal revealed that diamonds were exported from conflict zones through Geneva, Tel Aviv and Dubai, after which they ended up in Antwerp, their origins disguised and their true value underestimated. One of the companies that came under accusation was Omega Diamonds, which illegally exported diamonds from Central Africa to Belgium and avoided taxes. It was a high-profile case, brought to the public eye by a whistleblower named David Renous, a former employee.[202] According to Renous, Omega Diamonds was involved in a scheme in which diamonds were bought from Ascorp in Angola at undervalued prices. These diamonds were shipped through the United Arab Emirates and Switzerland before they ended up in Antwerp, with false certificates, from where they were sold at prices that were too high for what they were worth. According to Renous's presentation, the Angolan government was swindled out of $8 billion, and the plea was made to restitute this sum to Angola.[203] The Belgian government wanted to sue Omega Diamonds for violation of customs law, but the company managed to escape a huge fine after the Antwerp Court of Appeal decided in January 2017 that the Belgian system of import licences is in opposition to European law; as the presentation before the European Parliament has shown, however, the case might not be fully over.[204]

Stories of fraud such as that perpetrated by Omega Diamonds indicate that the diamond industry has once again entered a new era. The time when the trade in 'blood diamonds' enabled conflicting factions to fuel civil war in several African countries might officially have ended with the Kimberley Process, but geographical pockets remain in which illegal mining and trading in rough diamonds escape governmental control. Additionally, an awareness has grown that diamond mining causes detrimental effects to the environment. Considerations made by NGOs and other industry watchdogs no longer focus on Africa alone. The twentieth century has been dominated by the monopoly of De Beers and by blood diamonds, and the epicentres of both are found in Africa. But the twentieth century also saw the rise of new diamond fields in places that not many people expected: Russia, Canada and Australia. Furthermore, the traditional cutting industries of Amsterdam and Antwerp, which were centuries old, were challenged by new diamond-cutting centres in Israel and India. Antwerp's primacy as a commercial centre was challenged by the establishment of new diamond trading operations in the Middle and Far East. At the end of the twentieth century several of the structures that had been fundamental to the diamond industry were deconstructed, destroyed or rejected. Apartheid in South Africa was gone, the Holocaust had provided the final blow to Amsterdam as a diamond city of any significance, and the introduction of the Kimberley Process tried to clean up the trade in blood diamonds. The monopolistic position of De Beers, the dominant force in the diamond industry for more than a century, also began to crumble, not only because of the persistent competition from alluvial and industrial miners in several African regions, but because of the emergence of new large-scale players in the Western world. Perhaps for the first time in history, diamond mining was breaking loose from the confines of colonial exploitation.

6

Mining in the Western World:
The Twenty-first-century Collapse
of the World De Beers Created

*We mine above ground, below ground, along the courses of ancient
rivers, on coasts and under the sea, in four countries on two
continents, always in partnership with our host communities. We
work responsibly to make sure that, when diamonds are found, they
play a central role in the community's efforts to create jobs, improve
education and healthcare, and build infrastructure.[1]*

This statement, taken from the De Beers website, can be seen
as typical of the way in which the big diamond companies of
today appeal to the general public. It is too optimistic, designed
to counter twentieth-century criticisms of human exploitation. It also
attempts to persuade the consumer that, in spite of the loss of monopoly, De Beers still remains the global number one player in the diamond
industry. But in spite of such appeasing statements, the company founded
by Cecil Rhodes has a long history of colonial appropriation, collaboration with apartheid, oppressive labour regimes and involvement in blood
diamonds, and it could not suddenly have become the ethical, responsible
employer it now claims to be. After the collapse of the Soviet Union, De
Beers started to lose its position as the only diamond company that really
mattered. Events in Angola, Canada and Australia further eroded De
Beers' position and the company was gradually forced to come into line
with other industry players that started to advocate for more transparent
and ethical ways of doing business.

Today, the world of diamond mining is very different from the early
modern exploration of alluvial fields in India and Brazil, and from the
twentieth century's complete domination by De Beers. Official statistics
for 2018 on the Kimberley Process's website show twenty-one countries
producing diamonds.[2] Now diamonds are mined on every continent
except Europe and Antarctica, although further exploration of Russia's

Lomonosov field near Arkhangelsk might change that. In terms of weight, shown in illus. 89, Russia is the biggest producer, with 43,161,058.83 carats, a share of 29.1 per cent, followed by Botswana (16.4 per cent), Canada (15.6 per cent) and Australia (9.5 per cent). South Africa's old mines still produce a little over 99,000 carats, or 6.7 per cent, while Angola is not far off with a share of 5.7 per cent.[3] The old fields in Brazil and India have all but disappeared, while there was no official production in Indonesia. In terms of financial value, the picture is a bit different (see illus. 90). Russia still tops the ranking, with a share of 27.5 per cent, but Botswana's share of 24.4 per cent comes closer, while Australia's share is much lower, with 1.3 per cent, only half the share of Lesotho, which produces much less in terms of weight. This, of course, has everything to do with the quality of diamonds, which can best be assessed by comparing price per carat ratio (us$/carat). The most valuable stones come from Namibia (469.4), Liberia (401.8) and Lesotho (291.5). The cheapest, mainly industrial diamonds, come from the DRC (8.3), Australia (12.9) and the Central African Republic (22.7).

In 2018 Brazil's rough diamonds were worth u.s.$219/carat, and India's $215/carat, relatively high numbers which show that history still counts for something. While countries with a long diamond history are still yielding these precious stones, and new producing countries are emerging, today's diamond mining has become a truly global affair, which is reflected in the number of companies in control of mining and whose activities often extend over various continents. This last chapter deals with the loss of De Beers' monopoly, by looking at the emergence of diamond-mining industries in Russia, Australia and Canada, and the renewed efforts to find diamondiferous kimberlites near the old alluvial fields of Asia and South America.

The Retreat to Botswana

By the end of the twentieth century the monopoly that De Beers enjoyed in the diamond industry, and the control it had over the mining and selling of rough diamonds worldwide, was a thorn in the side of both the mining companies who tried to be pretenders to the throne and the American authorities. During its diamond reign, De Beers had come under severe scrutiny for two reasons. The first was political and had everything to do with the company's activities in countries with dubious regimes and long-lasting violent strife.[4] The second was economic. While De Beers' involvement in the apartheid system was occupying the attention of miners, activists and politicians, the u.s. Department of Justice had been increasing pressure on the company.

De Beers was indicted by an American court for a first time in 1945, accused of violating the Sherman Antitrust Act of 1890. The De Beers cartel was accused of circumventing the Act by selling to American sightholders in London and by its construction of a web of three hundred different companies and corporate aliases to enter the United States.[5] The Justice Department dismissed the case in 1948, but this was only the beginning of legal troubles for De Beers in the USA.[6] The company was prosecuted for a second time in 1974, when De Beers and two American companies were accused of price fixing and secretly partitioning the American market for low-grade industrial diamond grit. De Beers' corporate web proved again difficult to disentangle, but sufficient evidence was brought forward to settle with De Beers Industrial Diamonds in Shannon,

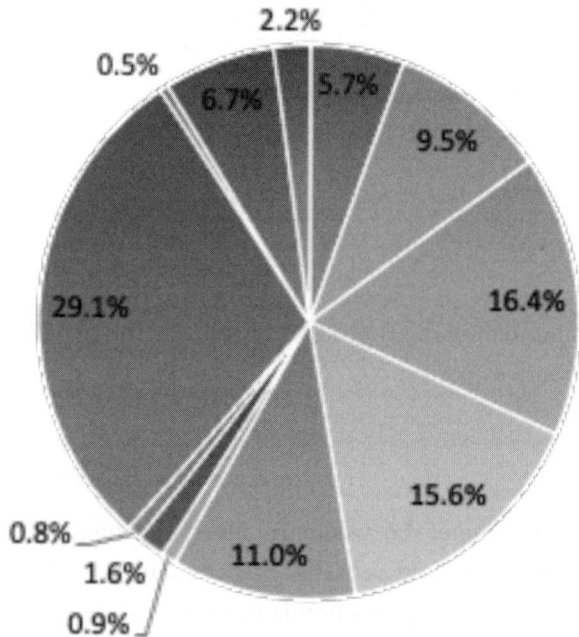

- Angola
- Australia
- Botswana
- Canada
- D. R. Congo
- Lesotho
- Namibia
- Other
- Russian Federation
- Sierra Leona
- South Africa
- Zimbabwe

89 National share in official global rough diamond production in weight in carats, 2018.[7]

- Angola
- Australia
- Botswana
- Canada
- D. R. Congo
- Lesotho
- Namibia
- Other
- Russian Federation
- Sierra Leona
- South Africa
- Zimbabwe

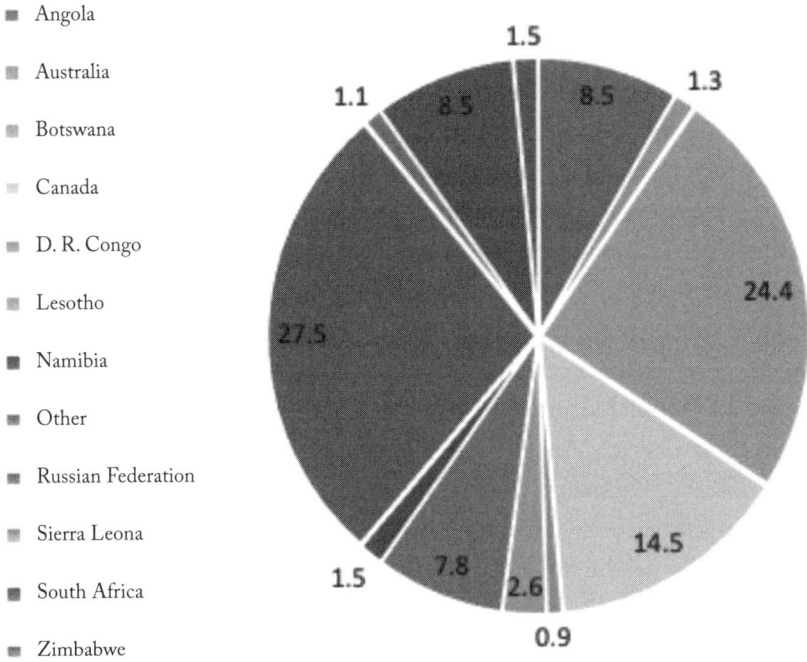

90 National share in official global rough diamond production in financial value in
u.s. dollars, 2018.[8]

Ireland, for a sum of $40,000.[9] It was a small victory, and the main com-
pany in South Africa had remained beyond reach of the American legal
system for a second time.[10] Undeterred, De Beers was forced to appear
before an American court for a third time in 1994, through its Swiss subsidiary De Beers Centenary AG. The company and General Electric were
accused of price fixing and of secretly dividing the market for synthetic
diamonds. Together, they controlled about 80 per cent of the market in the
commodity.[11] While General Electric was acquitted, De Beers was not let
off the hook, and the case dragged on until De Beers pleaded guilty and
accepted a fine of $10 million.[12] It was a major defeat for the enterprise,
and the beginning of the legal defeat of De Beers in the United States.
In 2001 two lawsuits on price fixing had been filed in New Jersey and
New York, and five others followed in Arizona, California and New York.
De Beers' cartel was accused of monopolization and the artificial maintenance of high prices.[13] Plaintiffs included diamond buyers purchasing
directly from De Beers, as well as a group of jewellers and retailers who

purchased from sightholders. At first De Beers kept up its usual defence to challenges from American jurisdiction, denying any direct involvement in the American market, but the defeat in 2004 made the company change course, and the following year a settlement was reached for $295 million. De Beers appealed in 2011, without result, and a final request for the case to be reviewed was denied in 2012. De Beers promised to comply with U.S. law and consequently was able to operate directly on the American market, which accounted for 45 per cent of global sales in jewellery.[14]

It was an important evolution, as the world of diamonds in 2012 was no longer the exclusive domain of De Beers. Diamond production had globalized with the discoveries of immensely rich diamond deposits in Canada, Australia and Russia, where new mining companies were formed. De Beers managed to strike a deal for Russian diamonds early on, but it was cancelled by the European Commission in 2010. In Australia producers had agreed to sell through De Beers' CSO, but they left in 1996. De Beers was a latecomer in Canada, and the country's two main diamond mines operated outside of the cartel. De Beers had lost its monopoly in production, but also in sales, and suffered from new and dynamic competition. The marketing director of mining company Rio Tinto in Australia remarked that 'nobody realizes about De Beers – just how moth-eaten they really are. Their arrogance has bred inefficiency. They have not adjusted to business realities.'[15] Nonetheless they tried: in 2011 Anglo-American bought the 40 per cent share of the Oppenheimer family in De Beers, ending the chairmanship of Harry's son Nicky Oppenheimer.[16]

The biggest move, though, was the company's relocation to Botswana. The country had gained independence in 1966, before which time it was known as the Bechuanaland Protectorate. In 1967 and 1968 two kimberlite pipes were discovered: the Orapa, second largest in the world, and the Letlhakane (see illus. 36). De Beers established Debswana, a partnership with the state, to explore these mines, but the best was yet to come, when the Jwaneng mine, then the world's richest diamond mine, entered its productive phase in 1982 (illus. 91). The three mines contained high-quality diamonds, and by 2007 Orapa and Letlhakane had produced 15.5 million carats, and the Jwaneng mine a little over 26 million. The total is higher than South Africa's entire historical production.[17] It was no surprise, perhaps, that in 2006 De Beers established a separate

Diamond Trading Company in Botswana to sort, classify and value the diamonds there.[18] Seven years later, in 2013, the system of sales on sights was transplanted from London to Gaborone, Botswana's capital, following a ten-year agreement with the government. Employees were transferred, new offices were built and a new corporate structure was created, in which De Beers was owned by two shareholders, Anglo-American (85 per cent) and the government of Botswana (15 per cent).[19]

In 2021, De Beers is mining in four countries. In South Africa, it operates the Voorspoed and Venetia open-pit mines (see illus. 36), but the latter, South Africa's highest-producing mine, is in the process of going underground.[20] Mining at the Namaqualand alluvial deposits has been suspended, while De Beers sold most of its historical mines to Ekapa Minerals in 2016.[21] In Botswana, the equal partnership between De Beers and the government, Debswana, operates four open-pit mines: Damtshaa, Letlhakane, Orapa (the world's largest open-pit mine) and the Jwaneng, which yields on average the most valuable diamonds. In Namibia, an equal partnership with the state, Namdeb, the successor of CDM, is work-ing at offshore and coastal deposits using five vessels, with a sixth under construction.[22] Canadian activities are divided over two mines in the Northwest Territories – Snap Lake and Gahcho Kué, the latter only entering its productive phase in 2016 – and the Victor mine in Ontario (see illus. 99).[23] Total production was estimated to occupy about a third of the global sales market for rough diamonds. De Beers still sells to 101 selected sightholders, with thirteen accredited buyers and three sight-holders for industrial diamonds, buying at sights held ten times per year simultaneously in Gaborone, Kimberley and Windhoek.[24]

Diamonds under the Snow of Russia's Far East

The waning of De Beers' monopoly was not only due to direct attacks on the company and its ethical policy, it had to do with geography. There were still areas where it was difficult for De Beers to control mining, mainly the alluvial sites in West and Central Africa. Similarly, artisanal mining as it continued in Brazil, Borneo and India yielded so little profit that De Beers, even though it obtained certain concessions in these countries, decided against establishing mining operations. But there were other dia-mond deposits that escaped control by De Beers, and some were so rich

91 Jwaneng mine, Botswana, 2020.

that they tipped the balance in favour of oligopoly. Angola is one example, and the state company Endiama is a mining giant, while Russia is another. In 2018 Russian diamonds accounted for 29.1 per cent of global production in weight, and 27.5 per cent in financial value, making the country the largest producer of diamonds on earth. The success story of Russian diamonds began to take shape during the 1950s, when Soviet prospectors discovered very rich kimberlite pipes in the Sakha Republic (formerly Yakutia), in the Russian Far East, but the presence of diamonds in Russia had already been noticed more than a century earlier.[25]

In 1830 a Dutch newspaper reported that diamonds had been found in the Ural Mountains, 'not inferior to those from Brazil'.[26] The article added that Professor M. van Engelhardt had already visited that region four years earlier. Moritz von Engelhardt (1779–1842) was a naturalist working at the University of Dorpat (now Tartu in Estonia) between 1820 and 1830, and he had indeed undertaken a scientific journey to the Urals in 1826. Upon his return he wrote a letter to his university rector in which he pointed out mineralogical similarities between the area he visited and the Brazilian diamond region, suggesting diamonds might be found in the Urals. The letter was originally published in the *Journal de St Petersbourg* but found its way to the international press: 'the platinum sand of Nijny-Toura, which belongs to the royal factory at Koushra, bears a striking resemblance to that of Brazil, in which diamonds are usually found.'[27]

The Dutch newspaper *Groninger Courant* continued the story by attributing the first discovery of a diamond in Russia to a thirteen-year-old boy named Paul Popov, made in June 1829 during an expedition undertaken by the famous Prussian explorer, geographer and naturalist Alexander von Humboldt (1769–1859). The previous year he had been invited by the Russian minister of finance, whose father was a mineralogist, to go to the Urals to investigate gold and platinum deposits for the tsar. Humboldt, who had already travelled extensively in South America, was struck by geological and mineralogical similarities between Brazilian mountains and the Urals, although his comparison between rock structures in the Old and the New World did not bring him to the conclusion that there might be diamonds in the Urals.[28] Perhaps Humboldt's meeting with Engelhardt in Dorpat changed his mind and, before he set out, Humboldt promised the tsarina he would bring back some precious stones for her.[29] One of the participants in the expedition was Adolphe de Polier, a French officer in Russian service, member of the Russian Academy of Science and husband of a wealthy Russian countess, Varvara Petrovna. Like Humboldt, de Polier was convinced of the existence of Russian diamonds and instructed several men to look for them on the land near Yekaterinburg, which led to Popov's discovery.[30]

After Humboldt's expedition, several diamonds were found in the Ural Mountains, all between 1.5 and 5.5 carats. In 1836 a French magazine wrote that, thus far, only 35 diamonds had been found.[31] The dominant opinion was that these discoveries had scientific merit but were of no commercial value: the stones were small and occurred only rarely, while some doubted whether the Ural diamonds were genuine.[32] No further efforts were undertaken to establish a mining industry, and the Bolshevik government contented itself with selling jewellery and diamonds that had been confiscated after the Revolution of 1917. A scientific programme to compare the geology of the world's diamonds fields with that of the USSR was set up in 1937, and one of its participants was a geologist named Vladimir Sobolev (1908–1982).[33] More than a century after Humboldt had looked for diamonds in the Ural Mountains, Sobolev, a former student at the Leningrad Mining Institute, published a monograph in which he predicted the existence of diamonds in Yakutia in Russia's Far East, based on a comparison with South Africa.[34]

Shortly after the end of the Second World War, the Soviets made diamond prospecting a priority, as they were hoping to cater for their demand for industrial diamonds from domestic deposits instead of purchasing them through cso in London.[35] In 1948 a team that had set out from Irkutsk discovered the first Yakutian diamond in a tributary of the Nizhnaya Tunguska river. The expedition soon moved on to explore the Vilyuy river, where a diamond was found in August 1949 by Grigorii Fainshtein. A permanent settlement was created at Nyurba on the banks of the Vilyuy (see illus. 92) to coordinate all efforts in the hunt for diamonds, but activities only accelerated when kimberlite was discovered at the Olyenok river, north of the Vilyuy, leading to the development of the Leningrad kimberlite pipe.[36] These discoveries had immediate repercussions on the international diamond market, and the Belgian diamond workers' union communicated that Soviet purchases had fallen from between 8,000 and 9,000 carats of diamonds each month in 1949 to 40 carats in January 1950, with none at all in February and March. There were rumours in Antwerp that the Soviets had either discovered large deposits or a more efficient way of producing synthetic diamonds.[37]

Activities at the Leningrad pipe remained secretive, and the first official discovery of a diamondiferous kimberlite pipe was reported in 1954, when a geology student and war hero named Larisa Popugaeva discovered the Zarnitsa pipe. Initially the discovery was not recognized as hers and she was even fired from her job at the All-Union Geological Institute in Leningrad, now St Petersburg, but she was later reinstated.[38] New discoveries soon followed, reported in secret code. When Yuri Khabardin found the Mirny ('Peace') kimberlite pipe in July 1955, he sent a coded telegram to the Ministry of Geology with the message that 'we smoked the pipe of Peace, the tobacco is excellent.'[39] The Mirny pipe indeed contained a relatively high percentage of diamonds of gemstone quality. The mine became operational in 1957 and was closed in 2004. Today it is the second largest man-made hole on the planet, after the Bingham Canyon copper mine near Salt Lake City (illus. 93).

Within ten days of the Mirny discovery, the Udachnaya pipe ('Success') was found, which turned out to be very productive and rich in gem-quality diamonds (illus. 94). Before the end of 1956 more than

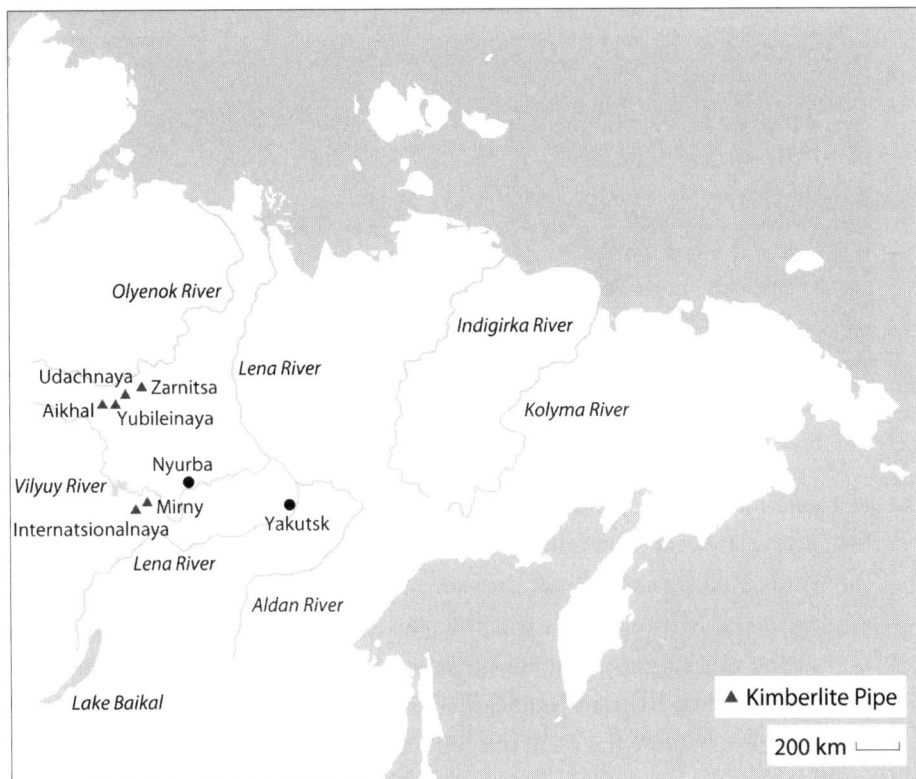

92 Diamond deposits in Siberia.

five hundred kimberlite pipes had been located, although not all of them were diamondiferous. The most important ones were the Sytykanskaya pipe, which was discovered in 1955 and entered production in 1979, the Twenty-Third Party Congress pipe (1959 and 1966), the Aikhal pipe (1960 and 1962), which is 450 km from Mirny and practically in the Arctic Circle, the Internatsionalnaya (1971), near Mirny, and the Yubileinaya (1975; illus. 95).[40] In 1998 some 1,000 kimberlite pipes were known to exist: 150 of these contain diamonds, with seven able to produce diamonds in a manner that has proven to be commercially viable.[41]

The potential impact of these Russian finds was not immediately recognized abroad. In 1956, under the headline 'Large diamond fields in Siberia? Dutch diamond circles not worried', a Dutch newspaper quoted two diamond merchants dismissing news from Yakutia as perhaps nothing more than propaganda.[42] But it was much more than that. When Nikita Krushchev took office as first secretary in 1953, he declared that a Soviet

93 Mirny mine, Siberia, 2014.

diamond industry should be fully developed.[43] At the 21st Party Congress, held a year later, the Yakutalmaz Trust was established (a combination of the words Yakutia and *almaz*, Russian for diamond). This was to begin mining at the Mirny pipe. It was the start of a period of industrialization of the mining area, with severe consequences for the environment and the local non-Russian people, the Vilyuy. The town of Mirny, on the Irelyakh river, became the main mining settlement, and other settlements

94 Udachnaya mine, Siberia, 2004.

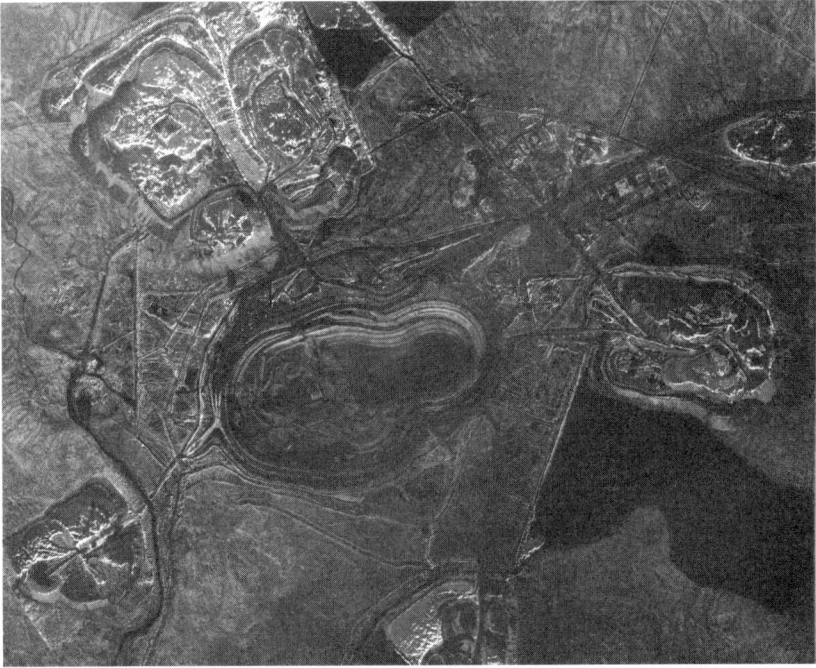

95 Yubileinaya mine, Siberia, 2020.

were built at Aikhal, Udachnaya and Irelyakh. From 1956 onwards, tens of thousands of labourers came to work in the diamond industry.[44] Many of them came from Ukraine, Belorussia and the European part of Russia, leading to the growth of the local population.[45] Soviet propaganda, however, focused more on images in which nature and industry went hand in hand (illus. 96).

On the Vilyuy river at Chernyshevskiy, northwest of Mirny, the Vilyuy Hydroelectric Station, a dam and power plant, was built to provide the mining towns with electricity, and a state farm system was expanded to provide food.[46] All these investments were necessary, but life remained hard. Yakutia is vast, remote and isolated due to the lack of a transportation network. A winter climate reigns for seven months, and Yakutia's climate has been dubbed the 'most severe of the inhabited world', with average temperatures varying between -43.5°c in January and 19°c in July.[47] The weather makes machinery freeze, steel snap, and the summer thaw necessitates the use of steel poles driven into the permafrost when constructing buildings. Not only were the climatological circumstances harsh, work was as well. The local mining management was given a great deal of freedom in how it operated, as long as rough diamonds kept arriving in Moscow. Yakutalmaz's first offices in Mirny were set on fire, and a strike broke out during the first year of mining there.[48] None of this discouraged the government, now fully aware of the diamond potential in the Asiatic part of the USSR, but it was soon realized that further financial investment was needed. Industrial diamonds were needed at home, but it was perhaps time to consider selling Russian gem-quality diamonds abroad.[49]

The Soviets and De Beers

To sell diamonds on the international market, the USSR needed to strike a deal with De Beers, whose CSO controlled the world's diamond trade. De Beers was worried about the developments behind the Iron Curtain. It had been the company's policy to reach agreements with outside producers to buy up production, something they had practised with a great deal of success in Africa, but the Soviet Union was of a different order. In 1957, when Harry Oppenheimer succeeded his father as De Beers' chairman, he sent his cousin Philip to Moscow to negotiate the Soviets' inclusion into the diamond cartel. De Beers' offer to buy all of Russia's gem-quality diamonds at renegotiable prices was accepted, although it was always a risky deal for the South Africans, as no one really knew how much the Yakutian pipes were producing: 'Soviet trading statistics do not itemise the level of diamond exports – if they exist.'[50] The details of the agreement negotiated by Philip Oppenheimer remained secret as well. When Western media reported on the deal in early 1960, they pointed out that it was a remarkable alliance, but one that guaranteed stability of current price levels for diamonds.[51]

The deal was renegotiated each year, duly communicated by Western media, but the political context became increasingly difficult.[52] South Africa and the Soviet Union had suspended diplomatic relations in 1957, right before Philip flew to Moscow, after the South African government accused the Soviets of a communist conspiracy aimed at overthrowing the apartheid government. Soviet foreign policy at the time aimed at driving a wedge between the West and its African colonies, and the USSR was considered a natural ally by several African anti-colonial movements.[53] Pressure mounted after the Sharpeville massacre of 21 March 1960, but

96 USSR stamp: Yakut Autonomous Soviet Socialist Republic, 1972.

it was only in 1963 that Harry Oppenheimer announced the agreement with the Soviets had come to an end. The *Daily Mail* reported the next year that 'no more Russian diamonds are to be sold by De Beers', stating that the company was 'angry at the Soviet support for the boycotting of South African trade'.[54]

Secretly, however, the agreement remained in effect, through a company named City East-West Ltd, which channelled Soviet diamonds through London.[55] Harry Oppenheimer admitted in 1978 that the only reason for secrecy had been the Soviet desire to stay out of the spotlight, and Harry's son Nicky later explained that ideological differences were put aside for commercial interest.[56] In exchange for selling 90 to 95 per cent of its gem-quality rough diamonds, the Soviets received hard currency and a supply of high-grade industrial diamonds from De Beers, which it needed but could not produce itself: 5 per cent of Soviet gemstone production was exempt from the agreement and was cut and polished in the Soviet Union or in other Eastern European countries.[57]

The agreement guaranteed De Beers continued control over the diamond market and prices, and gave them some political leeway in Africa. Angolan independence put the MPLA in charge in 1975, and they soon questioned the existing deal with De Beers. Soviet officials managed to convince the Angolan government not to switch to the competition.

Both the USSR and De Beers agreed to cooperate more closely from 1976 onwards, through an exchange of technology. A Soviet engineer was sent to the Letseng mine in Lesotho, and in return a group of De Beers personnel was allowed to visit one of the Soviet kimberlite pipes.[58] The Soviets had been able to improve the diamond-selection process through a method called X-ray luminescent separation, which relied on the emission of light by diamonds when exposed to X-rays. Machinery can use that process to separate diamonds of smaller sizes from their surrounding ore than the industry was able to do before.[59]

The Soviet Union was well aware that the vastness of their diamond deposits gave them a powerful negotiating position against De Beers, and at times they tested De Beers' patience, particularly in the early 1970s. In 1973 the *Financial Times* reported that the USSR was exploring the idea of selling directly to Antwerp.[60] A faction within government also wished to develop a domestic cutting industry. At the time, only three Soviet cutting factories, in Moscow, Smolensk and Kiev, were operational, each employing between 2,000 and 4,000 workers. Under the name Kristall, 24 cutting factories were set up, but proved unable to process Soviet production, which was still expanding and too large to be processed domestically.[61] Still shrouded in mystery, Yakutia's diamond fields were estimated to produce 10.3 million carats in 1977.[62] That year Harry Oppenheimer declared that De Beers had paid more than $500 million to the Soviet Union for its diamonds.[63] A great deal of the Soviet exports during the 1970s were 'silver bears', stones of high purity, silver colour and a size of up to 0.25 carats before cutting. For De Beers to absorb this additional production, time was needed, as well as a new marketing campaign. Silver bears were set in 'eternity rings', given by husbands to their wives as a symbol of 'enduring love' and 'rekindled romance'.[64] The irony was not lost on later scholars: 'to meet Soviet needs for hard currency, a South African corporation persuaded American men to buy their wives a luxury good with no practical value.'[65]

After the Communist Collapse

In 1988 Mikhail Gorbachev altered the organization of Russian mining, with both the gold and diamond mining industries being brought under the umbrella of the Administration of Diamonds and Gold (Glavalmazzoloto).[66] Two years later, De Beers made a deal with the

Soviet government that was roughly the same as previous agreements, but which also included a $5 billion loan to the government to invest in the diamond industry, with Soviet diamond stock as a guarantee. In May 1990, Boris Yeltsin was elected as chairman of the Supreme Soviet of the Russian Soviet Federative Socialist Republic, against Gorbachev's will, and he immediately protested that Russia had not been consulted about the diamond deal. A power struggle broke out in which the Soviet government, the Russian Parliament and the Republic of Sakha (former Yakutia) all claimed legal ownership over Sakha's diamonds. The collapse of the Soviet Union further fuelled these diamond wars.[67]

A minerals law issued in February 1992 promised the republics and local governments a more equal share in mining profits, and a month later Boris Yeltsin promised Sakha, now an autonomous republic within Russia, and whose mineral deposits were so crucial to the Russian economy, 20 per cent of the profits of gem-quality diamond sales and full profits for its industrial stones. It caused a rift between Yeltsin and the Parliament, which felt Sakha was given too much, and which tried to stop the establishment of Alrosa, Almazy Rossii-Sakha (Diamonds of Russia and Sakha), a joint-stock company that was responsible for diamond mining, sorting, grading, cutting and marketing.[68] Originally Russia and Sakha each owned 32 per cent, Alrosa's 50,000 employees 23 per cent, eight local governments 1 per cent each, and a social security fund for the military owned 5 per cent.[69] Profits were to be divided accordingly. Yeltsin managed to issue a special decree, bypassing Parliament in the creation of Alrosa. When the company finally came into being in 1993, Russian fears grew that Sakha got the better deal and that it would use its share in Alrosa to build its own cutting industry, to the detriment of existing factories in Russia. Sakha had indeed begun to set up its own cutting factories in 1991, and three years later Tuymaada Diamond had nine hundred employees in six factories.[70] Today, Tuymaada Diamond advertises itself as 'the largest producer of polished diamonds in the Republic of Sakha', buying rough stones directly from Alrosa.[71] There are also cutting industries still active in former Soviet republics such as Armenia, which remain tied to the global diamond commodity chain.[72]

The Republic of Sakha managed to use its political influence and economic riches to negotiate a better position in relation to Russia, but the latter retained a major share in Alrosa, which continued to grow in the following years. By mid-1996 it was clear that Alrosa had gained control over Russia's diamond production, despite heavy internal resistance, mainly coming from state officials who had worked at governmental organizations hitherto responsible for diamond production and export, such as the Committee of Precious Metals and Precious Stones, or Gohkran, the state repository for precious metals and stones that was established in 1996. The monopolistic position of Alrosa was not accepted by everyone, particularly considering the company's close link to Sakha's government. The growing independence of Sakha, fuelled by its importance to Russia's finances, was met with resistance within Russia's political class, as too much self-government for Sakha could set a dangerous precedent.

The deal between Russia and De Beers came under heavy internal attack as well. Ever since the collapse Russia had become a difficult partner for De Beers, as it used different channels through which it sold rough gem-quality diamonds on the market outside of the cartel. In 1994 this led to the fear that the old adage of never-declining prices for rough diamonds, protected by De Beers since the early days of its inception, would finally come to an end.[73] Negotiations were taking place between Russia and De Beers in 1995, with the agreement delayed by internal political forces in Russia that did not want a victorious Alrosa–De Beers tandem. Perhaps the most ferocious opposition came from the association that represented Russia's domestic cutting industry. One of the main obstacles was Alrosa's promise to end cutting on consignment, the practice by which Sakha rough diamonds were sent abroad for cutting, after which they returned to Russia to be sold as Russian-cut stones.[74] Voices lamenting the control of a foreign company over Russia's own diamond deposits were never silenced completely either, but in November 1998 the *Financial Times* reported that a deal had been reached: Alrosa promised to sell at least $550 million dollars' worth of rough diamonds through De Beers, representing half of Russia's financial value of production, while it could sell 5 per cent of this production outside cso.[75] It was a welcome deal for both sides. Russia needed money, while De Beers had been hit hard two years earlier by the decision of Australian producer Ashton Joint Venture (AJV) to abandon the sales cartel, reducing De Beers' control to 60 per cent of the market.[76] Nicky Oppenheimer, chairman of De Beers between 1998 and 2012, declared that the financial crisis in Asia and subsequent decline in demand forced producers to work together, and it was in De Beers' interest to reduce Russian sales outside the cartel to an absolute minimum.[77]

In 2002 the European Commission judged that the deal between the two largest producers of rough diamonds was a breach of antitrust legislation. De Beers proposed to fade out Russian purchases and fully stop them in 2009, but Alrosa objected and a legal battle ensued. The Commission's original decision, however, was upheld in 2010. Alrosa was listed on the Moscow Stock Exchange in 2011. A 16 per cent stake was sold by Russia two years later; currently the Russian Federation holds 43.93 per cent of the company, the Sakha Republic 25 per cent, district administrations of Sakha 8 per cent and other legal entities and individuals 23.07 per cent.[78] By that time De Beers had relocated to Botswana, and in 2015, both De Beers and Alrosa were among the co-founders of a new producers' association. Alrosa had already developed its own marketing arm in 1996, the United Selling Organization in Moscow, which now took full care of sorting, evaluating and selling Russia's diamonds.[79]

Alrosa had become big by controlling the production of Russian diamonds, but as early as its establishment in 1992 the mining company had been looking for opportunities to expand its activities, both domestically and internationally. In 1997 it became a partner holding a 33 per cent share in the Catoca Mining Company, which was exploiting the Catoca pipe in Angola (see illus. 82).[80] At home, Alrosa quickly developed an interest in three diamondiferous fields that had originally been discovered in 1979 in the Arkhangelsk Kimberlite Province of European Russia, near the White Sea: the Zolotitskoye, Kepinskoye and Verkhotinskoye fields.[81] Zolotitskoye was deemed to contain commercially viable diamond deposits, which were named the Lomonosov deposits. Severalmaz, a closed joint-stock company, was founded in 1992 to develop the Lomonosov cluster, located within the Zolotitskoye field, which was considered viable with an initial estimate of 50 per cent gem-quality stones.[82] Alrosa started to prospect the area in the late 1990s, and eventually secured 99.6 per cent of Severalmaz. The Alrosa subsidiary currently employs more than 1,600 people in Lomonosov, 'Europe's largest primary diamond deposit', which consists of six kimberlites, most still awaiting further development. Mining activities are taking place at two pipes, the Arkhangelskaya (since 2005), with a production of 1.37 million carats in 2014, and the Karpinskogo-1, where mining started in 2014.[83] Other promising mining projects came into the hands of other companies: the Grib diamond mine, for example, changed ownership various times and was sold by Lukoil in 2016 for $1.45 billion, without being fully operational.[84]

The results of further prospecting in Russia's Far East by Alrosa have also contributed to heightened production, such as the Nyurba open-pit mine, operational since 2001, and the Botuobinskaya kimberlite pipe, discovered in 1994 and entering production in 2015, the first new Russian pipe to do so in ten years. Its estimated reserve is 71 million carats, a little more than half of the world's diamond production in 2014.[85] Apart from establishing production at newly discovered deposits, Alrosa's main twenty-first-century challenge has been the transformation of several of the older open-pit mines into underground operations, such as those at Internatsionalnaya (1999), Aikhal (2005) and Mirny (2009).[86] Conversion started at the Udachnaya pipe in 2014. By the time the underground mine reaches its expected capacity, it will have become Russia's largest diamond mining site.[87]

Gems in the Australian Bush

By the early 1850s Australia had gained some independence from the British Empire, but it was still formally a colony when a gold rush drove many adventurers to New South Wales and Victoria on Australia's south-eastern coast.[88] In January 1853 *The Times* reported that the surveyor-general of New South Wales had found a fine diamond of 0.75 carats in one of the gold-digging areas.[89] Several later reports on diamond discoveries were fake, such as the news published by the *Melbourne Argus* in 1869 about a diamond the size of a 'turkey's egg', which made it into the British press. The egg turned out to be a crystal.[90] The same year, the *Glasgow Herald* published an extensive article on the state of diamond exploration in Australia. Prospectors were working on the Cudgegong river (see illus. 97), where some steam machinery was used, but discoveries were also reported near Sebastopol in Victoria and Christchurch in New Zealand.[91] At least one diamond, weighing 5.625 carats, was sent from the Cudgegong area to Harry Emanuel in London to be cut and polished, but whether Emanuel had any further involvement in Australian diamonds is not known.[92]

From time to time the media reported on additional alluvial finds in Queensland (1887), South Australia (1894) and Tasmania (1899).[93] In

1898 several English newspapers reported on a 'wild rush' taking place at diamond fields in the Nullagine area in the state of Western Australia, a known gold field.[94] Several Australian miners had returned from prospecting in the Klondike or from the gold and diamond fields in South Africa, and brought back experience and a thirst for fortune. Albert F. Calvert claimed that 'I, myself, was to the best of my belief the first to detect in 1891, the presence of diamonds in the Nullagine conglomerates' (Calvert would then have been a nineteen-year-old 'gentleman explorer'). The *Financial Times*, however, was not convinced by Calvert's statements: 'lest the historian of the future should find himself at a loss in crediting the proper person with the honours of the "find", Mr. A. F. Calvert, abandoning his customary reserve and modesty, has bashfully stepped into the limelight.'[95] All in all, digging in New South Wales remained modest, and total production of the late 1800s and early 1900s has been estimated at about half a million carats, with about half of that mined at Copeton (170,000 carats) and Bingara (35,000 carats) (see illus. 97).[96] There was also some exploration in Western Australia, but only a few hundred diamonds turned up, none heavier than 3.5 carats.[97]

As in Russia, these early alluvial discoveries did not unearth Australia's full potential, and no diamond mining industry developed. A breakthrough only came decades later, in 1939, when two scientists named Arthur Wade and Rex Prider discovered a geological analogy between South African kimberlite and Western Australian lamproite, a type of volcanic rock that differs substantially from kimberlite.[98] The idea that rocks other than kimberlite could be diamondiferous was very promising, and was later taken up by scientists for other rocks such as nephelinite and basanite.[99] It took two more decades before Prider's findings culminated in the discovery of diamonds in lamproite, bizarrely enough in a region named Kimberley.[100]

By 1967 Australia's mineral potential had drawn the attention of Union Minière (UMHK), which was looking to expand internationally after their assets in the Congo had been nationalized by Mobutu. UMHK sent prospectors to Canada and Australia, and was quickly joined by Tanganyika Concessions Ltd (TCL), a British-Rhodesian company that had been one of the founding partners of UMHK. TCL had experience in mining in Northern Rhodesia (Zambia) and the North Katanga (the later Congolese Tanganyika province).[101] TCL established a branch in

Melbourne in 1969, Tanganyika Holdings Ltd (THL), and the two companies agreed UMHK would focus on base metals and THL on precious metals and diamonds.[102]

In May 1969 UMHK placed an advertisement in the *Sunday Times* looking for 'exploration geologists for field operations in Western Australia'. Applicants were instructed to send their letters to Mr E. Tyler of Tanganyika Holdings Ltd, Gresham Street, London.[103] Ewen Tyler had been a geology student at the University of Western Australia, where he had known Rex Prider, the scientist working on lamproite. After finishing his studies, Tyler went to work at the biggest gold mine in Tanzania. Two years before returning to Australia, Tyler provided UMHK with help in setting up a base there. When he did return himself, in 1969, Tyler brought Tanganyika Concessions and their interest in diamonds with him.[104] Before the end of the year more Australians had taken an interest in diamond exploration, after diamonds had been found in the Lennard river, near Ellendale in the Kimberley region.[105]

In September 1969 Rees Towie, chairman of Northern Mining Corporation (NMC), a company specializing in the extraction of iron ore, nickel and tin, had a pivotal conversation with Norman Stansmore, an engineer who had worked in South Africa. Stansmore told Towie that his great uncle had been part of an expedition into the Simpson Desert in 1896. When the group reached a spot two days' travel from Halls Creek in East Kimberley, the uncle accidentally shot himself and died. A large diamond was found on his body. Towie met up with his old school friend Ewen Tyler in 1972 and, enthused by Stansmore's story, decided to join forces with Tyler and a group of companies prospecting for diamonds in Kimberley, to create the Kalumburu Joint Venture.[106] In 1975 Conzinc Riotinto of Australia (CRA) joined the group, which was renamed Ashton Joint Venture (AJV). Ewen Tyler remained its chairman until 1990.[107] The joint venture started to explore the Kimberley region, with CRA emerging in 1977 as the managing company, but no commercially viable diamond deposits were found in the first years of operation.[108]

The same year that the Kalumburu Joint Venture was founded, a young geologist named Maureen Muggeridge (1948–2010) moved to Perth, where she found a job with Tanganyika Holdings and later married Rees Towie's son. In July 1979, while she was six months pregnant, Maureen discovered diamonds in a small river in Kimberley that flows

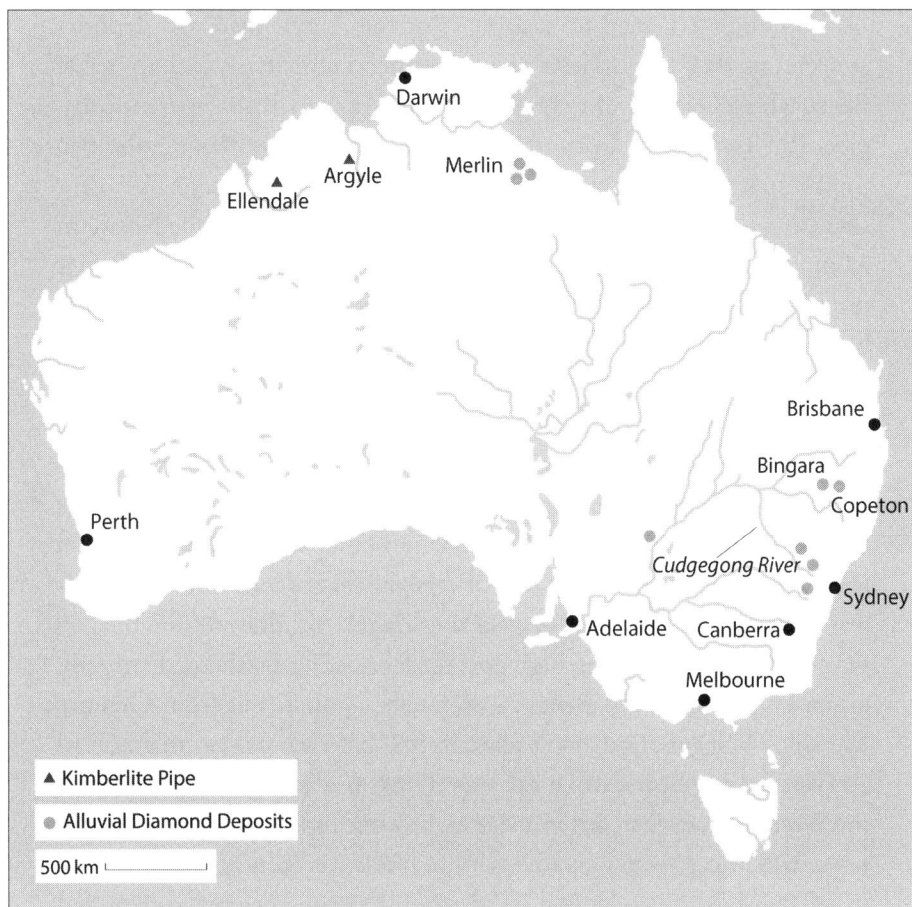

97 Diamond deposits in Australia.

into Lake Argyle. These were savannah lands, where temperatures could be as high as 45°c during the wet season. The competition was nearby, and Maureen hid her further efforts to find the source of the Smoke Creek diamonds: 'it all had to be hush-hush. You couldn't say you were looking for diamonds because that would spark too much interest.'[109] Further research showed that Maureen Muggeridge had discovered Australia's first (and at the time of writing only) economically viable diamondiferous lamproite pipe, the Argyle pipe (AKI), 25 kilometres (15 mi.) upstream from Lake Argyle (see illus. 97 and 98). This was 25 years after Larisa Popugaeva had found the first Russian kimberlite pipe.[110] Initially, it was believed that the Argyle deposits were kimberlitic, until further research showed that the host rock was Prider's diamondiferous lamproite.[111]

Although AJV tried to keep news of the Argyle diamond deposits as secret as they could, news reached concerned parties, including De Beers, which held shares in both CRA, through CRA's British parent company Rio Tinto Zinc Corporation (RTZ), and Ashton Mining, the two most important partners of the venture; in 1981 CRA held a 56.8 per cent share in AJV, and the Ashton Mining Group 38.2 per cent, while Northern Mining possessed a 5 per cent share.[112] Forecasts in 1981 predicted a yearly production between 20 and 25 million carats when the AKI pipe would be operational: 10 per cent gem-quality, 30 per cent near-gem and the remainder industrial. Argyle's deposits could be so rich in industrial diamonds as to provide for half the world's production. Further sampling of the lamproite demonstrated that the predicted ratio of carats per tonnes of earth was higher than expected.[113] It was not surprising that De Beers wanted to incorporate Argyle's production as rapidly as possible within their single-selling operation, CSO. The high yield of industrial diamonds was particularly interesting, considering Zaïre's withdrawal from the CSO in 1981 and the continuing high cost for fabricating synthetic diamonds, a market in which De Beers faced heavy competition from General Electric.[114] Negotiations took place in 1981 between CRA, as manager of Argyle, and De Beers, while AJV was trying to reach an agreement with the Western Australian government at the same time.[115] De Beers, hoping to control prices, found an adversary in Northern Mining, which aimed to sell its share of production independently, while the government had to deal with the parliamentary opposition, which was not happy to give control over mining to a company that was to a large extent controlled by foreigners – the South Africans of De Beers and the Malaysians involved in Ashton Mining. Nevertheless, a deal was struck that gave control over mining to AJV, in exchange for a system of royalty payments and the promise to construct a township for the mineworkers near Kununurra. CRA agreed with De Beers to enter single selling, on the same terms as most outside producers, thus preserving a small part of production for sales outside CSO, perhaps to cater for a local cutting factory in Perth.[116]

The preservation of a certain weight of diamonds to be processed locally was important to appease those arguing for strong economic protectionism, as political voices in India had been doing as well in an effort to preserve their own cutting industry. This stance was first defended by the opposition, but when they won the next elections, they changed course

98 Argyle mine, Australia, 2010.

and decided to go with the existing marketing agreement. It soon became clear, however, that the prospect of a cutting factory was an empty promise. Another source of friction was that AJV decided to fly their workers in from Perth, rather than constructing a township, as they had promised. The government decided to use the money reserved as compensation for the township to buy Northern Mining, which had been part of a takeover, to create a minor government participation in AJV through the Western Australian Diamond Trust (WADT).[117] Before the end of 1989, CRA and Ashton Mining had acquired control over WADT, giving De Beers the control over Argyle they wanted.[118] Open-pit mining at AK1 began in 1985 and production expanded rapidly, with 43 million carats mined in the peak year of 1994, 40 per cent of that year's global production in weight.[119] On average, Argyle diamonds are not of great quality, brown to near-white, with a mean size of less than 0.1 carats. The largest diamond mined at Argyle weighed 42.6 carats.[120] Argyle is very valuable because of the enormous size of its deposit, and the fact that it is the world's only consistent source for pink diamonds, producing more than 90 per cent of the world's supply.[121]

The agreement between Ashton Joint Venture and De Beers was renewed in 1986, allowing AJV to sell 25 per cent of production outside cso, and again in 1991, when De Beers also permitted independent sales of Argyle's pink diamonds. This almost unprecedented liberty led to the establishment of AJV's own marketing agency, with branches in Antwerp and Mumbai.[122] The high production of small diamonds at Argyle turned out to be the catalyst that made India's cutting industry the biggest in the world. Indian diamond workshops had existed in the early modern period but had become insignificant internationally by the time Indian diamond fields were exhausted in the nineteenth century, with output being sold domestically. Several Jain entrepreneurs attempted to set up trade operations in Antwerp during the interwar period, but it was only after the end of the Second World War and Indian independence in 1947 that several Indian businessmen, mainly Jains from Palanpur in Gujarat, set up firms there. The Indian government forbade imports of polished diamonds and jewellery, which led to a revival of the domestic cutting industry, relying on rough diamonds brought in from Antwerp. Lower labour costs enabled Indian factories to finish small stones that even the cutting industry in the Kempen could not process at a profit. Belgian cutters were recruited to train Indian diamond workers, and several Palanpuri firms managed to establish connections with the world's most important consumer market for jewellery, the United States. In the early 1960s Indian import restrictions were lifted, and the cso accepted several Indian entrepreneurs as sightholders.[123] Indian trade networks managed to reach a dominant position in Antwerp, with the concentration of 70 per cent of the city's current diamond trade in the hands of about three hundred Gujarati families.[124] The size of the cutting industry in India went from 30,000 cutters in 1967 to more than a million in 2004, while Antwerp's number of diamond workers shrank from 15,000 in 1965 to less than 150 in 2008.[125]

Independent trade in Australian diamonds contributed to the rise of India's cutting industry, but it also was an important step towards the demise of the De Beers' monopoly, and in 1996 AJV left the cso. Four years later the Argyle mine still produced an impressive 26.5 million carats.[126] The AJV was now reduced to two partners: Rio Tinto, which owned 59.7 per cent, and Ashton Mining Ltd., which held a 40.2 per cent share.[127] De Beers was not yet ready to accept defeat and made a bid to take over Ashton Mining in 2000, which was countered by a bid from Rio Tinto.[128] The Australian government was not keen on De Beers regaining control of Argyle's mining management, and Rio Tinto came out as victorious.[129]

The takeover bids had already pointed out diminished production and Rio Tinto, now the mine's sole owner, initiated Argyle's conversion into an underground block cave mine in 2005. The project was completed in 2013 and led to a reduction in employees to a total of 499, 43 per cent of which were locals from East Kimberley. By that time, alluvial and open-pit mining at Argyle had produced more than 800 million carats of rough diamonds. According to Rio Tinto, the conversion was to guarantee the continuation of mining with an average production of 20 million carats per year.[130] Reality, though, was harsher and Argyle's reserves have been going down so much that the decision was made to close the mine in 2020, rendering Australia's diamond future uncertain.[131]

While Argyle has produced the bulk of all of Australia's diamonds, efforts were made over the years to establish other viable lamproite pipe operations, particularly at Ellendale, where diamondiferous lamproite had been found in the early 1970s (see illus. 97). Two pipes, Ellendale A and B, managed by the Kimberley Diamond Company (KDC), became operational in 2003. Ellendale became famous for producing about half the world's supply of yellow diamonds, and KDC entered into a sales agreement with Tiffany's in 2010 to market these stones. Production at Ellendale entered a problematic phase in 2009, with the closure of Ellendale B.[132] Ellendale A was closed in July 2015, after KDC failed to pay its royalties to the government. One hundred workers lost their jobs, and KDC went into administration.[133] The parent company purchased the Lerala yellow diamond mine in Lesotho, financed by Chinese capital.[134] Later that year the Russian oligarch at the head of KDC was arrested at Sydney Airport, accused of providing misleading information to the stock market.[135] In January 2017 news came out that Australia's minister of mines was looking for a new operator to reopen Ellendale, after the mining companies paid $150,000 out of their mining rehabilitation fund for an environmental clean-up.[136] The Western Australian government announced in 2019 that they were in the process of leasing out tenements on the Ellendale mine again, with two Australian companies currently involved.[137] The minister responsible claimed that 'the department [of Mines, Industry Regulation, and Safety] consulted extensively with stakeholders including local government, Aboriginal interests, the police and pastoralists', a statement very much in line with present-day considerations on the impact of diamond mining on its immediate surroundings.[138]

One of the companies involved in the renewed Ellendale project is Gibb River Diamonds.[139] Its name clearly refers to its interest in developing alluvial mining prospects. Whether they will be successful remains an open question, but they are joining a long line of companies whose hopes of discovering new alluvial deposits had never disappeared since Australian diamond production had fully taken off in the 1980s. Only rarely were such hopes fulfilled. Between 1988 and 1995 about 7 million carats of diamonds were mined at the Bow river diamond field, 20 kilometres (12 mi.) northeast of the Argyle pipe.[140] Rio Tinto managed the Merlin alluvial fields in the Northern Territory, about 900 kilometres (560 mi.) from Darwin and located on sacred Aboriginal lands, between 1997 and 2003 (illus. 97).[141] During that time Australia's largest diamond, a white stone of 104.73 carats named Jungiila Bunajina ('Star Meteorite Dreaming Stone') was found.[142] Maureen Muggeridge left Tanganyika Holdings to pursue diamond exploration with her own Paramount Mining Corporation (PMC), but her unexpected death in 2010 also meant the end of PMC.

Adventures in Arctic Canada

In the spring of 1542 Jacques Cartier, the famous explorer whose voyages to North America were the basis for French claims on Canada, left Cap Diamant in Québec to return to his motherland. With him, he brought what he believed to be gold and diamonds, 'shining like sparks of fire when the sun illuminates them'.[143] The precious cargo turned out to be nothing more than iron pyrite and mica.[144] Cartier's misjudgement was immortalized in the French proverb 'faux comme un diamant du Canada' ('fake as a Canadian diamond'), an expression already mentioned by cosmographer André Thevet in the sixteenth century.[145] It would take several centuries before the realization that there was nothing fake about diamonds in North America. At the end of the eighteenth century, Jewish diamond trader Joseph Salvador had retreated to his plantation in South Carolina. In correspondence with his well-known scientific cousin Emmanuel Mendes da Costa in London, the latter suggested that the rivers on Salvador's lands might contain gold and precious stones, brought downstream from the Appalachian Mountains.[146]

Da Costa was not entirely wrong, and from the 1840s onwards small diamonds were sporadically found in the gold-digging areas of Georgia,

North Carolina, South Carolina and Alabama, all in the Appalachians. In the 1850s, after the great gold rushes of California and Oregon, a small number of diamonds were found in abandoned gold deposits.[147] A couple of diamonds were found in the Great Lakes region in the late nineteenth century, the largest weighing 21.25 carats.[148] Further minor discoveries were made in other states, with many rumours and false stories circulating, but nothing resulting in an exploitable diamond mine. In 1871, with diamond fever spreading internationally following the discoveries in South Africa, an employee of the Diamond Drill Company in San Francisco and his Kentucky cousin pretended to discover large finds of precious stones in the Rocky Mountains, which led to the establishment of several diamond companies, but their fraud was exposed in 1872.[149] Kimberlite was discovered in Kentucky fifteen years later.[150] Thus far, 27 of the USA's 50 states have produced diamonds, but these discoveries only carry scientific interest and have no commercial value.[151] It was calculated that, between 1908 and 1918, diamonds with a total worth of $27,749 (about £7,910) were mined on American soil. This amounts to roughly the same value as rough diamond production of Australia for the same period, but it is dwarfed by South African production for those years, which amounted to a value of almost £77.5 million.[152]

Today, at the Crater of Diamonds Park in Arkansas, the site of a former diamond mine, tourists can look for their own diamonds.[153] The only other diamond mine that has been operational in the USA was located in the State Line district, where the USA's most significant diamond discovery was made in 1959. The district is situated on the Colorado-Wyoming border, not far from the place used in the 1871 hoax. The State Line district is now the country's largest diamondiferous kimberlitic area and has yielded more than 130,000 industrial and gem-quality diamonds, although a small mine was only operational between 1996 and 2003. The largest diamond produced there weighed 23.8 carats.[154]

While American diamond mining did not amount to anything, history took a very different turn in Canada. Diamonds were found in Ontario in 1863 and 1920, followed by the finds of several small stones in Saskatchewan in 1962.[155] During the 1960s and '70s, further prospecting resulted in the location of kimberlites in Ontario, the Canadian Arctic Archipelago and Saskatchewan, where Monopros, a De Beers subsidiary, found a diamondiferous kimberlite pipe in 1989.[156] Although the discovery of these kimberlites did not lead to the discovery of rich deposits, it attracted the interest of other companies. The Texan company Superior Oil hired Canadian geologist Chuck Fipke to look for gems in North America. He located kimberlites in Colorado, but they did not contain commercially viable diamond deposits. Fipke went to Canada, where he established, with Superior's help, Dia Met, and focused on the Lac de Gras area north of Yellowknife in the Northwest Territories (see illus. 99). The Northwest Territories are sparsely populated, with only 39,460 inhabitants in an area of 1,183,084 square kilometres (nearly 500,000 sq. mi.). Lac de Gras is situated in the tundra, above the tree line.[157]

For several years no diamonds turned up, and Superior Oil abandoned its efforts to find them.[158] Fipke, however, continued and had a breakthrough when he decided to fly over the lake in a helicopter. It was then that he realized the kimberlite pipe was hidden underneath the lake. He brought in the Australian mining company BHP as a partner to provide additional investment, and by 1991 Dia Met had found the pipe and 81 diamonds.[159] News spread, and a diamond rush brought Monopros and more than fifty smaller companies to the Lac de Gras area, where in excess of 8 million hectares (19 million ac) of land was claimed for diamond exploration.[160] Some of the smaller 'junior' companies grouped their efforts, as was the case for DHK Diamonds, whose major partner was Rio Tinto. Competition was hard, with the presence of several international mining giants, and it was a matter of being the first to shift from exploration to exploitation. BHP had taken a head start, and their site was the first to have a processing mill, but Rio Tinto hoped it would catch up.[161]

The race for diamond exploration resulted in three major mines in the Northwest Territories, each operated by a big company (see illus. 99). The first to become operational was BHP's Ekati mine (meaning 'Fat Lake' in the local Tåîchô language), which was discovered in 1992. It is situated on leased Crown lands and consists of six open pits and two underground operations. Between its inauguration in 1998 and 2009, the mine has produced 40 million carats of rough diamonds.[162] In the reports submitted to the government assessing the impact of mining, BHP projected it would employ 830 people over a timespan of 25 years, and agreed to hire in Yellowknife, first from local indigenous populations, then from the local non-indigenous, and as a third option, other Canadians would be considered.[163] In 1999 BHP agreed to sell 35 per cent of its production through

De Beers, but the three-year contract was not renewed, and instead BHP sold its production through its offices in Antwerp.[164] The mine was sold in 2012 to the Dominion Diamond Corporation (DDC), formerly known as Harry Winston Diamond Corporation, after one of the early junior prospecting companies, Aber Diamond Corporation, purchased a majority in Harry Winston Inc.[165] They currently hold an 88.9 per cent share of the mine, as well as a 65.3 per cent claim on the neighbouring area. In 2013 the Ekati cluster produced 1.17 million carats, 20 per cent of which were industrial diamonds.[166] The largest diamond yet found at Ekati, weighing 186 carats, was sold for $2.8 million in 2016.[167]

Canada's second mine is the Diavik mine, also in the Lac de Gras area, discovered in 1994 and operational since 2003, in which year Canadian production jumped from 5 to 11 million carats (illus. 100).[168] It was discovered by Eira Thomas, the 'queen of diamonds', then a young geologist working for her father's company Aber. The mine was developed as a joint venture between Aber and Rio Tinto. DDC currently owns 40 per cent and Rio Tinto 60 per cent of a mine considered the 'highest-grade cluster of diamond pipes in the world'.[169] Diavik's production numbers passed 100 million carats in May 2016, and it is currently Canada's largest diamond mine.[170] Both mines are still expanding, contain a relatively high amount of gem-quality diamonds and produce the bulk of Canada's stones. They have also proven to be a crucial challenge to De Beers. At a time when the label of 'blood diamonds' had a strong impact on the public view of diamonds, Canada's reserves offered a clean alternative, and De Beers was not involved in the management of the country's biggest mines. It was another step towards De Beers' loss of its monopolistic position, but in 1999 the company did manage to purchase a diamond mine from Winspear Diamonds, one of the junior companies, at Snap Lake (see illus. 99).[171] The Snap Lake mine was the first underground diamond mine in Canada, and De Beers' first mine outside Africa. It is established on a kimberlite dyke rather than a pit.[172] De Beers currently operates two other diamond mines in Canada, the Victor mine in northern Ontario, and the Gahcho Kué mine in the Northwest Territories, which started production in 2016. Their reserves were estimated in 2007 at 75.9 million carats, 2.5 million carats less than the reserve at the Ekati mine.[173] Canada's three main diamond mines are all situated on the tundra of the Northwest Territories and are only accessible by air or winter ice roads.

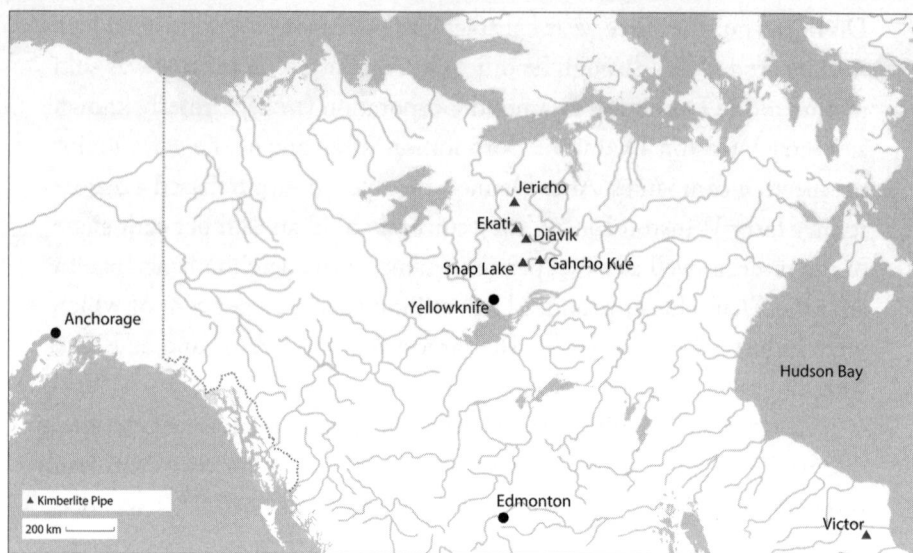

99 Diamond deposits in Canada.

In 2008 Ekati, Diavik and Snap Lake employed 2,500 people directly, producing 14 million carats valued at $2.08 billion.[174]

Canada produced about 14.8 million carats in 2008, making it the world's fifth largest supplier of rough diamonds that year in terms of weight.[175] Canadian stones are of good quality and on average were worth $152.3 per carat in 2008.[176] Four new companies were exploring the Northwest Territories in 2016, hoping to find new deposits.[177] Prospecting led to expanded production, and in 2018 Canada's production grew to 23.2 million carats, which meant a rise of 57 per cent within a decade, largely due to De Beers' expanded activities.[178]

The presence of diamonds in Canada and Russia has led scientists and field prospectors to speculate about the idea that diamond deposits could even occur further north. Russia has already placed a claim before the UN on a part of the Arctic Ocean it considers diamondiferous, the Lomonosov Ridge, which is disputed by Denmark and Canada.[179] In 2013 it was announced that kimberlites had been found on Antarctica, although it remains unclear whether these contain diamonds in a viable quantity.[180] Additionally, no mining is allowed on Antarctica, a prohibition that is unlikely to change anytime soon, particularly as in the twenty-first century the environmental impact of diamond mining has become an important consideration.

Never-ending Hopes on the Old Fields

Diamond mining in the twenty-first century is much more widespread than it has ever been. De Beers has lost its monopoly, Endiama and Alrosa are equal players in the field, which is still dominated by a small number of industrial companies operating open and underground pit mines built on kimberlite pipes, and there is an unknown mass of artisanal miners who continue to siphon riverbeds in the hopes of finding just what they need to improve their lives. The geographical theatre where all the mining is taking place is also larger than it has ever been; diamonds are being mined in Russia, Canada and Australia, and none of the African countries that revealed their shiny treasures since the late nineteenth century have been depleted of their diamondiferous reserves. The old glory of diamond mining in India, Borneo and Brazil pales in comparison to the large-scale industrial activities that are unfolding in many other places. But enough persons remain who hope that, in spite of the nineteenth-century downward spiral that continues to this day, the old mining areas have not quite shown everything they have. This continuing hope still attracts individual miners and small companies to diamond fields that have been active for centuries.

100 Diavik mine, Canada, 2016.

The hopes of those still working rivers in India, Borneo and Brazil are not merely based upon desire and fantasy.[181] The better geological understanding of the occurrence of diamonds in kimberlite after the discovery of diamonds in South Africa was applied to find similarities in other regions. At the end of the twentieth century, potentially diamondiferous kimberlites and lamproites have been located in several places in India, fuelling the hope that there might still be a future for Indian diamond mining.[182] In spite of these discoveries, however, only one kimberlite/lamproite occurrence is exploited commercially today, the Majhgawan diamond mine, 25 kilometres (15 mi.) from the city of Panna.[183] It is managed by a state company, the National Mineral Development Corporation (NMDC), founded in 1958, which also controls a number of iron ore mines. Environmental issues led to temporary closures,[184] and although the mine has a yearly production capacity of 84,000 carats, production has always been substantially lower, with a production of only 9,317.21 carats in 2009 and 26,989.58 in 2012, when NMDC employed 199 persons at their diamond mine. An approximate total of 1,005,064 carats had been mined at Majhgawan by that time.[185]

Government sources estimated in 2005 that the country's reserves were around 4.6 million carats.[186] Ongoing research, often on behalf of mining multinationals, has led to much higher estimates, and Anglo-Australian mining giant Rio Tinto began preparing to open a second diamond mine in India, the Bunder Project in Bundelkhand (Madhya Pradesh), where a diamond deposit of an estimated 27.4 million carats of diamonds has been located. The state of India approved the project in 2013, but in 2016 Rio Tinto decided to abandon it, doubting its viability. It came into the hands of the Madhya Pradesh government, which decided in June 2019 to auction the project, with several mining companies said to be interested, including the NMDC national company.[187] In December 2019 the mine was sold to an Indian multinational headquartered in Mumbai.[188] Rio Tinto has also discovered a potential diamond deposit in the south of Chattisgarh, in the Bastar region in central west India, located to the south of the unexploited area between the historical diamond mines of Wairagarh, Golconda and the sites on the Mahanadi (see illus. 5). Currently, no plans are scheduled for any exploitation as the region is considered too unsafe politically, with Maoist rebels highly active. The local government of Chattisgarh, however, has permitted several companies to explore areas further north, in the Korba Hills.[189] India's difficulties in setting up any structural operations can be seen in the production of the decade between 2009 and 2018, when 287,979.75 carats of diamonds were mined, representing a financial value of about $55 million – less than a third of Brazilian production for those years.[190]

Diamond production in Borneo had already been in decline for a long time. Even though Indonesian independence in 1949 had changed the political control of diamond mining on the island, the Dutch did not give up their economic interest in their former colony, and the Indonesian government decided it could continue to use Dutch diamond expertise. Joseph Asscher, scion of the famous Dutch Jewish diamond family, was in Jakarta in June 1965 negotiating with the government to exploit South Kalimantan's diamond mines as a joint venture between the Netherlands and Indonesia. Asscher, who remarked that mining thus far had taken place only in a 'very primitive manner', would bring the know-how and investments in trucks, jeeps, draglines and machines for washing, all to be imported from the Netherlands. He also promised to sell Indonesian stones in Amsterdam, while the Indonesians were to ensure the modernization of mining and good management. Asscher further hoped to develop diamond mining on Lombok and Sumatra.[191]

Interested in the proposition, the Indonesian government replied that circumstances were forcing them to seek wider control over its diamond mines, pointing out that Borneo was one of the few places where diamond mining was still ungoverned. They estimated that in the Cempaka district, 1,500 carats of rough diamonds were found per week, of which only five hundred were polished and traded in Martapura (illus. 101). The rest was smuggled to buyers in Java, Singapore, Bangkok and Hong Kong. By enhancing their grasp on the diamond mines with Dutch assistance, the Indonesians hoped to gain $200 million per year, as 90 per cent of the diamonds were considered of gemstone quality.[192] The cooperation with Asscher quickly led to, or coincided with, the discovery of a large diamond of 166.7 carats, estimated to be worth a million guilders. It had been found by a collective of 42 diamond miners, all belonging to the local Dayak people, and it was offered to President Sukarno, who promptly declared that South Kalimantan was richer in diamonds than South Africa's Kimberley region, and that the stones were of better quality. The miners received as a reward preferential treatment on the next pilgrimage to Mecca, and the discovery instigated so much excitement in Martapura that fires broke out, which were said to have caused as much damage as the value of the discovered stone.[193] Sukarno named the diamond the Tri Sakti, meaning the three principles, referring to Indonesia's pillars: political freedom, a culture based on Indonesian tradition and an independent economy.[194] The stone was cut by Asscher in Amsterdam, who showed the polished stone of 53 carats to the president, before it was sold to private owners, partially to cover Indonesian state debt.

Despite Asscher's offer and the optimistic presidential declarations about diamond deposits and modernization, the mining industry in Borneo remained in the same state as it had been for many years, with the persistence of traditional alluvial mining. In 1979 the discovery of a diamond of 30 carats led to a diamond fever attracting 4,000 adventurers to the fields.[195] In the 1980s fewer than five hundred miners were active at Cempaka on average, many of them Muslim farmers who took up diamond digging in the hope that a lucky discovery might pay for a pilgrimage to Mecca.[196] The realization grew that exhaustion was nigh, but in spite of the pessimistic undertone, periodic attempts to raise foreign capital for modernization continued. Unsurprisingly, Dutch firms, deprived both of their former colony and of the primacy of Amsterdam as a diamond centre, showed most interest. The Amsterdam Diamond Association decided to offer support for a modern diamond-cutting factory in Martapura.[197] During the 1970s a state-supported company named P. T. Aneka Tambang started to work in the Rian Kanan river, and although results were mixed, an Australian and an English company were lured to Borneo to mine for diamonds in a joint enterprise with it.[198] Eventually the companies merged to become Aneka Tambang (Antam), and their presence on the diamond fields has continued as a rare exception. Their report for 2013 shows that they held a 20 per cent stake in the Cempaka Diamond Project, processing alluvial diamonds in southeast Kalimantan, near Martapura (see illus. 14). The other 80 per cent was controlled by Gem Diamonds Ltd, registered in the British Virgin Islands, which owned diamond mines in Lesotho and Botswana.[199] For that year, the Kimberley Process statistics do not show any numbers for official Indonesian production, but in the five years between 2005 and 2009, the last year for which the Kimberley Process website contains data, 128,139.23 carats were produced in Indonesia, a 0.02 per cent share of world

101 Diamond mining, Cempaka, pre-1950.

production, 0.05 per cent when considering financial worth, indicating that Indonesia's diamonds were of a better quality than average.[200]

While activities continue at a low level in India and Borneo today, there are also countries in Asia that still hope to join the ranks of the diamond producers, particularly China, which has an association with diamond production that goes back to the nineteenth century. In 1874 two Frenchmen claimed they had located diamond deposits near Yi-Tchéo-Fou.[201] This place can be identified as Ichou in the Shandong province, and it is not that far from the Changma diamond field discovered in the twentieth century.[202] According to an early twentieth-century work on precious stones, these French travellers were struck by the curious way in which the Chinese mined for diamonds by walking around wearing sandals with soles made of rice straw. The sharp, pointy edges of diamonds attached themselves to the soles, and when they judged their sandals sufficiently armed, they plucked the diamonds out.[203] Marcel Bardet wrote that Germans found out about diamond deposits in Shandong in 1896.[204] This might very well be true, as Germans had obtained the right to construct a railway in 1898 that would pass through Ichou.[205]

Six areas have been known for producing diamonds since the 1960s. Four are alluvial fields and two are kimberlite pipes, one near Fuxin in the province of Liaoning, about 600 kilometres (373 mi.) northeast of Beijing, and another near Changma in the Shandong province, 500 kilometres

(310 mi.) south of the capital. The Changma diamond region is China's richest. Alluvial diamonds have been known to exist in Shandong since the 1940s, and the province contains at least ten diamond-holding kimberlites, although their commercial potential remains unsure. A first mine, Red Flag No. 1, now overgrown by peanut trees, yielded 20,000 carats of diamonds between 1970 and 1981. A second mine produced 31,000 carats in 1985. Total Chinese production for that year was estimated at somewhere between 300,000 and 500,000 carats, 15 per cent of which were of gem quality.[206] In 2002 open-pit mining in Shandong was transformed into underground mining. Production in the thirty years up to 2006 might have been as high as 1.6 million carats, with an estimated reserve of 9.7 million carats.[207] Since China joined the Kimberley Process in 2003, official production has been 416,992.11 carats between 2004 and 2013, but with a substantial decline over that period, as production was 74,029 carats in 2004 and 1,050 carats in 2013. China remains, officially, a very small producer, with 99 carats mined in 2018, and the country relies to a large extent on imports for the gemstone diamonds and industrial stones it needs.[208]

The future mining plans of Asian deposits remain very uncertain, and the same can be said about plans in South America. The problem in Brazil was that no primary deposits, like the African kimberlites, had been discovered, something that only changed in the last century. Since 1967 more than three hundred kimberlitic intrusives have been found, but very few of them turned out to be actual kimberlites and not one contained exploitable diamond deposits.[209] In recent times, while artisanal mining continues both in Minas Gerais and Bahia, the beautifully preserved historical mining towns are now the main appeal of these areas. The diamond and gold regions around Ouro Preto and Diamantina have become UNESCO world heritage sites, while the Bahian fields were turned into a national park, the Chapada Diamantina, a green mountainous area of about 1,520 square kilometres (587 sq. mi.). The old mining town of Lençóis, which had a population of 11,445 in 2015, is now a popular starting point for adventure travel into the park, where archaeological remains of nineteenth-century mining sites are an important attraction.[210] But as individual miners have not abandoned hopes, neither has the state. The Geological Survey of Brazil (CPRM) was founded in 1969, with shared state and private ownership. Several of its eight offices throughout the country supervise projects in diamond digging in Bahia (Santo Inácio), as well as in the states of Rondônia, Mato Grosso

102 Alluvial diamond mining near Diamantina, Brazil, 2003.

103 Alluvial diamond mining near Diamantina, Brazil, 2003.

(near Diamantino and Cuiabá, see illus. 20), Roraima and Minas Gerais.[211] In 1997 the CPRM's data indicated that there were fifteen active and three abandoned diamond mines in Brazil, and 365 active *garimpos* (293 abandoned). Additionally, it counted 18 unexplored deposits and 98 prospects, making for a total of 792 diamondiferous sites.[212]

Several years ago the Brazilian company Lipari Mineração received permission to start a mining operation at the Braúna project site, in the northeast of Bahia, about 10 kilometres (6 mi.) away from the city of Nordestina. Twenty-two kimberlites were found there during the 1980s, and in January 2016 the company announced an investment of £46 million in the hopes of opening Brazil's first kimberlite mine. They projected an annual yield of 225,000 carats for the first seven years of open-pit mining, after which underground operations would begin.[213] It is a very ambitious number, as Brazil officially produced a total of 232,685.17 carats in the five years from 2011 to 2015.[214] In their newsletter from May to July 2016, the company announced that 'Mina Braúna é realidade' ('Mina Braúna is a reality').[215]

Next to efforts to set up industrial operations, individual miners or small groups are still looking for diamonds in the riverbeds of the old diamond district. I visited a diamond field located a few hours drive from Diamantina in 2003, where miners were working the river as they had done for hundreds of years, their only modern equipment a machine to extract river soil (illus. 102 and 103). In the decade between 2009 and 2018, Brazil produced 968,584.5 carats of diamonds, with production rising in the last couple of years, jumping from 31,825.6 carats in 2015 to 183,515.7 in 2016. The two following years saw a yearly production of more than 250,000 carats.[216]

Brazil was not the only country in South America to contain diamond deposits. The presence of diamonds in Guyana has been known since at least the last decades of the nineteenth century. A substantial number of the miners who came to what was then British Guiana were African Americans, coming to the fields by boat. Foreign companies interested in Guyana's gold and minerals, of which there were forty in 1955, also dug up diamonds.[217] In the decade between 2009 and 2018, Guyana's diamond fields produced 771,401.12 carats, a number about 197,183 carats lower than Brazilian production for those years. Generally, however, Guyana's diamonds sold for better prices than Brazilian stones.[218]

In Venezuela, diamonds had been found in the early twentieth century, and by 1948 the country was producing between 13,000 and 34,000 carats per year, 75 per cent of which were of gemstone quality.[219] There were periodic diamond rushes and sporadic discoveries of big diamonds, such as the Liberator, a stone of 155 carats found in 1943, bought by American jeweller Harry Winston, who also had the Vargas diamond cut into several smaller stones.[220] In 1969 about 8,000 diamond-thirsty adventurers rushed to the remote village of San Salvador de Paul, on the border with Brazil.[221] Recent data for Venezuela's diamond production is not available, as the country withdrew from the Kimberley Process in 2008. The KP website still provides some statistics for the years after, but official output was very low, at 7,730.37 carats in 2009 and 2,099.10 carats in 2010.[222] Following a visit by the chairman of the Kimberly Process to Caracas, Venezuela was readmitted in 2016, in spite of ongoing smuggling and clandestine mining operations in the Amazon jungle.[223]

Epilogue: About Human Rights and Environmental Considerations

> His heavy desire extended to diamonds ... during the six years
> of his rule, one would have thought he had intended to empty
> all of Europe of diamonds, and to buy the complete produce
> of Golconda and Brazil.[1]

This quotation comes from a story published at the end of the eighteenth century about a black boy from Borneo who had become the favourite of the commander of the eunuchs in the Ottoman Empire. When the commander died in 1746, the boy, Bekir Aga, was named as his successor and the story goes that, together with a young slave and an Armenian merchant, Bekir started to become active in the diamond trade in the hopes of amassing enough of a fortune to retire to Cairo. It is not known what became of the boy, and whether the story was true. But it shows that diamonds fuelled dreams of social mobility for a long time, dreams that may have been realized by a lucky few, but which were shared by so many.

Diamond mining has a long and bloody history. For most of this time diamonds were extracted through slavery or other forms of human exploitation. In the twentieth century they have fuelled bloody conflicts in the heart of Africa, which became such a visible catastrophe that diamond producers and NGOs addressed the problem by establishing the Kimberley Process to guarantee the origins of rough diamonds and their conflict-free nature. It has been a laudable effort to halt abuse at the mining sites, but membership of the Kimberley Process remains voluntary, while malicious companies still manage to circumvent regulations established by the KP through smuggling or hiding a diamond's true origins. The late twentieth-century global upturn in diamond mining, and De Beers' loss of its monopoly, have contributed to the pressure put upon

Africa's blood diamonds by providing cleaner alternatives, but it has also led to the realization that a focus on the role played by rough diamonds in African wars is insufficient when dealing with the impact diamond mining has left on our planet.

Ian Smillie, a Canadian development professional who was one of those who helped to formulate the KP system, has drawn attention to the fact that the focus on African blood diamonds has led to the neglect of human rights issues related to global diamond mining. Many diamond deposits throughout history have been alluvial, which means that masses of artisanal miners have been drawn to these deposits to operate within some sort of 'casino economy', fuelled by dreams of a lucky find.[2] I visited a mining site in Brazil in 2003, where a small group of men was digging for diamonds in the Jequitinhonha river on behalf of local investors. Their wages were based on a percentage of the mined diamonds, but after mining for more than a year they had not found anything (illus. 102 and 103). They lived in improvised huts several hours' drive from Diamantina. They brewed their own liquor, the well-known Brazilian *cachaça*, and the one woman who lived with them officially took care of the household chores, such as cooking and washing, but it was clear that she was also expected to offer sexual services. The practice is reminiscent of the participation of ballet dancers and waitresses from Irkutsk in Russia's diamond expeditions of the 1950s, brought there to pleasure the men.[3]

While slavery is long gone from Brazil, it is clear that many of the miners still active are trapped in a demoralizing economic system relying on unfulfilled fantasies. This also applied to India more than a century and a half earlier. When Irish geologist Valentine Ball published a survey on mining in India, the use of enslaved workers had already been outlawed for decades, and yet he remarked that 'it would almost seem, in fact, that, except under a system of slavery, the diamond cannot be worked for profitably in India. The present system, though not so called, practically amounts to much the same thing.'[4] Like all artisanal miners that came before and after, the Brazilians I met had dreams about finding the one exceptional diamond that would allow them to leave the muddy diamond fields. Throughout history, men and women have shared this dream all over the world, a dream that has so often been abused by those in control, and Ball's remark still rings true for several mining operations across the world. Smillie estimated that currently about 16 per cent of rough diamonds are produced by artisanal miners.[5] In 2013 the World Bank concluded that 100 million people, artisanal miners and their families, depended on small-scale mining of diamonds, gold and other precious commodities, compared to the seven million depending on industrial mining.[6] A major problem is that most of them operate in the margins, without access to a number of vital needs such as healthcare or education, while the work is hazardous to their health, as miners often work knee-deep in rivers in remote areas and their working days are long. Miners not only suffer from exhaustion but from sexually transmitted diseases caused by the practice of using women as sex slaves. In Ghana's Akwatia diamond region, HIV prevalence in 2004 was twice as high as the national rate.[7] Miners cohabitating at alluvial sites in wet circumstances also suffer from outbreaks of disease, such as the pneumonic plague near the mining town of Zobia in the DRC's Oriental province, in the north of the country, where sixty miners died and 350 were infected just days after reopening the site in early 2005.[8]

Child labour remains a widespread and controversial problem in the world of artisanal mining. Part of the controversy is that institutions from the West often dictate a desire to eradicate child labour in other parts of the world without fully acknowledging its historical role in spreading it through colonial rule, or the fact that many Western countries today benefit from child labour elsewhere.[9] While Western concerns with child labour should certainly be placed in their proper historical, economic and political contexts, it must be said that the abuse of children in mining is widespread. In 2003 the International Labour Organization estimated that one million children were involved in small-scale mining and quarrying, while in certain areas, such as Sierra Leone's gold and diamond districts, 80 per cent of the population aged between nine and eighteen were involved in mining.[10] The persistence of child labour has been linked to economic impoverishment and the lack of political action to eradicate these practices.[11]

Although in most countries with alluvial deposits artisanal mining is regulated through licence fees and rent payments, research in Sierra Leone has shown that miners often resort to illegal mining because fees are too high. Furthermore, governments have a hard time controlling mining in the often remote and spatially dispersed diamond deposits.[12] It creates something of a vicious circle, as clandestine mining lowers governmental mining revenues, diminishing capital that could be applied to improve the living circumstances of artisanal miners. Diamond companies often maintain a presence on these alluvial fields, and their direct contacts with artisanal miners outside governmental control further corrodes human rights for the miners, who often do not receive fair prices for the diamonds they dig up. The situation was similar in Tanzania: 'unpaid and unfed, the only way to earn money from this punishing drudgery is to smuggle unearthed gems out of the mine and past the mine owner, before selling the raw stone to one of the many dealers in the town.'[13] Several NGOs, such as the Diamond Development Initiative in 2005, were established outside the KP framework to deal with human rights and environmental issues.[14]

The present-day exploitation of children is not exclusive to mining. Research has shown that in Indian diamond workshops, adults and children alike often work in dire circumstances, which led to several outbursts of protest in the early twenty-first century.[15] Today, only a small segment of the workforce enjoys a steady salary, but 80 per cent is paid between 1 and 25 rupees (equivalent to $0.013 and $0.33) per stone they polish. Circumstances are such that it has been found that suicide rates in Gujarat are at unprecedented heights.[16] In spite of laws that abolished child labour, the practice is still ongoing, and a 2018 Reuters report on suicides among diamond workers contains an interview with the mother of a boy who started as a diamond worker when he was sixteen, but who later committed suicide.[17]

The purpose of this book has been to show the remarkable continuity with which mining labour has been extracted from a lower class of workers and enslaved men and women. The evidence makes it abundantly clear that there has always been exploitation. A small elite of local rulers, sultans and rajas, kings and queens, emperors, followed by colonial administrators, governors and viceroys, and later also bourgeois capitalists, monopolists and industrialists, have never stopped trying to control the flow of rough diamonds. Locating diamond mines, however remote they were from the civilized world, and limiting access for groups of adventurers digging on their own account, has been a recurring component of diamond mining throughout history. Another has been the control over labour. At several times mining was free for all, provided taxes were paid. More common was the desire to fully control mining by using wage labourers or enslaved men, women and children. Often this workforce was kept in isolation, in closed compounds or guarded camps, to stop thievery and smuggling, but also out of a simple lack of respect for human life. Governments and private companies have, always and everywhere, sought recourse to regimes of forced labour, and the impoverished peasants in early modern India, the enslaved Africans in colonial Brazil and the racially abused wage labourers in South Africa have paved the way for a present-day class of underpaid or clandestine miners who are digging for diamonds in Africa, India and Brazil. While slavery has been formally abolished, the abuse of human rights has not ceased, and the extortion of labour is commonplace in many of today's diamond fields. Such practices have been able to persist in the world of diamonds because the flow in rough diamonds is controlled by a very select and secretive group of mining companies. The third thread that this book has aimed to analyse is exactly that, the control that institutions have been able to exercise over the worldwide trade in rough diamonds, from the East India Company and the Portuguese colonial authorities, to Cecil Rhodes, Ernest Oppenheimer and De Beers, and today's mining giants, such as Alrosa, Endiama and, still, De Beers. By arranging deals, fixing prices and supply, and hiding the manner in which rough diamonds are obtained with a cloak of secrecy, the select few have not only been able to control the market of diamonds for centuries, they managed to obscure the blood and sweat that were shed in order to extract the most precious of stones from the earth.

Mining has harmed those who have tried and are trying to gain their livelihood by looking for diamonds, but it has also had an enormous impact on the population living in diamondiferous areas. In South Africa, local communities were overturned from a very early stage through the use of migrant labour and the conversion of local economies to cater exclusively for the diamond mining sites. A similar evolution took place in regions of Namibia, Angola, West Africa and the DRC. In 2001, for example, under the pretext of wildlife preservation, the Botswana government decided to resettle San bushmen living in the Central Kalahari Game Reserve to camps where hunter-gathering activities were impossible, in order to make way for diamond mining.[18] A diamond mine was opened on San ancestral land in 2014.[19]

Diamond diggers in Brazil regularly venture into indigenous territories in the Amazon, leading to violent clashes.[20] In 1999 a diamond rush brought more than 3,000 diggers into the Roosevelt Indian Reserve, home of the Cinta Larga tribe. The *Village Voice* wrote in 2010 that $2 billion worth of rough diamonds had been mined there since 1999.[21] In 2004 at least 29 *garimpeiros* were killed by members of the Cinta Larga, whose first contact with outsiders dates from 1914, when they met with former U.S. president-turned-traveller Theodore Roosevelt.[22] Mining on indigenous lands is an illegal act and the government set up roadblocks to keep the miners out, without much success. The 2004 massacre was picked up by media all over the world, and journalists exposed a trail of governmental corruption, fraud and smuggling. A diamond trader was arrested at JFK Airport in 2004 carrying 1,170 carats of diamonds without a Kimberley certificate.[23] Although diamond mining has been suspended in the Roosevelt Indian Reserve since 2010, there is no doubt that illegal mining and smuggling continues, with stones taken into Venezuela and Guyana. The battle with mining in Brazil's indigenous areas is rendered more difficult by the dire financial state of FUNAI, the country's governmental agency responsible for its indigenous population. It allocated on average $52 per individual in 2014, which makes clandestine mining not only interesting to miners and international traders but to members of indigenous tribes, and at the end of 2015 Brazilian federal police arrested a number of people following an investigation into diamond smuggling in the state of Rondônia.[24]

In Australia diamonds were mined on Aboriginal lands. Australia's Aboriginal population has suffered a great deal since British colonization. Their lands were taken, they had no representation in Australian politics for a long time, their life expectancy is substantially lower than Australia's average, and they have less access to higher education. In short, they lack access to basic human services, while Australia's mineral boom has so often led to occupation of their lands. While the lack of a supra-local or national hierarchy in Aboriginal leadership has rendered it difficult to take a united stance, Aboriginals have opposed the development of several mineral extraction sites, notably against the development of the Argyle diamond mine in the 1980s, as the site was on Aboriginal land with great spiritual meaning. Theoretically it was protected through the Cultural Heritage Act of 1972, but legislation foresaw alternative use for certain sites, under which pretext diamond mining could establish itself at Argyle. Minor sums of compensation were paid to several Aboriginal owners, not more than 0.15 per cent of diamond sales revenues, but things changed only when Rio Tinto vouched to improve its relationship with the Aboriginals in 1995. Negotiations culminated in the Argyle Diamonds Agreement of 2004, guaranteeing contractually bound financial compensation to be allocated for Aboriginal development, no more destruction of cultural sites without the owners' consent, and a maximization of Aboriginal employment at Argyle.[25] At first the agreement appeared to be beneficial for the communities living near the Argyle mine, and Aboriginal employment at the mine went from 8 to about 25 per cent.[26] Later, though, financial mismanagement of the 25 million Australian dollars paid in royalties to the Aboriginal landowners, and declining production, caused new concerns among the local communities, who remained in the dark about the future of mining when it was known that the Argyle mine would be closing in 2020.[27]

Problems with mining companies destroying sites and stealing land, often in the slipstream of colonialism, have been at the heart of mining in most places outside of Europe, and are ongoing today. They are not confined to the mining of diamonds. As recently as September 2020, the chief executive of Rio Tinto was forced to resign, with two other colleagues, after the company blew up a sacred 46,000-year-old Aboriginal site at Juukan Gorge to make room for an iron ore mine – even though the company did not own the land.[28]

Similar problems regarding land ownership, dislocation and environmental damage to ancestral lands can also be found in Canada's Northwest Territories, although higher employment and economic prosperity have been cited as some of the few positive consequences of the interaction between large-scale mining companies and indigenous communities.[29] More generally, Canada's diamond mining activities have been welcomed as a necessary break with colonial or colonial-inspired mining practices in the southern hemisphere – even though the argument for continued subjugation of indigenous communities can still be made. The obligation to deliver Impact Benefit Agreements to include native populations in mining considerations, however, has not cancelled out an evolution in which traditionally important economic activities, such as fishing, trapping and hunting, have been threatened by the environmental and social impact the diamond mines have on the local socio-economic fabric.[30] Positive aspects of mining, however, disappear when a mine closes, strengthening the image of local dependency on international mining companies.

The historical inequalities stemming from land appropriation remain unresolved, and the guarantees given by the state and the mining companies to indigenous populations in Canada and Australia can be considered a form of paternalism that creates a dependency of locals on the companies. There is no denying that natural wealth is extracted from appropriated land and sent abroad, mostly by foreign multinationals, and that that situation is the same in Australia, Canada, South Africa, Botswana, the Congo and elsewhere. One of the main problems remains that diamond mining represents huge corporate interests, often negotiated or exploited in cooperation with local governments. In the case of Russia, for instance, the local population in Sakha had some success in exposing negative aspects of industrial diamond mining through political activism after the fall of the Soviet Union, but the movement disappeared in the late 1990s, unable to deal with Alrosa's economic and political power in the region, and the threat of the loss of work in case activism was pushed too far.[31]

104 Alluvial diamond mining near Koidu Town, Sierra Leone, 2020.

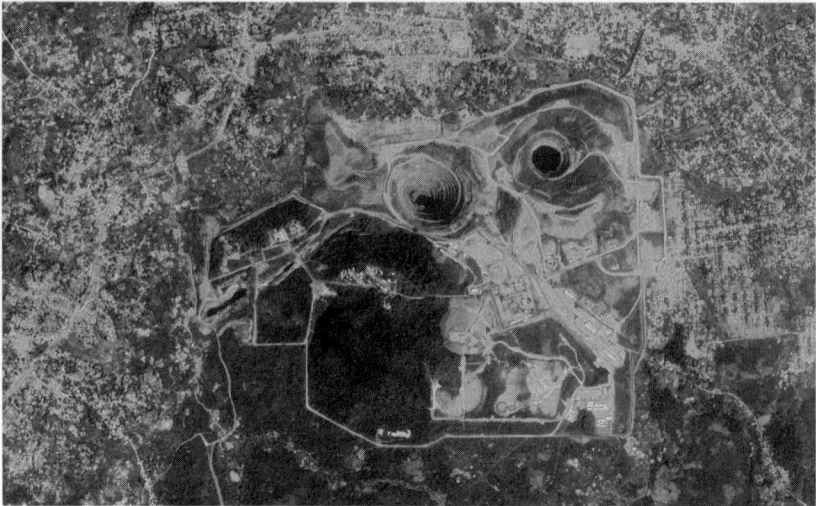

105 Kimberlite pipes near Koidu Town, Sierra Leone, 2020.

The growing concern with human rights has been one of the major additions to the mining process, even if judgement on whether it is merely a cosmetic operation to sell clean diamonds to the public or a genuine worry remains open. Another concern that has become much more important in recent years is that of a negative ecological impact. In Canada, research on caribou migration and the conduct of tundra-breeding birds has shown no considerable behavioural change caused by mining. However, the fact that such research is undertaken in the first place and is brought into negotiations between companies and the government demonstrates a changing approach to mining.[32] Additionally, mining agreements in both Canada and Australia include specific arrangements for reducing vegetation loss due to mining and the monitoring of water quality. In Namibia, the search for marine diamonds off the coast has led to concerns about disturbance to the habitats of seabed organisms.[33]

Diamond mining has had a negative impact on animal life in India. Panna, in the state of Madhya Pradesh, about 380 kilometres (236 mi.) from the state capital Bhopal, has long been famous for its diamond mines. Today these are being explored by the National Mineral Development Corporation (NMDC), but an environmental monitoring panel has demanded a halt to mining operations because the mines are located within the Panna National Park, one of India's tiger reserves. The right to mine in a reserve has been part of an ongoing legal battle.[34] Currently, 25 tigers live in the park, and part of NMDC's tactic is to use the presence of tigers to keep individual artisanal miners out of the area. As a consequence, whole villages where families of diamond diggers have been living were displaced.[35] Newspapers have reported in 2020 how hard it still is to locate Panna's small diamond mines, and the illegal activities of locals mining on private land and in the areas of jungle and forest outweigh legal mining, leading to regular police raids in which shovels, diesel machinery and other mining equipment is confiscated.[36] In legal operations, as many as a hundred people can work in one location, for a fee of 100 to 200 rupees per day, the equivalent of £1.24–£2.48, hired by contractors and landowners, forced into mining as the collection of forest revenues is no longer allowed.[37] The situation in Panna is representative of the complex interplay of government interest, mining interest and ecological impact, as well as societal consequences.

Part of the problem is that great numbers of artisanal diggers are drawn to alluvial diamond fields in the hope of bettering their lives, and that many of their activities remain unregulated, leading to excesses that are detrimental both for the diggers themselves and the environment. For some, the principal damage to the environment is not done by the industrial mining activities of the large companies, but by these numerous small-scale alluvial digging operations. Diggers transport river soil, alter river courses and strip the environment of its vegetation, destroying farmland in the process. Ian Smillie points out that a search for Koidu Town in Sierra Leone on Google Earth not only shows the two kimberlite pipes currently exploited but a landscape punctured by man-made craters and ponds (illus. 104 and 105).[38] Similar examples can be found surrounding several Brazilian settlements with a historical record of artisanal mining.[39]

Today, the growing concern with both the environment and the human rights of diggers and the surrounding local population, although it is undoubtedly used by companies to sell more and officially cleaner diamonds, is still a step in the right direction.[40] Most large companies now have part of their website dedicated to sustainability and environmental and social concerns. The challenge to reconcile ecological impact with societal concerns remains one of the main issues, while debates on land appropriation techniques that have their roots in colonial practice will never be silenced. In Ghana, the government has started educational programmes to create awareness among gold and diamond diggers of environmental damage and health hazards, while it has been suggested that the formation of mining cooperatives would create a better financial environment for diggers, enabling a more sustainable management of alluvial diamond fields.[41] In Sierra Leone, land reclamation initiatives try to convert some mining areas back to farmland, acknowledging that a possible solution for economic progress in the diamond mining zone may lie in linking agricultural production more closely to the mining economy. It is an approach that aims at addressing both environmental and socio-economic issues.[42] These efforts might improve the lot of many, but despite continuing pressure by NGOs and advertising campaigns guaranteeing consumers that they are buying a product of sustainable and clean mining, for many people working in the diamond mining industry these precious stones have never shone, and their lustre offers nothing more than a distant promise of betterment, still only achievable through blood, sweat and tears.

References

1 William Crookes, 'The Romance of the Diamond', *North American Review*, CLXXXVII/628 (1908), pp. 371–8. Crookes was one name in a long list of people who attempted to make synthetic diamonds. Robert M. Hazen, *The Diamond Makers* (Cambridge, 1999), pp. 25–8.

2 John P. Rafferty, 'Kimberlite Eruption', www.britannica.com, accessed 4 May 2020.

3 C.H., 'Why Diamond Production May Be About to Peak', 9 March 2017, www.economist.com, accessed 4 May 2020. Only 15 per cent of all kimberlite pipes are diamondiferous, and most of these cannot be exploited in a viable manner.

4 The fact that diamonds are nothing more than carbon was discovered by Smithson Tennant in 1796. Smithson Tennant, 'On the Nature of the Diamond', *Philosophical Transactions of the Royal Society of London*, CXXXVII/1 (1797), pp. 123–7. An allotrope is a term to indicate one of various physical forms an element can have. Charcoal and diamonds, for instance, are both allotropes of carbon.

5 Joshua M. Garber et al., 'Multidisciplinary Constraints on the Abundance of Diamond and Eclogite in the Cratonic Lithosphere', *Geochemistry, Geophysics, Geosystems*, XIX/7 (2018), pp. 2062–86. The estimate amounts to a quadrillion ton: a one with fifteen zeroes. Maya Wei-Haas, 'A Quadrillion Tons of Diamonds Lurk Deep Inside Earth', www.nationalgeographic.com, 17 July 2018.

6 'Presolar' means they have been formed before the sun existed.

7 Roy S. Lewis, Tang Ming, John F. Wacker, Edward Anders and Eric Steel, 'Interstellar Diamonds in Meteorites', *Nature*, CCCXXXVII (1987), pp. 160–62; and Masaaki Miyahara et al., 'Unique Large Diamonds in a Ureilite from Almahata Sitta 2008 TC3 Asteroid ', *Geochimica et Cosmochimica Acta*, CLXIII (2015), pp. 14–26.

8 An interesting take on the undeserved position of diamonds as the number one of precious and semiprecious stones can be found in Robert N. Proctor, 'Anti-agate: The Great Diamond Hoax and the Semiprecious Stone Scam', *Configurations*, IX/3 (2001), pp. 381–412.

9 Godehard Lenzen, *The History of Diamond Production and the Diamond Trade* (New York, 1970), pp. 20–21.

10 Quoted in Nichola Erin Harris, 'The Idea of Lapidary Medicine: Its Circulation and Practical Applications in Medieval and Early Modern England: 1000–1750', PhD thesis, Rutgers University, 2009, p. 170.

11 While diamonds have been valued on these four elements for centuries, an official and internationally accepted grading scheme was developed in the 1930s by the Gemological Institute of America. See '4Cs of Diamond Quality', www.gia.edu, accessed 4 May 2020.

12 Another 20 per cent is cut in another style. 'The Diamond Insight Report 2019: Diamonds and Love in the Modern World', p. 26, www.debeersgroup. com, accessed 4 May 2020.

13 The weight of one carat has not always been exactly the same everywhere and throughout time, and at times other units of weight were used in other regions.

14 Of which 19 million came from the Democratic Republic of the Congo, 18 million from Russia and 14 million from Australia. 'Mineral Commodity Summaries 2018', p. 55, www.usgs.gov, accessed 4 May 2020.

15 National Archives The Hague (hereafter NATH), 2.05.80: Archief van het Ministerie van Buitenlandse Zaken te Londen (Londens Archief) en daarmee samenhangende archieven, (1936) 1940–1945 (1958), N°3007: Stukken betreffende de doorvoer via de ambassade te Washington van per diplomatieke koerier vanuit Portugal verzonden diamanten, deels bestemd voor NV Philips, deels voor Nederlandse vluchtelingen, en een partij bestemd voor de schrijver M. Mok in Engeland, 1941–1942.

16 Humberto Fernández-Morán Villalobos, 'Method of Making Diamond Knives' (patented 22 June 1965), patents.google.com, accessed 4 May 2020.

17 Donald W. Olson, 'Diamond (Industrial)', in *u.s. Geological Survey, Mineral Commodity Summaries, January 2016*, ed. Joyce A. Ober (Reston, VA, 2016), pp. 56–7.

18 For the history of synthetic diamonds, see Hazen, *The Diamond Makers*. For the part of General Electric, see Thomas F. O'Boyle, *At Any Cost: Jack Welch, General Electric, and the Pursuit of Profit* (New York, 1998), pp. 277–331.

19 Nazanin Lankarani, 'Lab-grown Diamonds? This New Paris Jeweler Says They're the Future', *New York Times*, 11 September 2018.

20 See www.lightboxjewelry.com, accessed 4 May 2020.

21 Lankarani, 'Lab-grown Diamonds?'

22 As quoted in Martin Thomas, *Violence and Colonial Order: Police, Workers and Protest in the European Colonial Empires, 1918–1940* (Cambridge, 2012), p. 265.

23 Crookes, 'The Romance of the Diamond', p. 375. The quote continues on a misogynistic tone, 'just to win a few stones wherewith to deck my lady's finger! All to gratify the vanity of woman! "And," I hear my fair reader remark, "the depravity of man!"'. The expression is reminiscent of words uttered by Winston Churchill in 1891. Dorothy O. Helly and Helen Callaway, 'Constructing South Africa in the British Press, 1890–92: The *Pall Mall Gazette*, the *Daily Graphic*, and *The Times*', in *Imperial Co-Histories: National Identities and the British and Colonial Press*, ed. Julie F. Codell (Cranbury, NJ, 2003), pp. 125–44 (p. 135).

24 A number of scholars have already written important cultural and economic histories of the finished product. Good examples are Marcia Pointon, *Brilliant Effects: A Cultural History of Gem Stones and Jewellery* (New Haven, CT, 2009); and Marcia Pointon, *Rocks, Ice and Dirty Stones: Diamond Histories*

(London, 2017). See also the work of Joan Evans, *A History of Jewellery, 1100–1870* (New York, 1953); and Herbert Tillander, *Diamond Cuts in Historic Jewellery, 1381–1910* (London, 1995), who focus on the historical evolution of jewellery. A recent book on the early history of diamonds is Jack Ogden, *Diamonds: An Early History of the King of Gems* (New Haven, CT, 2018), which provides an overview of the early modern history of Indian diamonds, with a focus on the development of trade and cutting. The attention is still more on the cultural aspects of the finished product than on mining management and labour circumstances. Similar in range and topic, but focusing on the nineteenth and twentieth centuries, is Rachelle Bergstein, *Brilliance and Fire: A Biography of Diamonds* (New York, 2016).

25 David Jeffries, *A Treatise on Diamonds and Pearls* (London, 1751), p. 66.

26 Not to be confused with industrial diamonds.

27 For the role played by mining in the history of South Africa, see Martin Meredith, *Diamonds, Gold and War: The British, the Boers, and the Making of South Africa* (New York, 2007); and Jade Davenport, *Digging Deep: A History of Mining in South Africa* (Johannesburg, 2013).

28 'De Beers, Six Others Form Diamond Producers Association', www.miningweekly.com, 28 May 2015; see also the website of the DPA at www.diamondproducers.com, accessed 4 May 2020. The seven DPA members are Alrosa (Russia), De Beers (South Africa, Canada, Botswana, Namibia), Dominion Diamond Corporation (Canada), Lucara Diamond Corporation (Botswana), Petra Diamonds (South Africa, Tanzania), Gem Diamonds (Lesotho, Botswana) and Rio Tinto (Australia, Canada).

29 See kimberleyprocessstatistics.org, accessed 4 May 2020.

30 'The Diamond Insight Report 2019', p. 7, www.debeersgroup.com, accessed 4 May 2020.

31 An overview with additional information on all the bourses can be found on the website of the WFDB, www.wfdb.com, accessed 4 May 2020.

32 'The Diamond Insight Report 2019', p. 4.

33 The neglect of land ownership rights when diamonds were found somewhere was already a factor in the absolutist regimes of the ancient, medieval and early modern Indian kingdoms and sultanates, but became particularly shameless with European colonialism and its aftermath.

34 Jillian Ambrose, 'Ecotricity Founder to Grow Diamonds "Made Entirely from the Sky"', *The Guardian*, 30 October 2020.

35 Two important elements of this dark side are not, or hardly, addressed in this book, and both have to do with crime. The first is theft, which is discussed in Pointon, *Rocks, Ice and Dirty Stones*, pp. 171–202. The focus is on finished diamonds and jewellery. The second is smuggling, which is hard to assess due to a lack of source material and changing ideas of what exactly constitutes smuggling. An interesting study on the phenomenon is Simon Harvey, *Smuggling: Seven Centuries of Contraband* (London, 2016), which deals with a variety of commodities and historical periods.

36 Today, child labour is mostly thought of in non-European context, but European countries have a long history of exploiting children for labour, both

domestically as well as in the colonial context. Mining has been an important sector in this regard. For a study on nineteenth-century Britain, see Danielle Kinsey, 'Atlantic World Mining, Child Labor, and the Transnational Construction of Childhood in Imperial Britain in the Mid-nineteenth Century', *Atlantic Studies*, XI/4 (2014), pp. 449–72.

I ASIAN DIAMONDS: THE DISCOVERY OF A LUXURY COMMODITY, 50 CE–1785

1 John Keats and Paul Wright, eds, *The Poems of John Keats* (Ware, 1994), p. 18.
2 'Golconda', www.merriam-webster.com, accessed 4 May 2020.
3 Arun Kumar Biswas, 'Gem-minerals in Pre-modern India', *Indian Journal of History of Science*, XXIX/3 (1994), pp. 389–420 (p. 392).
4 Earl Marshal, 'A Description of the Diamond-mines, as It was Presented by the Right Honourable, the Earl Marshal of England, to the R. Society', *Philosophical Transactions (1665–1678)*, XII (1677–8), pp. 907–17 (pp. 908, 913).
5 Carl Ritter, *Die Erdkunde von Asien*, 21 vols (Berlin, 1817–59), vol. IV (1836), p. 343. Another one of those fathers, Alexander von Humboldt, was to play an important role in the discovery of Russian diamonds.
6 R. Shamasastry, trans., *Kauṭilya's Arthaśāstra* (Bangalore, 1915), p. 115. A discussion of the manuscript, its composition, its rediscovery and a new translation into English can be found in Patrick Olivelle, *King, Governance, and Law in Ancient India: Kauṭilya's Arthaśāstra* (Oxford, 2013). The reference to the superintendent's responsibilities can be found on p. 109.
7 Shamasastry, *Kauṭilya's Arthaśāstra*, pp. 115, 343.
8 CE stands for Common Era. For Olivelle's argumentation, see Olivelle, *King, Governance, and Law*, pp. 26–9. Based on his view, I have adopted a starting date of 50 CE for this chapter.
9 Ibid., p. 123.
10 A good example of linguistical confusion. This might very well be the same place as Ritter's Wairagarh.
11 Biswas, 'Gem-minerals', p. 403.
12 The *Bṛhatsamhitā*, a Sanskrit text that dates from the sixth century, mentions eight diamondiferous sites in India, all different from the sites mentioned in the Arthaśāstra. R. P. Kangle, *The Kauṭilya Arthaśāstra. Part III: A Study* (Delhi, 1965), p. 86.
13 For the claim on Ptolemy's diamond river, see Biswas, 'Gem-minerals', p. 409.
14 Corey Abshire, Dmitri Gusev, Ioannis Papapanagiotou and Sergey Stafeyev, 'A Mathematical Method for Visualizing Ptolemy's India in Modern GIS Tools', *e-Perimetron*, XI/1 (2016), pp. 13–34 (p. 32).
15 Berthold Laufer, 'The Diamond: A Study in Chinese and Hellenistic Folklore', *Publications of the Field Museum of Natural History. Anthropological Series*, XV/1 (1915), pp. 32–4.
16 Lionel Casson, 'Patterns of Seaborne Trade in the First Century A.D.', *Bulletin of the American Society of Papyrologists*, XXI/1–4 (1984), pp. 39–47.

17 Pliny the Elder, *The Natural History*, ed. John Bostock (London, 1855), Book 35, Chapter 15.

18 Ibid.

19 Sharae Deckard, *Paradise Discourse, Imperialism, and Globalization: Exploiting Eden* (New York, 2010), p. 134.

20 Samuel Purchas, *Hakluytus Posthumus; or, Purchas His Pilgrims*, 5 vols (London, 1625), vol. III, pp. 108–12.

21 J. Thorley, 'The Development of Trade between the Roman Empire and the East under Augustus', *Greece and Rome*, XVI/2 (1969), pp. 209–23 (p. 221).

22 Vimala Begley, 'Arikamedu Reconsidered', *American Journal of Archaeology*, LXXXVII/4 (1983), pp. 461–81.

23 Leonard Gorelick and John A. Gwinnett, 'Diamonds from India to Rome and Beyond', *American Journal of Archaeology*, XCII/4 (1988), pp. 547–52 (pp. 548–9).

24 Casson, 'Patterns of Seaborne Trade in the First Century A.D.', pp. 39–47.

25 Lenzen, *The History of Diamond Production*, pp. 1–8, 15–25.

26 Laufer, 'The Diamond', p. 45. Although it is not clear to what extent Ethiopia was seen as a source of diamonds.

27 Lenzen, *The History of Diamond Production*, pp. 21, 35–41.

28 Hakim Mohammad Said, ed., *Al-Beruni's Book on Mineralogy: The Book Most Comprehensive in Knowledge on Precious Stones* (Islamabad, 1989), pp. 75–80.

29 Nachum Gross, ed., *Economic History of the Jews* (New York, 1975), p. 158.

30 See Salvatore Ciriacono, 'Il diamante a Venezia tra la fine del medioevo e il secolo XVIII: Tecniche, produzione, competizione internazionale', *Nuova rivista storica*, XCVIII/1 (2014), pp. 199–224.

31 Lenzen, *The History of Diamond Production*, pp. 60–61.

32 Annelies De Bie, 'The Paradox of the Antwerp Rose: Symbol of Decline or Token of Craftsmanship?', in *Innovation and Creativity in Late Medieval and Early Modern European Cities*, ed. Karel Davids and Bert de Munck (Farnham and Burlington, VT, 2014), pp. 269–94 (p. 271). See also Ludo Vandamme and John A. Rosenhøj, *Brugge diamantstad: diamanthandel en diamantnijverheid in Brugge in de 15de en de 20ste eeuw* (Beernem, 1993). For Italian presence in Bruges, see Peter Stabel, 'De gewenste vreemdeling: Italiaanse kooplieden en stedelijke maatschappij in het laat-Middeleeuwse Brugge', *Jaarboek voor middeleeuwse geschiedenis*, IV (2001), pp. 189–221.

33 For a short introduction to the references to gemstones in the work of early Arabian scholars, see William John Sersen, 'Gem Minerals in Early Arabic Literature', *Mineralogical Record*, XXVI/4 (1995), pp. 43–8.

34 Aloys Sprenger, trans., *El-Mas'údí's Historical Encyclopaedia entitled 'Meadows of Gold and Mines of Gems' Translated from the Arabic* (London, 1841), p. 269.

35 Said, ed., *Al-Beruni's Book on Mineralogy*, pp. 75–80.

36 Ibid., p. 80.

37 Laufer, 'The Diamond', pp. 6–21.

38 Ibid., p. 10.

39 Ibid., pp. 7–10.

40 For a discussion, see Friedrich Hirth, 'The Mystery of Fu-Lin', *Journal of the American Oriental Society*, XXXIII (1913), pp. 193–208.

41 Jamel Eddine Bencheikh and André Miquel, ed. and trans., *Les Mille et Une Nuits*, vol. IV: *Sindbad de la mer et autres contes des Mille et Une Nuits* (Paris, 2002), pp. 340–466.

42 Deckard, *Paradise Discourse*, p. 134.

43 Marco Polo, *Il Milione*, ed. Antonio Lanza (Pordenone, 1991), cap. CXXXVIII.

44 Geneviève Bouchon and Anne-Laure Amilhat-Szary, eds, *Le Voyage aux Indes de Nicolò de' Conti (1414–1439)*, trans. Diane Ménard (Paris, 2004), p. 317.

45 Gordon Mackenzie, *Manual of the Kistna District in the Presidency of Madras* (New Delhi, 1990), p. 246. Sacrifice and other religious rituals were common in India's diamond mines (illus. 7). Rituals have continued to play a role in diamond mining up to today, see for instance Lorenzo D'Angelo, 'God's Gifts: Destiny, Poverty, and Temporality in the Mines of Sierra Leone', *Africa Spectrum*, LIV/1 (2019), pp. 44–60.

46 Bouchon and Amilhat-Szary, eds, *Le Voyage aux Indes de Nicolò de' Conti*, p. 117.

47 The Catalan Atlas, six vellum leaves mounted on wooden panels, is preserved at the Bibliothèque Nationale Française in Paris. See 'Ciel & Terre: L'Atlas Catalan', www.bnf.fr. The panels of the Atlas can also be consulted at 'The Cresques Project', www.cresquesproject.net. Both accessed 4 May 2020.

48 The English translation was published on the website of the Cresques Project at 'Catalan Atlas Legends > Panel VI'.

49 Ruslan Kostov, 'The Mineralogical Knowledge of the Ancient Bulgarians According to Some Medieval Sources', *Annual of the University of Mining and Geology 'St Ivan Rilski'*, XLVI/1 (2003), pp. 87–92 (p. 90). See also Abdulmamad Iloliev, 'The Silk Road Castles and Temples: Ancient Wakhan in Legends and History', in *Identity, History and Trans-nationality in Central Asia. The Mountain Communities of Pamir*, ed. D. Dagiev and C. Faucher (Abingdon, 2019), pp. 91–105. Spinel is a coloured crystal in the form of an octahedron. Only a small amount of spinels are of gemstone quality. They have been used in jewellery since Roman times but were often confused with rubies. Historically, they were found in Afghanistan, Myanmar and Ceylon. See Richard W. Hughes, 'The Rubies and Spinels of Afghanistan: A Brief History', *Journal of Gemmology*, XXIV/4 (1994), pp. 256–67.

50 W.K.B. Loftus, H. S. Simpson and M. J. King, 'Recovery Plant Practice at De Beers Consolidated Mines, Kimberley, with Particular References to Improvements Made for the Sorting of Final Concentrates', *Journal of the South African Institute of Mining and Metallurgy*, VII/9 (1970), pp. 317–28 (p. 319).

51 Polo, *Il Milione*, p. 214: 'e non crediate che gli buoni diamanti si rechino di qua tra gli Cristiani; anzi si portano al Gran Cane, ed agli re e baroni di quelle contrade che hanno lo gran Tesoro.'

52 Ishrat Alam, 'Diamond Mining and Trade in South India in the Seventeenth Century', *Medieval History Journal*, III/2 (2000), pp. 291–310 (p. 293).

53 Ciriacono, 'Il diamante a Venezia'. See also Hans Pohl, *Die Portugiesen in Antwerpen (1567–1648): Zur Geschichte einer Minderheit* (Wiesbaden, 1977);

and Jean Denucé, 'Het Huis Affaytati', *Antwerpsch Archievenblad*, 2nd series, IV (1929), pp. 218–24 for foreign trading communities in Antwerp involved in the diamond trade. For a case study of an Antwerp firm with a branch in Venice since the late sixteenth century, see Christina M. Anderson, 'Diamond-studded Paths: Lines of Communication and the Trading Networks of the Hellemans Family, Jewellers from Antwerp', in *Gems in the Early Modern World: Materials, Knowledge and Global Trade*, ed. Michael Bycroft and Sven Dupré (London, 2019), pp. 65–86.

54 Venetian merchants had been established in Istanbul for a very long time, their presence dating back to the Byzantine period. See Silvano Borsari, *Venezia e Bisanzio nel XII secolo: I rapporti economici* (Venice, 1988); and Donald M. Nicol, *Byzantium and Venice: A Study in Diplomatic and Cultural Relations* (Cambridge, 1988). For the general decline of Venetian presence in the Mediterranean, see Maria Fusaro, *Political Economies of Empire in the Early Modern Mediterranean: The Decline of Venice and the Rise of England, 1450–1700* (Cambridge, 2015).

55 James C. Boyajian, *Portuguese Trade in Asia under the Habsburgs, 1580–1640* (Baltimore, MD, 2008), p. 135.

56 Michael Limberger and Christophe Vielle, 'Het land waar de peper groeit: De eerste Zuid-Nederlandse contacten met India', in *Het wiel van Ashoka: Belgisch-Indiase contacten in historisch perspectief*, ed. Idesbald Goddeeris (Leuven, 2013), pp. 19–34 (p. 28). See also John G. Everaert, 'Soldaten, diamantairs en jezuïeten: Nederlanders in Portugees-Indië voor 1590', in *Souffrir pour Parvenir: De wereld van Jan Huygen van Linschoten*, ed. R. Van Gelder, J. Parmentier and V. Roeper (Haarlem, 1998), pp. 87–91.

57 S. V. Satyanarayana, 'Diamonds in the Deccan: An Overview', in *Deccan Heritage*, ed. H. K. Gupta, A. Parasher-Sen and D. Balasubramanian (Hyderabad, 2000), pp. 135–56 (p. 147).

58 Jan Huyghen van Linschoten, *Itinerario, Voyage ofte Schipvaert van Jan Huygen van Linschoten naer Oost ofte Portugaels Indien* (Amsterdam, 1596). Diamonds and other precious stones are discussed between pp. 104–10.

59 T. R. de Souza, 'A New Account of the Diamond Mines of the Deccan', in *Mediaeval Deccan History*, ed. A. R. Kulkarni, M. A. Nayeem and T. R. de Souza (Mumbai, 1996), pp. 124–34 (p. 124).

60 This mountain might well be the same as de' Conti's diamondiferous mountain.

61 Linschoten, *Itinerario*, p. 104: 'de diepte van een mans lenghte'.

62 Johan Verberckmoes and Eddy Stols, *Aziatische omzwervingen: het levensverhaal van Jacques de Coutre, een Brugs diamanthandelaar 1591–1627* (Berchem, 1988), pp. 171–4.

63 Kolipaka Srinivas, 'Diamond Industry and Trade in Medieval Andhra', *International Journal of Research in Economics and Social Sciences*, V/4 (2015), pp. 140–55 (pp. 141–2). These choices for mining management were essentially the same as those made later in other contexts.

64 Seema Singh, 'Over Sea Trade of Golconda During the 17th Century', MA thesis, Aligarh Muslim University, 1986, p. 12.

65 Karin Hofmeester, 'Economic Institutions and Shifting Labour Relations in the Indian, Brazilian, and South African Diamond Mines', in *Colonialism, Institutional Change, and Shifts in Global Labour Relations*, ed. Karin Hofmeester and Pim de Zwart (Amsterdam, 2018), pp. 67–107 (pp. 70–71).

66 Verberckmoes and Stols, *Aziatische omzwervingen*, pp. 171–4. Similar accidents also occurred in the alluvial diamond fields in Brazil and Africa. For the practice of *sati* through European eyes, see Pompa Banerjee, *Burning Questions: Widows, Witches, and Early Modern European Travellers in India* (New York, 2003).

67 Pieter van der Aa, *La galerie agréable du monde* . . ., 66 parts in 27 vols (Leiden, 1729). For more information on the work of de Hooghe and its use by van der Aa, see Benjamin Schmidt, *Inventing Exoticism: Geography, Globalism, and Europe's Early Modern World* (Philadelphia, PA, 2015), pp. 200–204. For an extensive study on Pieter van der Aa, see P. G. Hoftijzer, *Pieter van der Aa (1659–1733): Leids drukker en boekverkoper* (Hilversum, 1999).

68 Pieter van der Aa, *La galerie agréable du monde* . . . *Cette Partie comprend le tome premier des Indes Orientales* (Leiden, 1729), pp. 5–6.

69 A geologist who published a report on India's diamond mines in the late nineteenth century believed the Ramulkota and Raolconda mines were the same. Valentine Ball, *The Diamonds, Coal and Gold of India: Their Mode of Occurrence and Distribution* (London, 1881), pp. 19–20.

70 Jean-Baptiste Tavernier, *Les six voyages de Jean-Baptiste Tavernier, Chevalier Baron d'Aubonne, qu'il a fait en Turquie, en Perse, et aux Indes, Pendant l'espace de quarante ans, & par toutes les routes que l'on peut tenir, accompagnez d'observations particulieres sur la qualité, la Religion, le gouvernement, les coûtumes & le commerce de chaque païs; avec les figures, le poids, & la valeur des monnoyes qui y ont cours*, 2 vols (Paris, 1676), vol. II, p. 293.

71 Ibid., p. 296.

72 Ibid.

73 Alam, 'Diamond Mining', p. 300. In her article on diamond labour, Karin Hofmeester provided a few more contemporary accounts confirming this image. Karin Hofmeester, 'Working for Diamonds from the 16th to the 20th Century', in *Working on Labor: Essays in Honor of Jan Lucassen*, ed. Marcel van der Linden and Leo Lucassen (Leiden, 2012), pp. 19–46 (pp. 25–8).

74 Tavernier, *Les six voyages*, vol. II, p. 296.

75 Ibid., p. 304.

76 Ibid.

77 Ibid., pp. 304–7.

78 Ibid., pp. 308–11.

79 Ibid.

80 A copy of de Lange's report was included in the Dutch colonial registry for 1663, which was published as J. A. van der Chijs, ed., *Dagh-register gehouden int Casteel Batavia vant passerende daer ter plaetse als over geheel Nederlandts-India Anno 1663* (Batavia and The Hague, 1891), entry 31 July 1663, pp. 368–72.

81 Ibid., p. 369: 'van immemoriale tyden af'.

82 Pointon, *Rocks, Ice and Dirty Stones*, pp. 179–80.

83 Ibid., p. 180, mentions that the Cholmley brothers, well-known English seventeenth-century diamond merchants, refused to buy 'lasks', but that others did.

84 Gedalia Yogev, *Diamonds and Coral: Anglo-Dutch Jews and Eighteenth-century Trade* (Leicester, 1978), p. 140.

85 Van der Chijs, *Dagh-register*, pp. 368–9.

86 Marshal, 'A Description of the Diamond-mines', p. 910.

87 The last mine was described in most detail by de Lange. Van der Chijs, *Dagh-register*, pp. 369–72.

88 Ibid.

89 Ibid.

90 The Jewish merchant Salvador Rodrigues, discussed below, is one example.

91 Abul Fazl Allámi, *The Aín I Akbari*, trans. H. S. Jarrett, 3 vols (Kolkata, 1891), vol. II, pp. 125, 159, 231.

92 Nirmal Kumar Bose, *The Structure of Hindu Society* (Hyderabad, 1975), p. 45.

93 On the Mughal interest in Khokhra's diamonds, see Mathura Ram Ustad, 'Akbar and Jahangir's Attraction in the Diamonds of Kokhra', in *Proceedings of Indian History Congress: 57th Session*, ed. S.Z.H. Jafri and Aniruddha Ray (Chennai, 1996), pp. 392–3.

94 Henry Beveridge, ed., *The Tuzuk-i-Jahangiri; or, Memoirs of Jahangir*, trans. Alexander Rogers (London, 1909), pp. 314–16.

95 H. Blochmann, 'Notes from Muhammadan Historians on Chutia Nagpur, Pachet, and Palamau', *Journal of the Asiatic Society of Bengal*, XL/2 (1871), pp. 111–19 (pp. 115–16).

96 Annemarie Schimmel, *The Empire of the Great Mughals: History, Art and Culture* (London, 2004), p. 35; and Gérard Toffin, 'Brotherhood and Divine Bonding in the Krishna Pranami Sect', in *The Politics of Belonging in the Himalayas: Local Attachments and Boundary Dynamics*, ed. Joanna Pfaff-Czarnecka and Gérard Toffin (New Delhi, 2011), pp. 144–66 (p. 150). Maratha state-building had originated in the Bijapur sultanate and was to pose a serious threat to the Mughal Empire in the eighteenth century. See John F. Richards, *The New Cambridge History of India*, part 1, vol. V: *The Mughal Empire* (Cambridge, 1993), pp. 205–81.

97 Richards, *The New Cambridge History of India*, pp. 137–8.

98 On Mir Jumla's career as a 'portfolio capitalist', see Sanjay Subrahmanyam, *The Political Economy of Commerce: Southern India, 1500–1650* (Cambridge, 2002), pp. 322–7. His military accomplishments are the focus of J. N. Sarkar, *The Life of Mir Jumla, the General of Aurangzeb* (New Delhi, 1979).

99 Biswas, 'Gem-minerals', p. 405.

100 Tavernier, *Les six voyages*, vol. II, p. 311.

101 Marshal, 'A Description of the Diamond-mines', p. 909.

102 Radhika Seshan, *Trade and Politics on the Coromandel Coast: Seventeenth and Early Eighteenth Centuries* (Delhi, 2012), p. 32.

103 Richard Burn, ed., *The Cambridge History of India*, vol. IV: *The Mughul Period* (Cambridge, 1937), pp. 269–72.

104 Kaushik Roy, *Warfare in Pre-British India, 1500 BCE to 1740 CE* (London, 2015), pp. 180–82.

105 Van der Chijs, *Dagh-register*, p. 370.

106 Tavernier, *Les six voyages*, vol. II, p. 248.

107 Ibid., p. 305.

108 Iradj Amini, *The Koh-i-Noor Diamond* (New Delhi, 1994), pp. 225–8.

109 Richards, *The New Cambridge History of India*, pp. 205–81.

110 For an extensive analysis of the Maratha's conquest and establishment of rule, see Stewart Gordon, *The New Cambridge History of India*, part II, vol. IV: *The Marathas, 1600–1818* (Cambridge, 1993).

111 Jaswant Lal Mehta, *Advanced Study in the History of Modern India, 1707–1813* (Slough and Elgin, IL, 2005), pp. 107–9.

112 Various books have been written on the Koh-i-Noor. For a recent and comprehensive analysis, see William Dalrymple and Anita Anand, *Koh-i-Noor: The History of the World's Most Infamous Diamond* (New York, 2017). The Peacock Throne was the Mughal throne in Delhi, commissioned by Emperor Shah Jahan and richly ornated with gemstones. After Nader Shah took it, the throne was lost. See Susan Stronge, 'The Sublime Thrones of the Mughal Emperors of Hindustan', *Jewellery Studies*, X (2004), pp. 52–65.

113 Dalrymple and Anand, *Koh-i-Noor*, pp. 51–2.

114 Originally it weighed 190 carats, but after it was analysed in England it was found to be flawed, leading to its cutting by two of the foremost employers of the Amsterdam firm of Moses Coster, in a workshop specifically built for this purpose in London. Dalrymple and Anand, *Koh-i-Noor*, pp. 229–32.

115 How the diamond made it from the hands of Nader Shah to various rulers and eventually to the Sikh maharajah Ranjit Singh in the Punjab in 1813 is narrated in Dalrymple and Anand, *Koh-i-Noor*, pp. 93–128.

116 See Chapter Two.

117 Thomas Motte, 'A Narrative of a Journey to the Diamond Mines at Sumbhulpoor, in the Province of Orissa; By Thomas Motte, Esq. Undertaken in the Year 1766, by the Direction of the late Lord Clive, then governor of Bengal', *The Asiatic Annual Register; or, a view of the history of Hindustan, and of the politics, commerce and literature of Asia, For the Year 1799. Miscellaneous Tracts* (London, 1800), pp. 50–86 (p. 77).

118 Boyajian, *Portuguese Trade in Asia*, passim.

119 Ibid., pp. 181–2.

120 Even though there is still discussion about the size of Portuguese trade with India between 1580 and 1640, when both the VOC and the EIC were taking over. Boyajian believes that Portuguese traders conducted more trade than is commonly accepted, a hypothesis that is challenged by other scholars such as Om Prakash. While he does not deal specifically with diamonds, see Om Prakash, *The New Cambridge History of India*, part II, vol. V: *European Commercial Enterprise in Pre-colonial India* (Cambridge, 1998), pp. 37–9.

121 Femme S. Gaastra, *The Dutch East India Company: Expansion and Decline* (Zutphen, 2003).

122 On a contemporary description of port activities of Machilipatnam, see William Methwold, 'Relations of Golconda: Relations of the Kingdome of Golconda and Other Neighbouring Nations Within the Gulfe of Bengala (1625)', in *Relations of Golconda in the Early Seventeenth Century*, ed. W. H. Moreland (London, 1931), pp. 1–49 (pp. 36–8).

123 Søren Mentz, 'English Private Trade on the Coromandel Coast, 1660–1690: Diamonds and Country Trade', *Indian Economic and Social History Review*, XXXIII (1996), pp. 155–73.

124 Alam, 'Diamond Mining', pp. 305–6. W. P. Coolhaas, *Generale Missiven van Gouverneurs-Generaal en Raden aan Heren XVII der Verenigde Oostindische Compagnie*, vol. I: *1610–1638* (The Hague, 1960), p. 390.

125 Alam, 'Diamond Mining', p. 297.

126 Tijl Vanneste, *Global Trade and Commercial Networks: Eighteenth-century Diamond Merchants* (London, 2011), p. 44. For the historical role of Goa in the gem trade in general, see João Teles e Cunha, 'Hunting Riches: Goa's Gem Trade in the Early Modern Age', in *The Portuguese, Indian Ocean and European Bridgeheads, 1500–1800: Festschrift in Honour of Prof. K. S. Mathew*, ed. Pius Malekandathil and Jamal Mohammed (Tellicherry, 2001), pp. 269–304.

127 For an overview of the continuing trade in jewellery in Portuguese India, see George D. Winius, 'Jewel Trading in Portuguese India in the XVI and XVII centuries', *Indica*, XXV/1 (1988), pp. 15–34.

128 Lenzen, *The History of Diamond Production*, p. 91; and T. R. de Souza, 'Goa-based Portuguese Seaborne Trade in the Early Seventeenth Century', *Indian Economic and Social History Review*, XII/4 (1975), p. 438. The cruzado was a Portuguese silver coin, worth about 400 reis at the time. The real was the basic Portuguese currency, both in real and account money. For the mid-seventeenth century, the mentioned amounts correspond to about £3.5 million British pounds and a little over £5,000 British pounds. These estimates are based on exchange courses for the period that can be found in John J. McCusker, *Money and Exchange in Europe and America, 1600–1775: A Handbook* (Chapel Hill, NC, 1978), p. 108.

129 Edgar Samuel, 'Diamonds and Pieces of Eight: How Stuart England Won the Rough-diamond Trade', *Jewish Historical Studies*, XXXVIII (2002), pp. 23–40 (pp. 26–7).

130 For a detailed overview of the history of the readmission of the Jews in England, see David S. Katz, *The Jews in the History of England, 1485–1850* (Oxford, 1994), pp. 107–44.

131 Yogev, *Diamonds and Coral*, pp. 82–5.

132 Samuel, 'Diamonds and Pieces of Eight', p. 27.

133 Ibid., pp. 27–9.

134 Candidates who wanted to move to India as free merchants had to obtain permission from the EIC, and the Company's Court Minute Books contain many such requests. As long as the candidate promised with an oath to uphold the Company's rules, paid a fee and was able to have two references, it seems that until 1770 the Company granted the request of 'any applicant

who had some backing among the Company's stockholders'. Yogev, *Diamonds and Coral*, p. 163. For concrete examples, see Vanneste, *Global Trade*, pp. 113–14, 154–8.

135 Even though the worst was yet to come after Louis XIV revoked the Edict of Nantes, which had granted Huguenots religious freedom, in 1685. On the Huguenot diaspora, see Owen Stanwood, *The Global Refuge: Huguenots in an Age of Empire* (Oxford, 2020).

136 For a good and detailed biography of the life of Jean Chardin, see Daniel van der Cruysse, *Chardin le Persan* (Paris, 1998). For his travels, see Ronald W. Ferrier, *A Journey to Persia: Jean Chardin's Portrait of a Seventeenth-century Empire* (London, 1996). The first volume of Chardin's *Voyages du chevalier Jean Chardin en Perse et autres lieux de l'Orient* was published in 1686. Over the next decade two successive editions of his *Voyages* were published in England, along with reprints of his *Le Couronnement de Soleiman Troisième* (first published in 1671). In 1711, with the publication of the four-volume edition of his *Voyages*, Chardin provided a full and authoritative account, and abbreviated editions followed in rapid succession, testifying to a nearly insatiable European interest in oriental studies and culture. By the time of his death in 1712 Chardin's writing had earned him the praise of Gibbon, Montesquieu and Voltaire.

137 See Edgar Samuel, 'Gems from the Orient: The Activities of Sir John Chardin (1643–1713) as a Diamond Importer and East India Merchant', *Proceedings of the Huguenot Society*, XXVII/3 (2000), pp. 351–68, particularly p. 361. The Salvadors were one of the most successful Sephardic diamond trading families. A son of a third brother, Francis Salvador Junior, and his two sons Joseph and Jacob, were very successful in their own regard, although Joseph would end his life impoverished on an American plantation. They were involved in an eighteenth-century cross-cultural diamond trading network that connected London, Amsterdam, Antwerp and Lisbon. For an analysis of this network, see Vanneste, *Global Trade*.

138 Rosalind Bowden, 'The Letter Books of John and Nathaniel Cholmley, Diamond Merchants', *North Yorkshire County Record Office Review*, 67 (2001), pp. 6–57 (pp. 6–7).

139 Samuel, 'Diamonds and Pieces of Eight', pp. 33–4. For Jewish settlement in Chennai and their involvement in diamond trade, see Walter J. Fischel, 'The Jewish Merchant-colony in Madras (Fort St George) during the 17th and 18th Centuries: A Contribution to the Economic and Social History of the Jews in India', *Journal of the Economic and Social History of the Orient*, III/1 (1960), pp. 78–107, and III/2 (1960), pp. 175–95.

140 Yogev, *Diamonds and Coral*, pp. 89–91.

141 Ibid., p. 94. The diamond trader Joseph Salvador wrote two pamphlets under the pseudonym 'Philo-Patriae' in which he provides arguments on behalf of Jewish naturalization, which was proposed through the 'Jew Bill' of 1753, a law that, in spite of the efforts of the influential Salvador and others, was revoked after the public clamour it created. Philo-Patriae, *Considerations on the Bill to Permit Persons Professing the Jewish Religion to be Naturalized by Parliament* (London, 1753); and Philo-Patriae, *Further Considerations on the Act to Permit*

Persons Professing the Jewish Religion, to be Naturalized by Parliament (London, 1753). See also T. W. Perry, *Public Opinion, Propaganda and Politics in Eighteenth-century England: A Study of the Jew Bill of 1753* (Cambridge, MA, 1962).

142 Yogev, *Diamonds and Coral*, pp. 85, 95.

143 Ibid., p. 91, and Samuel, 'Gems from the Orient', p. 354.

144 Josiah Child, *A New Discourse of Trade, Wherein is Recommended several weighty Points relating to Companies of Merchants. The Act of Navigation. Naturalization of Strangers. And Our Woollen Manufactures. The Balance of Trade . . .* (London, 1698), p. 142.

145 See Philip Lawson, *The East India Company: A History* [1993] (Abingdon, 2013), pp. 51–6.

146 Yogev, *Diamonds and Coral*, pp. 94–102.

147 See, for instance, Arthur Attman, *Dutch Enterprise in the World Bullion Trade, 1550–1800* (Göteborg, 1983). For an analysis of the eighteenth-century bullion trade in the context of Jewish diamond traders, see Tijl Vanneste, 'Commercial Culture and Merchant Networks: Eighteenth-century Diamond Traders in Global History', PhD thesis, European University Institute, Florence, 2009, pp. 181–7. For a case study of English traders attempting to smuggle Portuguese bullion out of Lisbon, see Tijl Vanneste, 'Money Borrowing, Gold Smuggling and Diamond Mining: An Englishman in Pombaline Circles', *e-Journal of Portuguese History*, XIII/2 (2015), pp. 80–94.

148 For the trade in coral, see Francesca Trivellato, *The Familiarity of Strangers: The Sephardic Diaspora, Livorno, and Cross-cultural Trade in the Early Modern Period* (New Haven, CT, 2009), pp. 224–50. This important monograph analyses a cross-cultural network involving Jewish and Indian diamond traders. For the use of coral in jewellery, see Pointon, *Brilliant Effects*, pp. 107–12, 127–44. For an insight into Mediterranean coral fishing, see Olivier Lopez, 'Coral Fishermen in "Barbary" in the Eighteenth Century: Between Norms and Practices', in *Labour, Law, and Empire: Comparative Perspectives on Seafarers, c. 1500–1800*, ed. Maria Fusaro, Bernard Allaire, Richard Blakemore and Tijl Vanneste (Basingstoke, 2015), pp. 195–211.

149 The measures that were taken later included the abolition of import and export duties (1676). The free port status made Livorno one of the most prosperous Mediterranean port cities. For a detailed analysis, see Corey Tazzara, *The Free Port of Livorno and Transformation of the Mediterranean World, 1574–1790* (Oxford, 2017).

150 Yogev, *Diamonds and Coral*, p. 125.

151 Verberckmoes and Stols, *Aziatische omzwervingen*, pp. 194, 242–3.

152 Ibid., p. 129.

153 Yogev, *Diamonds and Coral*, pp. 132–4 (p. 134).

154 For the role London played as the main European supply centre of uncut Indian diamonds within a specific eighteenth-century cross-cultural diamond trade network, see Vanneste, *Global Trade*, particularly pp. 67–122. For an overview of the Anglo-Indian diamond trade institutions during their prime in the eighteenth century, see Yogev, *Diamonds and Coral*, pp. 124–68.

155 See Vanneste, *Global Trade*, pp. 95–122. For an extensive analysis of the Ashkenazi Prager firm, see Yogev, *Diamonds and Coral*, pp. 183–274.

156 Academics have relied on different theoretical models to explain growing international and intercultural trade in the Middle Ages and the early modern period. For the use of game theory, see Avner Greif, *Institutions and the Path to the Modern Economy: Lessons from Medieval Trade* (Cambridge, 2006). For a reliance on institutional economics, see Oliver E. Williamson, *Markets and Hierarchies: Analysis and Antitrust Implications – A Study in the Economics of Internal Organization* (New York 1975), as well as Douglass C. North, *Institutions, Institutional Change and Economic Performance* (Cambridge, 1990). Examples of network analysis in the historical context are Gunnar Dahl, *Trade, Trust and Networks: Commercial Culture in Late Medieval Italy* (Lund, 1998), Xabier Lamikiz, *Trade and Trust in the Eighteenth-century Atlantic World: Spanish Merchants and their Overseas Networks* (Woodbridge, 2010), Trivellato, *The Familiarity of Strangers*, and Vanneste, *Global Trade*. The latter two references look at specific intercultural diamond trade networks in the early modern period. Yogev asserted that 'partnerships between Jews and non-Jews were frequent, especially among the bigger merchants'. Yogev, *Diamonds and Coral*, p. 148.

157 Victoria Hutchings, 'Hoare, Sir Richard (1648–1719)', www.oxforddnb.com, accessed 4 May 2020. For Levy Moses's permission to go to India, see British Library, India Office Records (hereafter BL/IOR), B/62: Court Minute Book EIC 55 (1732–1733), entry 14 November 1732.

158 Accounts of their business dealings are preserved in the archives of the Hoare bank. Archives C. Hoare & Co., London (hereafter AHL), HB/I/II: *An account of diamonds bought and sold by Sir Richard and Henry Hoare in partnership with Marcus Moses, 1707–08.*

159 BL/IOR, B/68: Court Minute Book EIC 68 (1744–1746), entry 5 December 1744.

160 AHL, CT/2: Invoices for diamonds and other precious stones consigned to Charles Turner, East India merchant (and bank customer), 1764–1770.

161 BL/IOR, L/AG/50/5/5: *Agreement between Sir Robert Nightingale acting for George Drake, and Anthony da Costa acting for Joseph James Osorio, connected with their partnership at Fort St. George in the diamond trade, December 1721.*

162 The Diamond Fund can be visited as permanent exhibition in the Kremlin, www.gokhran.ru, accessed 4 May 2020).

163 Parts of the history of the Orlov Diamond remain unclear. The Armenian merchant and the Iranian man, said to be a millionaire, might be the same. How the French soldier got it, and from whom, is not exactly clear either. The Orlov might be the same diamond as another famous Indian cut, the Great Mogul, which disappeared also in the middle of the eighteenth century. Pointon, *Rocks, Ice and Dirty Stones*, pp. 54–5, 96; Ogden, *Diamonds*, pp. 308–10; and Edwin W. Streeter, *Precious Stones and Gems: Their History and Distinguishing Characteristics*, 2nd edn (London, 1879), p. 131.

164 For an analysis of the acceptance in English high society of prominent Sephardic diamond merchants, with Joseph Salvador as a concrete example, see Vanneste, *Global Trade*, pp. 130–35. For the life of Joseph Salvador, see

Maurice Woolf, 'Joseph Salvador 1716–1786', *Transactions and Miscellanies of the Jewish Historical Society of England*, 21 (1962–7), pp. 104–37.

165 Bruce Lenman and Philip Lawson, 'Robert Clive, the "Black Jagir", and British Politics', *Historical Journal*, XXVI/4 (1983), pp. 801–29.

166 On the early modern understanding of friendship, see Luuk Kooijmans, *Vriendschap en de kunst van het overleven in de zeventiende en achttiende eeuw* (Amsterdam, 1997).

167 Bruce P. Lenman, 'The East India Company and the Trade in Non-metallic Precious Materials from Sir Thomas Roe to Diamonds Pitt', in *The Worlds of the East India Company*, ed. H. V. Bowen, Margarette Lincoln and Nigel Rigby (Woodbridge, 2002), pp. 97–110 (pp. 108–9).

168 Ogden, *Diamonds*, pp. 194–7. See also Gérard Mabille, *Les Diamants de la couronne* (Paris, 2001).

169 P. J. Marshall, *East India Fortunes: The British in Bengal in the Eighteenth Century* (Oxford, 1976). The term *nabob* derived from Urdu and was used to refer to East India Company servants who had become rich in India, suggestively through corrupt and shady methods. Later, it was more generally applied for men who had amassed wealth in the Orient. J. Albert Rorabacher, *Property, Land, Revenue, and Policy: The East India Company, c. 1757–1825* (London, 2017), p. 274.

170 See Tillman W. Nechtman, *Nabobs: Empire and Identity in Eighteenth-century Britain* (Cambridge, 2010), particularly the two last chapters, pp. 140–220. See also Tillman W. Nechtman, 'Nabobinas: Luxury, Gender, and the Sexual Politics of British Imperialism in India in the Late Eighteenth Century', *Journal of Women's History*, XVIII/4 (2006), pp. 8–30; Tillman W. Nechtman, 'A Jewel in the Crown? Indian Wealth in Domestic Britain in the Late Eighteenth Century', *Eighteenth-century Studies*, XLI/1 (2007), pp. 71–86; and Romita Ray, 'All that Glitters: Diamonds and Constructions of Nabobery in British Portraits, 1600–1800', in *The Uses of Excess in Visual and Material Culture, 1600–2010*, ed. Julia Skelly (Farnham and Burlington, VT, 2014), pp. 19–40.

171 For this evolution, see Yogev, *Diamonds and Coral*, pp. 169–80.

172 Ibid., p. 173.

173 Ibid., pp. 174–5.

174 Ibid., pp. 169–80.

175 Mentz, 'English Private Trade on the Coromandel Coast'. See also Søren Mentz, *The English Gentleman Merchant at Work: Madras and the City of London, 1660–1740* (Copenhagen, 2005). Smuggling is not only hard to analyse from the historians' point of view, in early modern times it was often a weapon in mercantilist competition between states, and a widespread phenomenon. For this 'culture of smuggling', see Felicia Gottman, *Global Trade, Smuggling, and the Making of Economic Liberalism: Asian Textiles in France, 1680–1760* (Basingstoke, 2016), pp. 63–77. Gottman's work is one of the few extensive case studies on a smuggled commodity. The Coromandel coast might have been particularly interesting, because off the coast, particularly in the Gulf of Mannar separating mainland India from Ceylon, pearls were harvested, and these could be used to purchase diamonds. See Sanjay

Subrahmanyam, 'Noble Harvest from the Sea: Managing the Pearl Fisheries of Mannar, 1500–1925', in *Institutions and Economic Change in South Asia*, ed. Sanjay Subrahmanyam and Burton Stein (Oxford, 1996), pp. 134–72.

176 The main commercial centre in Gujarat was Surat. Jainism is one of India's three oldest religions, next to Hinduism and Buddhism, with enlightenment through nonviolence as an essential component. G. Ralph Strohl, Umakant Premanand Shah and Paul Dundas, 'Jainism', www.britannica.com, accessed 4 May 2020.

177 Makrand Mehta, *Indian Merchants and Entrepreneurs in Historical Perspective* (Delhi, 1991). For Shantidas Zaveri see pp. 91–114; for Virji Vora see pp. 53–64. There are only a few other Jain merchants active in gemstone trade who we know about, for instance the Jain scholar, poet and gemstone dealer Banarasidas (1586–1643), whose father had been a jewel trader as well. More research is needed on the careers of Jain merchants like him. Suraiya Faroqhi, *The Ottoman and Mughal Empires: Social History in the Early Modern World* (New York, 2019), pp. 176–7.

178 Robert Challe, *Voyage fait aux Indes Orientales par une Escadre de six Vaisseaux commandez par Mr. Du Quesne, depuis le 24 Février 1690, jusqu'au 20 Août 1691, par ordre de la Compagnie des Indes Orientales*, 3 vols (Rouen, 1721), vol. II, p. 121: 'ils s'habillent comme les Banians, parlent leur Idiome aussi-bien qu'eux, vivent & mangent avec eux & comme eux, font leurs mêmes cérémonies: en un mot, ceux, qui ne les connoissant pas, les prennent pour de vrais Banians.'

179 Ibid., pp. 123–5.

180 F. W. Stapel and Baron van Boetzelaer van Asperen en Dubbeldam, eds, *Pieter Van Dam's Beschryvinge van de Oostindische Compagnie*, 7 vols (The Hague, 1927–54), vol. II (1932), pp. 174–6.

181 Marshal, 'A Description of the Diamond-mines', p. 915. The Telugu are an ethnicity with a distinct language of their own, which belongs to the family of Dravidian languages, the world's fourth largest group with 175 million native speakers in South Asia. B. Krishnamurti, 'Telugu', in *The Dravidian Languages*, ed. Sanford B. Steever (London, 2015), pp. 202–40.

182 Van der Chijs, *Dagh-register*, pp. 368–72. Brahmins belonged to a Hindu caste of priest, but were also known to be agriculturalists. G. S. Ghurye, *Caste and Race in India* (London, 1932), pp. 15–18.

183 Tavernier, *Les six voyages*, vol. II, pp. 330–32.

184 Ibid., pp. 336–7.

185 The problem with the merchant circuits established overland is that, as a general rule, historians are much less aware of their functioning due to a lack of source material. This can be related to the fact that most of the documents in European archives related to early modern trade have focused on the maritime component of it, at the expense of the overland routes. See Sushil Chaudhury, 'Trading Networks in a Traditional Diaspora: Armenians in India, *c.* 1600–1800', paper submitted for presentation at Session 10, 'Diaspora Entrepreneurial Networks, *c.* 1000–2000' of the XIIIth International Economic History Congress, Buenos Aires, 22–26 July 2002, p. 3.

186 Coolhaas, *Generale Missiven*, vol. i, pp. 186–7. Aceh is a part of the Indonesian island of Sumatra.

187 As an Armenian settlement, it was named after Old Julfa, in present-day Azerbaijan but one of the most important cities of medieval and early modern Armenia. Today, New Julfa is part of Isfahan, and still harbours one of the largest Armenian diasporic communities in the world. Ina Baghdiantz-McCabe, 'Princely Suburb, Armenian Quarter or Christian Ghetto? The Urban Setting of New Julfa in the Safavid Capital of Isfahan (1605–1722)', *Revue des mondes musulmans et de la Méditerranée*, 107–10 (2005), pp. 415–36. For an insight into the current situation, see Saeed Rezaei and Maedeh Tadayyon, 'Linguistic Landscape in the City of Isfahan in Iran: The Representation of Languages and Identities in Julfa', *Multilingua*, xxxvii/6 (2018), pp. 701–20. A classic study is Edmund Herzig, *The Armenian Merchants of New Julfa, Isfahan: A Study in Pre-modern Asian Trade* (Oxford, 1991).

188 The raw silk was brought into Mediterranean trading circles by the Armenians. For an extensive study on the Armenian trading networks centred on New Julfa, see Sebouh D. Aslanian, *From the Indian Ocean to the Mediterranean: The Global Trade Networks of Armenian Merchants from New Julfa* (Berkeley, CA, 2011). For more on the Shah's commercial policies, including the establishment of New Julfa, see Rudolph P. Matthee, *The Politics of Trade in Safavid Iran: Silk for Silver, 1600–1730* (Cambridge, 1999), pp. 61–90.

189 Generally the Armenian diaspora was linked to the Mediterranean and the Indian Ocean, with only few expansions into northwestern Europe. For an overview, see Sebouh Aslanian, *From the Indian Ocean*, pp. 44–85. For Marseilles specifically, see Olivier Raveux, 'Entre réseau communautaire intercontinental et intégration locale: la colonie marseillaise des marchands arméniens de la Nouvelle-Djoulfa (Ispahan), 1669–1695', *Revue d'histoire moderne et contemporaine*, lix/1 (2012), pp. 83–102. London only became part of this diasporic world in the last decades of the seventeenth century, with about forty Armenian traders living in the city in the 1690s. Sebouh D. Aslanian, 'Trade Diaspora versus Colonial State: Armenian Merchants, the English East India Company, and the High Court of Admiralty in London, 1748–1752', *Diaspora*, xiii/1 (2004), pp. 37–100 (p. 46).

190 See Sushil Chaudhury and Kéram Kévonian, eds, *Les Arméniens dans le commerce Asiatique au début de l'ère moderne* (Paris, 2018); and Bhaswati Bhattacharya, 'Armenian European Relationship in India, 1500–1800: No Armenian Foundation for European Empire?', *Journal of the Economic and Social History of the Orient*, xlviii/2 (2005), pp. 277–322. From India, Armenian networks extended as far as Manila. Bhaswati Bhattacharya, 'Making Money at the Blessed Place of Manila: Armenians in the Madras-Manila Trade in the Eighteenth Century', *Journal of Global History*, iii/1 (2008), pp. 1–20.

191 No systematic study has been written on the Armenian involvement in the early modern diamond trade, but the references in the following pages allow for a general impression of the importance of Armenian trading networks

in the early modern Asian diamond trade. For a case study, see Evelyn
Korsch, 'The Scerimans and Cross-cultural Trade in Gems: The Armenian
Diaspora in Venice and its Trading Networks in the First Half of the
Eighteenth Century', in *Commercial Networks and European Cities,
1400–1800*, ed. Andrea Caracausi and Christof Jeggle (London, 2014),
pp. 223–39, 293–8.

192 Beinecke Rare Book and Manuscript Library, Yale University (hereafter
BRBML), John Chardin Correspondence and Documents, Gen MSS 216, Series
1, Folder 7: Letters from Sr John Chardin, with some accounts, &
from some Jews: Letter of John Chardin to Daniel Chardin, London,
24 April 1697: 'l'esprit defiant des Armeniens ne leur permet pas de remetre
leurs affaires a personne.'

193 The story is told by Robert Challe in his travel journal. Challe, *Voyage fait
aux Indes Orientales*, vol. II, pp. 372–83. See also Jacques Rougeot, 'Le "Journal
d'un voyage" de Challe', *Revue d'histoire littéraire de la France*, LXXIX/6 (1979),
pp. 1025–9 (p. 1026).

194 Challe, *Journal d'un voyage fait aux Indes Orientales*, vol. II, pp. 381–2: 'fatigué,
& rebutté de tant de chicannes inconnues dans son Païs'.

195 Coolhaas, *Generale Missiven*, I, p. 201.

196 BRBML, John Chardin Correspondence and Documents, Gen MSS 216, Series
1, Folder 12: Sir John Chardin's Letters (1686–1706): Letter of John Chardin
to Daniel Chardin, London, 5 April 1693: 'nous ne sommes pas de marchands en comparaison d'eux'. For a more general overview of the presence of
Armenian merchants and their activities within the framework of the EIC,
see Vahé Baladouni and Margaret Makepeace, eds, *Armenian Merchants of
the Seventeenth and Early Eighteenth Centuries: English East India Company
Sources* (Philadelphia, PA, 1998).

197 BL/IOR, B/40: Court Minute Book 36 (1690–1695), entries on 20 and 24
February 1690. For a short analysis of the relationship between the EIC and
the Armenian trade diaspora in India, see Ruquia Hussain, 'The Armenians
and the English East India Company', *Proceedings of the Indian History
Congress*, LXXIII (2012), pp. 327–34. For an extensive look at Armenian dealings with the EIC in the second half of the eighteenth century, see Aslanian,
'Trade Diaspora versus Colonial State'.

198 Ibid., p. 50. Of course, Armenian settlement in India was far from new, as
Armenians had been established there for centuries, but the agreement led
to a growing Armenian migration from Persia to India. Aslanian, 'Trade
Diaspora versus Colonial State', pp. 46–50. Calendar must have been one of
the most important Armenians in London, as John Chardin remarked in 1697
that the trade of the Armenians, which had begun to flourish in London,
was at a low after Calendar's death. BRBML, John Chardin Correspondence
and Documents, Gen MSS 216, Series 1, Folder 7: Letter of John Chardin
to Daniel Chardin, London, 24 April 1697. Calendar's will is preserved at
the British National Archives in Kew (hereafter NAK), Prerogative Court
of Canterbury and related Probate Jurisdictions: Will Registers (1384–1858),
Prob 11/434/167: Will of Coja Panous Calendar, 24 September 1696. The

family's name is also known as Ghalandarian. Aslanian, 'Trade Diaspora versus Colonial State', p. 46.

199 BL/IOR, B/40: Court Minute Book EIC 36 (1690–1695), entry on 6 June 1694 is an example of a transaction in lead involving Calendar.

200 Ibid., entry on 15 March 1695.

201 BL/IOR, B/40: Court Minute Book EIC 36 (1690–1695), entry on 7 January 1691.

202 BL/IOR, B/62: Court Minute Book EIC 55 (1732–1733), entry on 10 October 1733.

203 For the Sceriman family, see Korsch, 'The Scerimans and Cross-cultural Trade in Gems'; and Aslanian, *From the Indian Ocean*, pp. 150–58.

204 For an extensive study of the Livorno branch of the Sceriman family, and its involvement with precious stones, see Massimo Sanacore, 'Splendore e decadenza degli Sceriman a Livorno', in *Gli Armeni lungo le strade d'Italia: Atti del Convegno Internazionale (Torino, Genova, Livorno, 8–11 marzo 1997)* (Pisa and Rome, 1998), pp. 127–60.

205 Korsch, 'The Scerimans and Cross-cultural Trade in Gems', p. 235.

206 The full story has been analysed ibid., pp. 235–6.

207 The Franco family was one of the Sephardic Jewish families that gained a lot of financial success in the diamond–coral trade through Livorno. See Katz, *The Jews in the History of England*, pp. 176–7.

208 Korsch, 'The Scerimans and Cross-cultural Trade in Gems', pp. 235–6.

209 Ibid., p. 236, for the transaction.

210 This case can be found at Archivio di Stato di Livorno (hereafter ASL), Governatore e Auditore, Atti Civili Spezzati e Lettere (1629–1815), No. 2211.

211 This case can be found at ASL, Governatore e Auditore, Atti Civili del Governatore Alessandro Del Nero, No. 694 (1719).

212 It was not at all uncommon for merchants to settle commercial disputes in courts. See Tijl Vanneste, *Intra-European Litigation in Eighteenth-century Izmir: The Role of the Merchants' Style* (Boston, MA, and Leiden, forthcoming). The Alucan story is discussed in more detail in Sanacore, 'Splendore e decadenza degli Sceriman', and is also referred to in Korsch, 'The Scerimans and Cross-cultural Trade in Gems', pp. 236–7.

213 Sprenger, trans., *El-Mas'údí's Historical Encyclopaedia*, pp. 59–60.

214 'Adam's Peak', www.britannica.com, accessed 4 May 2020; see also Deckard, *Paradise Discourse*, p. 133. For a nineteenth-century description of Adam's Peak, see William Skeen, *Adam's Peak: Legendary, Traditional, and Historic Notices of the Samanala and Srí-Páda, with a Descriptive Account of the Pilgrims' Route from Colombo to the Sacred Foot-print* (Colombo, 1870).

215 For a discussion of Odoric's claims about Sri Lanka, see Ananda Abeydeera, 'Italian Traveller and Missionary: Odoric of Pordenone's Journey to Ceylon', *Deutsches Schiffartsarchiv*, XXV (2002), pp. 11–18. For an account of Odoric's travels in Asia, see Bernard Hamilton, 'Western Christian Contacts with Buddhism, *c.* 1050–1350', *Studies in Church History*, LI (2015), pp. 80–91.

216 James Emerson Tennent, *Ceylon, An Account of the Island: Physical, Historical, and Topographical with Notices of its Natural History, Antiquities and*

Productions, 2 vols (London, 1860), vol. 1, p. 38. 'Caswini' was the Arab scholar Al-Qazwini (1203–1283). For an analysis of some of Al-Qazwini's work, see Persis Berlekamp, *Wonder, Image, and Cosmos in Medieval Islam* (New Haven, CT, 2011).

217 Henri Cordier, ed., *Les voyages en Asie au XIVe siècle du bienheureux frère Odoric de Pordenone Religieux de Saint-François* (Paris, 1841), pp. 222–32.

218 Deckard, *Paradise Discourse*, p. 134.

219 Said, ed., *Al-Beruni's Book on Mineralogy*, p. 80.

220 L. K. Spencer, S. David Dikinis, Peter C. Keller and Robert E. Kane, 'The Diamond Deposits of Kalimantan, Borneo', *Gems and Gemology*, XXIV/2 (1988), pp. 67–80 (p. 67).

221 Ibid., p. 68. Henri-Jean Schubnel, 'Other Producers', in *Diamonds: Myth, Magic, and Reality*, ed. Jacques Legrand (New York, 1980), pp. 180–87.

222 Thomas Suárez, *Early Mapping of Southeast Asia* (Singapore, 1999), p. 185.

223 'Sambas and Pontianak Sultanates', in *Southeast Asia: A Historical Encyclopedia, From Angkor Wat to East Timor*, ed. Ooi Keat Gin (Santa Barbara, CA, 2004), p. 1170.

224 For these sultanates, see ibid., pp. 211–12, 1170–71.

225 *Historische Beschryving der Reizen, of Nieuwe en Volkome Verzameling van de Allerwaardigste en Zeldzaamste Zee- en Land-Togten ter Ontdekkinge en Naspeuringe Gedaan* (Amsterdam, 1759), XVIII, p. 152: 'het Land der Wilden'.

226 NATH, 1.04.02: De Archieven van de Verenigde Oostindische Compagnie, 1602–1795, No. 4855: *Kopie-beschrijving van de staat van de VOC-handel in Borneo, in het bijzonder van Banjarmasin, door Johan Andries, baron van Hohendorff, raad extraordinaris* (1757).

227 'Letter of John Saris to the Right Worshipful the East India Company', Bantam, 4 December 1608, in *Letters Received by the East India Company from its Servants in the East, Transcribed from the 'Original Correspondence' Series of the India Office Records*, vol. 1: *1602–1613*, ed. F. C. Danvers (London, 1896), pp. 20–23.

228 Jack Ogden, 'Diamonds, Head Hunters and a Prattling Fool: The British Exploitation of Borneo Diamonds', *Gems and Jewellery*, XIV/3 (2005), pp. 67–9. It was not uncommon for early modern sources to use 'Flemming', which is the term used for the inhabitants of Flanders in present-day Belgium, for Dutch people as well.

229 L.C.D. Van Dijk, *Neerland's vroegste betrekkingen met Borneo, den Solo-Archipel, Cambodja, Siam en Cochin-China* (Amsterdam, 1862), p. 2.

230 Ibid.

231 *Act of Cession and Handing Over of Landak and Sukadana (Borneo) between the Netherlands East India Company (the Netherlands), and Bantam, signed at Surasuang*, 26 March 1778.

232 Tivadar Posewitz, *Borneo: Its Geology and Mineral Resources* (London, 1892), p. 398.

233 Edward Balfour, *Cyclopaedia of India and of Eastern and Southern Asia, Commercial, Industrial and Scientific: Products of the Mineral, Vegetable and*

Animal Kingdoms, Useful Arts and Manufactures, 3 vols, 2nd edn (Chennai, 1871), vol. II, p. 90.

234 Spencer et al., 'The Diamond Deposits of Kalimantan, Borneo', pp. 67–80 (p. 70).

235 François Farges and Thierry Piantanida, *Le Diamant Bleu* (Neuilly-sur-Seine, 2010). Because the stone was recut, there is still some doubt as to the identification of the Hope with the French Blue.

236 A good book that elucidates the stone's history, but at the same time debunks the myth, is Richard Kurin, *Hope Diamond: The Legendary History of a Cursed Gem* (New York, 2007).

237 Lenzen, *The History of Diamond Production*, p. 16.

238 For trade connections between these areas, see Lenzen, *The History of Diamond Production*, pp. 1–8, 15–25.

239 Harlow, *The Nature of Diamonds*, p. 117.

240 C. Scott Littleton, ed., *Gods, Goddesses, and Mythology*, vol. VI: *Inca–Mercury* (New York, 2005), p. 735.

241 Lenzen, *The History of Diamond Production*, p. 21.

242 Ibid.

243 Ibid.

244 Ibid., p. 20.

245 Garcia da Orta, *Colloquios dos Simples e Drogas: Edição publicada por deliberação da academia real das sciencias de Lisboa. Dirigida e annotada pelo Conde de Ficalho socio effectivo da mesma academia* [1563] (Lisbon, 1891), pp. 195–6.

246 Ibid.

247 A practice that would last throughout the Mughal period. Europeans only managed to get hold of prestigious diamonds through plunder and unrightful appropriation.

248 For these overland routes, see Lenzen, *The History of Diamond Production*, pp. 35–41.

249 Evans, *A History of Jewellery*, pp. 53–5, 61.

250 Karin Hofmeester, 'Diamonds as Global Luxury Commodity', in *Luxury in Global Perspective: Objects and Practices, 1600–2000*, ed. Bernd-Stefan Grewe and Karin Hofmeester (Cambridge, 2016), pp. 55–90 (p. 69).

251 The acknowledgment of Agnès Sorel as the first goes back to the nineteenth century at least. Pierre Jaubert, *Dictionnaire raisonné universel des arts et métiers: contenant l'histoire, la description, la police des fabriques et manufactures de France et des pays étrangers: ouvrage util a tous les citoyens*, 5 vols (Lyon, 1801), vol. II, p. 529.

252 Hofmeester, 'Diamonds as Global Luxury Commodity', p. 69.

253 As quoted in Lenzen, *The History of Diamond Production*, p. 23. See also Anna M. Miller, *Gems and Jewelry Appraising: Techniques of Professional Practice* (New York, 1988), p. 2.

254 Lenzen, *The History of Diamond Production*, p. 23

255 Glenn Klein, *Faceting History: Cutting Diamonds and Colored Stones* (Bloomington, IN, 2005), pp. 40–41.

256 Colette Sirat, 'Les pierres précieuses et leurs prix au xve siècle en Italie, d'après un manuscrit hébreu', *Annales: Économies, Sociétés, Civilisations*, xxiii/5 (1968), pp. 1067–85 (p. 1078).

257 Karin Hofmeester, 'Shifting Trajectories of Diamond Processing: From India to Europe and Back, from the Fifteenth Century to the Twentieth', *Journal of Global History*, viii/1 (2013), pp. 25–49 (pp. 30–31).

258 Samuel Tolansky, *The History and Use of Diamond* (London, 1962), p. 71.

259 Evans, *A History of Jewellery*, p. 96.

260 The manuscript and the story are discussed in Marcel Tolkowsky, *Diamond Design: A Study on the Reflection and Refraction of Light in a Diamond* (London and New York, 1919), pp. 17–19. Tolkowsky also gave no credibility to the story but did consider that van Berken might have contributed some techniques leading to a higher symmetry in the form of polished diamonds.

261 See Vandamme and Rosenhøj, *Brugge Diamantstad*, p. 21. The facade of a building on Antwerp's most famous shopping street, De Meir, contains a statue of van Berken holding a diamond in his hand.

262 The translation of the original French comes from Tolkowsky, *Diamond Design*, p. 17.

263 Piero Pazzi, *I diamanti nel commercio nell'arte e nelle vicende storiche di Venezia* (Venice, 1986), pp. 13–14. For an overview on the existing evidence on cutting techniques before the fifteenth century, see Ogden, *Diamonds*, pp. 79–82; and Marjolijn Bol, 'Polito et Claro: The Art and Knowledge of Polishing, 1100–1500', in *Gems in the Early Modern World*, ed. Bycroft and Dupré, pp. 223–57.

264 Benvenuto Cellini, *The Autobiography of Benvenuto Cellini*, trans. Anne Macdonell (New York, 2010), p. 170.

265 Bartholomeo di Pasi, *Tariffa de i pesi, e misure corrispondenti dal Levante al Ponente, e da una terra, e luogo all'altro, quasi per tutte le parti dil mondo: con la dichiaratione, e notificatione di tutte le robbe, che si tragono di uno paese per l'altro* [1503] (Venice, 1557), pp. 166, 178, 180, 186; see also Hofmeester, 'Shifting Trajectories', p. 34.

266 Lenzen, *The History of Diamond Production*, pp. 71–5.

267 Felixarchief Antwerp (City Archives Antwerp (hereafter FAA), BE SA 174784: Gebodboeken A Bis (1 January 1439–31 December 1496), f. 15v.

268 FAA, BE SA 166831: Schepenregisters (1 January 1491–31 December 1491), f. 132r.

269 For the consultation of the goldsmiths, see FAA, BE SA 61783, Ambachten Boek (1 January 1563–31 December 1588), No. 4487. For the ordinance, see FAA, BE SA 174877, Stadsplakkaten (1 January 1542–31 December 1599), *Ordonnantie van de Diamantsnijders* (25 October 1582). The Antwerp archives contain a number of additional regulations and laws on the guild, issued between 1583 and 1798.

270 FAA, BE SA 424023, Vierschaar (1 January 1501–31 December 1600); several occurrences can be found in November and December 1582.

271 Henri Heertje, *De Diamantbewerkers van Amsterdam* (Amsterdam, 1936), p. 15.

272 On 20 February 1534 a diamond cutter from Ghent was accused of being an Anabaptist. FAA, BE SA 174785, Gebodboeken A (1 January 1489–31 December 1539), f. 193r.

273 Hofmeester, 'Shifting Trajectories', p. 37. Both cities tried for a long time to establish a cutting industry that could compete with those in Amsterdam and Antwerp, but they never succeeded.

274 For the three stages, see Ogden, *Diamonds*, pp. 79–80.

275 The London cutting factories of the late nineteenth century, for instance, paid cutters, for a twelve-hour working day, between 35 and 75 shillings a week, polishers 40 to 120 shillings and cleavers 50 to 130 shillings. Ogden, *Diamonds*, p. 180.

276 Ibid., pp. 125–6.

277 For an overview of the finishing process, see Tolansky, *The History and Use of Diamond*, pp. 56–69. The powder was a residue product from the bruting.

278 Heertje, *De Diamantbewerkers*, p. 21. F. Leviticus, *Geïllustreerde Encyclopaedie der Diamantnijverheid* (Haarlem, 1908), pp. 200–204.

279 Thomas Nicols, *Lapidary; or, The history of pretious stones: With cautions for the undeceiving of all those that deal with Pretious Stones* (Cambridge, 1652), p. 53.

280 Tolansky, *The History and Use of Diamond*, pp. 74–6.

281 For the evolution of the use of diamonds in jewellery during this period, see Evans, *A History of Jewellery*, pp. 103–25.

282 Hofmeester, 'Diamonds as Global Luxury Commodity', p. 70. In her article, Hofmeester linked the growing relationship between diamonds and femininity to the large number of female monarchs at the time, but later eighteenth-century discourse shows a strong connection in perception between commerce, luxury and femininity. See, for instance, Catherine Ingrassia, *Authorship, Commerce, and Gender in Early Eighteenth-century England: A Culture of Paper Credit* (Cambridge, 1998).

283 Evans, *A History of Jewellery*, p. 125.

284 Ibid., p. 130.

285 For a general discussion of early modern assessments of diamonds, see Marcia Pointon, 'Good and Bad Diamonds in Seventeenth-century Europe', in *Gems in the Early Modern World*, ed. Bycroft and Dupré, pp. 173–96.

286 Dalrymple and Anand, *Koh-i-Noor*, pp. 42–3.

287 For an overview of jewellery in relation to the Mughal emperors, see Kim Siebenhüner, 'Precious Things in Motion: Luxury and the Circulation of Jewels in Mughal India', in *Luxury in Global Perspective*, ed. Grewe and Hofmeester, pp. 27–54. For a more general analysis, see Kim Siebenhüner, 'Approaching Diplomatic and Courtly Gift-giving in Europe and Mughal India: Shared Practices and Cultural Diversity', *Medieval History Journal*, XVI/2 (2013), pp. 525–46. For Mughal knowledge of cutting, see Taylor L. Viens, 'Mughal Lapidaries and the Inherited Modes of Production', in *Gems in the Early Modern World*, ed. Bycroft and Dupré, pp. 259–79.

288 The growing participation of Europeans in the Indian diamond business not only changed the whole trade pattern but led to a better knowledge of the diamond mines in India through the survival of several commercial journals and diaries.

289 Everaert, 'Soldaten, diamantairs en jezuïeten', pp. 89–91. The article contains a few more examples. See also references in Vanneste, *Global Trade*, p. 43.

290 Jean de Thévenot, *Les voyages de Mr. de Thevenot aux Indes Orientales, Contenans une Description exacte de l'Indostan, des nouveaux Mogols, & des autres Peuples & Païs des Indes Orientales; avec leur Moeurs & Maximes, Religions, Fêtes, Temples, Pagodes, Cimetiéres, Commerce, & autres choses remarquables*, 3rd edn (Amsterdam, 1727), vol. v, p. 296: 'le roi [the sultan of Golconda] veut que les bons Ouvriers y demeurent . . . il fait même loger des joualiers dans son Palais . . . Les ouvriers du Château sont occupez aux pierreries communes du Roi, qui en a une si grande quantité que ces gens-là ne peuvent presque travailler pour aucune autre personne'.

291 Tavernier, *Les six voyages*, vol. II, pp. 328–9.

292 Ibid., p. 328.

293 Ogden, *Diamonds*, p. 329.

294 City Archives Amsterdam (hereafter CAA), 5075: Archief van de Notarissen ter Standplaats Amsterdam (hereafter CAA/5075), Notaris G. van Bruegel, No. 3496: Minuutacten van attestation (1669–1670), 15 March 1670, pp. 330–32: 'welcke const vant werck oock altijd naer de subtielheijd x const betaelt'.

295 Ibid. This confirms the higher remuneration for cleavers.

296 Ibid.

297 Ad van der Woude, 'The Volume and Value of Paintings in Holland at the Time of the Dutch Republic', *Art in History, History in Art: Studies in Seventeenth-century Dutch Culture*, ed. David Freedberg and Jan de Vries (Santa Monica, CA, 1991), pp. 285–330 (pp. 300–301).

298 CAA/5075, Notaris Jacobus Snel, No. 3602B: Minuutacten en afschriften (1681–1686), 29 September 1685, p. 311.

299 Heertje, *De Diamantbewerkers*, p. 22.

300 CAA/5075, Notaris Daniel van den Brink, No. 10300: Minuutacten (1735), 23 November 1735, f. 352; see also Heertje, *De Diamantbewerkers*, pp. 15, 25–6.

301 Erve van Putten and Bast Boekhoudt, *De zingende koddenaar, queelende verscheide nieuwe liederen, die hedendaags gezongen werden* (Amsterdam, 1774), pp. 61–2. The title of the song is 'De Vrolykheyt vol Verdriet, of het Hedendaagse Leven en Bedryf, der Diamant Sneyers en Slypers, zynde een Zamen-spraak', which means 'The Cheerfulness filled with Sadness, or the Contemporary Life and Profession of Diamond Cutters, being a Conversation'.

2 SLAVERY AND MONOPOLIES: DIAMONDS IN COLONIAL BRAZIL, 1720–1821

1 FAA, Insolvente Boedelskamer James Dormer, 1B1742, Francis and Joseph Salvador to James Dormer, London, 28 September 1753.

2 For a study on the cross-cultural diamond trade network that developed around these traders, see Vanneste, *Global Trade*.

3 For an overview of Brazil's early colonization by the Portuguese and an analysis of the functioning of indigenous societies, see Jorge Couto, *A Construção do Brasil. Ameríndios, Portugueses e Africanos, do início do povoamento a finais de Quinhentos* (Lisbon, 1997). Cabral's experiences were related in the famous

letter sent to Portugal by Pero Vaz de Caminha. For a critical edition, see Maria Beatriz Nizza da Silva, *A carta de Pero Vaz de Caminha. Estudo crítico de J. F. de Almeida Prado* (Rio de Janeiro, 1965).

4 Cláudia Damasceno Fonseca, *Des terres aux villes de l'or: Pouvoirs et territoires urbains au Minas Gerais (Brésil, XVIII siècle)* (Lisbon, 2003), pp. 48–52.

5 Arquivo Nacional da Torre do Tombo, Lisbon (hereafter ANTT), Corpo Cronológico, Parte 1, Maço 84, No. 109: Carta de Filipe Guilhem dando parte ao rei que, indo a porto Seguro para descobrir algumas minas, descobrira além de um grande rio, uma serra amarela que resplandecia como o sol, São Salvador, 20 July 1550.

6 W. L. von Eschwege, *Pluto Brasiliensis: Eine Reihe von Abhandlungen über Brasiliens Gold-, Diamanten- und anderen mineralischen Reichtum, über die Geschichte seiner Entdeckung, über das Vorkommen seiner Lagerstätten, des Betriebs, der Ausbeute und die darauf bezügliche Gesetzgebung u.s.w.*, 2 vols (Berlin, 1833), vol. II, p. 105.

7 André João Antonil, *Cultura e Opulencia do Brasil por suas drogas, e minas, Com varias noticias curiosas de fazer o Assucar; plantar, & beneficiar o Tabaco; tirar Ouro das Minas; & descubrir as da Prata* (Lisbon, 1711), pp. 131–2.

8 Neusa Fernandes, *A Inquisição em Minas Gerais no século XVIII* (Rio de Janeiro, 2000), p. 54.

9 A.J.R. Russell-Wood, *The Black Man in Slavery and Freedom in Colonial Brazil* (New York, 1982), p. 110. The 'fifth', or 'quinto' in Portuguese, was an old royal tax of 20 per cent applied on commodities obtained through mining and war loot. It was also applied on the enslaved. For its application in Brazil, see Manoel S. Cardoso, 'The Collection of the Fifths in Brazil, 1695–1709', *Hispanic American Historical Review*, XX/3 (1940), pp. 359–79.

10 Eddy Stols, *Brazilië: Vijf eeuwen geschiedenis in dribbelpas* (Leuven, 1996), p. 264.

11 Arquivo Público Mineiro, Belo Horizonte (hereafter APM), Secretaria de Governo da Capitania (Seção Governmental) (hereafter APM/SG), Cx. 125, Doc. 30: Informa sobre uma representação de Bernardo Fonseca Lobo, que descobriu uma lavra de diamantes no Serro Frio e ainda acudiu, com seus escravos arrematados, uma sublevação de pessoas contra o pagamento de impostos, n.p., n.d. Although the exact location remains a mystery, Lobo was probably working in a small river near the future diamond capital of Tejuco, the Rio Caetemirim, a side stream of the Jequitinhonha. As is the case for most archival references in the Portuguese and Brazilian archives, documents such as this one have been catalogued under a descriptive title that does not necessarily appear exactly that way on the document itself. In those cases, I have decided to preserve that title. When the archival document in question does have a specific title, it has been put in italics.

12 APM/SG, Cx. 125, D. 32: Silvestre Garcia do Amaral, Informa que ele foi morador muitos anos na capitania e que examinando umas pedras para D. Lourenço de Almeida certificou que eram diamantes, foi-lhe no entanto pedido segredo agora muitas pessoas se apresentam como os descobridores das pedras pede que seja lhe passada certidão de que é o verdadeiro descobridor, n.p., n.d.

13 APM/SG, Cx. 2, D. 10: Atestado passado por João Marques Bacalhau, desembargador da Casa da Suplicação, referente a chegada no porto de Lisboa de uma frota vinda do Rio de Janeiro, trazendo notícias dos diamantes encontrados em Minas, Lisbon, 10 January 1732. This means that Amaral's petition is from approximately the same date, while Lobo's was made earlier.

14 'Sobre o descobrimento dos diamantes na Comarca do Serro Frio. Primeiras administrações', *Revista do APM*, VII/1 (1902), pp. 251–63.

15 Augusto de Lima Júnior, *História dos Diamantes nas Minas Gerais* (Rio de Janeiro, 1945), pp. 19–20.

16 'Sobre o descobrimento'.

17 Biblioteca Nacional, Lisbon (hereafter BNL), Codices e Fundo Geral dos Manuscritos (hereafter BNL/CFGM), Cod. 4530, f. 280: Letter D. Lourenço de Almeida to the Crown, Vila Rica de Ouro Preto, 2 December 1729.

18 Letter Francisco da Cruz to Francisco Pinheiro, Vila Real, 3 August 1729, in *Negócios Coloniais Uma Correspondência Comercial do Século XVIII*, ed. Luis Lisanti, 4 vols (São Paulo, 1973), vol. 1, p. 322.

19 In 1729 £3 6s represented the equivalent of a buying power of £660–£990 today. Robert D. Hume, 'The Value of Money in Eighteenth-century England: Incomes, Prices, Buying Power – and Some Problems in Cultural Economics', *Huntington Library Quarterly*, LXXVII/4 (2015), pp. 373–416 (p. 381).

20 BNL/CFGM, Cod. 4530, ff. 282r–84v and 310r–16v: Regimento do Governador da Capitania de Minas Gerais para a lavra de diamantes da Comarca do Serro Frio, Ouro Preto, 26 June 1730.

21 A.J.R. Russell-Wood, 'Technology and Society: The Impact of Gold Mining on the Institution of Slavery in Portuguese America', *Journal of Economic History*, XXXVII/1 (1977), pp. 59–83 (p. 59).

22 APM, Secretaria de Governo da Capitania (Seção Colonial) (hereafter APM/SC), Cod. 33: Registro de portarias, regimentos, bandos, cartas, provisões, termos . . . e autos de arrematação (exploração de diamantes) (1729–1755), ff. 6r–7v. Letter by the ouvidor of Serro do Frio, Vila do Príncipe, 2 February 1732.

23 Due to both forced and free interracial sexual contacts, a varied population quickly came into being in colonial Brazil. This led to differentiated racial treatment on the basis of skin colour and (perceived) descendancy, and different possibilities for social betterment. A person of mixed descent ('mulato' or 'pardo') could be free, while in Portuguese 'negro' and 'preto' were pretty much used as synonyms for 'escravo'. In any case, most of the categories were considered 'black' to a degree and hence subject to racist and colonial oppression. For an analysis of the position of persons of mixed descent between the extremes of white freedom and black enslavement, see Mariana L.R. Dantas, 'Picturing Families between Black and White: Mixed Descent and Social Mobility in Colonial Minas Gerais, Brazil', *The Americas*, LXXIII/4 (2016), pp. 405–26. For an analysis of ethnic categorizing in colonial America, see Eduardo França Paiva, *Dar nome ao nove: uma história lexical da Ibero-América*

entre os séculos XVI e XVIII (as dinâmicas de mestiçagens e o mundo do trabalho) (Belo Horizonte, 2015).

24 'Sobre o descobrimento', pp. 259–60.

25 APM/SC, Cod. 33, ff. 9r–10r: Regulation issued by D. Lourenço de Almeida, Ouro Preto, 22 April 1732: 'se possa minerar Diamantes em todos os Rios, e terras da Comarca do Serro do Frio, como ate aqui se fes'.

26 APM/SC, Cod. 33: Letter André de Mello e Castro, Ouro Preto, 16 April 1733 (ff. 12r–3r) and 2 December 1733 (f. 15r).

27 'Sobre o descobrimento', p. 262: 'as pessoas inuteis ou perniciosas'.

28 ANTT, Manuscritos do Brasil, L.15, ff. 10v–1: Letter Conde das Galvêas to Martinho Mendonça de Pina e Proença, Ouro Preto, 19 July 1734.

29 Copies of these regulations were included in an anonymous eighteenth-century manuscript on the history of Brazilian diamond mining, *História Chronológica*. Regulations issued by Rafael Pires Pardinho, Tejuco, 8 November 1734 (f. 127r) and 27 December 1734 (f. 128r). For the full reference of this manuscript, see n. 84 below.

30 Arquivo Histórico Ultramarino, Lisbon (hereafter AHU), Conselho Ultramarino Brasil/Minas Gerais (hereafter AHU/CUMG), Cx. 28, D. 2296: Representação dos povos das Minas sobre o lamentável estado em que a cap-itação tem posto as minas, cuja decadência e grande, pedindo que as quatro comarcas sejam beneficiadas, n.p., *c.* 1734. See also Joaquim Felício dos Santos, *Memórias do Distrito Diamantino da Comarca do Sêrro Frio* (Rio de Janeiro, 1956), p. 78.

31 Júnia Ferreira Furtado, *Chica da Silva e o contratador dos diamantes: o outro lado do mito* (São Paulo, 2003), p. 33.

32 For the early stay of de Oliveira in Minas Gerais, see Furtado, *Chica da Silva*, pp. 74–9. AHU/CUMG, Cx. 37, D. 3024: Certidão do auto de rematação do con-trato de extração dos diamantes, realizado entre Gomes Freire de Andrade, governador das Minas e João Fernandes de Oliveira, que o rematou por 4 anos.

33 Ibid.; see also APM/SC, Cod. 1: Registro de alvarás, cartas patentes, provisões, confirmações de cartas patentes, sesmarias e doações (1609–1799), ff. 173r–7r: *Condizóes para a extracáo dos Diamantes aprovada pello Senhor General Gomes Freire de Andrada*, Ouro Preto, 20 June 1739.

34 Furtado, *Chica da Silva*, p. 80.

35 AHU/CUMG, Cx. 41, D. 3324: Carta de Gomes Freire de Andrade, governador de Minas Gerais, a D. João V expondo as dificuldades experimentadas pelos contratadores da companhia de diamantes, Ouro Preto, 12 June 1741.

36 'Sobre os irmãos Felisberto e Joaquim Caldeira Brant', *Revista do APM*, IV (1899), p. 812.

37 *História Chronológica*, ff. 178r–81r.

38 Santos, *Memórias*, p. 104; and Diogo Pereira Ribeiro de Vasconcelos and Carla Maria Junho Anastasia, eds, *Breve descrição geográfica, física e política da capitania de Minas Gerais* (Belo Horizonte, 1994), p. 238.

39 Furtado, *Chica da Silva*, p. 85; Júnia Ferreira Furtado, 'O labirinto da fortuna: ou os revezes na trajetória de um contratador dos diamantes', in *História:*

fronteiras, ed. Eunice Nodari, Joana Maria Pedro and Zilda M. Gricoli, 2 vols (Florianópolis, 1999), vol. 1, pp. 309–20 (p. 312).

40 AHU/ CUMG, Cx. 58, D. 4912: Carta do ouvidor a informar o rei dos excessos cometidos pelo contratador dos diamantes Felisberto Caldeira Brant e das diligências feitas sobre o assunto, n.p., 1752 (erroneously given as 1751); AHU/CUMG, Cx. 60, D. 5044: Ofício do governador de Minas, José Antonio Freire de Andrada para Diogo de Mendonça Corte Real, no qual dá conta da queixa apresentada pelo contratador dos diamantes, capitão Felisberto Caldeira Brant sobre o desaparecimento de diamantes do cofre, Ouro Preto, 8 September 1752; AHU/CUMG, Cx. 60, D. 5017: Carta de Sancho de Andrade Castro e Lanções, intendente dos diamantes da comarca do Serrio Frio, expondo ao rei D. José I os fundamentos da queixa de que formulava contra o contratador Felisberto Caldeira Brant, Tejuco, 5 August 1752.

41 Lima Júnior, *História dos Diamantes*, p. 199; Furtado, 'O labirinto da fortuna', p. 318.

42 *Deducçaó Compendiosa*, f. 319v: 'um homem summamente rustico; summamente simples e taó demente que . . . havia arrematado hum contrato que absolutamente naó podia cumprir'. This anonymous manuscript is very similar to the *História Chronológica*. For the full reference, see n. 84 below.

43 See Vanneste, *Commercial Culture*, pp. 285–93.

44 The trading monopoly will be discussed further below.

45 ANTT, Col. Leis, Maço 4, No. 144: *Decreto Real*, 11 August 1753.

46 Charles R. Boxer, *The Golden Age of Brazil, 1695–1750: Growing Pains of a Colonial Society* (Berkeley, CA, 1962), p. 223.

47 See the excellent book on her by Júnia Ferreira Furtado, which has been translated as *Chica da Silva: A Brazilian Slave of the Eighteenth Century* (New York, 2009). See also Mara Angélica Alves Pereira, Vânia Gico and Nelly P. Stromquist, 'Chica da Silva: Myth and Reality in an Extreme Case of Social Mobility', *Iberoamericana*, v/17 (2005), pp. 7–28. Acclaimed musician Jorge Ben wrote a song about her, released on his seminal album *África Brasil* (Philips, 1976).

48 For overviews of the transatlantic slave trade, see David Eltis and David Richardson, *Atlas of the Transatlantic Slave Trade* (New Haven, CT, 2015) and Herbert Klein, *The Atlantic Slave Trade* (Cambridge, 2010). For connections between Brazil and Angola established through enslavement, see Roquinaldo Ferreira, *Cross-cultural Exchange in the Atlantic World: Angola and Brazil during the Era of the Slave Trade* (Cambridge, 2012).

49 'Slave Voyages: Trans-Atlantic Slave Trade – Database', www.slavevoyages. org, accessed 4 May 2020.

50 Jacob Gorender, *Escravismo Colonial* (São Paulo, 1978), p. 457.

51 APM, Casa dos Contos, No. 1062: Tejuco: Intendência dos diamantes (1734–1741): *recebimento da capitação de 1734*.

52 *História Chronológica*, f. 51r. Alcide d'Orbigny, a nineteenth-century French scientist, claimed that 6,000 slaves were working in the diamond district in 1776. Alcide d'Orbigny, *Voyage dans les deux Amériques* (Paris, 1854), p. 137.

53 In the nineteenth century more slaves came from the Congo. For these percentages, see Laird W. Bergad, *Slavery and the Demographic and Economic History of Minas Gerais, Brazil, 1720–1888* (Cambridge, 1999), pp. 150–56.

54 Rodrigo de Almeida Ferreira, 'Técnicas de trabalho nos serviços diamantíferos e sociabilidade na demarcação diamantina', *Anais da VI Jornada Setecentista*, 1 (2005), pp. 531–9 (p. 532).

55 Michael Kevane, 'Gold Mining and Economic and Social Change in West Africa', in *The Oxford Handbook of Africa and Economics*, vol. II: *Policies and Practices*, ed. Célestin Monga and Justin Yifu Lin (Oxford, 2015), pp. 340–53.

56 Eduardo França Paiva, 'Bateias, Carumbés, Tabuleiros: Mineração Africana e Mestiçagem no Novo Mundo', in *O trabalho mestiço: maneiras de pensar e formas de viver – séculos XVI a XIX*, ed. Eduardo França Paiva and Carla Maria Junho Anastasia (São Paulo, 2002), pp. 187–207.

57 Vanneste, 'Women in the Colonial Economy'. For the economic activities of free black and mixed-race women, see Júnia Ferreira Furtado, 'Pérolas negras: mulheres livres de cor no Distrito Diamantino', in *O trabalho mestiço*, ed. França Paiva and Junho Anastasia (São Paulo, 2002), pp. 497–512.

58 For an extensive overview of their activities, see Vanneste, 'Women in the Colonial Economy'.

59 Ibid.

60 Ibid. For the activities of women in the diamond district in a broader context, see Luciano Figueiredo, 'Mulheres nas Minas Gerais', in *História das mulheres no Brasil*, ed. Mary del Priore (São Paulo, 2008), pp. 141–88; and Luciano Figueiredo, *O Avesso da Memória: Cotidiano e trabalho da mulher em Minas Gerais no século XVIII* (Rio de Janeiro, 1993). For the development of agricultural networks supplying the diamond district with food, see A. A. Carrara, *Minas e Currais: Produção rural e mercado interno de Minas Gerais, 1674–1807* (Juiz de Fora, 2007). For a study on women in the nearby gold mining regions, see Kathleen J. Higgins, *'Licentious Liberty' in a Brazilian Gold-mining Region: Slavery, Gender, and Social Control in Eighteenth-century Sabará, Minas Gerais* (University Park, PA, 1999).

61 This chart has appeared earlier in Tijl Vanneste, 'Women in the Colonial Economy: The Agency of Female Food Sellers in Brazil's Diamond District', *Tijdschrift voor Genderstudies/Journal of Gender Studies*, XVIII/3 (2015), pp. 255–72 (p. 261). It is based on the author's calculations using data from historical sources, mainly the *História Chronológica*. For the contract periods between 1740 and 1771, the given number per period is applicable for each year, as no information for a specific year within such period was available.

62 Letter Francisco da Cruz to Francisco Pinheiro, Vila Real, 17 May 1730, in Lisanti, *Negócios Coloniais*, vol. I, pp. 323–5 (p. 324).

63 The original letter can be found as AHU/CUMG, Cx. 108, D. 8571: Ofício do intendente geral dos diamantes, João da Rocha Damas e Mendonça para o secretário de estado da marinha e domínios ultramarinos, Martinho de Melo e Castro, no qual remete as relações de todos os habitantes da demarcação diamantina, Tejuco, 15 January 1775.

64 For an analysis of Julião's work in this context, see Silvia Hunold Lara, 'Carlos Julião and the Image of Black Slaves in Late Eighteenth-century Brazil', *Slavery and Abolition*, XXIII/2 (2002), pp. 125–46. He also had a few images of *negras e tabuleiro*. Reproductions of Julião's images can be found in Carlos Julião, *Riscos illuminados de figurinhos de brancos e negros dos uzos do Rio de Janeiro e Serro do Frio* (Rio de Janeiro, 1960).

65 BNL, Colecção Pombalina (hereafter BNL/PBA), Cod. 691, ff. 1–11: *Regimento para os administradores do contrato de dos diamantes*, 2 August 1771. For a detailed description, see Júnia Ferreira Furtado, *O livro da capa verde: o regimento diamantino de 1771 e a vida no Distrito Diamantino no período da real extracção* (São Paulo, 1996).

66 This information was taken from the late eighteenth-century writings of José Joaquim Rocha, published as José Joaquim Rocha, *Geografia Histórica da capitania de Minas Gerais*, ed. Maria Efigênia Lage de Resende (Belo Horizonte, 1995), p. 134; Furtado, *O livro da capa verde*, p. 118; and Raimundo José da Cunha Matos, *Corografia histórica da Província de Minas Gerais (1837)*, 2 vols (Belo Horizonte, 1981), vol. I, p. 371.

67 João Luís Ribeiro Fragoso, *Homens de grossa aventura: acumulação e hierarquia na praça mercantil do Rio de Janeiro, 1790–1830* (Rio de Janeiro, 1992), p. 106.

68 *Regimento para os administradores do contrato de diamantes*, art. XXXVIII and XXXIX.

69 Furtado, *O livro da capa verde*, p. 45.

70 AHU/CUMG, Cx. 117, D. 9237: João da Rochas Dantas e Mendonça, informando Martinho de Melo e Castro sobre a remessa de mapas contendo a relaçao de diamantes e pessoal relativo ao referido serviço, Tejuco, 22 January 1781.

71 Johannes Baptiste von Spix and Carl Friedrich Philipp von Martius, *Reise in Brasilien auf Befehl Sr. Majestät Maximilian Joseph I. Königs von Baiern in den Jahren 1817 bis 1820*, 3 vols (Munich, 1828), vol. II, p. 443.

72 Fernandes, *A Inquisição em Minas Gerais*, p. 66.

73 Laura de Mello e Souza, 'Violência e práticas culturais no cotidiano de uma expedição contra quilombolas: Minas Gerais, 1769', in *Liberdade por um fio: história dos quilombos no Brasil*, ed. João José Reis and Flavio dos Santos Gomes (São Paulo, 1996), pp. 193–212 (pp. 194–6).

74 *História Chronológica*, f. 42v.

75 For the restriction of clerics, see *História Chronológica*, f. 64r; for the inventories, see Furtado, *O livro da capa verde*, p. 48.

76 Caio César Boschi, 'Sociabilidade religiosa laica: as irmandades', in *História da Expansão Portuguesa*, vol. III: *O Brasil na Balança do Império (1697–1808)*, ed. Francisco Bethencourt and Kirti Chaudhuri (Lisbon, 1998), pp. 352–71.

77 For an extensive study on the most important brotherhood for enslaved Africans, see Julita Scarano, *Devoção e escravidão: a irmandade de Nossa Senhora do Rosário dos Pretos no distrito diamantino no século XVIII* (São Paulo, 1976).

78 It is very interesting to notice that the architectural style of these colonial mining churches was repeated in the churches built later in Benin and Nigeria by formerly enslaved men and women who had returned to Africa in

the beginning of the nineteenth century. See André de Oliveira, 'A história perdida da arquitetura brasileira dos retornados à África', www.elpais.com, 1 June 2018.

79 Scarano, *Devoção e escravidão*, pp. 79–95.

80 Ibid., p. 92.

81 Ibid., p. 83.

82 Ibid., p. 80.

83 The most famous *quilombo* in Brazil was that of Palmares, in Pernambuco, which existed between 1630 and 1695. At its zenith it was a small society with several thousands of inhabitants, many refugees from the sugar plantations. See Stuart Schwartz, 'Mocambos, Quilombos, e Palmares: A Resistência escrava no Brasil colonial', *Estudos Econômicos*, XVII (1987), pp. 61–88. It has been translated into English as Stuart B. Schwartz, 'Rethinking Palmares: Slave Resistance in Colonial Brazil', in *Slaves, Peasants, and Rebels: Reconsidering Brazilian Slavery*, ed. Stuart B. Schwartz (Urbana, IL, 1992), pp. 103–36. An outstanding graphic novel narrating the history of Palmares was published in 2017: Marcelo D'Salete, *Angola Janga: Uma História de Palmares* (São Paulo, 2017). An English translation came out in June 2019.

84 For an overview of society during the contract years, see Rodrigo de Almeida Ferreira, *O descaminho dos diamantes; relações de poder e sociabilidade na demarcação diamantina no período dos contratos (1740–1771)* (Belo Horizonte, 2009). These two manuscripts were largely written by the same person, and they overlap a great deal. While the *História Chronológica* is more concerned with mining and contains copies of a great deal of relevant laws and ordnances, the *Dedução Compendiosa* is more about the trade and events related to the trading monopoly. There are sufficient indications to assume it was written by, or in the name of, the marquês de Pombal, particularly personal and anti-semitic comments against Francis Salvador and the remark that, to solve the crisis following the clandestine activities of Caldeira Brant, the author (Pombal) could 'stay locked in my office without being interrupted [for eight days]'. The quote can be found in BNL/PBA, Cod. 695, ff. 306-80: *Dedução Compendiosa dos Contractos de Mineração dos diamantes; dos outros contractos da Extracção delles; dos cofres de Lisboa para os Payzes Estrangeiros; dos perigos em que todos laboravam e das Providencias, comque a elles occorreo o senhor Rey Dom Jozeph para os conservar*, n.d., on f. 324r: '[oito dias] em que pude estár fechado no Meu Gabinete sem ser interrompido'. For the animosity between Salvador and Pombal, see Vanneste, 'Money Borrowing'. The other manuscript can be found at BNL/CFGM), Cod. 746: *História Chronológica dos Contratos da Minerassão dos Diamantes dos Outros Contractos de Extracsão delles dos Cofres de Lisboa para os Paizes Estrangeiros dos Abuzos em que todos laborarão, e das Providencias com que se lhe tem occorrido ate o anno de 1788*, n.d. The manuscript has been published without additional explanation or analysis by an anonymous author as 'Do descobrimento dos diamantes, e diferentes methodos, que se tem praticado na sua extracção', *Anais da Biblioteca Nacional*, LXXX (1960), pp. 9–251.

85 John Mawe, *Travels in the Interior of Brazil, particularly in the gold and diamond districts of that country* (London, 1813), p. 313.

86 Spix and Martius, *Reise*, vol. ii, p. 442.

87 Mawe, *Travels*, p. 320.

88 Auguste de Saint-Hilaire, *Viagem pelo Distrito dos Diamantes* (Belo Horizonte, 1974), p. 16.

89 Dos Santos, *Memórias*, p. 159.

90 Affonso Ávila, *Minas Gerais: Monumentos históricos e artísticos: circuito do diamante* (Belo Horizonte, 1995), p. 287.

91 *História Chronologica*, ff. 36r–9v.

92 Mawe, *Travels*, pp. 219–37.

93 Unfortunately, Mawe did not include an illustration of these carts in his work. The water wheel depicted in illus. 27, which was only included in a later publication of Mawe's travel writings, was for pumping the river dry, similar as the one shown in illus. 23. The two innovations described by Mawe – carts and cylinders – were probably a technical answer to the declining numbers of enslaved labourers.

94 AHU/CUMG, Cx. 118, D. 9374: Carta de D. Rodrigo José de Menezes, governador de Minas, informando Martinho de Melo e Castro, entre outro assuntos, sobre a desordem que campeia nos serviços diamantinos, Ouro Preto, 24 June 1782.

95 AHU/CUMG, Cx. 118, D. 9350: Carta de D. Rodrigo José de Menezes, governador de Minas, informando Martinho de Melo e Castro sobre a necessidade que há em que algumas companhias de infantaria guarneçam Vila Rica a fim de protegerem as cofres da tesouraria geral e da intendência, Ouro Preto, 15 April 1782.

96 Dos Santos, *Memórias*, p. 98.

97 Spix and Martius, *Reise*, vol. ii, pp. 445–6.

98 Waldemar de Almeida Barbosa, *Dicionário Histórico-Geográfico de Minas Gerais* (Belo Horizonte, 1971), p. 205. Another example is the town of Milho Verde.

99 For the story of one employee of the Royal Extraction involved in smuggling in the 1780s, see André Figueiredo Rodrigues, 'Os "extravios que tão continuados têm sido . . .": contrabando e práticas comerciais ilícitas nas atividades do contratador João Rodrigues de Macedo', *Locus: Revista de História*, xi/1–2 (2005), pp. 1–20.

100 See Kenneth Maxwell, *Conflicts and Conspiracies: Brazil and Portugal, 1750–1808* (Cambridge, 1973), pp. 84–114.

101 Virgínia Maria Trindade Valadares, 'Elites mineiras setecentistas: conjugação de dois mundos (1700–1800)', 2 vols, PhD thesis, Universidade de Lisboa, 2002, vol. i, p. 295.

102 Ibid., p. 299. For agriculture, see José Newton Coelho Meneses, 'Produção de alimentos e atividade econômica na comarca do Serro Frio – Século xviii', in *Anais do ix Seminário sobre a Economia Mineira*, ed. H.E.A. Cerqueira, 2 vols (Belo Horizonte, 2000), vol. i, pp. 123–46.

103 AHU/CUMG, Cx. 58, D. 4806: Requerimento de João Fernandes de Oliveira, possuidor de muitas fazendas de criação de gado em Minas Gerais,

solicitando a D. João V a mercê de ordenar que só ele possa fazer uso das ditas terras, comprometendo-se a continuar a produzir bom gado, n.p., 5 January *c.* 1751. Meneses, 'Produção de alimentos', p. 125. See also Carlos Magno Guimarães and Liana Maria Reis, 'Agricultura e escravidão em Minas Gerais (1700–1750)', *Revista do Departamento de História da* UFMG, I/2 (1986), pp. 7–36.

104 For a thorough study, see Valadares, 'Elites mineiras setecentistas'.

105 Dos Santos, *Memórias*, p. 104.

106 For an overview of diamond mining in Goiás, see Ernst Pijning, 'Illusive Gems: The Disappearance of Diamonds from Goiás', *História Revista*, V/1–2 (2000), pp. 11–23. See also 'Do descobrimento dos diamantes', pp. 153–9.

107 Luís Palacín, *O Século do Ouro em Goiás 1722–1822: Estrutura e Conjutura numa Capitania de Minas* (Goiânia, 1994), pp. 52–4.

108 Francis de Castelnau, *Expédition dans les parties centrales de l'Amérique du Sud, de Rio de Janeiro à Lima, et de Lima au Para; exécutée par ordre du gouvernement français pendant les années 1843 a 1847, sous la direction de Francis de Castelnau: Histoire du voyage*, 6 vols (Paris, 1850), vol. II, p. 232.

109 Richard Burton, *Explorations of the Highlands of the Brazil; with a Full Account of the Gold and Diamond Mines*, 2 vols (London, 1869), vol. II, p. 153. Barbosa, *Dicionário*, p. 389. On the life and ideas of Richard Burton within the context of his time, see Dane Kennedy, *The Highly Civilized Man: Richard Burton and the Victorian World* (Cambridge, MA, 2005).

110 Barbosa, *Dicionário*, p. 453.

111 Clarete Paranhos da Silva, *O Desvendar do Grande Livro da Natureza: Um Estudo da Obra do Mineralogista José Vieira Couto, 1798–1805* (São Paulo, 2002), pp. 57–70. He discussed his findings about the area in José Vieira Couto, *Memoria sobre as Minas da Capitania de Minas Geraes* [1801] (Rio de Janeiro, 1842), pp. 113–38.

112 Barbosa, *Dicionário*, pp. 321, 389–95.

113 Several fears were expressed in a Portuguese document that discussed the possible establishment of a trading monopoly in Brazilian diamonds. AHU/CUMG, Cx. 28, D. 2295: *Condições para o estabelecimento do comércio dos diaman-tes*, n.p., *c.* 1734; see also Jeffries, *A Treatise on Diamonds*, p. 66.

114 AHU/CUMG, Cx. 28, D. 2295: *Condições*.

115 NAK, State Papers, 89/37, ff. 166–8: Lord Tyrawley to the Duke of Newcastle, Lisbon, 2 May 1732.

116 Both letters were included in AHU/CUMG, Cx. 28, D. 2295: *Condições*.

117 Yogev, *Diamonds and Coral*, pp. 110–20.

118 A story that can be found in different sources, including Jeffries, *A Treatise on Diamonds*. See the reference in the travel journal of Richard Burton: Burton, *Explorations*, vol. II, p. 108.

119 Ibid.

120 AHU/CUMG, Cx. 28, D. 2295: *Condições*.

121 AHU/CUMG, Cx. 37, D. 3024: Certidão do auto de rematação do contrato de extração dos diamantes. See also Furtado, *Chica da Silva*, p. 82.

122 See above.

123 For a merchant's take on the events, see *A Genuine Account of the Present State of the Diamond-trade in the Dominions of Portugal, With some Authentic Pieces. In a Letter from a Merchant in Lisbon to his Correspondent in London* (London, 1754).

124 Archives Diplomatiques. Ministère de l'Europe et des Affaires étrangères, La Courneuve, Mémoires et Documents Portugal, vol. 11: *Recueil de Pieces sur les Diamants du Brezil*, p. 341: 'l'un leurs acheptont toutes les diaments Bruts, cétoint . . . Sebastien Vanderton fils d'Ernest Vanderton Natif d'Anvers lapidaire de profession, très experimenté dans ce commerce'. Yogev, *Diamonds and Coral*, p. 121, suggests that the Vandertons did hold a monopoly.

125 Vanneste, *Global Trade*, pp. 52–3.

126 *Deducçaó Compendiosa*, ff. 308v–11v.

127 Vanneste, 'Money Borrowing'.

128 Yogev, *Diamonds and Coral*, pp. 118–19.

129 *Deducçaó Compendiosa*, f. 311r: 'os seus sinistros conselhos' and 'cauzou ao dito Famozo Hebreo huma grande alegria'.

130 Ibid., f. 326v.

131 Fernando de Castro Brandão, *História Diplomática de Portugal, uma cronologia* (Lisbon, 2002), p. 144; and C. Bille, *De tempel der kunst of het kabinet van den heer Braamcamp* (Amsterdam, 1961).

132 Vanneste, 'Money Borrowing'.

133 A copy of the contract was included in the *História Chronológica*, ff. 230v–33v.

134 FAA, Insolvente Boedelskamer James Dormer, 1B1743, Joseph Salvador to James Dormer, London, 1 April 1757.

135 L.M.E. Shaw, *The Anglo-Portuguese Alliance and the English Merchants in Portugal, 1654–1810* (Aldershot, 1998), p. 89.

136 'Gore, John (*c.* 1689–1763), of Bush Hill, Mdx.', www.historyofparliament-online.org, accessed 4 May 2020. On David de Purry in Lisbon and his links with the government, see Agostinho Rui Marques Araújo, 'Das Riquezas do Brasil aos Gastos e Gostos de um Suiço em Lisboa. David de Purry, um amigo de Pombal (1709–1786)', *Revista da Faculdade de Letras*, 11 (2003), pp. 109–37.

137 A copy was included in *História Chronológica*, ff. 238r–9r.

138 *Deducçaó Compendiosa*, ff. 341v–2r.

139 Ibid., f. 340v: 'corporaçaó dos Hebreos'.

140 For more on the family history, see C. J. De Bruyn Kops, 'De Amsterdamse verzamelaar Jan Gildemeester Jansz', *Bulletin van het Rijksmuseum*, XIII/3 (1965), pp. 79–114. Jan's son was an art collector who had purchased several paintings that had belonged to Gerrit Braamcamp earlier. See also the recent thesis on the family by Inger Wesseling, 'The Gildemeesters: A Family's Strategies for Commercial Success and Upwards Social Mobility during the 18th Century', MA thesis, Leiden University, 2019.

141 A copy was included in *História Chronológica*, ff. 239v–43r.

142 Hofmeester, 'Shifting Trajectories', p. 38.

143 Tijl Vanneste, 'Les privilèges de l'industrie du diamant brésilien au dix-huitième siècle', in *Die Ökonomie des Privilegs, Westeuropa 16.–19. Jahrhundert*,

ed. Guillaume Garner (Frankfurt, 2016), pp. 465–83 (pp. 478–9); and Kenneth Maxwell, *Marquês de Pombal, paradoxo do iluminismo* (São Paulo, 1996), pp. 44–57.

144 *Dedução Compendiosa*, f. 346r.

145 Marquis de Bombelles, *Journal d'un ambassadeur de France au Portugal (1786–1788)*, ed. Roger Kann (Paris, 1979), pp. 129–30.

146 BNL/PBA, Cod. 691, ff. 18r–v: *Letras sobre o contrato dos Diamantes que há para pagar, e dias dos seus vencimentos*, 1770.

147 'Do descobrimento dos diamantes', pp. 77–8.

148 Paulo Jorge, whose father was Milanese, was mentioned as one of the men who were part of Pombal's commercial bourgeoisie. Catia Brilli, 'Coping with Iberian Monopolies: Genoese Trade Networks and Formal Institutions in Spain and Portugal During the Second Half of the Eighteenth Century', *European Review of History*, XXIII/3 (2016), pp. 1–30 (p. 9). It is sometimes complicated for those years to establish who was involved in the monopoly, as it was often surrounded with some degree of secrecy. This must be one of the reasons that some academic literature cites the involvement of the Amsterdam-based Bretschneider brothers in the Brazilian monopoly during the 1770s, even though I could not find any archival source mentioning them. There was, however, a Jan Adam Bretschneider active in Amsterdam as a merchant in glass, who published an advertisement in the *Leydse Courant* on 10 May 1775, in which he put his whole business up for sale.

149 David Rabello, *Os Diamantes do Brasil na regência de Dom João (1792–1816): um estudo de dependência externa* (São Paulo, 1997), p. 177.

150 Fernande Jorge Dores Costa, 'Crise financeira, dívida pública e capitalistas (1796–1807)', MA thesis, Universidade Nova de Lisboa, 1992, p. 289. Some of them belonged to the families of da Cruz-Sobral, Quintela and Bandeira.

151 FAA, Insolvente Boedelskamer James Dormer, 1B1701, Thomas & Adrian Hope to James Dormer, Amsterdam, 3 August 1747, 21 August 1747 and 21 April 1749. See also M. G. Buist, *At Spes non Fracta: Hope & Co., 1770–1815; Merchant Bankers and Diplomats at Work* (The Hague, 1974), pp. 384–5.

152 For the detailed story of the loan, see Buist, *At Spes non Fracta*, pp. 383–427.

153 Ibid., p. 513.

154 Patrick Wilcken, *Empire Adrift: The Portuguese Court in Rio de Janeiro, 1808–1821* (London, 2005).

155 For the settling of loan accounts, see Rabello, *Os Diamantes*, pp. 125–228.

156 José Luís Cardoso, 'A New Contribution to the History of Banco do Brasil (1808–1829): Chronicle of a Foretold Failure', *Revista Brasileira de História*, XXX/59 (2010), pp. 165–89.

157 Harry Bernstein, *The Brazilian Diamond in Contracts, Contraband and Capital* (Lanham, MD, 1986), pp. 81–123.

158 Herbert H. Kaplan, *Nathan Mayer Rothschild and the Creation of a Dynasty: The Critical Years, 1806–1816* (Stanford, CA, 2006), p. 7. See also Lord Justice Cohen, 'Levi Barent Cohen and Some of his Descendants', *Transactions (Jewish Historical Society of England)*, XVI (1945–51), pp. 11–23.

159 Kaplan, *Nathan Mayer Rothschild*, p. 16. A Dutch historian asserted he was one of the most important Jewish figures in the Netherlands in the second

half of the eighteenth century: Jozeph Michman, *The History of Dutch Jewry during the Emancipation Period, 1787–1815* (Amsterdam, 1995), pp. 15–16.

160 Alexandre José Mello Moraes, *Historia do Brasil-Reino e Brasil-Imperio*, 2 vols (Rio de Janeiro, 1871), vol. 1, pp. 40–41.

161 Bernstein, *The Brazilian Diamond*, pp. 100–103.

162 Considering the existence of illegal activities, the actual number might have been substantially higher.

163 This yearly average is significantly lower than Brazil's yearly average today, which is only a tiny fraction of global production and is close to India's present-day yearly production in terms of weight. Of course, Brazil's diamonds from the eighteenth century were of higher gemstone quality than either Brazilian or Indian diamonds today.

164 Until 1790 the data comes from the eighteenth-century *História Chronológica* as transcribed in 'Do descobrimento dos diamantes', pp. 35–6. Data for the other years was taken from Eschwege, *Pluto Brasiliensis*, pp. 391–6. Eschwege also included the numbers for the period before 1790, which were the same as those from the 'Do descobrimento dos diamantes'. For the six mining contracts issued between 1740 and 1771, no yearly production numbers are available, only the total of diamonds mined per contract. I used those numbers to come up with yearly averages, which were then applied to the relevant years.

165 Lenzen, *The History of Diamond Production*, p. 125.

166 Eschwege, *Pluto Brasiliensis*, pp. 125–6.

167 Tijl Vanneste, 'The Eurasian Diamond Trade in the Eighteenth Century: A Balanced Model of Complementary Markets', in *Goods from the East: Trading Eurasia, 1600–1800*, ed. Maxine Berg, Hannah Hodacs, Felicia Gottman and Chris Nierstrasz (Basingstoke, 2015), pp. 139–53 (pp. 147, 149).

168 'Do descobrimento dos diamantes', p. 79.

169 Hofmeester, 'Diamonds as Global Luxury Commodity', p. 83

170 The exact genesis of this cut and Mazarin's role therein remains somewhat obscure. Ogden, *Diamonds*, pp. 168–70. See also Tolkowsky, *Diamond Design*, pp. 21–2.

171 Tolkowsky, *Diamond Design*, p. 22.

172 Ogden, *Diamonds*, pp. 170–72.

173 Jeffries, *A Treatise on Diamonds*, p. 30.

174 Evans, *A History of Jewellery*, p. 149.

175 These could be variations on older styles, and take many forms, such as oval, pear, heart or table. The choice for an irregular cut could have to do with the specific form of the rough stone, or with a specific consumer's demand. Tolansky, *The History and Use of Diamond*, pp. 76–80.

176 Evans, *A History of Jewellery*, p. 152.

177 Morag Martin, *Selling Beauty: Cosmetics, Commerce, and French Society, 1750–1830* (Baltimore, MD, 2009), pp. 93–4. The period of the French Revolution and its aftermath was tumultuous and characterized by two big stories. The first was the well-known affair of the diamond necklace that took place between 1784 and 1786, and the second the theft of the French Crown

Jewels in 1792. For the first, see Pointon, *Brilliant Effects*, pp. 147–78; for the second, see Germaine Bapst, *Histoire des joyaux de la Couronne de France d'après des documents inédits* (Paris, 1889), pp. 447–576.

178 Evans, *A History of Jewellery*, p. 151.

179 Pointon, *Rocks, Ice and Dirty Stones*, p. 143.

180 Ibid.

181 *Amsterdamse Courant*, 12 August 1730.

182 *Oprechte Haerlemsche Courant*, 17 August 1730.

183 For the idea of complementarity of Europe's diamond centres, see Vanneste, 'The Eurasian Diamond Trade'.

184 Hofmeester, 'Shifting Trajectories', p. 38.

185 De Bie, 'The Paradox of the Antwerp Rose', pp. 269–93.

186 D. Schlugleit, 'De Strijd om de Ambachtsregelingen in het Diamantvak te Antwerpen in 1754', *Bijdragen tot de Geschiedenis*, new series, XXII/9 (1931), pp. 42–9.

187 For diamond cutting in London, see Ogden, *Diamonds*, pp. 171–2, 183–4.

188 Jeffries, *A Treatise on Diamonds*, p. 101.

189 Tillander, *Diamond Cuts*, pp. 136, 167, 182; Jeffries, *A Treatise on Diamonds*, p. 152; and Hofmeester, 'Shifting Trajectories', p. 34.

190 Bleue-Marine Massard, 'La Manufacture Royale de Taille de Diamant (1779–1787) ou La volonté de doter la France d'un nouvel art sous Louis XVI', MA thesis, Université Paris IV Sorbonne, 2011.

191 FAA, Insolvente Boedelskamer van der Meeren, 1B2352, C. van Hogerwoert to M. van der Meeren, Amsterdam, 28 February 1735: 'onse vrinden die hier aen smousen of Joden maackelen of beunasen . . . in plaats van dat aen eerlyke Christenen te zenden'. The term 'smous', probably derived from Yiddish, was an antisemitic slur used to refer to Jews.

192 Schlugleit, 'De Strijd om de Ambachtsregelingen'.

193 Heertje, *De Diamantbewerkers*, pp. 22–3.

194 Ibid., p. 23: 'alzoo het ons onmogelijk is, volgens onze aangebore aart, gelijk de Jooden doen, onze kost te winnen met Schoenen schoon maken, of met Kammen en Brillen, en oude Kleeren te kopen en ons te behelpen gelijk de Zwijnen, 10 of 12 in een hok.'

195 ANTT, PT/TT/RED/A: Real Extracção de Diamantes das Minas no Brasil – A Direcção de Lisboa (1764–1807), PT/TT/RED/A-A/001: Fábrica de Lapidação de Diamantes. Recibos dos lapidarias, 1806–1807.

3 THE ROLLERCOASTER TOWARDS INDUSTRIAL MODERNITY, 1785–1884

1 Burton, *Explorations*, vol. II, pp. 104–5.

2 The remark was included in a synopsis of an article by Dr John Shaw that originally appeared in the *Cape Monthly Magazine* (September 1870). John Shaw, 'The Geology of the Diamond Fields of South Africa', *Nature: A Weekly Illustrated Journal of Science*, III (November 1870–April 1871), pp. 2–3 (p. 3). It was repeated in slightly different wording in the *Sunday Times*, 13 November

1870. On Shaw, see William Beinart, *The Rise of Conservation in South Africa: Settlers, Livestock, and the Environment, 1770–1950* (Oxford, 2003), p. 119.

3 For a recent study on the meaning of diamonds in the context of nineteenth-century imperial and Victorian Great Britain, see Adrienne Munich, *Empire of Diamonds: Victorian Gems in Imperial Settings* (Charlottesville, VA, 2020).

4 For the Battle of Plassey and its impact on British colonialism and territorial expansion, see Sekhar Bandyopadhyay, *From Plassey to Partition: A History of Modern India* (New Delhi, 2004), pp. 1–65. For a discussion of the role of Robert Clive in colonial policies and his relationship with the diamond trader Joseph Salvador, who advised Clive in policy matters in the early 1760s, see Vanneste, *Commercial Culture*, pp. 276–8.

5 Bandyopadhyay, *From Plassey to Partition*, p. 44.

6 It was not a coincidence that Thomas Motte's mission to Sambalpur took place a year later (see Chapter One).

7 FAA, Insolvente Boedelskamer James Dormer, IB1743, Francis & Jacob Salvador to James Dormer, London, 24 November 1747.

8 G. W. Forrest, 'The Siege of Madras in 1746 and the Action of La Bourdonnais', *Transactions of the Royal Historical Society*, 3rd series, II (1908), pp. 189–234. For the involvement of Salvador and Dormer, see Vanneste, *Commercial Culture*, p. 98. It seems their attempt failed, and a few years later they tried to control the Brazilian diamond monopoly, in which they ultimately also failed.

9 Bandyopadhyay, *From Plassey to Partition*, pp. 49–50.

10 Ibid., pp. 51–65.

11 Dalrymple and Anand, *Koh-i-Noor*, pp. 173–88.

12 Ibid., pp. 219–28.

13 'Koh-i-Noor: India Says It Still Wants Return of Priceless Diamond', www.bbc.co.uk, 20 April 2016, and 'Return the Kohinoor to Lahore: Pakistan Minister', www.thehindu.com, 11 April 2019.

14 Historiography on the event does not agree on death toll and the conscious effort of the British to murder Indians. Saul David, *The Indian Mutiny* (New York, 2002) provides a classic account. Amaresh Mishra labelled the British answer to the mutiny as a 'holocaust' and estimated that it led to 10 million deaths in the decade following 1857. Amaresh Mishra, *War of Civilisations: India, 1857 AD*, 2 vols (New Delhi, 2008).

15 Bandyopadhyay, *From Plassey to Partition*, pp. 66–183.

16 More information can be found on their website. See 'Geological Survey of India', mines.gov.in, accessed 4 May 2020.

17 Ball, *The Diamonds, Coal and Gold of India*, pp. 14–16.

18 Ibid., p. 14.

19 The place had been visited by geologists in the early nineteenth century as well. Ibid., pp. 16–18.

20 Ibid., p. 18.

21 Ibid., p. 19.

22 Ibid., p. 21.

23 Rasanada Tripathy, *Crafts and Commerce in Orissa* (Delhi, 1986), p. 55.

24 A history of the mining in the region is given by Ball, *The Diamonds, Coal and Gold of India*, pp. 39–44.

25 Ibid., pp. 25–38 (p. 38).

26 'The Diamond Mines of Sumbulpore', *New World*, III (6 November 1841), pp. 299–300.

27 Bhagwan Das Gupta, *A History of the Rise and Fall of the Marathas in Bundelkhand, 1731–1804: Based on Original Sources* (Delhi, 1987).

28 Ball, *The Diamonds, Coal and Gold of India*, pp. 50–54.

29 Louis Rousselet, *L'Inde des rajahs: voyage dans l'Inde centrale et dans les présidences de Bombay et de Bengale* (Paris, 1875), p. 440. The Bengal reform movement was better known as the 'Bengal Renaissance' and was an intellectual movement that advocated forms of Western-inspired freethinking, but also fostered nationalist and anti-British sentiment. See, for instance, Susobhan Chandra Sarkar, *Bengal Renaissance and Other Essays* (New Delhi, 1970); and David Kopf, *British Orientalism and the Bengal Renaissance* (Berkeley, CA, 1969).

30 Rousselet, *L'Inde des rajahs*, pp. 440–41; and Abshire et al., 'A Mathematical Method for Visualizing Ptolemy's India', p. 33.

31 Rousselet, *L'Inde des rajahs*, pp. 442–3.

32 Ibid.

33 Observors had made similar remarks about the Brazilian alluvial mines.

34 Ball, *The Diamonds, Coal and Gold of India*, p. 46.

35 Ibid., p. 51. Ball failed to mention the title of the newspaper, the date of publication and the name of the author.

36 Ibid., pp. 51–2.

37 Hofmeester, 'Working for Diamonds', p. 42.

38 Ball, *The Diamonds, Coal and Gold of India*, p. 57.

39 'Sambas and Pontianak Sultanates', p. 1170.

40 In 1938 both Divisions were united under a general government of Borneo, with the capital in Banjarmasin. See Robert Cribb, *Historical Atlas of Indonesia* (Richmond, Surrey, 2000), p. 129. For an overview of developments in Borneo during the nineteenth century, see Graham Irwin, *Nineteenth-century Borneo: A Study in Diplomatic Rivalry* (The Hague, 1955).

41 Mary Somers Heidhues, 'Chinese Organizations in West Borneo and Bangka: Kongsis and *Hui*', in *'Secret Societies' Reconsidered: Perspectives on the Social History of Modern South China and Southeast Asia*, ed. David Ownby and Mary F. Somers Heidhues (Armonk and London, 1993), pp. 68–88 (pp. 70–76).

42 H. Blink, *Nederlandsch Oost- en West-Indië Geographisch, Ethnographisch en Economisch beschreven*, 2 vols (Leiden, 1907), vol. II, pp. 360–62.

43 Posewitz, *Borneo*, pp. 401–2. Posewitz's discussion on diamonds can be found on pp. 379–406. Another report that mentioned diamonds is R.D.M. Verbeek, *Die Eocänformation von Borneo und ihre Versteinerungen* (Cassel, 1875).

44 Posewitz, *Borneo*, p. 381.

45 D. de Loos, *Gesteenten en Mineralen van Nederlandsch Oost-Indie*, vol. II: *Diamant en Edele Metalen* (Haarlem, 1889), p. 5.

46 J. Rueb, 'Diamanten op Borneo', *Economisch-Statistische Berichten: Algemeen Weekblad voor Handel, Nijverheid, Financiën en Verkeer*, II/99 (1917), pp. 867–9 (p. 869).

47 Max Bauer, *Edelsteinkunde*, 3rd edn (Leipzig, 1932), p. 281.

48 Rueb, 'Diamanten op Borneo', p. 869.

49 'De Diamantwinning', *Het Vaderland*, 6 May 1930.

50 Posewitz, *Borneo*, pp. 481–3.

51 'Exploratie van diamantvelden op Borneo', *Het Nieuws van den Dag voor Nederlandsch-Indië*, 26 September 1919.

52 De Loos, *Gesteenten*, p. 7.

53 Rueb, 'Diamanten op Borneo', p. 869.

54 Ibid.

55 Ibid.

56 Posewitz, *Borneo*, pp. 404–5.

57 Ibid., p. 405.

58 Ibid., p. 401.

59 Ibid., p. 405.

60 Ibid., p. 397.

61 Ibid., p. 398. Later that century, the town of Martapura became the main diamond finishing centre of Borneo.

62 Posewitz, *Borneo*, p. 397.

63 John Crawfurd, *History of the Indian Archipelago: containing an account of the manners, arts, languages, religions, institutions, and commerce of its inhabitants*, 3 vols (Edinburgh, 1820), vol. III, p. 493.

64 Ibid.

65 Illus. 30 clearly shows that Brazilian production numbers dropped significantly during the early nineteenth century.

66 Eschwege, *Pluto Brasiliensis*, p. 155.

67 Biblioteca Antonio Torres, Diamantina, *Resolução da Assembleia Geral Legislativa*, 25 October 1832.

68 Dos Santos, *Memórias*, p. 397: 'sombrio, melancólico'.

69 Marcos Lobato Martins, 'A Mineração de Diamantes e a Administração Geral dos Terrenos Diamantinos: Minas Gerais, Décadas de 1830–1870', *Revista de História*, CLXVII (2012), pp. 129–63 (pp. 134–5).

70 Dos Santos, *Memórias*, p. 403: 'lei que julgamos excelente'.

71 For an analysis of slavery and its abolition in the local context of Minas Gerais, see Bergad, *Slavery and the Demographic and Economic History of Minas Gerais*.

72 Lobato Martins, 'Mineração', pp. 137–9.

73 For the reference to the Caldeira Brant family, see Burton, *Explorations*, vol. II, p. 125.

74 Ibid., pp. 121–2.

75 Ibid., p. 104.

76 APM, Presidência da Província – Seção Provincial (hereafter APM/SP),

No. 1007: Originais de ofícios e mais papéis dirigidos ao Governo sobre indústrias e terrenos diamantinos, 1863, f. 60r.

77 Ibid., ff. 126–7: 'gente da baixa condição'. These archives contain more references to similar mining rushes.

78 APM/SP, No. 551: Registro de ofícios e mais atos do Governo sobre terrenos diamantinos, 1854–1866: 'pessoas que na maior parte são da peor classe da sociedade'.

79 Lobato Martins, 'Mineração', p. 144.

80 APM, Delegacia dos Terrenos Diamantinos, No. 13: Repartição de Terrenos Diamantinos – Matrícula de lotes arrendados (1886–1913), p. 196. For the life and presidential tenure of Kubitschek, see Robert J. Alexander, *Juscelino Kubitschek and the Development of Brazil* (Athens, OH, 1991).

81 Burton, *Explorations*, vol. II, pp. 98–100.

82 Marco Lobato Martins, 'A presença da fábrica no "grande empório do Norte": surto industrial em Diamantina entre 1870 e 1930', *Anais do IX Seminário sobre a Economia Mineira*, I (2000), pp 281–304 (p. 290).

83 Ibid., p. 290; and Paul Walle, *Au Brésil État de Minas Geraes (Préface de M.E. Levasseur)* (Paris, 1916), pp. 29–30. Walle visited Brazil as leader of a French commercial mission. He went to different places, including the diamond district, and claimed that Brazilian diamonds were of superior quality to South African stones.

84 A collection of these letters was published as Nicolaas Verschuur, *Brieven uit Brazilië* (Amsterdam, 1989).

85 'Sobre o descobrimento', p. 260.

86 Spix and Martius, *Reise*, vol. II, pp. 608–9.

87 José Martins Catharino, *Garimpo Garimpeiro Garimpagem* (Rio de Janeiro, 1986), pp. 53–70.

88 Alex Robinson, *Bahia: The Heart of Brazil's Northeast* (Guilford, CT, 2010), p. 234.

89 'A Diamond Mine', *The Penny Satirist*, 25 October 1845, and 'Discovery of a Diamond Mine', *Morning Post*, 17 November 1845.

90 Published as B. M. da Silva Acauã, 'Relatorio dirigido ao governo imperial, em 15 de Abril 1847, pelo inspector geral dos terrenos diamantinos da província da Bahia, o Sr. Dr. Benedicto Marques da Silva Acauã, membro correspondente do Instituto', *Revista Trimensal de Historia e Geographia, ou Jornal do Instituto Historico e Geographico Brasileiro*, IX/2 (1869), pp. 227–60.

91 Ibid.

92 Bauer, *Precious Stones*, p. 179.

93 Harry Emanuel, *Diamonds and Precious Stones: Their History, Value, and Distinguishing Characteristics with Simple Tests for their Identification*, 2nd edn (London, 1867), p. 59.

94 Lenzen, *The History of Diamond Production*, pp. 131–3.

95 Jozsef Garai, Stephen E. Haggerty, Sandeep Rekhi and Mark Chance, 'Infrared Absorption Investigation Confirms the Extraterrestrial Origin of Carbonado Diamonds', *Astrophysical Journal Letters*, DCLIII/2 (2006), pp. 153–6.

96 Janusz Konstanty, *Powder Metallurgy Diamond Tools* (Amsterdam, 2005), p. 2.

97 Marc W. Herold, 'The Black Diamonds of Bahia (Carbonados) and the Building of Euro-America: A Half-century Supply Monopoly (1880–1930s)', *Commodity of Empire*, Working Paper No. 21 (London, 2013). Black diamonds had been found in very small quantities in North Carolina and were also mined in Borneo.

98 Marc W. Herold and Samuel Rines, 'A Half-century Monopoly (1880–1930s): the Black Diamonds (carbonados) of Bahia and Jewish Merchants', *Revista Ciências Administrativas*, XVII/1 (2011), pp. 13–54 (p. 36).

99 Ibid., p. 25.

100 For a detailed analysis, see Norman Etherington, *The Great Treks: The Transformation of Southern Africa, 1815–1854* (Abingdon, 2014).

101 Meredith, *Diamonds, Gold and War*, p. 7.

102 Historically, colonizers used the pejorative and racist terms 'Hottentots' for the Khoi and 'Bushmen' for the San.

103 On the development of South Africa's colonial racial order, see Timothy Keegan, *Colonial South Africa and the Origins of the Racial Order* (London, 1996).

104 Linda Waldman, *The Griqua Conundrum: Political and Socio-cultural Identity in the Northern Cape, South Africa* (Oxford, 2007), p. 58.

105 Jan van der Stoep in conversation with Mr Cecil le Fleur and Captain Johannes Kraalshoek, 'Do Minorities Need Cultural Rights? The Case of the Griqua People in South Africa', in *From Our Side: Emerging Perspectives on Development and Ethics*, ed. Steve de Gruchy, Nico Koopman and Sytse Strijbos (Amsterdam, 2008), pp. 75–86 (p. 78).

106 For an in-depth analysis of the development of the Griqua people during those years, see Martin Chatfield Legassick, *The Politics of a South African Frontier: The Griqua, the Sotho-Tswana, and the Missionaries, 1780–1840* (Basel, 2010). This work is based on Legassick's doctoral thesis submitted at UCLA in 1969.

107 Waldman, *The Griqua Conundrum*, pp. 63–9.

108 This game, allegedly originating from Asia but played in many parts of the world, consists in repeated throwing and catching of five stones – or, originally, astragali, hucklebones or knucklebones of goat or sheep. The game is still known as knucklebones in the English language today. It is one of the oldest games of chance, its existence several millennia old. Linguistical confusion and the disappearance of the rules of games throughout time makes it very difficult to trace the precise origins of games in time and place, and it does not always allow for comparison. What is commonly accepted is that the throwing of animal bones in the air was related both to foretelling the future and to games – both dealing with chance and probability. See Florence Nightingale David, *Games, Gods, and Gambling: A History of Probability and Statistical Ideas* [1962] (Mineola, NY, 1998), pp. 2–5.

109 Later, Hond was arrested for illegal diamond buying, for which he spent some time in prison. Afterwards he returned to the Netherlands. Héritte

had a collection of precious stones and had published a treatise on it in 1867. Geoffrey Lynfield, *In Search of Gustav: The Story of the Lilienfeld (later Lynfield) Family Covering the Last 200 Years* (New York, 2005), p. 79. Marian Robertson, *Diamond Fever: South African Diamond History, 1866–9, from Primary Sources* (Cape Town, 1974), p. 232.

110 Robertson, *Diamond Fever*, pp. 69–84. Other versions of the Eureka's discovery exist, but according to Robertson, this is the most plausible one. In 1967 De Beers bought the stone and donated it to the people of South Africa. It is currently in the Kimberley Mine Museum.

111 Ibid., p. 36.

112 As quoted ibid., p. 69.

113 Ibid., pp. 66–8.

114 As quoted ibid., p. 125.

115 Emanuel appears in J. Culme, *The Directory of Gold and Silversmiths, Jewellers and Allied Traders, 1838–1914* (London, 1987). See also Charlotte Gere and Judy Rudoe, *Jewellery in the Age of Queen Victoria: A Mirror to the World* (London, 2010).

116 As quoted in Robertson, *Diamond Fever*, p. 138. For Atherstone, see 'Atherstone, William Guybon', *Encylopaedia Brittanica* (New York, 1911), vol.11, p. 845.

117 As quoted in Robertson, *Diamond Fever*, pp. 123, 132–3.

118 Ibid., p. 137.

119 James R. Gregory, 'Diamonds from the Cape of Good Hope', *Geological Magazine*, v/54 (1868), pp. 558–61 (p. 561).

120 James R. Gregory, 'Discovery of Diamonds, Etc., at the Cape', *Geological Magazine*, vi/61 (1869), pp. 333–4.

121 See Robertson, *Diamond Fever*, p. 162. Gold had been discovered north of the Limpopo river in 1868, leading to a gold rush. Meredith, *Diamonds, Gold and War*, p. 135.

122 'The Precious Stones of Australia', *The Star*, 20 February 1869.

123 'Gregory', *A Dictionary of South African English on Historical Principles* (Oxford, 1996), p. 266.

124 'Kaapkolonie', *Nieuwe Rotterdamsche Courant*, 22 May 1869. They had taken the news from a newspaper from Cape Town, *Kaapsche Volksblad*, 19 April 1869.

125 The Lilienfelds played an important role as traders and miners in South Africa's early diamond history. For more information, see Lynfield, *In Search of Gustav*.

126 *Graaff-Reinet Herald*, 24 March 1869.

127 Robertson, *Diamond Fever*, p. 194.

128 'European Items', *The Star*, 12 May 1871.

129 William J. Morton, *South African Diamond Fields and the Journey to the Mines* (New York, 1877), p. 10.

130 Robertson, *Diamond Fever*, p. 202; Jerome L. Babe, *The South African Diamond Fields* (Kimberley, 1976), p. 19.

131 Robertson, *Diamond Fever*, p. 206.

132 'The Diamond Valley', *Western Times*, 1 November 1870.

133 Frederick Boyle, *To the Cape for Diamonds: A Story of Digging Experiences in South Africa* (London, 1873), p. 86.

134 Robertson, *Diamond Fever*, p. 133.

135 Babe, *South African Diamond Fields*, pp. 19–22.

136 Meredith, *Diamonds, Gold and War*, pp. 24–5.

137 Babe, *South African Diamond Fields*, p. 48.

138 Robertson, *Diamond Fever*, pp. 173–92.

139 Meredith, *Diamonds, Gold and War*, pp. 22–6.

140 Colin Newbury, *The Diamond Ring: Business, Politics and Precious Stones in South Africa, 1867–1947* (Oxford, 1989), pp. 9–17.

141 Charles A. Payton, *The Diamond Diggings of South Africa: A Personal and Practical Account* (London, 1872), p. 156.

142 Babe, *South African Diamond Fields*, pp. 37–9.

143 Robertson, *Diamond Fever*, pp. 209–32.

144 Lynfield, *In Search of Gustav*, pp. 98–100; Gardner F. Williams, *The Diamond Mines of South Africa: Some Account of their Rise and Development* [1899] (New York, 1902), pp. 165–8.

145 Robertson, *Diamond Fever*, pp. 209–32.

146 A. E. Coleman, 'Life in the Diamond Fields', *Harper's Magazine*, XLVI (December 1872–May 1873), pp. 321–36 (p. 327).

147 Williams, *The Diamond Mines*, pp. 172–5. This would become the Big Hole. Illus. 40, as well as several others obtained from the same database, were labelled as originating from around 1900. All evidence suggests these were made earlier, perhaps as early as 1872. Compare, for instance, the 1872 print in *The London Illustrated News* (illus. 4) with illus. 40.

148 Ibid., p. 168.

149 'Diamond Land', *Penny Illustrated Paper*, 16 September 1871.

150 Babe, *South African Diamond Fields*, p. 70. William H. Worger, *South Africa's City of Diamonds: Mine Workers and Monopoly Capitalism in Kimberley, 1867–1895* (New Haven, CT, 1987), p. 15. While there were Chinese, Indian and Malay migrants working in Kimberley, with some exception these were mainly active in professions that supported the mining economy, but not so much as miners. 'No available evidence points to any Chinese having worked as a diamond diggerer although many survived as shopkeepers and laundreymen, living in the Malay Camp on the outskirts of the town.' Melanie Yap and Dianne Leong Man, *Colour, Confusion and Concessions: The History of the Chinese in South Africa* (Hong Kong, 1996), pp. 47–8. The Malay camp was a community founded by Malay transport drivers.

151 Payton, *Diamond Diggings*, p. 107.

152 Babe, *South African Diamond Fields*, p. 23.

153 Payton, *Diamond Diggings*, pp. 106–7. Payton later became a British diplomat, was stationed in Mogador (Morocco) and became one of the founders of Genoa Cricket & Football Club, the present-day football team Genoa F.C. in Italy. The term *kafir* comes from the Arabic word for unbeliever. In the colonial context of nineteenth-century South Africa it designated someone belonging to the Bantu people, although it could be used more as a slur

exclusively to denigrate someone. See A. J. Christopher, '"To Define the Indefinable": Population Classification and the Census in South Africa', *Area*, XXXIV/4 (2002), pp. 401–8.

154 Payton, *Diamond Diggings*, pp. 103, 114.

155 Quoted ibid., p. 26.

156 Ernest Cohen, 'Mittheilungen an Professor G. Leonhard', *Neues Jahrbuch für Mineralogie, Geologie und Palaeontologie* (1872), pp. 857–61; see also E. J. Dunn, 'On the Mode of Occurrence of Diamonds in South Africa', *Quarterly Journal of the Geological Society*, XXX (1874), pp. 54–60 (p. 54).

157 H. Carvill Lewis, 'The Genesis of the Diamond', *Science*, VIII/193 (1886), pp. 345–7.

158 These rules, 24 in total, were reprinted in Boyle, *To the Cape for Diamonds*, pp. 402–3.

159 Ibid., pp. 119–22.

160 Worger, *South Africa's City of Diamonds*, p. 18.

161 Anneke Higgs, 'The Historical Development of Diamond Mining Legislation in Griqualand West during the Period 1871 to 1880', *Fundamina*, XXIV/1 (2018), pp. 18–56 (p. 19).

162 Payton, *Diamond Diggings*, p. 5.

163 Meredith, *Diamonds, Gold and War*, pp. 33–4.

164 'A Growl from the Diamond Fields', *The Times*, 8 February 1872.

165 Todd Cleveland, *Stones of Contention: A History of Africa's Diamonds* (Athens, OH, 2014), p. 52.

166 'A Growl from the Diamond Fields'.

167 Rob Turrell, 'The 1875 Black Flag Revolt on the Kimberley Diamond Fields', *Journal of Southern African Studies*, VII/2 (1981), pp. 194–235 (p. 200).

168 Newbury, *Diamond Ring*, p. 22.

169 Payton, *Diamond Diggings*, p. 139.

170 Cleveland, *Stones of Contention*, p. 52.

171 Ibid., p. 53. For a study on black labour in the colonial context during the second half of the nineteenth century in Natal, see Keletso E. Atkins, *The Moon Is Dead! Give Us Our Money! The Cultural Origins of an African Work Ethic, Natal, South Africa, 1843–1900* (Portsmouth, NH, 1993). While the analysis does not deal with mining labour, the author's findings on how insertion into the colonial labour market was perceived socially and culturally by the communities participating in it are equally relevant for the communities participating in the early migrant labour to the diamond mines.

172 John Pampallis, *Foundations of the New South Africa* (Cape Town, 1991), p. 24.

173 Robert Vicat Turrell, *Capital and Labour on the Kimberley Diamond Fields, 1871–1890* (Cambridge, 1987), pp. 18–19. Cleveland's numbers were higher, as he estimated 15,000 to 35,000 non-white workers residing in Kimberley, a number that rose to 50,000 to 80,000 in the following years. Cleveland, *Stones of Contention*, p. 52. The difference can be partially explained by the fact that labourers residing in Kimberley also worked in the other mines nearby.

174 Oswald Doughty, *Early Diamond Days: The Opening of the Diamond Fields of South Africa* (London, 1963), p. 182.

175 Cleveland, *Stones of Contention*, p. 53.

176 Ibid., p. 57. This created labour shortages elsewhere; it was, for instance, one of the reasons behind disruptions in the colonial labour market of Natal around 1873. Atkins, *The Moon Is Dead!*, p. 132.

177 Payton, *Diamond Diggings*, p. 165.

178 Turrell, *Capital and Labour*, p. 31.

179 Doughty, *Early Diamond Days*, p. 190.

180 John Angove, *In the Early Days: The Reminiscences of Pioneer Life on the South African Diamond Fields* (Kimberley, 1910), pp. 67–9.

181 'South Africa', *Glasgow Herald*, 8 February 1872.

182 Turrell, *Capital and Labour*, pp. 27–9.

183 Ibid., pp. 28–9.

184 For an extensive analysis of the development of racist stereotypes and the growing racial antagonism in the diamond mines during its early history, see Paul G. Lawrence, 'Class, Colour Consciousness and the Search for Identity: Blacks at the Kimberley Diamond Diggings, 1867–1893', MA thesis, University of Cape Town, 1994.

185 Payton, *Diamond Diggings*, p. 139.

186 Ibid., p. 141. Exeter Hall was a building on the Strand in London, where anti-slavery movements regularly met. Payton's chapter on indigenous labour was entitled 'our coloured labourers'. Payton, *Diamond Diggings*, p. 137. When he referred to his own workers, Payton regularly used racist terms such as 'my boys' or 'my two darkies'. Ibid., p. 145.

187 Turrell, *Capital and Labour*, pp. 100–102. In spite of everything, throughout the 1870s some black and Asian claimholders remained and managed to become rich before selling their claims.

188 Ibid., p. 50.

189 Jade Davenport, 'Colonial Mining Policy of the Cape of Good Hope: An Examination of the Evolution of Mining Legislation in the Cape Colony, 1853–1910', MA thesis, University of Cape Town, 2009, pp. 52, 55.

190 Turrell, *Capital and Labour*, pp. 34–5.

191 Higgs, 'The Historical Development', pp. 31–2.

192 Turrell, *Capital and Labour*, pp. 34–6 (p. 35). For the establishment of alternative forms of government by diggers during the same period, see ibid., pp. 36–42.

193 Ibid., p. 12.

194 All of these technical innovations are discussed in Williams, *Diamond Mines*, pp. 229–31.

195 Turrell, *Capital and Labour*, pp. 12, 35.

196 Ibid., pp. 52–6.

197 Ibid., pp. 63–4.

198 Ibid., p. 58.

199 For a complete analysis, see ibid., pp. 49–72.

200 For an overview of the legislation on diamond mining introduced by the three different administrative regimes between 1871 and 1880, see Higgs, 'The Historical Development'.

201 Alois S. Mlambo and Neil Parsons, *A History of Southern Africa* (London, 2019), p. 115; see also I. B. Sutton, 'The End of Coloured Independence: The Case of the Griqualand East Rebellion of 1878', *Transafrican Journal of History*, VIII/1–2 (1979), pp. 181–200. The same turbulent period saw the outbreak of the Anglo-Zulu War (1879) and the First Boer War (1880–81). While the Zulu force was defeated, the Boer army managed to re-establish the independent Transvaal Republic – until their defeat in the Second Boer War. Meredith, *Diamonds, Gold and War*, pp. 86–104. On the First Boer War, also dubbed the Transvaal Rebellion, see John Laband, *The Transvaal Rebellion: The First Boer War, 1880–1881* (London, 2005).

202 Anthony Trollope, *An Old Man's Love* [1884] (London, 1993), p. 68.

203 Heertje, *De Diamantbewerkers*, p. 25.

204 Ibid.

205 Ibid., p. 26.

206 Daniël Metz and Karin Hofmeester, 'Amsterdam Diamantstad: Een nieuwe industrie', in *Een Schitterende Erfenis: 125 jaar nalatenschap van de Algemene Nederlandse Diamantbewerkersbond*, ed. Karin Hofmeester (Zutphen, 2019), pp. 13–33 (p. 20).

207 Ibid., p. 26.

208 Ibid., p. 28.

209 Heertje, *De Diamantbewerkers*, pp. 27–30.

210 Ibid., pp. 31–41.

211 Eric Laureys, *Meesters van het Diamant: De Belgische diamantsector tijdens het nazibewind* (Tielt, 2005), pp. 49–50.

212 Evans, *A History of Jewellery*, p. 182.

213 'Holland and the Hollanders [Second Paper]', *Harper's New Monthly Magazine*, XLIV (December 1871–May 1872), pp. 349–64 (p. 351).

214 Karina Sonnenberg-Stern, *Emancipation and Poverty: The Ashkenazi Jews of Amsterdam, 1796–1850* (London, 2000).

215 Karin Hofmeester, *Jewish Workers and the Labour Movement: A Comparative Study of Amsterdam, London and Paris, 1870–1914* (London, 2004), p. 14.

216 'Holland and the Hollanders', p. 351.

217 Some managed to move up the socio-economic ladder, while others were doomed to keep working in the unhealthy factories. For an overview of the opportunities taken and missed by Amsterdam's Jewish population in relation to diamonds, see Saskia Coenen Snyder, '"As Long as It Sparkles!": The Diamond Industry in Nineteenth-century Amsterdam', *Jewish Social Studies*, XXII/2 (2017), pp. 38–73. Coenen Snyder successfully demonstrated that the upward mobility of a part of the Jewish proletariat would have been impossible without the diamond.

218 For an overview of the union's early history, see Margreet Schrevel, 'Een stem in het kapittel. Diamantbewerkers organiseren zich', in *Een Schitterende Erfenis*, ed. Hofmeester, pp. 35–55.

219 For the ADB and the worldwide union, see Martine Vermandere and Karin Hofmeester, 'Internationale solidariteit uit zelfbehoud: Antwerpen onttroont Amsterdam', in *Een Schitterende Erfenis*, ed. Hofmeester, pp. 79–101.

220 Some argue that it was Morse, together with his foreman, who invented the first bruting machine in the 1870s, although this is disputed by Tolkowsky, who was of the opinion that it originated in Antwerp or Amsterdam. Tolkowsky, *Diamond Design*, p. 24; 'The Pioneer Lapidary: Death of H. D. Morse, the Wellknown Dealer in Diamonds', *New York Times*, 4 January 1888.

221 For an extensive study, see Thomas Figarol, 'Le district industriel de Saint-Claude et le monde du diamant à l'âge de la première mondialisation (années 1870–1914)', PhD thesis, Université de Besançon, 2015.

222 Heertje, *De Diamantbewerkers*, pp. 144–6.

223 Coenen Snyder, '"As Long as It Sparkles!"', p. 61.

4 BUILDING A WORLDWIDE EMPIRE: THE CENTURY OF DE BEERS, 1884–1990

1 'United States Court of Appeal for the Third Circuit. Shawn Sullivan; Arrigotti Fine Jewelry; James Walnum, on behalf of themselves and all others similarly situated, v. DB Investments, Inc; De Beers s.a.; De Beers Consolidated Mines, Ltd; De Beers a.g.; Diamond Trading Company; cso Valuations a.g.; Central Selling Organization; De Beers Centenary a.g. . . . Reargued En Banc on February 23, 2011', pp. 11–12, www.uscourts.gov, accessed 5 May 2020.

2 Kanfer, *Last Empire*, pp. 153–6, 161, 171–5.

3 Newbury, *Diamond Ring*, pp. 40–43.

4 Worger, *South Africa's City of Diamonds*, pp. 30–37.

5 Morton, *South African Diamond Fields*, p. 83.

6 Turrell, *Capital and Labour*, p. 82.

7 Worger, *South Africa's City of Diamonds*, pp. 42–3.

8 Turrell, *Capital and Labour*, pp. 81, 105. Martin Lilienfeld himself, a brother of Gustave and Leopold Lilienfeld, operated out of London. On the Lilienfeld firm, see Lynfield, *In Search of Gustav*.

9 In 1860 Amsterdam was home to five cutting factories. The biggest one, containing 538 mills, employed up to 925 diamond cutters and was owned by the Posno family. 'Nederlandsche Diamant-industrie', *Java-bode*, 7 January 1860. Five years later, a newspaper reported that the Posno firm had gone out of business, leading to the unemployment of four hundred cutters. 'Brieven uit Nederland', *Bataviaasch handelsblad*, 21 December 1864.

10 Turrell, *Capital and Labour*, pp. 80–82 and 111–16.

11 Newbury, *The Diamond Ring*, p. 27.

12 Turrell, *Capital and Labour*, p. 116; Stefan Kanfer, *The Last Empire: De Beers, Diamonds, and the World* (New York, 1993), pp. 53–8 (Barnato) and 67–8 (Robinson).

13 Gold mining was to become one of the other major extraction industries at the end of the nineteenth century, and its history of mining and labour bears many similarities to the diamond mining industry. For Robinson, see Robert V. Kubicek, 'The Randlords in 1895: A Reassessment', *Journal of British Studies*, xxi/2 (1972), pp. 84–103. Charles Harvey and Jon Press, 'The City and

International Mining, 1870–1914', *Business History*, XXXII/3 (1990), pp. 98–119 (pp. 110–11).

14 On these first efforts of Rhodes, see Turrell, *Capital and Labour*, pp. 82–7.

15 Worger, *South Africa's City of Diamonds*, p. 221. See also Robert I. Rotberg, *The Founder: Cecil Rhodes and the Pursuit of Power* (Oxford, 1988), pp. 199–201.

16 Payton, *The Diamond Diggings*, p. 138.

17 Cleveland, *Stones of Contention*, p. 63.

18 Ibid.

19 Ibid., pp. 63–4; Turrell, *Capital and Labour*, pp. 94–100.

20 Quoted in Turrell, *Capital and Labour*, p. 98.

21 Christopher M. Paulin, *White Men's Dream, Black Men's Blood: African Labor and British Expansionism in Southern Africa, 1877–1895* (Trenton, NJ, 2001), pp. 170–73.

22 Turrell, *Capital and Labour*, pp. 146–7. John M. Smalberger, 'I.D.B. and the Mining Compound System in the 1880s', *South African Journal of Economics*, XLII/4 (1974), pp. 247–58.

23 For more on the compounds, see Turrell, *Capital and Labour*, pp. 155–63. For the early history of the compounds, see also Rob Turrell, 'Kimberley's Model Compounds', *Journal of African History*, XXV/1 (1984), pp. 59–75; and Alan Mabin, 'Labour, Capital, Class Struggle and the Origins of Residential Segregation in Kimberley, 1880–1920', *Journal of Historical Geography*, XII/1 (1986), pp. 4–26.

24 Zélie Colvile, *Round the Black Man's Garden* (Edinburgh and London, 1893), p. 266. For more on Colvile, see Cheryl McEwan, *Gender, Geography and Empire: Victorian Women Travellers in West Africa* (Abingdon, 2000).

25 Ibid.

26 Ibid., p. 267.

27 Williams, *Diamond Mines*, p. 258.

28 For a detailed analysis see V. L. Allen, *The History of Black Mineworkers in South Africa*, vol. I: *Mining in South Africa and the Genesis of Apartheid, 1871–1948* (London, 2005).

29 Linda Weiss, 'Exceptional Space: Concentration Camps and Labor Compounds in Late Nineteenth-century South Africa', in *Archaeologies of Internment*, ed. Adrian Myers and Gabriel Moshenska (New York, 2011), pp. 21–32.

30 Lenzen, *The History of Diamond Production*, p. 151.

31 Williams, *Diamond Mines*, pp. 240–41.

32 Turrell, *Labour and Capital*, p. 150; Newbury, *The Diamond Ring*, pp. 76–8.

33 Newbury, *The Diamond Ring*, pp. 76–82.

34 Colvile, *Round the Black Man's Garden*, p. 266.

35 Turrell, *Labour and Capital*, p. 159.

36 Alie Emily van der Merwe, 'Health and Demograhpy in Late Nineteenth Century Kimberley: A Palaeopathological Assessment', PhD thesis, Leiden University Medical Centre (2010).

37 Several late nineteenth-century photographs dealing with the racial abuse of 'strip and search' were analysed in Marcia Pointon, 'De Beers's Diamond Mine in the 1880s: Robert Harris and the Kimberley Searching System', *History of Photography*, XLII/I (2018), pp. 4–24.

38 Worger, *South Africa's City of Diamonds*, pp. 147–87.

39 Turrell, *Labour and Capital*, pp. 134–8.

40 Ibid., pp. 138–43.

41 A quote from James Brown, one of the leaders of the Combined Working Men's Committee, published in the *Daily Independent* on 26 April 1884 and reproduced in Turrell, *Labour and Capital*, p. 143.

42 As quoted in Turrell, *Labour and Capital*, p. 143.

43 Worger, *South Africa's City of Diamonds*, pp. 203–19.

44 Cleveland, *Stones of Contention*, pp. 77–8.

45 The news made it to many British newspapers. An extensive report, including an engraving of the mine with the shaft on fire, appeared in 'Fire in the De Beers Diamond Mine', *Illustrated London News*, 18 August 1888. The *York Herald* confirmed in its article 'The Mining Disaster in South Africa', which appeared on 14 July 1888, that over five hundred men were rescued and published a list of all the white men killed, but unsurprisingly failed to name the black miners who had died.

46 'Terrible Fire in a Mine. Great Loss of Life', *Daily Telegraph*, 13 July 1888.

47 Ibid.

48 Newbury, *The Diamond Ring*, p. 87; Turrell, *Capital and Labour*, p. 207.

49 For a more detailed account of the story, see Turrell, *Capital and Labour*, pp. 206–27; Newbury, *The Diamond Ring*, pp. 86–95; and Worger, *South Africa's City of Diamonds*, pp. 191–236.

50 'Mr. Barney Barnato Drowns Himself at Sea. His Body Recovered', *Evening News*, 15 June 1897.

51 For an extended analysis, see Thomas Pakenham, *Scramble for Africa: White Man's Conquest of the Dark Continent from 1876 to 1912* (New York, 1991), pp. 336–57, 372–92, 487–503, 641–56. See also John Cooper, *The Unexpected Story of Nathaniel Rothschild* (London, 2015), pp. 73–82, for an analysis of Rothschild's involvement in the mining amalgamation in Kimberley and the interest of Rhodes in the gold mining operations at the Rand.

52 Colin Newbury, 'The Origins and Function of the London Diamond Syndicate, 1889–1914', *Business History*, XXIX/I (1987), pp. 5–26 (p. 20).

53 'The Jagersfontein and South African Diamond Mining Association, Limited', *Financial Times*, 26 September 1889.

54 Worger, *South Africa's City of Diamonds*, pp. 274–8.

55 Newbury, *The Diamond Ring*, p. 158.

56 Cooper, *The Unexpected Story*, pp. 73–4.

57 Gardner Williams had published his book on the diamond mines in 1899. His son Alpheus F. Williams became a general manager for De Beers and in 1932 he also published a book on diamond mining in South Africa, in which he showed a great interest in the geological aspects of diamond mining. Alpheus F. Williams, *The Genesis of the Diamond*, 2 vols (London, 1932).

58 Newbury, *The Diamond Ring*, pp. 107–31.

59 Ibid., p. 125. Strikes were sometimes reported in the British newspapers. In an article titled 'Natives on Strike in the De Beers Mines', the *Financial Times* informed its readers on 9 June 1905 that 2,300 black miners had gone on strike at the Dutoitspan mine; 53 had already been arrested.

60 A. E. Van Der Merwe, I. Ribot, D. Morris, M. Steyn and G.J.R. Maat, 'The Origins of Late Nineteenth-century Migrant Diamond Miners Uncovered in a Salvage Excavation in Kimberley, South Africa', *South African Archaeological Bulletin*, LXV/192 (2010), pp. 175–84. For a study on migrant labour at the gold mines during the same period, see Alan H. Jeeves, *Migrant Labour in South Africa's Mining Economy: The Struggle for the Gold Mines' Labour Supply, 1890–1920* (Kingston, ON, and Montreal, QC, 1985).

61 'The Wealth of Kimberly. How Diamonds Are Found. The Enormous Profits', *Evening Telegraph*, 1 March 1900.

62 'South Africa and Its Problems: The Diamond City', *Daily Telegraph*, 25 December 1900.

63 'The Labour System in Kimberley', *The Times*, 29 January 1901. See also 'African Mines', *Illustrated Police News*, 29 July 1899, which summed up the abuse suffered by miners at the hands of the overseers, including being forced to work when ill and regular assaults, although the article attributed the violence to the Zulu guards.

64 'Chinese Labour', *The Times*, 9 February 1905. See also Peter Richardson, 'The Recruiting of Chinese Indentured Labour for the South African Gold-Mines, 1903–1908', *Journal of African History*, XVIII/1 (1977), pp. 85–108.

65 Jonathan Crush, 'Scripting the Compound: Power and Space in the South African Mining Industry', *Environment and Planning D: Society and Space*, XII/3 (1994), pp. 301–24 (p. 306).

66 Mahmood Mamdani, *Citizen and Subject: Contemporary Africa and the Legacy of Late Colonialism* [1996] (Princeton, NJ, 2018), pp. 256–7.

67 This picture and various others were published as 'Guarding a Diamond-mine in South Africa: Night and Day Precautions in a Native Workers' Compound', *Illustrated London News*, 27 February 1932.

68 Ibid.

69 Lenzen, *The History of Diamond Production*, p. 158.

70 Turrell, *Labour and Capital*, pp. 74–5. Barney Barnato had been a walloper before he became rich.

71 Ibid., p. 75. For the Salomons family, see Vanneste, *Commercial Culture*, pp. 153–5. One of the family's foremost diamond traders was Israel Levin Salomons, also known as Yehiel Prager, active in London in the second half of the eighteenth century. For an extensive analysis of his activities, see Yogev, *Diamonds and Coral*, pp. 183–274.

72 Newbury, 'The Origins and Function', pp. 6–8.

73 These included the firms of Porges, Dunkelsbühler, Barnato and Mosenthal. Newbury, 'The Origins and Function', p. 7.

74 Ibid., p. 9.

75 Both Alfred Beit and Julius Wernher were instrumental in Rhodes's business successes of the 1880s. Colin Newbury, 'Cecil Rhodes, De Beers and Mining Finance in South Africa: The Business of Entrepreneurship and Imperialism', in *Mining Tycoons in the Age of Empire, 1870–1945*, ed. Raymond Dumett (Farnham and Burlington, VT, 2009), pp. 85–108 (pp. 97–9).

76 For two short periods the firm of V. A. Litkie & Co. was also a partner. Newbury, 'The Origins and Function', p. 9.

77 Ibid. The Central Mining & Investment Corporation (CMI) was founded in 1905 by Wernher, Beit & Co., and both firms were shareholders of one another. The purpose of CMI was to collect investments for gold mining near Johannesburg. See Raleigh Trevelyan, *Grand Dukes and Diamonds: The Wernhers of Luton Hoo* (London, 2012), pp. 181, 244–5.

78 Newbury, 'The Origins and Function', p. 11.

79 De Beers' monopoly no longer exists today, but the company is still a huge force to be reckoned with and continues to organize the sale of its production the same way. See Chapter Six.

80 Ibid., pp. 13–16.

81 Ibid., pp. 11–13.

82 Ibid., pp. 5–17.

83 Newbury, 'Cecil Rhodes', p. 103.

84 Newbury, 'The Origins and Function', pp. 13–15, 18. See also illus. 69.

85 For the development of advertisements in the French cosmetics industry between 1750 and 1830, see Martin, *Selling Beauty*, pp. 52–72.

86 For an extensive overview of the development of the concept of the engagement ring, see Pointon, *Rocks, Ice and Dirty Stones*, pp. 151–67.

87 'Incomparable Display of Diamonds!', *Evening Star*, 15 December 1898.

88 Ibid.

89 Ibid.

90 Louis Waefelaer, 'The Richest Diamond Mine in the World', *San Francisco Sunday Call*, 21 March 1909. I am grateful to Marcia Pointon for providing me with the reference to the article.

91 Ibid.

92 'Diamonds More Dear', *New York Tribune Illustrated Supplement*, 16 October 1904.

93 Ibid.

94 Ibid.

95 On the Second Boer War, see Iain Smith, *The Origins of the South African War, 1899–1902* (London, 1996).

96 In 2015 and 2016 efforts were made to remove a statue of him at Oxford University. See Yussef Robinson, 'Oxford's Cecil Rhodes Statue Must Fall – It Stands in the Way of Inclusivity', *The Guardian*, 18 January 2016. The #Rhodesmustfall movement at Cape Town University demanded the removal of his statue at the university, which led to the statue's removal in April 2015. The event ignited a larger debate on statues that celebrated figures who had participated in violent and racist colonial oppression. Amit Chaudhuri, 'The Real Meaning of Rhodes Must Fall', *The Guardian*, 16 March 2016.

97 Mark Twain, *Following the Equator: A Journey around the World* (Hartford, CT, 1898), p. 710.

98 For an overview of the events surrounding the development of the Premier mine's operations, see Newbury, *The Diamond Ring*, pp. 172–87.

99 Pointon, *Rocks, Ice and Dirty Stones*, pp. 37–8. Botha became the first prime minister of an independent Union of South Africa in 1910 and was one of the protagonists behind the development of the apartheid system.

100 *Soerabaijasch handelsblad*, 14 January 1908.

101 In the picture, the middle stone in the top row is the Cullinan I, cut as a pendeloque with 74 facets, weighing 530.2 carats. Until 1992 it was the largest cut diamond in the world. The Cullinan II, on its left, has a cushion-cut. Pointon, *Rocks, Ice and Dirty Stones*, pp. 37–8. The Asscher family, still in the diamond business today, rose to prominence during the *Kaapse Tijd* and became famous for the invention of the 'Asscher cut', an alternative cut based on table diamonds that was mostly popular among Western elites in the Art Deco period. For the family business, see their website at www.royalasscher. com, accessed 5 May 2020.

102 Newbury, *The Diamond Ring*, pp. 172–87.

103 Dario Gaggio, 'Diamond Industry: Industrial Organization', in *The Oxford Encyclopedia of Economic History*, ed. Joel Mokyr, 5 vols (Oxford, 2003), vol. I, pp. 79–82 (p. 80); see also Alfred A. Levinson, 'Diamond Sources and Their Discovery', in *The Nature of Diamonds*, ed. George E. Harlow (Cambridge, 1998), pp. 72–104 (pp. 86–7).

104 'German South-west Africa', *The Times*, 23 April 1900. For an overview of the short-lived German colonial empire between 1884, when the Berlin Conference divided Africa between the European colonial powers, and 1919, when the Treaty of Versailles ended the German imperialist project following the cessation of the First World War, see Sebastian Conrad, *German Colonialism: A Short History* (Cambridge, 2012). The book was originally published in German as *Deutsche Kolonialgeschichte* (Munich, 2008). For an overview of German South West Africa, see pp. 38–42 in the English translation.

105 'German South-west Africa'.

106 For an overview of the colonial activities of the SWAC and their efforts to attract German investors, see Richard A. Voeltz, *German Colonialism and the South West Africa Company, 1894–1914* (Athens, OH, 1988).

107 'Diamonds in German South-west Africa', *Aberdeen Journal*, 14 December 1906. The Strip did possess some diamonds, although not in great quantities and at the time no structural exploration was developed there.

108 Levinson, 'Diamond Sources', p. 88. This came a year after the end of a genocide on the Nama and Herero by German colonial troops. See David Olusoga and Casper W. Erichsen, *The Kaiser's Holocaust: Germany's Forgotten Genocide and the Colonial Roots of Nazism* (London, 2010).

109 The production numbers in carats come from Lenzen, *The History of Diamond Production*, p. 160. He obtained his numbers from Percy Wagner's account and from Wilhelm von Humboldt-Dachroeden, *Die deutsche*

Diamantenpolitik (Jena, 1918). There was no reliable data for 1909 and 1910 for the South African mines.

110 'Germany's Diamond-studded Sands: A Golconda in the Desert', *Illustrated London News*, 6 March 1909.

111 For the DKG, see Franz Göttlicher, *Koloniale Gesellschaften und Verbände* (Koblenz, 2003).

112 For an anecdotal account of the early history of Namibian diamonds, see Olga Levinson, *Diamonds in the Desert: The Story of August Stauch and his Times* (Tafelberg, 1983). Stauch was to lose most of his fortune during the Great Depression. The first reports on the discovery of diamond deposits made it to British newspapers in June 1908, although these initial articles did not contain much information. See, for instance, 'Discovery of a Diamond Field', *Exeter and Plymouth Gazette*, 27 June 1908.

113 'Diamond Mining in German South-west Africa: The Question of a Consolidated Company', *Financial Times*, 21 November 1908.

114 'Diamonds in German South-west Africa: Government Regulations', *Financial Times*, 15 December 1908.

115 Victor L. Tonchi, William A. Lindeke and John J. Grotpeter, *Historical Dictionary of Namibia*, 2nd edn (Lanham, MD, 2012), pp. 78–9.

116 S. E. Katzenellenbogen, 'British Businessmen and German Africa, 1885–1919', in *Great Britain and Her World, 1750–1914: Essays in Honour of W. O. Henderson*, ed. Barrie M. Ratcliffe (Manchester, 1975), pp. 237–62 (pp. 252–4).

117 Tonchi et al., *Historical Dictionary*, pp. 77–8.

118 Katzenellenbogen, 'British Businessmen', p. 253.

119 Ibid., pp. 252–4.

120 'Diamonds in German South-west Africa. Price Agreement Said to be Unnecessary', *Financial Times*, 9 July 1909.

121 Lenzen, *The History of Diamond Production*, p. 160.

122 *Algemeen Handelsblad*, 25 April 1910. The involvement of Coetermans, a big name in Antwerp's diamond industry, and his downfall, was described by one of his descendants in an eccentric, but at times enjoyable book: Vincent Mercier, *Prins Diamant: Het tragische verval van een wereldimperium* (Leuven, 2013).

123 Leviticus, *Encyclopaedie*, pp. 40–46. Heertje, *De Diamantbewerkers*, pp. 146–51.

124 Laureys, *Meesters van het Diamant*, pp. 50–51.

125 Not much academic research has been done on the diamond industry of the Kempen. An example is Eric Meylemans, 'De tewerkstelling in de diamant-industrie in de Zuiderkempen', thesis, Economische Hogeschool Limburg, 1984. More information can be found on the website of the local diamond centre, www.briljantekempen.be, accessed 5 May 2020.

126 The industry went into decline during the 1960s, unable to deal with the competition abroad. The last of the old factories to close was Slijperij Lieckens in Nijlen, in 1985. Today their old factory building has been restored. 'Vroegere diamantslijperij Lieckens in Nijlen wordt gerestaureerd', www.onroerenderfgoed.be, accessed 5 May 2020. For the current state of the site, see also 'Diamantwerkplaats Lieckens met waterput', inventaris.onroerenderfgoed.be, accessed 5 May 2020.

127 Heertje, *De Diamantbewerkers*, pp. 150–51.

128 Steven Press, 'Sovereignty and Diamonds in Southern Africa, 1908–1920', *Duke Journal of Comparative and International Law*, XXVIII (2018), pp. 473–80 (p. 478).

129 Newbury, *The Diamond Ring*, pp. 187–94.

130 After the demise of De Beers' monopoly, commercial agreements between the biggest producers became more important again in regulating the diamond industry. See Chapter Six.

131 Ibid., pp. 194–7.

132 Kanfer, *Last Empire*, pp. 192–4. See also Colin Newbury, 'Spoils of War: Sub-imperial Collaboration in South West Africa and New Guinea, 1914–20', *Journal of Imperial and Commonwealth History*, XVI/3 (1983), pp. 86–105.

133 Colin Newbury, 'South Africa and the International Diamond Trade, Part One: Sir Ernest Oppenheimer, De Beers and the Evolution of Central Selling, 1920–1950', *South African Journal of Economic History*, X/2 (1995), pp. 1–22 (p. 3); Newbury, *The Diamond Ring*, p. 212.

134 Newbury, *The Diamond Ring*, pp. 212–16.

135 Michael Coulson, *The History of Mining: The Events, Technology and People Involved in the Industry that Forged the Modern World* (Petersfield, Hampshire, 2012), pp. 233–5.

136 Tolkowsky, *Diamond Design*, p. 24. Later, as with all machinery, bruting machines advanced technologically. In 2007 the U.S. Patent office granted a patent to an entrepreneur from Ahmedabad in Gujarat for a laser bruting machine: Arvindbhai Lavjibhai Patel, 'Laser Bruting Machine' (patented 30 October 2007), patents.google.com, accessed 4 May 2020.

137 Ogden, *Diamonds*, pp. 125–6.

138 A copy of the patent is included at the end of his PhD. Marcel Tolkowsky, 'Research on the Abrading, Grinding or Polishing of Diamonds', PhD thesis, University of London, 1920. A scan of the dissertation can be downloaded at the e-theses online service of the British Library, ethos.bl.uk, accessed 5 May 2020.

139 Tolkowsky, *Diamond Designs*.

140 Tolkowsky did not include a culet in his design, but many modern brilliants have one. The number of 57 includes the single facet at the top. Older brilliant cuts that were fashionable during the eighteenth and nineteenth centuries are referred to as 'old brilliant cut', 'old European cut' or 'old mine cut' (illus. 15 and 17).

141 Robert J. Wueste, 'Brilliant Cut Diamond' (patented 2 March 2004), patents.google.com, accessed 4 May 2020. For an example of a fairly recent study, see Ilene M. Reinitz et al., Modeling the Appearance of the Round Brilliant Cut Diamond: An Analysis of Fire, and More About Brilliant', *Gems and Gemology*, XXXVII/3 (2001), pp. 174–97.

142 Several of the formerly famous European cutting companies advertise their own particular brilliant cut. Amsterdam-based Coster diamonds, for instance, in business since 1840, promote their own 201-facet brilliant cut, the Royal 201. 'Cut', www.costerdiamonds.com, accessed 5 May 2020. A

relatively recent study acknowledged the ongoing importance of Tolkowsky's ground-breaking work, but also pointed to updated scientific work using more modern technology such as high-resolution microscopes. J. R. Hird and J. E. Field, 'Diamond Polishing', *Proceedings: Mathematical, Physical and Engineering Sciences*, CDLX/2052 (2004), pp. 3547–68.

143 Klein, *Faceting History*, pp. 94–5.

144 'Marcel Tolkowsky, 92, A Retired Gemologist', *New York Times*, 15 February 1991. For the current family business and its history, see the firm's website at www.tolkowsky.com, accessed 5 May 2020.

145 'Het Smokkelen van Juweelen', *Het Nieuws van den Dag voor Nederlandsch-Indie*, 3 November 1930: 'listiger dan de mannen'.

146 Lenzen, *The History of Diamond Production*, p. 171.

147 For the Russian situation, see Sean McMeekin, *History's Greatest Heist: The Looting of Russia by the Bolsheviks* (New Haven, CT, 2009), pp. 54–72.

148 'Sovjet-Rusland en de nood van de diamantwerkers', *Het Volk*, 2 November 1920.

149 Lenzen, *The History of Diamond Production*, p. 172.

150 The firms of Wernher, Beit & Co. and Mosenthal, Sons & Co. were no longer part of it, instead there were, next to Anglo-American, three other newcomers: L. Breitmeyer & Co., Bernheim and Dreyfus & Co.; Lenzen, *The History of Diamond Production*, pp. 173–4. These firms all had a history that connected them with DBCM in the late nineteenth century. See Colin Newbury, 'Technology, Capital, and Consolidation: The Performance of De Beers Mining Company Limited, 1880–1889', *Business History Review*, LXI/1 (1987), pp. 1–42 (p. 39). Ludwig Breitmeyer had first been an agent for Wernher, Beit & Co. in Kimberley, then a partner. Newbury, 'The Origins and Function', pp. 13–14.

151 For the activities of these companies, see Chapter Five.

152 Newbury, *The Diamond Ring*, pp. 247–61.

153 'De Beers and Diamonds', *Financial Times*, 7 January 1926.

154 Newbury, *The Diamond Ring*, p. 265.

155 J. S. Kotze, 'Geskiedenis van die Wes-Transvaal Diamant Delwerye', MA thesis, University of Port Elizabeth, 1972, p. 123.

156 Theodore Gregory, *Ernest Oppenheimer and the Economic Development of Southern Africa* (Cape Town, 1962), p. 171.

157 Based on information in Lenzen, *The History of Diamond Production*, pp. 172–6, and Newbury, 'South Africa, Part One', passim.

158 The quote comes from a letter published under the name 'a son of Africa' to *The Star* on 3 October 1928. The excerpt was included in T. P. Clynick, *The Lichtenburg Alluvial Diamond Diggers, 1926–1929*, African Studies Seminar Paper 149 (University of the Witwatersrand, 1984), which provides a good account of the circumstances of the Lichtenburg diggings.

159 L.C.A. Knowles and C. M. Knowles, *The Economic Development of the British Overseas Empire*, 3 vols (London, 1936), vol. III, pp. 230–31.

160 Clynick, *The Lichtenburg Alluvial Diamond Diggers*, pp. 4, 7.

161 Ben Fine and Zavareh Rustomjee, *The Political Economy of South Africa. From Minerals-Energy Complex to Industrialisation* (London, 1996), p. 143.

162 Newbury, *The Diamond Ring*, p. 271.

163 Lenzen, *The History of Diamond Production*, p. 178.

164 Ibid., p. 181.

165 Newbury, 'South Africa', p. 4.

166 'De Beers Mine's New Interests', *The Times*, 21 March 1931.

167 Lenzen, *The History of Diamond Production*, p. 181.

168 Ibid.

169 Ibid.

170 Taken from data in Lenzen, *The History of Diamond Production*, pp. 179, 182–83, 185. Columns 7 and 8 were taken from data in Newbury, 'South Africa, Part One', p. 17. The Mandatory Administration of South West Africa included the quota of CDM. For DICORP, the percentage is the financial share held by each company, while for DPA, it represents the production quota that indicates how much of total sales in London will be covered by a particular producer.

171 For the establishment of the DPA, see Newbury, *The Diamond Ring*, pp. 252–332.

172 Lenzen, *The History of Diamond Production*, p. 182. Diamond production in these countries is analysed in Chapter Five.

173 Ibid., p. 181.

174 Newbury, 'South Africa, Part One', pp. 5, 10. The system of 'sights' still exists today.

175 Laureys, *Meesters van het Diamant*, pp. 40–41.

176 An Indian publication from 1930 suggests there was still some mining activity in Panna at the time. Hofmeester, 'Working for Diamonds', p. 43.

177 'Nederland', *Sumatra Post*, 15 April 1919. Bornean diamonds were the subject of several parliamentary debates.

178 'Diamantzoeken op Borneo', *Bataviaasch Nieuwsblad*, 11 October 1921.

179 Diamantwinning op Borneo', *Het Nieuws van den Dag voor Nederlandsch-Indie*, 26 January 1918; 'Exploitatie van de diamant-velden op Borneo', *Het Nieuws van den Dag voor Nederlandsch-Indie*, 22 September 1919; and 'Het gebrek aan ruw diamant en de Nederlandsche diamant-ontginningen op Borneo', *Het Centrum*, 1 April 1920.

180 'Diamanten op Borneo', *De Locomotief*, 7 March 1918.

181 'Koelie-Polak', *De Tribune*, 20 September 1919; 'Een beraamde tribunistische aanval', *Het Volk*, 19 September 1919.

182 'De diamanten van Borneo', *Bataviaasch Nieuwsblad*, 12 December 1918; and 'Diamant-industrie van Martapoera', *De Preanger Bode*, 4 June 1922.

183 J. Thomas Lindblad, *Between Dayak and Dutch: The Economic History of Southeast Kalimantan 1880–1942* (Dordrecht, 1988), p. 182.

184 'Borneo', *De Graafschap-Bode*, 23 December 1927.

185 'Diamantzoeken op Borneo', *Bataviaasch Nieuwsblad*, 11 October 1921.

186 Much later, Australia and Canada incorporated measures to guarantee indigenous employment at their mining sites, a policy that still came a

considerable time before official recognition that mining in both countries had relied on stealing indigenous land. See the Epilogue.

187 'Diamantwinning', *Algemeen Indisch Dagblad*, 21 December 1923.

188 'Geld voor groepsgemeenschappen', *Bataviaasch Nieuwsblad*, 7 February 1938; and 'Volksraad', *Het Nieuws van den Dag voor Nederlandsch-Indië*, 9 July 1932.

189 'Diamanten in Borneo', *Het Nieuws van den Dag voor Nederlandsch-Indië*, 21 December 1925.

190 'Productie van goud, zilver en diamant in Ned.-Indië in de periode 1913–1939', *Soerabaijasch Handelsblad*, 28 December 1940.

191 'Diamanten op Borneo', *De Locomotief*, 7 March 1918.

192 'Inheemsche diamantnijverheid op Borneo', *Het Vaderland*, 7 December 1932.

193 For the alleged discovery of the primary deposit, see 'Diamant op Zuid-Borneo: Het moedergesteente gevonden', *Algemeen Handelsblad*, 27 December 1932; 'De diamanten van Borneo: Onderzoek op primaire vindplaats', *Soerabaijasch Handelsblad*, 13 March 1934; and 'De Zuid-Borneodiamant', *Haagsche Courant*, 5 May 1934.

194 Frank G. Carpenter, 'The Richest Man in East Asia: A Visit to Lan Win Hong, the Multi-millionaire of Kwantung', *Deseret News*, 19 January 1901.

195 'Diamant-winning op Borneo', *Het Nieuws van den Dag voor Nederlandsch-Indië*, 3 November 1930.

196 'Diamanten gevonden in het Martapoerasche', *De Telegraaf*, 11 November 1930, referred to them also as 'foreign Easterlings in our Indian Archipelago'.

197 Herold and Rines, 'A Half-century Monopoly', pp. 19–20.

198 S. Hartveld, *Schetsen uit Brazilië* (Antwerp, 1921), p. 30.

199 Ibid.: 'de afgewerkte brillanten zijn tamelijk goed geslepen'. This is reminiscent of Indian preoccupations with weight (illus. 10).

200 *De Juweelenstoet, Le Cortège des Bijoux, The Jewels Pageant* (Antwerp, 1923).

201 The diamond was named after the then-president of Brazil, Getúlio Vargas (1882–1954). Sydney Ball and Paul F. Kerr, 'The Vargas Diamond', *Gems and Gemology*, iii/9 (1941), pp. 135–6.

202 Ibid.

203 The information came from an interview with Jules Sauer published at the website of the virtual People's Museum in São Paulo. 'Pedalando para longe do terror', www.museudapessoa.net, 10 November 2005.

204 'Jules Sauer, Brazilian "Gemstone Hunter," Dies at 95', www.timesofisrael. com, 3 February 2017. The obituary is mistaken in referring to 1939 as the year of his escape. Amsterdam Sauer still exists as a company in Rio de Janeiro, with their website at www.sauer1941.com, accessed 5 May 2020. Sauer wrote a number of books, such as *The Eras of the Diamond* (Rio de Janeiro, 2003); *Emeralds Around the World* (Rio de Janeiro, 1992); and *Brazil: Paradise of Gemstones* (n.p., 1982).

205 For a good recent general study of the Holocaust, see Laurence Rees, *The Holocaust: A New History* (London, 2017).

206 See the official report commissioned by the Belgian federal government on the confiscation of Jewish goods in Belgium, 'De bezittingen van

de slachtoffers van de Jodenvervolging in België. Spoliatie Rechtsherstel Bevindingen van de Studiecommissie: Eindverslag van de Studiecommissie betreffende het lot van de bezittingen van de leden van de joodse gemeenschap van België, geplunderd of achtergelaten tijdens de oorlog 1940–1945 (2001)', pp. 95–118, www.combuysse.fgov.be, accessed 5 May 2020. For the Dutch situation, see A. J. van der Leeuw, 'Die Aktion Bozenhardt & Co.', in *Studies over Nederland in oorlogstijd*, ed. A. H. Paape (The Hague, 1972), vol. I, pp. 257–77. See also Bies van Ede and Paul Post, *De Diamantenroof: Hoe hoge Nazi's met Diamanten uit België en Nederland naar Zuid-Amerika vluchtten* (Utrecht, 2016). The 60,000 carats are mentioned on p. 128.

207 NATH, 2.05.80, No. 3026: Stukken betreffende de diamantindustrie en de handel in en inlichtingen over uit Nederland afkomstige diamanten, 1942–1945: Letter Dutch Embassy Washington to Dutch Ministry of Foreign Affairs in London, Washington, 9 December 1942.

208 Ibid.

209 David De Vries, *Diamonds and War: State, Capital and Labor in British-ruled Palestine* (New York, 2010), p. 20.

210 Laureys, *Meesters van het Diamant*, pp. 151–63.

211 Ibid., p. 158.

212 Ibid., p. 161.

213 See Barak D. Richman, 'How Community Institutions Create Economic Advantage: Jewish Diamond Merchants in New York', XXXI/2 (2006), pp. 383–420. For the Belgian flight to New York, see Laureys, *Meesters van het Diamant*, pp. 167–71.

214 Ibid., pp. 171–7.

215 Jules Sauer, for instance, was not active in the diamond industry at that time.

216 For a comparison, see a conference paper from 2017 by Pim Griffioen, 'The Fate of the "Diamond Jews" of Antwerp and Amsterdam, 1940–1945: A Historical Comparative Overview', www.academia.edu, accessed 5 May 2020.

217 For a historical overview of the Jewish diamond industry of Amsterdam during German occupation, see Dawn Skorczewski and Bettine Siertsema, '"The Kind of Spirit that People Still Kept": VHA Testimonies of Amsterdam's Diamond Jews', *Holocaust Studies: A Journal of Culture and History* (2018), pp. 1–23 (pp. 4–6).

218 Ibid., p. 5.

219 Ibid.

220 'Translation of Document NO-1278 Prosecution Exhibit 440. Letter of defendant Mummenthey to defendant Baier, 8 June 1944, concerning proposal to set up a diamond cutting factory in Bergen-Belsen because the Dutch Jews have been deported from concentration camp Hertogenbosch, Netherlands', in *Trials of War Criminals before the Nuernberg Military Tribunals under Control Council Law No. 10: Nuernberg October 1946–April 1949*, 15 vols (Washington, DC, 1950), vol. V, pp. 639–41.

221 Ibid.

222 Skorczewski and Siertsema, '"The Kind of Spirit that People Still Kept"', pp. 5–6. Some of the personal stories of the 'Diamond Jews' survived through

oral testimony, but also through publications. There is, for instance, the story of Ina Soep, who fell in love in Bergen-Belsen with Jaap Polak. She was the daughter of Abraham Soep, owner of one of Amsterdam's biggest diamond-cutting factories before the war. See Jack Polak and Ina Soep-Polak, *Steal a Pencil for Me: Love Letters from Camp Bergen-Belsen and Westerbork* (Scarsdale, NY, 2000). Recently a study appeared that narrates the story of the children of these 'Diamond Jews'. While many of their parents died, 44 out of the 46 so-called 'diamond children' survived the Holocaust. Bettine Siertsema, *Diamantkinderen: Amsterdamse Diamantjoden en de Holocaust* (Hilversum, 2020). Research for the book made extensive use of interviews with surviving children as well as video recordings of interviews made during the 1990s.

223 NATH, 2.05.80, No. 3567: Stukken betreffende verzoeken van Nederlandse diamantbewerkers om tewerk te worden gesteld in verschillende landen, 1941–1944: Legation of the Netherlands to Ministry of Foreign Affairs, Caracas, 15 October 1941: 'de Venezolaanse Regeering bevordert de immi-gratie van deskundigen in het diamantvak wijl zij hoopt daardoor de Venezolaanse diamantmijnen tot ontwikkeling te kunnen brengen. Zij heeft daarom aan den Venezolaanschen Consul te Marseille opdracht verstrekt de paspoorten van de lieden . . . te viseeren'.

224 Much can be said about the extent to which the Allied forces were aware of the Holocaust. One of the dominant stories in historiography has long been that, while Allied intelligence was aware of the existence of Auschwitz from an early stage, they misunderstood the true nature of the camp. Michael Fleming has written a very insightful analysis on this question and has con-cluded that there was an earlier awareness of the Holocaust than previously thought. Michael Fleming, *Auschwitz, the Allies and Censorship of the Holocaust* (Cambridge, 2014).

225 Two English-language films on the battle for industrial diamonds were released in 1942 (*Enemy Agents Meet Ellery Queen*, dir. James P. Hogan) and 1959 (*Operation Amsterdam*, dir. Michael McCarthy).

226 Newbury, *The Diamond Ring*, p. 346.

227 Edward Jay Epstein, *The Rise and Fall of Diamonds: The Shattering of a Brilliant Illusion* (New York, 1982), pp. 93–6.

228 De Vries, *Diamonds and War*, p. 130.

229 Newbury, *The Diamond Ring*, pp. 345–6.

230 Gerhard T. Mollin, *Die USA und der Kolonialismus: Amerika als Partner und Nachfolger der belgischen Macht in Afrika, 1939–1965* (Berlin, 1996), pp. 63–5.

231 Kanfer, *Last Empire*, pp. 227–31.

232 For these companies, see Chapter Five.

233 Newbury, *The Diamond Ring*, pp. 333–49.

234 After Mobutu Sese Seko came to power in 1965, Congo was renamed as Zaïre (until 1997) and became an important ally of the West.

235 For the revival of Antwerp, see Laureys, *Meesters van het Diamant*, pp. 331–86. For Amsterdam's misfortunes, see Laureys, *Meesters van het Diamant*, pp. 398–404. Several of the surviving diamond dealers or their family members in Belgium and the Netherlands attempted restitution of lost goods.

236 'De Amsterdamsche Diamant Industrie', *Nieuwe Courant*, 27 March 1946. Much has been written trying to explain why such a large degree of Dutch Jews were murdered in the Netherlands (75 per cent), compared with France (25 per cent) and Belgium (40 per cent). According to the important study by Pim Griffioen and Ron Zeller, explanations need to be sought in the fact that the Netherlands were run by a civilian German administration, while Dutch officials who wanted to keep things running smoothly, Dutch police and the Dutch Jewish Council all played their part. Pim Griffioen and Ron Zeller, 'Comparing the Persecution of the Jews in the Netherlands, France and Belgium, 1940–1945: Similarities, Differences, Causes', in *The Persecution of the Jews in the Netherlands, 1940–1945*, ed. Peter Romijn et al. (Amsterdam, 2012), pp. 55–92.

237 Laureys, *Meesters van het Diamant*, pp. 391–8. For a personal memoir by the granddaughter of one of New York's diamond dealers, see Alicia Oltuski, *Precious Objects: A Story of Diamonds, Family, and a Way of Life* (New York, 2011). For an anthropological study of Manhattan's diamond district, see Renée Rose Shield, *Diamond Stories: Enduring Change on 47th Street* (Ithaca, NY, 2002). For an insight into the temporary diamond industry in Cuba, see Herman Portocarero, *De Diamantdiaspora: Een verborgen geschiedenis tussen Antwerpen en Havana* (Antwerp, 2019).

238 For an overview of the downfall of the wartime cutting centres, see Laureys, *Meesters van het Diamant*, pp. 391–8.

239 For these pre-war efforts, see de Vries, *Diamonds and War*, pp. 16–26. David de Vries's monograph is the most extensive study on the development of the diamond industry in Palestine and Israel. A shortened version of his look at the relocation to Mandate Palestine in the war can be found in David de Vries, 'Burnishing the Rough: The Relocation of the Diamond Industry to Mandate Palestine', in *Borders and Boundaries in and around Dutch Jewish History*, ed. J. Frishman, D. J. Wertheim, I. de Haan and J. J. Cahen (Amsterdam, 2011), pp. 143–54.

240 For the wartime negotiations and the proposal of a limited industry, see De Vries, *Diamonds and War*, pp. 26–64.

241 Laureys, *Meesters van het Diamant*, p. 396; De Vries, *Diamonds and War*, p. 240.

242 Laureys, *Meesters van het Diamant*, pp. 394–7.

243 Ibid., p. 388.

244 De Vries, *Diamonds and War*, p. 243.

245 Ibid., pp. 247–8.

246 For the agreement, see ibid., pp. 240–48. For the changing economic context, see ibid., p. 235.

247 Mildred Berman, 'The Location of the Diamond-cutting Industry', *Annals of the Association of American Geographers*, LXI/2 (1971), pp. 316–28 (p. 326).

248 For more present-day information, see the website of the Israeli diamond industry at www.israelidiamond.co.il, accessed 5 May 2020.

249 NATH, 2.10.62: Netherland Forces Intelligence Service [NEFIS] en Centrale Militaire Inlichtingendienst [CMI] in Nederlands-Indië, No. 1790: Stukken

betreffende tijdens de Japanse bezetting verborgen en verdwenen sieraden en juwelen, 1947: Bureau voor Oorlogsschade, Afd. Restitutie, Batavia to Hoofd Japanse Zaken in Batavia, Batavia, 9 October 1947. The letter contains a Dutch translation of Lim Kang Tjoean's original letter.

250 'Diamantslijperijen in Zuid-Borneo', *De Locomotief*, 16 March 1948.

251 For the long and century-old fight against Dutch colonial rule, see Piet Hagen, *Koloniale oorlogen in Indonesië: Vijf eeuwen verzet tegen koloniale overheersing* (Amsterdam, 2018).

252 In this regard, the Dutch government was no different from many Western governments who refused to give up economic interest in countries they had colonized but that had become independent.

253 See Bipan Chandra, Mridula Mukherjee, Aditya Mukherjee, K. N. Panikkar and Sucheta Mahajan, *India's Struggle for Independence, 1857–1947* (New Delhi, 1988); and Yasmin Khan, *The Great Partition: The Making of India and Pakistan* (New Haven, CT, 2007).

254 Hofmeester, 'Working for Diamonds', p. 43.

255 Hofmeester, 'Shifting Trajectories', p. 45. For the role of these family connections and the involvement of the Palanpuri Jain traders in diamonds, see Sebastian Henn, 'Transnational Entrepreneurs, Global Pipelines and Shifting Production Patterns: The Example of the Palanpuris in the Diamond Sector', in *The Global Diamond Industry: Economics and Development*, ed. Roman Grynberg and Letsema Mbayi, 2 vols (Basingstoke, 2015), vol. II, pp. 87–115.

256 This affected the nascent Palestine diamond industry that had been exporting their finished goods to India. De Vries, *Diamonds and War*, p. 237.

257 Hofmeester, 'Shifting Trajectories', pp. 45–6. Berman, 'The Location of the Diamond-cutting Industry', p. 326.

258 For the history of Rosy Blue, see 'Rosy Blue India's Historic Journey', www.rosyblue.in. See also Sallie Westwood and Annie Phizacklea, *Transnationalism and the Politics of Belonging* (Abingdon, 2000), p. 73. For the family's financial position in Belgium, see their entry at the website listing the richest Belgians: 'Familie Mehta (Rosy Blue)', www.derijkstebelgen.be. Their capital is estimated at 271.3 million euros. For the 2016 trial, see Mark Eeckhaut, 'Geen genade voor frauderende diamantairs', www.destandaard.be, 18 May 2016. All accessed 5 May 2020.

259 S. P. Kashyap and R .S. Tiwari, 'Shaping Industry in Surat: Characteristics of Firms by Size', *Economic and Political Weekly*, XIX/34 (1984), pp. M99–M103 (p. M99).

260 For Australia's diamond production, see Chapter Six.

261 Hofmeester, 'Shifting Trajectories', p. 47.

262 Berman, 'The Location of the Diamond-cutting Industry', p. 326.

263 Lenzen, *The History of Diamond Production*, pp. 184–5.

264 De Vries, *Diamonds and War*, p. 236.

265 Newbury, 'South Africa and the International Diamond Trade – Part Two: The Rise and Fall of South Africa as a Diamond Entrepôt, 1945–1990', *South African Journal of Economic History*, XI/2 (1996), pp. 251–84 (pp. 252, 260).

266 Newbury, 'South Africa, Part Two', pp. 253–6.

267 Newbury, 'South Africa, Part One', p. 17.

268 Newbury, 'South Africa, Part Two', pp. 268–70.

269 Ibid., p. 251.

270 Pointon, *Rocks, Ice and Dirty Stones*, p. 166. During the war N. W. Ayer had organized several campaigns for De Beers around the patriotic theme of 'Fighting Diamonds'. See Jessica L. Ghilani, 'DeBeers' "Fighting Diamonds": Recruiting American Consumers in World War II Advertising', *Journal of Communication Inquiry*, XXXVI/3 (2012), pp. 222–45.

271 For a detailed analysis, see Peter Carstens, *In the Company of Diamonds. De Beers, Kleinzee, and the Control of a Town* (Athens, OH, 2001).

272 John Knight and Heather Stevenson, 'The Williamson Diamond Mine, De Beers, and the Colonial Office: A Case-study of the Quest for Control', *Journal of Modern African Studies*, XXIV/3 (1986), pp. 423–45.

273 Ian Smillie, *Diamonds* (Cambridge and Malden, MA, 2014), p. 142.

274 Rosemarie Mwaipopo, '*Ubeshi* – Negotiating Co-existence: Artisanal and Large-scale Relations in Diamond Mining', in *Mining and Social Transformation in Africa: Mineralizing and Democratizing Trends in Artisanal Production*, ed. D. F. Bryceson, E. Fisher, J. B. Jønsson and R. Mwaipopo (New York and Abingdon, 2014), pp. 161–76. Mwaipopo links the story of Williamson to later developments in Tanzanian diamond mining.

275 Mwaipopo, '*Ubeshi* – Negotiating Co-existence', p. 167.

276 Ibid. The numbers originally came from Jay Epstein.

277 For an extensive study of the compounds in South West Africa, see Robert J. Gordon, *Mines, Masters and Migrants: Life in a Namibian Compound* (Johannesburg, 1977).

278 For a historical overview of South Africa's apartheid, see Nancy L. Clark and William H. Worger, *South Africa: The Rise and Fall of Apartheid* (London, 2004).

279 For UN policy against apartheid, see *The United Nations and Apartheid, 1948–1994* (New York, 1994).

280 See Chapter Six.

281 Kanfer, *The Last Empire*, p. 265.

282 For a detailed analysis, see V. L. Allen, *The History of Black Mineworkers in South Africa*, vol. I: *Mining in South Africa and the Genesis of Apartheid, 1871–1948*, and vol. II: *Apartheid, Repression and Dissent in the Mines, 1948–1982* (London, 2005).

283 Tom Lodge, *Mandela: A Critical Life* (Oxford, 2006), p. 83.

284 Kanfer, *Last Empire*, pp. 237, 281–95.

285 Ibid., pp. 312–14.

286 Several of the buildings used to house black miners were preserved for years after apartheid had ended. Svea Josephy, 'Fractured Compounds: Photographing Post-apartheid Compounds and Hostels', *Social Dynamics*, XL/3 (2015), pp. 444–70.

287 Mamdani, *Citizen and Subject*, p. 258.

288 Ibid., pp. 258–9. The most extensive academic account on the living circumstances of the Cape Town hostels is Mamphela Ramphele, *A Bed Called Home: Life in the Migrant Labour Hostels of Cape Town* (Claremont, 1993).

289 'Why 7-month Shifts Suit an Honest Man', *Sunday Times*, 8 February 1976.
290 Ibid.
291 Ibid.
292 Ibid.
293 Ibid.
294 Ibid.
295 Ibid.
296 M. D. Dewani, 'De Beers and Apartheid', *Economic and Political Weekly*, XXIII/41 (1988), pp. 2094–5.
297 Ibid.
298 V. L. Allen, *The History of Black Mineworkers in South Africa*, vol. III: *Organise or Die: 1982–1994* (London, 2005). See also Raphaël Bativeau, *Organise or Die? Democracy and Leadership in South Africa's National Union of Mineworkers* (Johannesburg, 2017), the first major study on the NUM and the role it played in ending apartheid rule.
299 Cleveland, *Stones of Contention*, p. 120.
300 Ibid., pp. 120–21.

5 THE ENDURING ATTRACTION OF ALLUVIAL MINING, 1884–2018

1 Ian Fleming, *The Diamond Smugglers* (London, 1957), p. 81.
2 *Verhandelingen van het Bataviaasch Genootschap, der Konsten en Weetenschappen* (Rotterdam and Amsterdam, 1786), vol. IV, pp. 545–8.
3 W. L. Ritter, 'De Diamant, eene Borneosche overlevering uit de XVIIIde eeuw', *Tijdschrift voor Neêrlands Indie*, III (1840), pp. 595–632 (pp. 603–9).
4 'Borneo: Eenige reizen in de Binnenlanden van dit Eiland, door eenen Ambtenaar van het Gouvernement, in het jaar 1824. Diamantmijnen te Soengie-Roentie', *Tijdschrift voor Neêrlands Indie*, I (1838), pp. 81–4.
5 'The Banjarmasin Diamond, Anonymous', www.rijksmuseum.nl, accessed 5 May 2020.
6 *Leeuwarder Courant*, 18 June 1858.
7 De Loos, *Gesteenten*, p. 9.
8 I. M. Krol, 'De Borneo-diamant, haar voorkomen, winning en bewerking', *De Ingenieur*, XXXIV/39 (1919), pp. 707–9 (p. 708): 'deze maat is nog een overblijfsel uit den Sultanstijd, toen de steenen van en boven dit gewicht aan hem moesten worden afgeleverd.' Three carats, however, was the wrong number, as earlier sources mention a threshold of five carats.
9 Posewitz, *Borneo*, p. 390.
10 Ibid. Such claims are reminiscent of colonial ideas in Brazil about the skills of men and women that had come from the Costa da Mina in prospecting for diamonds (see Chapter Two).
11 'Diamanten in W. Borneo', *Het Nieuws van den Dag voor Nederlandsch-Indië*, 10 January 1926; and *Nieuwsblad van Friesland*, 17 September 1929.
12 The remainder of the island is now part of Malaysia (known as East Malaysia), and also contains the Sultanate of Brunei.

13 'Indische Diamanten: Kansen op nieuwe diamantwinning op Borneo', *Sumatra Post*, 23 March 1932.

14 'Borneo: Een diamant-geschiedenis', *Nieuw Rotterdamsche Courant*, 14 July 1921.

15 M. D. Teenstra, *Beknopte Beschrijving van de Nederlandsche Overzeesche Bezittingen*, 3 vols (Groningen, 1852), vol. II, p. 438.

16 Dirk Willem Bosch, *Geschied- en Aardrijkskundige Beschrijving van Neêrlands Oost- en West-Indische Bezittingen* (Amsterdam, 1844), p. 147.

17 In Borneo, a *kongsi* of Chinese miners turned into the self-governing Lanfang Republic, which was suppressed by the Dutch in 1884. Mary Somers Heidhues, *Golddiggers, Farmers, and Traders in the 'Chinese Districts' of West Kalimantan, Indonesia* (Ithaca, NY, 2003), pp. 65, 124–5.

18 'De Diamanten van Borneo', *Bataviaasch Nieuwsblad*, 12 December 1918.

19 Hendrik Tillema, *Apo-kajan: Een filmreis naar en door Centraal-Borneo* (Amsterdam, 1938).

20 Sacrifice before work was also a common practice on the Indian diamond fields, as were other religious rituals (illus. 7).

21 'Gemengd Indisch Nieuws', *Het Nieuws van den Dag voor Nederlandsch-Indië*, 14 August 1929; and 'De diamantwinning', *Het Vaderland*, 6 May 1930.

22 Spencer et al., 'Diamond Deposits', p. 74.

23 Ronald E. Seavoy, 'The Religious Motivation for Placer Diamond Mining in Southeastern Kalimantan, Indonesia', *Journal of Cultural Geography*, III/2 (1983), pp. 56–60.

24 For a thorough overview on Congolese diamond mining, see the different contributions in Laurent Monnier, Bogumil Jewsiewicki and Gauthier de Villers, eds, *Chasse au diamant au Congo/Zaire*, Cahiers Africains: Afrika Studies 45–6 (Tervuren, 2001).

25 German colonial policy led to the establishment of German South West Africa, while Britain held colonies in the south and the north – the old Rhodesian dream had been to connect the two.

26 See Raymond F. Betts, *The Scramble for Africa: Causes and Dimensions of Empire* (Lexington, MA, 1972); Muriel Evelyn Chamberlain, *The Scramble for Africa* (London, 1974); Bernard Porter, 'Imperialism and the Scramble', *Journal of Imperial and Commonwealth History*, IX/1 (1980), pp. 76–81.

27 For an overview, see Adam Hochschild, *King Leopold's Ghost: A Story of Greed, Terror and Heroism in Colonial Africa* (London, 1998). This brutal colonial rule is epitomized by the famous photographs of Congolese plantation workers whose hands were severed as punishment.

28 See, for instance, 'The Congo Atrocities', *Evening Telegraph*, 21 November 1906.

29 Joseph Conrad, *Heart of Darkness* [1902] (London, 1973), p. 44. Hochschild, *King Leopold's Ghost*, pp. 142–9 discusses the role of *Heart of Darkness* in this regard, as well as the porytayed racism. A strong rebuttal of the novella in terms of fostering stereotypes was given by Chinua Achebe in a 1975 lecture, later published as China Achebe, 'An Image in Africa: Racism in Conrad's Heart of Darkness', in *Heart of Darkness, An Authoritative Text, Background and Sources Criticism*, ed. Robert Kimbrough (London, 1988), pp. 251–61.

30 'Het Congo Vraagstuk', *De Volksstem*, 12 June 1907.

31 Vincent Viaene, 'Reprise-remise: De Congolese identiteitscrisis van België rond 1908', in *Congo in België: Koloniale cultuur in de metropool*, ed. Vincent Viaene, David van Reybrouck and Bambi Ceuppens (Leuven, 2009), p. 43–62.

32 Frans Buelens and Danny Cassimon, 'The Industrialization of the Belgian Congo', in *Colonial Exploitation and Economic Development: The Belgian Congo and the Netherlands*, ed. E.H.P. Frankema and F. Buelens (London, 2013), pp. 229–50.

33 Thomas Ryan was a financier who started working for a dry goods firm in Baltimore in 1870. When his death was reported in 1928, he was labelled as 'the largest individual holder of Congo diamond fields', while he also played a role in the American Tobacco Company and the British Tobacco Company. 'Sixty Million Will of U.S. Financier', *Daily Mail Atlantic Edition*, 25 November 1928. He was succeeded by his son Clendenin Ryan. The Guggenheims had built a fortune through their involvement in U.S. railways and the metallurgy industry. Laureys, *Meesters van het Diamant*, p. 457. For the rise of the SGB, see Isidore Ndaywel è Nziem, *Histoire générale du Congo: De l'héritage ancien à la République Démocratique* (Paris, 1998), pp. 28–30.

34 Richard Derksen, 'Forminiere in the Kasai, 1906–1939', *African Economic History*, XII (1983), pp. 9–65 (p. 52).

35 Ibid., p. 51.

36 Ibid., p. 63.

37 Georges Arnaud, 'Les mines de diamant du Congo Belge', *Annales de Géographie*, XXXIV/187 (1925), pp. 90–91. In South America production of 1922 was estimated at 160,000 carats in British Guiana and 60,000 in Brazil.

38 Information on the meeting between Jadot and Guggenheim came from an article on Firmin van Brée, who had accompanied Jadot to Brussels and became the SGB's 'diamond man'. He was made director of Forminière in 1925 and its chairman in 1932, the year of Jadot's death. 'Know Your Competitors – XXXIV. Firmin van Brée: Diamonds', *Financial Times*, 24 October 1956.

39 Raymond Leslie Buell, *The Native Problem in Africa*, 2 vols (New York, 1928), vol. II, p. 554. Buell was a Harvard academic who visited the Congo during the 1920s. See also Cleveland, *Stones of Contention*, p. 103.

40 Arnaud, 'Les mines de diamant', p. 90. See also 'Know Your Competitors'. The article stated that, in 1925, 25,000 Congolese labourers were active in Kasaï's alluvial diggings.

41 Todd Cleveland, 'A Minority in the Middle: Ethnic Baluba, the Portuguese Colonial State, and the *Companhia de Diamantes de Angola* (Diamang)', in *Minorities and the State in Africa*, ed. Michael U. Mbanaso and Chima J. Korieh (Amherst, MA, 2010), pp. 195–216 (p. 199).

42 Cleveland, *Stones of Contention*, pp. 115–16.

43 Mafulu Uyind-a-Kanga, 'Mobilisation de la main-d'œuvre agricole: la dépendance de la zone rurale de Luiza des centres miniers du Kasai et du Haut-Katanga industriel (1928–1945)', *African Economic History*, XVI (1987), pp. 39–60.

44 Arnaud, 'Les mines de diamant', pp. 90–91.

45 Buell, *The Native Problem*, vol. ii, pp. 533–4.

46 David Northrup, *Beyond the Bend in the River: African Labor in Eastern Zaire, 1865–1940* (Athens, oh, 1988), pp. 131–8.

47 Jules Marchal, *Travail forcé pour le cuivre et pour l'or* (Borgloon, 1999), p. 10.

48 Willemina Kloosterboer, *Involuntary Labour since the Abolition of Slavery: A Survey of Compulsory Labour throughout the World* (Leiden, 1960), p. 134.

49 Derksen, 'Forminiere', p. 55; Buell, *Native Problem*, vol. ii, p. 538; and Cleveland, *Stones of Contention*, pp. 103, 106.

50 Derksen, 'Forminiere', pp. 55, 58–60.

51 A monopsony is a market situation in which there is only one buyer for a commodity, but multiple sellers.

52 Cleveland, *Stones of Contention*, p. 103; Derksen, 'Forminiere', p. 59.

53 Buell, *Native Problem*, vol. ii, p. 538.

54 Cleveland, *Stones of Contention*, p. 113.

55 Arnaud, 'Les mines de diamant', pp. 90–91.

56 As quoted in Michel Merlier, *Le Congo de la colonisation belge à l'indépendance* (Paris, 1962), p. 122.

57 Buell, *Native Problem*, vol. ii, p. 509.

58 Congo's now-abandoned Shinkolobwe mine produced most of the uranium used by the usa to bomb Nagasaki and Hiroshima. Tom Zoellner, *Uranium: War, Energy, and the Rock that Shaped the World* (New York, 2009), pp. 2–3. For a more thorough study of the American efforts to obtain Shinkolobwe's uranium and export it out of the country without drawing attention, see Susan Williams, *Spies in the Congo: America's Atomic Mission in World War ii* (New York, 2016). Williams shows that the American secret service (oss) used official inquiries into diamond smuggling as a way of hiding inquiries into uranium smuggling. Williams, *Spies in the Congo*, pp. 95–100.

59 Laureys, *Meesters van het Diamant*, p. 44.

60 Ibid.

61 Daleep Singh, *Francophone Africa, 1905–2005: A Century of Economic and Social Change* (New Delhi, 2008), p. 241.

62 Laureys, *Meesters van het Diamant*, pp. 44–7.

63 Todd Cleveland, *Diamonds in the Rough: Corporate Paternalism and African Professionalism on the Mines of Colonial Angola, 1917–1975* (Athens, oh, 2015), p. 27; W. G. Clarence-Smith, *The Third Portuguese Empire, 1825–1975* (Manchester, 1985), pp. 129–30. For Burnay, see Nuno Miguel Lima, 'Henry Burnay no contexto das fortunas da Lisboa oitocentista', *Análise Social*, xliv/192 (2009), pp. 565–88.

64 Cleveland, *Diamonds in the Rough*, pp. 30–38.

65 Clarence-Smith, *The Third Portuguese Empire*, p. 130.

66 Jeremy Ball, *Angola's Colossal Lie: Forced Labor on a Sugar Plantation, 1913–1977* (Leiden, 2015), p. 60.

67 Jorge Varanda, 'Crossing Colonies and Empires: The Health Services of the Diamond Company of Angola', in *Crossing Colonial Historiographies: Histories of Colonial and Indigenous Medicines in Transnational Perspective*, ed. Anne Digby, Waltraud Ernst and Projit B. Mukharji (Cambridge, 2010), pp. 165–84.

68 Cleveland, *Diamonds in the Rough*, p. 34.

69 Carlos Fieremans, *Het voorkomen van diamant langsheen de Kwango-rivier in Angola en Zaïre* (Brussels, 1977). Michiel C. J. de Wite and Edmond Thorose, 'Diamond-bearing Gravels along the Lower Kwango River DRC', in *Geology and Resource Potential of the Congo Basin*, ed. Maarten J. de Wit, François Guillocheau and Michiel C. J. de Wit (Heidelberg, 2015), pp. 341–60. The border between the Congo and Angola has not been drawn by the colonial governments of Belgium and Portugal with a division of diamond deposits in mind, which has created an interesting situation from the point of view of mining management and control. For an anthropological study of this region, see Filip de Boeck, 'Borderland Breccia: The Mutant Hero in the Historical Imagination of a Central-African Diamond Frontier', *Journal of Colonialism and Colonial History*, I/2 (2000), pp. 1–43.

70 Cleveland, *Diamonds in the Rough*, pp. 38–9.

71 The most detailed analysis of Diamang's labour system comes from Cleveland, *Diamonds in the Rough*, pp. 42–211.

72 Ibid.

73 Cleveland, *Stones of Contention*, pp. 99–103.

74 Todd Cleveland and Jorge Varanda, '(Un)healthy Relationships: African Labourers, Profits and Health Services in Angola's Colonial-era Diamond Mines, 1917–1975', *Medical History*, LVIII/1 (2014), pp. 87–105.

75 Todd Cleveland, 'Miners in Name Only: Child Laborers on the Diamond Mines of the *Companhia de Diamantes de Angola* (Diamang), 1917–1975', *Journal of Family History*, XXXV/1 (2010), pp. 91–110.

76 For an extensive overview of this debate, see Diogo R. Curto, 'The Debate on Race Relations in the Portuguese Empire and Charles R. Boxer's Position', *e-Journal of Portuguese History*, XI/1 (2013), pp. 1–42.

77 Laureys, *Meesters van het Diamant*, p. 46.

78 Newbury, *The Diamond Ring*, pp. 248–9. Due to the secretive nature of these dealings, historians have a hard time agreeing on the exact chronology. Clarence-Smith mentions 1922 as the year when Barnato Bros. entered Diamang, while Colin Newbury places it in 1924. Newbury also claimed Oppenheimer went to Angola in 1923, which is hard to reconcile with the publication of the news in English newspapers as early as January 1923. The *Cambridge History of Africa* did not mention Barnato's share (20 per cent) at all but referred instead to the 17 per cent held by Anglo-American. Clarence-Smith, *The Third Portuguese Empire*, p. 129; Newbury, *The Diamond Ring*, p. 248; and A. D. Roberts, ed., *The Cambridge History of Africa*, vol. VII: *From 1905 to 1940* (Cambridge, 1986), p. 256. The fact that Barnato Bros. had obtained a share in Anglo-American in the same period further complicated matters.

79 'Big Congo Diamond Deal: The Angola Company, Barnato and Anglo-American Auspices', *Financial Times*, 11 January 1923.

80 The Krijn firm had been involved in the earlier attempt to obtain a monopoly in the trade in German South West African diamonds and possessed a great deal of expertise.

81 'Congo Diamond Industry: Anglo-American Corporation', *Financial Times*, 7 June 1922.

82 Laureys, *Meesters van het Diamant*, pp. 71–5.

83 'Diamant-industrie: Besprekingen te Brussel', *Het Vaderland*, 16 October 1931; 'Uit de diamantnijverheid', *Algemeen Handelsblad*, 19 July 1932; and 'Diamond Corp. en verkoop van Congo-diamant', *Algemeen Handelsblad*, 3 July 1934. The article 'Diamond Pact' in the *Financial Times* of 28 September 1933 cited the *Algemeen Handelsblad* to report that an agreement between Oppenheimer and Forminière had been reached.

84 Heertje, *De Diamantbewerkers*, pp. 175–213.

85 Under impulse of several scholars, connected to the International Institute of Social History in Amsterdam, and Karin Hofmeester in particular, there is a renewed interest in the nineteenth- and twentieth-century history of Amsterdam's diamond workers. See, for instance, the recent publication on the Dutch diamond workers' union, Hofmeester, *Een Schitterende Erfenis*.

86 Albert E. Kitson, *Report on the Discovery of Diamonds at Abomosa, Northwest of Kibbi, Eastern Province, Gold Coast* (Accra, 1919).

87 For a historical overview, see Christopher R. Decorse, *An Archaeology of Elmina: Africans and Europeans on the Gold Coast, 1400–1900* (Washington, DC, 2001). For the British military conquest of the Ashanti Empire, see Robert B. Edgerton, *The Fall of the Asante Empire: The Hundred-year War for Africa's Gold Coast* (New York, 1995).

88 On the history of gold mining in Ghana, see Gavin Hilson, 'Harvesting Mineral Riches: 1000 Years of Gold Mining in Ghana', *Resources Policy*, XXVIII (2002), pp. 13–26.

89 Hilson, 'Harvesting', pp. 19–22.

90 Emmanuel Ofosu-Mensah Ababio, 'Mining and Conflict in the Akyem Abuakwa Kingdom in the Eastern Region of Ghana, 1919–1938', *Extractive Industries and Society*, II (2015), pp. 480–90 (p. 483).

91 Kevin Shillington, ed., *Encyclopedia of African History*, 3 vols (New York, 2005), vol. I, p. 979; see also 'Diamonds in West Africa', *Financial Times*, 27 February 1924.

92 Beatty (1875–1968) was an Irish American mining engineer and entrepreneur who would later also invest in diamond mining in Namaqualand and Sierra Leone. John Phillips, 'Alfred Chester Beatty: Mining Engineer, Financier, and Entrepreneur, 1898–1950', in *Mining Tycoons in the Age of Empire, 1870–1945*, ed. Dumett, pp. 215–38.

93 Peter Greenhalgh, *West African Diamonds, 1919–83: An Economic History* (Manchester, 1985), p. 40.

94 Ibid., pp. 36–40; 'West African Diamond Syndicate', *Financial Times*, 21 August 1923.

95 'The West African Diamond Syndicate', *Financial Times*, 21 December 1925.

96 A first litigation was reported in 'Diamonds in West Africa', *Financial Times*, 27 February 1924. Greenhalgh, *West African Diamonds*, pp. 41–2.

97 For an overview, see Greenhalgh, *West African Diamonds*, pp. 62–8.

98 William Burnett Harvey, *Law and Social Change in Ghana* (Princeton, NJ, 1966), pp. 71–2.

99 Roger S. Gocking, *The History of Ghana* (Westport, CT, 2005), p. 295.

100 See Emmanuel Ofosu-Mensah Ababio, 'Mining and Conflict in the Akyem Abuakwa Kingdom in the Eastern Region of Ghana, 1919–1938', pp. 480–90.

101 Emmanuel Ofosu-Mensah Ababio, 'Mining in Colonial Ghana: Extractive Capitalism and its Social Benefits in Akyem Abuakwa under Nana Ofori Atta I', *Africa Today*, LXIII/1 (2016), pp. 23–55 (pp. 28–33).

102 Phillips, 'Alfred Chester Beatty', pp. 231–2.

103 For an overview of benefits, which included the arrival of electricity and the application of mining revenue by the Ofori Atta to build schools and fund scholarships abroad, see Ofosu-Mensah, 'Mining in Colonial Ghana', pp. 34–48.

104 Greenhalgh, *West African Diamonds*, p. 45.

105 Newbury, *The Diamond Ring*, p. 287.

106 In South Africa, they held one-third of Cape Coast Exploration Ltd. Greenhalgh, *West African Diamonds*, p. 46.

107 'Sierra Leone's New Diamond Field', *Journal of the Royal Society of Arts*, LXXXV/4430 (1937), pp. 1043–5.

108 Greenhalgh, *West African Diamonds*, p. 52.

109 F. H. Hatch, 'Description of a Diamondiferous Gem Gravel from the West Coast of Africa', *Geological Magazine*, IX/3 (1912), pp. 106–10.

110 Greenhalgh, *West African Diamonds*, pp. 71–3.

111 For an overview, see Ibrahim Soumah, *Les Mines en Guinée: Comment ça fonctionne* (Paris, 2010).

112 Edward Wharton-Tigar, *Burning Bright: The Autobiography of Edward Wharton-Tigar* ([London], 1987), p. 132. Wharton-Tigar worked for Selection Trust before and after the war. He was a British spy during the Second World War and died in 1995. 'Edward Wharton-Tigar, 82, British Agent', *New York Times*, 26 December 1995.

113 A.J.A. Janse, 'A History of Diamond Sources in Africa: Part II', *Gems and Gemology*, XXXII/1 (1996), pp. 2–31 (p. 8).

114 Cleveland, *Stones of Contention*, p. 100.

115 Janse, 'A History, Part II', pp. 9–10.

116 This period was chosen because information for the two groups is available for those years.

117 Sylvie Bredeloup, 'La fièvre du diamant au temps des colonies (Afrique)', *Autrepart*, XI (1999), pp. 171–89 (pp. 174–5).

118 Magbaily C. Fyle, *Historical Dictionary of Sierra Leone* (Lanham, MD, 2006), pp. 185–6.

119 David John Harris, *Sierra Leone: A Political History* (Oxford, 2014), p. 34. Bredeloup, 'La fièvre', pp. 176–7. See also H. L. van der Laan, *Sierra Leone Diamonds: An Economic Study Covering the Years 1952–61* (Oxford, 1965).

120 Marcel Bardet, *Géologie du Diamant*, vol. II: *Gisements de diamants d'Afrique* (Paris, 1974), pp. 172–212 for numbers related to the Ivory Coast. For the

circulation of the miners and the measures taken, see Bredeloup, 'La fièvre', pp. 174–9.

121 'Diamantsmokkel in Sierra Leone neemt enorme vormen aan', *Leeuwarder Courant*, 18 June 1955: 'veel diamant verdwijnt via Beyrouth of Zwitserland achter 't Ijzeren Gordijn.'

122 A series of interviews that Ian Fleming, author of the James Bond books, conducted with John Collard, one of the organisation's members, led to a series of articles in the *Sunday Times*, and the publication of *The Diamond Smugglers*.

123 Based on data from Greenhalgh, *West African Diamonds*, pp. 38–9, 54.

124 Ian Fleming, *The Diamond Smugglers* (London, 1957), p. 118.

125 Madelaine Drohan, *Making a Killing: How and Why Corporations Use Armed Force to Do Business* (Toronto, 2003), pp. 67–93. Kamil published his memoirs as Fred Kamil, *The Diamond Underworld* (New York, 1979).

126 This also applied to the indigenous peoples of in Australia and Canada, but the nature of twentieth-century mining operations there did not lead to forced labour. The problems had more to do with the stealing of indigenous land.

127 A good example is Babatunde Zack-Williams, 'Diamond Mining and Underdevelopment in Sierra Leone, 1930/1980', *Africa Development/Afrique et Développement*, xv/2 (1990), pp. 95–117.

128 2006 Minerals Yearbook: Ghana ([usa], 2009); and the 'Annual Global Summary: Production, Imports, Exports and kpc Counts' for 2015 and 2018, kimberleyprocessstatistics.org, accessed 5 May 2020.

129 For the years after independence, see Roger Causse, 'Le diamant en Guinée (situation en 1957–1958)', in Pierre Legoux et André Marelle, *Les mines et la recherché minière en Afrique occidentale* (Paris, 1991), pp. 213–29. The same volume also contains an overview of diamond extraction in Ivory Coast: René Malaurent, 'Chronique de la Saremci (1945–1962) ou le diamant en Côté-d'Ivoire', pp. 230–60. See also *L'Afrique d'expression française et Madagascar* (Paris, 1985), p. 107; and 'Annual Global Summary: Production Imports, Exports and kpc Counts' for 2015 and 2018.

130 For a detailed historical overview, see Frost, *From the Pit to the Market*.

131 Cleveland, *Stones of Contention*, p. 148.

132 William Reno, *Corruption and State Politics in Sierra Leone* (Cambridge, 1995), p. 118; see also H. L. van der Laan, *The Lebanese Traders in Sierra Leone* (The Hague, 1975).

133 Reno, *Corruption and State Politics*, p. 106; and Cleveland, *Stones of Contention*, p. 149.

134 Reno, *Corruption and State Politics*, pp. 115–24.

135 For an overview of the two conflicts, and the role played by diamonds, see Ian Smillie, *Blood on the Stone: Greed, Corruption and War in the Global Diamond Trade* (London, 2010), pp. 79–114.

136 Cleveland, *Stones of Contention*, p. 150.

137 Greg Campbell, *Blood Diamonds: Tracing the Deadly Path of the World's Most Precious Stones* (New York, 2004), pp. 40–41, 51–2. The Mandinka are an ethnicity of about 11 million, living in Mali, Guinea, Senegal, Ivory Coast, Gambia, Burkina Faso, Liberia and Sierra Leone.

138 'Viktor Bout Sentenced to 25 Years in Prison', *The Guardian*, 5 April 2012.

139 Campbell, *Blood Diamonds*, pp. 75–8.

140 Ibid., p. 54.

141 Lansana Gberie, *A Dirty War in West Africa: The RUF and the Destruction of Sierra Leone* (Bloomington, IN, 2005), pp. 118–55.

142 Sebastian Junger, *Fire* (New York, 2001), pp. 175–98.

143 'Charles Taylor Found Guilty of Abetting Sierra Leone War Crimes', *The Guardian*, 26 April 2012.

144 Smillie, *Blood on the Stone*, pp. 113–14.

145 Lydia Polgreen, 'Diamonds Move from Blood to Sweat and Tears', *New York Times*, 25 March 2007. For a more general analysis of Sierra Leone's present--day diamond economy, see Nina Engwicht, 'The Local Translation of Global Norms: The Sierra Leonian Diamond Market', *Conflict, Security and Development*, XVIII/6 (2018), pp. 463–92.

146 See www.koiduholdings.com, accessed 5 May 2020. The company is owned by BSG Resources of the controversial Israeli businessman and mining entrepreneur Beny Steinmetz. See Ian Cobain and Afua Hirsch, 'The Tycoon, the Dictator's Wife and the $2.5bn Guinea Mining Deal', *The Guardian*, 30 July 2013.

147 Amelia Hill, 'Bin Laden's $20m African "Blood Diamond" Deals', *The Guardian*, 20 October 2002.

148 See Norrie MacQueen, *The Decolonization of Portuguese Africa: Metropolitan Revolution and the Dissolution of Empire* (London, 1997); and Lincoln Secco, *A Revolução dos Cravos e a crise do império colonial português: economias, espaços e tomadas de consciências* (São Paulo, 2004).

149 Smillie, *Blood on the Stone*, pp. 63–78.

150 Cleveland, *Diamonds in the Rough*, p. 214.

151 Manuel Ennes Ferreira, 'Nacionalização e confisco do capital português na indústria transformadora de Angola (1975–1990)', *Análise Social*, XXXVII/162 (2002), pp. 47–90.

152 Cleveland, *Diamonds in the Rough*, p. 215.

153 Christian Dietrich, 'UNITA's Diamond Mining and Exporting Capacity', in *Angola's War Economy: The Role of Oil and Diamonds*, ed. Jakkie Cilliers and Christian Dietrich (Pretoria, 2000), pp. 275–93.

154 Smillie, *Blood on the Stone*, pp. 70–73.

155 Alex Vines, *Angola Unravels: The Rise and Fall of the Lusaka Peace Process* (New York, 1999), p. 191.

156 For an overview, see ibid., pp. 191–217.

157 'Final Report of the UN Panel of Experts on Violations of Security Council Sanctions against UNITA: The "Fowler Report", s/2000/203', www.globalpolicy.org, 10 March 2000.

158 Jake H. Sherman, 'Profit vs. Peace: The Clandestine Diamond Economy of Angola', *Journal of International Affairs*, LIII/2 (2000), pp. 699–719 (p. 707).

159 Smillie, *Blood on the Stone*, p. 71.

160 Ibid., pp. 74–5. See also Ben Smith, 'Meet the Mogul', www.nymag.com, 4 May 2007, accessed 5 May 2020.

161 'Annual Global Summary: Production, Imports, Exports and KPC Counts' for 2005 and 2018.

162 Christian Dietrich, 'Inventory of Formal Diamond Mining in Angola', in *Angola's War Economy*, ed. Cillers and Dietrich, pp. 141–72 (p. 142).

163 In 2018, just before the introduction of the licensed cooperatives, about 4,800 artisanal miners were active in the diamond region. 'Angola tem mais de 4.800 garimpeiros, mais de 230 cooperativas de garimpo artesanal aguardam licenciamento', www.novojornal.co.ao, 3 July 2018; see also Armando Sapalo, 'Jovens dinamizam exploração de diamantes na Lunda-norte', www.jornaldeangola.sapo.ao, 12 August 2017.

164 'Angola Might End Semi-industrial Diamond Mining', www.thediamond-loupe.com, 16 January 2020. Endiama's news agency still issues news that the cooperatives might be part of the solution, even though the number of licences will be smaller in the future. 'Ana Feijó, alerta Cooperativas inativas vão perder Licenças', www.endiamaimprensa.com, 20 November 2019.

165 Cristina Udelsmann Rodrigues and Ana Paula Tavares, 'Angola's Planned and Unplanned Growth: Diamond Mining Towns in the Lunda Provinces', *Journal of Contemporary African Studies*, xxx/4 (2012), pp. 687–703.

166 Rafael Marques, *Diamantes de Sangue. Corrupção e Tortura em Angola* (Lisbon, 2011), translated into English as *Blood Diamonds: Corruption and Torture in Angola* (n.p., 2011).

167 'The Case of Rafael Marques de Morais', globalfreedomofexpression. columbia.edu, accessed 5 May 2020.

168 David N. Gibbs, 'Dag Hammarskjöld, the United Nations, and the Congo Crisis of 1960–1: A Reinterpretation', *Journal of Modern African Studies*, xxxi/1 (1993), pp. 163–74 (pp. 163–7).

169 The circumstances of the murder and the involvement of the CIA and the Belgian government have remained controversial for years. Gerard Soete, a former colonial policeman, admitted on Belgian television that he had made Lumumba's body disappear in sulphuric acid. Ludo De Witte, *The Assassination of Lumumba* (London, 2001), first published in Dutch in 1999. An interview with the daughter of Soete, in which she showed the journalist a tooth that belonged to Lumumba, stirred a great deal of controversy in 2016. Jan Antonissen and Hanne van Tendeloo, 'De moord op Lumumba: de dochter van de lijkruimer spreekt', *Humo*, 16 January 2016.

170 For an assessment of the DRC under Mobutu, see Mabiengwa Emmanuel Naniuzeyi, 'The State of the State in Congo-Zaire: A Survey of the Mobutu Regime', *Journal of Black Studies*, xxix/5 (1999), pp. 669–83. For the political system relying on favours, see Winsome J. Leslie, *Zaïre: Continuity and Political Change in an Oppressive State* (Boulder, CO, 1993).

171 For a recent article on growing calls to deal with this persistent past of political and economic Western colonialism in the specific context of Belgium and DRC, see Neil Munshi, 'Belgium's Reckoning with a Brutal History in Congo', *Financial Times*, 13 November 2020.

172 Smillie, *Blood on the Stone*, pp. 120–23.

173 Filip De Boeck, 'Domesticating Diamonds and Dollars: Identity, Expenditure and Sharing in Southwestern Zaire (1984–1997)', *Development and Change*, XXIX (1998), pp. 777–810 (p. 784).

174 Filip De Boeck, '*Garimpeiro* Worlds: Digging, Dying and "Hunting" for Diamonds in Angola', *Review of African Political Economy*, XXVIII/90 (2001), pp. 549–62 (pp. 554–5).

175 For a detailed analysis based on ground research, see De Boeck, 'Domesticating Diamonds'; and De Boeck, '*Garimpeiro* Worlds'.

176 For a short history of Kisangani after independence, see Jean Omasombo, 'Kisangani: A City at its Lowest Ebb', in *Urban Africa: Changing Contours of Survival in the City*, ed. Abdou Maliq Simone and Abdelghani Abouhani (Dakar, 2005), pp. 96–119. For Kisangani's diamond deposits, see pp. 105–9.

177 Ibid., p. 106.

178 Smillie, *Blood on the Stone*, p. 124.

179 Conflict has never ceased completely and the east of the country, bordering Uganda and Rwanda, remains extremely vulnerable. See Jason Stearns, *Dancing in the Glory of Monsters: The Collapse of the Congo and the Great War of Africa* (New York, 2011). See also Jason Burke, '"The Wars Will Never Stop": Millions Flee Bloodshed as Congo Falls Apart', *The Guardian*, 3 April 2018.

180 Ingrid Samset, 'Conflict of Interests or Interests in Conflict? Diamonds and War in the DRC', *Review of African Political Economy*, XXIX/93 (2002), pp. 463–80 (pp. 470–72). For the Congo wars, see also Walter C. Soderlund, E. Donald Briggs, Tom Pierre Najem and Blake C. Roberts, *Africa's Deadliest Conflict: Media Coverage of the Humanitarian Disaster in the Congo and the United Nations Response, 1997–2008* (Waterloo, ON, 2013). See also Hugues Leclercq, 'Le Rôle économique du diamant dans le conflit Congolais', in *Chasse au diamant*, ed. Monnier, Jewsiewicki and de Villers, pp. 47–78, for an economic analysis of the role of diamonds in the Congo wars. Leclercq provides detailed data on the export of Congolese diamonds to Rwanda and Uganda in the 1990s.

181 Ingrid J. Tamm, *Diamonds in Peace and War: Severing the Conflict-diamond Connection* (Cambridge, MA, 2002), p. 15, and 'Sifting Through a Dark Business', *Newsweek*, 12 July 2003.

182 Aryn Baker, 'Inside the Democratic Republic of Congo's Diamond Mines', *Time*, 27 August 2015.

183 Patience Kabamba, 'A Tale of Two Cities: Urban Transformation in Gold-centred Butembo and Diamond-rich Mbuji-Mayi, Democratic Republic of the Congo', *Journal of Contemporary African Studies*, XXX/4 (2012), pp. 669–85; see also Jean-Luc Piermay, 'Naissance et évolution d'une ville post-coloniale: Mbuji-Mayi (Zaïre): acteurs et enjeu fonciers', in *Espaces disputes en Afrique Noire: pratique foncières locales*, ed. Bernard Crousse and Emile Le Bris (Paris, 1986), pp. 133–43.

184 Jessica E. Kogel, Nikhil C. Trivedi, James M. Barjer and Stanely T. Krukowski, eds, *Industrial Minerals and Rocks: Commodities, Markets, and Uses*, 7th edn (Littleton, CO, 2006), p. 420.

185 For the role of diamonds in armed conflict, see Päivil Lujala, Nils Petter Gleditsch and Elisabeth Gilmore, 'A Diamond Curse? Civil War and a Lootable Resource', *Journal of Conflict Resolution*, XLIX/4 (2005), pp. 538–62; see also Joseph Hummel, 'Diamonds are a Smuggler's Best Friend: Regulation, Economics, and Enforcement in the Global Effort to Curb the Trade in Conflict Diamonds', *International Lawyer*, XLI/4 (2007), pp. 1145–69.

186 The quote comes from Lucinda Saunders, 'Rich and Rare are the Gems They War: Holding De Beers Accountable for Trading Conflict Diamonds', *Fordham International Law Journal*, XXIV/4 (2000), pp. 1402–76 (p. 1476). For a history of the Kimberley Process, see Franziska Bieri, *From Blood Diamonds to the Kimberley Process: How NGOs Cleaned Up the Global Diamond Industry* (Farnham and Burlington, VT, 2010).

187 Ibid., p. 185.

188 Audrie Howard, 'Blood Diamonds: The Successes and Failures of the Kimberley Process Certification Scheme in Angola, Sierra Leone and Zimbabwe', *Washington University Global Studies Law Review*, XV/1 (2016), pp. 137–59.

189 Jacob W. Chikuhwa, *Zimbabwe: The End of the First Republic* (Bloomington, IN, 2013), p. 410.

190 Mugabe became the country's leader immediately after independence in 1980 and was deposed in November 2017. He died almost two years later. For a recent assessment of Mugabe, see the essays in Munyaradzi Mawere, Ngonidzashe Marongwe and Fidelis Peter Thomas Duri, eds, *The End of an Era? Robert Mugabe and a Conflicting Legacy* (Bamenda, 2018).

191 Rumu Sarkar, *International Development Law: Rule of Law, Human Rights, and Global Finance* (Oxford, 2009), p. 344.

192 Chikuhwa, *Zimbabwe*, p. 413.

193 Misha Gupta, *The 'Invisible Hand', De Beers, and Emerging Markets* (Cergy-Pontoise, 2011).

194 That was the situation in 2018.

195 For an overview on Zimbabwean diamonds, the failure of KP's policy and human rights abuse at Marange, see *Reap What You Sow: Greed and Corruption in Zimbabwe's Marange Diamond Fields* (Ottawa, 2012); Andrew H. Winetroub, 'A Diamond Scheme Is Forever Lost: The Kimberley Process's Deteriorating Tripartite Structure and Its Consequences for the Scheme's Survival', *Indiana Journal of Global Legal Studies*, XX/2 (2013), pp. 1425–44; and Katie Farineau, 'Red Diamonds: Chinese Involvement in Zimbabwe', *Harvard International Review*, XXXV/1 (2013), pp. 28–30. For Anjin, a Chinese military defence industry, see Chikuhwa, *Zimbabwe*, pp. 415–16.

196 'Annual Global Summary: Production, Imports, Exports and KPC Counts' for 2013 and 2015.

197 'Mugabe: Government Will Now Own All Zimbabwe's Diamonds', www.aljazeera.com, 4 March 2016, accessed 5 May 2020.

198 'Annual Global Summary: 2015 Production, Imports, Exports and KPC Counts'.

199 Nathan Munier, 'Diamonds, Dependence and De Beers: Monopoly Capitalism and Compliance with the Kimberley Process in Namibia', *Review of African Political Economy*, XLIII/150 (2016), pp. 542–55.

200 See Nigel Davidson, *The Lion that Didn't Roar: Can the Kimberley Process Stop the Blood Diamonds Trade?* (Acton, 2016).

201 Ritu Sarin, 'Rosy Blue also in HSBC List: Diamond Dealers are Tax Haven's Best Friends', www.theindianexpress.com, 7 April 2016. The company has also been mentioned in the Panama and Paradise Papers. Ritu Sarin, 'Paradise Papers: on All Black Money Lists Leading Diamond Firm Rosy Blue Is Back', www.theindianexpress.com, 8 November 2017. Both accessed 5 May 2020.

202 Renous gave a presentation in the European Parliament on 20 June 2018. The PowerPoint document can be downloaded on the website of Ana Gomes, member of the European Parliament for the Portuguese Socialist Party between 2004 and 2019. David Renous, 'Omega Diamonds Case in Belgium: An Opportunity to Repatriate Assets to Angola', www.anagomes. eu, accessed 5 May 2020.

203 Ibid.

204 For Swiss leaks and the Omega case, see David Leigh, James Ball, Juliette Garside and David Pegg, 'HSBC files: Swiss Bank Hid Money for Suspected Criminals', *The Guardian*, 12 February 2015. Around the same date, a similar article appeared in *Le Monde*.

6 MINING IN THE WESTERN WORLD: THE TWENTY-FIRST-CENTURY COLLAPSE OF THE WORLD DE BEERS CREATED

1 Quoted from the De Beers website, 'A Diamond's Journey', www.debeersgroup.com, accessed 5 May 2020.

2 None of the USA's diamond deposits are economically viable. The Central African Republic has been suspended from the KP. The last year for which the KP website has provided data for the CAR was 2012, when production was 365,916.63 carats and the ratio of U.S. dollars per carat 169.79. 'Annual Global Summary: 2012 Production, Imports, Exports and KPC Counts'.

3 As most Russian diamonds come from Sakha, Russian production was included in the Asian percentage.

4 The two main examples are, of course, South Africa's apartheid and blood diamonds.

5 Epstein, *The Rise and Fall of Diamonds*, p. 202.

6 Dale J. Montpelier, 'Diamonds are Forever? Implications of United States Antitrust Statutes on International Trade and the De Beers Diamond Cartel', *California Western International Law Journal*, XXIV/2 (1993), pp. 277–344 (pp. 294–6).

7 This is the most recent data available, from 'Annual Global Summary: 2018 Production, Imports, Exports and KPC Counts'. The category 'other' contains twelve countries with numbers under 1 per cent, including Brazil (0.17 per cent), India (0.03 per cent), Cameroon, Central African Republic, Republic

of the Congo, Ghana, Guinea, Guyana, India, Ivory Coast, Liberia, Tanzania as well as China (which officially produced 99 carats in 2018).

8 'Annual Global Summary: 2018 Production, Imports, Exports and KPC Counts'.

9 Ibid., pp. 296–7.

10 David E. Koskoff, *The Diamond World* (New York, 1981), p. 325.

11 Keith Bradsher, 'U.S. Indicts G.E. and De Beers in Diamond Pricing', *New York Times*, 18 February 1994.

12 Mark R. Joelson, *An International Antitrust Primer: A Guide to the Operation of United States, European Union and Other Key Competition Laws in the Global Economy* (Alphen aan den Rijn, 2006), p. 131. For the 1994 case, see also Janine Farrell-Robert, *Glitter and Greed: The Secret World of the Diamond Cartel* (St Paul, MN, 2003), pp. 161–4. For the third case, see 'United States v. General Elec. Co., 869 F. Supp. 1285 (S.D. Ohio 1994)', www.law.justia.com, accessed 5 May 2020.

13 'United States Court of Appeal for the Third Circuit', pp. 14–15 (see the opening quote of Chapter Four).

14 Carli Cooke, 'De Beers Studies U.S. after 60-year Ban in No. 1 Market', www.bloomberg.com, 15 August 2012; and Anthony DeMarco, 'De Beers Seeks a Return to the U.S., Moves Diamond Operations to Botswana', www.forbes.com, 15 August 2012.

15 From a private conversation with author Tom Zoellner, quoted in Tom Zoellner, *The Heartless Stone: A Journey through the World of Diamonds, Deceit, and Desire* (New York, 2006), p. 150.

16 Richard Wachman, 'Anglo American Gains Controlling Stake in De Beers', *The Guardian*, 4 November 2011.

17 Janse, 'Global Rough Diamond Production', p. 109.

18 Helen Thomas, 'Botswana Readies for Diamond Trade', *Financial Times*, 19 February 2013.

19 Alexandra Wexler, 'De Beers Left London for Botswana, Transforming Lives and a Sleepy City', *Wall Street Journal*, 27 April 2016.

20 'The Group', www.debeersgroup.com, accessed 5 May 2020.

21 'Finsch', www.petradiamonds.com, accessed 5 May 2020; see also Janse, 'Global Rough Diamond Production', p. 109. Petra Diamonds, one of the partners in Ekapa, currently owns the Williamson mine in Tanzania.

22 For Namibia, see Daniel R. Kempton and Roni L. Du Preez, 'Namibian-De Beers State-Firm Relations: Cooperation and Conflict', *Journal of Southern African Studies*, XXIII/4 (1997), pp. 585–613; see also John J. Gurney, Alfred A. Levinson and H. Stuart Smith, 'Marine Mining of Diamonds off the West Coast of Southern Africa', *Gems and Gemology*, XXVII/4 (1991), pp. 206–19. Offshore diamond mining in Namibia led to the accidental discovery in 2008 of the Portuguese vessel *Bom Jesus*, which had left Lisbon in March 1533. Part of its cargo belonged to the extremely wealthy Fugger family. Francisco J. S. Alves, 'The 16th-century Portuguese Shipwreck of Oranjemund, Namibia. Report on the Missions Carried Out by the Portuguese Team in 2008 and 2009', www.patrimoniocultural.gov.pt, accessed 5 May 2020.

23 'Mines', www.debeersgroup.com, accessed 5 May 2020.

24 'Customer Directory', gss.debeersgroup.com, accessed 5 May 2020.

25 Often, Sakha is incorrectly thought of as part of Siberia. John Tichotsky, *Russia's Diamond Colony: The Republic of Sakha* (London, 2000), p. 21.

26 *Groninger Courant*, 5 January 1830.

27 'Account of the Discovery of Diamonds in Russia. In a Letter from St Petersburgh', *Edinburgh Journal of Science*, II (1830), p. 261: 'la sable de platine de Nijny-Toura appartenant à la fabrique de la couronne Koushra, offre une resemblance frappante avec celui du Brèzil, où l'on trouve ordinairement les diamans'. See also 'Mines de diamans', *Revue Encyclopédique*, XLV (1830), pp. 460–61. Reference to this article was made by other contemporary sources, such as John Murray, *A Memoir on the Diamond: Including its Economical and Political History* (London, 1831), pp. 29–30. Engelhardt's scientific findings were published as Moritz von Engelhardt, *Die Lagerstätte des Goldes und Platini im Ural-Gebirge: Untersuchungen* (Riga, 1828); and Moritz von Engelhardt, *Die Lagerstätte der Diamanten im Ural-Gebirge: Untersuchung* (Riga, 1830).

28 Alexander von Humboldt, *Essai géognostique sur le gisement des roches dans les deux hémisphères* (Paris, 1823).

29 Engelhardt, *Lagerstätte der Diamanten*, p. 8; Wulff, *The Invention of Nature*, p. 204.

30 For an extensive description of von Humboldt's Russian expedition, see Andrea Wulf, *The Invention of Nature: Alexander von Humboldt's New World* (New York, 2015), pp. 201–17. One of the expedition's members, Prussian mineralogist Gustav Rose, published his travel experiences as Gustav Rose, *Mineralogisch-geognostische Reise nach dem Ural, dem Altai und dem Kaspischen Meere* (Berlin, 1837). For de Polier, see 'Полье, граф Адольф Антонович это [Polier, Count Adolf Antonovich de]', dic.academic.ru, accessed 5 May 2020.

31 'Russische Diamanten', *Bredasche Courant*, 11 September 1832; *Mémorial encyclopédique et progressif des connaissances humaines, ou annales des sciences, lettres et beaux-arts; des arts industriels, manufactures et métiers; de l'histoire, la géographie et les voyages* (1836), vol. VI, p. 359.

32 An English translation was published as Max Bauer, *Precious Stones: A Popular Account of their Characters, Occurrence and Applications, with an Introduction to their Determination, for Mineralogists, Lapidaries, Jewellers, Etc. with an Appendix on Pearls and Coral* (London, 1904), p. 231.

33 Edward I. Erlich and W. Dan Hausel, *Diamond Deposits: Origin, Exploration, and History of Discovery* (Littleton, CO, 2002), pp. 9–10.

34 Vladimir S. Sobolev, *Petrology of Traps of the Siberian Platfrom*, Proceedings of the Arctic Institute 43 (Leningrad, 1936) [in Russian]. N. V. Sobolev, 'Preface: Contribution of Vladimir S. Sobolev to the Study of Petrology of the Lithosphere and Diamond Genesis', *Russian Geology and Geophysics*, L (2009), pp. 995–8.

35 Daniel R. Kempton and Richard M. Levine, 'Soviet and Russian Relations with Foreign Corporations: The Case of Gold and Diamonds', *Slavic Review*, LIV/1 (1995), pp. 80–110 (p. 87).

36 Erlich and Hausel, *Diamond Deposits*, pp. 10–11.

37 'Sovjet Rusland en Diamant', *Amigoe di Curaçao: Dagblad voor de Nederlandse Antillen*, 3 May 1950.

38 Erlich and Hausel, *Diamond Deposits*, p. 11. She published her findings with her supervisor as Natalya N. Sarsadskikh and Larisa A. Popugaeva, 'New Data on the Manifestation of Ultramafic Magmatism in the Siberian Platform', *Razvedka Nedr*, 5 (1955), pp. 11–20 [in Russian].

39 Tichotsky, *Russia's Diamond Colony*, p. 111.

40 Erlich and Hausel, *Diamond Deposits*, pp. 12–13.

41 Levinson, 'Diamond Sources', pp. 96–7.

42 'Grote diamantvelden in Siberië? Ned. Diamantkringen niet verontrust', *De Telegraaf*, 6 March 1956.

43 G. A. Vvedensky, 'Progress in the Soviet Diamond Industry', *Bulletin of the Institute for the Study of the USSR*, VI (1959), pp. 17–21.

44 Tichotsky, *Russia's Diamond Colony*, p. 102.

45 Susan A. Crate, 'Co-option in Siberia: The Case of Diamonds and the Vilyuy Sakha', *Polar Geography*, XXVI/4 (2002), pp. 418–35 (p. 422).

46 Ibid., pp. 421–2.

47 'Sakha', www.britannica.com, accessed 5 May 2020.

48 Tichotsky, *Russia's Diamond Colony*, pp. 103–4.

49 Ibid., p. 104.

50 'De Beers to Market Soviet Diamonds', *Financial Times*, 19 January 1960.

51 '"Don't Fight It – Join It"', *The Economist*, 23 January 1960.

52 'Diamond Pact with Russia', *The Times*, 19 January 1960; 'Soviet Diamond Agreement Renewed', *Financial Times*, 19 January 1961; 'Soviet Diamond Agreement Renewed', *Financial Times*, 5 December 1961; and 'Soviet Diamond Agreement', *The Times*, 6 December 1961.

53 Daniel R. Kempton, 'Russia and De Beers: Diamond Conflict or Cartel?', *South African Journal of International Affairs*, III/2 (1995), pp. 94–131 (pp. 99–100).

54 Charles Lloyd, 'De Beers Stop Red Diamond Sales', *Daily Mail*, 16 May 1964.

55 Kempton and Levine, 'Soviet and Russian Relations', pp. 87–8.

56 Kurt M. Campbell, *Soviet Politics towards South Africa* (Basingstoke, 1986), p. 102; and Tichotsky, *Russia's Diamond Colony*, pp. 105–6.

57 Debora L. Spar, *The Cooperative Edge: The Internal Politics of International Cartels* (Ithaca, NY, 1994), p. 67.

58 Kempton, 'Russia and De Beers', pp. 102–3; Campbell, *Soviet Politics*, p. 103.

59 J. Danoczi and A. Koursaris, 'Development of Luminescent Diamond Simulants for X-ray Recovery', *Journal of the Southern African Institute of Mining and Metallurgy*, CVIII (2008), pp. 89–97. The technology is still being developed today in Russia. Bourevestnik, part of the company that now hold rights to mine diamonds in Russia, filed a patent of X-ray luminescent separation of minerals in November 2013, granted the following year as a Russian patent. See Leonid Vasilievich Kazakov et al., 'Method for X-ray Luminescent Separation of Minerals and X-ray Luminescent Separator for

Carrying Out Said Method' (patented 6 November 2014), patents.google. com, accessed 5 May 2020.

60 'Soviet Union to Market Diamonds through Antwerp', *Financial Times*, 17 July 1973.

61 'Where Have Russia's Diamonds Gone?', *Russian Politics and Law*, XXXV/1 (1997), pp. 69–82 (p. 74). The factory in Smolensk opened in 1963 and still employs more than 2,000 workers today. See 'About', www.kristallsmolensk. com, accessed 5 May 2020.

62 A.J.A. Janse, 'Global Rough Diamond Production since 1870', *Gems and Gemology* (2007), pp. 98–119 (p. 101).

63 Campbell, *Soviet Policy*, p. 103.

64 Kempton and Levine, 'Soviet and Russian Relations', p. 88; Sara Kohles, 'Diamond Rings: Capitalizing on Social Trends', *Financial History*, 105 (2013), pp. 29–31.

65 Kempton and Levin, 'Soviet and Russian Relations', p. 98. Forpton and Levine, 'Soviet and Russian Relations', p. 88.

66 Tony Warwick-Ching, *The International Gold Trade* (Cambridge, 1993), pp. 159–60.

67 Kempton and Levin, 'Soviet and Russian Relations', p. 98. For the diamond wars, see Daniel R. Kempton, 'The Republic of Sakha (Yakutia): The Evolution of Centre-periphery Relations in the Russian Federation', *Europe-Asia Studies*, XLVIII/4 (1996), pp. 587–613 (pp. 591–4).

68 Ibid., pp. 592–3.

69 Kempton and Levine, 'Soviet and Russian Relations', p. 100.

70 Kempton, 'The Republic of Sakha', pp. 593–4.

71 The quote was taken from their website, www.tuymaadadiamond.com, accessed 5 May 2020.

72 H. G. Broadman, ed., *From Disintegration to Reintegration: Eastern Europe and the Former Soviet Union in International Trade* (Washington, DC, 2005), p. 341.

73 Tichotsky, *Russia's Diamond Colony*, p. 269.

74 For an overview of these turbulent years, see ibid., pp. 235–82.

75 Arkady Ostrovsky, 'Russia Welcomes Diamond Deal with De Beers', *Financial Times*, 4 November 1998.

76 See below.

77 Ostrovsky, 'Russia Welcomes Diamond Deal with De Beers'.

78 'Russian Diamond Miner Alrosa Raises $1.3 bln in Share Sale', www. reuters.com, 28 October 2013; Andrew W. Kramer, 'Alrosa, a Russian Rival to De Beers, Enters Public Trading', *New York Times*, 30 October 2013; and '2014 Annual Report', *Alrosa Annual Report* (2014), www.alrosa.ru.

79 'The United Selling Organization (USO) of ALROSA', www.alrosa.ru, accessed 5 May 2020. The name USO is so reminiscent of De Beers' CSO that it might have been conceived as a reminder to De Beers that their days of monopoly were over.

80 Kari Liuhto and Jari Jumpponen, 'Russian Corporations and Banks Abroad', *Journal of East European Management Studies*, VIII/1 (2003), pp. 26–45 (p. 36).

81 V. K. Garanin, G. P. Kudryavtseva, T. V. Possoukhova, M. Tikhova and E. M. Verichev, 'Two Types of the Diamondiferous Kimberlites from the Arkhangelsk Province, Russia', in *Mineral Deposits at the Beginning of the 21st Century*, ed. Adam Piestrzyński et al. (Lisse and Abingdon, 2001), pp. 955–8.

82 *Encyclopeaedia of Russian Business, 1995: Developments and Overviews: Industrial Review* (New York, 1995), pp. 226–7.

83 'PJSC Severalmaz', www.alrosa.ru, accessed 5 May 2020. For Arkhangelsk's diamond deposits, see also D. V. Verzhak and K. V. Garanin, 'Diamond Deposits in Arkhangelsk Oblast and Environmental Problems Associated with their Development', *Moscow University Geology Bulletin*, LX/6 (2005), pp. 20–30.

84 'Lukoil Concludes Agreement to Sell Grib Diamond Mine', www.lukoil.ru, 2 December 2016. Archangel Diamond Corporation, the original owner, was an international company that also attempted to prospect for diamonds in Finland, without any success. 'Europe's First Diamond Mine Planned in Finland', www.investinfinland.fi, 9 April 2014.

85 Svetlana Shelest, 'Botuobinskaya Comes Online (Rapaport Magazine)', www.alrosa.ru, accessed 5 May 2020. The original article appeared in *Rapaport Magazine* in April 2015.

86 'Mining', www.alrosa.ru, accessed 5 May 2020.

87 'ALROSA Plans to Produce 40 Mln Carats by 2020', www.tass.com, 27 June 2014. On Alrosa's website it is still stated that conversion of Udachnaya will be completed by 2015. 'Operations', www.alrosa.ru, accessed 5 May 2020.

88 Graeme Davison, Stuart Macintyre and John B. Hirst, *The Oxford Companion to Australian History* (Oxford, 1998), pp. 283–5.

89 'Diamonds in Australia', *The Times*, 10 January 1853.

90 'The Diamond Discoveries in Australia', *Nottinghamshire Guardian*, 15 October 1869; and 'The Great Australian Diamond', *The Times*, 3 November 1869.

91 'Diamond-mining in Australia', *Glasgow Herald*, 2 December 1869.

92 'Diamonds and Other Gem Stones in Australia', *Otago Daily Times*, 3 March 1870.

93 Erlich and Hausel, *Diamond Deposits*, p. 24.

94 Several English-language newspapers reported the rush on 15 October 1898, including 'Diamond Rush in Westralia', *Daily Mail*; 'Diamonds in Westralia', *Financial Times*; and 'Diamond Mining in Australia', *Morning Post*.

95 Albert F. Calvert, 'The Diamond Rush in Western Australia', *The Standard*, 17 October 1898; and 'Diamonds in Australia', *Financial Times*, 22 October 1898.

96 'Diamond', www.resourcesandenergy.nsw.gov.au, accessed 5 May 2020. The website is part of the New South Wales Department of Primary Industries.

97 Department of Minerals and Energy, *Gemstones in Western Australia: Geological Survey of Western Australia* (Perth, 1994), p. 8.

98 B. H. Scott Smith and E.M.W. Skinner, 'Diamondiferous Lamproite', *Journal of Geology*, XCII/4 (1984), pp. 433–8. Subsequent research has located diamondiferous lamproites in Arkansas, Zambia, India, China and Ivory Coast. Erlich and Hausel, *Diamond Deposits*, pp. 139–42.

99 The idea led to renewed exploration in New South Wales in the 1990s. L. M. Barron, S. R. Lishmund, G. M. Oakes, B. J. Barron and F. L. Sutherland, 'Subduction Model for the Origin of Some Diamonds in the Phanerozoic of Eastern New South Wales', *Australian Journal of Earth Sciences*, XLIII (1996), pp. 257–67.

100 Roger H. Mitchell and Steven C. Bergman, *Petrology of Lamproites* (New York, 1991), p. 5.

101 Georges Nzongola-Ntalaja, *The Congo from Leopold to Kabila: A People's History* (London, 2002), pp. 31–2.

102 Ewen W. J. Tyler, 'Australia's New Diamond Search', in *Transactions of the Fourth Circum-Pacific Energy and Mineral Resources Conference*, ed. M. K. Horn (New York, 1986), pp. 597–612. See also *Tanganyika et Union Minière* (Amsterdam, 1954); and 'Tanganyika Concessions Limited', *Daily Mail*, 18 December 1968.

103 'Tanganyika Holdings Ltd.', *Sunday Times*, 11 May 1969.

104 Tony Thomas, 'Argyle, the Gleam in Ewen Tyler's Eye', 7 June 1991, www.afr.com, accessed 5 May 2020.

105 W. J. Atkinson, 'Diamond Exploration and Development in Australia', in *Mining Latin America: Mineria Latinoamericana*, ed. K. B. Smale-Adams (London, 1986), pp. 1–16 (pp. 3–4).

106 The stories of Stansmore and Towie were reported in Stephen Bartholomeusz, 'A Chance Lead to a Diamond Trail', *Sydney Morning Herald*, 2 January 1981. The article dubbed the NMC as 'the only all-Australian partner in a project that could easily be the world's biggest diamond mine'. Other partners in Kalumburu were Belgian Sibeka, in which De Beers held a share, London Tin (future Malaysia Mining Corporation, linked to the CSO), and Australian Jennings Industries. For a transcript of the parliamentary discussion on Kalumburu and other diamond-related matters, see 'Senate 17 November 1978, 31st Parliament, 1st Session', www.historichansard.net, accessed 5 May 2020.

107 See ibid. on the beginning of Ashton. For the further involvement of Ewen Tyler, who joined Ashton in 1978, see 'Digging for Diamonds in the Rough', todayspaper.smedia.com.au, accessed 5 May 2020. The article originally appeared in the *Australian Financial Review* on 26 June 2018.

108 Atkinson, 'Diamond Exploration', p. 4.

109 The story of Maureen Muggeridge, as well as this quote, is taken from her obituary: Gerry Carman, 'Diamond Mine Trailblazer Dies', *Sydney Morning Herald*, 26 November 2010. She passed away when she was 62, still prospecting for diamonds in Western Australia.

110 The diamond deposits of Arkansas are also found in lamproite.

111 Smith and Skinner, 'Diamondiferous Lamproite', p. 435.

112 Dave Cox, 'Argyle Diamonds: The Political Economy of a Lost Resource', *Australian Journal of Political Science*, XXXI/1 (1996), pp. 83–98 (p. 91). The most important company involved in Ashton Mining Group was Ashton Mining Ltd, which held a 24.2 per cent share of AJV, and of which the Malaysia Mining Corporation, controlled by the Malaysian government, was the

most important shareholder (45.65 per cent in 1991). Jennifer L. Carr, *Major Companies of the Far East and Australasia, 1991/92*, III: *Australia and New Zealand* (London, 1991), p. 12.

113 Cox, 'Argyle Diamonds', pp. 91–2.

114 H. M. Thompson, 'Argyle, De Beers, and the International Diamond Market', *Minerals and Energy: Raw Materials Report*, 11/3 (1983), pp. 24–39.

115 The official agreement between AJV and the Western Australian government was solidified in the 'Diamond (Argyle Diamond Mines Joint Venture) Agreement Act 1981', www.legislation.wa.gov.au, 4 December 1981, accessed 5 May 2020. The Act is still in force; its most recent version dates from 18 March 2011 and can be consulted on the website of the Western Australian Department of Justice.

116 Cox, 'Argyle Diamonds', pp. 90–94.

117 Ibid., p. 96.

118 Ibid.

119 Bain & Co., *The Global Diamond Industry: Lifting the Veil of Mystery* (2011), p. 10.

120 James Shigley, John Chapman and Robyn K. Ellison, 'Discovery and Mining of the Argyle Diamond Deposit, Australia', *Gems and Gemology*, XXXVII/1 (2001), pp. 26–41 (p. 38).

121 Ibid., p. 38.

122 Colin White, *Strategic Management* (Basingstoke, 2004), p. 370; and 'Argyle Diamond Mine Leaving De Beers Cartel', *New York Times*, 8 June 1996.

123 Hofmeester, 'Shifting Trajectories', pp. 44–7; and Sebastian Henn, 'Transnational Entrepreneurs and the Emergence of Clusters in Peripheral Regions: The Case of the Diamond Cutting Cluster in Gujarat (India)', *European Planning Studies*, XXI/11 (2013), pp. 1779–95.

124 Laureys, *Meesters van het Diamant*, pp. 412–14.

125 Hofmeester, 'Shifting Trajectories', p. 47.

126 Shigley et al., 'Discovery', p. 40.

127 Rio Tinto was the result of the merger in 1995 between RTZ and its Australian subsidiary CRA. 'History. The Year 1995. The Modern Rio Tinto Group is Born', www.riotinto.com, accessed 5 May 2020.

128 'Reasons for Decision Ashton Mining Ltd. In the matter of Ashton Mining Ltd [2000] ATP 9', ww.takeovers.gov.au, 10 October 2000.

129 'Rio Tinto's £234m Argyle Bid Trumps De Beers', *The Independent*, 30 August 2000; 'De Beers Trumps Rio in Bid War for Ashton Mining', *The Independent*, 12 October 2000; and Neil Behrmann, 'Rio Tinto Buys 49% Ashton Stake, Beating Out Rival Bidder De Beers', *Wall Street Journal*, 7 November 2000.

130 'Argyle Diamond Mine – Underground Project 110 km South of Kununurra, East Kimberley: Report and Recommendations of the Environmental Protection Authority', www.epa.wa.gov.au, November 2005. See also 'Rio Tinto 2013 Sustainable Development', www.riotinto.com, accessed 5 May 2020.

131 Courtney Fowler, 'Rio Tinto Argyle Diamond Mine's Future May Decide Fate of Australian Industry', www.abc.net.au, accessed 5 May 2020.

132 Anne Lim, 'Tiffany's Ellendale Mine in the Kimberly Strikes Yellow Diamond Gold', www.theaustralian.com.au, 7 November 2013.

133 Nick Evans, 'Precious Little Left to Salvage from Ellendale Diamond Mine', www.thewest.com.au, 12 July 2015.

134 Ben Hagemann, 'Kimberly Diamonds Shifts to Africa', www.australianmining.com.au, 1 July 2015.

135 Ben Hagemann, 'Kimberley Diamonds Former Chairman Arrested', www.australianmining.com.au, 16 September 2015.

136 Ben Collins, 'Minister Moves to Reopen Ellendale Diamond Mine and Avoid Environmental Costs', www.abc.net.au, 27 January 2017.

137 'New Lease of Life for Former Ellendale Diamond Mine', www.mediastatements.wa.gov.au, 19 December 2019.

138 Ibid.

139 'Ellendale Overview', www.gibbriverdiamonds.com, accessed 5 May 2020.

140 See V. W. Fazakerley, 'Bow River Alluvial Diamond Deposit', in *Geology of the Mineral Deposits of Australia and Papua New Guinea*, ed. F. E. Hughes (Melbourne, 1990), pp. 1659–64; and Kogel et al., *Industrial Minerals and Rocks*, pp. 421–2.

141 For the question of Aboriginal rights and how these finally made it into mining discourse, see the Epilogue.

142 Kogel et al., *Industrial Minerals and Rocks*, p. 422.

143 Jacques Cartier, Robert Lahaise and Marie Couturier, eds, *Voyages en Nouvelle-France* (Montreal, 1977), pp. 146–7: 'lorsque le soleil les éclaire, ils brillent comme s'ils étaient des étincelles de feu'.

144 Robert Melançon, 'Terre de Caïn, âge d'or, prodiges du Saguenay', *Voix et Images*, v/1 (1979), pp. 51–63 (p. 56).

145 Ibid., p. 57.

146 BL, Add. Ms. 28542, ff. 98–9, Letter E. M. da Costa to Joseph Salvador, London, 6 March 1786. For the relationship between da Costa and Salvador, see Vanneste, *Global Trade*, pp. 167–70.

147 Bauer, *Edelsteinkunde*, p. 462.

148 Ibid., p. 463.

149 Robert Wilson, *The Explorer King: Adventure, Science, and the Great Diamond Hoax – Clarence King in the Old West* (New York, 2006).

150 J. S. Diller and G. F. Kunz, 'Is There a Diamond-field in Kentucky?', *Science*, x/241 (1887), pp. 140–42.

151 For an overview, see Erlich and Hausel, *Diamond Deposits*, pp. 14–24; and Bauer, *Edelsteinkunde*, pp. 461–4.

152 The conversion of U.S. dollars to British pounds was done for the year 1932, when Bauer's work appeared in print. The financial value of the mined rough diamonds is related, of course, not only to the total weight but to the quality of diamonds. Bauer, *Edelsteinkunde*, pp. 427, 453, 464.

153 'Crater of Diamonds State Park', www.arkansasstateparks.com, accessed 5 May 2020. For more on the history of Arkansas diamonds, see

Farell-Robert, *Glitter and Greed*, pp. 100–114. The mine was shut down in 1927, and talks were held to reopen it during the Second World War, but these never amounted to anything. Ibid., pp. 105–7.

154 W. Dan Hausel, *Geology and Mineralization of the Cooper Hill Mining District, Medicine Bow Mountains, Southeastern Wyoming* (Cooper Hill, WY, 1994). See also 'Wyoming State Geological Survey', www.wsgs.wyo.gov, accessed 5 May 2020.

155 L. D. Cross, *Treasure under the Tundra: Canada's Arctic Diamonds* (Victoria, BC, 2011), p. 110.

156 Erlich and Hausel, *Diamond Deposits*, p. 26.

157 William J. Couch, 'Strategic Resolution of Policy, Environmental and Socio-economic Impacts in Canadian Arctic Diamond Mining: BHP's NWT Diamond Project', *Impact Assessment and Project Appraisal*, XX/4 (2002), pp. 265–78 (p. 266).

158 See Vernon Frolick, *Fire into Ice: Charles Fipke and The Great Diamond Hunt* (Vancouver, BC, 1999); and Kevin Krajicek, *Barren Lands: An Epic Search for Diamonds in the North American Arctic* (New York, 2002).

159 Matthew Hart, *Diamond: The History of a Cold-blooded Love Affair* (London, 2001), pp. 71–86.

160 Levine et al., 'Diamond Sources', pp. 250–51.

161 Hart, *Diamond*, pp. 87–116.

162 Dan Zlotnikoc, 'A Northern Star: Canada's First Diamond Mine Celebrates a Milestone', *CIM Magazine*, III/7 (2008), pp. 40–43.

163 Couch, 'Strategic Resolution', p. 271.

164 Russel Shor, 'A Review of the Political and Economic Forces Shaping Today's Diamond Industry', *Gems and Gemology*, XLI/3, pp. 202–33 (p. 209).

165 Bernard Simon, 'Company News: Aber Mine of Canada Buys Control of Harry Winston', *New York Times*, 3 April 2004.

166 Donald W. Olson, 'Diamond, Industrial', *U.S. Geological Survey 2013 Minerals Yearbook* (2015).

167 H. Falck, S. Cairns, M. Robb and L. Powell, *2016 Northwest Territories Mineral Exploration Overview: November 2016* (Yellowknife, NT, 2016), p. 5.

168 Janse, 'Global Rough Diamond Production', p. 109; see also James E. Shigley et al., 'Mining Diamonds in the Canadian Arctic: The Diavik Mine', *Gems and Gemology*, LII/2 (2016).

169 Hart, *Diamond*, p. 116.

170 Cairns et al., *2016 Northwest Territories*, p. 3.

171 Hart, *Diamond*, p. 123.

172 G. H. Read and A.J.A. Janse, 'Diamonds: Exploration, Mines and Marketing', *Lithos*, CXII/supplement (2009), pp. 1–9 (p. 3).

173 Janse, 'Global Rough Diamond Production', p. 112.

174 Rebecca Hall, 'Diamond Mining in Canada's Northwest Territories: A Colonial Continuity', *Antipode*, XLV/2 (2013), pp. 376–93 (p. 379).

175 'Annual Global Summary: 2008 Production, Imports, Exports and KPC Counts'.

176 Ibid.

177 Cairns et al., *2016 Northwest Territories*, pp. 6–8.
178 'Annual Global Summary: 2018 Production, Imports, Exports and KPC Counts'.
179 'Partial Revised Submission of the Russian Federation to the Commission on the Limits of the Continental Shelf in Respect of the Continental Shelf of the Russian Federation in the Arctic Ocean. Executive Summary 2015', www.un.org, accessed 5 May 2020.
180 G.M. Yaxley et al., 'The Discovery of Kimberlites in Antarctica Extends the Vast Gondwanan Cretaceous Province', *Nature Communications*, IV (2013), Article No. 2921.
181 For a look at the continuing association of Indian diamond mining with mythology and religion, see Kuntala Lahiri-Dutt and Arnab Roy Chowdhury, 'In the Realm of the Diamond King: Myth, Magic, and Modernity in the Diamond Tracts of Central India', *Annals of the American Association of Geographers*, CVIII/6 (2018), pp. 1620–34.
182 Abhijeet Mukherjee and K. S. Rao, 'Diamond Potential in India and Exploration Strategies to be Adopted', in *Mining Challenges of the 21st Century*, ed. A. K. Ghose and B. B. Dhar (New Delhi, 2000), pp. 307–18.
183 T. K. Rau, 'Panna Diamond Belt, Madhya Pradesh – A Critical Review', *Geological Society of India*, LXIX/3 (2007), pp. 513–21.
184 See the Epilogue.
185 'Diamond Mining Project, Panna', www.nmdc.co.in, accessed 5 May 2020.
186 'Detailed Information Dossier on Diamond in India. Geological Survey of India 2011', www.employee.gsi.gov.in, p. 9, accessed 5 May 2020.
187 'Rio Tinto Gifts Bunder Diamond Project in India to Government of Madhya Pradesh', www.riotinto.com, 7 February 2017. For news on the auction plans, see 'India's Gov't to Auction Off Bunder Diamond Project', www.thediamondloupe, 5 June 2019.
188 'Bunder Diamond Mine in India Has New Owner', www.thediamondloupe.com, 16 December 2019.
189 'Rio Tinto Finds Diamond Reserves in Bastar, but Says Can't Mine due to Maoist Problem', www.indianexpress.com, 24 January 2014.
190 See the 'Annual Global Summary: Production, Imports, Exports and KPC Counts' for those years.
191 'Asscher gaat in Zuid-Borneo diamantmijn exploiteren', *Het Vrije Volk*, 8 June 1965; and 'Reuze-diamant op Borneo gevonden', *Limburgsch Dagblad*, 5 November 1965.
192 'Indonesie wil controle op diamantwinning', *Algemeen Handelsblad*, 3 November 1966.
193 'Edelsteen', *Algemeen Handelsblad*, 28 September 1965.
194 'Miljoenendiamant op Borneo gedolven', *Nieuwsblad van het Noorden*, 4 November 1965.
195 Spencer et al., 'Diamond Deposits', p. 74.
196 Ronald E. Seavoy, 'The Religious Motivation for Placer Diamond Mining in Southeastern Kalimantan, Indonesia', *Journal of Cultural Geography*, III/2 (1983), pp. 56–60.
197 'Diamant', NRC *Handelsblad*, 25 April 1979; and 'Diamant', *Limburgsch*

Dagblad, 2 October 1979.

198 Spencer et al., 'Diamond Deposits', p. 67.

199 '2013 Laporan Tahunan. Annual Report. Managing Reality Overcoming Uncertainty', pp. 230–31, www.antam.com, accessed 5 May 2020.

200 See the 'Annual Global Summary: Production, Imports, Exports and KPC Counts' for those years. In 2018 there was no official diamond production in Borneo, according to the 'Annual Global Summary'.

201 Jean Escard, *Les pierres précieuses* (Paris, 1914), p. 142.

202 Paul Barré, 'Les chemins de fer Asiatiques (suite et fin)', *Revue de Géographie*, XXIV/48 (1901), pp. 131–7 (p. 134).

203 Escard, *Pierres précieuses*, p. 142.

204 Marcel Bardet, *Géologie du Diamant*, vol. I: *Généralités* (Paris, 1974), p. 158.

205 Barré, 'Chemins de fer Asiatiques', p. 134.

206 Peter C. Keller and Wan Guo-dong, 'The Changma Diamond District, Mengyin, Shandong Province, China', *Gems and Gemology*, XXII/1 (1986), pp. 14–23.

207 Kogel et al., *Industrial Minerals and Rocks*, p. 422.

208 'Annual Global Summary: 2018 Production, Imports, Exports and KPC Counts'.

209 Erlich and Hausel, *Diamond Deposits*, p. 6.

210 The website for the park can be found at www.guiachapadadiamantina.com.br, accessed 5 May 2020. See also Samir S. Patel, 'Diamond Rush: Nineteenth-century Wildcatters Left their Marks on Brazil's Landscape', *Archaeology*, LX/2 (2007), pp. 53–8.

211 See their website at www.cprm.gov.br, accessed 5 May 2020. On the Santo Inácio project, see Luiz Carlos de Moraes and José da Silva Amaral, 'Diamante de Santo Inácio Estado da Bahia', rigeo.cprm.gov.br, accessed 5 May 2020.

212 Iran F. Machado and Silvia F. de M. Figueirôa, '500 Years of Mining in Brazil: A Brief Review', *Resources Policy*, XXVII (2001), pp. 9–24 (p. 19).

213 Geraldo Bastos, 'Mina entrará em operação na BA', atarde.uol.com.br, 17 January 2016. For the Lipari company, see their website at www.lipari.com.br, accessed 5 May 2020.

214 See the 'Annual Global Summary: Production, Imports, Exports and KPC Counts' for those years.

215 'Mina Braúna é Realidade', www.lipari.com.br, accessed 5 May 2020.

216 See the 'Annual Global Summary: Production, Imports, Exports and KPC Counts' for those years.

217 Barbara P. Josiah, *Migration, Mining, and the African Diaspora: Guyana in the Nineteenth and Twentieth Centuries* (New York, 2011).

218 See the 'Annual Global Summary: Production, Imports, Exports and KPC Counts' for those years.

219 Paul F. Kerr, Donald L. Graf and Sydney H. Ball, 'Carbonado from Venezuela', *American Mineralogist*, XXXIII/1–2 (1948), pp. 251–3.

220 'Diamant-ontginning in Venezuela', *Amigoe di Curacao*, 25 January 1945. For an individual account of an adventurer drawn to the prospect of shining

diamonds in Brazil and Guyana during the 1950s, see Victor G. C. Norwood, *A Hand Full of Diamonds: Further Adventures and Experiences in the Jungles and Diamond Fields of Guiana and Brazil* (London, 1960).

221 'Diamant-rush in Venezuela', *Nederlands Dagblad*, 16 August 1969.

222 See the 'Annual Global Summary: Production, Imports, Exports and KPC Counts' for those years.

223 Girish Gupta, 'Venezuela Rejoins Global Anti-"Blood Diamonds" Group', www.reuters.com, 18 November 2016. The annual global summaries of the Kimberley Statistics website do not contain any data on Venezuela since the country's readmission. See kimberleyprocessstatistics.org, accessed 5 May 2020.

EPILOGUE: ABOUT HUMAN RIGHTS AND ENVIRONMENTAL CONSIDERATIONS

1 *Algemeene Oefenschoole van Konsten en Weetenschappen: Zesde Afdeeling. Dertiende deel* (Amsterdam, 1782), p. 389.

2 Smillie, *Diamonds*, pp. 149–50.

3 Jiří Strnad, 'The Discovery of Diamonds in Siberia and other Northern Regions: Explorational, Historical, and Personal Notes', *Earth Sciences History*, x/2 (1991), pp. 227–46 (p. 235); Grigorii Fainshtein, *Behind Us the Cities Will Arise* (Irkutsk, 1988), p. 90 [in Russian].

4 Ball, *Diamonds*, p. 57.

5 Smillie, *Diamonds*, p. 147.

6 'Artisanal and Small-scale Mining', www.worldbank.org, 21 November 2013, accessed 5 May 2020.

7 Kaakpema Yelpaala and Saleem H. Ali, 'Multiple Scales of Diamond Mining in Akwatia, Ghana: Addressing Environmental and Human Development Impact', *Resources policy*, xxx/3 (2005), pp. 145–55 (p. 153).

8 'DR Congo Plague Outbreak Spreads', news.bbc.co.uk, 23 February 2005. For analysis of the recent outbreak of ebola, which was also influenced by the unhealthy and violent circumstances of alluvial diamond mining in Sierra Leone, see Paul Farmer, *Fevers, Feuds, and Diamonds: Ebola and the Ravages of History* (New York, 2020).

9 To this can be added that, for most of history, Europe's nations also made extensive use of it. See Hugh D. Hindman, ed., *The World of Child Labor: An Historical and Regional Survey* (London, 2009). For an analysis of change in the nineteenth century, see Elisabeth Anderson, 'Policy Entrepreneurs and the Origins of the Regulatory Welfare State: Child Labor Reform in Nineteenth-century Europe', *American Sociological Review*, LXXXIII/1 (2018), pp. 173–211. For present-day Western prejudice, see Tracy McVeigh, 'UN's Ban on Child Labour Is a "Damaging Mistake"', *The Guardian*, 18 December 2016.

10 Frost, *From the Pit to the Market*, pp. 101–4.

11 See, for instance, Gavin Hilson, '"Once a Miner, Always a Miner": Poverty and Livelihood Diversification in Akwatia, Ghana', *Journal of Rural Studies*, XXVI/3 (2010), pp. 296–307.

12 Sigismond A. Wilson, 'Sierra Leone's Illicit Diamonds: The Challenges and

the Way Forward', *GeoJournal*, LXXVI/3 (2011), pp. 191–212.

13 Richard Human, 'Tanzanite Trouble', www.newint.org, 2 April 2006.

14 See www.ddiglobal.org, accessed 5 May 2020.

15 Farell-Robert, *Glitter and Greed*, pp. 46–7. The book discusses India's diamond cutters more extensively between pp. 45–60.

16 Roli Srivastava, 'Death by Diamonds: Suicides Wipe the Shine off India's Gem Trade', www.reuters.com, 10 July 2018.

17 Ibid. For laws against child labour, see Rumani Saikia Phukan, 'Child Labour in Diamond Industry Continues Despite Abolition', www.mapsofindia.com, 8 February 2015.

18 Ian Taylor and Gladys Mokhawa, 'Not Forever: Botswana, Conflict Diamonds and the Bushmen', *African Affairs*, CII/407 (2003), pp. 261–83; see also Kenneth Good, *Diamonds, Dispossession, and Democracy in Botswana* (Woodbridge, 2008).

19 'Botswana Government Lies Exposed as Diamond Mine Opens in Bushman Land', www.survivalinternational.nl, 4 September 2014.

20 The Amazon is an immense international region, where illegal activities are very hard to control. Political borders are porous, and miners come from and go to neighbouring countries. For an academic approach, see Marjo de Theije and Marieke Heemskerk, 'Moving Frontiers in the Amazon: Brazilian Small-scale Gold Miners in Suriname', *European Review of Latin American and Caribbean Studies/Revista Europea de Estudios Latinoamericanos y del Caribe*, 87 (209), pp. 5–25.

21 Graham Rayman, 'A New York Operator's Trail of Blood, Bankruptcy, and Brazilian Diamonds', www.villagevoice.com, 9 March 2010.

22 Mario Osava, 'Rights-Brazil: Violence Stains National Day of Indigenous Peoples', www.ipsnews.net, 19 April 2004. Roosevelt, president between 1901 and 1909, published an account of his travels there. Theodore Roosevelt, *Through the Brazilian Wilderness* (New York, 1914).

23 Rayman, 'A New York Operator's Trail of Blood'. For a summary of the story, see Shawn Gerald Blore, ed., 'The Failure of Good Intentions: Fraud, Theft and Murder in the Brazilian Diamond Industry', *PAC Occasional Paper*, 12 (2005), pp. 25–7, www.impacttransform.org, accessed 5 May 2020.

24 'Extração illegal de diamantes em RO é destaque no Jornal Hoje', redeglobo. globo.com, 8 December 2015. For a recent follow-up showing the persistence of clandestine mining, see Felipe Abreu and Luiz Felipe Silva, 'O garimpo illegal numa das maiores reservas de diamantes do planeta', *Folha de S. Paulo*, www.folha.uol.com.br, 27 September 2015.

25 Ciaran O'Faircheallaigh, 'Social Justice, Aboriginal Leadership and Mineral Development in Australia', in *A Twenty-first Century Approach to Teaching Social Justice: Educating for Both Advocacy and Action*, ed. R.G.J. Ill (New York, 2009), pp. 207–30.

26 Michael West and Suzanne Smith, 'Diamonds Are Not Forever: Indigenous Communities Grapple with End of the Mining Boom', www.abc.net.au, accessed 5 May 2020.

27 Ibid.
28 Ben Butler, Lorena Allam and Calla Wahlquist, 'Rio Tinto CEO and Senior Executives Resign from Company after Juukan Gorge Debacle', *The Guardian*, 11 September 2020; and Lorena Allam, '"Devastated" Indigenous Owners say Rio Tinto Misled Them Ahead of Juukan Gorge Blast ', *The Guardian*, 12 October 2020.
29 Colleen M. Davison and Penelope Hawe, 'All That Glitters: Diamond Mining and Tåîchô Youth in Behchokö, Northwest Territories', *Arctic*, LXV/2 (2012), pp. 214–28.
30 For a critical approach, see Hall, 'Diamond Mining'; and Richard J. DiFrancesco, 'A Diamond in the Rough? An Examination of the Issues Surrounding the Development of the Northwest Territories', *Canadian Geographer*, XLIV/2 (2000), pp. 114–34; see also Patricia J. Fitzpatrick, 'A New Staples Industry? Complexity, Governance and Canada's Diamond Mines', *Policy and Society*, XXVI/1 (2007), pp. 93–112, for a more positive assessment.
31 Crate, 'Co-option in Siberia'; see also Susan A. Crate and Natalia Yakovleva, 'Indigenous People and Mineral Resource Extraction in Russia: The Case of Diamonds', in *Earth Matters: Indigenous Peoples, the Extractive Industries and Corporate Social Responsibility*, ed. Ciaran O'Faircheallaigh and Saleem Ali (Sheffield, 2008), pp. 222–44. For a detailed assessment of the impact of mining on the local Vilyuy in Sakha, and a comparison with Canadian institutions to protect the indigenous population, see Susan Crate, *Cow, Kin, and Globalization: An Ethnography of Sustainability* (Lanham, MD, 2006), pp. 221–88.
32 Couch, 'Strategic Resolution', p. 271; Adam C. Smith, John A. Virgl, Damian Panayi and Allison R. Armstrong, 'Effects of a Diamond Mine on Tundra-breeding Birds', *Arctic*, LVIII/3 (2005), pp. 295–304.
33 J. Rogers and X. C. Li, 'Environmental Impact of Diamond Mining on Continental Shelf Sediments off Southern Namibia', *Quaternary International*, XCII/1 (2002), pp. 101–12.
34 P. Naveen, 'Tigers Vanished from Panna after Diamond Mines Were Shut: Madhya Pradesh Authorities', www.timesofindia.indiatimes.com, 2 October 2014; and Neeraj Santoshi, 'Close Diamond Mining in Panna Tiger Reserve by 2017: Panel', www.hindustantimes.com, 22 September 2014.
35 Personal communication with Dr Bhanumathi Kalluri, at the time working for Dhaatri – A Resource Centre for Women and Children, www.dhaatri.org, accessed 5 May 2020.
36 'Illegal Diamond Mines Raided in Panna Reserve', www.timesofindia.india-times.com, 9 February 2020.
37 Personal communication with Dr Bhanumathi Kalluri.
38 Smillie, *Diamonds*, p. 148.
39 See, for instance, Ricardo Junior de Assis Fernando Gonçalves and Marcelo Rodrigues Mendonça, 'Trabalho e garimpo: atividade garimpeira de diamantes na Comunidade de Douradinho no município de Coromandel/ MG', *Espaço em Revista*, XIV/1 (2012), pp. 86–95.
40 For a recent academic overview, see Koen Vlassenroot and Steven Bockstael,

eds, *Artisanal Diamond Mining: Perspectives and Challenges* (Ghent, 2008).

41 R. K. Amankwah and C. Anim-Sackey, 'Strategies for Sustainable Development of the Small-scale Gold and Diamond Mining Industry of Ghana', *Resources Policy*, XXIX/3 (2003), pp. 131–8.

42 Roy Maconachie and Tony Binns, '"Farming Miners" or "Mining Farmers"?: Diamond and Rural Development in Post-conflict Sierra Leone', *Resources Policy*, XXIII/3 (2007), pp. 367–80.

Select Bibliography

Alam, Ishrat, 'Diamond Mining and Trade in South India in the Seventeenth Century', *Medieval History Journal*, III/2 (2000), pp. 291–310

Allen, V. L., *The History of Black Mineworkers in South Africa*, 3 vols (London, 2005)

Bergstein, Rachelle, *Brilliance and Fire: A Biography of Diamonds* (New York, 2016)

Bieri, Franziska, *From Blood Diamonds to the Kimberley Process: How NGOs Cleaned Up the Global Diamond Industry* (Farnham and Burlington, VT, 2010)

Bycroft, Michael, and Sven Dupré, eds, *Gems in the Early Modern World: Materials, Knowledge and Global Trade* (London, 2019)

Cleveland, Todd, *Diamonds in the Rough: Corporate Paternalism and African Professionalism on the Mines of Colonial Angola, 1917–1975* (Athens, OH, 2015)

—, *Stones of Contention: A History of Africa's Diamonds* (Athens, OH, 2014)

Coenen Snyder, Saskia, '"As Long as It Sparkles!": The Diamond Industry in Nineteenth-century Amsterdam', *Jewish Social Studies*, XXII/2 (2017), pp. 38–73

Dalrymple, William, and Anita Anand, *Koh-i-Noor: The History of the World's Most Infamous Diamond* (New York and London, 2017)

De Bie, Annelies, 'The Paradox of the Antwerp Rose: Symbol of Decline or Token of Craftsmanship?', in *Innovation and Creativity in Late Medieval and Early Modern European Cities*, ed. Karel Davids and Bert de Munck (Farnham and Burlington, VT, 2014), pp. 269–94

De Boeck, Filip, '*Garimpeiro* Worlds: Digging, Dying and "Hunting" for Diamonds in Angola', *Review of African Political Economy*, XXVIII/90 (2001), pp. 549–62

De Vries, David, *Diamonds and War: State, Capital and Labor in British-ruled Palestine* (New York and Oxford, 2010)

Epstein, Edward Jay, *The Rise and Fall of Diamonds: The Shattering of a Brilliant Illusion* (New York, 1982)

Erlich, Edward I., and W. Dan Hausel, *Diamond Deposits: Origin, Exploration, and History of Discovery* (Littleton, CO, 2002)

Evans, Joan, *A History of Jewellery, 1100–1870* (New York, 1953)

Farrell-Robert, Janine, *Glitter and Greed: The Secret World of the Diamond Cartel* (St Paul, MN, 2003)

Ferreira Furtado, Júnia, *Chica da Silva: A Brazilian Slave of the Eighteenth Century* (New York, 2009)

Frost, Diane, *From the Pit to the Market: Politics and the Diamond Economy in Sierra Leone* (Martlesham, Suffolk, 2012)

Greenhalgh, Peter, *West African Diamonds, 1919–83: An Economic History* (Manchester, 1985)

Hart, Matthew, *Diamond: The History of a Cold-blooded Love Affair* (London, 2001)

Hazen, Robert M., *The Diamond Makers* (Cambridge, 1999)

Hofmeester, Karin, ed., *Een Schitterende Erfenis: 125 jaar nalatenschap van de Algemene Nederlandse Diamantbewerkersbond* (Zutphen, 2019)

—, 'Shifting Trajectories of Diamond Processing: From India to Europe and Back, from the Fifteenth Century to the Twentieth', *Journal of Global History*, VIII/1 (2013), pp. 25–49

Kanfer, Stefan, *The Last Empire: De Beers, Diamonds, and the World* (New York, 1993)

Kempton, Daniel R., 'Russia and De Beers: Diamond Conflict or Cartel?', *South African Journal of International Affairs*, III/2 (1995), pp. 94–131

Knight, John, and Heather Stevenson, 'The Williamson Diamond Mine, De Beers, and the Colonial Office: A Case-study of the Quest for Control', *Journal of Modern African Studies*, XXIV/3 (1986), pp. 423–45

Krajicek, Kevin, *Barren Lands: An Epic Search for Diamonds in the North American Arctic* (New York, 2002)

Kurin, Richard, *Hope Diamond: The Legendary History of a Cursed Gem* (New York, 2007)

Lenzen, Godehard, *The History of Diamond Production and the Diamond Trade* (New York, 1970)

Mawe, John, *Travels in the Interior of Brazil, particularly in the gold and diamond districts of that country* (London, 1813)

Meredith, Martin, *Diamonds, Gold and War: The British, the Boers, and the Making of South Africa* (New York, 2007)

Monnier, Laurent, Bogumil Jewsiewicki and Gauthier de Villers, eds, *Chasse au diamant au Congo/Zaire*, Cahiers Africains: Afrika Studies 45–6 (Tervuren, 2001)

Munich, Adrienne, *Empire of Diamonds. Victorian Gems in Imperial Settings* (Charlottesville, VA, 2020)

Mwaipopo, Rosemarie, '*Ubeshi* – Negotiating Co-existence: Artisanal and Large-scale Relations in Diamond Mining', in *Mining and Social Transformation in Africa: Mineralizing and Democratizing Trends in Artisanal Production*, ed. D. F. Bryceson, E. Fisher, J. B. Jønsson and R. Mwaipopo (New York and Abingdon, 2014), pp. 161–76

Newbury, Colin, *The Diamond Ring: Business, Politics and Precious Stones in South Africa, 1867–1947* (Oxford, 1989)

Ogden, Jack, *Diamonds: An Early History of the King of Gems* (New Haven, CT, 2018)

Oltuski, Alicia, *Precious Objects: A Story of Diamonds, Family, and a Way of Life* (New York, 2011)

Pointon, Marcia, *Brilliant Effects: A Cultural History of Gem Stones and Jewellery* (New Haven, CT, 2009)

—, *Rocks, Ice and Dirty Stones: Diamond Histories* (London, 2017)

Proctor, Robert N., 'Anti-agate: The Great Diamond Hoax and the Semiprecious Stone Scam', *Configurations*, IX/3 (2001), pp. 381–412

Robertson, Marian, *Diamond Fever: South African Diamond History, 1866–9, from Primary Sources* (Cape Town, 1974)

Said, Hakim Mohammad, ed., *Al-Beruni's Book on Mineralogy: The Book Most Comprehensive in Knowledge on Precious Stones* (Islamabad, 1989)

Samuel, Edgar, 'Diamonds and Pieces of Eight: How Stuart England Won the Rough-diamond Trade', *Jewish Historical Studies*, XXXVIII (2002), pp. 23–40

Shield, Renée Rose, *Diamond Stories: Enduring Change on 47th Street* (Ithaca, NY, 2002)

Smillie, Ian, *Blood on the Stone: Greed, Corruption and War in the Global Diamond Trade* (London, 2010)

Taylor, Ian, and Gladys Mokhawa, 'Not Forever: Botswana, Conflict Diamonds and the Bushmen', *African Affairs*, CII/407 (2003), pp. 261–83

Tichotsky, John, *Russia's Diamond Colony: The Republic of Sakha* (London and New York, 2000)

Tillander, Herbert, *Diamond Cuts in Historic Jewellery, 1381–1910* (London, 1995)

Tolansky, Samuel, *The History and Use of Diamond* (London, 1962)

Trivellato, Francesca, *The Familiarity of Strangers: The Sephardic Diaspora, Livorno, and Cross-cultural Trade in the Early Modern Period* (New Haven, CT, 2009)

Turrell, Robert Vicat, *Capital and Labour on the Kimberley Diamond Fields, 1871–1890* (Cambridge, 1987)

Vanneste, Tijl, *Global Trade and Commercial Networks: Eighteenth-century Diamond Merchants* (London, 2011)

Vlassenroot, Koen, and Steven Bockstael, eds, *Artisanal Diamond Mining: Perspectives and Challenges* (Ghent, 2008)

Worger, William H., *South Africa's City of Diamonds: Mine Workers and Monopoly Capitalism in Kimberley, 1867–1895* (New Haven, CT, 1987)

Yogev, Gedalia, *Diamonds and Coral: Anglo-Dutch Jews and Eighteenth-century Trade* (Leicester, 1978)

Acknowledgements

This book is the result of a long journey into the world of diamonds. I want to thank Eddy Stols, who was the first to set me on the trail of Brazilian precious stones. He gave me the opportunity to spend some time at the Universidade Federal de Minas Gerais, where I met an inspiring group of historians, and I am grateful for the time spent with Eduardo França Paiva and Júnia Ferreira Furtado, often in the company of Bart Vanspauwen. Later I continued to work on diamonds but shifted to early modern trade, which resulted in a PhD at the European University Institute in Florence, and I am lucky to have had the supervision of Diogo Ramada Curto and Anthony Molho. The other members of the jury, Maxine Berg and Jan de Vries, provided me with more than enough encouragement to stay focused on diamonds.

It was always a pleasure to meet colleagues working on similar topics, and my conversations with the participants of the 'Gems in Transit' workshop in Warwick in 2015, which was continued in Amsterdam, Utrecht and Antwerp in 2016, were very inspirational for the writing of this book. Thank you, Michael Bycroft, Sven Dupré, Marjolijn Bol, Karin Hofmeester and particularly Marcia Pointon, who was always generous in sharing information and advice. I am equally fortunate to have met Liliane Hilaire Perez and Evelyne Oliel-Grausz, who helped to enhance my knowledge on Jewish history and on the history of technology. I also am very much obliged to Petra van Dam and Al Angharad Williams for reading versions of the manuscript, and generously giving me their time, feedback and encouragement. I am equally indebted to the anonymous peer reviewer who provided many useful suggestions and criticisms.

I was lucky to be able to spend time on this book while enjoying the pleasure of exchanging ideas with Maria Fusaro, Richard Blakemore, Erika Kuijpers and my colleagues at the Vrije Universiteit Amsterdam. This book could not have been written in its current form without the conversations I had with Tracian Meikle, who helped me realize that there can be activism in being a scholar. I could obviously not have done this without the support of friends and family. I have very much appreciated the wamth of Yassine Khoudja, Eva Schmitz, Andrea Capecci, Phil Baber, Gray Akotey, Olivia Somsen, Adrian Olivet, Alice Barthelemy, Marlène Dewaere, Orfee Melsen, Roberto Verdecchia Schneider, Sander de Vries, Nienke Elbertse, Elisabeth Enthoven and everyone at L'Affiche, Henk Sleijfer, Michel Hesp, Chaim Wannet and the rest of SBK.

Finally, my love and gratitude go to the person I owe the most to, Trees de Geest, and to Rosa Sijben, who decided she was going to walk with me through life. I could never have finished this without them.

I have dreamed of writing a general history of diamond mining for many years, and I am greatly indebted to everyone at Reaktion Books, helping me out with what seems like infinite patience. Thank you, Ben Hayes, Michael Leaman, Amy Salter

Maria Kilcoyne and Alex Ciobanu. I am particularly grateful to my editor, Phoebe Colley, for her infinite patience and meticulous work on the text, and Susannah Jayes, for her work on the picture selection, which I kept changing until the very last moment.

I always wanted this book to be a complete narrative and an interesting read. As to the first aim, I know I have failed, so I can only hope I have succeeded with regards to the second.

Photo Acknowledgements

The author and publishers wish to thank the organizations and individuals listed below for authorizing reproduction of their work:

Alamy: pp. 57 (Frederick Reglain), 266 (imageBROKER); author: pp. 201, 273, 313, 314; Pieter van der Aa, *La galerie agréable du monde*: p. 34; Arquivo Histórico Ultramarino, Lisbon: pp. 86, 94, 95; Biblioteca Nacional de Portugal, Lisbon: p. 251; Biblioteca Nacional do Brasil, Rio de Janeiro: pp. 135, 217; Bibliothèque Nationale de France, Paris: pp. 30, 75; Boston Public Library: p. 188; British Library, London: pp. 52, 152, 157; Eugène Caustier, *Les entrailles de la terre*: p. 195; *Evening Star*: p. 193; Louis Figuier, *Les nouvelles conquêtes de la science*: p. 139; Google Earth: pp. 282, 287, 323, 324; *Harper's New Monthly Magazine*: p. 56; *Illustrated London News*: pp. 17, 199; Carlos Julião, *Riscos Iluminados*: pp. 96, 97; Kempens Erfgoed (Collectie Schitterend Geslepen): p. 202; John Mawe, *Travels in the gold and diamond districts of Brazil*: p. 99; John Mawe, *Travels in the interior of Brazil*: p. 102; Mugar Memorial Library, Boston University: p. 175; Nationaal Archief, The Hague: pp. 168, 187 (Collectie Spaarnestad), 189 (Collectie Spaarnestad), 234 (Collectie Spaarnestad), 256; Nationaal Museum van Wereldculturen, Amsterdam: pp. 227 (TM-10014322), 244 (RV-A440-f-136), 311 (TM-10007447); New York Public Library: p. 218; Picryl: pp. 146, 150, 155, 161; Rijksmuseum, Amsterdam: pp. 47, 50, 71, 77, 148, 149, 151, 153, 154, 159, 160, 165, 177; Louis Rousselet, *L'Inde des Rajahs*: p. 125; Johann Moritz Rugendas, *Malerische Reise in Brasilien*: p. 132; Shutterstock: pp. 70 (DiamondGalaxy); Rosa Sijben: pp. 6, 74; Rosa Sijben and Boetie Zijlstra: pp. 22, 63, 80, 142, 247, 285, 297, 306; Smithsonian National Museum of Natural History: p. 8; Johannes Baptiste von Spix and Carl Friedrich Philipp von Martius, *Reise in Brasilien*: p. 101; Stadsarchief, Amsterdam: p. 197; Isaac Taylor, *A Nutshell of Knowledge*: p. 36; Wellcome Collection: pp. 179 top and bottom, 180; Wikimedia Commons: pp. 11 (Junkyardsparkle/CC0 1.0 Universal Public Domain Dedication), 138 (James St. John/CC BY 2.0), 196 (Paul Parsons (paul.parsons@hyphen.co.za/CC BY-SA 3.0), 203 (Lubor Ferenc/CC BY-SA 4.0), 226 (Ministry of Information of Indonesia/ Public Domain); 265 (Mummane/CC BY-SA 4.0, 286 top (Staselnik/CC BY-SA 3.0), 286 bottom (Stepanovas/CC BY-SA 3.0), 289 (USSR Post/Public Domain), 299 (Reise-Line/CC BY-SA 3.0), 307 (NASA/METI/AIST/Japan Space Systems, and U.S./Japan ASTER Science Team/Public Domain); Gardner F. Williams, *The Diamond Mines of South Africa*: p. 174; Yale University Library: pp. 176, 181 top and bottom.

Index

Illustration numbers are indicated by *italics*